Weather Bird

Weather Bird

JAZZ AT THE DAWN OF ITS SECOND CENTURY

GARY GIDDINS

OXFORD

UNIVERSITY PRESS

2004

OXFORD

UNIVERSITY PRESS

Oxford   New York
Auckland   Bangkok   Buenos Aires   Cape Town   Chennai
Dar es Salaam   Delhi   Hong Kong   Istanbul   Karachi   Kolkata
Kuala Lumpur   Madrid   Melbourne   Mexico City   Mumbai   Nairobi
São Paulo   Shanghai   Taipei   Tokyo   Toronto

Copyright © 2004 by Gary Giddins

Published by Oxford University Press, Inc.
198 Madison Avenue, New York, New York, 10016
www.oup.com

Oxford is a registered trademark of Oxford University Press

Library of Congress Cataloging-in-Publication Data
Giddins, Gary.
Weather bird : jazz at the dawn of its second century
/ Gary Giddins.
p. cm.
Includes index.
ISBN 0-19-515607-2
1. Jazz—History and criticism.   2. Performing arts.   I. Title.
ML3507.G53   2004
781.65—dc22   2004000654

1 3 5 7 9 8 6 4 2
Printed in the United States of America
on acid-free paper

FOR LEA, DEBORAH, AND ALICE
AND FOR ROBERT CHRISTGAU

AND IN MEMORY:

LESTER BOWIE
NICK BRIGNOLA
JAKI BYARD
BENNY CARTER
ROSEMARY CLOONEY
TOMMY FLANAGAN
JOHN LEWIS
BUDDY TATE

In bygone times a feeling for nobility was always maintained in the art of music, and all its elements skillfully retained the orderly beauty appropriate to them. Today, however, people take up music in a haphazard and irrational manner. The musicians of our day set as their goal success with their audiences.

       —Athenaeus, The Learned Banquet *(c. 200 c.e)*

Music awakens time, awakens us to the finest enjoyment of time; music awakens—and thus has moral value. Art has moral value, in that it awakens. But what if it does the opposite? What if it dulls us, puts us to sleep, opposes all action and progress? Music can do that too; it knows very well the power of opiates. A gift of the Devil, my dear sirs; opiates make for lethargy, inflexibility, stagnation, slavish inertia. There is something uncertain about music, gentlemen. I tell you that music is, by its very nature, equivocal. I do not exaggerate when I insist that it is politically suspect.

       —Thomas Mann, The Magic Mountain

The shaking air rattled Lord Edward's membrana tympani; *the interlocked* malleus, incus *and stirrup bones were set in motion so as to agitate the membrane of the oval window and raise an infinitesimal storm in the fluid of the labyrinth. The hairy endings of the auditory nerve shuddered like weeds in a rough sea; a vast number of obscure miracles were performed in the brain, and Lord Edward ecstatically whispered "Bach!"*

       —Aldous Huxley, Point Counter Point

Anyone can make the simple complicated. Creativity is making the complicated simple.   *—Charles Mingus*

Everybody has the blues. Everybody longs for meaning. Everybody needs to love and be loved. Everybody needs to clap hands and be happy. Everybody longs for faith. In music, especially this broad category called jazz, there is a stepping-stone to all of these.

       —Martin Luther King, Jr.

Contents

Introduction and Acknowledgments

The sense of enlargement of life may be so uplifting that personal motives and inhibitions, commonly omnipotent, become too insignificant for notice, and new reaches of patience and fortitude open out. Fears and anxieties go, and blissful equanimity takes their place. Come heaven, come hell, it makes no difference now!
   —*William James,* The Varieties of Religious Experience

It is now 40 years since I found in Louis Armstrong specifically and in jazz in general a substitute for the God of my fathers—though I didn't realize it at the time. If, as William James argues, an authentic religious experience is one that permanently transforms, unlike, say, the cheap tickets to holiness provided by a variety of hallucinogens in my college years, then the Armstrong conversion seems to have held pretty well. It transfigured my adolescence and has governed most of what I've made of my adulthood. Of course, the limits of my talent had something to do with this. I didn't abandon my childhood ambition of becoming Hawthorne because I hooked onto something better. A writer will write and the only question is the subject. For a long time, I fought against criticism as a capitulation; sometimes, I fight still. But then I return to Armstrong and company and know I'm right, or in any case still locked in the bonds of worship. The trouble with choosing your own god is that it chooses you in turn, and there you are, come heaven, come hell.

My parents' home was not especially musical, beyond a few popular singers and bands: albums by Sinatra, Belafonte, Ted Heath, various cha-cha-cha and mambo ensembles with sexy covers. Yet as progressive Spockian suburbanites determined to raise the sights of their children, they also invested in—along with World Book Encyclopedia and an unabridged Webster, purchased in installments—two bulky Reader's Digest anthologies of classical music. Inexplicably, that company declined to honor conductors: only in small print on the disc-labels could one find their names, from Sir Adrian Boult and Rene Leibowitz to the more obscure Massimo Freccia and—unforgettable name—Odd Gruner-Hegge. The music did its job, however, despite its mostly negative connotations in my adolescent circles. I shut the door and merrily conducted the first Brandenburg, Mozart's G-minor symphony, *Le Sacre du Printemps*, the Eroica, Italian, and Pathetique symphonies. That habit and my inclination to memorize long passages led my parents to the sorry conclusion that I had a talent for music making when my true gift lay in record playing. Thus followed lessons on a succession of instruments until the most patient of instructors conceded that I was hopeless. My ability to read the bass clef paralleled that of a four-year-old confronted with Faulkner; as notes flew off the treble staff, I sheepishly intoned, "Every good boy does fine."

Rock and roll soon entered the picture: Little Richard, Lloyd Price, Fats Domino, Ray Charles, Jackie Wilson, Dee Clark, the Coasters, Bobby Darin, Sammy Turner, the Five Satins, the Diamonds, the Shirelles, Buddy Holly, Bo Diddley, Bobby Day, Bobby Rydell, Chuck Berry, Jimmy Jones, Marv Johnson, Johnny and the Hurricanes, and U.S. Bonds, among many others. They racially integrated my world in a way the neighborhood, movies, and TV did not. My friends and I marveled that most of our favorites were Negroes, to us an unknown and estimable breed—so dapper in their tailored tuxedos and high-swept conks. We debated which of them looked the coolest and wondered what they were like. The only Negroes we knew were women, deputized authority figures: maids, mothers' helpers—every home had one. Where did they disappear to every Thursday, maid's day off? Did they all go to Harlem? And what kind of place was Harlem that dispatched, dozens, perhaps hundreds of women to look after white households? What if our own mothers had to leave us to take care of Negro families? You don't read this sort of thing in Civil Rights histories, but that was the kind of conversation rife among twelve-year-olds in white upper-middle-class Long Island towns of the late '50s and early '60s.

Here I pay thanks to Pearl Hill, who came from Alabama—her father operated a chain of black movie theaters and wanted her out of there—to live with my family. A teenager herself (I wasn't as yet) and the object of my first irreconcilable crush, Pearl lived upstairs, and whenever she bought a new 45, I raced up to hear it: Little Richard grinding out "Shake a Hand," Lloyd Price thundering the scary saga of "Stagger Lee." On one occasion I was transported by a totally different music wafting down. The cover depicted a man with a smooth Indian-like face, eyes closed, sporting a madly plaid sports coat. Listening to the rhythm, which punched the beat without rocking it, and his voice, taking all the time in the world, I thought: This is deep stuff from a place I don't know anything about. A good seven or eight years would go by before I next encountered the name or music of B. B. King. The subject of jazz came up once when she wanted to impress a jazz fan she was dating, and asked me if Dizzy Gillespie pronounced his name with a hard or soft G; I had no idea. When I was 12 or 13, my mother gave her permission to take me with her on Thursdays to rock and roll matinees, at which point I suppose she became my governess. We went to the Apollo in Harlem, the Hillside in Queens, and the Brooklyn Paramount, cheering the acrobatic Isley Brothers and mimicking (one simply held one's nose) the hilarious nasality of Rosie and the Originals.

Suddenly, rock and roll went into a coma—as Little Richard turned to gospel, Buddy Holly died in an airplane crash, Jackie Wilson got shot, Elvis got drafted, Chuck Berry and Jerry Lee Lewis got arrested or blackballed, and Dee Clark, Lloyd Price, Fats Domino, and everyone else I liked disappeared, quite mysteriously, from the Top 40, to be replaced by parody acts like Fabian and novelty recitations of which "Big Bad John" still makes me shudder. In truth, boredom had also set in. Classical music, though, continued to hold my attention, and I eagerly sought guidance. Huxley's dazzling *Point Counter Point* sent me in search of Bach's B minor Suite for Flute and Strings (the clerk at Macy's, bless her, insisted I buy Antonio Janigro's I Solesti di Zagreb version, coupled with the fifth Brandenburg and featuring Jean-Pierre Rampal, a flutist then too little known to merit a sleeve mention) and prompted a fascination with the Beethoven quartets, especially the A Minor, through which, with the Guarneri String Quartet on the turntable and my first Kalmus Study Score in hand, I hoped to understand the radical sway that sped Huxley's anarchist Spandrell to suicide by firing squad. In Spandrell's maunderings over Beethoven, I also encountered the Lydian mode, years before I heard of George Russell. No one wrote more euphorically about music than Huxley, who abominated jazz as art, metaphor, and social disease. No one's perfect.

An enthusiastic review sent me in search of Virgil Thomson's *Four Saints in Three Acts*, the incomparable 1947 abridgement, of which I can still sing large segments from memory. A CBS special on Casals led me to the Bach cello sonatas; a piano teacher recommended *Rhapsody in Blue* (the symphonic Oscar Levant version). I can no longer recall who or what brought the Mass in B Minor into my life, but the reel-to-reel edition of Hermann Scherchen's 1959 recording—stately, slow, huge, rapturous— sent me reeling. I would hyperventilate so badly through the Kyrie that the Gloria would have to be postponed: The B Minor Mass loomed for me as the grandest achievement in Western civilization, the stick by which to measure everything else.

Still, those records represented a furtive passion, leaving the abyss vacated by rock and roll. Hanging out in the Village, I burrowed into the renascent folk boom, especially the rediscovered Delta bluesmen, dead (Robert Johnson) and alive: Son House, Skip James (eventually the first musician I ever interviewed), and Mississippi John Hurt (who one night in Boston asked to use the Martin D-18 I had saved for but could barely play, and later sat at our table and taught me to pick "Do Lord").

None of this quite did the trick. But Ray Charles made an album called *Genius + Soul = Jazz*, and I thought if Ray is jazz than that's the place to look, especially after I met a girl who said she liked jazz and when I said "me too," quizzed me, humming a tune and challenging me to name it. I could think of only two jazz titles, "One O'Clock Jump" and "Take Five," neither of which had I ever heard, but I crumpled my brow and scratched my chin, and said, "Um, it sounds a little bit like 'Take Five,' a little, maybe." She said, "You really *do* know jazz." Thank you, Lord.

A friend loaned me albums by Cannonball Adderley and Charles Mingus about which my mother remarked, "What is that? It sounds like they're tuning up." Surly as I was, I could mount no effective retaliation as I wasn't certain she was far wrong. Then came my first serious encounter with jazz, in New Orleans in the summer of 1963 (see the ensuing essay, "The Original Dixieland One-Step"), and a band billed as Emanuel Sayles and his Silverleaf Ragtimers featuring George Lewis, with Kid Howard, Big Jim Robinson, Joe Robichaux, Alcide "Slow Drag" Pavageau, and Joe Watkins, most of them unknown north of Mason-Dixon, their records—which my father would later enable me to buy—available only through mail-order. Manny Sayles was the gatekeeper ushering me into a new world.

On a Sunday in September before school started, I reluctantly accompanied my parents on a long drive to visit their friends, and spent the afternoon, as they talked, reading a stack of *Cue* magazines, one of which had a poll in which a dozen or so jazz critics named their top-ten albums. I memorized many of the titles, most especially the one that appeared on virtually every list: *The Louis Armstrong Story, Volume 3: Louis Armstrong and Earl Hines*. The long name interested me; in pop music, volume two contained second-draw stuff that didn't fit on the first, so why *Volume 3*? And who was Earl Hines? Above all: Louis Armstrong?—the beaming, perspiring guy who sang "Blueberry Hill" on Ed Sullivan? I had always enjoyed watching him, but was he a genuinely vital figure or a tourist attraction, like the other super-famous jazz musician of the day, Al Hirt? I bought the album, sneaked it into my collection, and bided my time until my sister and parents were out of the house.

And so I am sitting on the navy-patterned sofa in the den, scrupulously designed by my mother, with its ceiling of red damask wallpaper and oak beams, the walls fitted with a redwood chair-railing painted white, an oak floor with oak pegs, a brick fireplace to my left, and some ten or twelve feet before me a dark pine unit that housed the stereo, a television, and book shelves; and though this room disappeared in 1973 and my memory has slackened, it and the moment—not least a gentle, Indian-summer stillness in the air—are kept persistently vivid by the recollection of putting the platter on the turntable and returning to the sofa before the automatic tone arm descended to the first groove of "Basin Street Blues." I briefly describe that performance in the essay "Hot," included here, but when I first heard the opening measures with their tinkling celeste, my stomach sank and I groaned: This was worse than I feared, $2.79 down the drain. Yet almost immediately, a soft and gravelly, wordless crooning—truly "a kind of excellent dumb discourse"—emerged from what universe I could not imagine. After the final trumpet solo, which builds in spiritual increments, I was at the turntable before the next track began, and played it again, standing there, and then a third time, after which I lifted the platter and noticed a wet spot, a drop of water on the vinyl, and realized I was crying.

I returned the album to its place knowing, at fifteen, that I was in possession, as far as my provincial world was concerned, of a fairly astonishing secret. It was the B Minor Mass all over again; Louis Armstrong, the clowning TV personality, was Bach; and I was then and for some years to come defensive enough not to tell anyone. But, of course, everything had changed. The world was not as it seemed, genius was not confined to the realm of marble busts and high-school music rooms. It took me six months to listen to all of side one, in part because I played it only when no one else was around, and memorized each selection before moving to the next. "Weather Bird," the madman joust with Hines, made me laugh aloud. I did skip quickly over "No, Papa, No." But not "Muggles," which begins tediously, until midway in its string of solos Armstrong alights for one of the most dramatic entrances in musical history and turns a blues into his own Kyrie eleison; or "St. James Infirmary," an inspired rendition of a tune I knew from my immersion in blues and folk; or "Tight Like This," which was too confusing, head-spinning, fearsome, and weird to share indiscriminately with anyone—all that transgender japing as Armstrong erects a pyramid made of three increasingly blissed-out segments I assumed he could not surpass.

My jazz obsession waxed over those six months as I bought records, listened to the few hours of daily jazz broadcasting, read reviews, lost myself for hours at a time in Leonard Feather's *The New Edition of the Encyclopedia of Jazz*, and borrowed ID to gain admittance to the Village Vanguard and the Village Gate. I drifted increasingly into my own world, surreptitiously reading Modern Libraries and paperbacks in class or mentally improvising solos while the second-hand beat out another fifty-minute torment. Pretending to take class notes, I made lists of musicians I had heard or needed to hear. Or I'd fasten on a tune, improvising for days on end—"Airegin," "Criss Cross"—one chorus after another, bebopping relentlessly into oblivion. Only English engaged my interest—many days, I did not attend school at all. The Beatles arrived; I hardly noticed. Among dozens of albums I accumulated, there were more by Armstrong and I played them with the others in normal fashion—I could hardly wait to get the platters on the turntable, each one a mystery until spun, since, unlike pop, jazz was not much previewed on radio.

My sixteenth birthday fell on a Saturday, and by way of giving myself a present, I figured it was time to finally flip *The Louis Armstrong Story, Volume 3*. The punch line is this: "West End Blues" leads off side two. Armstrong had, in fact, surpassed "Tight Like This." Fortunately, the rest of the side, which I also played that afternoon, represented an unmistakable falling off—Louis had already exhausted me and it was consoling to know that, like Hercules, he was half god and half human. Years later Decca released an album of big-band Armstrong, *Rare Items*, annotated by Dan Morgenstern, which confirmed my suspicion that Armstrong is inexhaustibly exhausting and that there is nothing to be done except surrender. To borrow Harold Bloom's conceit, Armstrong invented the human in American music, supplanting the mechanics of ragtime and traditional polyphonic jazz as well as classical alloys (from Gottschalk to Dvořák to Gershwin) that attempted to create "serious" music from American folk sources, with a fluid, graceful, rhythmically unparalleled model on which a durable art grounded in individualism could flourish.

In Armstrong's world, it was no longer sufficient to merely master the trumpet or saxophone; instead, jazz musicians adapted their instruments as extensions of themselves, making each solo as distinct as a signature or fingerprint. At a 1966 concert on Randall's Island, Edmund Hall and Pee Wee Russell played a duet, and I could scarcely believe they were playing the same instrument, so utterly distinctive was each man's approach to the clarinet. By then I had learned, with immense satisfaction, that not only is character fate, but also style, timbre, and attack. Coleman Hawkins, Lester Young, Ben Webster, Bud Freeman, and Herschel Evans all played tenor saxophone and were of similar age and background, yet announced themselves unconditionally in the space of a few notes. Nor was this generational: for the same could be said of their successors, tenor players like Dexter Gordon, Sonny Rollins, Stan Getz, John Coltrane, Charlie Rouse, Wayne Shorter, Zoot Sims, Booker Ervin, and—here is the thing—*many others*. This apparently infinite well of personal expression quickened my fixation and deepened my resolve.

Which may not be the best preparation for writing jazz criticism. I recently asked pianist and broadcaster Marian McPartland what she listened for in the young musicians she actively encourages. She identified a range of technical abilities; when I mentioned originality, she thought for a moment and said, no, she didn't look for that. She was concerned with mastery of the form. Not me: I take a certain degree of mastery for granted (one doesn't review amateurs) and search for a core of singularity that, in jazz, frequently trumps conventional virtuosity. That approach may no longer be fair when the majority of them emerge not from diverse apprenticeships with acknowledged maestros, but from the classroom, where conformity is a virtue and requirement. In this atmosphere, individuality becomes a luxury, sometimes defined by geography. If you visit Des Moines and you go to a bar where someone is playing luminous piano in the manner of Hank Jones, you may feel you have stumbled into heaven. In New York, that same someone would be just a guy who plays Hank Jones; we've already got the original (from Vicksburg, Mississippi, by way of Pontiac, Michigan). Lester Young once said, "Originality's the thing. You can have tone and technique and a lot of other things but without originality you ain't really nowhere." Easy for him—he was also half god, half human.

Bill Crow tells a story in which Gene Quill walks off the stage at Birdland and a heckler tells him, "All you do is play like Charlie Parker," whereupon Quill holds out his alto and says. "Here, *you* play like Charlie Parker." I've heard the same story involving Richie Kamuca and Lester Young—it's probably generic. A lover of Beethoven's sonatas is pleased to encounter someone who plays them well, yet Parker or Young lovers decry a musician who can do the same. Interpretation, the lifeblood of classical music, is downgraded to imitation in jazz, beyond occasional attempts at orchestral repertory. One does grow weary as the generation of Rollins clones gives way to Coltrane clones followed by Shorter clones. We are, of course, spoiled, those of us who lived through the jazz eras in which individuality ruled.

In 1919, the Swiss conductor Ernest Ansermet, who premiered *The Soldier's Tale* and other early 20th-century musical benchmarks, reviewed a concert he attended in London by Will Marion Cook's Southern Syncopated Orchestra. He concluded his essay by comparing Cook's musicians, among them clarinet virtuoso Sidney Bechet, to "those figures to whom we owe the advent of our art," the 17th- and 18th-century pioneers "who made expressive works of dance airs, clearing the way for Haydn and Mozart." He suggested that Bechet's way was "perhaps the highway the whole world" would soon travel.

Ansermet was most prescient in his assumption that Cook's men were heralds of permanent artists like Haydn and Mozart, not the finished product. Within a decade the world would learn of Bechet, Armstrong,

Ellington, Bessie Smith, Hines, Beiderbecke, Hawkins, Fletcher Hender-son, Benny Carter, and other artists who fulfilled his prophecy. For a while jazz also fulfilled Adrian Leverkuhn's prognostication (*Doctor Faustus*) that "A great deal of melancholy ambition will fall away from art, and a new innocence, yes, a harmlessness, will emerge. Art will embrace the future, reclaiming its role as the servant of a community that encompasses far more than 'education' and that does not acquire culture, but perhaps is culture." As for that jarring word, *harmlessness*, recall Dr. Johnson's colloquy with Boswell:

> BOSWELL: Is not *harmless pleasure* very tame?
> JOHNSON: Nay, Sir, harmless pleasure is the highest praise. Pleasure is a word of dubious import; pleasure is in general dangerous, and pernicious to virtue; to be able therefore to furnish pleasure that is harmless, pleasure pure and unalloyed, is as great a power as men can possess.

Ansermet exulted at being present at genesis. We are not far removed from genesis now, though far enough to feel the pressing burden of history. Until recently, jazz critics were engaged in evaluating potential classics; now we are just as likely to review interpretations of, remakes of, and homages to those classics. When I began writing, it was possible to see five of the jazz grandees mentioned above. Jazz sustains its allure in part because so much early history continues on parade. But the longer the parade grows the harder it is to find a place in line.

The trade of writing about music hasn't changed in the nearly 200 years since it became a journalistic sideline. The trick is still to find con-crete images to describe and appraise non-verbal art and the feelings it engenders while sustaining one's youthful ardor and openness—despite the mellowing or wisdom or crankiness or despair or revelation that comes with age. The death of jazz, movies, literature, and civilization is as confidently predicted as the end of the world and the second coming. Sidney Bechet, in his posthumous memoir, offered a more realistic credo: "You got to be in the sun to feel the sun. It's that way with music too." It's that way with everything. Criticism is often a battleground between empathy and disdain. A musician once complained that my work is too emotional. He's right. Much as I admire the writing of categorical intel-lectuals, feeling is the only arbiter I completely trust. Like everyone else, I aspired to join William James's tough-minded tribe—just as I deter-mined to be one of those who, in Bertrand Russell's dictum, braved the future rather than retreat to the past. It didn't work out that way: As a critic, I am chiefly an enthusiast mired in the past and reliant on sensibility. This confession is not an apology, just fair warning to anyone who wandered out of the rain into these pages.

A vigorous art deserves and requires a disputatious criticism. Better to be wrongheaded and punitive from time to time than reliably soft, predictable, and accommodating. But with the eradication of antitrust laws and the selling out of the FCC, not to mention the retailing of art to corporate interests (through an insidious extension of copyright protection for what amounts to perpetuity), jazz has all but disappeared from commercial TV and radio. I concluded some time ago that I could not justify using the space allotted me in the *Village Voice* or other venues to caution readers against records they've never heard of. Much of my time was spent searching for performances and recordings I liked well enough to explore in essay form and that exemplified the art's liveliness. As a result, enthusiasm became a safe harbor and disputation a matter of personal grousing, except once in a while, usually when covering festivals that guarantee excuses to pick nits.

This selection of moderately revised pieces from a period of nearly 14 years is the fourth drawn principally from the Weather Bird column I began writing for the *Voice* in 1974 and discontinued at the end of 2003; it follows *Riding on a Blue Note*, *Rhythm-a-ning*, and *Faces in the Crowd*. Policy changes altered the kind of work done there, and I found myself drawn to other projects, as I had been for much of the '90s. I have nothing but gratitude for the *Voice*, which allowed me free rein and paid me well to pursue a kind of writing no other publication permitted. I had a long run and few complaints.

When Bob Christgau initially asked me to write the column, I thought it would co-exist namelessly with other writings in *Music*. But, of course, it had to have its own heading; I objected to *Jazz* because I was too sensitive to the implication—rampant in those days—that jazz and music were mutually exclusive. Most universities with jazz programs then, and quite a few now, inserted them in Folklore, African American, and English departments, anything but Music. So I reasoned: Let the banner be something neutral and personal. I chose Weather Bird mainly because the Armstrong-Hines record's blending of humor and drama, finery and thrills, like-mindedness and canny aggression, and its uniqueness (even now, after more than 75 years) incarnates the essence and peculiar logic of jazz. Moreover, it is the greatest of all jazz duets, and I had thought of criticism as a dialogue between writer and reader—that's the way it seemed to me, reading the great critics, their impressions fueling my own. It came as quite a shock to discover that many readers think criticism is merely a sermon to which they are obliged to respond with huzzahs or catcalls. Like George Brent in *Jezebel*: "I like my convictions undiluted, same as I do my bourbon."

Dialogue aside, the name also served as a quadruple pun—signaling Armstrong, New Orleans funerals ("Flee as a Bird to the Mountain"), Charlie Parker (Bird), the god of postwar jazz; and Bob Dylan ("You don't need a weather man to know which way the wind blows"), the swami of my generation, which I had vainly sought to engage. Part One, covering the not very gay '90s, is called "The Beige Decade," a paraphrase of Thomas Beer's summa of the 1890s, *The Mauve Decade*, so titled, because—he explained, restating Whistler—his was a pink era trying to be purple. The beige decade was a time in which white tried to be black and vice versa, indicating a large stride toward Duke Ellington's "fantasy" of a common ground for black and tan.

During most of those years I worked on two books, a biography of Bing Crosby and *Visions of Jazz*, and consequently was often on halftime at or on sabbatical from the *Voice*. With the books finished, I was ravenous to resume my old regimen; the reader will note that Part Two, representing the work of three years, is almost as long as Part One. I hardly need add that I've selected pieces that seemed to me worth revisiting and suppressed those that were more ephemeral or should never have seeped through my modem. It was a mostly pleasant surprise to reread the jazz festival reviews, which I had initially not planned on including. One of my more frequent complaints about the JVC Jazz Festival is that it rarely succeeds in summarizing the state of things, yet in retrospect it often appears to have done precisely that, one way or another. If the triptych of Armstrong pieces in the last section seems to close a circle, given the foregoing remarks, that outcome was not intentional. I'm not sure what triggered the renewed obsession: his centenary, my Crosby research, Ken Burns and Geoffrey C. Ward's *Jazz*, and a liner note assignment all played a part. Though none of this work has appeared in book form before, other essays about many of the same artists have; I hope that in each instance I've come up with something new.

All but 16 pieces and the introduction originally appeared in the *Village Voice*, and are copyright V.V. Publishing Corporation and reprinted by permission. I am indebted to several *Voice* editors who presided over the work included here: Chuck Eddy, Eric Weisbard, Joe Levy, and Doug Simmons, as well as the Editor in Chief, Don Forst. I take this opportunity to thank Diane Fisher, who first brought me into the paper in 1973. Chiefly, I thank Robert Christgau, the editor of the vast majority of these pages. This book is in part dedicated to him—a gesture that can hardly convey the immense satisfaction of working with him for so many years.

I'm grateful to John Rockwell and Fletcher Roberts for asking me to write the pieces that appeared in the *Arts & Leisure* section of *The New York Times*. I thank Fred Kaplan for bringing me to the short-lived magazine *Fi* and *The Absolute Sound*, which published a few of these reviews. I was honored when Benny Carter asked me to write an appreciation for his Kennedy Center Honor, and more so when he gave me a rare interview. Seth Rothstein of Columbia/Legacy convinced me to write liner notes, and I'm glad he did. Four essays were commissioned for books, and I am grateful to their editors and publishers: Eric Weisbard asked me to deliver a paper at the 2002 Experimental Music Project symposium in Seattle, and shrewdly persuaded me to expand it for *This Is Pop* (Harvard University Press); Geoffrey Ward requested "Parajazz" for his invaluable companion to *Jazz* (Knopf); Robert Wilson and Stanley Marcus included Ellington in *American Greats* (Public Affairs); and Bea Friedland recruited the introduction to Eddie Condon's *We Called It Music* (Da Capo).

It's a lucky writer who gets to eulogize two of his editors while they continue to flourish—formal appreciations of Sheldon Meyer (for the *New York Times Book Review*) and Robert Christgau (for the festschrift *Don't Stop 'til You Get Enough*) will reappear in a subsequent volume of my essays. The one written on the occasion of Sheldon's retirement proved to be way premature. This is our fifth book together—one neither of us anticipated when we worked on *Visions of Jazz*. I am delighted, as ever, to acknowledge the splendid support of OUP, especially music editor Kim Robinson, and a staff that includes the venerable Joellyn Ausanka, Eve Bachrach, Woody Gilmartin, copyeditor Patterson Lamb, cover designer Kathleen Lynch, and publicist Jordan Bucher. I was honored to be photographed by Herman Leonard, the George Hurrell of jazz photography, an incomparable master of lighting and indefatigable companion, who provided a memorable sojourn in New Orleans; my thanks as well to his indispensable aides, Jenny Bagert, Elizabeth Underwood, and Annie Ripper. Thanks also to Michael Anderson, who convinced me to go memoir-heavy in the preceding pages, and Steve Futterman, who encouraged me to keep some of those that follow.

I am grateful to have my interests represented by Georges Borchardt, Inc., and thank Georges and Anne Borchardt and DeAnna Heindel for working so hard for such meager commissions. My assistant Elora Charles, a classics expert who doubles as muse ("Shouldn't you be working on, uh, something?"), has taught me more about Alexander the Great and other ancients than I thought I wanted to know. Norma Salfarlie brings order from chaos. I am lucky to be embedded in a small but close family, and owe more than gratitude to Norman and Helen Halper, Donna and Paul Rothchild and my nieces, Lee and Jenny Rothchild; and Ronnie Halper and Marc Donner and my nephew, Aaron Donner. This book is largely dedicated, along with everything I do, to three women. My mother, Alice Giddins, is a beacon of independence and a lifelong inspiration. Deborah Halper is the love of my life and the soul of my work, which she actually reads, exceeding all marital obligations. Lea Giddins, having entered high school, writes more than I do, and not only doesn't get paid for it but has to suffer the indignity of grading. Yet she helps me more than I do her. But for Debbie and Lea, I'd play hooky all the time.

G.G.
April 2004

PART ONE

❖

The Beige Decade, 1990–2000

1 ❖ Tender Moments
(JVC 1990)

I didn't attend many events at the JVC Jazz Festival this year, in part because of other commitments and in part because there wasn't much I wanted to hear. From what I saw, the staid schedule was given a lackluster presentation. My sense of foreboding was triggered opening night when I noticed that the usual program was replaced by a JVC brochure in which pride of place was given not to greetings from the "organizer," George Wein, but to the sponsor, JVC president Hiroshi Sano. The general absence of Wein at the concerts was also notable: His enthusiasm can usually be counted on to impart a touch of festiveness. Too many of the disc jockey announcers, on the other hand, recalled Zippy: Hey, kids, are we having fun yet? One of them obliviously advised the audience to attend an Oscar Peterson concert that had been canceled weeks earlier. The venues were troublesome as usual, excepting the marvelous Weill Recital Hall. Most nettlesome was the rudeness of latecomers who, per usual, were encouraged to flounce in whenever they liked. Still, there were tender moments even amid the chaos, and lessons to be gleaned.

Dizzy Gillespie and his United Nations All-Star Orchestra were preceded by Marcus Roberts and a band so repressed by its own dignity it might have been playing conservatory etudes. The best pieces were an Ellington blues and an original called "The Cat in the Hat Comes Back," which featured an exacting, vigorous trumpet solo by Scotty Barnhard, who alone seemed determined to get some sparks flying. Roberts himself was most engaging in an unaccompanied version of Monk's "Misterioso," with supple guitar-like washes and a brief stride interlude, and even then his touch was chilly. Contrast Gillespie, who floated out playing a miked trumpet while the orchestra asserted the various rhythmic figures of "Manteca," turning Carnegie Hall from blue to Caribbean red. Having announced his own preeminence in a characteristically jostling solo, combining introspective timbre and dazzling pyrotechnics, restoring the inclination to dance and revel, he served as host for the specialty numbers that followed—James Moody hurtling through Gillespie's Afrocentric "Kush" and his own "Moody's Mood for Love" (for which Dizzy sang the woman's part); Paquito D'Rivera employing clarinet and alto on a "Latin American Suite" that also showcased Slide Hampton, Claudio Roditi, and a rousing young pianist from Panama named Danilo Perez; Jon Faddis and Gillespie splitting the atom on "And Then She Danced" from Gillespie's undervalued album *Jambo Caribe*. Flora Purim dispelled the magic, but a conguero named Giovanni Hidalgo restored it. The sound was boxy.

The sound was exactly what it's supposed to be at Carnegie Hall the following evening for a flamboyant set by the World Saxophone Quartet. The absence of amplification allowed all the nuances and dynamics to resound the way the players intended. After the opening theme, "Steppin'," David Murray reached back to his gospel past for a dedication to Nelson Mandela, played over a rigorous vamp stated first in real time and then in double time by Hamiet Bluiett's baritone, while Oliver Lake and Arthur Blythe meshed their altos in response. Oliver took the lead on "Sittin' on the Dock of the Play," defining a backbeat so palpable you could hear the drums that weren't there; Bluiett showed off his extravagant command in a cadenza to "Sophisticated Lady," melding pianissimo undertones, popped keys, stentorian barks, and siren whistles (all in dramatic service to Ellington's melody), before the ensemble filled out the release. A cadenza by Blythe led into a fast, swing riff with diverse voicings and a free episode. Murray, backed by humming chords, played top to bottom on a ballad, working up an array of blazing harmonics. Together and individually, the WSQ makes the blood roar.

I appreciated the opportunity to hear, on the same bill, Steve Reich and his ensemble performing *Music for Mallet Instruments, Voices, and Organ* and *Music for 18 Instruments*, two pieces written in the mid-'70s. But I'm not eager to hear them again. Imagine Red Norvo's "Dance of the Octopus" played repeatedly for an hour. The subtle shifts in rhythmic figures and the glacial articulation—especially in the latter piece, which combined four voices, cello, violin, and two clarinets with rotating pianists and xylophonists—were intoxicating for minutes at a time, occasionally conveying the white light given off by Gregorian chant. Yet at length, the goal seemed to be to induce a trance, the last thing I want from music. At times, the ceaseless malletting suggested a confluence of drills, a visit to the dentist. Yet the blending of clarinets and strings was tantalizing; arrangers could do some happy fishing in this pond.

Perhaps the week's most exhilarating surprise took place in direct contravention to what was intended. "An Evening of American Song," at Town Hall, promised restrained interpretations of all the usual suspects. But Barbara Lea, who was supposed to sing Berlin, Gershwin, and Porter, switched to Vincent Youmans—for the most part, obscure Vincent Youmans at that; and Ruby Braff and Dick Hyman, who were scheduled to perform songs from *My Fair Lady*, did for a while, then switched to Fats Waller and James P. Johnson. Two acts makes for a long first set. Gerry Mulligan, who wasn't aware of the changes, came out after intermission and announced that since we'd been hearing all that Berlin,

Gershwin, and Porter, he'd play his own material—which is what he'd been scheduled to do all along. A few Tin Pan Alleycats grumbled, but not for long. Mulligan was in peak form as player and composer. He introduced several new pieces from an upcoming album that had the tangy lyricism and rhythmic gait of his best work, among them "Lonesome Boulevard," which has the solid ease of a country air; "A Gift for Dizzy," a heady samba; "Sun on Stairs," which combines swing riffs with a delicate release; and his latest and fastest train song, "The Flying Scotsman." His satiny, expressive timbre remains unrivaled on baritone, his improvisations as lucid and coherent as his themes.

Of Mulligan's older pieces, "Line for Lyons" ("written in 1910 by Jelly Roll Morton," the composer announced), one of the most enduring melodies to come out of the cool era, was exceptional. Mulligan began his solo accompanied by Dean Johnson's bass and built to a sequence of nimble fours with drummer Dave Ratajczak. Bill Charlap, an intense robust pianist who favors rigorous rhythmic figures and knuckle-busting clusters, proved his mastery of dynamics by following the tumult with a quiet solo of his own. On his autobiographical lament, "I Never Was a Young Man," Mulligan sang the rueful lyric and the mike went dead, as it had done repeatedly during Lea's set. Throwing his head back, he managed to fill the hall anyway, and mused afterward, "I'm probably the only singer on Broadway who's not miked." He ought to have been given an evening to himself, quartet for one set and big band for the other.

Evenings given over to Jim Hall and Stan Getz were agreeable, though each was sabotaged by strings, real and synthesized. Pat Metheny served charmingly as an informal host for Hall, noting on behalf of the many participating guitarists, "We can all trace the biggest parts of our styles to Jim." The tribute provided the most elliptical of stylists an opportunity to revive several of his musical associations from the past 30-plus years. With Ron Carter, he played "Alone Together" and "St. Thomas"; with Bob Brookmeyer, a medley of "Skylark" and "Begin the Beguine," which found the rarely heard valve trombonist's conversational tone, proliferating ideas, and long phrases fully intact; with Mulligan, "All the Things You Are" (contrapuntal and fresh) and "Prelude to a Kiss." Hall's clarity and economy, his sliding pitches and dense harmonies were buoyant throughout. The program's pace was fatally skewed by two extended works that combined string quartet with a jazz rhythm section—a piece Hall wrote in college and a more recent opus by Don Thompson. A third piece for strings and Gary Burton—Astor Piazzola's "Laura's Dream"— had a pleasing romantic edge, but little spontaneity. The subsequent guitar duets came alive twice: John Scofield joined Hall on the old Coleman

Hawkins showstopper, "Sancticity," an outstanding vehicle; and Metheny contrasted his rangy riffs with Hall's tranquil chime-like notes and snare-like strumming on Jobim's "Chega de Saudade." Incredibly, a battery of photographers whose cannon roar devastated one piece after another invaded the concert. One photographer explained that this was a producer's idea, to get shots for a forthcoming album cover. Sol Hurok is spinning.

Stan Getz alternated between playing with his superb quartet (Kenny Barron, Alex Blake, Terri Lyne Carrington) and the quartet augmented by two synthesizers, played by Eddie Del Barrio and Frank Zottoli. The latter were present to perform virtually his entire new album, *Apasionado*, written by Del Barrio, Herb Alpert, and Getz. Getz's comeback after serious illness is cause for celebration ("I'm too evil to die," he told Mel Lewis), and he performed with vigor and ingenuity, but the album is second-rate; only on a blues did he slice decisively through the caloric fake strings. The quartet pieces were something else, of course. *Apasionado* may sell better this year (though that remains to be seen), but his other new album, *Anniversary*, is the one that will take permanent place among the Getz benchmarks. When he returned to that material, he blazed—the famous Getz sound variously smoky and electrifying, his alliance with Kenny Barron even more developed than on the album. A couple of times, he called for the mikes to be turned off, but the grateful applause of the audience didn't deter him from having them turned back on as he returned to yet another selection from *Apasionado*. As a result, he never sustained the head of steam he can build on a great night. But he came damn close at the end, following a galvanizing "What Is This Thing Called Love?" with an impassioned "Blood Count."

The big surprise of the week was the appearance by pianist Sir Charles Thompson in the Weill Recital series. Thompson achieved a secure, individual approach in the '40s and '50s, notably on recordings with Coleman Hawkins and Jimmy Rushing—he had edited down a glossary of swing techniques to a spare style of acute melodic ideas. At 72, he chose to use his hour for a musical memoir, recalling his associations with Charlie Parker, Lester Young, Hawkins, and others, and showed how firmly rooted he is in the Tatum/Wilson/Waller tradition. He described his solo on Hawkins's "Stuffy" (a Thompson original) as "the first time someone heard me and thought it was me playing and not Count Basie." He incorporated lovely stride episodes in an Ellington-Strayhorn medley, showed off his bop (cum Garner) sensibility on "Stella by Starlight" and "All the Things You Are," and played the entire Basie arrangements of "April in Paris" and "One O'Clock Jump," before closing with his "claim to fame," "Robbins' Nest." It was an eminently civilized presentation, nostalgic and compelling at the same time, the sort of epiphany that should make a jazz festival feel good about itself the next morning.

[*Village Voice*, 24 July 1990]

2 ❖ *Front Porch Blues*
(Colorado 1990)

Early in the first afternoon of music at Dick and Maddie Gibson's 28th annual Colorado Jazz Party, I found myself especially looking forward to the sets with Herb Ellis, hoping to hear some blues. Even before the party was off to an official start, at the Friday night musicians' jam, he got off a few lucid 12-bar strophes that made me realize how hungry I was for that southwestern minor-third twang, the gospel according to Charlie Christian. Ellis's phrases have an easy, loping quality that whisks you along; they are buoyed by familiar dissonances yet surprisingly un-fogged by cliché.

The opening sets on Saturday afternoon usually smack of warm-up time, and so it was when Snooky Young and Urbie Green played a duet on "When Your Lover Has Gone" and Flip Phillips and Kenny Davern followed with "Hindustan." It was when those same players, plus a rhythm section including Ellis, went into "Blues Walk," however, that the stakes went up a notch. Ellis let loose one chorus after another, grunt-ing in unison with his solo, his eyes shut and mouth distorted by the divine afflatus. Years ago people talked about his technical agility—this was the guy who nightly traded body blows with Oscar Peterson and earned a niche in the studios. But the most winning quality of his playing all Labor Day weekend was simplicity of technique and a corresponding inflation of feeling.

During a subsequent set, when Ellis sidled out of the verse to "The More I See You" into a backbeat pocket for the chorus, Maddie Gibson suggested his playing might reflect a salutary move, two years ago, from L.A. to Arkansas. I've never seen Arkansas, let alone his home, so there was nothing to stop me from imagining him just a-settin' and a-rockin' on his front porch, his knee crossed high on the other leg, unfurling blues choruses until the strings got too hot to touch. That was the image sug-gested when he laid back in his chair, face clenched, for a molasses-slow "Georgia on My Mind" and a chipper "Sweet Georgia Brown," backed by Bob Haggart's bass and Bruno Carr's drums. On another set, he joined with Carr, Major Holley, and pianist Roger Kellaway, but signaled them to lay out as he triggered a pumping, stop-time solo. When Kellaway got knee-deep into his own solo, Ellis motioned for bass and drums to drop out again, and countered Kellaway's flamboyance with his own bass line and choked chords. They were rocking.

In the early 1960s, when I first became enamored of jazz guitar, I got the wrong idea about Ellis, who will be 70 next August. His one slick and negligible effort with Charlie Byrd for Columbia was enough to put me off: Since I wasn't an Oscar Peterson fan, I failed to excavate there for early Ellis; and since his own albums for Verve and Epic (sessions with Buddy Tate and Stuff Smith) were out of catalogue—many still are—it remained for the Gibson parties, which I first attended in 1975, and the Concord Jazz series he began recording around the same time, to disabuse me of my prejudice. It's ironic, because for me, in the depths of my ignorance, the lineage of jazz guitar was pretty narrow—Christian to Barney Kessel (especially the Contemporary albums with the elusive flutist Marvin Jenkins) to Wes Montgomery, who had not yet sold out. If anyone had a stake in that lineup, it was Ellis, who came from Farmersville, Texas, and who, notwithstanding an apprenticeship with a couple of dim dance bands, was one of the first to build on Christian's accomplishment. But we are all victimized by the records that aren't available. Fortunately, Concord appears to be preparing everything for CD; look out for *Soft and Mellow, Montreux Summer 1979* (which has a characteristic "Georgia on My Mind"), and especially the neglected jewel, *Rhythm Willie*, in which Freddie Green chomps away at the rhythm, freeing Ray Brown to engage Ellis on his own linear turf. Verve and Epic need to air their archives, and someone ought to get Ellis into a studio now for a whole session of front-porch blues.

The Gibson weekends—some 35 hours of jam session music in three days—always revive my energy. This year Dick produced it in association with his youngest son, Josh, though Maddie helped as well. Having missed it last year, I was mildly surprised by two changes in the sociology of Denver. (1) Smoking was banned from the ballroom where the music is played. (2) Drinking is now permitted on Sunday nights. The wisdom of those priorities enhanced the music, which follows a fairly predictable evolutionary arc over the three days.

On Saturday, most of the pleasures are provided by individual solos, whether featured or in the midst of roaring vehicles by seven- or eight-piece bands. On Sunday, the ensemble begins to subsume the soloists, the sum dilating way beyond the parts. It's at that moment that the short hairs on the back of your neck certify the total transcendence of jam session music. On Monday, invariably the payoff day, individuals and ensemble are in perfect accord and revelations are commonplace. I suspect the change has something to do with the gradual equalizing of so many different musicians. At first you have 60 players, mostly from New York and California, but from several other places as well, reflecting a medley of backgrounds and career choices, from club circuit stardom to studio anonymity; from blues, swing, bop, stride, and traditionalism; from as far back as 1905 (Doc Cheatham) to at least as recently as 1954 (Scott Hamilton). A day later, most such distinctions have been abandoned and you have five-dozen musicians dealing with the present moment.

A few set pieces broke up the usual routine of small instrumental bands. Joe Williams was on hand as boy singer, fronting a handpicked group: Harry Edison, Snooky Young, Bill Berry, Jerome Richardson, and a tenor terror who never gets East, Red Holloway, in the front line; and Ross Tompkins, John Heard, and Panama Francis out back. Williams was in good voice and of stirring mettle, breaking up a regimen of blues, including "In the Evening" and "Shake, Rattle and Roll," with occasional ballads, and actually managed to outrage several people with the single-entendre lyrics of "Who She Do." Since neither the Gibsons nor Williams are funded by the NEA, they have nothing to worry about.

Peanuts Hucko was asked to choose 15 musicians for a Benny Goodman repertory band, and, while the leader felt obliged to apologize for severe limitations in rehearsal time, he might well have boasted about the shine they brought to the material. Most of the arrangements were by the Henderson brothers, plus well-chosen ringers by Mel Powell ("Oh, Baby"), Mary Lou Williams ("Camel Hop"), Eddie Sauter ("Scarecrow"), and Claude Hopkins ("I Would Do Anything for You"), as well as a Bob Haggart chart written to feature Irving Fazola during their days in the Bob Crosby band. Highlights included Phil Woods swaggering through "I Found a New Baby," Dan Barrett interpreting the Lou McGarity stop-time solo on "String of Pearls," and various chorus and half-chorus epics by Hucko, Randy Sandke, Warren Vaché, and Bob Cooper, whose resplendently cool tenor reflected more than a touch of ghostly Al Cohn heat. The one grievous lapse came during "Sing Sing Sing," when pianist Paul Smith decided to burlesque the great Jess Stacy solo. Smith generally tends to go for laughs, perhaps to disguise his execrable time (one musician said of Smith after another set, "He was three beats off the entire piece. Every time he hit four, we were still pedaling through one, two, and three"), but his usual litany of corny quotes was particularly vulgar in the midst of an otherwise persuasive performance.

Benny Powell and Buddy Tate, recent survivors of serious illness, played two of the most poignant solos. Powell, who was hospitalized most of last year for a kidney ailment, thanked everyone for sending cards and gifts, and ended, "I better shut up before I start crying." He transmuted the tears in a boldly imaginative "But Beautiful," the tone a tad wider than usual, but the ideas luminous and decisive, the drama prudently controlled. Tate is one of jazz's supermen, rebounding from one calamity after another (most recently a car accident), his Texas cry remaining untarnished. On "Billie's Bounce" and a featured solo on "Just Friends," his tenor roared: If the phrases seemed shorter, the time and resonance were yeoman—passionate, authoritative, swinging, and crested with patented shouts and moans, keeling down from the upper register. He played a duet with Scott Hamilton ("All of Me")—their first in two years—and the lockstep unison was gripping.

The two comedians of the weekend were Marty Grosz, whose canny guitar solos and vocals (he sings like Fats Waller) were preceded by straight-faced monologues, including one about a society band contractor, Bullets Auchincloss, who produces tea dances at Sing Sing (you had to be there); and Peter Appleyard, the Canadian vibraphonist and Goodman alum, who did spot-on impressions of Red Norvo, Terry Gibbs, Lionel Hampton, and Milt Jackson (in shades and listing way to the right).

Standout performances abounded: Benny Carter, unperturbed by a surge of arthritis in his neck, making "Misty" sound novel (no one else, not even Sarah Vaughan, not even Erroll Garner could do that) and "Out of Nowhere" sound easy; Phil Woods delivering an impassioned "Prelude to a Kiss" and exchanging blistering figures with Roland Hanna on "The Song Is You"; Slide Hampton, perhaps the most underrated bebop virtuoso soloist alive, approaching familiar material like "Body and Soul," "My Funny Valentine," and "Laura" with gambits so wily you didn't know what he was into until he'd already played a chorus of variations; the imperturbably personal Jimmy Knepper, inspired by or undeterred by Hampton's "Laura," following with one of his own; Kenny Davern elaborating the climaxes on "St. Louis Blues" (paced by Herb Ellis slapping the fret board), and chiming with Bob Wilber, whose own penchant for drama was realized with a painstaking "Memories of You"; Nick Brignola cheerfully transforming "Blues in the Closet," backed only by bassist Major Holley; plus Bob Cooper's mentholated "We'll Be Together Again," Scott Hamilton's shaded "Chelsea Bridge," Al Grey's mischievous "Don't Blame Me," and on and on. I've said nothing about the rhythm players, so I'll close with two words of rejoicing: Alan Dawson.

[*Village Voice*, 2 October 1990]

3 ❖ Chippin' Off the Old Block
(Javon Jackson)

Tenor saxophonist Javon Jackson was a 22-year-old student at the Berklee College of Music when he auditioned for Art Blakey in 1987. Blakey took him on, and three years later, when the roving graduate program known as the Jazz Messengers came to an end, Jackson had seniority among the band's sidemen. Tracing his early development on records is a gratifying game of cat and mouse. For one thing, his improvisations are short and efficient (he hasn't the time to outwear his welcome), and for another, he has crafted a cagey style from readily identifiable gambits associated with Sonny Rollins and Joe Henderson, among others. You keep waiting for an authoritative leap, a departure that lets you know the gifted student is now on his own road, and you get plenty of indications. Compare his solos on the title tracks of Blakey's *Not Yet* (Black Saint, 1988) and *Chippin' In* (Timeless, 1990). The former, five choruses long, starts with two modulated riffs, expands with Rollinsesque triplets and a fluent navigation through the low register, and finishes with a whirling Hendersonian arpeggio. It's a fine solo, but you can practically see the wheels turning.

On *Chippin' In*—not only the title track but also "Brain Stormin'," "Byrd Flight," "Love Walked In," and even "Kay Pea," where he applies Rollins's craggy low-end attack to the hypnotic midrange permutations of Prestige-era Coltrane—the influences are consolidated. You can still isolate the Rollins turnback or the Henderson riff-pattern, but his idiomatic control is richer—rhythmically halting units lead to flowing phrases gracefully draped over the chords at a precipitous tempo. The stylistic development on "Chippin' In" reverses that of "Not Yet," beginning with Henderson-like bluster and coming to earth with the short, charged, thematic figures reminiscent of Rollins. Yet the solo has a logic and vitality that comes from inside, which is one reason after you hear it, you want to hear it again. Within months, he went beyond that, as demonstrated by a quintet he introduced at the short-lived New York jazz club, Time Jazz, in February.

The musicians assembled for that engagement embody a shorthand history of hard bop, the style that dominates today's mainstream jazz. The old man of the group is Louis Hayes, who, having served with the Adderleys, Horace Silver, and Freddie Hubbard, is the drummer most identified with the idiom after Blakey himself. The band's baby, about whom much will be heard, is 20-year-old bassist Christian McBride (who has played with Hubbard and Benny Golson), the possessor of fleet fingers and a pre-amplifier-age tone that bounces off all the walls. In between are two more Blakey alums. The robust pianist James Williams taught at Berklee before his four-year stint as a Messenger, beginning in 1977, and has an admirable reputation for generously encouraging young musicians. Brian Lynch, a great section player who alternates between the jazz and Latin scenes, made his name with Horace Silver and played with most of New York's big bands before bringing his virtuosic Clifford Brown–inspired trumpet to the last edition of the Messengers.

Small wonder that the band clicked. The leader initiated two especially memorable dramas—the first on the immortal test piece for tenor saxophonists, "Body and Soul," which Jackson began working on in Denver, where he grew up and started playing clubs at 16. After an eight-bar cadenza, he charted the melody with his broad dark sound, spirited tremolos, and a persuasive lyric bite. Ballads always come late for even the most gifted jazz players—Jackson's version of "You've Changed" on the final Blakey album, *One for All* (A&M), is his most awkward moment on records, though he shines when the tempo picks up after the theme statement and he's on his own—and on "Body" his tone occasionally veered a bit flat. Yet his hefty sound and steady gait kept the chorus on track. Williams came in with a diverting riff and then picked out melody notes with such authority and power (including locked-hands harmony for a couple of bars) that when Jackson returned, sustaining the brighter tempo, he was plainly aroused. As Hayes supported him with finessed waves, he began with a discursive reference to "Blues in the Night" and swaggered—Rollins's headiness very much in the air—into a sustained closing cadenza built on the materials of the song yet capped with a reference to "The March of the Children" from *The King and I*.

That hard bop isn't nearly as monolithic as its detractors used to complain was made vitally clear on an ebullient version of Rollins's blues, "Tenor Madness." The three soloists took it in three different directions. Jackson roared, building his early choruses on discrete riffs, then generating longer phrases, bopping naturally between the lower and middle registers. Lynch likes to turn the rhythm around, displacing accents, and he succeeded to the extent that it was hard to hear the up beats; he superimposed his own time over that of the rhythm section, but he never got lost and, as Jack Webb says in *Pete Kelly's Blues*, they finished together. Williams focuses as hard on coherent phrases as on the chords, so that the harmonic structure is subordinated to his long and intense melodic figures. His firm touch makes the piano ring, and his use of rhythmic patterns in the bass augments everything he does in the treble. Also memorable were a "Star Eyes," complete with the old Walter

Bishop Jr. intro and an effective contrapuntal tenor-trumpet finale; and Jackson's "Kay Pea," on which Lynch once again juggled the beat and Williams opposed the ardor of his linear phrases with concentrated open fourths. McBride's spacious sound (all wood, all natural) and Hayes's diplomatic snare work never failed them.

Jackson is a shy, modest man and in some respects a shy, modest player. His best solos are crystal in design and geometrical in their logic; you can follow them easily, because he plots them with deliberation, never screaming when a murmur will do, never speeding when the traffic is already flowing. It is a remarkable thing to encounter a young musician who has nothing to prove except the ability to craft a telling improvisation, and in doing so reminding us that that's accomplishment enough.

[*Village Voice*, 12 February 1991]

4 ❖ *Heavy Mettle Thunder (Ronald Shannon Jackson)*

The trouble with most fusion is that nothing ever really fuses. A few surface aspects of jazz and rock are tacked together in a highly calculated manner that only confirms the suspicion that jazz-rock is more often than not an oxymoron—an exceedingly dull one at that. As a movement, fusion is to music what melting-pot civics is to sociology. Which is, I suppose, why it has a huge popular following and a minute body of critical confirmation. A unique situation: Fusion has been with us for a quarter of a century, twice as long as the Swing Era, but virtually all commentary is focused on things like equipment and technique or nostalgia. Yet one recalls, and even revisits, some of the rousing beginnings—Tony Williams's *Emergency!* (blemished by the leader's decision to sing), and the crushing sound-storms created by Miles Davis and John McLaughlin—and wonders anew at how its potential could so quickly be sapped of vitality and innovation.

And then there was that wholly surprising incursion of the harmolodic forces marshaled by Ornette Coleman. Suddenly the prophet of free jazz was notating parts for electric guitars and basses with the same meticulous zeal with which he had composed for chamber groups and symphony orchestra. The result was genuine fusion, in that you could not identify the generic parts, let alone separate them. The sound proved no more alluring to the masses than Coleman's original assaults on musical conventions, but he did generate a voluminous critical patronage. *Dancing in Your Head* was that rarest of birds, a new sound: Nothing like it had ever been heard before. Critics on both sides of the aisle recognized that and found something congenital to applaud. Coleman went far beyond the initial spurt with *Of Human Feelings, Song X, In All Languages*, and *Virgin Beauty*. Yet instead of expanding, his audience—critics and public alike—seemed to abate. He carved his own following from the larger tribes without winning over the mainstream in jazz or rock. Which wasn't surprising. His music was visionary and absolute and hard, too new to pass as anyone's idea of fusion. You could not smell the glue or see the nuts and bolts.

The two primary beneficiaries of Coleman's Prime Time band, James Blood Ulmer and Ronald Shannon Jackson, went further still. Something about the clashing wall-to-wall harmonies admitted all kinds of possibilities. When Ulmer created his masterpiece, *Odyssey*, everyone could distinguish the dense tableaux, the elements of jazz improvisation and rock rhythms, yet the result most often sounds like country music—the real thing, from down yonder. That recording remains an isolated gem; Columbia dumped Ulmer shortly after it was released, and none of his subsequent albums have had comparable impact. I suspect it would have remained isolated even if he had been able to turn out a whole series of follow-ups. Like Coleman, who returns to the fray only when he has something new, Ulmer has not been one for facile repeats. The same is true of Jackson, who, as expected, has devoted the most attention to the music's rhythms. His records throughout the '80s and '90s suggest a steady evolution in dealing with issues as mundane as sound engineering and as substantial as viable instrumentation and the coordination of composition and improvisation.

Jackson is an astounding drummer, as everyone agrees. In the muscularity of his playing, his scrupulous control of every skin and cymbal, his mathematician's ken for subdivision, and his capacity to draw on historic and international traditions of percussion, he has emerged as a kind of all-purpose new-music connoisseur who brings a profound and unshakably individual approach to every playing situation. Considering the wallop he added to recordings by Coleman, Ulmer, Cecil Taylor, and Last Exit, it's surprising he isn't entreated to do more free-lance work and that he remains relatively little known to musicians and fans who think Dave Weckl is God's own drummer. Well, maybe *Red Warrior* (Axiom) will help to change all that. It has the air of a breakthrough; all the elements have been refined and simplified, at least on the surface. No saxophones, no violins. The instrumentation is three guitars, two basses, and drums. In truth, the record sounds at first blush like heavy metal for intellectuals. I'd expect it to have greater appeal for the readers of *Guitar Player* than of *Down Beat*. Though if, like Coleman and Ulmer, he can amass only the audience he has created for himself, he'll end up with a more discerning crowd of his own.

You can spin the disc in one of two ways, and it's wise to give each a chance. At modest volume, the fastidiousness of the writing—Jackson is melodic without quite being lyrical—and the shape of the six pieces, as well as the variations of the guitar soloists, come across in a deft and non-threatening way. Give it the juice it deserves and clearly expects and *Red Warrior* will shake your home and everyone in the vicinity. At the center of each piece are Jackson's unanticipated changeups in the rhythm patterns—he divides, subdivides, and turns around the beat in so many ways you don't want to even try and count along. Let the musicians worry about that; they're getting paid to do it. Still, you can't miss the implacable conviction of his backbeats—now on the fourth beat, now the first, now on the second beat of alternate measures. On "Elders," every beat is a backbeat during the intro, then each of those is quartered; after a brief storm of *Ascension*-dimensions, followed by a muted guitar riff tapped with all the emotion of Morse code, he effects an incredibly spry and jumping swing riff on the snare, which, after a disarming bass solo, builds to an aroused rock-arrogant crescendo by the ensemble, which leads to a solo by the Fireball.

I don't know who of the three guitarists the Fireball is (the CD has no liner notes or solo information), but that's my shorthand for the guitarist who favors lots of reverb and overtones. I suspect he's Steve Salas, who plays with a rock band called Colorcode and was Jackson's guest on this session. The other guitarists are Jef Lee Johnson and Jack DeSalvo, and the bassists are Ramon Pooser and Conrad Mathieu. The title piece, an attractive eight-to-the bar power riff, gives each guitarist a solo (the Fireball last, of course), and their diversity underscores the album's improvisational variety. Two of them are heard in a canonical theme statement on "Ashes," to which Jackson soon adds a backbeat that has a punch reminiscent of Jimmy Crawford's bass drum in the 1930s Jimmie Lunceford band—which is to say, you feel it in the gut. Nothing is harder to sustain than a slow blues, and—though "Gate to Heaven" is festooned with the usual change-ups—the passages in which Jackson whacks alternate second beats while sustaining a shuffle rhythm have insuperable authority. He evens out the rhythm as he brightens the tempo, and, after the Fireball scrapes the frets, reprises the slow and ardent two-beat.

It's difficult to avoid the thought that *Red Warrior* would find an entirely different audience if the leader was white and 25 instead of black and twice that. On the other hand, if that were the case, the record would have been released on a rock label and I'd probably never know it existed. Strange the ways genrefication is still determined by racism, ageism, social class, and the vagaries of record distribution.

[*Village Voice*, 26 February 1991]

5 ❖ *Go Wes, Young Man (Mark Whitfield)*

You can't help but suspect that much of the delayed interest generated by Mark Whitfield, the talented 23-year-old no-frills jazz guitarist who made his Village Vanguard debut last week, is related to the surprising fact that he records for Warner Bros. I mean, how many critics, having registered the label affiliation, scanned the cover photos on his first album, *The Marksman* (young and clean-cut, brown suit and tasseled loafers, no socks, crouching or leaping, guitar at the ready, in quasi–Chuck Berry poses), and tossed it into the maybe-three-weeks-from-Thursday-if-nothing-else-comes-out-in-the-interim pile? Arriving from a company that construes jazz as stylish background music, which is to say polite fusion or, worse, Quincified sampling, Whitfield is as confounding as an IBM researcher who preaches the merits of the pencil: "Inexpensive and portable, doesn't require electricity or a printer, makes instant corrections and, with practice, can be moved as fast as a cursor. Could be *the* writing implement for the '90s."

Born on Long Island (legit bass in the school band), relocated to Seattle (jazz guitar in the school band), and polished around the edges at the Berklee School, Whitfield was discovered by George Benson, who may have heard something of his own younger self in Whitfield's traditional approach, taut electric sound, fluent chords, and enthusiasm. In a fascinating new instruction book for guitarists that can be read by civilians as well, *Exploring Jazz Guitar* (Hal Leonard), Jim Hall recalls students pumping John Lewis at the School of Jazz in Lenox, Massachusetts, about how they could make a living at jazz: Lewis responded, "Wait a minute! You've got it backwards. Being able to play jazz is your reward. There is no other pay-off." Whitfield plays as if he felt well rewarded. He's got a trick bag that includes fast strumming, parallel octaves, hard plucking, edgy riffs, and fierce double-timing, but his hole card is clarity.

Just how good he is became more apparent from his opening night at the Vanguard than from the record, or, more precisely, from a comparison between the two. Whitfield has come a long way in a year. He played several selections from the album, but with an earned mark-up in clout and radiance. Not that the album doesn't sustain a charm of its own. It accurately defines his thoroughly traditional repertoire, which consists almost exclusively of blues and ballads. (His first major gig was with organist Jack McDuff, who also gave Benson his initial shove; like Benson, Whitfield's playing is far too urbane to remain at ease in that restrictive genre.) Of the disc's six originals, "The Blues, From Way Back" is what it says, if you accept c. 1959 as "way back"; "Little Digi's Strut" is another 12-bar blues, but in eight; "The Marksman" and "Medgar Evers' Blues" cannily build on 16-bar constructions, the first in AABA song form, but both with the addition of eight-bar tag figures; "A Long Way from Home" and "Namu" are ballads. All three of the disc's standards were written by big band leaders: "The Very Thought of You" (Ray Noble), "In a Sentimental Mood" (Duke Ellington), and "No Greater Love" (Isham Jones).

The album suffers from sameness of tempo—after the opener, which is the title track, medium-up is about as heady as Whitfield gets. When he really comes alive—doubling time on "The Marksman," assembling dynamic riffs on "The Blues, From Way Back" and "Medgar Evers' Blues," displaying deft voicings on "In a Sentimental Mood" (somewhat reminiscent of George Van Eps) and "Namu"—he disarms you with his cool assurance. But live, he also exhibited a raw energy and a discerning lyricism that cut much deeper. Perhaps the most revealing performance was of Ray Noble's great song, "The Very Thought of You," which is merely efficient in the recorded version. The Cambridge-educated Noble is an unjustly eclipsed figure whose 1930s orchestras succeeded on both sides of the Atlantic; some of his songs proved especially appealing to musicians in the postwar era, including "I Hadn't Anyone Till You," "The Touch of Your Lips," and Charlie Parker's mantra, "Cherokee." "The Very Thought of You" is likely the best of them, a perfectly crafted melody that has always sat well with bass-baritone crooners (Arthur Prysock did it right), though perhaps the definitive version is the one Tony Bennett and Bobby Hackett recorded (on the former's *A Time for Love*). In the club, Whitfield established an unerring legato backbeat and picked the melody so gently he seemed to be discovering the tune's ascending cadences for the first time. Thirties ballads are now so old they're new, but musicians who can make you hear them as new are scarce. Even 25 years ago, you didn't often encounter such economy, patience, and respect for song in musicians as young as Whitfield.

He was born in the same period that took the lives of John Coltrane and Wes Montgomery; like Wynton Marsalis, whom he credits with "guidance" as well as for the use of his rhythm section on the album, Whitfield combines an appealing button-down candor with an arresting sense of accomplishment, in his person as well as his playing, that confuses the radicals because it appeals to the wrong people for the wrong reasons as well as the right ones. I find myself increasingly impatient with those who dismiss the conservatives who dismiss free jazz, just as I am with those who rant against free jazz or swing or bop or jazz repertory. The byword in the 1970s was eclecticism; maybe eclecticism in its mature phase is authenticity. In any case, the music itself is now so diverse that you don't see individuals spreading themselves as thin as they were wont to do back then. Whitfield is nothing if not authentic. My goodness, he opened the set with his way-back blues, even slower than on the record, wasting not a note and taking his time as though he had long since passed that stage when he might have felt the need to prove anything to anybody.

The blues bring out a lyric bite in Whitfield's playing, although the shape of his solos isn't innovative: He works up a riff for eight bars and goes for melodic resolution in the next four. But he's so sure about where he's going, and his timing is so good, you find yourself trusting him and paying increasingly close attention. His smooth tone recalls Montgomery and Benson, even Jimmy Raney and Kenny Burrell, but he mixes it up with personalized gambits—knuckle-busting double-time riffs that deserve the applause they invariably get, and brash strumming, often without a pick, Wes-style. Montgomery had a programmatic approach to solos—linear phrases often configured in octaves, followed by chords. On "Freddie Freeloader" (he also played "Bye Bye Blackbird," confirming the doctrine that every musician under 60 has memorized at least two albums by Miles Davis), Whitfield reversed the order and began with fast chords, almost as though he were warming up for the single-note improv that followed. He climaxed with an ardent riff that made his fingers a blur and had the audience cheering.

What's more, he's got a congenial band that shares his ability to dramatize slow blues. Pianist Peter Martin waited out the slower tempos, choosing his direction succinctly, though he was occasionally intrusive on the faster pieces. Tarus Mateen is the second bassist I've heard in as many months (Christian McBride was the first) who plays deep and dark in the low register, the Paul Chambers register, preferring an earthy four to the skittery virtuoso approach that has virtually dominated the instrument since the early '60s. And drummer Billy Kilson gets a hard chomping sound on the ride cymbal, fires up the turnbacks, and moves almost imperceptibly between his sticks and brushes in shading Whitfield's shifts from thumb to pick, or chords to single notes. The Vanguard hasn't seen the last of these guys. And if Warner treats his records (a second one has been planned) as more than a favor to George Benson, it might open the door for other players who play for the elation of playing. It won't be the first time, incidentally. Warner Bros. actually put out several good albums in the '50s and, on Reprise, in the '60s; the former may be the only domestic jazz series that has never been reissued. Well, I'm sure Quincy is working to rectify that even as we speak.*

[*Village Voice*, 19 March 1991]

*Not quite: To no one's great surprise, Whitfield's second album for Warner was a pop album that did nothing for his career but dim the ardor of his admirers. Realizing that the company did not have his best interests at heart, he switched to Verve, determined, he told me, to make it as "a straight-ahead jazz player."

6 ❖ *Jazz Danish*
(The Jazzpar Concert)

Denmark is neither the most nor least surprising nation in the world to sponsor the first international jazz prize. It has enjoyed direct contact with black music's perceived threat to European values since the first minstrel troupes visited almost 130 years ago. In the 1890s, Copenhagen was host to the Fisk Jubilee Singers and a black opera company; in 1903, Sousa brought over the cakewalk. Yet for half a century, at least until the 1920s, this famously liberal country, which behaved so bravely during the World War II occupation, shared the typical European paranoia about black music, characterizing it as the product of savages and worse. In his three-volume *Jazz i Danmark*, published in 1982 with a summary chapter in English, Erik Wiedemann identifies five myths that shaped the reception of jazz in Denmark: (1) racism—its creators were "sub-human"; (2) chauvinism—jazz, being primitive and exotic, represented a threat to European culture; (3) reverse racism—jazz can only be played by blacks because they are born with it; (4) biological democracy—jazz is a "natural" music because "everyone is born with it"; (5) aesthetic—jazz is folk, not art, music.

Although Denmark produced talented jazz players as early as 1924, when the first Danish jazz records were made, and had a resident big band (under the leadership of saxophonist Kai Evans) by 1927, general mastery of the music was resisted and delayed. According to Wiedemann, conservatory-trained musicians felt compromised by the technical and emotional demands of jazz and could not accept its revolutionary aesthetics as a western phenomenon. All the myths, as well as the reluctance to endorse jazz on its own terms, were exploded in the 1940s. The Nazis had a lot to do with it.

During the five years of the occupation, concerts by Danish jazz musicians proliferated, in part because of German injunctions against jazz, which thus came to symbolize resistance. From 1933, Wiedemann writes, "advocating jazz became part of the politics of anti-fascist culture." Worse, as far as the Nazis were concerned, Danes regularly sought news from the BBC, not Danish State Radio, which was then under German control. Since the early 1960s, Danish Radio, with its Radiojazzgruppen and Radioens Big Band, has been internationally celebrated for its work in jazz—Mercer Ellington named it as the repository for his father's unreleased music. But until the war, Danish Radio snubbed jazz. The Nazis changed that in 1944, forcing the station to offer jazz broadcasts in the vain hope of drawing listeners away from the BBC.

After the liberation, however, the jazz boom fizzled and Danish musicians who had become prominent in those years—violinist Svend Asmussen, pianist-singer Leo Mathisen, guitarist-bassist-trombonist Niels Foss, early bop trombonist Peter Rasmussen, Kaz Timmermann's Harlem Kiddies quintet—found themselves playing abroad more often than at home. Mathisen, a humorous performer who modeled his style after Fats Waller's, was reduced to playing lounge piano. Asmussen might have achieved stardom in the U.S., except that on the two occasions when Benny Goodman tried to bring him over, immigration refused him a visa. So what happened? Once again jazz in Denmark, now closely identified with the horrors and affronts of the occupation, was undermined by nonmusical factors. After the liberation, audiences no longer wanted to hear a music that reminded them of the dark days. Serious jazz lovers moved onto bebop; the general public went elsewhere.

In a way, the Jazzpar is also a response to nonmusical factors. The Scandinavian Tobacco Company created the prize after the Danish government banned cigarette advertising. The sponsor keeps a low profile at Jazzpar events. As Dan Morgenstern noted at the 1991 Jazzpar concert, after announcing next year's candidates, "We don't have anything like this in the United States, but if we did, you can bet the sponsor's name would be all over the stage, all over the music stands, all over everything." There were no women handing out sample weeds as in the days when Kool sponsored George Wein's New York festival. Of greater significance, the company exerted no influence on the jurors.

The event is unique in many ways. The Jazzpar is the only international jazz award; the jury for the first three years consisted of two Americans and three Europeans, plus Arnvid Meyer, the non-voting director of the Danish Jazz Center who presides, usually in silence, over the meetings. The monetary award, about $35,000 this year, makes it the biggest jazz prize in the world, and is exclusive of travel and other expenses incurred in performing and eventually recording the programs, which thus far have consisted primarily of new work. The Jazzpar itself is a statuette created by Jorgen Haugen Sorensen; the original is a huge sculpture on display in Copenhagen's Falkoner Centret, where the main concert takes place. The first recipient, in 1990, was Muhal Richard Abrams. This year David Murray was chosen by a committee made up of Morgenstern and myself (U.S.), Philippe Carles (France), Bert Noglik (Germany), and Wiedemann. (Don Cherry, Jackie McLean, Martial Solal, and Randy Weston were the other 1991 nominees.) One key stipulation is that the recipient perform with Danish bandleaders who may select additional international soloists. Those bands were selected by a Danish committee consisting of Wiedemann, Boris Rabinowitsch, and Ib Skovgaard.

The March 13 concert in Copenhagen (repeated in Odense and Aarhus) began with the Jens Winther Quintet featuring Al Foster. Winther, a 31-year-old trumpeter now living in New York, opened with a glacial cadenza of sustained rubato notes. As Foster kicked in on the toms and cymbals, it became a medium-tempo "Alone Together." He followed with two originals, "Peace Piece" (no relation to Bill Evans's) and "Scorpio Dance," which ably contrasted the leader's plush, laconic trumpet and the stormier arpeggiated style of tenor saxophonist Tomas Franck. The second band was something to write home about. Jasper Thilo, the Danish Radio Big Band's most admired soloist (he's also recorded a fine series of albums with Al Grey, Kenny Drew, and especially Harry Edison), put together a quintet with guest Hank Jones, who arrived the morning of the performance but glittered nonetheless. Most European jazz communities reflect the influence of the key American soloists who have toured or lived with them. Denmark learned saxophone from Coleman Hawkins in 1935 and Benny Carter in 1936. During the next 50 years, the country grew rich in American expatriate musicians, including Don Byas, Oscar Pettiford, Stan Getz, Ben Webster, Dexter Gordon, Horace Parlan, Brew Moore, Thad Jones, Ed Thigpen, and Doug Raney. The Thilo group reflects all this.

Thilo's tenor sax is squarely in the Hawkins-Webster-Byas tradition, warm and lush, lyrical and relaxed. Bassist Hugo Rasmussen has a huge thumping sound in the style of Pettiford, and guitarist Doug Raney, son of Jimmy Raney, has a deft, muted sound strikingly reminiscent of his father's. Thilo opted for a smart menu of standards from jazz and pop, including "You Leave Me Breathless," "Lover Come Back to Me," and "Tin Tin Deo." A reading of "Thou Swell" was reminiscent of the version the senior Raney recorded with Getz. But it was Jones who quietly hustled off with every number, changing from linear phrases to chords and back throughout "Chelsea Bridge," pumping up the action to a rollicking finish on "Shiny Stockings" (he and Thilo doubled time just enough to generate adrenalin), and displaying flowery open harmonies and broken chords on his patented arrangement of "Oh, What a Beautiful Morning."

The band invited to accompany Murray was Pierre Dorge's New Jungle Orchestra, an inspired choice. Dorge plays guitar and what the Art Ensemble used to call "little instruments." His compositions range over the international palette with particular attention to Africa and America, and are often transmuted by an epic, melancholy Scandinavian fervor. The New Jungle Orchestra averages 10 musicians (John Tchicai used to be a mainstay) and Dorge's music includes an impressive interpretation of *Peer Gynt* as well as the more typical improvisational festivities of *Brikama* and *Different Places Different Bananas*. His musicians entered one at a time (to Dorge's "Do Green Ants Dream?"), followed by Murray, and Horace Parlan, a resident of Denmark for 19 years. Dorge's dedication to the featured guest, "David in Wonderland," was an astute showcase, and was followed by Murray's dedications to his son, Mingus, "Shakill's Warrior," and brother, "Song for Doni." Murray's prolix, bursting tenor charged the band and audience—his high notes arching into the hidden register with deadly accuracy, his enamored ballads coursing with easy candor.

Like Denmark, Parlan has developed an approach to jazz that was dictated by a non-musical factor: polio, which resulted in the partial crippling of his right hand. From records alone, you can't tell how he surmounted that obstacle, but in concert you can see that he plays fluent linear passages with the left hand, while using his right (almost like drumsticks) for powerfully rhythmic chords. The highlight among Murray's new pieces was "Istanbul," which he said later was inspired by a stay at the hotel where Agatha Christie wrote *Murder on the Orient Express*. It opens with synthesized strings and arco bass, to which Murray adds his bass clarinet in unison with mallets. The piece sustains the opening drama—the quality of intrigue—throughout, and represents a distinguished addition to his work.

No less fascinating was Murray's collaboration with his brother Doni, a 27-year-old instructor of gospel choirs in Texas. Parlan opened with church tremolos and Doni threaded his voice through countless melismatic twists and turns. Soon, a genuine gospel blush was established on "Nobody Knows the Trouble I've Seen" and "Down by the Riverside," with David roaring the obbligato and the audience clapping on two. This was how Murray had begun, playing with his family's band in a Pentecostal Church (before Doni, who had never performed with David before, was allowed to join), and offered a rare glimpse into the roots of his music. The encore was the ever-mutating "Flowers for Albert." The rhythm section didn't give Murray quite the pulse he needed, but it didn't matter much since the headiest moments were two elaborate cadenzas, the first by trombonist Jorg Huge and the second by Murray— a full-rigged showcase of staccato blasts, multiphonics, endlessly roiling arpeggios, circular breathing, conversations between registers, and the rest. He closed with a definitive, hard-earned BLAM!

So, you ask, who are the candidates for the 1992 Jazzpar? The jurors (same as last year except Brian Priestley from the UK replaced Carles) nominated, in alphabetical order, Tommy Flanagan, Charlie Haden, Lee Konitz, Abbey Lincoln, and Albert Manglesdorff. The winner will be announced in May.*

[*Village Voice*, 2 April 1991]

*Konitz won; see "Grand-Lee," ch. 12 below.

7 ❖ *The Glow of Doc Cheatham (JVC 1991, Part One)*

Seven years ago, I wrote, "Few educated Americans can name even five jazz musicians under the age of 40." One measure of how quickly jazz evolves is that I can't imagine typing such a thing today. "Under 40" is the *idée fixee* of the current JVC Jazz Festival, two-thirds over as I write, and thus far the most genial and satisfying in years. Where racism and sexism wouldn't dare raise their shameful heads, ageism is casually flaunted. Two kinds of musicians predominate this year—under 40 and over 60. Players who came up in the '60s and early '70s must be on vacation somewhere; either that, or the programming has been done in collusion with *The New Republic* and other regressive think tanks that want to put those scarifying years . . . where? Behind us, of course.

Still, it isn't a bad thing to underscore a phenomenon that scarcely seemed imaginable seven years back. We have gone beyond Wyntonism.

Wynton himself has gone beyond Wyntonism, which was once defined by an earnest, even didactic, devotion to contained modernism. Marsalis, now at 30 a mentor, has led the way farther back into the future by coming to grips with the full meaning of his New Orleans heritage: As Bing Crosby once said, "Louis Armstrong is the beginning and the end of music in America." If the exhilarating goings-on at the season's most revelatory concert, the salute to Doc Cheatham at Town Hall, fairly represent the zeitgeist, three generalizations may be tendered. First, Armstrong is enjoying his most pervasive influence on the shape of contemporary jazz since the middle 1930s. Second, the capaciousness of jazz repertory, once thought to be an academic, possibly Europhile, certainly white adjunct to the important business of progressive improvisation, is embraced in all its luster by young black musicians, whose support is essential to its growth. Third, momentum is building out there, and you can feel it.

In the first matter, it should be noted that we are encountering the first generation of musicians raised in the post-Armstrong world. I suspect they are liberated by his absence in a way that was never possible for their predecessors. Of matter two, it must be remembered that jazz repertory is not merely the interpretation of written scores, but the witting embrace of discrete styles and movements. At the tribute to Cheatham, we had the spectacle of Jon Faddis, Dizzy Gillespie–inspired prodigy of the '70s; Wynton Marsalis, Miles Davis–inspired prodigy of the '80s; and Byron Stripling, leading Armstrong-legatee of the '90s, playing Pops, Pops, and more Pops—not just the tunes, mind you, but the feeling, the ideas, the erotic glow. To the degree that this concert could not have been brought off 10, 20, 30, or 40 years ago, it was profoundly contemporary. It was also stunningly optimistic, which is one reason I think people were enthusing about it days later. In the parade of veteran players, we confronted the passing scene; at the same time, we had reason to believe that their riches were in good hands. Not, I hasten to stress, because the younger players know "Struttin' with Some Barbecue," but because they respect the power that makes "Struttin'" worth knowing.

Cheatham, himself a figure unique to the post-Armstrong era, is an ideal focus for the pandemic assertion of jazz verities. Watching him, at 86, lean back on his chair, a rail-thin figure of absolute rectitude with his Zero Mostel forward-comb and festive jacket, the trademark amulet hanging from his trumpet, his arms raised high in marching band posture, elbows out like wings, producing a gently perfect tone, cultivated melodies, and insouciant swing, you couldn't help but recall that there never was another music in which a man could so unmistakably find the full measure of his gift so late in life. At least two other instances of this phenomenon presented themselves in the past two decades, and others may come to light. In 1969, at 86, ragtime pianist and songwriter Eubie Blake appeared from out of nowhere, a cipher in the history books; during the next 14 years, he brought an era back to life, in effect returning to us a part of history we had discarded and might never have recovered. A few years later, Joe Venuti, the nearly forgotten violinist of the '20s and '30s, was also back, playing with a vitality and adaptability that triggered a reassessment of his place and the nature of his art.

In one symbolic vignette of that era, Dick Gibson's Colorado Jazz Party presented Blake and Faddis in a performance of the older man's most famous song, "Memories of You." They were 93 and 23, and while the performance was stately enough, it was also forced, obvious in its appeal to ageist sentimentality, and therefore more cute than dramatic. That was not the case at Town Hall last week, where, despite the perorations of the undoubtedly well-meaning emcee, Phil Schaap, who could contain neither his infinite self-regard nor obtrusive minutiae, the cross-generational weave was more often than not natural as silk. The connective tissue of such veterans as Buddy Tate, Dizzy Gillespie, Harry Edison, Ruby Braff, Al Grey, and Britt Woodman helped bridge the generations, but no one could doubt that the evening's magnetic spell was stimulated by the contagiously impeccable Cheatham, who brushed off the inclination to patronize his seniority with an anecdote. In answer to the oft-posed request for his secret, he quoted his doctor, who instructed one of Doc's fans: "His secret is that his mother married his father." Then Cheatham sang and played one of Armstrong's songs of seduction, "I Double Dare You."

Cheatham's singing is one of the miracles of his autumnal career, a career that would be barely remembered had it ceased at 65. Although he heard King Oliver in the flesh and accompanied Ma Rainey and subbed for Armstrong at the Vendome Theater in Chicago in 1926, he was known as a lead player, which is to say that, beyond the grateful circle of musicians and bandleaders, he was hardly known at all. In the '40s, he dropped out of music, returning several years later to take up lead in Latin bands or ensemble trumpet in traditional jazz groups, like that of the DeParis Brothers. After a mid-'60s tour with Benny Goodman, he started appearing regularly in New York clubs and at festivals, and within a decade he was a fairly ubiquitous presence in the mainstream, an unassuming patriarch—he strolled unattended to his own tribute—who worked every kind of gig. Only in the last decade has he come into his own as a performer, as an entertainer. A man of unlimited charm, he might have mounted a successful career in cabaret, because the key to his tantalizing way with a song is a mastery of parlando, his fastidious sense of which notes ought to be crooned, spoken, or whispered.

He is so secure in himself that his originality is more accepted than marveled at, though there is something truly marvelous about his manifest distinctiveness. Cheatham's timbre on trumpet occasionally puts me in mind of Bill Coleman, and his love of Armstrong informs the clarity of his phrasing; but the total effect is sui generis. His vocal style suggests a vanished era, but no specific antecedents. The songs he adapts become his own because he intimately caresses the lyrics. It is difficult to imagine him singing a song that expressed a sentiment he didn't fully credit. Thus "I Double Dare You" becomes far more coquettish in Cheatham's reading than in Armstrong's, which was edged with the bravado of youth, and "It's the Little Things That Mean a Lot" becomes a discourse on the social contract. In his later years, Armstrong engagingly covered the Mills Brothers' 1946 hit, "I Guess I'll Get the Papers and Go Home," but I doubt if anyone but Cheatham could make it work as an ideal, non-cloying curtain closer.

The impact of what Cheatham has learned to do with a song was underscored by contrast with Byron Stripling's overripe performance of "On the Sunny Side of the Street," part of which was an Armstrong impersonation (he also played Armstrong's great solo, though at a tempo too fast to be fully effective). It was the damnedest thing of the evening—an immensely gifted young black jazz musician singing in the theatrical, pursed lips, rolling eyes style of prewar Negro entertainment, without a trace of condescension or embarrassment. Fifteen years ago, he would have been considered eccentric; 25 years ago, he'd have been called a Tom. One privilege of youth is the freedom to decode the past on your own terms. What Stripling might have learned by Cheatham's example, however, is that less is not merely more but of the essence. As a trumpet player, he already knows it. A still more impressive indication of Cheatham's genteel strength emerged in contrast to the teeming might of the three neo-Armstrongian lions in the instrumental arena. Here, more was definitely more.

The concert opened with Charlie Shavers's "Undecided" by a four-man rhythm section (Cyrus Chestnut, Howard Alden, Eddie Jones, Oliver Jackson), two altoists (Michael Hashim, Joey Cavaseno), and the three horsemen of the apocalypse. Almost immediately, you could see that as far as they were concerned bebop was to be banished this night. Stripling played it straightest; Faddis used broad glissandi, controlling the high notes that in the past have often controlled him; Marsalis growled and retarded the time. Then the trio essayed "West End Blues," Faddis and Stripling sharing the cadenza and Marsalis falling in on the theme, and it was hair-raising. Not as hair-raising as Armstrong's 1928 record, to be sure, but close, and something of a benchmark performance in the para-historical realm of jazz repertory. In the intensity of the homage, Stripling and Faddis each sustained a four-measure note, the latter also following though with Armstrong's downward arpeggios, while Marsalis achieved convincing authenticity in tone and Chestnut imparted a smart light-fingered interlude before the ride-out. For two choruses, the three trumpets ripped and smeared and echoed each other, and when they joined in apparently fortuitous unison passages, you could feel a cold wind on your brow. And that was just the second tune in a set that lasted 100 minutes.

Trombonists Al Grey, muted, and Britt Woodman, open, played a duet on "I'm Beginning to See the Light," followed by Grey's plunger-intoxicated "St. James Infirmary." Then, with those two riffing in the Basie mold, Buddy Tate, though looking frail and walking haltingly, romped with customary authority through "Jumpin' at the Woodside," his sound a little grayer than usual, but his energy high and his control absolute. Cheatham's full set with his regular band (Chuck Folds, Bucky Calabrese, Jackie Williams) plus Cavaseno closed the first half. The second half began with some changes in the rhythm section (rotund, ingratiating Arvell Shaw made his first appearance) and a parade of six trumpet players—the three horsemen, plus Marcus Belgrave, Harry Edison, and Dizzy Gillespie. Faddis clutched a black handkerchief in his right hand, a witty and credible touch, and Edison, with his perfect sense of space and proportion, underscored the axiom that every trumpeter who created something genuinely original in the 1930s did so by personalizing some aspect of Armstrong's precepts, in his case simplicity of line and attention to timbre.

Marsalis did something that was, in its way, as atavistic and unexpected as Stripling's vocal, and a lot more satisfying. Accompanied only by Wycliffe Gordon on tuba, he paid homage to Armstrong's mentor King Oliver, with a rendition of "King Porter Stomp," one of the two Jelly Roll Morton pieces that Oliver and Morton recorded as a duet in 1924. No one expects less of Marsalis, but it should nevertheless be noted that he did not play only the big band strain, which would have satisfied virtually any young brass player likely to essay that piece between, say, 1930 and 1990, but a complete transcription of the multi-strain work as originally composed for piano. The deed and execution were sublime, incarnating the message that Miles was a diversion for Wynton and that his truest claim to individualism may lie in the idiom of hometown euphoria that has lain dormant too long. The humorlessness that occasionally plagues his appearances was conspicuously absent tonight. Indeed, the level at which Marsalis is now performing is so far beyond that exhibited on his belatedly released albums of standards that his reputation seems to be hovering precariously in the gap.

Similarly, Faddis's recordings of his Faddisphere suggest nothing of his hard-won victory over high-note vulgarity in making his top register ring with purpose, or his success in muting the influence of Gillespie in favor of a more austere means of expression. Snooky Young, the premiere lead trumpeter and as much an influence on Faddis's approach to sound as Gillespie is on his style, usually eschews the high end when he steps out as soloist. For Faddis, that would be a draconian decision, and his superb performance at Town Hall shows it would be an unnecessary one. On a duet with Gillespie on "I Can't Get Started," he took his characteristic clean-up position, but avoided histrionics. The notes were punched cleanly, the phrases tracked dramatically, the power soaring honestly. As for Gillespie, he probably merits an annual JVC tribute, if only for his refusal to give himself a break. Unlike the Armstrong players, he is wedded to an approach that requires lengthy, knotty configurations of a different kind of intellectual, technical, and emotional stamina.

The producer, George Wein, introduced Ruby Braff, trumpet player number eight, and provided himself an opportunity to play piano. They skipped gingerly through "Yesterdays" and "The Man I Love," and on the former, Braff, comped by Howard Alden's guitar, seemed to start every phrase in a different register or chord, as though he were surrounding the melody from all sides. It was an interlude before the deluge: "Struttin' with Some Barbecue" by the entire cast. Usually, such finales are noisily perfunctory, but this one was the concert highlight, a distillation of all that preceded it, a concentrated epiphany concerning Armstrong's dominance and the possibilities of expression under that umbrella. Every player had his chorus, and every chorus was urgent and distinctive. Yet, three stood apart—Cheatham, because his euphonious chiming precision held its own among the fireworks; Faddis, because he crested the summit without losing his head; and Marsalis, because he packed his every measure with a crackerjack surprise, doubling, retarding, sculpting, and mewing each note. The shout from the audience that greeted his last hurtling arpeggio was the sound of jazz. A good enough sound on which to depart, yet the Doc reclaimed the night with his encore, "I Guess I'll Get the Papers," and during a tripping interlude in which he and Marcus Belgrave entwined their trumpets, you could see the whole jazz past and future unfurl before your eyes. And its name is Louis Armstrong.

[Village Voice, 9 July 1991]

8 ❖ Miles Ahead
(JVC 1991, Part Two)

The recent banner on the *Voice* cover that read "Best JVC in Memory" took me aback. The salute to Doc Cheatham was one of the best *concerts* in memory (anyway, the best since Sonny Rollins barnstormed Carnegie Hall with Roy Hargrove and Jim Hall in April), but I wrote that review when the festival was still in full swing, just before it took a nosedive in the much abused name of bebop, first in a staid set by the under-40s and then in a misguided tribute to Dexter Gordon. Yet there was a buzz this year, heightened by low expectations. Why, I can't say. Most of the performers were familiar, sound problems and rude latecomers were omnipresent, among them an unusual number of camera-jockey tourists. Maybe, it's this simple: For good and bad, and notwithstanding its conservative leanings, it was a jazz festival, largely unpretentious and guileless. The lesson of this particular generation of under-40s is not that they exist, but that they feel no compulsion to seek commercial prestige in the trappings of rock.

Which brings me to Miles Davis, who took a savage beating in the dailies: to Peter Watrous at the *Times*, "the problem seemed simple: Mr. Davis was incapable of sustaining more than a few notes at a time"; to Lee Jeske at the *Post*, his "set contained more noodling than a day at the Ronzoni factory." Indeed, beforehand I advised a non-musical colleague not to expect much. The word was out that Davis had agreed to play an evening of Gil Evans arrangements at Montreux in a couple of weeks, and I had observed on a couple of occasions the disparity between what he plays in New York and what he offers the more discerning audience in Europe. Yet the first phrases I scribbled into my virginal No. 800 Reporter's Note Book were: "long mid-register lines, wonderfully lyrical." In short, it was the most satisfying Davis performance I've heard since 1987 (in the Hague). He soloed at length and with what seemed to me obvious pleasure.

It may be true, as Jeske wrote, that he played "the same set he's been playing every year since 1985," but he also played the same set throughout most of the '60s, when no one was complaining, and I'm not convinced that the slow blues and "Time after Time," the peaks of his current book, are intrinsically inferior material to "Walkin'" and "Autumn Leaves." (For that matter, it might be remembered he took "Autumn Leaves" from Roger Williams, who is not intrinsically superior to Cyndi Lauper.) Of course, he looked strange: He wore a curly, shoulder-length wig and ostentatious clothing designed to show off his Mariah Carey waistline. But Davis's unembarrassed pleasure in showbiz is something I've always enjoyed. He has lately developed the habit of hoisting applause-signs with the first names of each musician in the band, occasionally the wrong sign, so that Deron Johnson got an ovation when Kenny Garrett completed a solo—not that anyone in the group would know who was being applauded when. And, as has been commonplace in recent years, he and his cohort engaged in a lot of shoulder-bumping, palm-slapping, deep crouching, and extensive promenading.

The band also came in for its share of knocks, deservedly in the case of Foley, the lead bassist, who had little to say and numerous episodes in which to say it. Excepting that, the sextet was a commendably tight and elemental unit. Garrett gets a gutsy, fervent sound on alto sax, and his solos complemented the more elusive, introverted improvisations of Davis; he occasionally plays to the gallery with coarse squawking, but he is never boring. Johnson is a find, a deft and modest keyboard player who mines the territory Herbie Hancock explored in the early '60s, bluesy figures alternating with big open chords. The flashpoint of the set came early, a slow biting blues that ideally supplemented B. B. King's opening set. Here the rhythm section—drummer Ricky Wellman, bassist Rich Patterson, and a restrained Foley—really shone, tendering a spare, surprise-filled backdrop for Davis to extend his jutting arpeggios and mournful sustained notes, sometimes open, sometimes muted. In this context, the sudden explosions—crashing cymbal, snapping bass—intensified the drama, and you had the feeling Miles wasn't walking on eggshells but through a minefield.

At other times, the sameness of rhythms—the equally distributed beats for long stretches—was numbingly dull. Is there any response to music more deadly than the dazed nodding of one's limbs because there is no nourishment for mind or body? Those moments were particularly annoying because they broke the concentration of an hour that was otherwise focused and provocative. I too wish Davis had another ballad in his pocket besides "Time after Time," but the piece continues to suit him. His extended variation was engraved with that bruised timbre reminiscent of the records with Gil Evans, and his use of space was characteristic, which is to say canny, seductive, brilliant. One might ask of Davis's critics what Freud asked of women, except that an obvious answer presents itself: What we might all have preferred is the more ambitious program that was being readied for Montreux. Even those of us who prefer Davis's noodles to almost anyone else's pasta would like to hear him aspire for the unreachable.

"Friends of Sassy: A Tribute to the Divine Sarah Vaughan" was amus-

ingly emceed by Bill Cosby. It was fairly short on recollections and anecdotes, yet misty-eyed all the same, because Vaughan is still very much
alive in memory and it was hard to believe she wouldn't saunter on
stage and take charge. Joe Williams sang a restrained "Misty," Dizzy
Gillespie played "Lover Man," and Roberta Flack whined "Tenderly,"
and that was pretty much it for the direct tributes. Shirley Horn performed "Sarah," a lovely gesture as much for the ailing Carmen McRae,
who wrote it, as for the object of its devotion. Opera singer Florence
Quivar ended the program with an ardent reading of "The Lord's
Prayer," though not with the melody Sarah sang, reminding us what
music would have lost had Vaughan been persuaded to pursue "legiti-
macy." Riding the crest of the evening was Billy Eckstine, who remi-
nisced, sang a couple of his greatest hits, plus "Lush Life" (backed by
tenors James Moody and Frank Wess), and demonstrated total control
of his vibrato. Flack descended into the pits with a rap version of "Prelude to a Kiss" and a song by Gene McDaniels that had me recalling,
for want of anything else to do, the festival debacles of Diahann Carroll
and Diana Ross. She did redeem herself with a fervent and persuasive
reading of George Jessel's "My Mother's Eyes," a ludicrous exercise in
mush that to my knowledge has only been essayed in jazz once, by Pee
Wee Russell, but which Flack magically transformed. What's next?
Dionne Warwick digging out "My Yiddische Mama"? No, Jackie Wilson
already did that.

   "One for Dexter" is best forgotten, except that an effort so consistently
muddled as this calls for some attempt at explanation. Midway, it occurred to me that this was the kind of tribute to modern jazz that a
reactionary like Stanley Dance might have produced if he were of a sufficiently sadistic nature. But in fact the producer was Gordon's widow,
Maxine Gordon, who subtitled the event, "The Gala World Premiere of
the BeBop Caravan." Shirley Scott served as music director for a program
that took an approach exactly opposite to the one in honor of Doc Cheatham. Those who have thrilled to Gordon chasing Wardell Gray, or declaiming "Soy Califa," or getting around with Bobby Hutcherson, or
delving into countless ballads know his music is ripe with earthy wit,
stalwart charm, and torrid pleasure. None of that was in evidence in this
particular caravan; nor was there much tenor saxophone playing or music composed by or associated with Gordon.

   Instead there were poems, skits, platitudes, and film clips from 'Round
Midnight, as if its protagonist and Gordon were indivisible, as well as
badly executed and, in some cases, badly written big band arrangements
and stultifying blackouts between acts. The latter were not merely the
result of bad planning (a light on stage would have prevented some of

the tripping over wires, though there was no reason why the next group couldn't be in place when the present one finished), but a peculiarity of the pervasive affectation. The tone was one of inside knowledge, precisely the kind of silly cliquishness that made the music offensive to the meeker jazz enthusiasts of the '40s. Instead of the sensual pleasure that was the cornerstone of Gordon's art, we got defensive self-righteousness. With all the attention accorded matters of race, you couldn't help but note that in the program (which wasn't distributed until intermission), all the black composers were identified, but not the white composers. Still, there were three savory moments: actor Arthur French's masterly recitation of Langston Hughes's Simple story in which the birth of bop is traced to the head-bopping of billy clubs; Bobby Hutcherson's radiant "Love Letters" on marimba; and, best of all, Barry Harris's exquisitely beautiful chorus on Ellington's "All Too Soon." Wouldn't it be nice if JVC paid tribute to Barry Harris—or will he have to be as old as Doc Cheatham?

[*Village Voice*, 23 July 1991]

9 ❖ Benny's Brood
(Rickey Woodard / Jesse Davis)

The 29th annual Gibson Jazz Party, held in Denver over the Labor Day weekend, got jump-started at Friday's preliminary musicians' jam. The rhythm section, as good as any of those heard during the 56 sets programmed over 60 hours during the following three days, consisted of Roland Hanna, Ray Brown, Herb Ellis, and Frank Capp, and the ancient tune was "How Come You Do Me Like You Do?" The first soloists to take a shot at it were Harry Edison, the seductive master of the cup mute; Al Grey, the swashbuckling trombonist; Spike Robinson, a Lestorian tenor saxophonist known in Denver and London but not in New York; and Glenn Zottola, a big band trumpeter with an increasingly Armstrongian bite.

Then Benny Carter stepped in, pacing himself at first with curvy elliptical phrases, and soon connecting them in pungent exclamations that slashed at the rhythm, poked open the all too familiar chords, and brought the room to a sudden respectful silence. Carter, at 84, defies expectations about the vigor of jazz elders, not because he can still do it well, but because he can still make it new. Though sequestered in a limbo beyond the prizes and huzzahs reserved for those who work in the educated European tradition and/or achieve comprehensive celebrity, he astonishes fellow musicians in part because age hasn't laid a glove on his stamina, technical aplomb, or creative edge.

He was followed to the mike by Rickey Woodard, one of five newcomers to the party, two of whom represented an infusion of relatively young blood: 26-year-old Jesse Davis, who has been much heard in New York during the past three years, and 36-year-old Woodard, who is little known outside of L.A. The recent release of their first records, on Concord Jazz, should alter their parochial reputations. Woodard plays tenor and, secondarily, alto sax in a style informed by a varied but aligned tribe of robust players who came up in the '50s; yet following Carter's lead, he played a solo that rippled with recognition of the master's odd lapidary leaps and semi-staccato transitions. Dick Gibson, who has an ear for unlikely affinities, programmed Carter and Woodard in a duet on Monday. The tune was "The More I See You" and the blend was provocative. Woodard's lucid doubling, varied once again by his emulation of Carter's timbre and concept, provided diligent responses in a series of sensational four-bar exchanges.

Woodard's presence struck a particular chord with me because I'd written about him in 1988, after an accidental encounter during a California visit. Leonard Feather and I had gone to hear a member of the Ray Charles band at the Comeback Inn ("the Vegetarian jazz club by the sea") in Venice, but the scheduled performer didn't show, so Woodard, also a member of Charles's reed section, filled in. We were impressed by his uncommon rapport with a tradition of such warm-blooded modernist tenors as Johnny Griffin, Hank Mobley, and George Coleman, which distilled his more expected debt to Coltrane. And never heard another word about him.

But Woodard was no mirage. Born and raised in Nashville, he apprenticed in his father's band, alongside his three siblings, an uncle, and a cousin, playing Top 40/r&b dance gigs in Tennessee, Kentucky, and Alabama. He turned to jazz about 15 years ago, and in 1979 relocated to L.A., where he was brought to the attention of Ray Charles, with whose orchestra he toured for seven years. Woodard married (and divorced) a Raelette and began pursuing a solo career that is now taking off with the release of *The Frank Capp Trio Presents Rickey Woodard*, with two more albums in the wings, one with Horace Silver and the other his own session for Candid.

Asked to name his favorite saxophonists, Woodard fired off a list of tenors that has an almost poetic consistency: "Ben Webster, Coleman

Hawkins, Gene Ammons, Sonny Stitt, Dexter Gordon, George Coleman, Hank Mobley, John Coltrane, Zoot Sims—those are my favorites." He has named his tenor and alto Pauline and Olita, though I can't remember which is which. The album with Capp, a mostly one-take party-like session, shows how coherent and sure he is on a ballad ("Polka Dots and Moonbeams") and on post-bop blowups ("Au Privave" and "Doxy," on which bassist Chuck Berghofer plays the vamp he created for Nancy Sinatra's immortal "These Boots Are Made for Walkin'"). But at the party, where he had to measure up to tunes he'd never played and in some instances had never heard, he leaned toward his grayer forebears, building his solos from the root of the harmonies, occasionally depending overmuch on riffs and quotations, but generally letting his lower notes swell and his top ones rip.

Gibson unhappily introduced him at one point with a gratuitous attack on Ornette Coleman (whose name continues to spur mainstreamers to the cross) and a preposterous but by now familiar claim for the current renaissance in milk-fed jazzpersons: "For the first time in 45 years," he said, "there are great young jazz musicians"—a statement undermined by the demographics of his own party and specifically by the fact that the band massed behind him at that moment consisted entirely of players (Randy Sandke, Carl Fontana, Howard Alden, Roland Hanna, John Heard, Ed Thigpen) who had come to jazz well within the past 45 years. Not to mention most of the musicians on whom Woodard and all the other neo-traditionalists have devised their own angles.

Consider Jesse Davis, who gamely pitched in on every tune hurled at him, including "The Sheik of Araby." Davis is a commanding saxophonist out of Parker and Adderley, who also made their mark in the past 45 years. His high-water work at the party included readings of "Alone Together" (with an empathic Ray Brown bass line) and "This Is Always" (with an equally empathic Milt Hinton bass line), but it was diverting to also hear him skip gingerly through the foreign territory of an old chestnut, registering the chords like a computer, and then hot-stepping his chorus. The party is invariably an education, and for Davis it was a chance to stand toe to toe with musicians he knew only on records or not at all. "Benny, Al Grey, Sweets, and Cooper—he is bad, bad!" (More about Bob Cooper later.)

Though not part of the Marsalis fold, Davis was born in New Orleans and came into contact with Ellis Marsalis during his senior year in high school, when he took courses at the Center for Creative Arts. "He asked me to play for him, a blues in F. I was playing all these Grover Washington licks. Ellis stopped me, told the band to jam, and took me downstairs to the library and made me a couple of tapes of Charlie Parker and Sonny Stitt." His inclination to pursue jazz in the first place was a happy accident: He had been twirling the radio dial a few months earlier, and heard an "alto burning"—Cannonball Adderley.

Later that same year, 1982, he moved to Chicago to attend Northeastern Illinois University. He worked with Von Freeman and Redd Holt and soaked up some of the AACM action ("I love Muhal's stuff, his writing, everything") before moving to New York in 1986 and enrolling in Rufus Reid's program at William Patterson College. During his second semester, he got a call from Illinois Jacquet, which led to a two-and-a-half year apprenticeship in a big band ("the man is a master, I'd thought he was a honker from the JATP stuff, but he is so much more"), followed by gigs with Panama Francis, Major Holley, Cedar Walton, and Rufus Reid. "I was playing at Augie's, a small club near Columbia, when two ladies—Janet Silesky and Leah Grammatica—walked in and hired me to open a new place, M.K.'s." A series of weekend appearances at that short-lived room and its successor, Time Cafe, helped establish him on the New York scene.

Davis made his initial recording with TanaReid (*Yours and Mine*, Concord Jazz), turning in a persuasive performance of "Warm Valley," which opens with a canny duet by Reid and Ralph Moore. Carl Jefferson was sufficiently impressed to sign him for his own date, *Horn of Passion*, one of the most impressive debuts in years. Smartly produced and recorded, it combines originals based on standard progressions with standard melodies, and offers exceptional playing by Mulgrew Miller as well. Davis tears through "Lover" changes on "Li'l Mack," produces an authentic hard bop jolt in his teaming with tenor saxophonist Antoine Roney on "Stop and Go," and flares his tone—à la Benny Carter via Cannonball—on "Violets for Your Furs." But the range of his promise is best suggested on two ballads: "Here's That Rainy Day," played in long meter with Latin and gringo rhythms and fierce doubling on the turnbacks, and "Star Dust," with an a cappella verse and lyrical chorus.

The party may have confirmed something of a sea change, as he arrived dreaming of Bird and left, like everyone else, talking about Benny Carter. "I tried to play like Charlie Parker, and couldn't," Davis said. "Then I tried to play like Cannonball, and couldn't. Then Stitt and I couldn't get past the first note—Stitt is bad. Bird is the main influence because he covers so many eras and styles in his playing. He stood for the tradition, and I figured if I studied enough Bird I'd get a hold of it. Now I want to concentrate on how I feel inside, my emotions, and bringing that out in what I play. Ultimately, I want to be like Benny. Not only has he achieved longevity, but his playing is always honest and beautiful, and harmonically he plays a lot of stuff. I'd say he's the ultimate jazz musician because he's always full of surprises. You'd never think a man who walks so slowly to the stage could get up there and kick ass on the horn like that. But his playing is so beautiful, it really inspires you." As we walked out of the musicians' room, Jimmy Knepper walked in shaking his head: "Those old cats are playing their asses off—John Frigo and, of course, Benny!"

But of the 57 musicians assembled this year, the one most talked about after Carter was undoubtedly Bob Cooper, enjoying his own renewal at 65. A veteran of the west coast scene (the Kenton band, numerous records under his own name and others, accompanist to his late wife, the good singer June Christy), Cooper demonstrated un unmistakable affinity for Al Cohn, whose broad attack and beaming ideas informed most of his appearances, including an a cappela duet with Carter on "All the Things You Are," a captivating "Hackensack," a cagily smooth solo on "There Will Never Be Another You," and a collaboration with Warren Vaché on "Yesterdays." Also unexpectedly notable were two new additions on piano, Eddie Higgins and Gerry Wiggins, who brought a romping boisterousness to their solos, and two duos that have become Gibson house bands: the tenors of Scott Hamilton and Flip Phillips and the clarinet and soprano sax of Kenny Davern and Bob Wilber—reason to call attention to three recent mainstream albums: Wilber and Davern's *Summit Reunion* (Chiaroscuro), Higgins's *Those Quiet Days*, with Kevin Eubanks and Rufus Reid (Sunnyside), and Hamilton's *Radio City*, with Wiggins (Concord Jazz).

[*Village Voice*, 17 September 1991]

10 ❖ *The Advocate*
(Eddie Condon)

Eddie Condon was a vigorous jazz activist whose barbed tongue and stubborn beliefs were powerful implements for spreading the jazz gospel as he interpreted it. Decades after his death, in 1973, the kind of music he championed was still widely known as Condon-style, though, inevitably, the prophet and his music receded into memory when the last practitioners passed on. They merit our respect all the same. Condon and the success he enjoyed recall a tremulous period in jazz history, when the racial divide was first breached and the very act of playing jazz or representing oneself as a jazz musician conveyed the thrill of anarchy. The suspicion of outlawry was real in the United States, where *Ladies Home Journal* blamed jazz for an increase in rape, and severe in the Soviet Union, where playing it was a criminal offense. Condon's career could hardly have been more unorthodox.

Though not an important instrumentalist or bandleader, Condon performed on many fine—even important—recordings and fronted countless bands. His accomplishments as a composer were few, yet he helped to codify an enduring school of jazz. He was a radical in his youth and a reactionary ever after, yet he won a lasting respect as one of jazz's most effective propagandists, heralding America's brave new music on the bandstand and off, as a musician, organizer, memoirist, broadcast personality, newspaper columnist, and club owner.

The Condon-style, also known as Chicago-Dixieland (a phrase he disliked), was born in the late 1920s, reached its apex a decade later, and sustained a popular following throughout the '40s and '50s, even though it had long since jettisoned all signs of progressive development. Indeed, predictability was part of its allure. What started out as a scrappy, everyman-for-himself music, hell-bent on capturing the drive and feeling of pioneer black jazz musicians, became a conservative backwater—a respite from the anxieties and cyclical rebellions of modernism. Played by small ensembles with a driving beat, Condon-style meant a loose-limbed music, inspired by the informality of the jam session and nourished by an intimate ambience that was far too tolerant of journeymen vocalists, roguish bandstand antics, and a petrified repertoire. But it was an honest music at its best, sometimes compellingly so, and it preserved an illusion of effortless musical camaraderie that comforted a generation.

Condon's personality mirrored his music. He worked hard at perfecting a mask of cynicism to hide the sentimentality lurking just below the surface. Had he been the scold he pretended to be, however, he could hardly have gotten away with as much mischief. A genuinely witty man, he made his impudence palatable even to his victims, who quoted Condon's jibes with pleasure. Some of his observations are among jazz's most familiar quotations. Condon on the French critic Hugues Panassié: "Who does the Frog think he is to tell us how to play? We don't tell him how to jump on a grape." On modern jazz: "The boppers flat their fifths. We consume ours." On Pee Wee Russell: "He's gaining weight—under each eye." On any number of singers: "He once tried to carry a tune across the street and broke both legs." *We Called It Music*, the first and most valuable of Condon's three books, includes several lines that have been repeated and rephrased so often most people no longer know where they originated—for example, his elegiac recollection of first hearing Bix Beiderbecke: "The sound came out like a girl saying yes."

In addition to being the entertaining memoir of a jazz musician, *We Called It Music*, subtitled "A Generation of Jazz" so that everyone would understand what *It* referred to, is a definitive statement on the first generation of white jazzmen and how they saw themselves in relation to the black innovators they emulated. Read today, half a century after the coming of modern jazz and in light of decades of myth-making revisionism, Condon's memoir brims with far more socio-musical ironies than were apparent on first publication, in 1947. Some of that irony was underscored by a strange supplementary chapter written for an English edition in 1962, and unavailable in the United States for 25 years.

The main text emphasizes the debt Condon's generation owed Louis Armstrong, King Oliver, Ethel Waters, and Bessie Smith—the royalty of the new kind of music. "When [Jimmy] McPartland mentioned King Oliver," Condon writes, "smoke came out of his eyes." The contemporary reader expects no less, but it should be noted that in Condon's early years jazz was popularly associated with Paul Whiteman, Irving Berlin, and George Gershwin. In recognizing the genius of authentic jazz players, Condon and friends were siding with a community of artists that was decidedly left of respectable. The pride that animates *We Called It Music* and similar jazz memoirs reflects the satisfaction of men who were considered outlaws in their youth and pioneers as adults. In addition to serving up anecdotal portraits of the titans in action (Oliver at Lincoln Gardens, Jimmie Noone playing for Ravel, Fats Waller preparing a record date), Condon captures the excitement of young acolytes learning and, in some cases, mastering a newborn art. He recounts with chauvinistic pleasure the arrival of Beiderbecke and Leon Roppolo, who proved that whites could express themselves through black music, and he celebrates the commingling of the Irish, Italians, Jews, and bluebloods who heeded its call.

There is a paradox here. If Condon and friends started out as avant-garde renegades ("One of the ladies told me it was just like having the Indians in town again"), intent on playing jazz despite the indifference of "the Republicans" who preferred saccharine fiddle bands, they soon became the most cautious of musical populists. The more respectable and intellectual jazz became, the more they relished their reputations as "natural" musicians—the kind who can readily identify with young Eddie's rather disingenuous question, "What's reading got to do with music?" At times, he seemed to regard jazz as little more than a folk art, a nonstop jam session sustained in an alcoholic mist; the children of the Volsted Act, he explains, inebriated themselves to show that no government could dictate sobriety.

That attitude proved contagious to fans suffering from unrequited nostalgia, as witness the gee-whiz prose occasionally served up by commentators in the liner copy of Condon's record albums: "A dozen good guys having a good time. That is, after all, what it is all about," or "This music *is* roadsters and girls and cutting classes and oranges." It also led to grumbling by distinguished players like Jack Teagarden and Pee Wee Russell, who blamed the Condon clique for stereotyping them and limiting their options. Yet Condon's best work had a spark of its own, and though he often "conducted" more than he played, his bands produced memorable work over many years by Russell, Vic Dickenson, Bobby Hackett, Billy Butterfield, Edmund Hall, Buck Clayton, Bud Freeman, Kenny Davern, and quite a few other Condon regulars.

Back in 1947, when Condon and Thomas Sugrue collaborated on *We Called It Music*, Condon was at the height of his fame as a jazz personality. His nightclub, which opened in 1945, met with great success, as did his Town Hall concerts, radio broadcasts, and records. Sugrue, a newspaper and magazine writer who wrote fiction, poetry, and a biography of the psychic Edgar Cayce, was responsible for the book's strictly historical (italicized) passages; they contain valuable information, but need to be read prudently. In excoriating the "theology" of the scholar's approach to jazz, he refuses to distinguish between quaint phrases like "licorice stick" and commonplace musicology on the order of "polyrhythm" and "glissandi." His contention that the piano was introduced in jazz in 1897, the year prostitution was legalized in the French Quarter of New Orleans, is as loony as his refusal to admit that racism helped to launch the Original Dixieland Jazz Band. Does anyone still believe that "prostitution mothered jazz" or that "the Negro is born with rhythm?" There are more mundane errors as well: Paul Whiteman commissioned *Rhapsody in Blue* (hardly "a tune," by the way) for Aeolian Hall not Carnegie; Duke Ellington made his New York debut at Baron Wilkins' Inn not the Kentucky Club; Condon did not produce the first integrated record date (the New Orleans Rhythm Kings session with Jelly Roll Morton is the most famous of those that preceded it); "jazz" and "swing" were not mutually exclusive musics. Minor factual errors aside, Sugrue's and Condon's dated notions have the anthropological value of showing firsthand some common images of jazz in the 1940s.

Condon's readers also deserve a warning about the opening section of the book, pertaining to his childhood. Stilted and jittery, it is filled with incidents of sadistic violence that are probably intended to convey a Tom Sawyer or Little Rascals flavor, but the relentless jokiness is tiresome, especially when it becomes apparent that Condon is unwilling to candidly address the subject of his family and upbringing, most especially as concerns his ambivalence about his father and his eagerness to leave home. The same problem obtains in the 1962 addition, "Major and Minor Chords," which was originally bannered as "answering in no uncertain manner the criticism he received on his recent tour of Great Britain." Again, the writing is jokey, mannered, and sentimental, with thudding one-liners, self-serving claims, and countless references to booze.

Between these opening and closing chapters, Condon's book comes splendidly alive. From the moment he gets his first banjo and leaves home to tour with a band (at 16), the memoir sparkles. In his description of traveling to Cedar Rapids to join Peavey's Jazz Bandits, Condon makes apparent his need to find a surrogate family in jazz and an outlet for his impish behavior. He vividly portrays his ascent into the mysterious musical culture that thrived in those "mackinaw days," when everyone seemed to be dancing, spooning, and playing music at countless lake resorts all over the Midwest. The insupportable claims that come later, such as his insistence that Benny Goodman didn't play real jazz at Carnegie Hall in 1938, or that by 1947 there were no more than 50 "first class players" (including Ralph Sutton and Johnny Blowers, of course, but not Charlie Parker and Dizzy Gillespie) must be read in the context of Condon's faith in the music that captured his imagination and liberated him from Momence, Indiana, in the early '20s. Credit him with keeping the faith and doing his damnedest to sustain some of the innocence at the heart of jazz as he first knew and loved it.

Condon kept active in the years following the appearance of *We Called It Music*. His nightclub changed premises in 1958—relocating from West 3rd Street to East 56th Street—and managed to survive until 1967, for an impressive run of 22 years. He collaborated on two more books: *Eddie Condon's Treasury of Jazz* (1956), a wide-ranging anthology of writings with an accent on literary flair, edited by Condon and Richard Gehman; and *Eddie Condon's Scrapbook of Jazz* (1973), a hugely entertaining collection of pictures and captions, collated by Condon and Hank O'Neal. From 1964 on, illness prevented him from traveling much, though he embarked on occasional tours and appeared from time to time in clubs and at festivals—his last performance was at a tribute to him at the Newport Jazz Festival–New York in 1972, the year before he died. Two years later, bassist Red Balaban opened a new jazz club called Eddie Condon's on 54th Street. The walls were covered with enlarged photographs of Condon and his favorite musicians; the music was Condon-style, plain and simple; and the place prospered through 1985—40 years after Condon opened his original saloon.

[*We Called It Music*, Da Capo Press, 1986, revised 1991]

11 ❖ *Martin Williams, 1924-1992*

It is inconceivable to me that anyone ever called Martin Williams, the tireless advocate and critic of America's native arts (primarily jazz, but also movies, newspaper comics, and TV), Marty. He wore the name Martin, much as he did his inevitable narrow ties, with a casual certitude he was wont to characterize as "insufferable egomania." He had, in a word, presence. Tall and trim, the slender neckwear accentuating the span of his military frame, and exceedingly vain of his good looks, he did not lend himself to diminutives of any sort; on the contrary, he was more martinet than Marty, yet more Martin than Mr. Williams. His death leaves a gaping wound in the field of jazz criticism and education, and in the lives of all who knew and learned from him. Martin had been undergoing radiation treatment for cancer, which left him vulnerable to the flu. He was found dead in his Alexandria, Virginia, home in the early hours of April 13, 1992.

Martin was my mentor—indeed, he instructed a whole generation: critics and listeners and teachers, even musicians, though some of his contemporaries took his measure too lightly, criticizing his austere prose and even questioning the depth of his affections. Others knew he was onto something important, a way of writing about jazz that eschewed familiar anecdotes about colorful semi-mythological musicians in favor of formal but accessible musical analysis. He accomplished this with a diction virtually shorn of metaphor and reminiscence. His ego notwithstanding, Williams's criticism is remarkably selfless. When he returned to writing in the early '80s, after a long and uneasy hiatus, I encouraged him to put more of himself in his work—if not a memoir then at least a personal expression of his involvement with music. He smiled and shook his head decisively. "I can't," he said. Thirty years ago, Whitney Balliett referred to him as a man "who *thinks* about jazz more than any other public observer," and Martin's prose did, in fact, suggest an ascetic's attempt to pose ideas and ask useful questions.

He first exerted a major impact as prolific contributor to and co-editor with Nat Hentoff of *The Jazz Review* (November 1958–January 1961), an unparalleled and lamentably short-lived attempt to apply the principles of the text-focused new criticism to jazz. Many talented writers were introduced in its pages, among them several musicians—Gunther Schuller, Cannonball Adderley, Dick Katz, Bill Crow, Cecil Taylor, Zita Carno. The magazine was often accused of humorlessness, but it ran hilarious parodies of jazzcrit and album cover art. Even its letters column proved

significant, for it opened the door to Sheldon Meyer, later Martin's publisher at Oxford University Press, and Dan Morgenstern, just beginning
to make his mark as a critic, editor, and historian.

In the mid-'60s, I developed a passion for Theater of the Absurd, and
thus it was the bannered attraction of new works by Beckett, Ionesco,
and Genêt that drew me to the *Evergreen Review*, where I discovered
Martin's key essays, the bulk of which became his masterpiece, *The Jazz
Tradition* (1970). What a revelation it was to find the same impassioned
yet cautious, persuasive voice examining the aesthetics of Monk *and* Morton, underscoring links rather than dissimilarities, inviting the listener
closer into the music with specific examples and non-musicological ex-
egeses. In those same years, he wrote television reviews for the *Village
Voice* (collected much later, in 1982, as *TV: The Casual Art*) and mocked
the snobbishness of most TV critics, sharpening his obsession with finding the right rhetoric to duly recognize what was uniquely American in
the arts. He often said he hoped to live long enough to hear a graduate
student answer the question "Who is America's greatest dramatist?" not
with O'Neill or Williams, but rather Griffith or Ford.

It may sound strange to say of a writer and editor with at least 20
books to his credit (including Macmillan's Jazz Masters series) that writing never came easy, but I'm certain it didn't. For him, writing was a
process of winnowing. He could be tersely eloquent, at times almost laid
back, as in *The Jazz Tradition*, *Jazz Masters of New Orleans*, *Where's the
Melody?*, *Jazz Heritage*, *Jazz in Its Time*, *Jazz Changes*, and the posthumous
Hidden in Plain Sight, but he could also be fastidious to a fault, honing
in on the essence of an issue (Hentoff once praised his ability to penetrate
"essences," an observation Martin treasured) but leaving it largely unex-
plored. Yet he was a born teacher, sometimes impatient, as he was quick
to acknowledge, but eager to share what he knew and to exchange ideas.

In 1974 and 1975, a few years after leaving journalism for a position
as director of the jazz and American culture programs at the Smithsonian, he created fellowships for young jazz critics. At an intensive series
of seminars, for which his faculty included Morgenstern, Albert Murray,
Jaki Byard, and David Baker, he hoped to encourage a new generation
of jazz writers who would take the field past what he considered his
own "amateur" status. I have explored ideas from those sessions (as well
as his books and conversation) in countless pieces. The fellows included
other young writers who would also contribute to the *Voice* music section
in the 1970s—notably Stanley Crouch, J. R. Taylor, and Peter Keepnews.
Even our editor, Robert Christgau, had come into Martin's sphere,
having taken his course at the New School, an encounter each recalled
with pleasure. We all recognized Martin's abiding influence. We were a

generation in part formed by him, able to quote him chapter and verse. Martin was genuinely astonished at that.

My respect for his pedagogical insights is wed to one of the many short notes he sent me over the years. (He usually called to discuss or take issue, and the call would begin coyly, in media res or with a one-word greeting; he rarely announced himself, and you didn't need more than a word to recognize his strong, faintly drawling voice. If he wanted to compliment you, however, he wrote a note—less emotional and more definitive.) Perhaps because I coveted his approval more than I knew, I kept my distance in the years when I felt most unsure of myself. But in 1977, I published an essay that seemed to me a personal breakthrough. The fact that Martin recognized it as such and wrote to say so served as an almost terrifyingly personal confirmation. When we went through divorces at the same time, we became more friendly and for a few years talked about something other than music: women. Once he called to express his sole regret about *The Jazz Tradition*, the omission of Bill Evans, which he hoped to rectify some day. He elaborated at length on Evans's importance and why he had been slow to gauge it, and then, offhandedly, just before hanging up, mentioned he was dating Helen Keane (Evans's manager and producer).

That was, in my experience, a rare instance of Martin's wit. He thought of himself as witty and had a hearty, exuberant laugh, but he was usually too dramatic to be genuinely funny. Of course, he could be acerbic as hell. Bryant Dupre, who later conducted an in-depth and unpublished interview with Martin, accompanied him and J. R. Taylor to a screening of *Intolerance*, an abiding landmark in Martin's aesthetic scheme. A segment of the audience giggled in derision. Choosing his moment, Martin said in a stage whisper that reverberated throughout the theater, "It's very fashionable to feel superior to silent films." Bryant says there wasn't a peep after that. Martin was imposing and uncompromising. When *The Smithsonian Collection of Classic Jazz*, the double-platinum mail-order anthology that is a virtual companion to *The Jazz Tradition*, was originally released, he was faulted for not being "objective": too much Monk or Ornette, too little someone else. Martin didn't equate "fair" with art. His selections reflected a lifetime of thinking about jazz aesthetics, of what was great and what was merely fad or fashion, and why.

The series of records Martin produced for the Smithsonian are among the smartest reissues ever offered. And because they sold so well, he was emboldened to make the case for another of his passions, comics and comic books. He particularly admired E. C. Segar, the creator of Popeye, who between 1929 and his death in 1938 (after which Popeye was, in

Martin's view, horribly corrupted) produced a serial epic of life during the Depression, including a bruising lampoon of totalitarianism—and, in some ways, a precursor of Art Spiegelman's *Maus*—called "Popeye's Arc," the subject of discussion in *Hidden in Plain Sight*. Needless to say, Williams also used his clout at the Smithsonian to advance the cause of jazz repertory. He loyally espoused the cause of Doug Richards, whose locally based band Martin believed merited a national forum, and mailed countless cassettes to spread the word. Martin's tenure at the Smithsonian was hardly smooth. Impatient with concessions, he butted heads more than once. But then he lived his whole life in opposition to received wisdom.

Martin Tudor Hansfield Williams was born in Richmond in 1924, the only child of a socially aspiring Virginia couple with "delusions of aristocracy," as he told Dupre. He dismissed his middle names as his mother's wayward idea of elegance. He was educated at the St. Christopher Episcopal Preparatory School (at 16, in 1941, he wrote in the school paper about his realization that Benny Goodman's band style derived from that of an obscure black orchestra leader named Fletcher Henderson) and the University of Virginia. To please his parents, he prepared to study law and, failing that, embarked on a short-lived career as a teacher of English literature. The high point of his Navy stint was not Iwo Jima, though he was present when the flag was raised, but the times he was on shore in Los Angeles and got to see Kid Ory and the fearsome Charlie Parker–Dizzy Gillespie band (which initially bewildered him). A few years later, a reluctant graduate student at Columbia, he had an epiphany while listening to Sidney Bechet: "I saw that the man and the instrument and the passion and the music were one. I had never realized it before. I was just staggered."

Largely on the basis of reviews Martin wrote for *The Record Changer*, a reactionary collectors' magazine, Whitney Balliett, who was leaving his post as jazz critic for the *Saturday Review* to move to the *New Yorker*, recommended him to the *Review*'s music editor, Irving Kolodin. Soon, Martin was also freelancing for *The American Record Guide*, *Down Beat*, and elsewhere (he wrote his first, seminal appreciation of Morton for Riverside Records to annotate the Library of Congress sessions), while supporting himself as an editor at the *Encyclopedia Americana*, where he met his wife Martha Coker. Little more than a decade separates his tenure at *The Jazz Review* and his recruitment by the Smithsonian, but in those years he permanently defined his credo, "A new country of any importance needs a new art, and we have one." His work remains vital and indispensable.

[*Village Voice*, 28 April 1992]

12 ❖ Grand-Lee
(Lee Konitz)

Is there any designation more debilitating to the commercial welfare of an artist than that of "musician's musician"? And is any jazz-man more closely identified with that universally respected yet marginalized breed than Lee Konitz? For 45 years, his work has been the subject of close analysis, imitation, high regard, and occasional bewilderment. In 1947, at age 20, he recorded his first acclaimed alto saxophone improvisations with Claude Thornhill's band: "Thrivin' on a Riff" and the splendid "Yardbird Suite," in which he alights with puckish alertness, a lowercase bird chirping in a timbre shy of vibrato though formidably songful. In those days he astonished simply by virtue of not mimicking (uppercase) Bird, while fully reflecting Bird's modernist breach in melody, harmony, and rhythm. Konitz's cool sound, a partial reflection of his clarinet studies with a member of the Chicago Symphony, was so much his own that a school seemed almost destined to grow around it.

As it happened, the dean turned out to be Miles Davis, who with Gil Evans and a select team of composers and players reconceived the Thornhill approach on a smaller and more adventurous scale, begetting that chimerical by-product of bop, Cool Jazz. Konitz was present as a key soloist—especially his shimmering contributions to "Move" and "Israel." But notwithstanding his subsequent alliance with Davis in 1951 (the only Prestige date on which Davis appeared as a sideman), when Konitz introduced his own "Hi-Beck" and George Russell's "Ezz-thetic," he had by now become closely enmeshed in the circle of musicians surrounding Lennie Tristano, a cult within the cult of modern jazz. The many recordings from that association, which sound like nothing else before or since, reconfirmed that daunting line in the dust between a song's melody and chords—Konitz's "Subconscious-Lee," based on "What Is This Thing Called Love?" is a classic example—and, in a spontaneous group improvisation that remained unreleased for decades, "Intuition," peered into the future of free jazz.

If Konitz's tone seemed too prim in the early years (Andre Hodeir called it "diaphanous"), it became prismatic as his overall approach matured. By 1961, when he recorded the incomparable *Motion*, with Elvin Jones and Sonny Dallas, it had weight and soul and dark depths of angst to match the clarion harmonic dazzle. Yet even *Motion*, which stands alongside Coleman's *Ornette!* and Coltrane's *Live at the Vanguard* as one of the landmark saxophone recitals of that era, was more admired than heard. A couple of years ago, a definitive version of the album was released on Japanese Verve with three new selections; it isn't available here because, in the words of a PolyGram executive, "Lee's records are a hard sell." Much of his best work was recorded during the past 30 years, including adaptations of Armstrong and Bartók, the creation of a new nonet, unaccompanied alto recitals, an album of duets (*The Lee Konitz Duets*, ingeniously produced by Dick Katz, reissued recently by Milestone), a remarkably fruitful and often perilous collaboration with Martial Solal, a quintet with Bob Mover, a reunion with Gil Evans, and more, a succession of new departures.

Small wonder then that the international jury for the 1992 Jazzpar voted him as third recipient (after Muhal Richard Abrams in 1990 and David Murray in 1991) of that prize, or that his performance in Copenhagen on March 27 was fascinating. The concert at the Falkoner Hotel was actually the third and last in a Jazzpar tour in Denmark, and like its predecessors included sets by the Jorgen Emborg Quintet, with bassist Steve Swallow, and the John Tchicai Quartet, with pianist Misha Mengelberg. Emborg's long and icy set consisted of originals plus "Over the Rainbow," and produced more agreeable tension in the build-ups by drummer Alex Riel and percussionist Lisbeth Diers and in the fleet, burbly electric bass solos by Swallow than in the restrained solos by the pianist-leader and saxophonist Fredrik Lundin. Mengelberg, a chain-smoking eccentric of short stature, hunched posture, and quick, antic moves, appeared carrying an ashtray and cigarettes and promptly stole the set by simulating the clash of broken dishes with his first chords; he had prepared the piano in advance. Tchicai, who focused on tenor yet reflected Konitz's influence even on that instrument, concluded a witty if bumpy performance (employing tape overlays and stage antics) with a rowdy version of Jelly Roll Morton's "Grandpa's Spells," though Tchicai himself was curiously reticent.

Konitz, on the other hand, was raring to go and commented acerbically beforehand about the prospect of playing "lead alto" with a big band. In truth, he might have been as well served with just a rhythm section, as the accompanying "all-star" Danish nonet, directed by saxophonist Jens Sondergaard, was never as electrifying as the alto solos. But the sonorities were pleasing and generally well played, and as often happens the written passages spurred the chief soloist to increasingly aggressive fancies—his tone richly hued, robust even when most quiet, his melodies often tender, yearning, supplicating, as in the closing passages of "Leewise," by Fredrik Lundin, one of four works debuted in the program. The opener, "Partout" by Ole Kock Hansen, began with an assertive Konitz cadenza and included solos by trombonist Erling Kroner and trumpeter Allan Botschinsky. The next piece brought the first chills of the evening, a saxophone duet by Konitz and Sondergaard on "Alone Together," a favored theme—it was the subject of a 15-minute suite on *The Lee Konitz Duets*. As the altos entwined, their instincts took over and the soaring and weaving created an inexorable logic.

The pianist Butch Lacy contributed "Skygger," a dedication to Konitz incorporating a poem (in Danish) by Peter Poulsen, and the pianist Peggy Stern, who has been touring with Konitz, took over the keyboard for her original "The Pazzenger," which had an alto-piano unison head. "She has also arranged one of my early hits," Konitz announced to mordant laughter, by way of introducing "Subconscious-Lee." Yet the highlight of the set and the piece most discussed later was the closing piano-alto duet on "Body and Soul," one of those standards that Konitz has played at and around dozens and probably hundreds of times. Once at a workshop at the old Jazzmania Society he defined the task of the jazz musician as an attempt to spontaneously create a perfect solo every time; one rarely succeeds, he added, but that was the goal. He played "Body and Soul" so deep inside the tune that it was more referential than explicit; the fragments of melody, the taut lyricism that brushed against the chords, poking them for a new angle of light and then basking in it before skittishly moving on to something else, was undiluted Konitz—intellectual, rigorous, austere, and beautiful.

That same evening the Jazzpar Committee, presided over by Arnvid Meyer and including as voting members Brian Priestley from the UK, Erik Wiedemann from Denmark, Werner Wunderlich from Germany, and Dan Morgenstern and myself from the land of Rodney King, announced the nominees for the 1993 prize: Kenny Barron, Carla Bley, Tommy Flanagan, Jimmy Heath, and Martial Solal. The winner, named this week, is Flanagan.

[*Village Voice*, 12 May 1992]

13 ❖ Swing to Black (Doc Severinsen)

When the siege of Johnny Carson sentimentality began to burgeon, my usually circumspect bride suggested we tape some of the final shows. Astonished, I asked her how many times she estimated we had watched *The Tonight Show* in the nine years we'd known each other. Neither of us had to hesitate before supplying the answer: never. We had never watched the entire show, not once. We had seen hundreds of Carson's monologues, of course, usually with pleasure and no little admiration (while noting that nothing dates more irrevocably than Carson's headline-scanning humor), but then switched off, assuming—after plenty of experience with his first 20 years—that the rest of the hour would be a procession of fading stars and hopeful starlets, pedestrian musicians and desperate comics, all selling something, usually non sequitur film clips. Sure, exceptions come to mind, nights I kept the sound off and read, awaiting Sonny Rollins or Sarah Vaughan or Stan Getz. But they were rare. Carson, the ardent jazz fan, preferred Pete Fountain.

So as much as I will miss Carson's reassuring professionalism, and as much as I loathe Jay Leno's tit-for-tat political humor, logorrheic add-ons to ill-timed jokes, and brothel-inspired decor, I can't say I've experienced the changing of the guard with any emotional upheaval. Carson's primary innovation, ignored amid all the crocodile hype, is that he took a live and loose-limbed, spontaneous *talk* show, in which the increasing number of guests bolstered the conviviality of the evening's chat, and replaced it with a militantly fastidious 44-minute comedy hour with occasional music, in which the guests on the Siberian wing of the couch sat quietly while the latest addition peddled his/her wares unmolested by impulsive wit or possible skirmish. Carson's less imaginative heirs assume that his way is the only way; most arrive at work with a stentorian announcer, raucously grateful audience, second-banana bandleader, and a lineup of Hollywood hucksters.

I won't much miss Doc Severinsen and his clothes either, but I do mourn the passing of some of what he represented. His leaving marks a more momentous end-of-era blip in the zeitgeist than Carson's, because the *Tonight Show* Band was the last network studio orchestra. Every TV station once had its own contract musicians, a combination of studio wizards and jazz soloists; the instrumentation was that of a Swing Era big band. If the conductors tended to be middle-of-the-road hacks, their primary responsibilities were to master split-second cues, back singers, and entertain the studio audience during commercials. Viewers tend to think of those bands in terms of five-second bites, but in fact they played off-camera a lot, and the studio audience's enthusiasm was earned and real.

For years, studio orchestras were enormous, a big band augmented by a complement of strings. Jackie Gleason carried a jazz group for private entertainment and a small philharmonic for his show. But when variety bit the dust and vaudeville was interred with Ed Sullivan, studio orchestras became regimental swing bands—of the sort that accompanied Merv, Dick, and Johnny—and the last popular vestige of the sound that dominated American popular music during the two decades preceding the rise of TV. As such, they also kept alive a whole school of singers and instrumental soloists who came of age in that era. A singer might prefer a trio for touring, but in a spot with Carson she could have the luxury of an orchestra—the colors, the opulence, the power.

The *Tonight Show* Band stood for other things as well, including the last barrier before the ultimate hegemony of rock. Musically, that counted for little; but it meant something emotionally and metaphorically as a connection with prewar culture. The ties were at least as profound as those between TV variety and theatrical vaudeville, or TV comedy and its antecedents in radio, or early radio and minstrelsy. More than any other people on earth, we are shaped by the superficial continuities of low art; it's what we have instead of politics. Sometimes, it's what we have instead of family: If the *Tonight Show* Band was the music of our parents, our parents have now receded one notch further into history. Flip the channel, and, at last, we see only ourselves. Pretty scary.

Jay Leno, who once promised irreverence, is now as safe a Republican presence as Bob Hope, formerly touted for his political humor. Arsenio is every bit as unctuous as Merv. The incredible shrinking Dennis Miller (whose hysterical giggle creeps out his own guests) wanted to be Mort Sahl but is settling for the narcissism of late Jack Paar. Letterman, the only original in the bunch, is no less a prisoner of format. If these guys are us, we may be in more trouble with our children than our parents were with theirs. The bands on these shows accurately reflect the pervasive lack of imagination and dubious purpose. The ostensible aim, if one recalls Steve Allen or early Parr, is entertainment. Yet Carson, who streamlined the program into a forum of light diversion, simultaneously turned it into a showcase for lean and hungry performers, a publicity machine, a chamber of commerce. The other hosts function similarly as handmaidens, and are neither interesting personalities, canny interviewers, or sparkling conversationalists. Excepting Letterman, they have little taste for anarchy.

The most puzzling aspect of some of the bands is that even as they eschewed Doc Severinsen's size, they imitated his most deplorable contribution to TV music—a revival of the funny hats syndrome or, in his case, funny suits. Funny hats were part of the presentation of Mickey Mouse bands in the dance band era of the '30s and '40s, for example Kay Kyser, who performed in a mortar board. Musicians were often assumed to be one step removed from clowns. Countless pop bands featured funny faces or funny rubber-leg walks or funny haircuts (notably Kyser's Ish Kabibble, completely forgotten until the Beatles came along and countless parents suddenly recalled his pudding-bowl do, also worn by Moe the Stooge). Sometimes band members performed with derby mutes on their heads or mimed femme singers. They played dummies or sharpies, drunks and womanizers or rubes and innocents. The most famous bandleader character on radio was Phil Harris, a hard-drinking, gregarious roustabout with a ready supply of jive.

In the early days of TV, onstage bandleaders were a sober breed, usually downright dull—Jose Mellis, Skitch Henderson, Milt DeLugg. Severinsen, more than anyone else, changed all that. A first-rate lead trumpeter and veteran of the Charlie Barnet and Tommy Dorsey bands (among others), he was a constant presence in the studios and on big band dates through the early '60s. He also served a long tenure on talk shows, playing under Henderson on Steve Allen's show and under DeLugg for Carson. When Carson anointed him leader, Severinsen was remade as a character musician, at the helm of a character orchestra. The fiction was no more detailed or deep than the primary conceit of his appearance. Every night he wore a ludicrous outfit. The band would be collectively referred to as ring-a-ding weirdos. When Doc was off-duty, his replacement, saxophonist and arranger Tommy Newsom, also had to play a role: the rube, the incredibly boring man. (How boring *is* he, Johnny?)

Another troubling aspect of the band was the lingering racism that had infected the studios for decades. The *Tonight Show* Band, under Skitch Henderson, helped to break the color bar by hiring Clark Terry and featuring him. (The Carson show, not his affiliations with Ellington and Basie, encouraged Terry to go out as a single, achieving long-delayed recognition as one of the great trumpeters and entertainers of his generation.) His was the only black face in the band until Snooky Young joined on the West Coast, yet Doc Severinsen took most of the solos, which he played in the manner of Harry James at the peak of high-note orgasm. The *Tonight Show* Band appeared to have only two black chairs. In the '80s, when Terry was long since gone, Ernie Watts integrated the reeds. I note with pleasure that the band Branford Marsalis leads for Leno has two nonblack chairs (as well as a woman), but since he's at the helm of an octet his racial ratio is a generous 25 percent. Another thing about Marsalis: He refuses to do funny hats (as did Billy Taylor as David Frost's bandleader and Bobby Rosengarden as Dick Cavett's), which may ultimately do him in—though man for man, Marsalis has the finest assemblage of musicians on a talk show since Hank Jones played solo on CBS mornings.

Still, Severinsen built a powerful orchestra, a precision instrument in the tradition of Lunceford and Basie, boasting some of L.A.'s best—in addition to Young and Watts, the "name" musicians included trumpeter Conte Candoli, saxophonists Bill Perkins and Pete Christlieb, pianist Ross Tompkins, and drummer Ed Shaughnessy. He raised to an insider's art the business of introducing guests with descriptive song cues, for example, "All the Things You Are" for Christine Jorgensen. With Carson's sponsorship, he never had to economize on instrumentation (Branford's octet is really a budget cutter's big band), and he commissioned an imposing book of arrangements by, among others, Tommy Newsom, Mike Barone, John Bambridge, and the great Bill Holman. Yet the band was frequently capsized by the leader's appalling taste: remember the touring outfit he called Now Generation Brass? Severinsen's good side came to the fore in 1986, with two rigorous albums for Amherst, *The Tonight Show Band with Doc Severinsen* and a sequel. Most of the material consisted of new versions of jazz classics, notably Barone's recasting of Charlie Barnet's Ellington-inspired "Skyliner" and Holman's fantasia on "The World Is Waiting for the Sunrise." *Volume II* is the richer set, but both discs are admirable, despite the leader's hogging of solos.

You could say Doc played the clown so that no jazz successor will have to, at least in the immediate future. Branford, whose first number with Leno was a backbeat version of Monk's "Criss Cross," can probably accompany anyone. For the present, rock has taken over the funny hats franchise—consider Paul Schaffer, whose I'm-so-hip-I'm-square routine and lemonade combo is postmod Ish Kabibble; or the histrionic house band on *Saturday Night Live*, which sports derbies and wide suspenders, and compensates for musical impotence with fierce limb-shaking. What could those groups or others like them bring to Ella Fitzgerald or Rosemary Clooney? That's the real significance of the last studio orchestra's departure: the passing of generations of entertainers who thought a plush backing was their proper due. These are leaner times.

[*Village Voice*, 9 June 1992]

14 ❖ *Lions in Summer (JVC 1992)*

An alluring melancholy pervaded the 1992 JVC Jazz Festival, as though the music, on the battlements at high tide, wanted nothing more than to linger in the warmth of its glorious past and customarily rattled present; one last and loving look before dawn breaks on the vacant shore. JVC itself is rattled, by competing interests and a dearth of sure-fire attractions. The nine-day commemoration was nothing like a sweeping or even discerning survey of the jazz terrain, but rather a stoic meditation on departed or ailing kings, with tributes proffered by followers, jesters, and a reassuring body of untried princes, only rarely by equals.

Opening with the first of two homages to Dizzy Gillespie, whose 75th year is receiving much of the recognition it deserves, JVC unfurled appreciations of gray eminences (Lionel Hampton, Illinois Jacquet, the Modern Jazz Quartet, Ray Charles) and the recently and not-so-recently departed: John Coltrane, Buck Clayton, John Carter, Clifford Brown, Thelonious Monk, and Stan Getz. Gerry Mulligan revived the 52- and 53-year-old recordings of the Miles Davis Nonet; Charlie Haden reconstituted the Liberation Music Orchestra; Nina Simone compensated for her no-show of several years ago; and the return of the Brecker Brothers proved that fusion, too, has its memorialists.

With the Knitting Factory and the mixed-media Fire Wall Arts Festival taking up the slack, JVC barely glanced at free jazz or parajazz. (What else are we to call it? New music sounds silly 30 years after the fact, and avant-garde isn't always accurate.) I think that's a mistake, generally and on principle, but I can't say I was distressed by it, not this year. In the nearly four decades George Wein has been producing America's primary summer jazz festival, he has tried just about everything twice; banishment one season usually means capitulation the next. Besides, with JVC '92, he achieved something relatively rare, a consistency of tone and purpose. Salutes to Coltrane and Carter notwithstanding, this party celebrated the mainstream, the political center. You did not get an invite unless you knew the changes, or at least conceded their supremacy. The festival, rife with players of every generation, focused on continuity.

Back in Newport days, when jazz was embarrassingly rich in kings, Wein could present its diversity almost exclusively in terms of royalty, from Armstrong and Ellington through Coleman and Taylor. Youth was often relegated to student bands, which produced remarkably few musicians of consequence. Now the music can no longer afford to marginalize its youth. The accent is perforce on sustenance—you know, traditional family values, the kind of stylistic competence that leads to personal distinctiveness, as opposed to groundbreaking innovation that leads to new musical movements. The epiphany for '92 may have been the moment at Town Hall when 87-year-old Doc Cheatham remarked of 18-year-old Nicholas Payton, "He reminds me so much of King Oliver"— this at the second tribute to Gillespie. Genius and anarchy, like Gillespie himself, at home recuperating from illness, were resting up as the second-liners carried on. *Have You Seen Sideman?*, the name of the suite

Bobby Bradford dedicated to John Carter, might have been JVC's theme. Sideman was everywhere.

Genuine excitement was more elusive. But it too was present, though hardly ever where you expected, which of course underscored the delight. Who is the most technically adroit and consistently inventive purveyor of authentic bebop trumpet around? Besides Gillespie, who continues to wear the crown and may yet again astound us? On the basis of "To Dizzy with Love" and "Trumpets for Dizzy," I suggest Red Rodney has no competition. Of the eminent trumpet players who played in the Charlie Parker quintets (Miles Davis, Fats Navarro, Kenny Dorham), Rodney alone survives, without bitterness or disillusionment, to reappraise and nourish the achievements of 40 years ago. When he made his comeback in the mid-'70s, bad teeth and the long layoff combined to limit him to one or two characteristic solos a set. A lot of paste has flowed under his bridge since then. His stirring return to form, first in tandem with Ira Sullivan and now with a band that boasts the extremely promising saxophonist Chris Potter, has offered several stunning episodes, not least his casually aggressive triumphs at the Gillespie tributes. Pouncing, striding large across the stage, wrapping his arms around colleagues (he actually provoked an onstage smile from Roy Hargrove, who despite his gleaming solos often looks as though he were doing penance), Rodney could barely contain his joy.

At "To Dizzy with Love"—after a brightly-lit "Ow!" that allowed everyone in the all-star orchestra (festivals justify themselves with such storied congregations) to flaunt a chorus—Freddie Hubbard leaped to the head of the line with two shining choruses on "Woody'n You," aiming his high notes and concentrating his crackling intensity on the turnbacks. After that, though, he appeared to devote himself to a private competition with Wynton Marsalis, whose discursive triplets and pungent growls were hardly prepossessing. They rebounded on "Bebop," probably the best of the orchestral performances conducted by Slide Hampton, who also served as emcee. Everyone took a chorus (Jackie McLean's was a scorcher) until Marsalis: he took two good ones, the second accompanied only by the lambent piano of Hank Jones, easily his best of the night. Naturally, Hubbard wanted two, too, his second accompanied only by the chatter of Marvin Smith's drums. Meanwhile, Claudio Roditi coolly limned the changes for melody, and Jon Faddis played hair-curling high notes, sculpting from them one truly extraordinary solo on "Blue and Boogie," which climaxed with an arpeggio that rocketed nearly out of sight before coming to ground with a series of Armstrongian descending phrases colored and contoured by bop harmonies.

Still, Rodney made the lasting impression, at first with what has become a signature performance, "I Can't Get Started"—long, lyrical figures occasionally reminiscent of Bobby Hackett, and spelled by the infallible Jones, who followed with his own reflections on "Lover Man." Then with canny variations on "Tour de Force" (Faddis and Hubbard felt impelled to quote "Jeepers Creepers"), leading to a bopsieland finish as the trumpets improvised en masse, and in his single, rolling chorus on "Bebop." Rodney was no less impressive two nights later at the convergence of 15 trumpeters, besting Marsalis (his oddly plodding phrases played with an excessively plumy sound) and Faddis (a savvy chorus of Gillespie-style dissonances dispelled by a frenzy of yelping) on the blues "Wheatleigh Hall," maintaining equilibrium amid the tumult, and still more rewardingly exchanging rollicking fours with Roy Hargrove on another version of "Woody'n You," this one a meeting of minds between the old bop master and the young lion who is perhaps best prepared to build on bop's pure and rigorous foundation.

"Trumpets for Dizzy" came closest of any concert to capturing the exhilaration of last year's salute to Doc Cheatham. Stage-managed by Faddis, it served as a catalog of styles, from the whispered aphorisms of Harry Edison to the punchy bravura of Nicholas Payton, all floated by the first-class rhythm section of Kenny Barron, Ray Drummond, and Victor Lewis. The most unexpected performance was turned in by Jimmy Owens, who produced a rich, centered sound on flugelhorn, carving his solos with fastidious care. A graduate of the Newport Youth Band, Owens has been a familiar figure on the New York jazz scene for 30 years, invariably showing up at jam sessions (his "Lo-Slo Bluze," performed at Radio City in 1972, with a climactic Charles Mingus bass solo, is very likely the first Newport–New York festival's best remembered performance) and loose-limbed concerts without having recorded a suitably persuasive album. An enterprising producer should help him do just that. Sure-footed, imaginative, lucid, he built his solos with the venturesome care of a blues singer. A highlight was a rather grand adaptation of Gillespie's celebrated medley of "I Can't Get Started" and "'Round Midnight": Marsalis, Edison, and Ryan Kisor handled the first, and Roditi and Owens the second, closing with a cadenza by Owens that sank so low the notes grew muzzy yet were resolved with much drama.

Most of the young players acquitted themselves well—Hargrove has yet to make a record as good as he is, but he has more fire than anyone else in his generation; Kisor has an elegant sound, expert time, and a fancy for rhythmic displacements; Michael Leonhart has diligent ideas but wants power and polish. Payton encourages proprietary feelings not only because he's 18, but also because he's on the verge of any number of possible futures. New Orleans bred and currently a member of Elvin Jones's band, he knows the changes well enough to discard them when a snappy riff will do the trick, and if his solos lack the formidable finesse of Kisor, they indicate a stark classicist's sense of direction.

The miracle man of the evening was Cheatham, who sang and played with typical élan, elbows akimbo, trumpet bell facing the moon, plating every note in gold, even finding a way to mug the hipsters in the cadenza to "A Night in Tunisia," by recapitulating the key melody-phrase and then abstracting it over a two-octave arpeggio. Everyone pays lip service to Doc, but few musicians seem inclined to actually learn from him. For example, he was the only musician who checked to see if his mike was alive and correctly positioned, greeted the audience, and announced his selections. The mystery men were Faddis and Marsalis, two brilliant performers who often undermine their gifts with transparent calculation. Faddis (an amiable host, incidentally) doesn't yet believe that the audience will love him if he doesn't climax every solo with dog whistles, though his stunningly intoned, controlled chorus of "West End Blues" proved he doesn't need them. Marsalis was too detached and clever (his "Tunisia" solo was an irritating three-note figure played over 24 bars) to let himself have much fun; even his beautifully played chorus of "I Can't Get Started," accented with patented Gillespie dissonances, was a bit heartless.

McCoy Tyner and his trio (bassist Avery Sharpe and drummer Aaron Scott) enjoyed an emphatic triumph in the first third of the tribute to Coltrane. Carnegie Hall's acoustics brightened in acknowledgment of the moment. It's not that Tyner played anything we hadn't heard before, but that he has been a looming presence for so long and the stylistic progenitor of so many other players that to hear him at the pinnacle of his powers is to discover again why he held a generation of pianists spellbound. From a pulsating "Giant Steps" to an unusually delicate "Someone to Watch over Me," he was in utter command of dynamics, tempo, voicings, and overall drama. Anyone who thinks the old new music never produced a hit should have heard the crowd roar when Tyner intoned the opening vamp to "My Favorite Things." Perhaps the peak of his set came with "Mr. P.C.," taken at a precipitous tempo with but one theme chorus to steady the nerves, and a striking unaccompanied passage in which he sustained a tumbling bass ostinato (occasionally hinting at the symmetry of stride) against a firestorm of trebly tremolos. He was too generous to his sidemen, but they were so attentive one understood why.

Elvin Jones's set was undoubtedly better than it sounded; Carnegie closed in on him, as though he were working in an echo chamber.

Everything was a haze, though Sonny Fortune managed to poke through with a variation on Coltrane's "Alabama" solo, and he and the leader built up a near-*Ascension* intensity on "Afro-Blue." Javon Jackson scored on the encore, a 16-bar blues with altered changes by none other than the amusing emcee, Bill Cosby. Then things got strange. Cosby told a story about buying *Ascension* when he was 19—he made being 19 the point of the whole story, yet when Cosby was 19, the new Coltrane album was Miles Davis's *Round About Midnight*; Cosby was starring in *I Spy* when *Ascension* came out.

Things got worse after he introduced "spiritual leader" Charles Lloyd. Warning, this is a minority opinion: the *Times* witnessed "miraculously graceful improvisations that had the audience pent up, waiting to explode into a standing ovation." They had me pent up as well. In one of the most tedious displays of empty virtuosity I've heard in years, Lloyd played an endless rubato cadenza that chortled all the way up and all the way down, again and again. Jones spent most of that time on mallets, eyeing Tyner for a window in which they could go into time. In his utterly ersatz manner, Lloyd pillaged middle-late Coltrane—"Chasin' the Trane," "Psalm"—but without Coltrane's heart, soul, or brains, without even the anxious lyricism that made *Forest Flower* a crafty and very popular '60s artifact and *Love In* a definingly campy debacle. He did retain the patented choreography: knee-bends, shimmying, body-waving. Cannonball had reason to keep him on a short leash.

With a recording of David Murray performing Bobby Bradford's suite *Have You Seen Sideman?* due shortly, I'm inclined to limit my comments on the performance at Equitable Auditorium. Murray and Bradford, supported by Fred Hopkins and Andrew Cyrille, produced an open, pealing quality reminiscent of the quartet Bradford once led with John Carter, though the contrast between Bradford's pensive trumpet and Murray's teeming tenor and bass clarinet is rewarding on its own terms. The pieces, ranging from a declarative blues called "Woodshedetude" to a cortege that is the title movement, were enticing; yet despite a high standard of performance, the quartet seemed insufficient to do justice to the entire piece. One longed for another instrument. Cyrille's nattering vamp on a clamped high-hat intruded on "A Little Tang," though he compensated in part with a rattling good solo.

Birth of the Cool is modern jazz's most enduring chimera. The Miles Davis Nonet had little commercial success in performance or on records until the sessions were released on LP with that famous obstetrical title, thereafter achieving immediate status as a classic and a watershed. Yet although the recordings represented a breakthrough for most of the participants, it is not at all clear what they gave birth to, beyond the reputations of those concerned. Davis, Gil Evans, Gerry Mulligan, John Lewis, Lee Konitz, Max Roach, and the rest went off in very different directions, and although some would be lured again by the premises behind a nonet or tentet, the shape of cool jazz had an entirely different countenance, symbolized by two foursomes—Mulligan's pianoless quartet in the West, and Lewis's Modern Jazz Quartet in the East. No, the fascination with the Davis recordings resides in the special radiance of those arrangements and performances, often imitated but never matched. Thus they are an ideal basis for investigative jazz repertory, and Mulligan has done a superb job in capturing the original sensuousness of the music while avoiding slavishness. The contemporaneity of his performances on record (on GRP) and in concert is striking. Even when the notes are the same, articulation makes them new.

Mulligan has expanded the instrumentation to 11 pieces by adding a second trumpet and a tenor saxophone. Whereas his record is loyal to Davis's concept, thanks to Wallace Roney's mimetic trumpet, and somewhat tempestuous in replacing Lee Konitz with Phil Woods, the concert restored Konitz to his original chair, but allowed Art Farmer to playfully remake the trumpet solos in his own upbeat, lyric fashion. What joy to hear the polyphonic weave in such unforgettable themes as "Israel," "Budo," "Move," "Jeru," and especially Evans's "Boplicity" and "Moon Dreams." The latter, based on an obscure melody by Chummy Mac-Gregor (Chubby to readers of the *Times*; Harry Morgan to fans of *The Glenn Miller Story*), received an especially sumptuous performance, a perfect unison statement for eight bars, followed by counterpoint in the second eight, as the theme is shaded and elaborated by the full complement, before that poetic finish with arco bass bonding brasses and reeds.

But Mulligan had much more up his sleeve than the nonet material. With Rob McConnell playing Bob Brookmeyer's valve trombone role on "Line for Lyons" (the quintessential '50s cool jazz theme), he revisited his own quartet and conveyed a whole era of romance through his uniquely captivating baritone sound, smooth as the surf and light as day. He adapted Farmer's festive blues "Blueport" for the larger ensemble, ending with exchanges in which Mulligan played four bars a capella and Farmer eight with rhythm, and vice versa. Forty years of the jazz life have not impaired their fundamental optimism, their humanistic approach. Sadly, the evening was marred by boxy acoustics. The reeds suffered least, which is why one of the most memorable performances was Mulligan's duet with Konitz on "Alone Together," accenting the distinction between the altoist's tensile bar-stretching figures and the baritonist's knowing virility. This was a moment—very hip, very cool.

And there were others. Abbey Lincoln was the standout at the Stan Getz tribute, bringing the most depth and emotion to an evening curiously bereft of Getz's actual music. The problem was probably unavoidable, as the major players he influenced are largely gone or in Europe. Nino Tempo performed an agreeable imitation, and Astrud Gilberto, in good voice and expertly accompanied, offered appealing renditions of "One-Note Samba" and "The Girl from Ipanema." Kenny Barron was denied a solo, yet he handsomely accompanied Lew Tabackin in a strenuous version of Billy Strayhorn's "Blood Count." Gary Burton, Charlie Byrd, and Scott Hamilton participated, as did, too briefly, the recently revamped Woody Herman Orchestra, directed by Frank Tiberi and offering glossy versions of "Keen and Peachy," "Early Autumn," and "Four Brothers." But it's not possible to leave this concert without noting Avery Fisher's appalling sound, which rendered Byrd and Hamilton inaudible, and Burton and much of the big band a fog of overtones. More distressing still was the unconscionably rude policy that distinguishes jazz from "serious" music: doors are kept open throughout the performance and stragglers are allowed to wander in and out at will.

B. B. King and Ray Charles were a thrill, paying homage to themselves, drawing on their vast repertoires for material they haven't worked in recent years, and keeping the shtick to a relative minimum. Nina Simone received a standing ovation after every number, but I think a sociologist could better explain her appeal to the overdressed white suburbanites who cheered ecstatically at all that African Earth-mother sing-along. I'm told that the Saxophone Encounters took flight in the second half, but I had left to admire the MJQ's reunion with Laurindo Almeida at Carnegie (they played the Adagio from Rodrigo's *Concierto de Aranjuez* and Lewis's "That Slavic Smile"): the tenor half was disappointing, with only Ricky Ford generating heat. Big Nick Nicholas was out of tune, and Joshua Redman, though holding his own, showed little of the gusto with which he won last year's Monk competition. My guess is this was a transitional festival: look at us, it says, this is where we are, floating blithely down the mainstream, losing leaders. Next year, the Redmans, Paytons, Hargroves, and Kisors should move closer to the front. It surely is time.

[*Village Voice*, 14 July 1992]

15 ❖ Yin, Yang, and Noir
(Oliver Lake / Charlie Haden)

Oliver Lake was nearly 30 when his first recordings made their way—via his own label, Passin' Thru—from St. Louis to New York. That was 20 years ago, and his subsequent career offers a kind of Baedeker of the era's jazz itinerary. First we encountered him, along with many promising musicians of the early '70s, in a collective (St. Louis's Black Artists Group), performing with a malleable ensemble that favored "little instruments" and modal subjects, or standing alone, an unaccompanied altoist with a distinctively stark, urgent style. He made the obligatory trip to Paris before settling in Brooklyn, part of an unusually mature generation of newcomers who were bred in all the new musics of the '60s, rock and soul as well as jazz, and could hear beyond them to previously established forms and functions. Although he mentioned Paul Desmond and Jackie McLean as early inspirations, Lake had a sound as individual as his hair, a tonsure circled by dreads. His timbre was cured in acid, but his intonation remained centered and sure. By the end of the '70s, he had recorded two sets of duets (notably *Buster Bee*, with Julius Hemphill), and embarked on a long alliance with drummer Pheeroan ak Laff.

Lake was a no less emblematic player for the '80s. Able to avoid the economically induced constraints of solos and duets, he formed flinty small groups that alternated guitarists (Michael Gregory Jackson, Kevin Eubanks) and pianists (Anthony Davis, Geri Allen). At the same time, he balanced two discrete groups that embodied the period's yin and yang: World Saxophone Quartet, of which he was a charter member, was perhaps the most characteristic serious band of the decade (in any case, the only one to make the Smithsonian's *Classic Jazz* update); and Jump Up, which recorded such titles as "Consume" and "Trickle Down Theory," and was a commercially aggressive and successful avant-reggae unit, employing vocals and a fancier dress code. Lake had a banner year in 1988: WSQ recorded *Rhythm and Blues* (Nonesuch); he appeared as "special guest" with a powerful left-of-mainstream rhythm section—Mulgrew Miller, Reggie Workman, Freddie Waits—on *Trio Transition* (DIW); and he produced one of the best albums under his own name, displaying quintet and large orchestra on *Otherside* (Gramavision).

The most luxurious piece on *Otherside*, "Dedicated to Dolphy," underscores the powerful influence Eric Dolphy has had on Lake's playing, a tie previously made manifest on his 1980 album, *The Prophet* (Black

Saint). They are ultimately different kinds of players: You can't separate Dolphy's approach to phrase and timbre from his comprehensive virtuosity; his jagged melodies and promethean trans-octave arpeggios reverberate with a robustness that borders on the romantic. Lake, a saxophonist of more modest means, tends to keep his emotions under wraps, his melodies sharpened by a caustic attack that, though no more violent than Dolphy's, is edgier in its spartan design. Yet the connection between them is significant. Lake not only favors the harsh and gaping arpeggios that were a Dolphy trademark, but has also expanded on the vocabulary he created on alto sax, much in the way James Newton has extended Dolphy's flute and David Murray his bass clarinet.

Lake hasn't had a new record for a while, but the recently issued *Virtual Reality* (Gazell), recorded late last year, should revive interest in this very singular stylist. It even suggests his continued ability to remain a representative jazzman for the '90s, including as it does four canny selections drawn from jazz repertory and a fifth so new the composer's own version has yet to be released. The setting is familiar enough, a guitar quartet, yet Lake's playing and choice of material conveys a discerning generosity, perhaps an increased accessibility. It's as though a decade of confronting the diverse audiences lured by WSQ and Jump Up have made it easier for him to court the rough jazz trade. Make no mistake: The album is not at all compromised. Lake simply leaps at the listener with a sense of play and determination that will not be denied. (Strangely, the packaging might be, with its portentous title, dour photo, and absence of composer credits on the box.)

The first four selections work so well together they constitute a de facto suite. Curtis Clark's "Jesus Christ" is an arresting Coltrane-inspired theme, an eight-bar blues played a second time with changes, then all 16-bars repeated by unison alto and guitar. Lake's tone is restive and alive; guitarist Anthony Pearson of Brooklyn follows engagingly with a compatibly metallic sound. The follow-up is a carol-like version of Mingus's "Fables of Faubus," in which Santi Debriano's scooped notes on bass echo those of Lake, who treats the piece (proof that good can come from evil) with pealing melodicism. The third track moves to an even higher plateau of reflective intensity in a performance of Dolphy's "The Prophet," trumping Lake's 1980 version (a quartet performance with trumpeter Baikida Carroll that opened with slipshod unity and proceeded with a blustery alto solo), establishing a nearly rhapsodic bent, threaded with gruff notes, purposeful rests, and references to the theme, and handsomely paced by ak Laff, who gets a bright touch from the snares and taps his way through all the spaces.

Bobby Bradford's blues "Shedetude" (introduced by the composer as

"Woodshedetude" when he performed it with David Murray at JVC, as the first movement of a new suite, *Have You Seen Sideman?*), recalls early Ornette in the way it filters bop phrases through postbop accents and hesitations. It's an excellent vehicle for Lake, who avoids the usual blues locutions (especially in his turnbacks) in an eight-chorus solo, and Pearson, who toys with riffs and displaced rhythms. The second half of the disc consists of three pieces by Lake, closing symmetrically with another empowering blues, "Jest a Little." His sound proves surprisingly flexible in his originals—long, fluent phrases in "Pop a Wheelie"—and in Rahsaan Roland Kirk's "Handful of Fives" (a welcome revival from *The Inflated Tear*), in which his alto sounds much like Kirk's stritch.

Perhaps the best way to encounter Charlie Haden's enchanting new album, *Haunted Heart* (Verve), is the way I first heard it, unencumbered by expectations. So in the spirit of the movie reviewer who can't refrain from giving away the ending, let me suggest that before you drift to the next paragraph, you buy the CD; refrain from examining the list of selections or personnel; set aside an hour; pour yourself a stiff drink; and listen. If you've heard his previous Quartet West albums, the 1987 *Quartet West* and the 1988 *In Angel City*, you may have some idea of what to expect; but if you haven't, it hardly matters. The superior new volume will focus attention on them retrospectively anyway.

Haden seems always to be involved in several projects at once, either as leader or sideman, and it's typical of his remarkable career that he is currently represented by three new releases, the others (recorded in 1990 and issued by Soul Note) being a reunion with Paul Bley and Paul Motian, called *Memoirs*, and something of a sequel to the much-admired *Silence*, with Enrico Pieranunzi and Billy Higgins, called *First Song*, both choice. The Quartet West records, however, have a different agenda, part philosophical speculation, part nostalgia, to revisit the mythic Los Angeles of the '40s and '50s—the L.A. of Raymond Chandler, noir movies, and Central Avenue; the L.A. that lured Haden from rural Missouri to the mean streets. He has said he thinks of each of Quartet West's three albums as scores for movies, music designed to make a case for the cultural richness of the postwar era and somehow revive it. With *Haunted Heart*, he's expanded on that notion to the point of casting three of his favorite sultry torch singers in crucial if supporting roles. And if that doesn't clinch the conceit, he begins the drama with a 37-second introduction lifted from the credits of *The Maltese Falcon*, plus transitional sounds of traffic (borrowed from the sound archives assembled for *Bugsy*).

The blending of old and new, which might have descended to the level of gimmickry if maneuvered by a heavier hand, is obviously note-worthy as a new wrinkle in sampling, as well as for the cool hand with which it is done. But to keep things in perspective, that's the secondary achievement of this album. The primary achievement is the break-through meeting of minds that is Quartet West: Ernie Watts, who seems on the verge of ubiquity now that he is liberated from the *Tonight Show* Orchestra, has never sounded more sensitive, his lithe sound and supple approach recalling the blend of hard and soft embodied in Hank Mob-ley's best work; Alan Broadbent (whose Maybeck recital is one of the best entries in the Concord Jazz series), has become a pianist of great subtlety, as well as the accomplished composer of suitably noir ballads; Lawrence Marable, one of the outstanding veteran drummers on the L.A. scene, remains as reflexively quick and empathic as Haden himself, the one bassist since Mingus who justifies most if not all his solos.

The material includes movie music by David Raksin (*The Bad and the Beautiful*), a big band theme (a startling transformation of Glenn Miller's "Moonlight Serenade"), bop milestones by Bud Powell and Lennie Tris-tano, and three exquisite ballad sequences—that is, they combine the quartet's ruminations with the original and complete recordings by Jo Stafford ("Haunted Heart," 1947), Jeri Southern ("Every Time We Say Goodbye," 1954), and Billie Holiday ("Deep Song," 1947). Those exceed-ingly seductive voices, set up as they are and carefully spaced, clinch *Haunted Heart* as one of the year's most evocative and sexiest records.

[*Village Voice*, 21 July 1992]

16 ❖ *Always True in Her Fashion (Peggy Lee)*

The first time I really listened to Peggy Lee was accidental. I'd bought a Benny Goodman set on Harmony, an old subsidiary of Columbia, got it back to the dorm late, put it on and soon fell asleep. The last thing I recalled hearing was "Why Don't You Do Right," and I dozed off hap-pily surprised because I didn't expect to hear any Billie Holiday on the album. I thought about it in class the next morning, and that evening some friends came by to hear this performance I raved about. We all agreed: Definitely an ace record—primo Lady Day. Only after they left and I looked at the small print did I discover that the singer was Peggy Lee: the platinum blonde with the mole on her right cheek to whom I had never tumbled and was now ready to dismiss as yet another Billie imitator, another minstrel.

Live and learn.

Probably it was the two-note bubble on the word "ri-ight" that girded my ignorant assumption, that and the thin voice and the legato time and the knowledge that Billie had sung early on with Goodman. Because Lee, though admittedly influenced by Holiday's sense of economy, swing, and ability to make the most of a small range, never sounded that much like her. They did share something profound, however, a candid vulnerability that draws you into the drama of what they sing and how they sing it. They slur notes, but their slurs have different pedigrees, even if they had monstrous childhoods in common. Read either of their lives and you may wonder if the slurs aren't a kind of musical recoiling, wounded sighs. The former Norma Deloris Egstrom of North Dakota, who started singing on radio at 14 in part to escape the ministrations of a wicked stepmother, sings in the clipped cadences of the cold country, the vowels rarely indulged, the timbre cool and coy, icily sexy, giving way to an intimate vibrato as she attains high notes she only pretends to find daunting. A noted perfectionist, Lee gets it right or she doesn't go for it. Yet you feel she's at constant risk.

Holiday had Lester Young, and Lee had her husband David Barbour, whose lilting guitar shadowed her with affection and clarity in the '40s, when just about everything she did hit the charts, especially the songs they co-composed—"I Don't Know Enough About You," "It's a Good Day," "What More Can a Woman Do?," "Mañana," even the straight blues, "Everything's Movin' Too Fast." Later she would collaborate with Sonny Burke on the score for *Lady and the Tramp* and write lyrics for Duke Ellington when he worked on *Anatomy of a Murder*. Along the way, she acted in a handful of movies, bagging an Oscar nomination for *Pete Kelly's Blues*. Every performer in Hollywood ought to thank her for waging the battle against the rodents at Disney who reaped millions in *Lady and the Tramp* video sales yet continue to drag her through courts rather than acknowledge a subsidiary rights clause in her prescient contract. When she finally wins in the higher courts—Disney keeps appealing— a barrier to equitable profit sharing will be blown off its hinges.

Lee is a credit to her race in other ways, and it is unseemly to blame her for capitalizing on opportunities once permitted those of Scandinavian rather than of African stock, though one suspects that her success in the pop arena is the only reason she is perennially ignored by the jazz press (even *The New Grove Dictionary of Jazz* lists Barbour, not Lee). Not the least considerable of her achievements is her enduring claim on songs from the blues underground—from Lil Green's "Why Don't You Do

Right," at the very beginning of her career, to Little Willie John's "Fever," at its very pinnacle. Covers they may be, steals they are not. She found her own way in those songs, as in the others, marrying wit and theatrics. She never embarrassed herself with them, and she doesn't embarrass her audience today, at 72, singing "Fever" while seated at Club 53 at the New York Hilton, where she is ensconced for a month.

One of the benefits of having a career that is now of 58 years duration is that she can pick and choose, drawing on hits that still work and combining them with songs that ought to be hits. During the past quarter-century, after the surprise bonanza of 1969's "Is That All There Is?" and before illnesses derailed her, Lee seemed as desperate as just about every other singer of her generation to cross over to the next, pickling herself in the trappings of over-designed glamour and ill-fitting Beatles ballads. The Club 53 engagement, however, achieves contemplative elegance in its simplicity. Though reliant on a wheelchair, she manages to walk to the throne situated in front of Mike Renzi's empathic quintet. And though her voice is diminished in strength and occasionally teeters on the more extended phrasings, she has accustomed herself to those limitations, betting on her intelligence, her gift for economy, to make every sigh and slur resonate with meaning. She rivets the audience's attention.

It is startling to see her. The platinum Cleopatra wig is in place, but the dark glasses of recent gigs are gone, and her face is much broadened and less tractable, the result of her several strokes. Yet the tender timbre of the voice is intact, the hushed phrasing, the minimalist (and North Dakotan) trust in thrift—the le note juste, the commanding posture, the easy wit. We are all in this together. Watch me as I guide you through this song. It isn't much and so easy we'll laugh about it afterward. But in fact she is often most moving when you least expect, as on the bridge to "S'Wonderful," when her laid-back phrasing takes on increased strength and seems to quell the bossa beat that gets the song started. She and her audience could scarcely hope for a better band than the one Renzi has organized. With Steve LaSpina on bass and drummer Peter Grant, the rhythm section paces her with a plush moderation, Renzi fitting the chords and periodically dressing them with a string synthesizer. Jay Berliner fleetly recalls Barbour on guitar, and Gerry Niewood (who made a splash in the '70s with Chuck Mangione) adds reeds and flute, often blending as one with Renzi.

Sometimes she settles for a near-parlando style, as on Jerome Kern and Dorothy Fields's neglected "Remind Me," backed only by Renzi, or even on "Fever," accompanied by bass and drums, conducting every phrase with a gesturing finger, yet for all the complicit humor in the conceit making the temperature rise all the same. Elsewhere she is more expansive: She has a lock on Cole Porter's "Do I Love You?" and "Always True to You in My Fashion," taken with her trademark Latin bounce and spelled by a soprano sax solo. Yet perhaps the finest moments of her opening night set were those blue-colored ballads in which she seemed to suspend each line of the lyrics from the pull of LaSpina's bass, notably Gershwin's "Our Love Is Here to Stay"; a shrewd and welcome revival of Lil Hardin Armstrong's "Just for a Thrill," phrased almost entirely in frugal sighs and expressive rests that subtly suggest Ray Charles, whose influence was no less apparent in her treatment of Sy Oliver's "Yes Indeed" and even in a new setting for "Why Don't You Do Right," now outfitted with a "Hit the Road, Jack" vamp.

If there was a failing to the set it was her willingness to curtail or undercut some of her requisite hits: "I Don't Know Enough About You" is too good to fob off in a chorus, no matter how many times she's done it, and since the miracle of Leiber and Stoller's tearjerker, "Is That All There Is?," is that she can make it work at all (no one else could), it hardly seems appropriate to enfeeble it now with jokes. On the other hand, "Mañana" deserves retirement; Mexicans didn't dig her my-seester accent in 1948, when it topped the charts amid a cluster of south-of-the-border anthems—and they had a point. Her closer, "I'll Be Seeing You," is, of course, foolproof. Not a dry eye in the house.

Lee is well represented on several recent CDs, though the Deccas have been slow to emerge from the vaults of MCA. Her entry in the Capitol Collector's Series, *The Early Years*, is one of the best. Unlike others in the series, it focuses on a specific period, 1945–50, giving most of the high-points. The drawback with other volumes (Kay Starr's, for one) is that they are more attuned to *Billboard* sightings than excellence. In Lee's case, at least in this period, the hits *are* excellent. All the selections were recorded with Dave Barbour's accompaniment, and they constitute as impressive a body of jazz-inspired pop as was created in the postwar era. A second volume, picking up with her return to the label in 1958, after a fruitful sojourn at Decca, has yet to materialize. A selection of her finest radio broadcasts has been issued as *Peggy Lee with the Dave Barbour Band* (LaserLight), and her beginnings as a big band chirp can be sampled on *Benny Goodman Featuring Peggy Lee* (Columbia).

For Capitol's 1959 *Beauty and the Beat!*, she was teamed by producer Dave Cavanaugh (in those days A&R men actually gave thought to such matters as artists and repertoire) with George Shearing's Quintet. The three instrumentals don't count for much, yet Shearing is cannily intuitive in following Lee's every move and making the most of those mir-agelike rests. She is scintillating throughout in a characteristically telling program that includes definitive versions of the two Cole Porter songs in her current show. One of two previously unreleased bonus tracks, Kern and Hammerstein's "Don't Ever Leave Me," is shudderingly stark, a genuine treasure reclaimed from the vaults. No less worthy is a British import, *It's a Good Day* (Parrot), compiled from Bing Crosby's radio shows by Geoff Milne, the former English Decca executive who recorded Crosby in his last years. Lee was a regular on the show in 1947 and 1948, and this anthology collects 14 performances by her, 12 duets with Crosby (including "Everything's Movin' Too Fast," a rare instance of Crosby singing blues; "You Came a Long Way from St. Louis," which she later refined for the Shearing album; and a rousing "I Got Rhythm" with violinist Joe Venuti), and a medley of 10 selections by Lee, Crosby, and Fred Astaire—on "A Fine Romance," they trade improbable bebop licks. Much of her best work needs to be reissued and surely will be as Lee is restored to her rightful place in the pantheon of indispensable singers.

[*Village Voice*, 18 August 1992]

17 ❖ Computer Wars (Robert Parker)

Among the finest early jazz recordings are those by the Clarence Williams Blue Five of 1924, in which Louis Armstrong and Sidney Bechet resolve by example such essential issues as the role of the soloist, dispositions toward repertoire, and ensemble infrastructure. Bechet held his own, occasionally besting Armstrong, which no one else would ever do. "Mandy, Make Up Your Mind" is a less than hair-raising but highly picturesque sample of their work, and it's unique for boasting the only sarrusophone solo on a jazz recording. The brass double-reed instrument (invented in 1865 and used primarily in military bands) came in a family assortment, descending in pitch from sopranino to contra-bass: Bechet wielded the bass version. Not surprisingly, given acoustical recording techniques of 1924, he produced a clamorous rumble suggesting the kind of internal combustion caused by bad diet. Unless, that is, you listen to the recording as reprocessed a few years ago by the Australian engineer Robert Parker.

On *Sidney Bechet*, one of 25 CDs in Parker's "Jazz Classics and Golden Years in Digital Stereo" series, picked up this year for American distribution by the New York company DRG, the sarrusophone chorus emerges with elucidative definition. You can hear the staccato tonguing and the ebullient motivation; the overall impression, once of frenzy, is now of audacious wit. Perhaps if Bechet had known the sound would travel so well over nearly 70 years, he might have tried the instrument a second time. In any case, this performance, along with virtually all of Parker's remastering, and that of other high-end jazz engineers such as John R. T. Davies in England and Jack Towers here, demonstrates that a great deal of information was packed into the grooves of waxen discs in the land before tape, and canny restoration brings it all back.

As sound reproduction has become increasingly complicated, an exquisitely simple idea has been lost: The shortest distance between performer and listener is a straight line. In the early days of recording, the musicians played into a horn attached to a needle that etched the sound into a platter. At home, the listener reversed the process: the needle mined the platter and transmitted the music through the short length of a tone arm and through a horn. The efficacy of that set-up was brought home to me recently during a visit with Bill Daugherty, an entertainer and collector of 78s and antique phonographs (he has 75 models). He played Caruso's "Serenata" on the Victor IV, a machine made between 1902 and 1920—his dates from 1908—and outfitted with a huge mahogany horn. The immediacy and richness of the sound was astonishing, vastly more realistic than the Soundstream Computer versions of the '80s. Daugherty says the wooden horn absorbs more surface noise than a metal one, and the medium-loud needle he uses (and changes every three records) is the right size for the grooves of that particular record.

Practical, his system is not. A Victor IV, if you can find an antiquarian with one in stock, goes for at least $3000; it will maximize the reproduction of a particular era's 78s; and you'd need the Coliseum to house the number of 78s that can be stored in a wall of CDs. But it points up the degree to which modern engineers find themselves going a long distance out of the way to come back a short distance correctly. Serious recordists are almost unanimously agreed that analogue is superior to digital, but those who take the time are finding ways to make digital more accurate. They develop needles to fill out the grooves of master 78s (the more snug the fit, the more information it can retrieve) and monitor the process so that essential musical data isn't destroyed with the surface noise, hiss, and clicks that the digital system can successfully abate.

The thing that has music lovers pulling their hair out is the computerized systems used by major labels, which usually are not operated by music lovers or by music lovers with audio reproduction skills. The labels refuse to acknowledge the work of engineers like Parker or Davies (even when they steal their work). Not only do these companies claim ownership of the jazz heritage, rather dubiously in some cases, but they also possess the master pressings that committed engineers need to get maximum results. It is obviously true that we experience sound subjectively (else there would be only one manufacturer of speakers); at a certain level—e.g., a comparison of two versions of the same performance as reprocessed by Parker and Davies—personal preference is the only arbiter. But sound is not so subjective that it can justify entire instruments being erased, muted, or thinned beyond recognition.

The latest catastrophe is Decca's *Ella Fitzgerald: The Early Years, Part 1*, yet another indication that the NoNoise system won't learn from its mistakes. A couple of years ago, Qualitron distributors imported the French Classics label, including the same performances by Fitzgerald and the Chick Webb Orchestra; the CDs are blighted with surface noise, but the music is realistic and lively. By contrast, the new Deccas are so clean the very traction of swing is gone. The trumpets especially are disemboweled; what were fortes are now squawks. Swing depends on nuance, on the way musicians breathe, on how they sound in the rooms in which they play. Without room ambience, without highs and lows, all that remains is a fixed midrange—cold, remote, and lifeless. There must be an agreeable midpoint between the noisy surfaces to which vinyl has long accustomed us and the arid reductions of digitalization.

Parker is one of the pioneers in navigating those shoals, and unlike his colleagues he has been singularly successful in promoting himself as well as his work. His photograph adorns several CDs in the DRG series, his name sometimes above the title. I can recall no other engineer, with the arguable exception of Thomas G. Stockham, Jr., who revivified Caruso, achieving comparable star status. Naturally, that aspect of Parker's success drives other engineers nuts. Indeed, his personal stamp is both the glory and the drawback of his albums; as anthologies, they reveal an eccentric taste in jazz and pop that, though almost always producing entertaining results, often overlooks the masterpieces one expects to find. During his recent visit to New York, I asked him about his technique and background.

Born in 1936 and raised in Sydney, Parker is the son of one of Australia's trailblazing radio engineers. He started collecting records at age 12 and soon learned how to remaster recorded performances. The LP was introduced in Australia in 1952, and three years later Parker bought a disc-cutter and experimented with transferring 78s to LP. In the '60s, record companies began using echo chambers to simulate stereo on mono recordings. Parker disdained the "electrically rechanneled for stereo" era, but not the idea; he figured they "were doing the wrong things for the right reasons." He took on the challenge of reproducing the spatiality of stereo, of re-creating the living presence of the ensemble. Using a cone filter, which splits the sound spectrum into a sawtooth effect, he fed the top half of the spectrum into one channel and the bottom half into the other.

Parker, who refers to himself wryly as an "impressionist," is quick to point out, "We're talking about artifacts, not absolutes." He argues, "It was never possible to make a completely accurate recording and it isn't now. Seventy-eights *are* crappy recordings, but they contain information that, if you can get it out, will give you better representation. I'm not interested in 78s—I'm interested in getting into the studio with the original performance, and you can hear more detail when the signal is spread beyond mono." Parker points to a changeover in the field in the '60s, when Wyndham Hodgson ("a hero"), the precision engineer who made jewel bearings for watches until he discovered how to design a stylus that accurately fit the grooves of records, founded the Expert Stylus Company in England.

Parker makes his transfers direct from 78s to digital (no quarter-inch tape), but does most of the equalization in analogue. All but about 3,000 of his 20,000 records are 78s, and he favors master pressings, as runoff discs "are terribly inferior to the original." Some of the odd choices on his albums reflect his ability to locate those masters. Though wary of criticizing producers, he is candid in expressing dismay about the Sonic Solutions NoNoise system, in use at Decca and RCA: "Disastrously ill-conceived, in my opinion. Tremendous loss of information in every example I've checked." He has reservations about the Cedar process, too, now employed at Sony, but finds it useful for declicking, although, he notes, both systems introduce distortion in their declicking phases. "If your objective is surface noise, they work, but if your objective is a vital performance, they don't." He blames the low quality of work at the majors on "computer-whizzes who don't listen to music" and "the quick-fix mentality." "Computers have no way of knowing if overtones are being lost forever, along with the instruments. You have to like the music and want to listen to it."

Of the 25 albums leased to DRG, the majority are jazz, and include city surveys—*New Orleans, Chicago, New York,* and *Kansas City*—that are distinguished by a mix of consensus masterworks and lesser numbers, some gems, others more in the line of pop novelties. One of the most revealing anthologies is *Hot Violins,* an exceptional survey that restores to catalogue two numbers by the neglected Eddie South (Columbia never even reissued him on LP). Also highly recommended are *Swing Groups 1931 to 1936,* which accents clarinetists and is marred only by a painful

Mezz Mezzrow solo; *Swing Big Bands 1929 to 1936*, a compelling argument for several overlooked performances by famous orchestras; *The Blues 1923 to 1933*, mostly the divas plus Jimmie Rodgers; and a sparkling introduction to the weird world of *British Dance Bands*, including the ever-timely "Masculine Women and Feminine Men" ("which is the rooster, which is the hen/it's hard to tell them apart toda-a-ay"), as sung by Ramon Newton of the Savoy Havana Band in 1926.

The CDs devoted to individual artists are not best-of sets, but lively samplers of Sidney Bechet, Jelly Roll Morton, Venuti and Lang, Nichols and Mole, Benny Goodman, Bix Beiderbecke, Bob Crosby, Johnny Dodds, and Clarence Williams (alas, not the Blue Fives). The best of the pop compilations are *Saucy Songs* (incomparable Mae West, Ethel Waters, and Bessie Smith), *Love Songs* (Armstrong, Waller, Crosby, and Richard Tauber), *Silly Songs* (very), and a volume of England's romantic balladeer and wartime casualty, *Al Bowlly with Ray Noble*. As DRG expands its Parker catalogue, much of the best is yet to come, including a Louis Armstrong volume, two collections of Bing Crosby, and two of King Oliver, which includes a transfer of "Dippermouth Blues" so vivid you may feel, as I did, that you are hearing the real Oliver for the first time.

[*Village Voice*, 8 December 1992]

18 ❖ Giant Step
(Jackie McLean)

Jazz sets that are strings of solos are tedious, except when they aren't. Jazz originals lack distinction, except when they don't. Hard bop is glaring and rigid, except when it isn't. In other words, all the axioms apply to the second rate, merely. When the giants come to town, all the conjectures about what makes so much jazz club action a deadening thing disappear. For those who remember all the years when you couldn't hear Jackie McLean at the Village Vanguard, years when he focused his attention on teaching, his appearances there now are simply too precious to miss. Last visit, he presented the final appearance of the quintet that included pianist Hotep Idris Galeta, and was made especially memorable by McLean's searing version of a Burt Bacharach tune, "A House Is Not a Home." A year and a half later, his music is someplace else entirely. But not really. Mastery is its own home and God bless the child that's got one.

McLean's primary home is his pitch, a curiously individual way of bending the tempered scale so that his every note is an expression of personality and vision. It's an adroit yet implacable force, directed at some elusively personal microtone left of center, and contiguous with a rhythmic sense that, with equal individuality, instinctively drags on the beat. The result is a shrewd and sensuous attack, as compelling as that of any vocalist, drawing you in and demanding attention with efficient ideas delivered as confidently as hammer blows. McLean's music is profoundly communicable; his musical posture—in his compositions as well as his improvisations—establishes a broad and overpowering mood. The job of his musicians is to augment his mood, delving into scales as he does, and writing music that elaborates his perspective. A good example is the auspicious debut of pianist Alan Jay Palmer, a student in the African American music department, which McLean founded and chairs, at the University of Hartford's Hartt School of Music.

At the Vanguard and for McLean's fine new album, *Rhythm of the Earth* (Antilles), Palmer brought in new pieces that somehow capture the McLean aura and the long history of his music. He wrote four of the album's eight pieces, and they are as emblematic of the leader's inclinations as, say, the music McLean's sidemen (especially Grachan Moncur III) produced for the classic Blue Note sessions of the early 1960s. Palmer's "Dark Castle" is a ballad etched in the sparked melancholy of McLean's acid pitch; "Sirius System" is a punching AABA power riff that drives his deft yet never glib bebop facility; and "Oh Children Rise" is that rarest of triumphs, a band vocal that works, because the soft, high-pitched unison singing has an unearthly quality and the melody mirrors McLean's inflections on saxophone.

Stronger still are McLean's originals: "For Hofsa" is a ballad written for his wife in a style that perfectly marries pitch and melody—that is, only a musician with McLean's subjective approach to timbre would be likely to invent such a melody; the title selection is a long, modal round-robin staged over the accents of vibraphonist Steve Nelson, played in a manner that recalls Bobby Hutcherson's work on McLean's *Destination Out!* nearly 30 years ago. In fact, the whole CD suggests a further rapprochement with the past, already anticipated in his recent Triloka albums. The front line includes trumpeter Roy Hargrove, relaxed and assured, and trombonist Steve Davis, a member of McLean's working band and a stylish, cogent improviser. The lean arrangements for seven musicians all underscore one incomparable motive: to burn with passion and conviction, to speak one's mind and save one's soul. No one fails the leader or the listener.

Similarly, the McLean sextet established its benign fever at the

Vanguard with the first notes of "Sirius System" and glowed all night. The soloists were decisive, and not all of them got solos every time out; the young bassist, Ernie Barnes, was charged with stoking the furnace, which is what bassists ought to do—no commercial interruptions, as Duke Ellington once characterized pieces that come to a thudding halt for a bass solo. Alan Palmer layered the surface with powerfully intoned chords, and drummer Erik McPherson orchestrated the heads, complemented the front men, and offered solos that sustained and ventilated the intensity of the performances. One highlight involved a sequence where, in lieu of the usual fours, McLean and Rene McLean alternated in a series of sax-drums duets.

During the more than 20 years that Rene has toured with his father's bands, he has become an increasingly persuasive player, but he has almost always reflected his father's impress. Recently, he seems to have come into a sound more genuinely his own. Whereas once he sounded like Jackie McLean on tenor, now he explores the more indigenous reach of the tenor, especially down below, and (conversely) the steeper altitude of the soprano. His solos are concentrated compilations of short, prodding figures, varied and strengthened with an intonation that recalls Coltrane in his *Meditations* period. He and McLean make a strong front line with Steve Davis, whose trombone solos are winning in their unassuming directness and fluent delivery. Jackie McLean is the unmovable center, however, penetrating every corner of his music, at times, as when he laced a swirling improvisation with barking gunshots, sounding like two men—as though he can barely contain what he knows.

[*Village Voice*, 22 December 1992]

19 ❖ *Vivid Multitudes* *(The Best Jazz Records of 1992)*

Travel, influenza, and the death of Dizzy Gillespie have all conspired to postpone the onerous task of a 10-best list into the Season of Clinton, which has already delivered a number of sprightly '93 releases by some of the very people listed below. The trick in looking back is not to work too hard at it. Go with the records that stand out vividly, that provoked multiple hearings or at least good and stable thoughts. Even so, know that you haven't listened to everything, and recognize the inevitable:

Immediately after your list goes into print, you will find the year's masterpiece buried in the sofa—still wrapped in cellophane with one of those annoying silver adhesives to ensure the absolute and utterly pointless sterility of the disc. The selections are arrayed alphabetically. Mea culpa in advance.

1. Muhal Richard Abrams, *Blu Blu Blu* (Black Saint). "Bloodline" and the title selection, a big production blues of the sort only Abrams can pull off (but hasn't since 1981's "Blues Forever"), are peaks in an album that demonstrates perhaps more convincingly than *The Hearinga Suite* that he is one of the leading big band composers of the day, not least because he makes his soloists shine.

2. Don Byron, *Tuskegee Experiments* (Elektra Nonesuch). A momentous debut. Byron's liquid clarinet is coolly lucid. His range, including standards by Ellington and Schumann, is less impressive than the unison sparkle he coordinates with guitarist Bill Frisell.

3. Rosemary Clooney, *Girl Singer* (Concord Jazz). The seemingly effortless jazz-pop big band vocal albums of the '50s and early '60s, now devoured by audiences first discovering Riddle and May, are summoned to memory by this nearly impeccable set, crafted for Clooney—whose always good-humored voice has matured to suggest an extraordinary candor—by pianist and arranger John Oddo.

4. Kenny Davern and Bob Haggart, *My Inspiration* (Musicmasters). Proof that consonance, too, can shake you up. Haggart's major-key orchestrations are glimmeringly old fashioned without being musty or nostalgic; Davern's clarinet fully exploits the opportunities, especially on "Brother, Can You Spare a Dime."

5. Jesse Davis, *As We Speak* (Concord Jazz). Not just a big step for the altoist, an unreconstructed post-Cannonball bebopper who quotes Bird, but the introduction of an expansive sextet with Robert Trowers's trombone and a rhythm section augmented by Peter Bernstein's guitar.

6. Tommy Flanagan, *Beyond the Bluebird* (Timeless). With a calm mastery that makes most other records seem fidgety, this reunion with Kenny Burrell is a meditation on their Detroit roots, with references to Bird and Thad Jones. It offers a sublime "Yesterdays" with a verse of unknown origin.

7. Stan Getz and Kenny Barron, *People Time* (Gitanes/Verve). The radiant tenor saxophonist's last recordings are among his most provocative and moving, but the main reason these duets are instant classics is the uncanny level of dialogue between Getz and Barron, who at times makes the piano thunder with romance.

8. Charlie Haden, *Haunted Heart* (Gitanes/Verve). The third Quartet West album is best, and not only because the latest excursion into noir

jazz actually drafts three of the sultriest torch singers of postwar cabaret. I'm twice grateful because it sent me searching for other Jeri Southern Deccas, including "I Thought About You Last Night," one of the most erotic records I've ever heard.

9. Julius Hemphill, *Fat Man and the Hard Blues* (Black Saint). The former chief composer for the World Saxophone Quartet organized a sextet of saxophonists and produced a lexicon of section riffs, from r&b as well as jazz. It suggests that his truest sound is not his alto but the massing of reeds.

10. Joe Henderson, *Lush Life* (Verve) and *The Standard Joe* (Red). The tenor saxophonist had a key year because of the former, a shapely inquiry into the music of Billy Strayhorn, with inspired work by four supporting musicians, including Wynton Marsalis. The trio album affirms the cause for celebration, with two extended approaches to "Body and Soul," and an alternative "Take the A Train."

11. Oliver Lake, *Virtual Reality* (Gazell). The suitelike intensity of the first four selections, including burnished interpretations of Mingus's "Faubus" and Dolphy's "Prophet," and the premiere of a blues from a Bobby Bradford suite (vide Murray) is especially rousing, but the whole album suggests an accessibility that ought to bring the tart-toned altoist a larger hearing.

12. Joe Lovano, *From the Soul* (Blue Note). His second album for the label fulfills the promise of his first; he even takes a rewarding shot, as every tenor saxophonist must, at "Body and Soul," though the finely etched detail of his "Portrait of Jenny" is more sumptuous and individual. Moreover, Lovano smartly brought together Dave Holland and the late Ed Blackwell.

13. Jackie McLean, *Rhythm of the Earth* (Birdology Antilles). A reaffirmation by the great altoist, whose "For Hofsa" stands squarely among his finest ballad performances and whose title selection recalls the glory days at Blue Note, this album also marks an impressive debut for pianist-composer Alan Jay Palmer.

14. Roscoe Mitchell, *After Fallen Leaves* (Silkheart). The man for all reeds, whom a reader has kindly reminded me once recorded on sarrusaphone (I had thought only Sidney Bechet had that distinction), is characteristically robust, oddly lyrical, and patently uncatagorizable in a recital that shifts direction every track.

15. Frank Morgan, *You Must Believe in Spring* (Antilles). If I came up with an idea as good as this—ballad duets with five pianists, each of whom also has a solo feature—I'd want everyone to know. The packagers elected to keep it a secret. Morgan's alto has an ethereal beauty especially well suited to ruminative melodies; his entrance on "You've

Changed" is deep. PS: Kenny Barron, Tommy Flanagan, Roland Hanna, Barry Harris, and Hank Jones.

16. David Murray, *Shakill's Warrior* (DIW), *David Murray Big Band* (DIW), *Death of a Sideman* (DIW). Musician of the year? Probably. What kind of a day is it that doesn't see the release of a new Murray album? As of December, he claimed 127 as a leader, which makes him, at 37, jazz's Simenon. Yet these albums are decidedly different additions. The first is a back alley quartet session, with a surprisingly restrained Don Pullen on organ. The second is his most winning orchestral album, especially the homages to Gonsalves, Young, and Webster. The third is Bobby Bradford's eight-part suite, far more diverting here than in its concert debut last summer.

17. Red Rodney, *Then and Now* (Chesky). Rodney's quintet with the remarkable altoist Chris Potter is one of today's most practiced. Bob Belden's arrangements contrive a new sheen for classics by Dizzy, Bird, Bud, and Dameron in the year's best purebred bop album—the solos and spirit dead on, in the pocket, authentic.

18. Artie Shaw, *The Last Recordings* (Musicmasters). My no-reissues rule gets somewhat bent here, since most of these stunning 1954 selections were briefly available at the time they were recorded. They offer the pinnacle of Shaw's virtuoso clarinet and document a combo with Hank Jones and Tal Farlow that found its own path between swing and bop.

19. Howard Shore and Ornette Coleman, *Naked Lunch* (Milan BMG). Okay, it sounds like movie music; yet it's hard to resist Coleman and strings—one naked, the other out to lunch. Imagine *Skies of America* with all the i's crossed and t's dotted. The music is better without the movie, a Cronenberg mishap.

The label of the year, conservative though it may be, is Verve-Antilles-Gitanes-Birdology-PolyGram, which also created the 10-CD cube, *The Complete Billie Holiday on Verve 1945–1959*, one of the year's most revelatory reissues, along with Mosaic compendia of the Nat Cole Trio (18 CDs) and Count Basie's 1959 Birdland band. Also outstanding are the 10 volumes of early Sun Ra discs on Evidence, making possible a long overdue evaluation. ECM brought out in one package the two *Jimmy Giuffre 3, 1961* sessions, and Carla Bley and Paul Haines's 1971 *Escalator over the Hill*. Rhino did best with *Aretha Franklin Queen of Soul*, the cream of her Atlantics. Columbia finally edited a decent selection of Franklin's earlier records as well. Otherwise, the most interesting Columbia reissues were in the Collector's Series, including long deleted albums by Jimmy Rushing, Tony Bennett, Jon Hendricks, and, yes, Martha Raye. Delmark reissued the 1940s Apollo sessions, including the undervalued Coleman

Hawkins collection, *Rainbow Mist*. Blue Note edited a canny *History of Art Blakey and the Jazz Messengers*, DRG imported the Robert Parker Digital Stereo series, and Denon began importing a scrupulously remastered edition of the Savoy catalog, including the long unavailable *Charlie Parker Story*, which documents the pivotal "Koko" session.

[*Village Voice*, 2 February 1993]

20 ❖ PG-13
(Rosemary Clooney)

It's amusing, in a dismaying sort of way, to watch the occasional pop critic of the '90s recapitulate the contempt for received wisdom that made much '60s criticism seem arrogantly self-satisfied. You know, the solemn young writers who have no intention of aging themselves, and who treat Dylan, Jagger, McCartney, and Fat Elvis (the one who lost the stamp election) as grizzled hacks who should have retired gracefully or died with the glow of flaming youth. After glimpsing Jagger, never a favorite of mine, on *Saturday Night Live*, I admit to sharing in the ridicule: why did he appear ludicrous, while Jimmy Witherspoon, his senior by two decades, was riveting at Fat Tuesday's last week, singing blues that were venerable when Jagger was born? Wasn't Jagger once touted as a kind of white bluesman? Did he forget everything he ever knew, or has he come to accept his own limitations? Witherspoon mentioned Jagger as playing a role in his receiving a Lifetime Achievement award from the Rhythm-and-Blues Foundation this week, an event certified with a ceremonial performance of his signature tune, "Ain't Nobody's Business."

A quarter of a century ago, critical derision was aimed at a generation of singers who, having apprenticed with and then supplanted big bands in the national affection, proceeded—with help from such producers as Mitch Miller, the Betty Crocker of pop song—to force-feed the public a diet of gooey novelties that dominated the charts in the early 1950s, providing ample justification for rock and roll and other mild anarchies. ("What have you got?" a Brando character responded when asked what he was rebelling against. No one would have understood him had he said, "Patti Page singing 'How Much Is that Doggie in the Window.'") Humbert Humbert, dining with Lolita in jukebox heaven, would later write of the "nasal voices of those invisibles serenading her, people with names like Sammy and Jo and Eddie and Tony and Peggy and Guy and Patty and Rex, and sentimental song hits, all of them as similar to my ear as her various candies were to my palate." He also noted that Lo was a "disgustingly conventional little girl."

Though the better and more experienced singers detested such drivel (Kay Starr on "Rock and Roll Waltz": "I almost had to take a Dramamine to do it"; Perry Como on "Hot Diggety": "I *hated* that ridiculous song"), they were often enriched by and forever allied with it. Jo Stafford had "Shrimp Boats" and Frank Sinatra, "Mama Will Bark." Irish Kentuckian Rosemary Clooney, as she points out to the audience at Rainbow & Stars grateful for the obligatory—and surprisingly swinging—chorus of "Come On-a My House," was importuned to sing an Armenian folksong with an Italian accent, accompanied by harpsichord. Number one record in the country, July 1951. Actually as many novelties were recorded in the early days of rock as before, and continued through the mid-'60s, a roster of purple people eaters, straitjacketed loonies, harmonizing chipmunks, and pious sermonizers of the American dream, among them such potential hall of famers as Jimmy Dean, Lorne Green, and Senator Everett Dirksen.

The current interest in the best of the prerock singers once lambasted as counterrevolutionary owes much to the realization that the songs they sing—beyond the once-fashionable hits that made them stars—are an incomparable treasure that no one else can mine as well. The repatriation of postwar singers and songs has had three overlapping stages. First was the recognition of Jo and Tony and Peggy, and others unmentioned in Humbert's rosary, as high-caliber artists. "We had *faces* then," Norma Desmond says in *Sunset Boulevard*; her musical counterpart today might justly insist, "We had voices"—evocative, distinctive, individual. Second was the need for great songs, reprised for their enduring melodies and colorful harmonies by jazz musicians who always acknowledged the fact that rock never filled the need for pliant ballads. Third was the eventual recognition of the manifest adultness of great lyrics. Perhaps you have to love and lose more than once, or crack your head on the pavement, to know what Larry Hart was writing about—to get past the cleverness of his internal rhymes to the deep feeling that animates his metaphors.

Thus many of us in our forties find ourselves responding to singers in a different way than we did even a decade ago. Instead of primarily appreciating timbre and melody, we begin to really hear the words— almost unintentionally. The ability to interpret them with credibility and power separates great pop singers from pretenders, who get by on good intentions, big pipes, and unctuous smiles. Rosie and Tony and Peggy and Carmen and even Frank and Ella are no longer the ubiquitous "invisibles" serenading us at every road stop. We go to hear them in part because they have become the songs; with rare exceptions their gifts seem to defy the comprehension of would-be heirs. Indeed, the aging process in which they and the songs are locked underscores the story-telling urgency of the best lyrics.

You could hardly ask for a better example than Rosemary Clooney's new album, *Do You Miss New York?*, her 17th for Concord Jazz. Its release coincides with her fifth annual February stay at Rainbow & Stars, a perfect blend of music and geography. The show, which draws its theme from the new album and also includes a heart-stopping rendering of "It Never Entered My Mind," is a celebration of her restored powers. The unmistakably earthy quality of her timbre has always suggested extraordinary candor, yet there is an almost chilling directness in what she can do. You might wonder what she could possibly bring to songs that have been done so often. Yet from the first note, you know you are in the grip of a singer who chooses her material wisely, knows it well, and makes it new. "We'll Be Together Again" seems to find its provenance in her maternal assurances, though one remembers that it also belongs to Sinatra. Her performance is additionally graced by an expert half-chorus by Bucky Pizzarelli and a remarkable full chorus by Warren Vaché that, if performed on a 1939 big band recording, would have been sufficient to secure a reputation. We don't listen as closely as we did then, but this solo and this album merit close inspection. The few awkward spots—the last line of "I Get Along Without You" sounds badly spliced (the room ambience disappears), Vaché's gliss at the close of "Gee Baby" is too cute, the duet with singer-guitarist John Pizzarelli (Bucky's son) doesn't jell—stand out, because the overall frankness invites and withstands scrutiny. It's a profoundly grown-up experience.

[*Village Voice*, 2 March 1993]

21 ❖ *Living Large* *(Bobby Watson)*

It couldn't have been his new album, *Tailor Made* (Columbia), that brought out SRO crowds for Bobby Watson's big-band debut at the Village Vanguard in mid-May, because it had hardly hit the streets and is something of a disappointment anyway. So credit the turnout to a vestigial jazz alertness periodically sweeping over Manhattan when something good is in the air. Musicians caught up in the presently fashionable winds (long may they blow) of big band repertory have a mission. But a musician who endures the trauma of organizing a big band to play his own new music has an obsession, one to be applauded and encouraged at every step. Soloing before or simply listening to the crashing brasses and swaying reeds, Watson exuded the kind of pleasure—it's almost sexual—unique to orchestral amplitude, which in jazz means a number in the very low two-figures.

With a rhythm section (augmented by Latin percussion) taken from his quintet, Horizon; an equally practiced reed section drawn from the 29th Street Saxophone Quartet (Watson is a member); and brasses boosted by the patented brilliance of Jon Faddis, Watson had reason to beam. The divisions swirled and coiled, lifting his fiery alto sax solos on crests and then floating them in pleasurable anticipation of crests to come. The straightforward, bop-inflected writing made up in limberness what it lacked in depth, and when the voicings got fancier, the mild stretches of balladic prettiness were direct and even ingenuous. This is an orchestra that takes its cue from the 1950s, not for the purposes of revival or homage, but to grasp again that moment when fluent bebop melodies and boisterous Latin rhythms found common cause. Several of the pieces—"Lafiya," "Old Time Ways," "Free Yourself"—advanced with storytelling logic and a deft concerto-like regard for the soloists. You'll want to catch this band on its return.

But what to make of the record, which is merely ripe with fine moments, like a souvenir of the real thing, yet never quite fulfills its promise? The packaging alone suggests corporate ambivalence about the project. Only after you buy it and examine the buried personnel listing does it become clear that *Tailor Made* is a big band album, and even then the soloists aren't properly identified. Watson writes that having an orchestra is the realization of "one of my life wishes," and then gives the close-enough-for-jazz warning—you've heard it at countless concerts: "The music you are hearing was laid down . . . without the benefit of advance rehearsals."

It's easy to empathize with the impulse behind that too familiar boast/ apology—a tribute to outstanding musicianship and a tale nearly as old as written music. Berlioz, who also had a thing for size, credited his "palpitating joy" and "wild audacity" for his persistence in plugging ahead with concerts despite musicians who bitched, "We shall never manage it. You know that we can have only two rehearsals, and it ought to have five or six; without an extraordinary delicacy of touch it will be torn into rags." Nothing in Watson's music requires such delicacy, except the nature of swing itself.

A more impressive boast would be, "Columbia added $1,500 to the budget so we could rehearse three hours before the tapes were turned on." Or, the band could have arranged to go into the studio Monday morning, after the gig; in effect, the Village Vanguard would have financed the equivalent of six rehearsals. Familiarity breeds swing. This was an issue even at the height of the big-band era. Frequently the Ellington or Herman bands would go into the studios to record new pieces, usually with exceptional precision. But after a few months on the road, the band would be captured, playing the same number, by a fan equipped with tape, disc, or wire, and by then the tempo had settled into an instinctive groove, the sections breathed in tandem, and the soloists had refined their routines. Ellington's "Take the A Train" would not be the perfect record it is if he (and trumpeter Ray Nance) hadn't tested it at an earlier session and revised it substantially.

With more time, Watson might have avoided the mistake of featuring himself throughout the album and not making better use of several powerful players. Not even Faddis gets much room to shine: I'm guessing that most of the few trumpet spots are by the less electrifying Terell Stafford or, in the case of "The Thing's [sic] You Do," Melton Mustafa. Pianist Steven Scott, of Horizon, sounds less conversant with the music than he did live—of the four pianists who appear on the record, James Williams acquits himself best on the one ballad, "Like It Was Before." More problematic are two undersized pieces—possibly excerpts from unfinished works—and an unaccountably large number of fade-outs, which are almost always infuriating. The worst instances are "Old Time Ways," which opens with a charmingly closely voiced episode for trombones and reeds, before the tempo moves up—the opening would have worked just as well reprised at the end; and "Free Yourself," which telegraphs the fade for a hapless minute or so, destroying the momentum Watson and the ensemble have built.

Reservations notwithstanding, the record can be recommended for the pleasures of a crack ensemble attacking fresh music sturdily constructed to show off the leader's increasingly boisterous alto. Like Cannonball Adderley before him, Watson is an ornithologist with a penchant for Benny Carter–like melody notes. On the first selection, an homage to Betty Carter, he threatens to explode in a breathless maze of customary ideas, but on the follow-up, "Old Time Ways," he breathes and expands and strains, and it's largely the excellence of this solo that underscores the disappointment of the fade-out. As a writer, he offers expertly conceived bop figures on "Conservation"; "Tudo Bem" comes to life in trumpet and (underrecorded) trombone passage; and the two mambos blaze— especially "Catch Me If You Can," another highlight of the Vanguard set, which clearly spurs the ensemble. Perhaps the next album should be recorded live. In any case, score *Tailor Made* as chapter one and hope that the maddening economics of jazz permit a book to follow. Anyone who wants his own big band deserves one.

[*Village Voice*, 25 May 1993]

22 ❖ *Gallic Swing (Stephane Grappelli)*

The 85th birthday tribute to Stephane Grappelli, at Carnegie Hall on June 9, was a triumph for the ageless violinist and the particular brand of jazz he has made his own. The swing he invokes is as decisive as a pendulum or an axe, a bright and inexorable thumping that subdivides every measure with four definitive blows, 128 per chorus. The music soars over those demarcations, charged by the beat, but it's difficult if not impossible to ignore the rigors of that ground rhythm; at times my own bobbing neck and those all around put me in mind of perpetual motion cranes pecking at water glasses. Periodically, you brake the action, the better to focus on the specific notes, but before you know it the chomp-chomp-chomp-chomp infiltrates an unguarded part of the brain, and the foot begins to tap, the elbow to twitch, and the neck to pitch forward. It's a kind of hypnosis.

Yet the mind won't submit unless the melodies are spun gold, beguiling you into security. Grappelli, an exceptionally elegant improviser, has focused for so long on a standing repertoire, notwithstanding numerous divagations, that the most miraculous aspect of his playing is how the rhythm continues to elicit consistently fresh and rewarding performances. Is there no end to "Honeysuckle Rose" and "I Got Rhythm"? For Grappelli, apparently not. Nearly 60 years after he and Django Reinhardt, taking off on Joe Venuti and Eddie Lang, provided Europe with its own jazz soul, he continues to show a rare feeling for melody amid the exhilarating pleasures of rhythm. An analysis of his solos, which rarely exceed two or three choruses, will reveal favorite and repeated patterns, but it won't explain his distinction as a performer fully in touch with the moment. Grappelli much prefers the spell of familiarity to the perils of novelty. Each 32-bar cycle of "Honeysuckle Rose" is a diverting ride home.

Which is not to say that Grappelli, at 85, has slipped into an autumnal phase. His playing is informed by an extraordinary vigor and spontaneity; on the other hand, he seems impatient with ballads, offering rubato meditations as preludes to his full-tilt rambles. Even as the leaves turn, he blows away the mist and restores to them a pulpy, verdant immediacy. A world unto himself, he remains the paterfamilias for a style of time-playing that, once the common coin of a generation, is now a specialty, a discrete mode of jazz classicism. In the '70s, when Grappelli recordings were issued in flocks, he all but drowned the delicacy of his art, and the ritual pleasures of his music often surrendered to glibness. But for a performer as energizing as Grappelli, records are often no more than souvenirs. The deluge reflected the glories of a second-act career.

In the 30 years after he relocated to England in 1939, Grappelli slipped out of the limelight—the postwar return to France and the reunions with Reinhardt tended to reinforce his second-banana stature. In 1969, he made his first visit to the United States, and the waxing of his international reputation has found him at the nexus of generations of string players, including pop comets like David Grisman and immutable graybeards like Yehudi Menuhin, as well as most jazz violinists and virtually every guitarist who can strum rhythm and find the notes to "Nuages." The Carnegie concert was characteristic: no piano except his own (highly ornamental, heavily harmonicized), and no drums. Grappelli appeared at the apex of a faultless trio with guitarist Bucky Pizzarelli and bassist John Burr. The Rosenberg Trio, three members of a Dutch Gypsy family playing two guitars and a bass and making their American debut, exemplified the textures and pulse of Quintette du Hot Club rhythm. Nigel Kennedy, impressively game if not yet sufficiently relaxed with the jazz lexicon, made a valiant contribution as well.

Indeed the concert, produced by Pat Phillips and Ettore Stratta, was better than its parts, a reminder of how luxurious concertized jazz can be. Most jazz concerts don't work, which is one reason much of the Downtown audience—burned by echo-chamber sound, inflationary prices, and amateur-hour theatrics—stays away. This concert was exemplary in its simplicity. A botch in the amplification system that delayed the program 15 minutes was suffered by the good-natured announcer Stan Martin, but when he was finally able to introduce the trio, the sound was warm, evenly balanced, and enveloping. Whether purely acoustic imaging would have been better still, I can't say. This mix left little room for complaint (only an unaccompanied bass solo was boxy), proving once again that the hall itself is not inimical to ably amplified jazz.

The trio performances were a celebration of embellishment, the melodies and harmonies of "All God's Chillun Got Rhythm," "I Thought

About You," "I Hear Music," and the rest assailed as rhythmical fantasies, the meshing of gears so smooth and effortless that a complicated piece (like "Night and Day") emerged no less naturally as a transformed Gallic romp than the more submissive standbys (like "Them There Eyes"). Grappelli produces a stately, sweet, and ringingly clear tone, settled in the midrange and rarely embroiled in double- or triple-stop chords. He is light-footed and modest, avoiding all strain and never overindulging a solo. His long white hair trails down his neck, and he plays seated, standing only to curtsy. He wore a flowered vest over a chartreuse shirt. Pizzarelli and Burr also wore flowered prints. They might have been conventioneers in Waikiki.

The Rosenbergs made a stunning debut, especially the lead guitarist Stochelo Rosenberg, who is perhaps the most proficient Djangologist since Bereli Lagrene. He inclines, however, to play every selection at numbing velocity, picking his phrases with icy precision and strumming up the fret board with locomotive energy. The sound of an acoustic guitar amplified by a pickup is the best of two worlds, combining the robust warmth of wood and the kinch-edged severity of electrified steel. The unity of the Rosenbergs suggests a much larger ensemble. Nous'che Rosenberg's rhythm guitar is as plush as a four-inch carpet and Nonnie Rosenberg's bass extends its depth. The three closed a blues by trilling in unison. On "Honeysuckle Rose" (which, like "Nuages," was heard twice), they accelerated in lockstep rigor. They know the changes; they *are* the changes. But they need to learn a ballad.

The second half showcased Pizzarelli's seven-string guitar, in a superb "Nuages," opening with an extended rubato cadenza, and mining the melody with a maturity, emotional resonance, and breathing room that the Rosenbergs could only intermittently suggest in their performance of the same piece—it was a lesson from the master that roared to a dynamic close with buoyant and full-bodied strumming. Burr was also impressive in unaccompanied variations on "Makin' Whoopee" and "In a Sentimental Mood." Grappelli played a piano medley that hovered barely aloof of the cocktail hour. Then Nigel Kennedy made the trio a quartet, playing all the solos and exchanging fours with Grappelli, who was determined to take a back seat to his guest. Kennedy made the most of dynamics—his sound can rise up like a siren—and repetition, and he engineered a series of riff-based solos, never so much as considering the possibility of a quarter-note rest. Still, what he lacked in swing, he made up for in persistence and excitement—occasionally the sort of excitement achieved by sawing a single phrase until applause sets in. The same violinist who recorded the most painstakingly slow version of the Tchaikovsky violin concerto imaginable could hardly contain his ardor in the throes of jazz. The highlight of his set with Grappelli was a funny, partly contrapuntal, dilatory two-violin arrangement of "Tiger Rag." For the finale, all seven musicians connected on "Sweet Georgia Brown" and "Undecided," the three guitars imparting the drive of the original Quintette du Hot Club, Kennedy clamping down on triple stops, and the serenely imperturbable Grappelli slipping deft ornamentation in any space not already taken.*

[*Village Voice*, 22 June 1993]

*Most of the concert, excluding the performances with Nigel Kennedy, was released on record as *Stephane Grappelli: "85 and Still Swinging"* (Angel).

23 ❖ A Surprise Banquet (JVC 1993)

When the peak of a nine-day jazz festival is scaled by a 75-year-old entertainer whose jazz associations over half a century have been at best tangential and at worst gratuitous, you can assume that the usual suspects flagged terribly or that said entertainer astounded. Lena Horne's sublime 30-minute performance at the tribute to Billy Strayhorn should become part of Newport/New York/Kool/JVC legend. And yet she wasn't the only one who performed at a level that may, as time goes by, also qualify as memorable. Thus what looked like thin gruel going in provided something of a banquet. Against all odds, the flagship of impresario George Wein's global operation turned out to be a modest success—not for the sweep and aspiration by which we usually evaluate it, but for incisive and animated musicianship. The Sound of Surprise surprised.

True, the perception may have been helped by diminished expectations. The piano recitals were gone, as were the crossover artists—Ray Charles, B. B. King—who ensure a certain boisterousness. Instead of three major hall concerts per evening, JVC '93 offered two or one. New music was conspicuously absent. Several young mainstreamers were pressed into jam session tableaux, but none received important debuts or showcases. A jazz festival, especially in this country, can no longer depend on headliners to draw a tip. (Miles, you are sorely missed.) Even Charles Lloyd, ringingly endorsed by some commentators last summer, failed to fill the tiny outpost of Merkin Hall. It looks as though future ballyhoo will emanate from the music's exuberant center, its common language, a language JVC will have to be increasingly creative in mining.

Opening night took place in two cities. While Gerry Mulligan and Betty Carter launched the festival proper at Carnegie, the press core and many musicians congregated on the south lawn of the White House for a mini-festival and presidential photo-op to be telecast on PBS in the fall. Although the invitation read, "On the occasion of the Fortieth Anniversary of the Newport Jazz Festival," the milestone proved a weak sister to the 25th anniversary event; that one was presented by President Carter, who set a tone of casual inclusiveness extending to and beyond the music, which ranged from Eubie Blake to Cecil Taylor. Taylor was present this time, too, but only as a member of the audience, along with Wein himself, who oddly enough was barely acknowledged by President Clinton, stiffly reading from a teleprompter.

Wynton Marsalis's Septet opened with a windy excerpt from *Citi Movement* and recouped with Ellington's "Play the Blues and Go," though both performances underscored the disparity between the leader, an increasingly riveting soloist, and his sidemen, who too often seem to be engaged in an exercise of connect the dots. And his was the only practiced band. There followed two fringe piano recitalists: Michel Camilo, who opened coherently and built to a showy finish, and Dorothy Donegan, who opened showily (Rachmaninoff) and finished in the same vein (Vincent Youmans); and two longer instrumental episodes, a swing jam and a bebop jam, fatally divided by a somnolent passage in which Herbie Hancock accompanied Joe Henderson, on a "Lush Life" that was mostly distracted arpeggios, and Grover Washington, on a tepid Hancock original.

The swing session included Clark Terry, Al Gray and a rhythm section made up of Dick Hyman, Charlie Haden (rarely heard in this context since the '60s), and Elvin Jones, and provided some reverberant drama when tenor saxophonist Joshua Redman intrepidly quoted the *Martha* fragment from Illinois Jacquet's "Flying Home" solo, only to be steamrolled by the master himself reclaiming the whole solo. The boppers— Red Rodney, Jon Faddis, Jimmy Heath, Henderson, and a rhythm section of John Lewis, Christian McBride, and Thelonious Monk, Jr., who emceed the evening—romped healthily through "A Night in Tunisia" and "Confirmation," with Lewis in especially aphoristic form. Also performing were three singers: Rosemary Clooney, who wittily chose her two selections for their lyrics ("Sweet Kentucky Ham," about going on the road, and "Love Is Here to Stay," which begins, "The more I read the papers/The less I comprehend"); Bobby McFerrin, who sang didactic scat (Horace Silver's "Peace") and invited the Clintons to visit his kids;

and Joe Williams, who led the finale with a medley of "Shake, Rattle and Roll," "Everyday," and "All Blues," during which the presidential saxophonist puffed two choruses, reminding us that we support him not for his music, but because his administration will focus on the economy instead of Iraq and bring a moral wisdom to Haiti, socialize health care, defend the rights of gays to be gay, and make Solomonic appointments to the Supreme Court.

Devoted as we are to Clinton and her lovely husband Bill, we couldn't help but notice that the overall pleasantness of the occasion (enhanced by food worked up from recipes by Clark Terry, Andrew Cyrille, and Milt Jackson) was needlessly marred by incredibly inconsiderate treatment of the press, dragooned into a kind of class system that had nothing to do with the relative significance of the critics themselves. Invitations were issued in tiers: At the top were critics invited with spouses to dinner and music, followed by those invited without spouses to dinner and music (e.g., me), followed by those invited to music only, followed by those invited to sit in what was euphemistically called a "press pool." This last group was kept waiting in a room until the food was safely carted away, and then situated at the rear, cordoned off by a velvet rope, although empty seats were visible at most tables.

Well, it was a relief to return to Manhattan, where people are judged entirely by the content of their character, even if the triptych of singers assembled at Town Hall was less than ideal. Nancy Marano and Eddie Montiero do Jackie and Roy better than anyone since Jackie and Roy. Montiero accompanies the vocal harmonies on a synthesizer accordion that enables him to play "bass" as well as "guitar," "piano," "organ," and "vibes" solos, all of which sounded preplanned. Their book includes jazz classics ("If You Could See Me Now," "Whisper Not," "Joy Spring"), but lacks jazz spontaneity. Anita O'Day virtually trips over her own spontaneity, deconstructing words into repeated eighth-note syllables and engaging her quartet in precipitous exchanges. The voice is thin and the intonation uneven, but her set grew in confidence and by the time she paid tribute to her past ("Let Me Off Uptown" and "Boogie Blues"), she was certifiably in tune for a wordless "Four Brothers" and an excellent goodbye theme, "I'll See You in My Dreams."

In between was Cassandra Wilson, whose often captivating set included "My One and Only Love," Robert Johnson's "Come On in My Kitchen," and several originals. Wilson has the sexiest contralto in years, the body language to back it up, and a favored sighing interval that stamps all of her songs with an unmistakable and original imprimatur. Why then is she perversely bent on alienating her audience? The sound, excellent for the others on the bill, became a maddening echo chamber for her, partly the result of her inexplicable use of electric bass. Lacking either microphone technique or articulation or both, she allows the words to bleed together—you wonder why she bothers to write lyrics if she doesn't want them understood. Wilson may be the last best hope for jazz singing: She is perhaps one step from greatness, but it's a big step, and I get the feeling she won't take it until she decides she really does want to communicate with the strangers arrayed before her.

Billy Strayhorn was a composer of exquisite miniatures, and the tribute to him at Avery Fisher was bound either to be exquisite itself or a flat disappointment. Mostly, it worked beautifully. Guitarist Howard Alden and trumpeter Warren Vaché played duet treatments of "Johnny Come Lately," "Smada," and "Lotus Blossom," the last preceded by Ellington's "Single Petal of a Rose." Supple, lyrical, in tune with each other, they inclined—perhaps because of the absence of bass and drums—toward long, breathless phrases; on "Smada" especially, a few rests might have strengthened the solos with a grander architectural design. Bobby Short, the amiable emcee who brightened the evening with a recital of all the members of the Copasetics, a club of professional and amateur dancers of which Strayhorn was president, joined the duo for a persuasive reading of "Your Love Has Faded." Joe Henderson, backed by Dave Holland and Al Foster, provided a harder edge than many in the audience desired, but played an expansive and creative set, beginning with a cool, evenly pitched theme statement of "Isfahan" in a performance that built to a clanging climax, and including a "Lush Life" ably shadowed by Holland and Foster, who soloed at length on a rambunctious "Take the A Train."

By way of introducing Lena Horne, Short repeated her warning to him, "Don't expect me to become a jazz singer overnight." But that's what she did. Ten days short of her 76th birthday, she appeared, a vision of sculpted beauty and earned glamour, before an audience already on its feet. She could have gotten away with anything, but she delivered on her fabled devotion to Strayhorn with a spellbinding salute of seven songs, including a couple of obscurities, and a recollection of the first time they met, at a performance of *Jump for Joy* in Los Angeles in 1942. She had been alone, and Ellington sent Strayhorn to her seat at intermission to make certain she was comfortable. He "looked like a lovely brown owl," she recalled.

Although she performed with several jazz orchestras in her early years, Horne found her métier on the stage, where she emoted not by the dictates of swing but through the autobiographical allowances of theater. Never as successful on records, where her mannerisms tend to intrude, she triumphed as an icon—the surviving performer who, bruited about, lives to tell the tale. What was most remarkable about her performance at JVC was the absence of the mannerisms and the celebration of self. Oh, she was stunningly theatrical, but she embraced the songs outright. Accompanied just by Jay Berliner's guitar, she produced a perfect chorus of "A Flower Is a Lovesome Thing," really opening up at the release, but pacing the whole performance as an aria, which in a dramatic context it might very well be.

Elsewhere, she was backed by a quintet led by Frank Owens with solos by saxophonist Jerome Richardson. She opened a bit nervously with "Maybe," which Strayhorn apparently wrote for her, but relaxed appreciably on "Something to Live For" and the 1941 "Love Like This Can't Last," a marvelous little-known song that deserves revival. Reminding the audience that "Jump for Joy" was a rare Ellington attempt at a protest song, she examined all its ambiguities, its black (in both senses of the word) humor, gospel ardor, and secular esprit. The first note of her ordained encore, Arlen's "Stormy Weather," was greeted with a roar that echoed through the rest of the festival. She closed on a sustained semifalsetto note I never imagined was in her repertoire. The astute audience thundered.

No one should have been asked to follow her. Mercer Ellington, leading the Ellington orchestra in a program of Strayhorn instrumentals, was the logical anticlimax, but proved even more disappointing than necessary. Weighted down with an extra percussionist and second keyboard, the ensemble was logy and unswinging, and the arrangements—some of them among Strayhorn and Ellington's most sublime inventions—were pointlessly revised. "Day Dream" is not improved by a brass vamp and plunger-mute trumpet solo; nor is "Take the A Train" enhanced by additional choruses.

The rest of the festival, or most of it, was loosely knit, jammed, and jazzy. (The exception was "The Jazz Connection: The Jewish & African American Relationship," at Avery, a concert proposed three years ago by the Jewish Presence Foundation that lay dormant until Wein offered to produce it, programming it in collaboration with musical director Randy Sandke and myself.) Wein, who has led various editions of the Newport All Stars over the past four decades, finally gave himself an evening on his own festival, and it is unlikely that he has ever employed a musician who more shamelessly and repeatedly plugged a new record. The irony is that the musicians were hard-pressed to recall the album's routines and compensated with a greater display of extemporaneous improvisation. Highlights included a slow blues with Illinois Jacquet, Warren Vaché's "What's New," Nicholas Peyton's "Struttin' with Some Barbecue," Doc Cheatham's "I've Got the World on a String," and Flip

Phillips (who described Django Reinhardt as a three-fingered Gypsy who only stole bowling balls) and Howard Alden's "Tears" and "Nuages." The presence of Phillips and Jacquet did not produce the half-expected JATP rumble, which was a relief, but spirited chase choruses were provided by Gerry Mulligan and Wynton Marsalis on "Bernie's Tune" and "What Is This Thing Called Love?" and the amazing Cheatham and Jon Faddis produced a warmly attentive harmonization of "Mood Indigo." Clark Terry and Al Gray also got to shine.

The celebration of Thelonious Monk and Charlie Parker, also at Town Hall, began in dire straits: a painfully clumsy 75-minute set of Monk's music led by bassist Larry Gales. Clark Terry said at the top, "This is the rehearsal," to which Gary Bartz replied, "He isn't kidding." With David Newman trying to find his notes, the heads sounded as though they'd been telegraphed from three separate cities. Little of the material was identified, and nothing at all was said of Monk. With Jaki Byard on piano, Bartz raised the ante a bit on "Ruby My Dear" and "In Walked Bud," but to little avail. The only musician who consistently distinguished himself was pianist Hilton Ruiz, who, prolix though he is, played aggressive, rollicking solos with richly intoned dynamics and a certainty untouched by the numb fumbling all around him.

Set two, dedicated to Parker, was the antithesis in every sense. A radiant cast celebrated Parker's memory, announced the tunes, and played the hell out of them. The ever inventive Red Rodney and Barry Harris served as the sparkplugs, aided by Bob Cranshaw playing a standup bass and drummer Mickey Roker. The three saxophonists were Charles McPherson, who turned the ballad "Bird of Paradise" into a medium cooker; Greg Abate, who seemed zealous on alto but made a convincing stab at tenor on "Donna Lee," and Jesse Davis, who roared through "Little Willie Leaps." Walter Bishop, Jr., recited his own poem, "Owed to Bird," by turns funny and moving ("he was our Christ after a fashion"), and took to the piano for "Yardbird Suite" and "Big Foot," playing with polish and big thumping chords.

(The Bird and Monk concert was scheduled opposite "Wynton and Jon," at Avery, the only difficult choice presented all week. The muted exchanges between Marsalis and Faddis on "UMMG" were the subject of much discussion. So, on a less imperial note, were the shenanigans of Lincoln Center, which demanded that Faddis's Carnegie Hall Jazz Band be renamed the JVC Jazz Festival Big Band as a precondition for Marsalis's participation. This seemed especially cheap, as JVC had no problem with Wein continuing to name his ensemble Newport. That was the least of it. Copies of a letter written by Rob Gibson, director of Lincoln Center Jazz, to certain members of the Classic Jazz Orchestra were circulated all week. In the letter, Gibson said he was firing all musicians over 30 in "an attempt on our part to try and get some of the younger musicians to learn more about this music and begin to play it with some authority. Obviously, we had that authority with you, and that's why this has been a tough one." The reasoning not only wants logic; it is discriminatory. When *Billboard's* Jeff Levinson inquired about the letter and its ramifications, the firings were rescinded and the musicians reinstated.)

The best jam of all was the tribute to Art Blakey. Ira Gitler, the associate producer, has a built-in jive detector when it comes to modern jazz playing, so the musicians he assembled were expected to play well—precise heads, bright and invigorating solos. Beyond that you get the luck of the draw, and this night was lucky indeed. It took half the opener, "Minor March," for the quintet of Jackie McLean, Donald Byrd, James Williams, Dennis Irwin, and Lewis Nash to mesh completely; then the magic took hold and never let up. McLean has been playing exceptionally well for the past couple of years, and yet there was a rare exhilarating quality to his playing this night—a diamond-hard brilliance that waxed through the first tune and the follow up, "Fidel," and then completely broke free on "Dig," where he continued beyond the expected caesura into an additional chorus that had the other musicians looking at him with unmistakable admiration. Byrd, on flugelhorn, was no less surprising, because he hasn't played with such care and finesse in two decades: His tone is thin, but he phrased with determination, avoiding licks and facile quotes. It was like being transported back to the Bohemia and Birdland to hear veterans of those years play with such tenacity and fire.

By contrast, the second set—with Curtis Fuller, Benny Golson, and Brian Lynch—was anticlimactic, and not helped by "Up Jumped Spring," which can be waltzed too easily into a state of hapless sappiness. Fuller's "A La Mode" was much better, with the trombonist interpolating Volga boatmen and Golson working fierce fragments against brass riffs; the hotpoint flashed during Mulgrew Miller's piano solo, when Elvin Jones clamped onto a piano figure and the two men fed off each other for the duration of the chorus.

The second half matched the opening set. Elvin and Dennis Irwin joined in a reassembled version of Blakey's great band of the early '80s, with Wynton Marsalis, James Williams, Bobby Watson, and Billy Pierce, and no sooner were they through the theme of "Webb City" than again the shades of time disappeared, along with the hassles of leading a band, and the soloists bounded into the open. Marsalis kept his solos short, sculpting them with economy, coherence, and dynamics, and seemed to inspire Watson to a heady rapture that was the essence of this band in its prime; he in turn inspired Pierce, who on Watson's "A Wheel Within a Wheel" pushed himself so resolutely into the changes that Marsalis, who had played a brief opening solo, came back for a second shot. On "E.P.A.," Jones pressed the ensemble and soloists every measure of the way, and Marsalis once again showed what a fiery player he can be when unimpeded by other responsibilities. Donald Harrison and Terrence Blanchard had to follow that, and succeeded by reproducing the solid ensemble coupling that distinguished their edition of the Jazz Messengers. When the entire cast was assembled for "Moanin'," much of the audience was clapping in time, an often boorish activity that in this context was well earned.

Those highs were not sustained through the subsequent concerts, testimonials to Birdland (Gerry Mulligan, John Lewis, Lee Konitz, Roy Haynes, Phil Woods, Gary Bartz, Barry Harris, Red Rodney, Jon Faddis, George Shearing, the Basie Orchestra conducted by Frank Foster) and Jazzmobile (Jesse Davis, David Sanchez, Ryan Kisor, Christian McBride, Nnenna Frelon, Bobby Watson's Horizon and Big Band), and obviously not because of the talent involved. Everyone played well, but no one played spectacularly well and by this point there had been enough inspiration to encourage us all to resist near beer. Still, it remains thrilling to hear the Basie brasses shake in unison, and Watson's orchestra, though overly dependent on de facto alto saxophone concertos, glows with vitality. The sound in the main halls, live but controlled for the most part, faltered toward the end, the inevitable result of overmiking. But balance of sound was not the sticking point. Latecomers were: Between selections, PLEASE CLOSE THE DAMN DOORS.

[*Village Voice*, 13 July 1993]

24 ❖ *Tremolos and Elegies (Cyrus Chestnut)*

By their tunes ye shall know them. So in welcoming pianist Cyrus Chestnut as he emerges from the ranks of accompanists into the limelight of leadership, let's begin with the tunes—those he writes and those he interprets. Last week he debuted with one trio at the Village Vanguard and with another on his first major album, *Revelation* (Atlantic). The 31-year-old, Baltimore-born, Berklee-graduated, and widely apprenticed pianist is a prolific composer, and he favors his own material. But not exclusively. The album's two exceptions suggest something about his range and taste.

The jazz genealogy of Jules Massenet's "Elegie" as one of Art Tatum's pet morsels is well known. Tatum elaborated the tune with characteristic élan, his variations partaking of stride bass, supersonic arpeggios, and a rubato close, all underscoring the source melody. Chestnut is less respectful of the original. He begins improvising over a pedal-bass, then buttresses himself with a descending four-chord figure that suggests nothing so much as the turnback for "Sweet Georgia Brown," which is his immediate set-up for Massenet's tune. The pop reference is echoed in the introduction of a standard old-time four-note descending bass vamp. He wails on that and then on the chord changes he has adduced, kicking into overdrive with propulsive riffs and, unlike Tatum, completely escaping the gravitas of the original. Chestnut reprises the tune only at the end, as a head, incorporating the four-note vamp on piano before a quick and not inelegant fade. In stately contrast, "Sweet Hour of Prayer" is an old hymn sweetly played, peeled of all complexity, with a slow-motion Bach mordent as the kicker.

During his opening Vanguard set, Chestnut announced that as a product of the Baptist church he often plays hymns. He chose "Greater Thy Faithfulness," opening slow and alone, vamping into time, and then launched a brief cadenza that salvaged the performance. It wasn't a first-rate set, often the case with Tuesday night openings, but perhaps exacerbated in this instance by a houseful of press and record company people. He seemed to lose his concentration during the one other non-original, "For All We Know," which he established with soulfully dawdling block chords, spiked with skittering forays that recalled Hampton Hawes, before sacrificing his momentum to a bass solo and never quite recovering it. Yet it confirmed his deliberation in choosing material that speaks to him. How, at century's end, does a young jazz pianist go about crafting a career or even a presence? In the absence of a riveting original style, his material may be decisive.

Chestnut does have his own style, though his persona is evident in his technical skill and the uses to which he puts it, not in an extensive reordering of fundamentals. You could pick him out in a blindfold test because of his rhythmic inventiveness (his drive and predilection for time changes); his insistence on making a trio act like a trio (he emphasizes group dynamics, refusing to delegate solos to fill out a set); his canny use of details to revitalize familiar phrases; his attraction to the extreme octaves, especially the plink-plink high notes; and his penchant for tremolos, a signature he is in danger of overdoing, though played right it could turn into a selling point. Like many players of his generation, Chestnut consolidates instrumental styles prevalent in the late '50s and early '60s. He sounds more like the pianists who immediately preceded Bill Evans and McCoy Tyner than those who immediately followed them, and he is practically untouched by free jazz. Yet a monochromatic quality occasionally overtakes his playing, less on the record than in concert, and you wonder why contemporary pianists frequently settle for limited harmonic spectrums.

He reminds me a bit of Wynton Kelly, another outstanding accompanist (Kelly served Dinah Washington, Chestnut Betty Carter) known for his rhythmic ingenuity. Unfortunately, Kelly was never able to exploit his gifts when he went out on his own. His quartet with Wes Montgomery should have developed into a major force, but the same commercial interests that shanghaied Montgomery saddled Kelly with the fashionable soul-funk of the mid-'60s. Unlike Montgomery, his career went nowhere, and he didn't live long enough to find himself again. Chestnut does not have Kelly's personal problems, and arrives at a time when he probably won't be tempted by his professional compromises. Today, the clarity and suppleness of Kelly and Sonny Clark and Hampton Hawes and Bobby Timmons is once again highly valued, and so is the two-fisted brio of Ray Bryant and Phineas Newborn, Jr., and even Dave Brubeck and Ahmad Jamal. Yet the difficulty of carving out a niche is as great as ever.

Chestnut's ace in the hole is his original material, and the primary pleasure of *Revelation* is the way he thinks through his own tunes. The dazzling opener, "Blues for Nita," isn't a blues at all, but rather a cheerful 34-bar AABC song with a pleasantly ominous bass line that comes to the fore in the performance's climactic episode: a tremolo sustained with altered dynamics for some 44 ringing measures, the left hand shifting from chords to a bass walk before teaming with the right in a well-earned crescendo. It may remind you of the way organist Jimmy Smith could keep you hanging on a drone until you noticed you weren't breathing. Also contributing to the character of the piece is an introduction, reprised as a transition, that ties a 4/4 riff to a 5/4 vamp, the break signaled by drummer Clarence Penn's cymbal swipe and bell. The entire eight-chorus performance moves with auspicious finesse, and typifies Chestnut's affinity for off-center shapes, transitions, and time changes. (At the Vanguard, with bassist Rodney Whitaker and drummer Carl Allen, he played Allen's "Alternate Thoughts" in an undulating 5/4: 1960 lives.)

"Lord, Lord, Lord" opens with tremolos and is configured in a conventional 32-bars, but the A sections are divided between an earthy bass vamp (weighty tone, played by Christopher J. Thomas) and light, cosmopolitan piano chords. The release uses slap bass to suggest stride and finishes with a glittery arpeggio. All the thematic elements in the composition are sustained in improvised choruses. Similarly, a whizzing swinger called "Macdaddy" employs stop-time for half the A sections, reflected in punching riffs throughout the solo, and contrasted with the more melodic and rhythmically legato release. The premature ending is a diverting surprise. So is the brief "Revelation," a piano solo in the key of Monk. Every pianist has to play something Monkian, and this one has all the edges and angles, the close chords, a nearly impenetrable transition, another premature ending, and a reference to "Well You Needn't" in the bridge. At the Vanguard, Chestnut said he plays this differently every time, and sure enough that performance had whispers of a boogie bass and a clattering of minor seconds.

The album peters out, possibly a victim of too much cleverness: "Cornbread Pudding" is just what it sounds like, a revival of circa-1960 food songs, but the elongated blues-with-a-bridge structure takes a while to get going and is weakened by a dull bass solo before Chestnut's one good chorus. The only true ballad, "Proverbial Lament," withers under the strain of forced lyricism—I half expected to hear Keith Jarrett groaning in the background. But I've saved for last the exceptional "Little Ditty," which is neither little nor ditty. In the context of the album, the piece is entirely characteristic—not merely a blues, but a blues with an eight-bar bridge and a two-bar hesitation at the tail of every chorus, and an improv that boasts a 12-measure tremolo, lots of high-note plinking, parallel lines, an interpolation of "Rockin' in Rhythm," sustained motives, resolute swing, and a tag ending that would be corny if it weren't played with such ingenuous enthusiasm. This is the piece that most recalls Wynton Kelly, because it is the most direct and the most solidly grounded in bebop harmonies. Yet it represents only one direction for Chestnut, whose trajectory will be well worth following.

Revelation is beautifully recorded. Chestnut produced himself, with engineer Jim Anderson, and the music was recorded on a two-track analog system. Rather poignantly, considering the postproduction cosmeticizing that has become increasingly rampant, he posts the credo: "Complete takes only, with no additional mixing or editing." From the first notes—piano and a sibilant swipe of the cymbal—the sound is robust, warm, and accurate.

[*Village Voice*, 8 February 1994]

25 ❖ *The Power and the Reticence (JVC 1994)*

Competing big bands, controlled jam sessions, piano duets, salutes, jazz al fresco, Duke Ellington and Dave Brubeck, Ray Charles and Mel Tormé. Where the hell are we—the Newport Jazz Festival of 1958, the Newport-in-New York Festival of 1972, Nice, New Orleans, a Savoy Ballroom of the imagination? No, we're right here on the sun-scorched terra firma of New York City in 1994, where the JVC Jazz Festival gazes stoically at the future through a rear-view mirror. Satchel Paige had it wrong: Always look back, because if you're lucky, your old and just possibly better self may be gaining on you.

The iconoclast in me wants to catalog what JVC ought to be, especially by example of what Europe routinely offers in the way of summertime jazz festivals—at Norway's Kongsberg Festival, where I dropped in for a day, the performers included the Art Ensemble of Chicago, Randy Weston, Steve Coleman, bluesman Johnny Copeland, and opera singer Barbara Hendricks, who presented an evening of songs from Ellington's three Sacred Concerts in the local church. But you've heard that spiel before and, in any case, the reporter in me prefers to honor that most resilient of impresarios, George Wein, for once again taking cheapjack and making Jack Daniel's. I'm not referring to the more adventurous afternoon concerts, a welcome return to the street events of Newport's early years in New York, but to hall-bound exhibits that transcended expectations. Not for the first time has a schedule that looked tepid on paper produced magic in the playing. You've heard that spiel before, too, yet this year the surprises were a little more intense than usual.

For example, Dick Hyman. I know, I know—you hear the name and your blood tingles, the short hairs vibrate, the heart hammers. But Hyman's fastidious tribute to himself at Town Hall was a charmer from near-beginning to end. As *Newsday*'s Gene Seymour noted, JVC and its predecessors have done particularly well with homages to undercelebrated jazz veterans with strong ties to New York, from Eddie Condon and Roy Eldridge to Gil Evans and Buck Clayton and Doc Cheatham, whose 1991 evening was a fiesta of synergy and excitement. Hyman's night was relatively discreet, chamber-like, and drummerless. As pianist and organizer, he had been a pioneer of jazz repertory in the '70s, so I expected him to essay James P. Johnson, Jelly Roll Morton, and Scott Joplin. But aside from Fats Waller's "Sweet Savannah Sue," he played straight improvisational fantasies on standards—mostly very old standards, by Tchaikovsky and Hines and Ellington, among others.

Roger Kellaway and Derek Smith, with whom he has performed four-handed piano improvs for many years at Dick Gibson's jazz parties and Hyman's annual 92nd Street Y series, were present for duets and trios. Howard Alden and Bob Haggart joined with him in airily swinging renditions of "Idaho" and "Dardanella," and Frank Wess inspired a reverential hush with the Lestorian edge he imparted to "Just You, Just Me" and two relatively avant-garde selections, "A Time for Love" and "(Meet) The Flintstones." A show-and-tell highlight was a droll resume of Hyman's career, illustrated with recordings, including movie scores, commercials, pop novelties, collaborations with Charlie Parker, Benny Goodman, Johnny Mathis, Arthur Godfrey, Tony Bennett, and a cage full of canaries: "In those days," he said, "I'd come over and wash your floors for scale." But the lynchpin of the evening was the indefatigable Ruby Braff, lately recovered from serious illness.

Hyman's playing can get awfully stiff-necked left to its own classically schooled devices, which was the case with his opening solo on "What Is This Thing Called Love?" Then Braff came out, and before they had finished eight bars of "Sophisticated Lady," the hall was awash in a roseate glow. Given Braff's idiosyncratic approach to rhythm and melody, it's hard to believe he was often dismissed as a mere traditionalist in the early days. His notes are less played than sculpted, sustained beyond expectation or peremptorily cut off. Every aspect of his pitch is controlled, from attack to decay. The melody notes peal like great bells or small chimes, and his asymmetrical phrasing keeps rhythm in a kind of swinging suspension. He didn't sound like Armstrong on "My Monday Date" or like Beiderbecke on "Sunday," yet he managed to impart both—the power and the reticence. In arousing Hyman's acute antennae, he brought the duets to a state of grace.

Intimations of grace were also palpable at the Carnegie Hall tribute to the recently retired shepherd of the night flock, the Reverend John Garcia Gensel, who, as Jimmy Owens observed, is usually associated with memorials to the dead; he did not have to follow Orpheus to get his tribute, if one may apply Greek mythology to Lutheran orthodoxy. Gensel had become so much a part of the jazz community that he'll be as hard an act to follow at Saint Peter's as Johnny Hodges was in the Ellington band. American clergymen may look more like Elmer Gantry and less like Father O'Malley every day, but Gensel revives one's agnostic faith. For one thing, he always had time; for another, he created a remarkably nondenominational and nonjudgmental space. Not knowing one reversed collar from another, I once called him when I was writing a piece on the Catholic theologian Hans Kung. After explaining the difference between Catholics and Lutherans (for one example, his wife Audrey), he promised a reading list and phone numbers, and delivered that day. He and Audrey are returning to Pennsylvania; like everyone else, I'll miss them.

The concert was emceed by Bill Cosby and stage-managed by Ira Gitler, and went seamlessly, considering the large number of musicians. As with Hyman's concert, the mood was reminiscent of the Town Hall broadcasts Eddie Condon presented in the '40s, or afternoon jams at the Newport Jazz Festival—breezy, fast, and generous with good feelings, long but not too long. Among my souvenirs: Cheatham aiming at the chandelier and acing his compatriots, *again*; Gerry Mulligan entering "These Foolish Things" obliquely and sustaining his lyricism and legato time; Roy Haynes using an overhand grip to motor "Take the A Train"; Jimmy Owens and Lew Tabackin dramatically reviving Ellington's homage to Gensel, "The Shepherd"; Robert Trowers's burnished open horn and Dennis Wilson's pitch-perfect plunger mute in a trombone duet on "Just a Closer Walk with Thee"; Hilton Ruiz's expansive "Lush Life," complete with parallel-hands block-chord cadenza; Barry Harris's silken, clichéless rendering of "Get Happy" (memo to George: consider a JVC tribute to Harris and Marian McPartland, who can converse as well as play); solos by Jon Faddis, Wallace Roney, Jimmy Heath, and Lew Soloff. When the last band screwed up the four-bar exchanges, Harris inserted a bar of "Cocktails for Two."

Still, the concert for which this festival will probably be remembered was billed as "A Historic First Meeting," and that's what it was: Jon Faddis's Carnegie Hall Jazz Band on Avery Fisher's stage right and Wynton Marsalis's Lincoln Center Jazz Orchestra on stage left. Alone, neither band has been much noted for bruising excitement, and the idea of a battle between repertory bands sounds like a bad joke: the legendary battles of the '30s were as much about exciting new material as spick-and-span execution. Well, forget all that. Neither band is exclusively concerned with classic repertory, and yet three exhilarating payoffs were achieved on precisely that turf: Marsalis's Ellington triptych, climaxing with "Dance of the Floreodores" from the *Nutcracker*, preceded by a murderously swinging "Happy Go Lucky Local" and a simmering episode from *Afro Bossa* and concluded by a James Carter cadenza consisting largely of a few well-aimed blasts; Faddis's adaptation of Gillespie's "Things to Come," for which Marsalis crossed the stage to take his turn with the trumpet soloists, who achieved unison grandeur in a series of brass tuttis that suggested the handiwork of arranger Slide Hampton; and both bands together on a version of "Battle Royal" that Ellington prepared for his collaboration with Basie, *First Time!*

But though Marsalis occasionally seemed riled by Faddis's easy demeanor and made a few testy remarks, always followed by second-thought protestations of respect, this was not the 1937 Webb-Goodman bout, not a fight to the death, not really a fight at all. Only the audience can declare a knockout in one of these set-tos, and the splendidly involved throng at Avery Fisher decidedly refused every invitation to enmity—applauding, cheering, stomping, and laughing at successful conceits, and merely applauding or chuckling at unsuccessful ones. Rarely did the bands cross into each other's realms, which is one reason the evening was so satisfying. Marsalis's music was rooted in Ellington; Faddis's in Gillespie. One of Faddis's smartest moves was responding to the Ellington triptych with a sumptuously arranged ballad, "It Never Entered My Mind," arranged by Renee Rosnes, featuring muted brasses and flutes and supple episodes for reeds and trombones. That was not the desperate parry of a bloodied opponent.

The only extra-musical tension came when Marsalis brought out singer Milt Grayson for a mild reading of Billy Eckstine's "Jelly Jelly." The audience was receptive but hardly thrilled. Faddis joked about the unfairness of introducing a singer when he didn't have one. So he sang himself, a recurring falsetto-and-basso-profundo blues in the manner made familiar by Gillespie and James Moody. Terrible: despite my fondness for vaudeville, I thought he sacrificed badly needed momentum. But the audience, impressed by his temerity or his unpretentiousness, approved in thunder. Marsalis muttered, "I'm not gonna imitate a woman. We're just gonna stand up here and swing." He later told Faddis, "You should've stayed with comedy." Which made me wonder how an artist who knows Armstrong and Ellington as well as Marsalis came to think that the majesty of the blues and a sense of humor are mutually exclusive.

No one needed to be defensive. Marsalis proved himself an exceptional conductor, holding the ensemble in the palm of his hand, and possibly setting to rest, at least for the time being, the conductor controversy at Lincoln Center, since they could scarcely hope to find anyone better. Except for an Ellington-like original that took a long time getting nowhere, he never let the energy flag, and his sections sang in radiant unison. Faddis has a broader if in some ways more conventional book, but he also produced precision work and let the soloists fly: One of the evening's biggest ovations went to Frank Wess, who essayed the old Count Basie vehicle, "Blue and Sentimental."

Battle ethics notwithstanding, there was a winner: the jazz audience. This concert brought back big band fever like nothing I've seen in 25 years. People streamed out of the hall as though they'd seen the glimmer of a new day. Maybe they had.

[*Village Voice*, 19 July 1994]

26 ❖ *Leonard Feather, 1914–1994*

Leonard Feather, who passed away on September 22, 1994, nine days after his 80th birthday, always insisted that John Hammond was the most important of all jazz critics. That's not surprising if you recall that Feather, who was Hammond's junior by four years, initially made his way through the British jazz world in the early '30s, when Hammond's articles in *The Gramophone* and *Melody Maker* were stirring the jazz waters as no English-speaking critic had or would again until Feather himself took up the sword for modern jazz in New York a decade later. Hammond encouraged him to make the move, in 1935; 20 years later, he helped midwife publication of Feather's *Encyclopedia of Jazz*. Yet it was also Hammond with whom Feather conducted the most vitriolic of several public feuds.

Hammond was the prototype writer-activist, enforcing his critical pronouncements with a regimen of recording, promoting, producing, and general agitation, mostly on behalf of new talent and new movements— he helped launch the Swing Era. He was also unstinting in his devotion to civil rights, in and out of the music biz. With varying degrees of success, Feather would follow his lead, adding his by no means negligible abilities as lyricist (occasionally aided by his wife, Jane) and composer. Indeed, his early years here were devoted almost exclusively to producing, arranging, and composing. Not until the early 1940s, when he became associated with *Metronome* and *Esquire*, did he begin to function primarily as a critic.

Yet while Hammond could never entirely disentangle criticism from engagement, and quickly fixed himself in the corporate world, Feather— though often entangled himself—had the intellect and independence of a critic born. Over the amazingly long, prolific, and frequently cantankerous and controversial run of his career, he decisively supplanted Hammond as jazz's most forceful critic and chronicler. That assertion may surprise some who know my own allegiance to Martin Williams,

who was often at Leonard's throat, and my distance from Leonard's
workaday opinions, which from the mid '60s on could be found mostly
in the *Los Angeles Times*. Yet all of us, even Martin (who contributed to
one of Feather's encyclopedia yearbooks), had to acknowledge his work
and be grateful for his industry. I would measure his preeminence chiefly
on four fronts.

1. His most influential book, the second edition of *The Encyclopedia of
Jazz*, published by Horizon in 1960 as *The New Encyclopedia of Jazz*, remains a cornerstone of jazz historiography. Despite errors (mostly birth-
dates) and rivals, from Chilton to Grove, it is unmatched in its critical
breadth and autonomy, and for ancillary sections that approach the subject in myriad ways—musicological, sociological, even anthropological.
At the time of his death, he was working on a biographical encyclopedia
with Ira Gitler, formatted for the Oxford Companion* series and foregoing the editorial apparati and photographs of the Horizon volumes.
A singular aspect of Feather's encyclopedias (four volumes and two yearbooks) was the accent on stylistic influence and musicians' perspectives;
in forms he submitted to musicians, he attempted to suss out the generational and lateral connections that soon became a constant in jazz
criticism. After the original *Encyclopedia*, in 1955, Feather edited two revealing yearbooks that have been combined in one volume by Da
Capo—check out the study of audience demographics, the history of the
record industry, profiles of critics and DJs. More than any other critic,
Feather took the subject whole.

2. In 1949, Feather published his first book, a shocking-pink $2 pa-
perback with a tiny picture of his head ("the first critic to herald the new
movement in jazz") under the title, *Inside Be-Bop*. It opened, hilariously,
with six epigrams eviscerating bebop, including one from Hammond,
who at the time found the whole subject of modern jazz anathema. Only
103 pages, it had an incalculable impact, making the case for Charlie
Parker and Dizzy Gillespie biographically, historically, and musically.
Even by today's standards the transcriptions are exemplary. Feather was,
together with Barry Ulanov (the field's Aquinas), one of two esteemed
bop heralds. Gitler recalls his early work as humorous, irreverent. In any
case, he got the first book out. And though later generations of critics
rebuked it and him for missing the boat on Thelonious Monk (I say he
needed a fall-guy to underscore the evaluative weight of his endorse-
ments), he captained the ferry that brought Parker and company to port.
Inside Be-bop is probably the most plagiarized book ever published about
jazz, as Leonard was quick to note. I told him that much of the stealing

---

*The Biographical Encyclopedia of Jazz appeared in 1999.

was inadvertent: The book's central ideas passed so quickly into the realm of received wisdom, they were iterated by writers with no idea of their provenance. During the same conversation, I suggested he contact Da Capo about a reprint. When the deal was done, I asked if he would add a new introduction, you know, to clear the air about Monk. He said he'd think about it, but in the end he could concede only that although he might have devalued him, others did the reverse. Another idol he could not bear was Jelly Roll Morton.

3. Feather invented the "blindfold test," originally for *Metronome* and then *Down Beat*, which copyrighted it—a sore point for him—and continues to publish it. I seem to recall his saying that he did something similar on his popular live-audience radio show, *Platterbrains*. Eventually, he took a revised and renamed version with him when he joined the staff of *Jazz Times*. The significance of the blindfold test exceeds its entertainment value. It added a phrase to the language and a dimension to the issue of critical authority, demonstrating that people often judge a work of art differently when they don't knew who signed it. Over decades, Feather embarrassed scores of musicians who thought that race and gender were audible, or that studio men can't improvise, or that big names are invariably identifiable. His tests occasionally made news (one with Monk and several with Miles Davis leap to mind), or evinced a political edge, as when mainstreamers dumped on or defended the avant-garde or, in the early years, the "moldy figs" of jazz traditionalism that Feather often reviled. Which of us hasn't run the test on friends or ourselves? I recall an evening when a colleague dissed Zoot Sims, whom an hour later I slipped onto the turntable—he guessed one favorite tenor after another, ultimately conceding that Zoot "could play." I exhausted some of my own prejudices after flunking a similar test.

4. Not even Hammond championed civil rights more ardently than Feather, especially when he relocated to Los Angeles, and with his great friend Benny Carter as his guide, went to work on Jim Crow in the musicians union and movie studios. His revelations of systemic racism were eye-openers, and instigated important changes. What is perhaps not as well remembered is his service on behalf of women musicians, whom he tirelessly represented in his writings and as a producer. He helped to introduce Dinah Washington (who enjoyed hits with several of his blues lyrics) and Sarah Vaughan; produced all-women jazz ensembles in cooperation with Mary Lou Williams and Beryl Booker; and helped, among several others, Mary Osborne, Vivian Garry, and Vi Redd, who introduced his lyric to "Anthropology" and his canniest blues, "I Remember Bird." One of his wittiest pieces, "Mound Bayou," with lyrics by Andy Razaf, was a minor hit for Helen Humes.

Those accomplishments seem to me paramount, but there were other aspects to his influence. A careful, clear writer and solid researcher, he opened a lot of slick magazines to jazzcrit. He wrote hundreds of liner notes and produced dozens of records (*Pre-Bird Mingus* and *Sonny Rollins Trio and Brass* among the classics) and anthologies. He consulted on movies and TV shows. He wrote, with Jack Tracy, one of the first and funniest of the jazz joke-and-parody books, *Laughter from the Hip*. His much-revised *The Book of Jazz*, with its frequently imitated "The Anatomy of Improvisation" and emphatic reproofs of New Orleans primitivists, was an academic standby for years. Leonard was a sober writer, sometimes dour. He had little patience with the glib hyperbole that is forever uncovering "perfect" solos and dubbing every musician "jazz's greatest" this or that. As a result, he sometimes appeared exceedingly cool, which is one reason much of his best work can be found in the relaxed personal essays collected in such books as *From Satchmo to Miles*. As a composer, he was inordinately proud of having written pioneering attempts at jazz waltzes and dodecaphony. Those efforts are largely forgotten, but B.B. King still gets his biggest laugh of the night singing the stop-time chorus of Leonard's "How Blue Can You Get?"

I met him in 1975, at Dick Gibson's jazz party, and we saw each other two or three times a year after that. Shortly before our first encounter, I had come across his venomous exchange with Hammond over Duke Ellington's work in the early 1940s, which Hammond scorned and which Feather represented as a publicist. I considered Feather's fierce response, "Heil Hammond" (this in 1943), one of the most powerful polemics I'd ever read. Yet when I mentioned it to Leonard, he at first denied writing anything with such a headline, and later dismissed it as the gross excess of impetuous youth. In truth, he was never more forceful than when angry, and by the time I got to know him, he was living down a reputation as a tough customer—the guy Muggsy Spanier allegedly cold-cocked before recording "Feather Brain." At the 1975 party, a couple of bop veterans who had not encountered him in years, sniped from a distance about his demeanor—beady eyes, watchful of all the musicians out to Muggsy him. But those slights were forgotten when the same musicians could no longer resist rehearsing old times with him, remarking afterward how much he had mellowed.

He looked mellow enough, and scarily ageless—one of those men who never gain any weight or lose any hair. Tall, reserved, unimposing in manner, he was remarkably steadfast. Well into his seventies, he was driving to the clubs, flying to the festivals, sailing on the cruises, and filing review after review with no sign of ennui, though his taste increasingly favored the flashily virtuosic over the expressively idiosyncratic.

He was completely focused on music, and unapologetically acerbic in his asides. When I last saw him, in the spring, he had begun to weaken, dispirited by the 1993 earthquake that forced him and Jane to vacate their Sherman Oaks home. He had been in a coma for most of the past month, but went out with his boots on—not with a pen in his hand, but with Benny Carter at his hospital bedside every day, playing jazz records.

[*Village Voice*, 11 October 1994]

27 ❖ After the Ball
(Gerry Mulligan / Maria Schneider)

Big bands were so closely associated with dancing during the Swing Era that their revival in the 1950s—by which time bop had produced a more meditative jazz listener and rock and roll had parted dancers from swing rhythms and each other—required something new in the way of justification, e.g., music qua music. Motivation no longer came from dance-floor customers or smiling baton-wielding bandleaders who couldn't read music, but from the needs of orchestrators and musicians bred in modern jazz yet ardent in their belief that big is better. The transitional period was perhaps symbolized by the firing of Count Basie from the Camel Rock and Roll Party because, in Alan Freed's immortal words, "musically [Count] has the greatest band in the country, but it isn't a dance band."

Basie, Ellington, and Woody Herman achieved new musical plateaus as the '60s dawned, but dancers who stubbornly clung to each other in the face of twists and frugs still found safe haven in their plush ensembles. Although Herman openly disdained dancers, all three courted them, and generally offered the same "book," or repertory, whether or not the audience was seated. Ellington had been composing listener-intensive music all along, and by 1940 many people were disinclined to dance even to his dance music for fear of missing something. Two decades later, the difference between Ellington's dance and concert music was often illusory. I attended a 4-H Club show at which he played almost the same set for the concert half as for the dance half; the only difference was they removed the rows of folding chairs for the latter.

The soon-parodied line went, "Will big bands ever come back?" But they were all over the place. Stan Kenton orchestrated Wagner for the progressive music crowd. Ghost bands with smiling baton-wielding bandleaders and nostalgia-laden books provided sweet memories for those who lamented Major Glenn Miller and the best years of our lives. Hey kids, why not go into the rec room to watch American Bandstand, so mom and I can enjoy Lawrence Welk? It became customary for pop singers who had graduated from the bands to re-record the old songs with lush orchestras scripted by such luminaries as Nelson Riddle, Billy May, Van Alexander, Sy Oliver, Benny Carter, and Ralph Burns—in that setting, big bands were so much the norm they were almost invisible.

Still, a purely musical big band was a risky proposition, despite the growing number of powerfully individual writers, among them George Russell, Gil Evans, Thad Jones, Gerry Mulligan, Ernie Wilkins, Frank Foster, Bill Holman, Neal Hefti, Johnny Mandel, and Gerald Wilson. If anyone could make a go of it, Gerry Mulligan was a likely candidate. A bona fide jazz celebrity steeped in the big bands since his teens, when his first arrangements were accepted by Gene Krupa, he later wrote for Elliot Lawrence, Claude Thornhill, and Kenton. He had the temperament to lead a big band, the personality to charm an audience, and, for a while, the backing of Norman Granz and Verve. In case anyone doubted his intentions, he called his 1960 ensemble the Concert Jazz Band.

Bill Kirchner, a musician and writer (he annotated Mosaic's invaluable *Complete Solid State Recordings of the Thad Jones/Mel Lewis Orchestra*), has now selected a dozen pieces for the Mulligan entry in Verve's Jazz Masters series. Given the company's success with box sets, a complete edition of Mulligan's five Concert Jazz Band albums and the rumored trove of unreleased performances should be high priority. Even so, Mulligan's *Jazz Masters 36* is cause to reconsider an ensemble that not only produced its own classics but set in motion the big band resurrection of the '60s and continues to inform that of the '90s—witness Maria Schneider's debut *Evanescence* (Enja) and her long-running Monday night gig at Visiones.

The first order of business for a concert band was to reevaluate the relative importance of swing, melody, and harmonic voicing. The constant foxtrot-four had become excruciatingly dull, which made tempo changes, contrary meters, and rubato cadenzas increasingly attractive. The blending of instruments across the divide of reeds, brasses, and rhythm produced bolder colors, cluster harmonies, richer and headier brews. Longer melody lines suggested the linearity of improvised solos. Needless to say, all these "innovations" were part of Ellington's music from about 1927. But Ellington had made a separate peace with the music world, and few staff arrangers with dance bands could do more than pay homage with borrowings. Mulligan gave them oxygen.

Ironically, the administrative duties of bandleading kept him from writing more than one arrangement for the CJB, but Mulligan had something of an alter ego in the trombonist who succeeded Chet Baker and Art Farmer in his pianoless quartet. Kirchner astutely describes Bob Brookmeyer as "a totally personal mixture of the gutbucket and the cerebral." Known as a trombonist whose instrument had valves instead of a slide and as an occasional pianist (duets with Bill Evans), Brookmeyer became a prominent arranger through his work with the CJB, his contributions ranging from the briskly swinging clarity of "You Took Advantage of Me," with its now-you-see-it-now-you-don't ensemble backing, including a radiant chorus by the reeds, to the close harmonies of "Manoir de Mes Reves" and the cool wit of "Big City Blues," with its piano and clarinet opening, plus Clark Terry—with whom Brookmeyer later formed an unjustly neglected quintet—and Jim Hall.

The CJB didn't have a pianist per se; Mulligan and Brookmeyer took turns when necessary. But it had a staunch rhythm section in bassist Bill Crow and the gently but decisively propulsive drummer Mel Lewis. Not the least significant upshot of the band was Lewis's decision to relocate from Los Angeles to New York. Within three years of the Concert Jazz Band's 1963 demise, Lewis and Thad Jones took Mulligan's gambit another step and created the Monday night orchestra at the Village Vanguard, which in their absence celebrates its 29th anniversary at the Vanguard all this week. Brookmeyer, who became the band's music director after Jones left, was in the original lineup—his serial "ABC Blues" and "Willow Tree" were among the band's early gems.

Other composers, old and new, gloried in the CJB's precision and in the opportunity to set off Mulligan's endlessly supple baritone sax, which could assume almost as many colors as the ensemble. At Mulligan's suggestion, Al Cohn added the exhilarating Ellington/Webster-influenced ensemble chorus to "Lady Chatterley's Mother" and expanded "Blueport" from Mulligan's quartet version, opening it up for exciting exchanges between Mulligan and Clark Terry. In adapting his own "Israel" from the Miles Davis Nonet, John Carisi added a chorus in which the trumpets play Davis's original solo. Johnny Mandel, another graduate of Elliot Lawrence's band (and Basie's and Herman's), was just beginning to establish himself as a film composer—the triple-meter "Barbara's Theme," from *I Want to Live*, is darkly beautiful.

One of the most celebrated CJB performances was George Russell's update of his "All About Rosie," originally something of a concerto for Bill Evans, but in Mulligan's performance a burnished play of light and dark, satin and steel, with glowing precision in all the sections, especially the reeds. Gary McFarland was unknown at 28, when he turned up at a

1961 rehearsal with two pieces, "Weep" and "Chuggin," profoundly influenced by Ellington and Strayhorn. At the time of his tragic death 10 years later, his reputation had been sullied by several trite projects. But the McFarland that Mulligan put on his way was an impressive writer (Verve and Impulse are overdue in reissuing *The Jazz Version of How to Succeed in Business, Point of Departure,* and *The October Suite*), with a rare ear for melody and the ability to layer rhythms in the wind sections. Like Brookmeyer and Jones, McFarland developed Ellington's love of harmonic density, employing what the influential arranger and educator Rayburn Wright called "grinds"—major and minor seconds woven into the voicings.

The rather sudden ascension of Maria Schneider during the past year provides a singular expansion of the circle. She has studied with Wright, who died in 1990, as did her former husband and co-bandleader, John Fedchock (and Kirchner, Sy Johnson, Dave Berger, among many others). She later worked extensively with Brookmeyer, who introduced her to Mel Lewis, whose orchestra premiered several of her pieces. Then she went to work writing for Gil Evans, whose influence is especially conspicuous, though she has also absorbed Ellington, Russell, and Jones.

Schneider has plenary gifts. She's a fine conductor, as she demonstrated in her Carnegie Hall Jazz Band commission, "El Viento," eliciting bright dynamics and an even rhythmic keel from the ensemble. As a writer, her greatest strength is in the rich vertical dressing of harmonies that swell in discerning, spacious clouds of sound. During moments on a recent night at Visiones, where her 17-piece orchestra appears every Monday with no cover charge (that can't last forever), the whole orchestra, breathing as one, managed to suggest the motionless vapor of Evans's harmonies and a nearly florid exuberance. She voices guitar in unison with the ensemble or piano, and frequently changes the reeds, so that the double-alto, double-tenor, baritone line is breached by flute, soprano sax, clarinet, bass clarinet, in sundry combinations. She is generous to soloists (including Tim Hagans on trumpet, Rick Margitza and Mark Vinci on reeds), who return the favor with deliberation, prompted by the dramatic settings she devises for them. A good composer can fill the air with few instruments, and Schneider drew captivating moments from just two or three players at a time.

Her choices in standards are unexpected ("Days of Wine and Roses," "Over the Rainbow"), and the originals are generally more compelling, especially "Evanescence," the Evans-inspired title selection from her impressive debut CD, which begins modestly with bass, guitar, brushes, and achieves a powerful, piquant Spanish cast; "Wyrgly," which climaxes in a display of guitar-synth effects and ensemble jubilance; and a distinctive, haunting triple-meter pastoral theme called "Green Piece," which recalls the score from *High Noon*. Schneider builds her themes on ostinatos and vamps, in part because her melody lines aren't especially strong. But she understands the texture of the orchestra as few young composers do, and at 34, her promise is enormous.

[*Village Voice*, 7 February 1995]

28 ❖ *Redefining Dizzy* (The Carnegie Hall Jazz Band / Lalo Schifrin)

Jazz repertory without messianic passion will be nothing more than the recycling of hits for monied subscribers—cf. the New York Philharmonic. But the movement is so new, the repertory so ambiguous, and the audience so impressionable that we're unlikely to step into that bear trap any time soon. Almost everyone in the movement has a case to make, however much at odds it may be with commerce. When the ensemble that evolved into the Lincoln Center Jazz Orchestra performed Ellington's long neglected *Anatomy of a Murder*, it proved a point: the audience came, heard, and was conquered, and the piece's place in jazz discourse was redefined. Other examples abound.

The Carnegie Hall Jazz Orchestra has been circumspect about the past, making its primary contribution in the commission of new works, including revisions of classic arrangements that needed no such help. Its "Trumpet Tribute" on February 23, however, made a compelling case for reconsideration of *Gillespiana Suite*, the five-movement concerto grosso Lalo Schifrin wrote for Dizzy Gillespie in 1960, and, by extension, of their entire collaboration. Schifrin conducted; music director Jon Faddis played the Gillespie role; and Frank Wess (flute) and Dick Oatts (alto) shared the responsibilities of Leo Wright, the only woodwind in the original performances. The orchestra's reading of a difficult score was crisp and aggressive, at times sensationally evocative.

For years, Faddis has argued that Gillespie achieved a peak of performance in the late '50s and early '60s, and that the album *Gillespiana* represented a kind of zenith. Yet that period was often ignored or patronized as a popularizing aftermath to Gillespie's revolutionary work in the previous decade. *Gillespiana*, in particular, has suffered a nebulous critical history during the past 35 years, infrequently discussed or even mentioned in appraisals of Gillespie's accomplishment—including my own. But Faddis has now made his case, and a second look is in order.

Gillespiana was highly regarded at the time of its release, and often cited by people who were drawn to jazz because of it. Indeed, 1960 was a major year for Gillespie. In late fall, Verve announced a year-long promotion by offering free copies of his *A Portrait of Duke Ellington* to the first 5,000 who wrote in for it, but queries ran many times that, and in the end everyone got it for a buck. Two weeks later, Schifrin combined Gillespie's quintet, in which he played piano, and an ensemble of brasses and rhythm to record *Gillespiana*. The results encouraged the label to seek a date at Carnegie for a formal debut. No prime-time bookings were available, so the March 4, 1961, concert was called "Genius at Midnight," and a bronze head of Gillespie prominently displayed. Auxiliary highlights included the premieres of Gillespie's "Kush" and Schifrin's variations on "A Night in Tunisia" ("Tunisian Fantasy").

Gillespie also made news that year when Tulane University canceled a contract with his quintet because he wouldn't replace Schifrin with a black pianist—his manager, Joe Glaser, and the union backed him up in refusing to refund Tulane's deposit. He broke the house records at San Francisco's Jazz Workshop in the summer, and returned for an unprecedented eight-week booking. The fan-driven competition between Gillespie and Miles Davis, who unseated him in the *Down Beat* critics' poll in 1958 and 1959, was briefly decided in Gillespie's favor: they tied in 1960, and Gillespie won in 1961, by one vote. But the victory was illusory, as was the success of *Gillespiana*, although it triggered a second work by Schifrin, *The New Continent*, which (with Benny Carter conducting) debuted at Monterey in 1962 and was recorded a few weeks later. Limelight didn't release it for three years.

Again the reviews were enthusiastic, but by 1965 jazz was rent on one side by rock and on the other by the avant-garde, and Gillespie was no longer deemed the center of anything. Even Davis's sales began to flag. The two major works with Schifrin were long overlooked—Verve coupled *Gillespiana* with the Carnegie concert on CD in late 1993; *The New Continent*, also controlled by Verve, has never been reissued. Yet the latter offers, in "The Conquistadors," one of Schifrin's most appealing themes, and in "Atlantis" and "The Chains," solidly structured concerti for Gillespie—their recurring figures rousing him to some of his slyest improvising of the era. When he breaks loose on—or of—"The Chains" (the introductory thumping unhappily recalls the galley drums in *Ben Hur*), he crackles, twisting notes over a bright rhythm and blues canter that carries him into a trumpet cadenza that, though less than a minute long, should be considered in any accounting of unaccompanied brass solos.

The neglect isn't entirely hard to understand. As Faddis has pointed out, *Gillespiana* was a rare example of the mentor taking a cue from the student. Few recordings in jazz history or in the LP era had the romantic provenance of the collaborations between Davis and Gil Evans. Everyone wanted to follow in their steps, even Louis Armstrong. (At least Gillespie and Schifrin beat Davis and Evans to Carnegie, by more than two months.) Gillespie first encountered Schifrin in 1956, while touring Buenos Aires—a lucky break for Schifrin, who was living in Paris at the time and visiting South America—and offered him a job. Schifrin, who had won arranging and piano prizes in Argentina in his teens, took him up in 1960, and spent three years in the quintet—*On the French Riviera*, for septet, is probably their best-known work together. For all the educational variety of his background (his father was concertmaster of the Buenos Aires Philharmonic and his teachers included Messiaen and a student of Schoenberg), he was no more able to match Evans's indigenous blend than Gillespie could Davis's dark moody drama.

The Davis-Evans records helped define the period. In contrast, Schifrin's suite was a tribute to Gillespie, a summing up rather than a manifesto, a concerto that finds its power in provoking the soloist while suggesting the range of his historical achievement in big bands, modern harmonies, Afro-Cuban rhythms, and more. Still, it successfully avoids pastiche, maintaining genuine excitement in the dialogue of ensemble and soloists (how promising Leo Wright was in those years, before he relocated to Europe). Nor does he fail to create memorable tableaux that, absent Evans's cloudlike chords, have an arresting quality of their own— the flute and trombones in "Blues," with its cannily altered changes; the elephant shrieks of "Africana," in which Gillespie begins his solo in what is for him the lower register, and, over a dramatic landscape of conga and timbale rhythms and brass tuttis, plots a muted solo of enormous wit and responsiveness to the ensemble's contrary theme. His imagination never falters.

Schifrin was also undervalued for a dumber reason: his great success in Hollywood. A rhythm vamp in the "Toccata" that exuberantly concludes *Gillespiana*, and the 5/4 bass figure in the second movement of *The New Continent* each prefigure the theme that established him as a comer in that arena—the 1966 5/4 intro for *Mission Impossible*, the one TV suspense-show theme since *Peter Gunn* and *Dragnet* that everyone seems to know, and like them the source of a hit single and two best-selling albums. Schifrin told Royal S. Brown (*Overtones and Undertones*, University of California Press) that he went west not for the money but because movies gave him a chance to combine his classical and jazz training. His long affiliation with Don Siegel and Clint Eastwood, in addition to such films as *The Cincinnati Kid*, *Bullitt*, and *Cool Hand Luke*, helped re-establish the neonoir sound in the '60s and '70s. He stirred much interest for bringing jazz techniques back to Hollywood; *Down Beat* even proclaimed his 1965 *Once a Thief* the first jazz score since *I Want to Live*—forgetting Ellington's *Anatomy of a Murder*, John Lewis's *Odds Against Tomorrow*, Leith Stevens's *The Gene Krupa Story*, Freddie Redd's *The Connection*, and *The Cool World*, with a Mal Waldron score partly improvised by Dizzy Gillespie.

Critics have a way of sniffing at jazz musicians who make it elsewhere, however, and as the tone changed from encouragement to derision, Schifrin's Hollywood efforts were dismissed as "slick hack work" and his jazz tainted by association. He went a long way in justifying the disrepute in his 1977 reunion with Gillespie, *Free Ride* (Pablo), an abomination that is all vamps and fades, notwithstanding several glimmerings of Gillespie's cunning. Surprisingly, his 1995 CD series, *Jazz Meets the Symphony* (Atlantic), is less inventive than his best film scores; these tributes to Gillespie, Davis, Armstrong, Ellington, and others, though often entertaining and always well played, smack of precisely the unconsidered tours of nostalgic benchmarks that many people fear will be jazz repertory's endgame. The collage style (what's the meaning of the Garner-esque "Sleepy Time Down South" or the *Rhapsody in Blue* segue to "Someday" in the Armstrong medley?) come off as glib and arbitrary.

Yet Schifrin remains true to his master ("I have had many teachers, but only one master," he has said of Gillespie), as he proved in the dynamic performance of *Gillespiana*. The orchestra was totally in his grasp, despite his self-imposed double duty of having to cross back and forth from the piano. One way to measure how good the Carnegie Hall Jazz Band has become is to compare it with the 1961 Carnegie Hall recording. Many members of that all-star unit appeared on the album and had more time to drill than Faddis's orchestra. Yet there were no wobbly sonorities and missed cues evident (as there are in the "Genius at Midnight" performance), as Schifrin plotted the dense brasses and clattering rhythms, cleared them away for quiet patches, comped alertly at the piano, and painstakingly set up the soloists, all of whom—Wess, Oatts, trombonist Steve Turre, drummer Lewis Nash—exceeded the challenge.

Faddis was magnificent in what at times sounded like a personal coming-out—he honored Gillespie with a measure of individuality he never permitted himself when standing in Gillespie's shadow. He floated beyond the triplet patterns of "Prelude"; understated the half-valved muted effects but hit squarely the high muted note Gillespie rang on "Blues"; crafted a cadenza on "Africana" with imperial logic; and, beginning in the lower middle register, cautiously forged the splendid climax of "Toccata," as the ensemble shouted the final figures.

The concert's other episodes were less conclusive: a jam session centered upon Clark Terry; a mosaic of Miles Davis themes arranged by Slide Hampton and featuring Wallace Roney; and an uneven if often exciting assemblage of Louis Armstrong pieces arranged by Randy Sandke—including astute adaptations of "Hotter than That" and "Tight like This," the latter heating to a boil as Faddis played Armstrong's first chorus, unison trumpets took the second, and they came together for the third with Faddis overlaying a high-note counterpoint. The rhythm section (Cyrus Chestnut, Peter Washington, Nash) firmly grasped the music and Sandke outfitted the selections with regard to their origin, though his tendency to append brief codas to the Armstrong solos made for anticlimactic endings.

Gillespiana Suite was everything jazz repertory ought to be. In confirming the vitality of the work as a concert piece, it encouraged one to return to the record with new regard, which in turn makes the possibility of another live performance even more desirable. If fear of repetition discourages an encore (unlike audiences for European classics, who prefer what they know by heart, the jazz rep audience is suspicious of repeats), the Carnegie Hall band might take a look at *The New Continent*. Faddis would have a blast with it.

[*Village Voice*, 14 March 1995]

29 ❖ *The Swinging Cowboy (Herb Jeffries)*

As the imposing six-foot-plus frame of Herb Jeffries emerged from the stairwell of the Village Vanguard shortly before his first set on Sunday night, the audience began to applaud, murmuring, "Eighty-three? Is that what 83 looks like?" With luck, yes: His wife Regina confirmed his birth date as September 24, 1911. Resplendent in a white dinner jacket and embroidered shirt, Jeffries acknowledged the reception, embraced numerous friends, parried remarks on the order of, "Remember when we met in the Sherman Hotel in 1939?" and took a seat to listen to his pickup quartet open the set with "In a Mellow Tone." Reluctant to leave the audience for the stage, he finally sauntered to the mike, by which time the Vanguard was no longer a nightclub. It was proprietress Lorraine Gordon's jazz salon. Even the paying customers—if there were any— must have felt they had lucked into a private party.

And half an hour later, as he reached back for a black Stetson and pulled loose his bow tie, it wasn't even a jazz party. Jeffries has returned from obscurity courtesy of Warner Western, the label that signed him in 1994 to record cowboy songs. It's a cinch you won't see anyone else on their roster—Sons of the San Joaquin, Red Steagall, Michael Martin Murphey—here, but after all none of them spent four years in the Duke Ellington band. Gordon, who didn't know of the cowboy record when she inquired into his whereabouts, simply wanted the peerless ballad singer who drifted from sight in the '60s. His highly enthusiastic Nashville sponsors, also present, wanted to hear some of the record. In the end, he satisfied both parties, his patter full of convincing arguments about the historical synergy between jazz and country. His own background as a bronco buster helps to explain why he now emerges as a genre-buster.

Jeffries grew up in a mixed neighborhood in Detroit, where he learned to ride horses and speak Yiddish. He never endured discrimination or even thought of himself as an African American until he went out into the world and, like Julie in *Showboat*, discovered the unwritten law about one drop of black blood. "In our community," he told me, "there were only three black families and I'm not including myself for the simple reason that, while most people identify me as being black, I'm actually Irish-Italian and I have a great-grandmother who was Ethiopian—which is Semitic, not African. Yet I've been identified as being Afro-American, which is okay with me. It's made my life very interesting."

In 1933, he joined the Earl Hines Orchestra in Chicago, and toured the South, a devastating experience. "I was appalled. I had lived in a multicultural neighborhood in which we *shared* the culture, and had never seen people discriminate against each other. We played in the backs of warehouses in Florida, Alabama, Mississippi, and sheriff's buses would come behind us and follow us to the border. Blacks couldn't go to theaters, they had to have their own little 10-row theaters, and there were thousands and thousands of these segregated mushroom theaters throughout the south, where blacks went to see white cowboy pictures. I said, 'My god, black children can't relate to being a cowboy because there are no black cowboys,' and yet they were very obviously a part of our history. It's been estimated that one-third of all cowboys were black.

So I got it in my mind to go to California and find someone to make some black cowboy pictures."

His ticket was provided by Blanche Calloway, who hired Jeffries away from Hines just before her band embarked on a road tour that took them through the South and on to Los Angeles. (He was replaced in the Hines band by the very young Billy Eckstine, who sang in the same register as Jeffries, thereby necessitating no alterations in the arrangements.) Unable to raise financing from black businessmen or Chicago policy barons, he finally convinced an Irishman named Jed Buell—who had made the notorious *Terror of Tiny Town* (the only all-midget western)—to produce the first black cowboy movie, *Harlem on the Prairie*, shot in five days in 1936 at a cost of $70,000. Jeffries starred and composed his own theme song, "I'm a Happy Cowboy," the lead track on his new album—on which, Jeffries observes, Warner expended one year and $250,000. He made four other westerns, including *The Bronze Buckaroo*, a title conceived to undermine the producer's propensity for the word *Harlem*.

There are many examples of singers who translated musical success into movie careers. Jeffries reversed the process. He was little known when he arrived in Hollywood, and his contributions to cinema—"These were not B movies; C at best"—didn't make him a household name. But they were popular in black theaters, and they brought him to the attention of Duke Ellington. "He contacted me and said, 'I just played the Apollo with your picture, *The Bronze Buckaroo*. Would you be interested in doing a theater tour with my band?' So I joined Ellington and did a magnificent theater tour, plus club dates like the Sherman Hotel in Chicago, and a few other wonderful, wonderful engagements he played." In his memoirs, Ellington recalls that Jeffries was initially "inclined to the falsetto." But "between shows, while everybody else was playing poker, Herb would be ad-libbing and doing imitations all over the place . . . One day he was doing his imitation of Bing Crosby, when Strayhorn and I both said in unison, 'That's it! Don't go any further. Just stay on Bing.'"

Jeffries fills in the story: "Duke thought Bing was one of the greatest baritones of all time. When I first went with Duke's band, I was sort of a tenor, up in that range. But Ellington used to talk so much about the mellow, rich, baritone voice of Crosby, and I began to lower my range. Then I started listening to his records, and he became sort of my guru. One day Ellington heard me doing an impersonation on 'Where the Blue of the Night,' and he said, 'That's the voice I want you to record with!' So I started using that timbre, but I didn't want to be an imitator of Crosby, so while I used his lower register, which was all milk and honey,

I also developed a dramatic voice with a little more volume to avoid an impersonation."

The result, "Flamingo," was arranged by Strayhorn and recorded for RCA during Christmas week of 1940, but not released until the following summer, when it proved a huge and enduring hit—Warner estimates sales of 14 million over time. It became Jeffries's theme song and the name of the nightclubs he opened in the south of France in the 1950s, which were featured in an uncommonly probing discussion of his career and experience with racial prejudice in *Life* in 1951. Yet if "Flamingo," a ballad by Ted Grouya and Edmund Anderson (whose Monday-night visit to the Vanguard included onstage joshing about the correct lyrics to the song), paid the band's bills and launched the singer's career, other numbers introduced by Jeffries are Ellington masterworks: "I Don't Know What Kind of Blues I've Got" has Ellington's finest lyric and is crooned with a suave yet haunting cool far removed from Crosby even as it suggests the link between Crosby and Eckstine; the acerbic "Jump for Joy," lyric by Paul Francis Webster, is a taunting swinger, its sentiments expressed with smooth virile irreverence.

On the more conventional ballads—"Flamingo," "You, You Darlin'," and "There Shall Be No Night"—the baritone timbre combines with a high, tense, punctilious phrasing that suggests the tenors of an earlier era. In ballads, his impeccable diction is underscored by slightly orotund vowels, and a discriminating use of the Irish mordent, a la Crosby. After service in the army, Jeffries had several minor hits under his own name—"When I Write My Song," "The Four Winds and the Seven Seas," "Sophisticated Lady," and an evocative "Basin Street Blues" that opens with street-seller cries—before relocating to France for nearly 10 years.

The big surprise of the Vanguard sets, echoing the pleasures of his album, *The Bronze Buckaroo (Rides Again)*, is that Jeffries's pipes are as well preserved as his exterior. Indeed, when he rose from his stool to let out great climactic high-note flourishes, he also emoted prodigal sustained notes unmarred by waffling or overstated vibrato that have little if any precedent in his famous recordings of the '40s. The husky, loping phrases emanating from the cavern of his baritone are perfectly suited to the ambling simplicity of cowboy songs, but for an "Autumn Leaves" or a "My Funny Valentine" or an "I Got It Bad" or a "Sweet Lorraine" (the proprietress now in clover), he showed that the top range had a distinct glow of its own, and he could balance both halves of his range to tell his story, mining all the musical and lyrical elements as only the best balladeers can. In sets that were spontaneous, barely rehearsed, and incrementally robust, he was ably supported by pianist Dick Katz, bassist

Jamil Nasser, drummer Leroy Williams, and the young guitarist Peter Bernstein, whose obbligatos were deft and witting—during the cowboy songs, Jeffries put his hat on Bernstein's head whenever he soloed.

The record goes down easy as Old No. 7, and its brevity (10 songs, 28 minutes)—characteristic of Nashville, cheesy by jazz standards—will probably add to its goodwill, though a few solos in excess of eight bars would have emphasized the jazz-western nexus and given the album some heft. The arrangements are skillful, with efficient guitar solos, the requisite fiddling, a supple rhythm section, and vocal support by several western performers (including Rex Allen, Jr., and Sons of the San Joaquin), plus a teasing appearance by the Mills Brothers (actually Donald, the only living brother, and his son John)—Warner Western ought to resurrect them, too. The songs were well chosen: "You, You Darlin'" sounds more at home here than it did in Ellington's book; "Tumblin' Tumbleweeds," "Nine Hundred Miles," and "Back in the Saddle Again" (which got an extra entendre at the Vanguard, but not on the record) are foolproof; "Lonesome Rider Blues" has Jeffries's finest lyric and an impeccable performance by singer and ensemble. But the peak is "Cow Cow Boogie," an anthem of urban horsemen composed by Benny Carter and splendidly popularized by Ella Mae Morse. Ella Mae, move over. When he sang it at the Vanguard, Jeffries sidled directly from Carter's tune into "I Don't Know What Kind of Blues I've Got"—from whimsy to deep blues. Even without that fillip, the juxtaposition of Carter, the most cosmopolitan of musicians, and Gene Autry points to an overlooked connection.

From the mid-'30s, when Jimmie Rodgers recorded with Louis Armstrong, and the Hackberry Ramblers put a hillbilly imprimatur on "You've Got to Hi De Hi," and Bob Wills overlaid annoying falsetto cries on otherwise acceptable big band charts like "Big Beaver" and "Playboy Stomp," western musicians have used jazz licks, riffs, and solos. Two of the best examples are Merle Haggard's late-'60s tributes to Rodgers, *Same Train, A Different Time*, and Wills, *A Tribute to the Best Damn Fiddle Player in the World*, which have just been reissued by Koch. Haggard censored Wills's line "darkie raise the cotton, white man get the money," but he let his players kick their boots off. Still, none of them roamed as widely as Jeffries. The bronze buckaroo combines western swing, honky-tonk, cowboy songs, crooning, and an unmistakably global wit. He's a happy cowboy because he hasn't spent his whole life on the range.

[*Village Voice*, 4 July 1995]

30 ❖ *Festival Blues*
(JVC 1995)

No jazz festival in the world could compete with the combination of ace musicianship and star power that was New York's bounty during the last two weeks in June. You had your choice of Benny Carter, the Modern Jazz Quartet, Elvin Jones, David Murray, Javon Jackson, Kenny Burrell, Anita O'Day, Dick Hyman, Don Byron, Roy Hargrove, and Charnett Moffett in the upscale clubs alone. An additional 108 (so they say) bands were corralled by the Knitting Factory for the "What Is Jazz?" festival, featuring Cecil Taylor, Lester Bowie, Dewey Redman, Marty Ehrlich, Henry Threadgill, Evan Parker, Rashied Ali, and James Blood Ulmer. Parks and pubs likewise brandished their finest jazz wares.

And oh yeah, the JVC Jazz Festival was around, the presumed excuse for all this, with its gloried history and invincible publicity machine. Shall we be charitable and surmise that most of the major artists had already been booked for the aforementioned gigs, leaving JVC no options beyond Al Jarreau, the Ohio Players, a Russian rock band, and Helen Schneider? No, we shall not. Impresario George Wein didn't merely trim back; he zoned out. He had at his disposal two of the city's great concert halls plus Bryant Park. He had a couple of aging legends whose very appearances prompted vertical ovations. What he lacked was an idea or a theme that might manifest a concern for, love of, or interest in jazz. There were moments, yes—there always are. But calling those disparate events a festival is like calling the Republicans a party.

Wein kept a low profile, as is his wont except during jam sessions featuring musicians of the generation he most admires (these days, his own), but he was there at the gate to introduce Dee Dee Bridgewater at Carnegie—"one of the great privileges of my life." Appearing with Thad and Mel on Monday nights at the Vanguard 20 years ago, she was a poised and impending presence, the most capable jazz singer of her generation. Maybe it came too easy: After a taste of Broadway luster (*The Wiz*), she went disco, Hollywood, and abroad. Now, she was testing the waters for a record in the works with a barely tolerable French band and a selection of Horace Silver songs that permitted neither diversity nor intimacy. Didn't matter. The lady glowed, her vocal projection prodigal enough to survive unison heads with trumpet and sax. Bridgewater is a torrential scat singer, bristling with life, and her one ballad demonstrated her appealing upper-middle range and head tones. On a new version of

"Doodlin'," she displayed her ripe timbre scatting a trumpetlike solo directly into the mike.

After two decades, it was wonderful to see her. So why was she squeezed into a show headlined by two tenor saxophonists? And why weren't the saxophonists encouraged to perform together—isn't such an encounter the very thing that distinguishes a festival from the usual club gig? Joshua Redman could have used direct contact with the sotto voce meditations of Joe Henderson. His performance was frequently incoherent, driven almost exclusively by the thrills and chills of cold technique. On "The Oneness of Two," he switched to soprano for a more focused improvisation that built to an earnest Coltrane explosion, and on "Sweet Sorrow," one of his more intriguing originals, the rhythm section followed him with tangible spontaneity, dropping out for his big cadenza, which began with impressive siren wails and ended up a glossary of familiar tricks. His closing piece, which he described as "a walk on the wild side," was a cross between "Blue Trane" and "Harlem Nocturne."

Joe Henderson, backed by an attentive Brazilian quartet, expanded the Jobim repertoire of his recent *Double Rainbow* CD to suggest an autobiographical purview, from his best-known tune, "Recorda-Me," the bossa-influenced Blue Note classic that helped establish him in 1963, to "Lush Life" (unaccompanied), from the 1992 album of Strayhorn songs on Verve, which made him a bona fide star. Henderson has become an increasingly introverted player, understating phrases and reducing harmony to a succession of discrete ports, at each of which he ruminates with supple—sometimes silken, sometimes woolly—arpeggios. No romantic, he probes Jobim's book for modern mutations rather than wallowing in its opulent melodies. Even the most popular melody of the set, "Felicidade," proceeded from a jubilant exposition to a series of tangled arpeggios—from melody into pure abstraction. Henderson makes you sit forward in your chair rather than blowing you back—a novel approach.

The accent on tenors sent me racing down to the Knit for a midnight appearance by Archie Shepp, though truth to tell, I was mainly interested in the backing band of Jaki Byard, Richard Davis, and Alan Dawson, which had originated in the 1960s for producer Don Schlitten's Booker Ervin series on Prestige. It was not to be: unhappily, Dawson was in the hospital. But Michael Carvin, who sat in for him, was in imperial form, working mostly with brushes and using bass drum thumps to kick the rhythm and quiet the crowd. Byard was uncharacteristically reticent, and gave most of the trio solos to Richard Davis, whose wine-dark sound, radiant in every register, plucked or bowed, was one of the glories of the week. The humor and pleasure with which the three traded fours was a promise of the full-scale japes they would mount as Shepp (in Blues Brother garb) and Dick Griffin entered. Shepp's split-tones, intestinal timbre, and caustic swing were unmistakable, but soon his embouchure failed him and he began singing. By then, though, Byard had showed how a great rhythm section can make a faltering performance interesting. During Griffin's less-than-emphatic solo, Byard had the trio drop out, then signaled for just Davis to play back-up, then for Shepp to join in. Then he pumped big band riffs with both hands. For a few moments, everybody was rocking.

JVC had more accomplished singers the next night at Carnegie in Peggy Lee and Mel Tormé, each backed by a different Mike Renzi quintet. For her first New York appearance since 1992, Lee resembled a cross between Mae West and a Kabuki ghost, an apparition of pink and platinum perched on a floral patterned chair that might have been spirited out of a Victorian parlor or the closing scene of *2001*. As she began to croon "I Love Being Here with You," the corporeal reality took over. Ailing she was. Vocally impaired she was. But if her instrument was often no more than a husky whisper, her phrasing and intonation were exemplary. A medley of "That Old Feeling," "What's New," and the forgotten "Mr. Wonderful" had the quality of séance. Doing that she could have gone on all night. But as the set passed midpoint with a brooding "Fly Me to the Moon" and an exultant "Fever," she made a surprising turn toward the blues and gave three masterly examples of what perfect phrasing is all about on "See See Rider," "You Don't Know Baby," and the Lil Green anthem that made her famous, "Why Don't You Do Right." She concluded as always with "I'll Be Seeing You." As she walked slowly off, the throng was on its feet a lot longer than usual.

Mel Tormé may have more energy than he did a decade ago, and one feels churlish not to match his wattage. If he didn't have that spring in his step, that tenacity in his eyes, that clarity in his phrasing, he wouldn't get away with his tributes to the Big Band Era. (Moment of silence.) But he has and he does, so the good cheer was not quite dispelled by the utter familiarity of the set—"Opus One," "A Nightingale Sang in Berkeley Square," "Pick Yourself Up" (with his J. S. Bach interlude), "Star Dust," and the Tribute to Benny Goodman, complete with a "Sing Sing Sing" in which he plays drums. Of course, Peggy Lee's set was no less familiar. But because she lacks energy, we're content with the songs and the voice. Besides, it isn't the songs that wear out, but the shtick. From the guy who wrote a weekly show for Judy Garland, we expect something new. That aside, he was in excellent voice. Except on "Star Dust," the phrasing was sure, the lyrics underlined so that you couldn't help but register them, and the songs dressed in their verses, even "You Make Me Feel So Young" and "Memories of You."

Never have I spent a more incomprehensible evening in a concert hall than at "Garden of Evil," an Avery Fisher program that promised to showcase Johnny Mercer but shot most of its load plugging a similarly named book, set in Savannah, by John Berendt. If you hadn't read it, you didn't get it, though one of the many narrators might have cleared up what the book had to do with Mercer in a minute. Instead, jazz musicians and cabaret singers alternated with actors (introduced by a disembodied voice: "And now the lovely Miss Carrie Nye") who read on and on into the night. And the singers! Mercer loved jazz and jazz singing. So how to explain Anne Hampton Calloway, or Nancy Lamott, who clobbers a song in the hope it won't get up and clobber her back. Moments, there were few. I have never seen Bobby Short, in a suit but shirtless, more animated or in grander voice than detailing "The Weekend of a Private Secretary"; Harold Nicholas and Margaret Whiting defined charm in a duet on "Come Rain or Come Shine"; and in the concert's true salvation and one of the headier performances of the festival, Gerry Mulligan transfigured "I'm an Old Cowhand," "Dream," and "Midnight Sun," providing depth, swing, and, dare I say, beauty in a show that was more enthused about a transvestite who wiggled and a senior Rotary Club entertainer who didn't. Jeepers creepers.

Oscar Peterson suffered a stroke two years ago, so there was much concern as to whether he would retain the digital (can one still use that word, or is it doomed to mean just the opposite?) magic—the razzle dazzle of skittering arpeggios perfectly articulated yet barely sounded, or precipitous chords pounded out like explosive charges, and double-time runs that leap from the treble to the bass like a fugitive dodging bullets. Peterson is unimaginable without his technique, and though his left hand, confined to comping in the first set and laying out for most of the second, may still require recuperation, the right hand did all of the above, ably supported by mostly longtime accompanists, but undermined by sound that was unacceptably murky for Carnegie. The showstoppers were "Sweet Georgia Brown," in which he exchanged cadenzas with guitarist Lorne Lofsky, and "Satin Doll," with one of those ardently pounded out-chorus arrangements played with a heft no one else can quite approach. Bassist Niels Pederson was featured twice, unwinding robust phrases that swing from the lower register to the upper one in unbroken loops, like Mobius strips. By the time the second half was curtailed at Peterson's request, the audience was still hungry but satisfied.

Peterson's concert was the only one at which latecomers were required to enter the hall after a number was over. Why he and his audience were treated with a deference denied Peggy Lee and everyone else is a mystery.

The only possibility for a jam session at the festival was an 80th birthday party for Flip Phillips. But it wasn't a jam at all, nor was it much fun. Maybe they should have booked Town Hall, or put somebody in charge. The rigid pacing stymied the musicians: first you play a tune, then he plays one, then the other guy, but make sure nobody wanders outside the fixed rep of nine tunes. JVC is famous for bringing this sort of thing off—think of the Doc Cheatham soiree a few years back—but not tonight, Josephine. Only Kenny Davern, on "Sweet Georgia Brown" and "Comes Love," and the crafty Cheatham, on "Sweet Lorraine," burbled with the pleasure of sheer music making. Phillips was in complete possession of his old-master timbre, but the gorgeous sonority gave way to cursory inquiry on ballads such as "Cottage for Sale" (complete with the Billy Eckstine extension). The second half went to the Illinois Jacquet band.

Coming into the final stretch, it looked as though JVC would fold with a whimper. But history repeated itself as Duke Ellington and Count Basie engaged in a battle of the bands at Avery Fisher. Actually, Wynton Marsalis played Ellington and Jon Faddis played Basie, and it was a battle of the *repertory* bands, a concept fraught with irony. To reveal the outcome out front, Faddis outsmarted and outswung Marsalis every step of the way. The first mistake Marsalis made, after winning the toss, was going first. That meant no matter what he played all evening, the audience would subconsciously wonder how Faddis could top him and Faddis could choose his response at leisure. And he chose well—opening several pieces with brief tuttis that compelled attention, and then, after a dramatic pause, springing into a Basie canter that enforced instant foot-tapping or head-nodding before we knew where he was going. Usually, he was going to Basie's '50s book. Marsalis, who couldn't resist an obligatory comment about swinging, sounded curiously reluctant to swing for much of the evening, focusing his energies on the compound textures of Ellington-style writing, and though he turned in powerful performances—including a wry "Across the Track Blues"—the band never felt fully mobilized. If the evening hadn't been sullied with the bullshit promotion of a battle, it would have been easier to enjoy the pleasing contrast between musics that are texture- or rhythm-driven.

But Marsalis himself laid down the gauntlet, and Faddis, who hardly said a word first set, looked suitably warriorlike, and took chances, too. Marsalis rarely varied his tempo or outlook; Faddis swung convincingly at extreme tempos and in styles ranging from "Prince of Wails" and "Moten Swing" to "Shiny Stockings" to an unholy revision of "Sing Sing Sing" (sounded like Jim McNeely, although, foolishly, no arrangers or pieces were ID'd on either side), for which Dave Liebman was brought out. It went on too long, but at its peak—the ensemble deconstructing familiar riffs as Liebman screamed properly seditious phrases—broke through the gentility of jazz rep and reminded us how dangerous this music can be. Not surprisingly, it brought out Marsalis's Bob Dole side— in his only response to Faddis all night, he had his band holler for a few seconds of intended parody.

Marsalis visited the Basie book himself with "I Left My Baby," and Faddis, who stood in for Dizzy Gillespie last year, resurrected him in a "Manteca" designed for Steve Turre's conch shells—a rare exception to the Ellington and Basie rule. Another difference between the orchestras was more telling. Faddis leads a mostly middle-aged band (Frank Wess was unleashed at length), Marsalis a mostly 20- and 30-something band. One is filled with masterly players; the other with gifted musicians who have yet to achieve mastery. All of the trumpet players in the Lincoln Center Orchestra were impressive. But how in the world do you go up against a brass section as seasoned as Lew Soloff, Byron Stripling, Earl Gardner, and Randy Brecker? The same was true of Carnegie's trombones and reeds. Their rhythm section—Lewis Nash, Peter Washington, Kenny Drew, Jr., and Howard Alden—was killing.

But enough of makeshift institutional competition. Wein and JVC have something here, and if they are serious about developing big band clashes, let them enlarge the playing field. The consensus this year was in Faddis's favor. Fine: Next year let him go against the Vanguard Jazz Orchestra (baritone saxophonist Gary Smulyan will have a decision to make). Let the winner of that encounter go up against Gil Evans or Maria Schneider or David Murray or Illinois Jacquet or the real Basie orchestra the following year. Or is the whole point simply to advertise the resident bands of the houses that house the festival? I'm not optimistic, but that's partly because I saw where the festival booked Frank Foster for his last night as music director of the Count Basie Orchestra—an unpleasant Times Square joint called the Supper Club, accompanying a singer named Helen Schneider, whom I will bet George Wein would never have booked in the nightclub he used to run in Boston. You had to dig jazz to get in there.

[*Village Voice*, 18 July 1995]

31 ❖ *Young and Verbal*
(Carmen McRae)

Someone once claimed that nobody could impart more emotion and meaning to certain words—like *love*—than Billie Holiday. It was a compliment she relished. No question, she could penetrate the core of intention in any song, even a fatuous one: The phrase "me, myself, and I are all in love with you" is banal on paper, but what a buoyant declaration she makes of it. She wasn't the first, of course, but until the mid-'30s, Louis Armstrong focused his singing more on music than words, Bing Crosby was most expressive as a ballad singer, and Mildred Bailey explored a gentler dramatic range. The blues singers were relatively generic and, by Cafe Society standards, primitive, though not as dated as the torch singers, who made do with one overheated recipe for tears.

So whatever else Holiday achieved, she located meaning in songs while simultaneously freeing them from melodrama, and in that respect and others she was a beacon for Frank Sinatra, her exact contemporary, who pared singing down even further. In studying the precise message of a lyric, Sinatra defined the abyss between a good pop singer and a poor one: the good one subordinates instrument and technique to the art of interpretation; the poor one is too in love with the sound of his or her own voice to bother with the song.

Those paradigms have obvious ramifications for standard pop, but they apply no less stringently to jazz. No singer was more stubbornly verbal than Carmen McRae, who could inflect words as though she were giving them a tongue-lashing. Famously outspoken and even a bit frightening, McRae and her songs had a similarly tart appeal. You didn't necessarily turn to her for a profane insight into the songwriter's art, but you occasionally got one anyway. This is especially true of the numerous Billie Holiday tunes she covered. McRae owed an immense debt to Holiday, but that hardly explains the glee with which she returned not merely to the Holiday classics, but to the trifles as well. She took them to a new place. If Holiday made the word *love* shimmer with unrequited longing, McRae cast it in irony and caustic languor. Consider her 1965 live recording of "No More": Holiday sang "you ain't gonna bother me no more, no how" as if trying to key up her resolve, while McRae phrased the same line with dripping contempt, as if she had a gun in her purse. In a tour de force seven-minute "Love for Sale," she interpolated the joke, "You can see I'm the madam, right?" which served to remind any dunderhead not paying attention that the song is not the cry of universal womanly despair so many singers try to make of it—it's about commerce.

I grew up with the McRae of the '60s, and attended the 1965 Village Gate gig that produced the burnished, constantly surprising *Alive!* (Columbia). She was in her middle forties, but was still considered the hip young jazz singer (interestingly, Betty Carter, Abbey Lincoln, and Shirley Horn were all off the scene in those years), performing in jazz clubs with jazz musicians, and alternately recording with lavish string sections or small combos. I had mixed feelings: She hadn't the sonority of Sarah Vaughan or the swing of Ella Fitzgerald. She did have a cry in the back of her throat that parsed her phrases, a strange nasality that occasionally undermined her pitch, and an obstreperousness—which could be stifling on records and more so live. At a subsequent Dangerfield's engagement, she wasn't getting much respect, and coasted through the entire set smirking and inserting asides for the amusement of the help.

At some point in the '70s, I found *By Special Request* in a 99-cent cutout bin. It was a Decca album recorded in 1955, and I could hardly believe what I was hearing: a whole other Carmen, from the supper-club era, singing in a lilting, oddly sweet, even buttery voice. The Deccas are the least known of her recordings, because most of them have never been reissued on LP, let alone CD. But they range from trio to big band sessions, from songs about birds (with Ben Webster) to songs by Noel Coward, and they minutely document her development from an irreproachable interpreter of pop songs to a diva of unique regality, who still tells the story but in a voice that suggests no antecedent other than her younger self. The Deccas cover five years, from 1955 to 1960, from supper club to jazz club, and include about 175 sides. Some day, someone is going to issue this music in its entirety, but not soon. In the '70s, McRae herself helped Leonard Feather choose 32 selections for an anthology. In the last couple of years, more than half the total work has been issued on four CDs, all on Decca Jazz. *Here to Stay* combines 10 out of 12 numbers from *By Special Request*, her first album on the label, with 10 out of 12 numbers from the album she did with Ernie Wilkins's big band, her last on the label. *Carmen McRae Sings Great American Songwriters* ranges through the whole period, capably fulfilling its aspiration.

Now we have a new double-CD memorial collection, *I'll Be Seeing You*, and while the selection is constrained to fill in gaps (only the famous voice and piano recording of "Something to Live For," with composer Billy Strayhorn on piano, is repeated from the previous CDs), it serves as an exceptional survey of McRae's early approach. McRae came to Decca unknown to the world but with more than a decade of experience, much of it as a pianist or as a band singer with Benny Carter, Mercer

Ellington, and others. She had won the Apollo's amateur night contest in 1939, and was taken up by Irene Kitchings, the songwriter close to Billie Holiday, whom she worshipped and emulated. McRae had recorded eight unappealing sides for Bethlehem in late 1954, yet Decca believed she had star potential when it began recording her a few weeks later. They instantly scored with a pop single—"Whatever Lola Wants." Backed by the Dave Lambert Singers blurting "unh," the piece is pure kitsch, but note that McRae is at least as seductive as Gwen Verdon.

One of the first pieces recorded for the more discriminating LP market (if I read Feather's original notes correctly) was "I Can't Get Started." When she comes to the fill-in-your-own-name line, she sings "Frank Sinatra had me to tea," a significant choice as he had not yet been confirmed as God, though he had restructured his music during the previous 18 months. McRae understood what he was doing, and the entire collection recapitulates her determination to communicate every word and inference. No one has more plaintively unraveled "I'm Through with Love" than McRae, though everyone has tried—for that matter, no one else has clearly enunciated the words that for years I thought were "icy Frigidaire" (McRae puts an iron stop between "frigid" and "air"). On a jaunty if cursory reading of "If I Were a Bell," she shifts her intonation between the reference to "me and my quiet upbringing" and the rebellion that follows.

Later McRae may be deeper, but the increased roughness exacted a charge not required in these early performances, which scintillate with an animated glow, swing, clarity, and wit. This Carmen could reach posh nightclub audiences; I get the feeling the later Carmen wasn't much interested in trying. You can hear the difference in her authority—no one could mistake the Carmen of 1955 with the Carmen of 1957. The former is casually impeccable and the latter impeccably authoritative. Her 1955 performance of "Yardbird Suite" is richly melodic, more swing than bop, despite an intro taken from Miles Davis's "Walkin'." Her 1957 martini-dry version of Noel Coward's "Someday I'll Find You" relieves it of the sentimentality that has rendered it untouchable by anybody else except boozy tenors. This number and the rest of the Coward set (other than "I'll See You Again") is presently unreleased. Why has Decca gone this route when virtually every other label is attempting to restore original albums? In McRae's case, the company has the added commercial lure of their unavailability for more than 30 years.

On the other hand, there is a payback in this collection: what a radiant anthology of songs—one or two mediocrities, salvaged by the singer, but the rest top of the line—"Speak Low," "But Beautiful," "Ghost of a Chance," "Star Eyes," "Lush Life," "The Party's Over," and "East of the

Sun" from the first disc alone. She reminds you why the Bronislau Kaper movie theme "Invitation" was once popular; she gives "The Thrill Is Gone" a reading so incisive you wonder how it could have faded away. Two highlights are "Flamingo," long the property of Herb Jeffries and other baritones, underscoring her top notes and head tones (lusciously complemented by the many-hued timbre of Ben Webster) for a shimmering performance; and "Bye Bye Blackbird," in her hands a mocking swinger. Both songs are from another rarity, the *Birds of a Feather* album, arranged by Ralph Burns.

When McRae signed with Columbia and recorded her 1961 tribute to Holiday, one of the finest achievements of her career, she was already a grand dame in voice, if not yet in body. She still had the richness, the natural beauty. As the years went by, her work became increasingly erratic, possibly a consequence of her devotion to the words—in the absence of appropriate verbal inspiration, she fell back on personality and attitude. I don't care to argue with admirers who insist that she grew more profound with the years. But I don't think anyone can doubt that no matter how much she gained, she lost something, too. Whatever you think of her later work—wonderful in the late '60s and early '70s, I'd say, iffy afterward—*I'll Be Seeing You* is a revelation.

[*Village Voice*, 8 August 1995]

32 ❖ Three by Three (Tim Hagans / Dave Douglas / Roy Hargrove)

Jazz trios built around wind instruments don't quite scan. Exceptions from Sidney Bechet to Sonny Rollins to Leo Smith notwithstanding, the rules of jazz deportment dictate that a saxophonist is not fully dressed without a complement of three; nor is a trumpet star complete without a full rhythm team or a front-line partner. Such customs spring from the assumption that a brass player's chops cannot withstand a solo regimen unsupported by at least one other improviser, and from the fear that reprieve-choruses will be taken up by bassist or drummer. However emphatic the conception, the suspicion abides that the poor fellow has lost his fourth wheel. Judging from the appearance of three new trumpet trios, tricycles may soon make a comeback.

In each case, a different member of the rhythm section is missing, which is not to say he's missed. For the most part, the trumpeter escapes with his lip unbloodied, his head unbowed. Tim Hagans chooses the expected accompaniment—bass and drums—on *Audible Architecture* (Blue Note), a swarming, spirited tour de force that should raise his profile several notches. At 41, Hagans has been a sideliner for two decades, working at first with Stan Kenton, Woody Herman, and Thad Jones, and more recently with Joe Lovano, Maria Schneider, Marc Copland, and Bob Belden. His one previous Blue Note album, *No Words*, shows the impact of Miles Davis in model quintet and sextet settings—well played and plotted with good contributions from everyone, but generic all the same. The new record holds your attention from the start, despite or because of limited instrumentation. Hagans is persistent as a bee. Davis and Freddie Hubbard are his forbears, but his motific confidence and preference for the middle-high register also suggest Booker Little.

The opener, "I Hear a Rhapsody," is exemplary—his first turnback out of the theme introduces material he uses to thread his subsequent five choruses. He also draws on the melody, embellishing it with his own lyricism but never consigning it to the limbo of bebop disdain. Bassist Larry Grenadier provides diverse rhythmic patterns, including a half-time beat, while drummer Billy Kilson interacts steadily with the trumpet phrases, which grow longer and more complicated as the solo continues—Hagans hurtling from one chorus to the next, confident that bass and drums will mark the way. The bass solo reminds you why the trio format incites dread. Grenadier is good, but can any bass player sustain interest soloing every time out?

Hagans's waltz, "Jasmine in Three," features him in a light and comely mood, buoyed by responsive and patient drumming, and working at the nexus where dolorous Miles meets unrelenting Freddie. Davis's call is more apparent elsewhere. On the title track, "Audible Architecture," a 48-bar theme in which the first four of each 12 are treated as trumpet cadenzas, he flies on the wings of Milesian motifs, even quoting his master toward the end of his solo. A drums episode leads to a three-way exchange. "Garage Bands," a two-chord head played over an ostinato rhythm in a manner suggesting Eddie Harris's "Freedom Jazz Dance" (popularized by Miles), brings in Bob Belden, another Herman alumnus, better known as an arranger and bandleader. His tenor's heavy, gritty sound leans toward multiphonics and his call-and-response dialogue with Hagans is fervent. Kilson's solo recalls Joe Morello's way of maneuvering against the constraints of a rhythmic riff.

Belden's admiration for Wayne Shorter is apparent in the short, quizzical phrases with which he cobbles his statement on Hagans's "Shorts."

The almost canonical head of "Blues in MY Neighborhood," a 24-bar blues (8+8+8) constructed on a vamp that sounds like Horace Silver with more notes, recalls Davis's out-of-synch approach during his *Nefertiti* period. Hagans's four-chorus solo is creamy in its assurance and finishes with a chorus of arching high tremolos that spill effortlessly and without end. Belden begins his solo dragging his notes over the bar lines, before Grenadier signals the arrival of bar nine with one well-placed note. Kilson does the same at bar 17. With rhythm players like that, the soloist can proceed with confidence, and you have to wonder if the "lost" pianist mightn't cloud the interaction. "Drum Row" is given over entirely to a trumpet and drums duet, each responding to the other in 10-measure phrases—it's a study in equilibrium. The closer, "Whatever's Next," is a minute-long "Taps" for session's end.

Dave Douglas has become the preferred trumpet player of the downtown elite—despite uptown gigs with Horace Silver and Vincent Herring, he's best known for affiliations with Don Byron, Myra Melford, Anthony Braxton, John Zorn, Evan Parker, and others who flourish below Canal Street. Like David Murray, he leads several bands, including a quintet called New & Used (*Souvenir*, Knitting Factory Works), his String Group (*Parallel Worlds*, Soul Note), a sextet (the Booker Little homage, *In Our Lifetime*, New World), and the Tiny Bell Trio, which offers a surprisingly venturesome follow-up to its eponymous 1994 Songlines debut with *Constellations* (hat ART). Indeed, this album is pretty damn near irresistible; don't let the label's obscurity deter you from seeking it out. Douglas's music is more composed than Hagans's and one source of pleasure in Tiny Bell is the way its members phase in and out of unison, juggling the written and the improvised with an artlessness that belies the complexity of the pieces. Douglas's rhythms are catchy and buoyant and different. They cover much of Europe, from Spain to Bosnia, yet sustain a playful, heady second-line zest.

Deploying a rich, full trumpet sound in every register, Douglas plots his solos with decisive storytelling logic, supported in kind by guitarist Brad Schoeppach and drummer Jim Black. You don't miss the bass here, because Schoeppach fills the air around the trumpet, and Black underscores the exotic rhythms with a kit that makes liberal use of tambourines and blocks. If guitar and bass suggest a wry universality in their swing, Douglas embodies a universal approach to jazz trumpet with a glossary of half-cocked notes, growls, and blasts—the very language of '70s neo-classicism, but with a technical aplomb no one will dispute. All those attributes are displayed on the title selection, and then emphasized on "Unhooking the Safety Net" (he's good with titles), with its opening cadenza and a sort of Mediterranean march-dance that savors of Flamenco trumpet. The East European mode is felt on "Taking Sides," which combines unison and part writing, and the Spanish tinge permeates the extended "Maquiladora." In contrast, he offers a superb rendition of Herbie Nichols's "The Gig," which is built on hesitations that sound strangely European in this context, a thorny meditation on "Scriabin," and a reading of a Schumann duet subtitled by Douglas "mit Humor."

The most orthodox and familiar of the new trumpet trios is *Parker's Mood* (Verve), by the Roy Hargrove/Christian McBride/Stephen Scott Trio. Despite the democratic attribution of credit and several solo and duet performances, the trio numbers are done in the usual way (trumpet plus backing), except that solos are evenly distributed. The tunes are classic, the musicianship irreproachable, the motive worthy. So why the yawn? The album never comes alive. Constrained by adulation and short running times, these variations are devoid of the exhilaration that makes Charlie Parker our contemporary. Only pianist Stephen Scott delivers—his best solos are decisive, swinging, measured, and fit (helped no little degree by lively engineering). McBride is amazing, but amazing bass can't save a project like this, and at times (see "Marmaduke") even his four/four is too foursquare. Hargrove has to hold the fort, and though he plays clean, he also plays safe. The mute restrains him on "Dexterity," one-chorus limits do it everywhere else.

Curiously, Hargrove appears undermined by an all-star package that relieves him of full responsibility, while Hagans and Douglas have no alternative but to carry the ball. It's never the fourth wheel you miss, but the first.

[*Village Voice*, 24 October 1995]

33 ❖ *Different Drummer (Modern Jazz Quartet)*

Long ago, in the depths of adolescence, I stood shoulder to shoulder with a friend and future jazz critic at a Duke Ellington concert and dance. I had seen Ellington before, including a recent performance of virtually the same set—a point I made with jaded impatience to my friend, who was hearing him live for the first time. He turned on me with justifiable irritation for trying to divert his awe. Taking in his slack jaw and glazed eyes, as he stared at the bandstand, I recalled my own first encounter with Ellington, my own slack jaw and glazed eyes, and quickly recovered my sense of wonder. The first time with Ellington is, like the first time with sex or Charlie Chaplin or really good asparagus, epic. Later you may have to call up your purer self to defeat the deadening effects of sophistication.

A great concert is ultimately a collusion between artist and listener, in which the alertness of one is inseparable from that of the other. The musicians may savor the joys of a shining performance before a dull audience, just as a falling tree may crash through an uninhabited forest, but art truly burgeons when its nuances are shared. The Modern Jazz Quartet, now at the close of its 43rd year, opened the 1995 San Francisco Jazz Festival with a performance worth savoring—a performance that restored the wonder elicited by this longest-lived chamber ensemble at its best.

The MJQ is almost too good. Fixed snapping rhythms embellished with bells and chimes support contrapuntal melodies and compelling improvisation. Clipped, jabbing piano and vivid blues complement saturated sonorities augmented by bowed bass and accelerated vibraphone vibrato. A seductive book, assiduously reworked and enhanced for decades, transfigures popular songs into originals and vice versa. The downside is one's natural propensity to take it for granted, especially given how the ensemble's formality can overwhelm the very improvisations it frames, not least the controlled but always palpable tension between Milt Jackson's effusively carnal vibes and John Lewis's elusively rational piano. As musical director, composer, and arranger, Lewis sets the MJQ in motion, and one measure of his prowess is the way that he focuses Jackson's gift, enlarging its expressiveness by reining it in. A comparison with Ellington and Johnny Hodges is inescapable.

Enchantment was almost immediately apparent at the October 13 performance in San Francisco. The foursome appeared on stage at the Masonic Auditorium, high atop Nob Hill, in customary tuxedos to a customary standing ovation, which did not deter them from lifting off with a decisively chipper "Softly as in a Morning Sunrise." Sigmund Romberg's song, from a 1928 operetta, is so much a part of the jazz of the past 35 years that it's hard to recall that the MJQ claimed it as a standard as early as 1952 (recording it as the Milt Jackson Quartet), and introduced Lewis's arrangement, with a lick from Bach's *The Musical Offering* appended to the top, at the 1955 session for which Connie Kay made his recording debut with the band. Perhaps the opening selection was a subtle way of underscoring the evening's purpose: It was called "Dedicated to Connie," as is a recently released album, recorded in 1960 in Slovenia. The evening unfolded with a preponderance of pieces from early in the Quartet's history—Lewis film scores, bop and pop adaptations, *Porgy and Bess*, three Jackson blues, all from before 1960. Yet it peaked with a piece that germinated during the decade between 1964 and 1973.

Joaquin Rodrigo became the toast of Spain and a world-famous composer when he premiered his *Concierto de Aranjuez*, for guitar and orchestra, in Madrid in 1940; today, notwithstanding acclaimed recordings by Carlos Bonell, it is better known in this country for jazz extrapolations of its middle movement, and as a concerto for trumpet rather than guitar. In 1960, Miles Davis and Gil Evans adapted the Adagio as the centerpiece of *Sketches of Spain*. Four years later, Lewis adapted it for a collaboration by the MJQ and guitarist Laurindo Almeida. He continued to muse over the piece, however, reworking it for the Quartet in the late '60s (for *Space*, one of their two unjustly forgotten albums on Apple), and then as a concerto for quartet and orchestra for 1973's *In Memoriam*, perhaps the most plaintive work in the MJQ catalog. I had never heard the Quartet perform the piece live, and I had not heard any version as moving as the one they played at the Masonic.

Rodrigo's music is most powerful when it is simplest—in *Aranjuez*, he seemed to reduce all of Spanish music to a few basic phrases that evoke complicated responses, the way a folk tune can summon up a larger culture. Having associated the piece with mourning in *In Memoriam*, it is likely that Lewis was thinking of Kay in returning to it. The music shimmered like tall grasses. A perfect union of writing and improvising, it combined handsome still passages that reverberated with the repeated three-note figure on which the Adagio is built, and stirring unaccompanied cadenzas—a flooding of Milt Jackson's vibes, the sinuous fraternity of John Lewis's piano and Percy Heath's bowed bass. The audience, hip to every nuance, rose again, but it can hardly have been ready—at least I wasn't—for the sustained intensity of expression, for it was still early in the first set.

The ultimate John Lewis waltz, "Skating in Central Park" (from *Odds Against Tomorrow*), is also an indelible New York City melody, and not even Jackson, playing so aggressively as to challenge the stability of the bar lines, could undermine the sentiment. On Ann Ronell's "Willow Weep for Me" (Jackson: "If you don't know this song, you shouldn't be in here") and Charlie Parker's "Confirmation" (Jackson: "The greatest improvising jazz artist of our generation is Charlie Parker"), the organic genius of the Quartet—with its feints and thrusts, tuxedoed junctions and Saturday-night fish frys, stylish manners and unceremonious cool— illuminated how uniquely daring the MJQ remains 43 years later. Slack jaw, glazed eyes.

And a new drummer. That's the big story, of course, and the choice was as natural as it was inspired. Albert Heath, youngest brother of Percy Heath (and of Jimmy Heath), was one of the most tasteful and efficient drummers to come along in the late '50s, when he made his reputation with J. J. Johnson's quintet and the Art Farmer–Benny Golson Jazztet. Although he worked with many great musicians (most memorably with Dexter Gordon and the Heath Brothers), long stays in Scandinavia and California lowered his profile. His only album as a leader, the inventive *Kwanza*, is long out of print. In San Francisco, he was understated, keeping a powerful pulse without breaking a sweat. Connie Kay, though often remembered for his bells and cymbals, was most impressive in the austerity of his swing—he could steer the ship without moving a muscle beyond his wrists and feet, and you always knew there was a bass drum. Heath, finding his ground between Kay's economy and his own preference for an energetic shove, may ultimately recover the straight-ahead polish of Kenny Clarke, the MJQ's first drummer. In the meantime, he's perfectly swell. His eight-bar eruption on "Confirmation" elicited a confirmatory roar, and his very presence seemed to encourage a certain levity, as when in "I'll Remember April," Lewis expansively interpolated "When the Saints Go Marching In" and "In and Out the Window," and Jackson followed with an ad lib from "Rockin' in Rhythm."

The new double-CD album, *Dedicated to Connie* (Atlantic), is a find. Lewis chose this concert for release because he considers it representative of Kay's and the MJQ's best work ("never before or since has the Modern Jazz Quartet played better"). All the members of the ensemble believe their finest recordings are live albums, either *European Concert* or *Last Concert*, and *Dedicated to Connie* is of that quality. But it is also valuable as an index of the MJQ's repertoire as of 1960, some of which is rarely if ever performed, like the albums *The Pyramid* and *The Comedy*. The five pieces that would become part of *The Comedy* two years later, plus the earlier "Fontessa," which was cut from the suite before that album was made, were highlights of the 1960 concert. "La Cantatrice" actually seems melodically richer without the vocal, and "Columbine" and "Pulcinella" are performed with an intensity of expression not unlike that achieved with *Aranjuez* in San Francisco—as though they aren't just playing it, but learning it, loving it, meaning it.

[*Village Voice*, 14 November 1995]

34 ❖ They Never Went Away
(Big Bands)

The big band is the most imperial and recondite of 20th-century musical ensembles. Even jazz critics, who for reasons of close kinship have devoted far more serious attention to the big band than critics in pop or classical, are frequently ignorant of its workings. Orchestration, the least examined of the jazz arts, is widely regarded as a species of behind-the-scenes arcana, like film editing; only writers with distinctive styles and onstage roles—Ellington, Gil Evans—excite acclaim. Other arrangers of enormous talent are overlooked or, if they go Hollywood (and earn a living), patronized. Of the jazz whiz kids who jammed the musical landscape of the 1920s, Don Redman and Bill Challis are the least known, though one could argue that their influence was as decisive as that of the instrumentalists and singers now appearing on stamps.

Similarly, section men and lead players are treated as faceless technicians by those who wish there were soloists in every chair, even though it is often the "studio" musicians who make the orchestra roar. The role that section leaders play within a section and the role the section plays within the band are apparently as forbidding as higher mathematics. The soloists are the stars, understandably. But the others are inexplicably overlooked—a situation analogous to football fans knowing the quarterbacks and not the defensive linemen. Seventy-five years have passed since Paul Whiteman made dance bands glamorous and jazzy, 70 since Fletcher Henderson and Duke Ellington made them streamlined and jazzier, 60 since Benny Goodman made them fashionable and rich—yet their methods and devices remain less understood than they were in the Swing Era. The music itself is buried in a haze of nostalgia, invariably scored to that old, old refrain, "Will big bands ever come back?"

No, they won't, not in the image of, say, Benny Goodman arriving at *Hollywood Hotel*, reception directed by Busby Berkeley with the kind of pomp the Romans accorded Cleopatra. It's difficult to believe bandleaders were once megastars. In the '30s and '40s, almost all of the top white bands and many of the top black ones were lured to Hollywood, and the image of a man in a tuxedo waving a baton—not necessarily at his musicians—set hearts fluttering. Ava Gardner and Betty Grable married bandleaders. Of course, they divorced them, too.

But the demise of the Swing Era did not destroy the impulse to compose music for what had become an American institution, one that had long since forgotten its roots in marching bands and bandshell bands, but was increasingly eager to test the limits of brasses, reeds, and rhythm. As postwar economics bankrupted the traveling orchestras, "rehearsal" bands arose. Just as '20s dance band musicians attended after-hours jam sessions to play combo jazz, postwar studio musicians joined off-night ensembles to play big band jazz. It was soon apparent that in the absence of dancers (and dance halls), big bands could stretch in new directions. In the mid-'40s, Boyd Raeburn's adventurous band relied on financial help from other bandleaders for its brief survival; in the mid-'60s, the Thad Jones–Mel Lewis band was the hottest in New York because every Monday night it played the riskiest arrangements it had.

The '60s turned out to be a surprisingly prodigal period for big band music, with new voices (Gary McFarland, Oliver Nelson, Carla Bley) added to a chorus of veteran heavy-hitters, stretching all the way back to the near-beginning (Benny Carter and Duke Ellington). Staff arrangers employed by the Count Basie, Woody Herman, and Stan Kenton orchestras were writing concert and dance music, and even short-lived Monday night bands that didn't enjoy the miraculous survival of Jones-Lewis produced books of their own. Still, all that activity failed to create the sense of a coherent movement, and paradoxically fanned the perception that big band music was marginal and quixotic.

In *Big Band Renaissance* (Smithsonian), an expertly compiled and annotated five-CD collection of 75 recordings made between 1941 and 1991, Bill Kirchner issues a gentle polemic and a firm corrective to those for whom big band music is shrouded in the fog of Glenn Miller's reed section. His intention is to show how the death of the Swing Era liberated big bands, and to induce wonder at the postwar accomplishment. Kirchner is himself an arranger, bandleader, and saxophonist, and his choices are weighted to represent the arrangers—though the soloists are also here, from Charlie Parker to John Coltrane. It's easy to quibble with selections—and in a minute I will—but it must be said of this compilation (as was said of Martin Williams's *Smithsonian Collection of Classic Jazz*) that its strength derives from the integrity of the compiler. This is no faceless assortment. It has pride and prejudice—a point of view.

Kirchner divides his material into four groups: Road Bands (name bands, mostly); Part-Time Bands (so-called rehearsal orchestras); Studio Bands (assembled for recording projects); and Avant-Garde Bands. The last, something of a misnomer, is the only stylistic division: Each selection could have been included in one of the other three (e.g., Sun Ra as a road band, Charlie Haden as a studio band). This segregation suggests an uneasiness with avant-garde music, though it also provides one of the amusing juxtapositions—from Doc Severinsen's "Sax Alley" to Sun Ra's 1956 concerto for tympani, "A Street Named Hell."

Jay McShann's 1941 "Swingmatism" is a perfect way to start—it's an anthem that foretells the postwar aesthetic with a fresh unison attack and the first studio-recorded solo by 20-year-old Charlie Parker. The next tracks measure writers Eddie Sauter and George Handy's impatience with the constraints of dance band conventions and are followed by five heady Ellington selections that establish him as the presiding genius of postwar jazz, just as Martin Williams and Gunther Schuller's Smithsonian anthology, *Big Band Jazz*, established his preeminence in the earlier period. Daring voicings, modes, revitalized blues, and the merger of bop and swing are recurring ideas throughout the collection; all were achieved peerlessly by Ellington. Only Stan Kenton is represented by as many records, and if that sounds oppressive, give thanks for the variety of his writers, from Gerry Mulligan (the unique "Young Blood") to Bob Graettinger (the unique "A Trumpet").

Most performers and several selections are expected, though not as many as you'd think—Kirchner often goes for overlooked items, and he has resurrected more than a dozen treasures. Charlie Barnet's 1949 "Eugipelliv," written by Paul Villepigue combines sassy brasses, Latin percussion, and ominous soprano sax voice-leading, and augurs a dozen urban-crime film scores of the late '50s—in fact, you can almost hear Leonard Bernstein's Jets rumbling through it. In Harry James's "That's Thad," Thad Jones brings James and Corky Corcoran into the '60s, with a pulsating D-flat blues that plays affectionate swing locutions against bop harmonies. I had never heard Mike Crotty's Bartók-meets-"Noel," written for the U.S. Air Force Airmen of Note, or Sam Jones's big band from 1979, or the terrific passage in Kenny Clarke and Francy Boland's 1963 "Now Hear My Meanin'," in which trumpets are divided into Harmon- and cup-muted sections for a fixed point of interchange, while saxophones swarm in the foreground. And I'm convinced after hearing Sauter and Finegan's 1954 "The Loop" that Nelson Riddle heard it too.

Omissions? Whole divisions are absent: r&b orchestras, salsa orchestras, orchestras convened to back singers, European radio orchestras, jazz repertory orchestras. The one work by Bill Holman (a sly piece for Les Brown and Frank Rosolino) is insufficient testimony to his importance. Gil Evans has three arrangements (as many as Ellington), but while the inclusion of two versions of "Blues for Pablo" (one by Hal McKusick's nonet) is an editorial stroke, the third track, "The Barbara Song," great as it is, leaves unsampled his later work, which might have fit in with the avant-garde (e.g., "Zee Zee," "Relaxin' at Camarillo," "Little Wing"). Also absent is an example of George Russell's music of the past 35 years, though his glorious 1958 "Manhattan" is here complete. No selection is edited—extended pieces by Mingus, Don Ellis, and Monk-Overton are included. But not David Murray's big band or Julius Hemphill's or Maria Schneider's. Of course, the inclination to quibble underscores Kirchner's point: When the Swing Era died, big band music blossomed.

[*Village Voice*, 12 December 1995]

35 ❖ *Beyond the Rudiments (The Best Jazz Records of 1995)*

Now that the holiday cheer has dissipated, we may return to glum re-ality—a juncture I reach via a belated compulsion to conjure a 10-best list. This year I was surprised to discover that when I casually ticked off my favorite records, 10 or 12 seemed about right. Still, as I jostled my memory, the number of contenders doubled. Poring through the still segregated CDs of '95, I doubled the lot again—musing foggily, for ex-ample, over Peter Kowald's solo bass album (*Was Da Ist*, FMP). Let's give it a second spin. Just fine, though 70 minutes is a lot of bass. Try something new. Ahh, Dave Holland. Solo bass (*Ones All*, Intuition). Maybe a beer would help. No, it's 10 A.M. All right then, just how lusty *is* Hamiet Bluiett's *Young Warrior, Old Warrior*?

Yet when it was over and the pile was down to about 25 discs, the pleasures of rediscovery were stifled by despair. The state of jazz, to coin a phrase, reminded me once again of those '70s ruminations that pro-claimed a renaissance in short fiction on the grounds that so many could do it well. Jazz today boasts too many adequate players—a general level of musicianship good enough to impress academicians—and only a handful who promise a worthy future. Mid-decade has always been a peculiarly telling moment in jazz history: Armstrong landed in '25, swing in '35, bop in '45, hard bop in '55, new thing in '65, loft jazz in '75, and the neocons in '85. I'm not sure what '95 delivered beyond a none too subtle rebuke to those who would fetter this improvisational music with formal conventions.

Jazz may now have a seat at Lincoln Center's table, but the corre-sponding recognition that Jazz at Lincoln Center is to jazz what the New York Philharmonic is to the classics—no less, but also no more—should heighten the resolve of the working stiffs who are the lifeblood of an art that has played fast and loose with conventions all its days. Maybe in-stitutional jazz is this mid-decade's theme song: Lincoln Center, Carnegie

Hall, the Thelonious Monk Competition, numerous beneficiaries of Leila Wallace, the U.S. Postal system. Each has wrought its wonders. But has there been a musical breakthrough? Has there been a record everyone will stand and salute? For all the masterly recordings by established players, few if any were masterpieces, and with the possible exception of James Carter, whose *The Real Quietstorm* made many converts, none of the newcomers broke much ground. Yet excellence was available, and this alphabetical list indicates some of the pleasures to be had.

1. Kenny Barron, *Wanton Spirit* (Verve). With Roy Haynes and Charlie Haden at his back, the pianist snares "Take the Coltrane" and "Bebop" and lights their fuses. By contrast, the ballads merely glisten.

2. Hamiet Bluiett, *Young Warrior, Old Warrior* (Mapleshade). It's uneven—the war between horns and rhythm section isn't metaphorical enough. But it introduces Mark Shim, a gifted young tenor saxophonist who has been gigging in David Murray's big band and has signed with Blue Note, and Bluiett is in rare form—lusty, blustery, swinging, cantankerous.

3. Ruby Braff and Ellis Larkins, *Calling Berlin Vol. 1* (Arbors). Arbors Records is a small but growing outfit in Florida; of several mainstream operations launched in recent years, it has the narrowest, decisively pre-bop niche, which it fills surprisingly well. It takes nothing away from his albums for Concord Jazz and elsewhere to note that Braff's work for the label has surpassing urgency and luster. His long-awaited reunion with Larkins, a program of Irving Berlin, is by turns haunting and playful (dig the cover) and always supple and expressive—two cranks in a lovefest.

4. Anthony Braxton, *Charlie Parker Project 1993* (hat ART). The moldy Braxton controversy fades before these sextet performances, which are vital, good-humored, savvy, and impertinent. Bonus: Misha Mengelberg's delirious piano.

5. James Carter, *The Real Quietstorm* (Atlantic). The year has not dimmed its luster. His saxophones keep saying "make room," and his ideas justify the conceit of his huge sound.

6. Clusone 3, *I Am an Indian* (Gramavision). Reeds, cello, and percussion begin with a war whoop, a "Sing Sing Sing" rhythm, and the title song, written for Fanny Brice, and continue with Powell's "Celia" and Ellington's "Purple Gazelle." Sometimes the playfulness is silly, but mostly it warms the heart.

7. Dave Douglas, *Constellations* (hat ART). Though his trumpet is clarion, the real payoff of his Tiny Bell Trio is its unerring three-part inventions.

8. Chico Freeman, *Focus* (Contemporary). Supported by an ace

rhythm section, Freeman and Arthur Blythe swing harder than most of the prodigies and achieve a rare poignancy on Don Pullen's threnody, "Ah, George, We Hardly Knew Ye."

9. Charlie Haden and Hank Jones, *Steal Away* (Verve). In a critical, even miraculous work that says something new about folk songs and spirituals at the foundation of African American music, they circumvent glib reverence in favor of dedicated dread. It's a record for everyone.

10. Tim Hagans, *Audible Architecture* (Blue Note). A sideman's trumpet trio decodes tunes made to be pulled at both ends.

11. Jim Hall, *Dialogues* (Telarc). Frisell, Harrell, Lovano, more. The variety grows on you the way the guests grew on Hall and vice versa. Never a wasted note.

12. Javon Jackson, *For One Who Knows* (Blue Note). Cyro Baptiste's percussion salvo signals the start of something different, Terrasson and Haque top their own debuts, and Jackson—whose arrangements upset the usual head-and-solos schedule—has his hottest outing to date. "Paradox" is the smoothest homage to Sonny Rollins I know.

13. Abbey Lincoln, *A Turtle's Dream* (Verve). For more than half a century, a jazz diva was almost by definition a singer crying for her man. Lincoln has turned that around—never with greater emotional resolve than on this sublime album. (Of the new singers who turned up, the one I most anticipate hearing next year is Paula West, whose self-produced *Temptation* takes risks with repertoire that prove Lincoln isn't the end of the road.)

14. Joe Lovano, *Rush Hour* (Blue Note). The CD that won all the jazz mag awards has Rollins-like trios, Ornette-like quartets, a new suite with overcast strings arranged by Gunther Schuller, and the leader's stylistic generosity. Lovano's reputation for shrewd ambition is greatly bolstered here. (Another worthy example is "Somewhere" on Mike Manieri's uneven but often absorbing *An American Diary* [NYC].)

15. Charles McPherson, *Come Play with Me* (AR). A dynamic quartet recital finds McPherson escaping the body if not the shadow of Charlie Parker, and Mulgrew Miller firing up the kind of performance he failed to deliver on his own recent release. Compare this charged disc and the best of his more ornithological recordings, the reissued 1965 *Con Alma!* (Prestige).

16. Gerry Mulligan, *Dragonfly* (Telarc). From mournful ecstasy to breezy cool, Mulligan's essay in sustained lyricism is executed with a finesse that heightens each measure. "Brother Blues" and "Art of Trumpet" are distinguished arrangements, but the selections in which he, Warren Vaché, and John Scofield confide in each other almost make you feel like you're eavesdropping.

17. David Murray, *South of the Border* (DIW). If I keep waiting for Columbia to pick up its distribution I'll never get to comment on it. In a year that offered Murray's electrifying octofunk rockers, *The Tip* and *Jug-a-Lug*, and the alluring *Ballads for Bass Clarinet*, a new record by Murray's big band deserved a wider hearing. Recorded in 1992, a year after its eponymous predecessor (with its tributes to Paul Gonsalves, Lester Young, and Ben Webster), the new work is more contained and better executed. Butch Morris's conductioning is splendidly realized in the boomeranging glissandi and punchy riffs that support the terse soloists, among them James Spaulding, Don Byron, Frank Lacy, and Graham Haynes. The double tenors of Murray and Patience Higgins on a dreamily intoxicated "St. Thomas," the sustained buoyancy of "Happy Birthday Wayne Jr.," the spiraling pull of "Fling," and the full-blown bender by Murray on a revision of "Flowers for Albert" are among the highlights. Big band music is *supposed* to be sensuous.

18. Chico O'Farrill, *Pure Emotion* (Milestone). Afro-Cuban rhythms in the service of big-band arrangements that would be hip and gracious even without them.

Reissues. You would have no idea what you were getting from the packaging for John Coltrane's *Stellar Regions* (Impulse), yet it consists of unissued takes with the exception of "Offering," which appeared on *Expression*, the album released just after his death and the last he supervised. (According to the notes, "To Be," that album's flute and piccolo selection, was actually recorded at another date.) *Stellar Regions* provides the entire output of February 15, 1967, and helps to demystify the final period. What was everyone so afraid of back then? Far from sounding anarchic, Coltrane works over familiar scales and hymn-like melodies, sustaining bursts of rare intensity. "Configuration" is "Countdown" eight years later—no revelation, perhaps, but a spirited affirmation.

The year's most impressive audiophile CDs were Denon's Savoy Master Transfer Collection, a limited edition series, consisting thus far of 16 discs remastered with 20-Bit digital technology. The packaging is neat—a miniaturized cardboard LP-jacket containing the CD (designed to resemble an LP) in a tyvex sleeve, and a play sheet. A magnifying glass is required to read the jacket notes. The sound is full bodied and intimate—not least the long unavailable *Charlie Parker Story* (the "Koko" session). There are five other Parker volumes, as well as the terrific *Introducing Lee Morgan* (only 19 and playing the hell out of an upturned trumpet, with Hank Mobley and Hank Jones), Curtis Fuller's *Imagination*, Milt Jackson's *The Jazz Skyline*, the anthology *Opus De Bop*, and the indispensable Fats Navarro collection, *Nostalgia*. Forget surface noise: the '40s live again in these grooves—Navarro never sounded nearer.

Blue Note also came up with improved source material for a couple of classics, including the complete collaboration between Navarro and Tadd Dameron—a set that might have had wider appeal if the alternates were segregated on the second disc. The Bud Powell quintet is repeated here, along with Benny Goodman's "Stealin' Apples"; the liner notes by Carl Woideck are illuminating. *The Complete Aladdin Recordings of Lester Young* is a long delayed correction of Blue Note's flawed 1975 LPs. It includes the Nat Cole trio session from 1942, all of Young's Aladdins, and a sparkling Helen Humes session from 1945, with a previously unreleased instrumental. The recordings are vibrant, especially Young's twin masterpieces, "D.B. Blues" and "These Foolish Things."

Imagine a national weeklong WWII holiday. Instead of Christmas songs all you hear day and night is "I'll Be Seeing You," "I'll Walk Alone," "Amapola," "You'll Never Know," and "You'd Be So Nice to Come Home To." Actually, that's kind of what 1995 was like. I'm torn between hollering "enough" (surely it's time for a moratorium on "I Fall in Love Too Easily") and going back to the well for another round with the Ink Spots. It's certain than no other war in history with the arguable exception of the French Revolution produced as much good music (and equally certain that much of that music was by Jule Styne, who was conspicuously unrepresented by tributes). Among the many recent WWII anthologies, the Smithsonian's *You'd Be So Nice to Come Home To* is especially canny in skirting some of the clichés, and serves as companion to the Smithsonian's 1993 *We'll Meet Again: The Love Songs of World War II*, which has an excess of Brits. Better still and much jazzier is a five-CD set called *G.I. Jukebox*, consisting of 100 records made for the Armed Forces Radio Service. I bought it on an overseas flight—the only place you can purchase it because AFRS discs cannot be legally sold in the U.S. If you prefer to sing these songs, Hal Leonard has just published a discerning volume of sheet music, *I'll Be Seeing You*—50 songs and a historical timeline.

If you have a child or know a child, use him or her as a beard to buy Gene Seymour's book, *Jazz: The Great American Art* (Watts). It's intended for young people, but as a general primer, you could do a lot worse. As someone who was employed by Captain Kangaroo for one day, I'm in awe of writers who can write simple without writing down. Seymour hits the historical and musical high spots, touches on issues, and dabbles in personalities. He has a judicious perspective and manages to make his way from before Ma Rainey to beyond the AACM in 176 pages. For fully grounded adults, the jazz book of the year was *Hot Jazz and Jazz Dance* by Roger Pryor Dodge (Oxford). Dodge's essay, "Harpsichords and Jazz Trumpets," which, among other things, established Bubber

Miley on the critical map, has inspired generations of jazz critics. It was not generally known that Dodge wrote a great deal more than that, between the years 1929 and 1964; his son, Pryor Dodge, has rectified the matter. Dodge was a dancer (he studied with Nijinsky's teacher) who considered jazz the most significant development in classical music since Bach. He is endlessly meditative, querulous, and restive, pondering every facet of a performance for musical excellence and historical implications. Dodge attended the 1924 debut of *Rhapsody in Blue*, and declared it anti-jazz. He was on a tear for the next 40 years. Some of his best essays address the issues of jazz repertory and the divide between creativity and replication. How modern can you get?

[*Village Voice*, 16 January 1996]

36 ❖ *Lost and Found*
(Brian Barley / Andrew Hill)

A Canadian label that morosely calls itself Just a Memory has re-released three recordings from 1967 and 1970 that turn a belated spotlight on an obscure saxophonist named Brian Barley. A search of periodicals and books turned up not a single reference to him outside of discographies, so all I know of him is drawn from the blurb on his sole album as a leader—born in Toronto; took up saxophone under the influence of Lee Konitz; favored "Coleman, Coltrane, Dolphy, Rollins, and Shepp"; died "a tragic and accidental death" in June 1971, at 28. Not much. His playing on these CDs makes you want to know more.

The earliest is *Maynard Ferguson Sextet*, a radio transcription session coordinated with Ferguson's homecoming during Expo '67. This was a transitional period for Ferguson, whose long association with Roulette had ended in 1964, leaving him foundering among labels and alternating between big band and sextet. The Canadians hired him to stock both units with homegrown talent. In the sextet, they got a credible rhythm section and a front line comprising Ferguson's blaring trumpet, an untuned altoist, and the 24-year-old Barley, whose tenor saxophone displays a promisingly forthright middle register and a penchant for growls and pitch deviations. It's his blues solo over a walking bass on Mike Abene's "To and Fro" and his soul-style variations on an otherwise flat performance of Lanny Morgan's "Polecat" that make the album worth restoring. Yet there's little indication where Barley is going. The influence of Rollins is clear—perhaps Al Cohn as well. But the sonorities of the new music are hardly felt at all.

Nor were they heard three weeks later when Ferguson returned to the studio for *Maynard Ferguson Orchestra*, this time with 15 fellow Canadians (he expanded his usual 13-piece lineup by augmenting the rhythm section). Barley now shared tenor duties with an established musician, Nick Ayoub, a Stan Getz contemporary who had played with Ferguson as early as 1943. This is the better album—Ferguson needs an orchestra to stand up to his pyrotechnics, and the arrangements of "Take the A Train," "Frame for the Blues," "Whisper Not," and others are strong and characteristic (and uncredited). Barley, though, does not impress. His pitch is unsure and his ideas are merely responsive—often pedestrian, rarely inventive.

What a surprise, then, to come upon *Brian Barley Trio*, recorded by Radio Canada International three summers later. Now 27, he leads his own trio, playing his own music, and reflecting with unselfconscious clarity the most exciting developments of the jazz he'd matured with. In the U.S., some of those developments were old-hat by 1970—Coltrane died the summer Barley was gigging with Ferguson, and jazz was in bad shape commercially and aesthetically. Yet Barley embraces '60s innovations with fervor and imagination, his only bow to fashion an electric bass. In the liners, each of the musicians volunteered his favorites, and their utterly predictable lists read like a canon. Bassist Daniel Lessard named Ron Carter, Jimmy Garrison, and Scott LaFaro. Drummer Claude Ranger named Elvin Jones, Max Roach, and Tony Williams. Barley was no master—just a gifted player who knew who the masters were. Except for Dolphy, whose signature phrases I fail to hear in his work, his muses inform virtually every decision he makes. His blending and countering of their styles is dynamic: Rollins's discipline, Coltrane's zeal, Shepp's caustic sound, Coleman's scooped tones and quarter-note pitch. They flash across his solos like patterns of light and shadow.

The pleasure of this record is its ability to recall a precise era of musical confluence. The first three tracks are best. "Plexidance," based on eight-bar patterns, begins in Rollins's shadow—Barley's timbre, his theme, and the very context of a pianoless trio testify to the influence. But from the beginning of his solo, Ornette Coleman looms in the slurred notes and furtive pitch. As the improvisation builds, Barley adapts Archie Shepp's scraping timbre and swings with increasing ferocity, getting only slightly obstreperous toward the climax—and that a matter of dynamics—before relying once again on Rollins's patented thematic improvisation. "Shlucks" is an extended kaleidoscope that opens with a dirgelike theme—Ornette bleeding into Coltrane—with a return to caustic Shepp (drums verging away from Elvin and toward Sunny Murray), ultimately breaking into the freedom-now stratosphere of late Coltrane. The piece goes on, and though it occasionally wants coherence, lively moments arise like serendipitous adventures, as if Barley disdained doing any one thing for very long. Ranger's "Le Pingouin" is the most comical selection, a Woody Woodpecker riff dilated over an odd 24-bar (16 plus 8) structure. The tenor solo weds Shepp's sound and Rollins's ken for organization in handily built four-bar phrases.

Unhappily, the album droops in its finale. Barley plays soprano sax on "Two by Five," and chooses a far-too-obvious Eastern theme, the repetitiveness of which accentuates his relative listlessness on the instrument. Despite the moody quality of the theme and the gonging percussion, all of which is suitably outré, "Oneness" displays something of the timbre he exhibited in the days with Ferguson. In the late '60s and early '70s, many saxophonists in and out of big bands overhauled their styles to incorporate the innovations of Coltrane and others. Barley was different: He tried to define a personal music in which all the key influences of the era were absorbed as themes for his variations. He never secured so much as a footnote in jazz history, but this album is a worthy recovery from a bleak period and distant shore.

If Brian Barley's record thumps into the '90s as a time capsule from the '60s, so in a way does Andrew Hill. He doesn't have a new CD, but he's a living embodiment of the era when hard bop and politics and new music coalesced into a loose movement with Coltrane as saint, Shepp as orator, and Hill as outlying cult figure—a Herbie Nichols who would not give up or go away. Hill, who teaches at Portland State University in Oregon, has been through New York in recent years and has recorded admirably for Black Saint and Blue Note, but he is invariably associated with the years 1963–66, when Blue Note's Alfred Lion took a strong interest in him and recorded a series of provocative albums, among the knottiest of the period. When Mosaic boxed them, it included structural breakdowns of Hill's compositions, yet knowing what they are doesn't make counting them any more automatic. This is music of the head, and only in the most successful works, notably *Judgment* and *Point of Departure*, does the emotional power lift off from the mathematical precision that grounds each piece. *Point of Departure*, in particular, is a benchmark, covering the ground between modality and freedom. Hill is at his most communicative with an inspired cast that includes Dolphy (his last recording), Kenny Dorham, and Tony Williams.

Communication is always the issue with a musician as demanding as

Hill, and there is something preposterous about hearing him in a restaurant, where the slightest chatter or table noise can throw off your (but apparently not his) concentration. Still, his opening set at Iridium last week settled any fears that he might actually have learned a standard over the years, or written an AABA tune in which each letter represents eight bars. With attentive backing from bassist Santi Debriano and drummer Gene Jackson, who has his own take on Tony Williams, Hill tied several pieces into medleys, sustaining long rattling grooves with relentless, kneading riffs and tinkling treble figures and ringing minor seconds. I tried to count. But it was no use. If he played a 12-bar blues, it went over my head. Ultimately, the only thing to do was give in to the rhythms and repetitions, follow the change-ups, surrender to the sonority that long ago assimilated Monk, Powell, Taylor, Tatum, and Nichols. Brian Barley would have killed to play one night with Andrew Hill; the best of Hill's compositions—like those of Monk or George Russell—are so generous with options that soloists as constitutionally different as Dolphy and Dorham could play them any which way they chose and learn something about themselves in the process.

[*Village Voice*, 6 February 1996]

37 ❖ *Monk with Frets* *(Marc Ribot)*

Over no aspect of jazz is there so lusterless a uniformity as modern guitar. Before the war, you could count on the fingers of one hand the number of jazz musicians who could play it at all. But by 1960, Barney Kessel's manual was everywhere, and an army of eighth-note plectrists swarmed onto the scene. The few who really stood out, by virtue of doubling the lead or editing out notes or phrasing in octaves or adding or deleting strings or frets, were the blessed minority. Too many guitar players sounded like too many others. Mark Ribot's new CD, *Don't Blame Me* (DIW), sounds different—at least, from other guitarists. If you need a reference point, consider Thelonious Monk.

Ribot, a 41-year-old native of Newark, is a certifiable eclectic who has been circling the downtown irony school for more than a decade. A student of the Haitian classical guitarist and composer Frantz Casseus, he played in a Stax/Volt backup outfit in the late '70s and early '80s, as well as with Jack McDuff—apprenticeship in an organ combo is de rigueur for most guitarists and presupposes conventional chops. Five years with the Lounge Lizards secured him a downtown reputation. He replaced Arto Lindsay, whose untuned noise guitar had been so minutely controlled as to give the noirish ensemble nothing more jolting than a mild electric shock. Even so, Ribot's more educated attack threatened to give the Lizards a decorous glaze. In fact, he gave them more possibilities, including occasional banjo and cornet, as well as seasoned guitar vamps. His solos, which could be both metallic and twangy, were never four-to-the-bar jazz, even though he was in the same edition of the band as Curtis Fowlkes and Roy Nathanson—this was when the ensemble's fake jazz attitude was undermined often enough by real jazz to make the fakery seem an affectation rather than a style. He produced at least one coherent, original, blistering solo on "Voice of Chunk," from the album of that name.

Ribot joined with various interrelated avant-pop figures, including Fowlkes and Nathanson's Jazz Passengers, Tom Waits, Evan Lurie from the Lizards, Elvis Costello, John Zorn, and more than a dozen others. His most promising step was to organize bands of his own, Rootless Cosmopolitans and Shrek. With the former, he released a notable record in 1990, on which his key associates are Don Byron and Anthony Coleman, and the repertory covers Hendrix and George Harrison as well as two songs—"I Should Care" and "Mood Indigo"—that are known not least for brooding interpretations by Monk. *Rootless Cosmopolitans* offers mostly originals that shriek and rumble and clatter with unexpected amiability, but in the pause-and-conquer strategy of those two songs, especially the 77-second "I Should Care," Ribot suggested a new potential in his playing. *Don't Blame Me* delivers on it.

Here is a disc that consists chiefly of standards, and actually mines them for something beyond the usual glibness of theme and variations. Ribot maintains a respect for their songfulness that shuns wanton irony. He plays them as though the lead sheets were painted over a long wall in oversized notes, each note to be tested and accepted or rejected before moving to the next. Think of *Thelonious Himself*: Ap-ril-in . . . Paa . . . RISSSS. There's much of that here. Not to mention the repertory connection—five of the seven prewar standards have been recorded by Monk, a couple in parallel interpretations. The first track, "I'm in the Mood for Love," is the oddest. The melody itself is always suggestive of self-parody, and Ribot underscores his ambivalence by playing it as though his instrument were a bowed contrabass, integrating fragments of melody with exaggerated surface noise, as if that single chorus were the work of a deeply sincere amateur. It leads without pause into

"Noise #1," which sends patches of sound from one stereo speaker to the other.

By contrast, "Don't Blame Me" is played up in the treble range, and the articulation of melody is reminiscent of Monk's famous version on *Criss Cross*, complete with minor seconds and other dissonances and a percussive attack. Bass notes are used to back and fill the trebly improvisation, which is rarely more than an arpeggiation of the melody notes. Sometimes the attack has a knife-edge thrust. The tuning is Ribot's own. "Body and Soul" is taken similarly, but with a touch of conventional guitar in the phrasing, undermined by discordant asides. In one passage, the strings seem to shake; in another they ring in a manner reminiscent of Django. Nothing is smooth in these readings—even the easiest passes sound tough. "Solitude" is anti–Joe Pass, played with a spastic determination, some figures going from hammered high notes to whomping low ones, but always with judicious juxtaposition. "Dinah" opens with swinging plucked chords, as in reference to Monk's solo stride version, while the solo is a variation on a shave-and-a-haircut. Nowhere is his guitar technique or his homage to Monk more certain than on "These Foolish Things," in which he allows his twangy low notes to briefly gambol.

Throughout, Ribot tenders a sense of quiet amusement and accomplished discernment. His guitar seems to have not six strings but the two halves of a piano, the high notes and the low ones. His phrases are often chromatic figures that go from one extreme to the other, and his dynamics are founded on the contrasts between treble and bass. Another contrast he uses is between electric and acoustic. One of his finest performances is of Albert Ayler's "Ghosts," a theme that was initially mainstreamed by Basie, but is nevertheless rarely performed. Ribot handles it beautifully, at first with single notes, followed by strumming to set them off; but the single strings are made to seem electric and the strummed passages acoustic. "Spigot," an original, is based almost entirely on the give and take between two chords. "Bouncin' Around" shows off his rock and roll roots, as Ribot draws on Duane Eddy bass notes and ends with a jolting finish built on Chopin's funeral march—the only reference to death in a record filled with lively amusements.

[*Village Voice*, 14 May 1996]

38 ❖ The King
(Benny Carter)

In the early '90s, a woman from the Kennedy Center Honors called to pick my brain. The committee, she said, had decided that a jazz artist should be among the next group of honorees. At that time, Washington's awards for lifetime achievement in the performing arts had only recently become the dull joke they remain today. Good intentions had been subverted by TV, so that genius itself was insufficient to warrant recognition. Additional criteria included popularity and/or tokenism: The winners' circle required a woman, a black, a Jew or other ethnic, an unthreatening high-brow, a pop or film star. Everyone knew that. Yet I could hardly believe this woman's candor.

Peggy Lee had been suggested, she said. Was that a good idea? I told her Peggy Lee deserved all kinds of awards, but pointed out that she was a tangential figure in jazz and that genuinely great jazz figures ought to have priority. Such as? The obvious choice, I told her, was Benny Carter—a patriarchal but still vigorously active figure in his 80s whose achievement was beyond dispute.

She laughed: "That's so funny, I just hung up the phone with Quincy Jones and he said exactly the same thing."

"So what else do you need to know?"

"Well, I'm sure he's great, but we can't give a Kennedy Center Honor to Benny Carter."

"Why not?"

"This is for television. No one's ever heard of him."

They ignored jazz that year. Yet Hollywood forces led by Jones and Leonard Feather mounted a campaign on Carter's behalf, and, taking advantage of President Clinton's purported love of jazz, succeeded in getting him selected in 1996. Four years later, Clinton awarded him the National Medal of Arts.

Carter, who died on July 12, 2003, a month short of his 96th birthday, never lacked awards. The *New York Times* obit showed him sitting before a wall of plaques, statuettes, Grammys, citations, and medals. That he never achieved much popular renown was partly a result of career choices that buried him in Hollywood studios for two decades. His stylistic reserve—intellectual, introverted—didn't help. Jazz fans and critics often neglected him as well. Among musicians, however, he was known as The King. No one in jazz history—including Armstrong, Ellington,

Gillespie, Parker, you name him or her—was more universally admired by his brethren.

Much of the regard had to do with his demeanor, a sober mix of modesty and authority. He was invariably referred to as a gentleman, which meant two things: that his manners were impeccable and that you didn't mess with him. He could cut you on the bandstand and off, but sweetly and with a smile. I once saw him negotiate a record deal over dinner. An executive wanted him to forgo union-mandated arranger fees. Benny calmly changed the subject to the label itself; it wasn't one of those fly-by-night bargain operations, was it? "Absolutely not," the exec boasted. "We do not discount, everyone pays full-price." "And yet," Benny said, thoughtfully chewing, "you want a discount from me." End of discussion. While recording Carter's 1961 masterpiece, *Further Definitions*, the producer asked Dick Katz to put "a little more Basie" in his solo. Benny countered, "I want to hear more Dick Katz in that solo!" At the 1987 session with the American Jazz Orchestra, he interrupted a soloist who quoted a pop song, admonishing, "Please don't play other people's music when you're playing my music," which had the instant effect of making everyone focus more intently on their improvisations.

I was asked to write Carter's encomium for the Kennedy Center booklet, which follows. It is followed in turn by an interview I conducted at the time he performed with the American Jazz Orchestra. He was famously reticent with journalists. For example, being a gentleman, he agreed to an interview for Ken Burns's *Jazz*, but being Benny he gave him almost nothing to use. Off-mike, he was generous with his time and wisdom; on-mike, he seemed to find too many complexities lurking behind every question, inclining him toward monosyllabic responses. So this interview turned out to be a rarity—Benny's way, as Ed Berger (*Benny Carter: A Life in American Music*, by Morroe Berger, Edward Berger, and James Patrick is an essential work of jazz scholarship) explained to me, of thanking the AJO for a harmonious collaboration.

The Kennedy Center custodians never did reward Peggy Lee—or, for that matter, Rosemary Clooney (too overweight for the camera, a consultant told me), Sarah Vaughan, Miles Davis, John Lewis, Max Roach, Sun Ra, or *any major jazz figure of the postwar era*, save Dizzy Gillespie (and tangentially B. B. King and Ray Charles). Recipients whose careers began before the war were Benny Goodman, Count Basie, Frank Sinatra, and Ella Fitzgerald. If one figure in 2003 merits a medal from his government for meritorious service to the performing arts, it is Sonny Rollins. But even as I venture the suggestion, I can hear that woman in Washington cracking up.

1. The Kennedy Center Honors, 1996

If you would see his monument, look around. Benny Carter's gift is that capacious, his influence that acute, his presence that secure. Consider the unique range of his achievement.

Instrumentalist

Benny is the last member of a sextet of innovative musicians, all associated with jazz, who established the saxophone as an expressive, dominant instrument in 20th-century music. Sidney Bechet on soprano sax; Coleman Hawkins on tenor; Frank Trumbauer on the now obsolete C-melody; Harry Carney on baritone; and Johnny Hodges and Benny Carter on alto. In the years they struggled to master it, the sax was a vaudeville joke, played in a clipped staccato manner and considered incapable of fluent beauty or the rendering of a ballad. The Six resurrected Adolph Sax's ostracized 19th-century musical interloper.

Between them, Carter and Hodges developed the yin and yang of alto sax—Hodges's impassioned dynamism, Carter's cool lyricism. A composer at heart, Carter taught himself to improvise with unerring logic, his melodic lines flowing with an elegance and purity that seemed timeless in, say, 1933 ("Krazy Kapers"), and no less so in, say, 1985 ("Lover Man"). He was also an exceptional clarinetist ("Dee Blues," 1930) and trumpeter ("More Than You Know," 1939). Indeed, the most remarkable thing about his playing is its detachment from period fashions. Benny is always modern. For 20 years, until the arrival of Charlie Parker, he and Hodges dominated the instrument; half a century later, Carter, Hodges, and Parker remain its kings. Carter's arabesques and decorative swoops, ingenious melodic paraphrases, and originality are the quintessence of jazz at its most refined. He has also recorded memorably on tenor sax, soprano sax, trombone, and piano.

Composer/Arranger

The image, self-described, of the young Benny Carter seated on the floor, surrounded by pages of stock arrangements, trying to figure out how they were constructed, is the stuff of fable. By 1930, Carter was in the vanguard of composers for that singular American ensemble, the big band. Years before the Swing Era, he was an architect of the style and substance of orchestrating reeds and brasses and rhythm instruments. Writing for Fletcher Henderson, McKinney's Cotton Pickers, and Chick Webb, he redefined the idiom, tearing away the baroque ornamentation of the dance bands, streamlining rhythm, ordering a new parity between composition and improvisation in such classics as "Blues in My Heart," "Lonesome Nights," "Symphony in Riffs," and "When Lights Are Low." He emerged with Duke Ellington and Fats Waller as one of the most gifted songwriters to come from within the jazz world.

As an arranger, Benny had a special affinity for saxophones, and his passages for unison reeds became his trademark, endlessly imitated. He had that rare ability to notate a passage so that it swung with the spontaneity of an ad-lib solo. At the height of the New Music movement of the 1960s, one of the most highly regarded and discussed albums was his *Further Definitions*. As the band era ended, he was in constant demand to orchestrate recordings for numerous musicians and singers, including Count Basie, Sarah Vaughan, Joe Williams, Peggy Lee, Ella Fitzgerald, Benny Goodman, Lou Rawls, Carmen McRae, and Jo Stafford. His Western parody, "Cow Cow Boogie" (a collaboration with Don Raye and Gene de Paul), as sung by Ella Mae Morse, was a top-10 hit, as was his arrangement for Ray Charles of "Busted."

Bandleader

Inevitably, Benny would need a band of his own to sustain his independence. Under his direction, the Chocolate Dandies and McKinney's Cotton Pickers produced some of the most forceful jazz of the '20s and early '30s, but when he set out for Europe, in 1935, for a three-year tour with lengthy residencies in Paris, London, Scandinavia, and Holland, he really came into his own. Along with Coleman Hawkins, also touring the continent, Benny established new standards for European jazz. His influence was so pervasive that for decades young arrangers, altoists, and trumpeters in several countries mimicked him. In country after country, he formed exemplary orchestras, often transforming society bands into jazz bands. At the same time, he made a stand for integrated orchestras that would have lasting repercussions. His polymath approach was especially evident on the English "Swingin' at Maida Vale" session: He wrote four arrangements and three pieces, conducted, sang, played trumpet, alto, tenor, and clarinet.

Within a year of returning home, Benny organized one of the great orchestras of the Swing Era, though not an especially popular one. More intent on the music than on the vagaries of dance, he combined harmonic sophistication with deceptively urbane swing to fashion unforgettable numbers, such as "Melancholy Lullaby," "Sleep," "Savoy Stampede," "Slow Freight," and "Scandal in A Flat." Unlike many of his contemporaries he greeted Charlie Parker as an innovator and not a threat;

among the modernists he helped introduce in the 1940s were J. J. Johnson, Max Roach, Art Pepper, Dexter Gordon, and Miles Davis, who called him "a whole musical education."

Pioneer

Benny played a prominent if quiet role in civilizing Hollywood, crashing the racial barriers of the studio system and leaving the doors wide open behind him. He was the first African American to score major films and television shows, sometimes as a ghost. His mannerly but uncompromising disposition, married to his undeniable brilliance, breached a notoriously closed system. Among the films he worked on (and appeared in) are *Thousands Cheer*, *Panic in the Streets*, *Clash by Night*, *The Snows of Kilimanjaro*, *The View from Pompey's Head*, *Flower Drum Song*, and *Buck and the Preacher*. He scored two dozen television shows, including 35 episodes of *M Squad*. In 1978, Benny was inducted into the Black Filmmakers Hall of Fame, and in 1980, he received the Golden Scroll of the American Society of Music Arrangers.

Born in New York City on August 8, 1907, and raised in Harlem, Benny Carter has lived most of his life in Beverly Hills. Benny, who has long been known in musicians' circles as King, refuses to make any claims for himself. But we know him as a gentleman and an inspiration— as an artist of matchless originality and resourcefulness, whose cool pear-toned approach to swing is a world apart. Jazz is his cathedral.

2. Benny Carter and the AJO

Jazz musicians are not given to hyperbole. They've seen and heard too much and their standards are usually intractable. Yet in the seven days that Benny Carter rehearsed the American Jazz Orchestra, leading to an SRO concert on February 26, 1987, a lovely innocence seemed to bloom in the band's ranks, culminating in an outpouring of affection. In the minutes before the big event, several habitually laconic artists volunteered their feelings on the value of a week's lessons from the master. "This is the kind of night you dream about when you start playing and wonder if it will ever come your way," from a studio player with 20 years' experience. "This is one of the great nights of my life," from a virtuoso usually affiliated with the post-modernists. "There's a lot of excitement here tonight, something you don't see very often," from a senior member who has worked with practically everyone over four decades. "The incredible thing is that when you study these arrangements, you find something going on—a nuance, a voicing, a way of phrasing, something—in every measure," from the band's personnel manager. During the preceding week, at least half a dozen AJO members made another observation, almost always in the same words: "This music plays itself."

Carter supported the efforts of the AJO from the beginning, and his wisdom, seasoning, innovation, and generosity provided the band with a grounding and erudition—an authenticity—it could not otherwise have achieved. For Carter, the AJO offered the first chance in decades to conduct a program of his new and old music, played by a crack orchestra. At a panel on the evening before the concert (participants included Roy Eldridge and Milton Babbitt), the AJO's music director John Lewis remarked, "Benny Carter is a complete musician, which is rare. He knows every aspect of being a musician, the practical as well as the artistic." David N. Dinkins, then the Borough President of Manhattan, presented him with a proclamation and declared February 26, 1987, Benny Carter Day. In August, Carter and the AJO repeated the concert at Lincoln Center Plaza, followed by a third and final performance at the Smithsonian. From the beginning, Benny advised us that he was preparing a new suite, which the Orchestra would premiere. He worked on *Central City Sketches* up until the day of the concert (and after, for the purposes of the record), demonstrating a tireless concern with detail. During the weeks of preparation, John Lewis requested four Carter classics. Benny agreed on condition that John play piano. The pleasure John took in watching Carter work reminded us that every master has a master in turn.

GIDDINS: Where do you place big band music among the many musical things you do? I assume it's a luxury now.

CARTER: Well, of course it's a luxury. Actually, it's always been, even when I had a big band regularly, because I could never support it, nor could it support me. I always had to be doing some outside arranging to add to my income, and not only to add to my income, but to add to the money I could pay members of the orchestra. We certainly never made enough money to really cover the band's payroll. In the early years, I recorded with most of the bands around New York, and if I wanted a particular, good trumpet player who had to have a little more money, I'd pick it up. But I was very fortunate, because that was very rare. Even though they were worth more money, they seemed to be happy to join my band and play for whatever I could pay them. Not because they needed the work. I will say that there were occasions when I had to fire a couple of musicians to make them go with other people who

offered them so much more money. I was embarrassed to keep
them, and I knew they could use the money for themselves and
their families.

GIDDINS: You're self-taught as an orchestrator, aren't you?

CARTER: Partly. I did some studying after I went to Hollywood in
the early '40s. But prior to that, yes, I was self-taught.

GIDDINS: I find it almost incomprehensible that anyone could teach
himself to write the kind of arrangements you wrote for Fletcher
Henderson and McKinny's Cotton Pickers. Did you do it by listening?

CARTER: You can bet I listened! [laughs]

GIDDINS: How did you learn the mechanics of it?

CARTER: Well, you take those stock arrangements and you lay them
piece by piece on the floor and you get down on your knees and
study each part and then you start writing the lead trumpet first
and the lead saxophone first—which, of course, is really the hard
way. It was quite some time that I did that before I knew what a
score was [laughs], and of course after you know how to make a
score, well, you know the score. At that time, I didn't.

GIDDINS: Can you remember the first time you wrote an arrangement that you felt had your imprint on it?

CARTER: Oh, I've never thought of it having my imprint on it. I
don't really know what that means.

GIDDINS: You're not conscious of a Benny Carter style?

CARTER: No, I'm not. I've always felt that that was one reason for
the failure of my orchestras. Really. I thought they were probably
eclectic. I don't know, I think in the early days, when I played at
the Savoy Ballroom, in the late '30s and the early '40s, I was reaching for a hit record because that was the only thing that pushed
the big band, any big band, to success. Much of the time, I even
had other people doing arrangements for me.

GIDDINS: Did any of your records take off?

CARTER: Well, when you say "take off," that's a relative term, I
suppose. But about 1943, 1944, I had a couple of records like "Poin-
ciana" and "Malibu," which was one of my songs, and "Hurry,
Hurry," which was a pretty hot item with my former singer, the
late Savannah Churchill. I can't say that any of them really took off
though, no.

GIDDINS: You were aware, however, that there was a Benny Carter
style as an instrumentalist?

CARTER: Well, I guess so. I let other people point to that. Like somebody asked me yesterday in an interview, what did I feel my contribution had been. I said, I don't know. If I've made a contribution I would be very happy to know that, but I'll let somebody else say it. I don't know. And I'm not being modest, I really don't know. Contribution to what—to my livelihood?

GIDDINS: Creating a style, then, is not a conscious thing. It's something that develops when you play the best you can.

CARTER: Oh, yes, that's what I feel. You play, and what comes out comes out.

GIDDINS: Who were the arrangers that you studied when you were teaching yourself?

CARTER: Oh, I guess mostly they were the stock arrangers, people like Arthur Lang, and oh, there was one arranger that I liked so much, he scored for the Goldkette Orchestra, why doesn't his name come to me . . .

GIDDINS: Challis?

CARTER: Of course, Bill Challis! And then Archie Bleyer. I think Archie was the first one who made a four-part harmony common by use of the sixth in the major chord, and of course in the minor chord as well. So these people—I studied their arrangements, and of course I played them because I was playing with an orchestra then, Charlie Johnson's Orchestra. We played some stock arrangements, quite a number of them actually.

GIDDINS: Who else arranged for Charlie Johnson?

CARTER: Benny Waters. You know there were three saxophone players all of whom were named Benny—Benny Whittet, Benny Waters, and Benny Carter. Benny Waters did quite a bit of the arranging, and then I did some.

GIDDINS: What about saxophonists, who did you listen to?

CARTER: At the time, there weren't too many saxophonists to whom I *could* listen. I listened to Frankie Trumbauer and I was tremendously impressed with him. And he was still not really a jazz saxophonist, you know. And I was tremendously impressed with Wayne King—what did they call him, "the waltz king"? Yes, he played lovely saxophone. He wasn't a jazz saxophonist, but he played the instrument and he got a great sound out of it.

GIDDINS: You mentioned Elmer Williams the other day.

CARTER: Oh, Elmer played tenor. I admired him greatly. He had a wonderful sound.

GIDDINS: Was [Coleman] Hawkins an influence?

CARTER: Yes, yes, but I never tried to play like him. I couldn't. Of course, we sat side by side in the Fletcher Henderson orchestra for quite a little period, and he played tenor. So there were hardly any alto players around. There was Johnny [Hodges], who was my contemporary. I think we were the same age. I knew him, but not too well. As a matter of fact, I've never known Johnny too well. And I knew one other who is not as highly sung as he should be and that was Hilton Jefferson, who was a lovely player and a lovely man.

GIDDINS: Was [Don] Redman a good player?

CARTER: Yes, he was an excellent player. He was not really a jazz saxophonist either, I don't think—jazz being the term it is, I'll leave that to somebody else to say. But he was a multi-instrumentalist as well, as you know, and a fine writer.

GIDDINS: Were you aware of the fact that you and Hodges seemed to be emerging as the major voices in jazz alto at the same time?

CARTER: No, I didn't think about it.

GIDDINS: Does that evaluation, which is standard jazz history, seem accurate to you in retrospect?

CARTER: Well, I don't know. You see, there were many saxophone players that I heard in those days that I never hear about now, and nobody else hears about, and you wouldn't know their names if they were mentioned, because they didn't record and they just weren't heard by enough people. But there were some good players. My teacher, Arthur Reeves . . . when you say I was self-taught as an arranger, I was not *completely* self-taught as a saxophonist. I had a very fine teacher named Arthur Reeves and he was a great player. But I won't say he was a jazz player.

GIDDINS: Is it true you studied trumpet with Cuban Bennett and Bubber Miley?

CARTER: No, I didn't study with either of them, because I wasn't playing trumpet at that time. I didn't play trumpet until much later. After I left McKinney's Cotton Pickers—and Doc Cheatham and I both played with McKinney's—I got my own band together to play the Arcadia Ballroom on 53rd Street and Broadway. I think it was 1932, and Doc Cheatham was the lead trumpet player in the orchestra and he encouraged me to play trumpet because he knew that I loved it and I wanted to play it. He used to reach over his stand and hand me his trumpet and mouthpiece and tell me to go up to the mike and play. He practically made me do it. Most people would say, "Gee, that little whippersnapper, he better not touch my horn," you know. But Doc just loved to see me try, and he encouraged me and showed me a few things, and the mouthpiece you heard me play on today he gave to me in 1932. And that's the only mouthpiece I've ever had. Of course I have had a duplicate made, and at this point I'm not sure which is the original. The duplicate was made so well.

GIDDINS: You've never had trouble changing embouchure?

CARTER: The trouble isn't in changing embouchure. As I continue to say, the trouble is not devoting equal time to each instrument—that's the whole thing. It's no great feat to be able to play two instruments, even though they require different embouchures. It's a matter of just playing both instruments. If you can practice one hour a day, give 30 minutes to each instrument. If you can practice four hours a day, two hours to each instrument. And when you get on the bandstand at night, if you have to play four hours, play two hours on each instrument. But I've never been able to do that.

GIDDINS: Have you written music over the years for orchestras that you haven't had the chance to perform?

CARTER: No. If there was anything that I had written to perform, I would have done so even at my own expense.

GIDDINS: The film work you've done, is there material from that? A lot of people now are crafting suites from Korngold or Steiner scores and such.

CARTER: Yes, yes. There's some music—it may not be available because of the studios needing all of the space that they can get. Like the television studios, gee, they just eat up music. They just destroy scores and parts and everything. A lot of people don't know what they have there. The people who come into the studio don't know what's there.

GIDDINS: So you don't have them either.

CARTER: I don't have them either. Some things I have. I have tapes of some of the shows I've done—I have quite a number of tapes. But I don't have the music or the parts. I have some scores, but for the most part you don't think of keeping that stuff. You never think of what you'll do with it later.

GIDDINS: Are there pieces you've written that you're especially fond of?

CARTER: I like them all. I like them all, sure. After all, they're my babies.

[Kennedy Center Honors, 1996 / *Central City Sketches*, 1987]

39 ❖ Drum Dada
(Han Bennink)

Some performers, like Chaplin, are not ensemble players—you train the spotlight on them and hope for the best. No one who knows the 54-year-old Dutch drummer Han Bennink exclusively from the diverse recordings he has made over 35 years would put him in that category. Yet at the Knitting Factory's Bennink festival, which consisted of eight hour-long duets with as many partners over four nights, he emphasized his theatrical inclinations. Looking trimly Aryan with a close-cropped blond pate, he opened each set with a gunshot whack on the snare, attended his associates' initial forays with rudimental support, and then departed for the realm of Dada in a series of gestures, anarchic and funny, that transported the audience into a realm of prudent but grateful tittering. Boring he is not.

The presentation was far more musical and rewarding than it can possibly sound autopsied, but here goes. In practically every show, he did much or all of the following: accoutered himself in wooden clogs and, seated on the floor, played them like drums; placed a cymbal on his head and rang it like a gong; snapped scissors in rhythm; bunched sheets of newspaper percussively; rested his right foot on the tom-tom; deadened the snare with a towel; flipped, dropped, and threw away his sticks; carried the snare to the stage apron; placed the end of one stick in his jaw and rapped on it with the other; held the snare to his mouth and screamed; played the backside of the bass drum through his legs; produced various rattles, bells, and other noisemakers; pushed over parts of the traps and tossed cymbals in the air or threw them to the ground—always rhythmically, of course.

Bennink was recognized as a singular performer by the time he was 20, when word spread that at least one European drummer could swing and a covey of visiting players—mostly saxophonists, from Ben Webster to Sonny Rollins—took advantage. American listeners learned about him with the release of Eric Dolphy's 1964 *Last Date*, which also served to introduce Bennink's long-time collaborator, the older but compatibly eccentric pianist Misha Mengelberg. Bennink's work on that session was not overwhelming: Like Dr. Johnson's woman preacher, he scored by doing it at all. Representing a significant advance from such predecessors as Jorn Elniff, the Danish drummer who had backed Dolphy on his earlier European jaunt, he even made it to Newport in 1966. Four decades later, European drummers have come a long way, baby.

By Newport, Bennink had fully embraced the new music, expressed in duets with Mengelberg, and within a year the two men and Willem Breuker founded the Instant Composers Pool. Bennink soon appeared and recorded with Peter Brotzmann, Globe Unity Orchestra, Derek Bailey, Don Cherry, Marion Brown, Anthony Braxton, Peter Kowald, and many others. His (and Mengelberg's) 1982 Soul Note album with Roswell Rudd, *Regeneration*, was his most internationally acclaimed record since *Last Date*. Six years later he participated brilliantly in Cecil Taylor's Berlin duets, inspiring the pianist with his vivacious marchlike dynamics. More recently, he has deconstructed Irving Berlin as a member of the irresistible Clusone 3 (*Soft Lights and Sweet Music, I Am an Indian*), a knowing ensemble that works hard to disguise its pleasurable mainstream leanings, and recorded trios with Ray Anderson (*Cheer Up*) and duets with Dave Douglas (*Serpentine*), both of whom partnered him at the Knit.

For those who attended more than one performance (I caught five), a suspenseful subtext soon became apparent. How would each player hold Bennink's attention? The slide guitarist David Tronzo did well enough, but was nonetheless the sacrificial lamb in going first. He favored extended notes, often squeezed and vocalized, and managed to make himself heard by everyone except the hyperactive Bennink, who rolled over him like a catamaran. Beyond the Dada (did I mention yodeling? clackers? a tiny cymbal held against the mouth?), Bennink kept hope alive with a demonstration of conventional techniques that held the week together. Using march rhythms as a transitional resource, he alternated between strict time and free time, showing a particular fancy for two-beat patterns.

Like Buddy Rich, Bennink builds his solos on basics—paradiddles and ratamacues and rolls, stoked with speed and incremental dynamics to orgasm. By placing a towel on the snare, he effects a flat, crackling sound that complements the thunder he sustains on the bass drum. He can heighten the little-drummer-boy parade marches to a point of unholy aggression. Perhaps his most startling technique is the way he holds the left stick almost horizontal to the snare, effecting simultaneous rim shots amid rapid rolls or, conversely, controlled wind-downs. He is uncanny with brushes, snapping time along until he tires of it and kicks over the hi-hat. Andrew Cyrille, one of the guiding lights in the transition from bop to bop-doubt, embraced Bennink in a duel of cowbells, and switched to sticks for ingenious variations on four (I can recall no triplet or quintuplet rhythms all week—it was backbeat, four-beat, or no beat), that ultimately marched off into Bo Diddleyville. Significantly, Cyrille chose to follow Bennink's lead and when left briefly to his own devices measured time until the Dutchman bounced back.

Dave Douglas precipitated the most conventional set with an entrance that sounded more planned than the others, then rode a second-line beat with a thinly disguised "Surrey with the Fringe on Top," followed by a proudly anointed "Our Love Is Here to Stay," which prompted Bennink to sustain an ecstasy of swinging brushes and, inevitably, air-brushes. Unhappily, Douglas brought along an electronic gizmo that occasionally blighted the lucent timbre of his trumpet with pinched cries and two-note chords reminiscent of the Varitone, long thought to have expired with love beads. He got over it for a free episode that culminated in a march, followed by a rubato, abstract "'Round Midnight" and a 16-bar blues with Bennink nailing down the backbeat.

Ellery Eskelin, who in the space of a phrase can suggest the fuzzy toneless warmth of Ornette on tenor and the granite bark of Roscoe Mitchell on anything, induced Bennink to ching-a-ching-ching for a while, but in a short time both musicians moved to a steady, accentless time zone. Bennink upheld a fantastic Gamelan-like rhythm on snare and tom, Eskelin produced swing phrases in the top register, Bennink mimed cutting off his ear with scissors (crrritic!), Eskelin roared into banshee range, and they ended up in the midground of '60s free jazz, but with humor and without religion. Eskelin is presently represented by *Green Bermudas*, in which he uses a sampler on déclassé pop, and *The Sun Died*, a nod to Gene Ammons with Marc Ribot that will not please most of Ammons's fans, but will amuse students of harmolodics.

The most satisfying set featured Matthew Shipp, the provocative pianist now in a state of headlong maturation, who asks the important questions about melody and time and keyboard technique in a post-Cecil world and ventures to answer them. The reflexiveness he demonstrates with David S. Ware can be heard to advantage on Joe Morris's *Elsewhere* and in the hothouse challenge of Roscoe Mitchell (*Matthew Shipp Duo*). But neither disc quite captures the Brechtian drama with which he faced Bennink, not simply the Weillish melodies and 8/4 cadences, but his determination to stand up to the drummer, who seemed more determined than ever to command center stage. He rummaged through his bag of tricks, and Shipp responded with music-box melodies, the flight of a bumblebee, plucked strings, and a relentless recitation of "Tenderly," pounded out in the bass as though it were Rachmaninoff. With all the cymbal throwing, woodblock rattling, furniture moving, more and more "Tenderly," the duet mutated into a sporting event. Bennink, mighty damned tired of "Tenderly," did his best to kill it; he whistled, howled, crashed his chair down on his cymbals. Shipp pummeled away, then, finally, squirreled off into his own indigenous and most welcome figures, leading to a terrific unison rhythm when he adapted Bennink's patterns on piano. Bennink reprised shtick. Shipp reprised "Tenderly." They lock-stepped rhythms again, and went out with a lullaby. You had to be there, and I'm glad I was. But I can do without a tape.

[*Village Voice*, 11 February 1997]

40 ❖ On Their Own (Gerry Gibbs / Ravi Coltrane)

In the early '60s, a young pianist named Alice McLeod worked with Terry Gibbs—she made her recorded debut on his 1963 album, *Jewish Melodies in Jazztime* (Verve). Gibbs introduced her to John Coltrane, whom she married. The Gibbses later produced a son, Gerry, who was followed a year later by the Coltranes' second son, Ravi. The boys became fast friends, and when Gerry relocated from the West Coast to Queens in 1988, he found a nearby place for Ravi. Since that time, they have scratched at the New York scene, alone and together. Initially, each exploited familial ties: Gerry, a drummer, played with the Terry Gibbs–Buddy DeFranco Quintet; Ravi, a saxophonist, toured with Elvin Jones; both worked with Alice Coltrane. But they have long since made their own connections—Gibbs with John Campbell, Joe Henderson, and Joe Lovano; Coltrane with David Murray, Joanne Brackeen, Pete LaRoca, and Ryan Kisor. Now Coltrane is the featured guest on *The Thrasher* (Qwest), an impressive, at times almost giddily entertaining debut by the Gerry Gibbs Sextet.

At center stage is Gibbs's composing and arranging. The performers are consistent and fine, but the compositional gambits—the grids that parse and shade each man's contribution—sustain and steady them so adroitly that they sound as poised as road-savvy soloists in a big band. As with the best tunes of Horace Silver or Wayne Shorter, the writing governs the action. Though Gibbs lacks their melodic originality, he compensates with engaging voicings, change-ups and asides, frequent genre bending, and much interplay. The solos are measured, focused, even inspired—Coltrane and pianists Uri Caine and Billy Childs have rarely sounded better, and vibist Joe Locke is more appealing here than on his own debut.

Gibbs, a vigorous drummer armed with an arsenal of bells, whistles, chimes, horns, gongs, and blocks, has shown during his long stint at Visiones how much texture he can ring from a tentet; he is no less effective with six pieces. Maximizing Mark Feldman's violin, he savors the power of strings to enrich the ensemble fabric while invoking musical ghosts rarely indulged in jazz recordings. The title selection, written in memory of Don Pullen, is punched up with brief interludes of ersatz bluegrass violin and a pizzicato two-beat before slipping into jazz time, signaled with one of Gibbs's favorite alarums, a Rahsaan-style whistle. The cartoonish "Another Adventure with Mr. Fick" (Raymond Scott keeps emerging like a Freudian slip) has a stop-time theme, augmented with whistles and bells and ominous grunts (which rather overbake the joke in the last moments), as well as discrete childlike drum figures applied with candid affection to leaven swing's melting pot. That same piece offers one of Coltrane's better soprano saxophone solos—a confident, expanding, coherent statement that coolly assesses the time and, notwithstanding an abiding Wayne Shorter influence, suggests a timbre of his own.

Gibbs's "F Train to Bermuda" is an enchanting theme, and typifies his approach. As the first piece on the album, it is designed to show off all the players, yet is so tightly structured that it skirts the inevitability that accompanies what might have been a generic string-of-solos jaunt. Taken way up-tempo, it begins with an eight-note bass vamp played against a sustained tremolo, proceeds via a tenor saxophone break into the kind of rhythmic melody that can be played on drums, and takes flight as a calypso. Sax and piano breaks, rhythmic switcheroos, vamps, and set-ups recur throughout, and are pulled off as quickly as card tricks. Even at his busiest, Gibbs maintains a light, sure touch. Coltrane's tenor suggests the dry midrange of Hank Mobley with a whimper in the top notes. Rarely does he recall his father's style, though he comes close on "Love Letter to Dawna Bailey" (Gibbs's wife, who died in 1991 of sickle-cell anemia), bending notes in the upper register, but always with a softer affect. In addition to Coltrane's expressive solo, "Love Letter," the most compelling of the ballads, finds Locke playing succinctly in the manner of Milt Jackson, and finishes with a chorus neatly arranged for vibes, violin, drums, and piano. Gibbs understands that he doesn't have to use all the instruments all the time.

Two of the most surprising selections are adaptations. Gibbs has reconfigured John Coltrane's "Impressions" into a 58-bar piece, with a bridge in which he turns the rhythm around, setting up a two-bar scored figure that is in turn continued with a six-bar piano passage. This is succeeded by eight-beat unison episodes, first for tenor and bowed violin and then for piano and plucked violin. None of this gets in the way of the pithy solos (two choruses by Coltrane, one by Caine, and one by Gibbs and the ensemble), and it succeeds in putting the Debussy-derived fragment in a new light. This is an "Impressions" with almost as much theme as variation. Less successful is a brief "In a Sentimental Mood" that wisely makes no attempt to recapture the Coltrane-Ellington landmark. On the other hand, Ellington's "Rockin' in Rhythm" is treated in a fresh, synthetic manner (a second sax part is dubbed) that suits its roller-coaster verve—the voicings are humorously animated, Caine is outstanding, and the final section offers a novel way to stretch the tail-swallowing theme into infinity.

Coltrane is also well represented on a more conventional album by the quintet Grand Central, in which he shares the front line with saxophonist Craig Handy. Recorded in 1995, *Tenor Conclave* (Evidence) is a tribute to Hank Mobley, and except for the title selection avoids chase choruses and other ventures into tenor madness. It's a focused evaluation of Mobley's work as composer and saxophonist, particularly from the 1960 period of *Soul Call* (the source of four of nine titles), a breakthrough for Mobley in the year before he joined Miles Davis. Like Charlie Rouse, who replaced Coltrane in Monk's quartet, Mobley, who replaced Coltrane in Davis's band, was severely undervalued at the time. The consensus has shifted. If Mobley, a charter member of Art Blakey's Jazz Messengers and Horace Silver's Quintet, was one of the defining musicians of hard bop, he made his reputation by avoiding a hard sound. His playing never lost the tempering lyricism of Lester Young, apparent in the triplets and riffing turnbacks of his rhythmically adventurous Rollins-influenced style. He disarmed listeners by cloaking his knotty harmonies and angular rhythms in a smooth, unperturbed, pure-gin sound.

Coltrane is temperamentally closer to Mobley than the more caustic Handy, but the latter also navigates the middle range with deliberation and loping swing, and you won't have any trouble telling them apart. All but two selections are Mobley originals, among them the twin pinnacles, "This I Dig of You" and "Take Your Pick," two soberly celebrational ABAB songs that remind me of Freddie Redd's music for *The Connection* and are well served by a dual-tenor attack. On the first, Coltrane breaks up the rhythm as Mobley liked to do and unfurls sheets of 16th-notes with velvety assurance; on the second, a resourceful variation on "Green Dolphin Street," he toys with the source melody before spinning outward.

The presence of "Hank's Waltz," a good blues in six, says something about the impact of records, as Mobley's 1965 recording was first released posthumously, more than 20 years later—too late for older Mobley fans to pay much attention, but just right for Handy, who develops a telling slab of melody in his cleverest solo, and Coltrane, who quotes his father's improv on "Someday My Prince Will Come." Other effective moments include Handy's blistering incursion and the exchanges on "Tenor Conclave," Coltrane's dissonant opening and Mobley-out-of-Pres turnbacks on the 16-bar blues, "Soul Station," and his Shorter-influenced soprano on the Silver-inflected "East of the Village." The rhythm section (Billy Childs, Dwayne Burno, Cindy Blackman) is admirable, not least in its watchfulness on "If I Should Lose You." Of course, a cynic may complain that just about everything on this disc might have been heard 30 years before, and that's true to a point: But who would have recorded a tribute to Hank Mobley 30 years ago? No such nits can be picked regarding *The Thrasher*.

[*Village Voice*, 17 June 1997]

41 ❖ Classic Ambition (Wynton Marsalis)

Longer than *Don Giovanni*, *Aida*, or the combined playing time of Ellington's *Black, Brown and Beige*, Max Roach's *We Insist! Freedom Now Suite*, and Hannibal Peterson's *African Portraits*, Wynton Marsalis's *Blood on the Fields*, an oratorio that—like the latter three works—takes as its subject the African American slave experience, is, in short, long. The first question posed by a three-hour piece must be: Does it justify its length? Beethoven, attacked for self-indulgence in his Third Symphony, doubled the duration in his Ninth; time may tilt the scales for Marsalis as well. But the audience for the February 24 Lincoln Center Jazz Orchestra performance was unwilling to wait; some two-thirds of the sold-out house rose to its feet ("feet in the butt," the work proclaims, "beget recognition") and fled, greater clumps scurrying with each ensuing episode. Marsalis anticipated that response in an unusual opening plea for the house to stick. "It gets there," he pledged. I was reminded of the screening of Otto Preminger's *Exodus* during which Mort Sahl rose and petitioned the director, "Otto, let my people go!"

As a concert work, *Blood on the Fields* is an exercise in unqualified hubris, a discursive pastiche in which a broad range of influences is welded but not integrated, ingested but not digested. In substituting ambition for discipline, it underscores its composer's most glaring weaknesses—inability to configure a melody, clumsy didactic rhetoric, emotional coldness that arms itself against sentimentality with self-conscious cleverness. Marsalis, as *In This House, on This Morning* made arduously clear, lacks an internal editor. Nor does he have colleagues or friends to tell him that bigger isn't better, that it is no shame to hire a librettist, that he can't walk on water. What he does have is an inexplicable 1997 Pulitzer Prize for a 1994 work to validate the hype. He also has an album, recorded January 22–25, 1995 (according to Sony), which was slyly withheld from release until the prize was given; the CD libretto is identical to that in the 1997 concert program.

The three-disc set relieves the listener of the obligation to take it in all at once, yet absorption over time fails to alleviate *Blood on the Fields*'s repetitions and dullness, and the recording is additionally marred by undistinguished musicianship. All of which is especially perplexing considering the theme. A work that explores the middle passage, slavery, and freedom ought to have emotional resonance—it ought to illuminate the horror (as, for example, Peterson's superior oratorio does during the boy soprano's invocation in "The Middle Passage") and allow us to share in the jubilation (as, for example, Ellington's incomparable *Black, Brown and Beige* does in "Emancipation Celebration"). Otherwise, what's the point? White audiences are generally scared to death to say anything untoward about a work of art that concerns slavery. So the wisecracks that started to build in Avery Fisher Hall last February suggest the irreverence *Blood on the Fields* generates, and the record is more alienating.

It begins with a trumpet cadenza played in a kind of Harry-James-meets-Mannie-Klein Hollywood jazz style (cf. *Young Man with a Horn*), along with the first of many egregiously chanted lines intended as narrative cues, but droned with such affectlessness as to scream out for parody. Yet the succeeding orchestration illustrates one of Marsalis's undeniable strengths, his gift for mimicry. As a trumpeter, he has played Miles Davis, Louis Armstrong, Cootie Williams, and others with mixed success; as a composer, he has now assimilated without quite internalizing Ellington, Mingus, Horace Silver, Motown, New Orleans, Gillespie, Coltrane, the Art Ensemble of Chicago, and more. Stravinsky observed, "A good composer does not imitate; he steals," but at his best Marsalis imitates with brio and affection. If the use of seesawing arco bass to depict the rolling of ocean waves is a tad obvious, his use of dark muted brasses and Mingusian cacophony are distinctive, and he has come up with the striking technique of shoring up declarative vocals with bold instrumental figures. He juices the Horace Silver–style vamp on "Lady's Lament" with a tricky time signature, alternating four and five; builds the brasses and woodwinds voicings on "Oh What a Friend We Have in Jesus" up from the tuba; and subverts AABA form in the pleasurable "Juba" (sung by Jon Hendricks), a rhythm song that suggests a Professor

Longhair lick wedded to a hambone rhythm, by turning the bridge into a concluding chorus.

But the parts don't add up. The story concerns two slaves, an arrogant prince named Jesse and his humanizing woman, Leona, who represent the long road from anger and victimhood to acceptance and triumph. As characters, they are flat and frequently diffuse—the more they sing, the less convincing they are as flesh and blood or as carriers of ideas. Leona, especially, needs a passionate aria, but despite Cassandra Wilson's considerable ability in combining masks and head tones to maximize expressiveness, she simply does not have the material necessary to make the requisite impression. Marsalis's most powerful melodic idea, the "I will not slave for any man" quatrain (in "Plantation Coffle March") intoned by Miles Griffith as Jesse, is dropped without development.

Marsalis has thought much about his subject, and admirably skirts clichés while challenging false history. Jesse, for example, boasts of all the slaves he owned as an African prince. The white Slave Buyer is no Simon Legree caricature, but a robust citizen on a shopping spree. This last conceit turns on itself. Not only does the Buyer—arriving in a marketplace illuminated by a Gillespie Afro-Cuban jazz lick—speak 20th-century black lingo ("people, that's what I'm copping"), but, as sung by Hendricks, he swings harder and with greater joy than any black character in the work. Hearing him scat while the band rocks, you wonder—facetiously—if white slave traders invented jazz and observant slaves just picked it up. And if facetiousness has no place in a work like this, neither do what appear to be inside songwriter jokes—like the passing resemblance between the cadence for the phrase "Soul for Sale" and Porter's "Love for Sale," and between the phrase "Will the sun come out?" and Arlen's "When the Sun Comes Out."

The libretto is at times stuffy ("the bitter lash of failure"), prosaic ("let me bathe in the cool waters of your love"), inapt ("God don't like ugly" in a 19th-century gospel song), and downright silly ("Hawk at the mule / Of tragedy"), and the mosaic of musical borrowings, especially from Ellington and Mingus, is no more coherent. Less inspired than precocious and showy, Marsalis writes like a brilliant student who has mastered all the tricks at the cost of his own individuality. In the last third, which is no more creditable on record than at the end of the concert, he offers an ersatz Ellington song ("I have no heart, it's been crushed and torn by misery"), interpolates a violin reel, repeats his Juba theme, and closes with an instrumental, "Due North," that changes keys in the manner of Ellington's "Going Up."

Stanley Crouch observes in the liner notes that at 32, Marsalis's age when he debuted *Blood on the Fields*, neither Ellington "nor anyone else had written a work this ambitious." That's quite true, though only so far as jazz is concerned. But unlike Marsalis, Ellington, at 32, had written numerous classics, from "Black Beauty" to "Rockin' in Rhythm" to "Mood Indigo." He bided his time before attempting a large-form work on black history, abandoning an opera in the interim because it wasn't good enough. His subsequent magnum opus, *Black, Brown and Beige*, though widely misperceived, produced a number of enduring melodies, including "Come Sunday," the most hauntingly original hymn in contemporary music. A roll call of past Pulitzer winners (which does not include Ellington, Mingus, Lewis, Coleman, or any other jazz composer) in music, fiction, and theater will convince anyone that *Blood on the Fields* deserves to reside in that motley company. But if Marsalis allows pomp and circumstance to drown out the sound of his audience's tramping feet, he may be doomed to produce one white elephant after another. An avant-gardist can afford to chase crowds away. A classicist ought to heed his calling.

[*Village Voice*, 1 July 1997]

42 ❖ *Hard of Hearing (JVC 1997)*

The 25th edition of George Wein's New York jazz festival, now firmly sponsored by JVC, was all over the map, musically and geographically, including a series of potentially canny shows at the Kaye Playhouse that promised to look at neglected areas tangential to jazz. For the first two nights, though, good intentions were undone by what one observer called the Worst Wives Clubs. Ignorant of Rich Conaty or his radio show, "The Big Broadcast," I had foolishly assumed the concert of that name would be a look at '30s radio and maybe the Paramount movie series that celebrated it. But it was merely a vanity production, with Conaty producing comedy routines that caricatured the good old days as a dreary joke. A reasonably likable baritone named Allan Marks sang "I'd Rather Lead a Band" in a Batman mask (no explanation). A girl group proved that deedle-dee-dees do not the Boswells make. A boy group crooned all too soberly in spite of ceaseless mugging by a little guy in the middle.

There were compensations. It was a tonic to hear 80-year-old saxophonist Jerry Jerome unleash his magnanimous 1930s Hawkins-Webster sound on "Crazy Rhythm," and amusingly odd to see "the legendary Miss Dolly Dawn" (a septuagenarian Betty Boop, formerly of the 1930s George Hall band), sing, twinkle, and smile at the same time. Scott Robinson parsed "Star Dust" on saxophones, from soprano to contrabass, a pretty good stunt as stunts go. Herb Gardner and the Big Broadcasters brightened the evening immeasurably with accurate readings of '20s Ellington, Whiteman, and Casa Loma, peaking with Bennie Moten's riffed-out version of "Blue Room"—marred only by an obstreperous drummer who reminded me of the psycho drummer in Hitchcock's *Young and Innocent*. Enter Conaty's wife, Manhattan Mary, who sang with weird pitchless foghorn sonority while nervously pulling at a skirt that was split as far as it could go. I thought of a raft of old musicians' jokes, like: How can you tell that the woman ringing your doorbell is a singer? She's out of tune and doesn't know when to come in.

The Hoagy Carmichael retrospective had a fine cast plus illuminating anecdotes from the composer's son. To demonstrate Bix Beiderbecke's influence, the ensemble—Kenny Davern, Scott Hamilton, Randy Sandke, Dave McKenna, Michael Moore, Jackie Williams, and the show's producer, Howard Alden—romped through "Riverboat Shuffle" and "Davenport Blues." Davern played a radiant, slow-motion, shimmying "New Orleans," and Hamilton, after a mawkish verse, pushed deep into the chorus of "Star Dust." Everything went swimmingly until another singer-wife, Terrie Richards Alden, demonstrated the voice Blossom Dearie might have if awakened from a deep sleep without her sense of pitch. She had about five numbers to Davern's one, and what she did to "Skylark" shouldn't happen to a pigeon. I thought of a raft of old musicians' jokes, like: Dizzy Gillespie goes to heaven and is greeted by Charlie Parker, who raves about how peachy the heavenly band is, playing with the finest musicians who ever lived, good hours, a little wine at dinner, you name it, except one thing. What's that? Well, God's got this girlfriend. The craggy-voiced Bob Dorough made amends with a "Hong Kong Blues" he wouldn't do in Hong Kong; "Baltimore Oriole," which he recorded memorably 30 years ago; and the haunting "Winter Moon," Carmichael's last important song, long ignored by everyone except Art Pepper. During a sequence of songs Carmichael wrote for Louis Armstrong, Sandke soared on "Ev'ntide" and "Jubilee."

The great New York monuments to acoustic engineering could be put off no longer—and Aretha Franklin was singing gospel at Avery Fisher. Aretha, however, can't tolerate air conditioning, or so the rumor went as people wondered why the place was as sticky as Calcutta. Nor was she much interested in the soundboard or in singing a full set. She belted a few extravagant numbers from *Amazing Grace*, backed by her vocal group and full choir, in splendid voice, though fighting amplified rhythm instruments, and then disappeared so that Jesse Jackson could deliver a long, patronizing speech about AIDS. The program's true star turned out to be Chicago's Reverend Donald Parsons, who began his sermon (subject: Why didn't they persecute Mary Magdalene's partner?) with a snoozable dignity, building steadily to an electrifying climax of quaking fortissimos, the platitudes thundering like imprecations from Mount Sinai.

The Society of Singers' 80th birthday tribute to Lena Horne, also at Avery Fisher, was everything such a gala ought to be: none of those self-adoring Lord Webberized singers, more infatuated with their pipes than the songs they annihilate—just seasoned pros. Jazz, sparse as it was, provided most of the high points: Joe Williams singing the blues, Rosemary Clooney singing three Billy Strayhorn arrangements from *Blue Rose,* Billy Taylor treating "Take the A Train" as an undulating ballad, and Bobby Short rasping "Lush Life." The most exhilarating performer was Chita Rivera, who had opened on Broadway in *West Side Story* a few weeks before Horne opened in *Jamaica,* singing and dancing a number from *Chicago,* emitting almost as many sparks as Lena's eyes, which were displayed in several film clips and were no less dazzling when she finally took the stage for a chorus of "As Long as I Live."

The only drawback was you couldn't hear most of what was said, an augury. At Carnegie the next night, Geri Allen played a few measures of "Old Folks"—and when her trio kicked in, every note she and Ron Carter played was sucked into a painful, echoey din. Making things worse was her drummer, the slam-bang Lenny White, aided and abetted by the saboteur at the soundboard; during a bass solo, he had two ride cymbals and the hi-hat going at the same time. Proof it wasn't the hall arrived after a brief intermission, when in support of Joe Lovan's Celebrating Sinatra band, Al Foster discovered . . . brushes! Even with sticks, he was a model of elegance and discipline, not to mention collaboration. The full complement of strings and winds playing Manny Albam's arrangements gave much pleasure, not least a passage of "Someone to Watch over Me," as Lovano's high-note cries played against Judi Silvano's wordless vocal. By virtue of being audible, bassist Ed Schuller aced Ron Carter.

I left at intermission, missing a reportedly stupendous performance by Cassandra Wilson, for Herbie Hancock's New Standard All-Stars, taking another crack at a program that had been disastrous last time around. Avery Fisher's sound ranged from cloudy to soupy, badly muddying John Scofield's guitar, but the set's robust musicality could not be denied. The gimmick remains questionable: "Norwegian Wood" will always be

"Norwegian Wood" no matter how many chords you nail into it. The soloists rarely accessed the themes anyway. Michael Brecker was off on a tear on Stevie Wonder's "You Got It Bad Girl," and it was no mean pleasure to hear Hancock overcome his recently chronic reserve on Peter Gabriel's "Mercy Street" and especially Prince's "Thieves in the Temple," which in this arrangement sounded like one of Hancock's "Watermelon Man"–era funk tunes. His technical ingenuity and crystal touch were unmistakable in spite of the dampening fog he had to cut.

The most moving event of the week was the halting appearance of the partly paralyzed Barney Kessel at a Kaye Playhouse tribute. His wife read his prepared notes—a rosary of guitarists he had studied, from Eddie Lang to his fellow Oklahoman, Charlie Christian, with whom he once spent three days jamming. A dozen participants plucked and strummed in duets and trios, including Herb Ellis, who turned "Willow Weep for Me" into a mint-julep blues, followed by a Tal Farlow solo that bounded all over the fret board. Winard Harper's deft and witty drumming made a strong impression throughout the evening.

As alienating as the Kessel program was moving was the spectacle of McCoy Tyner fronting a string orchestra, conducted by John Clayton, to perform songs by Burt Bacharach. Shorn of whatever rhythmic interest Dionne Warwick and others once gave those cloying melodies, the result was stupefying. Clayton, somewhat apologetically, credited the idea to Tommy LiPuma, the record industry menace who specializes in convincing good musicians to play bad music—in this instance Tyner rendering two-note piano voicings in the manner of Peter Nero. Stay tuned for Cecil Taylor's variations on the Moody Blues.

Tyner looked like he might make it up in the second set, leading his trio, playing some quasi-stride, turning up the heat behind violinist John Blake, and welcoming—in addition to Wynton Marsalis and James Carter—Elvin Jones, whose drums were stationed as far from the piano as possible while remaining onstage. Still, there was a moment during "Cotton Tail," when Tyner and Jones mixed it up in something approaching a dialog. After that, Tyner folded his tent and played chords for the guests. Carter engaged in a full panoply of effects—triple-tonguing, growling, circular breathing, variations in timbre—in a largely successful attempt to avoid running changes on "In a Sentimental Mood"—an agreeable crowd-pleaser that had nothing on Coltrane's boudoir lament. Marsalis opened the evening crafting genial duets with John Lewis, who countered his long virtuoso cadences and circular glisses (effective on "I'll Remember April") with fierce swing and dedicated blues tonality.

The week's most inspiring musician was Nicholas Payton, because he makes me wonder about his future. Many musicians have learned Armstrong solos and played them with reasonable authenticity, but Payton uses Armstrong's music—the broad range of his style—to enhance his own, much as other young trumpet players take off from Miles or Freddie Hubbard. This makes him a closer relation to Cootie Williams or Buck Clayton or Ruby Braff, who forged original styles on Armstrong's foundation, and sets him apart from mere repertory players. After half a century of bop-inflected improvisation, the Armstrong model serves as a new and provocative resource. Perhaps inadvertently, Payton offered proof during his short set at Avery Fisher's Verve concert. He appeared with a solid post-bop quintet, including Jesse Davis and Anthony Wonsey, and opened with a generic post-bop head. He followed with an acceptable "How Deep Is the Ocean," complete with cadenza. So far, merely okay. He finished with "Wild Man Blues," suddenly roaring to life and taking the audience with him. In an improvisation of rips, slurs, and sighs, and an out-chorus on the edge of euphoria, he now sounded free to be himself. How he will amalgamate that prewar style with his modernist obligations is one of the few interesting questions the festival raised.

At a program of rediscovered pieces associated with Armstrong and Beiderbecke, produced by Sandke and George Avakian at Kaye, Payton was more rigorously confined by the repertory, but even here he made his mark, especially on "fantasy" pieces, like a version of Don Redman's "Stampede" arrangement in which Payton and Sandke represented an imagined coming together of Louis and Bix. The emotional power was underscored by the fact that they were playing trumpets owned by the mighty legends themselves. Much of the program consisted of pieces Beiderbecke recorded but never released, and he couldn't have asked more from the ensemble: Scott Robinson's C-melody fixed in the key of Tram; the drummer Alvester Garnett finessing the apposite style; and Ken Peplowski, Joel Hellany, and Dick Hyman easily superseding their models.

But this was Sandke's night—his arrangements caught the spirit of the Goldkette-Whiteman-Henderson era and his playing imparted Bix's brisk lyricism and quiet fire. On "Singin' the Blues" he and Payton created another fantasy séance (much abetted by Robinson's Trumbauer chorus, which Howard Alden Eddie Lang'd every step of the way). The Armstrong segment included Oliver-style arrangements, with two-trumpet breaks, and a "Weather Bird" that restored a secondary strain Armstrong wisely left off the record; it would have inhibited his jousting with Earl Hines. Sandke imbued the "Weather Bird" solo with a beauty and energy that bid fair as substitutes for the original's mad humor. Other Armstrong compositions testified to the prevailing impact Louis

Jordan had in the mid-'40s (in "Jive Don't Come from Kokomo," he even interpolated a Jordan lyric). Lost maybe, but no loss—Armstrong could no more do Jordan than vice versa.

Never has festival season seemed so segregated: history and the mainstream midtown; comers in Harlem or Bryant Park; tangentials at various clubs; the grizzled avant-garde downtown at Texaco's Knitting Factory festival. The alleged war between entrepreneurs—Wein and the Knitting Factory's Michael Dorf—existed only in the heads of people who enjoy that kind of thing, and maybe in the heads of the entrepreneurs themselves, though I doubt it. The Knit was packed every night and the midtown halls did better than expected. People went to hear the music they wanted to hear and didn't give a damn who sponsored it. If there was an embarrassment of riches, there was little conflict. The true embarrassment was the appalling sound at the main JVC halls, far worse than in the last few years. A blight on the music and the audience, it needs to be tackled whatever the cost in bruised egos—a ban against monitors and over-amplification might be a good start, but, of course, that will never happen.

[*Village Voice*, 15 July 1997]

43 ❖ = 2
(Wayne Shorter and Herbie Hancock)

Jazz duets got off to an awesome if taxing start, peaking early in 1928 with "Weather Bird," Louis Armstrong and Earl Hines's friendly fracas of capers and feints. We have long since grown too polite for that sort of thing. A contemporary duet between jazz musicians is more likely to represent an excess of understanding and support, often to the degree that one takes a backseat to the other—as in a sonata where the violinist gets all the good lines while the pianist props him up. In the last few years, the duet has become increasingly popular as a means of making diverse records at relatively low rent.

Diversity, however, is not what Wayne Shorter and Herbie Hancock had in mind when they embarked on *1 + 1* (Verve), a suite-like meditation that rewards scrutiny but demands patience, much patience. A reunion of two bent romantics who have spent much of the past 25 years eluding the implications of their enormous impact on jazz in the 1960s (when they worked together in the Miles Davis Quintet and on sundry recording projects), this much anticipated album was not conceived for easy listening or critical consensus. An album of absences, it has something to disappoint everyone. On the one hand, it is acoustic—soprano sax and piano—and highly melodic, with not even the echo of a funk backbeat. On the other, it is by no means a conventional jazz record, eschewing as it does blues, standard harmonic progressions, and swing. Its daunting sameness in tempo and mood can only be perversely deliberate, yet each piece is beautifully played and imaginatively conceived.

Despite the equality signaled in the title and underscored in graphics that alternate the two stars' names, as well as a fastidious division of compositional labor (three by Shorter, three by Hancock, three by both, and one ringer), this is Shorter's album. He sets the tone and temper for most selections. Hancock shadows him with delicacy and respect, constraining himself in his own solo passages. Excepting Hancock's "Joanna's Theme," it is a soprano sax sonata, and as such, an important album. Hancock, never shy, has been well represented in all facets of his talent. Shorter is another story: We have here his most expansive statement as an instrumentalist since *V.S.O.P.* 20 years ago, at least in an acoustic setting—he plays creditably on soprano, tenor, baritone, and alto throughout last year's popular but critically misperceived big band–fusion album *High Life.*

Shorter initially made his mark as a tenor saxophonist who found his bearings in the Rollins-Coltrane nexus, and developed a personal style at once authoritative and evasive—bold, pensive, not entirely of this world. On soprano, he created a different voice, a dreamily piping pitch-perfect articulation that owed little to Coltrane and even less to Lacy or Bechet: a gentle sound that retained the instrument's harsh edges and avoided the Middle Eastern wail. By the time he began focusing on soprano, he had already emerged as one of the most forceful and programmatic composers in jazz. His endlessly imitated Blue Note albums were invariably thematic, though the imposition of ideas sometimes overwhelmed his music. Countless musicians from Bach to Coltrane have composed for the greater glory of God, but only Shorter sought to express God's own purview, in *The All-Seeing Eye.* Pictorial intensity informs almost everything he does, not just the ornate color chords, but the fragmentation of line, the languor and repetition, the framing of unexpected notes—all designed to avert cliché and seize the moment. The link between the 1969 *Super Nova,* his first major work on soprano, and *1 + 1* is unmistakable. It's as though Weather Report, *Atlantis,* and the rest had never intervened.

Shorter's originals are perhaps (my impressions are still malleable) the most savory selections on *1 + 1.* The Burmese-inflected "Aung San Suu

Kyi" is bound to become a Shorter classic, fetching and memorable in the way of his most enduring melodies. Hancock vamps the head with a four-chord walk, not unlike Gershwin's "Prelude No. 2," pacing Shorter, who limns the melody in four and five measure phrases interspersed with rests. Most of the performance is composed, but Shorter's ad-lib section is darkly lyrical, and his climax, the first of several such on the album, is pitched high and dynamic. Even by his standards, "Diana" is wrought with unusual intervals, moving from a chromatic opening into ever wider leaps, mirroring his solo style in its fragmented rhythms, complemented by Hancock's sumptuous filling out of the harmonies. They commune discerningly on "Meridianne—A Wood Sylph," offering the illusion of call-and-response interplay, though the piece is virtually through-composed, and cannily plays with time; passages fluctuate between triple and duple and even quintuplet rhythms.

Let me break here to offer advice you won't need: Listening to the entire album at one sitting is a chore that undermines the singularity of the later pieces. Try three or four selections and take a breather. Just how conscious the sameness is can be gauged in part by the two longest tracks, which are alternate versions of the same piece; it has a shared byline and appears first as "Visitor from Nowhere" and later as "Visitor from Somewhere." Releasing alternate takes is hardly novel, but one can't help but wonder if the repetition here doesn't indicate either a paucity of material or a disinclination to set up another session or both. As it happens, the "Visitor" pieces are unevenly worthy: The material is weak and the pyramid-like structure takes a while to crest, but when it gets there—especially in the longer and superior "Somewhere"—the two men do achieve something of a joust, a fleeting contest of wits and virtuosity. After a heated climax, the wind-down sounds apologetically meek.

"Memory of Enchantment," Michiel Borstlap's winning entry in the 1996 Thelonious Monk competition, is the piece that precipitated the album. Shorter and Hancock performed it at the Kennedy Center event. A work suggesting the influence of Shorter though more straightforward in its melody, it is played with affection and tonal shading, rising to a passage of intense interaction. As usual, Hancock's impressionistic episodes feel like interludes. Here and elsewhere, he retreats at the point of breaking loose. Even on "Joanna's Theme," the saxophonist's raspy reading is more focused than Hancock's improvisation. Yet emerging from the rubato decorum of "Manhattan Lorelei," Hancock succinctly conveys the unfettered romanticism that is his premier gift, unfolding the layers of the piece all too briefly. Shorter returns with an unexpectedly playful melody before settling into the primary theme.

I referred earlier to the album as suite-like. But the suite is a form designed to abet variety, not a collection of adagios. What then to make of this odd disc? As an album, it is poorly paced and almost obsessively narrow. It can lay no claim to the ambiguities of mood music: The soprano is a penetrating instrument and Shorter uses high or strident notes to sculpt and mottle its sound. Taken whole, the album is as baleful as an overdose of Satie. Yet each piece on its own, some more than others, rewards attention for its depth of feeling and superb execution. In Ellington's frequently misapplied adage, *1 + 1* is beyond category—a challenging landmark in the careers of two artists who specialize in confounding expectations.

[*Fi*, September 1997]

44 ❖ *New Tunes for an Old Ax (Joe Morris)*

Joe Morris, the 42-year-old New Haven-born guitarist, is nothing if not original—he plays his weathered, compact black Gibson like an obsessive who can't be bothered with what fellow guitarists do. But his originality stems in part from the unlikeliness of his inspirations. He doesn't play generic guitar music, having adapted precepts, concepts, and even phrases from musicians who play piano, saxophone, and other instruments. This sort of thing is not unusual in jazz. Roy Eldridge sounded like no other trumpet player of the 1930s, because he siphoned many of his ideas from saxophonists, teaching himself to play as fast as they, but with the trumpet's special brilliance and range. Morris has gone to the avant-garde well to test the brink of improvisational reason, but at the same time developed a quintessential jazz-guitar tone, dark and dulcet, its vibrato squarely modulated and inimical to sonic overkill. If Ornette Coleman were Jim Hall he would be Joe Morris.

For three recent evenings at the Knitting Factory, Morris's trio offered a retrospective of his compositions, from the 1983 "Sweep Out" (on the vinyl-only *Wraparound*, self-released on the Riti label) to most of the pieces on the new *Antennae* (Aum Fidelity). His consistency was as impressive as his diversity—the records, mostly duos and trios with one solo and a couple of quartets, show that he's been working the same track for years. The conspicuous ringer is *Sweatshop* (Riti), a trio project recorded in 1988 and 1990, with electric bass guitar and a Hendrixian edginess that is wonderfully lustrous and direct. *Sweatshop* may be the easiest point of entry for many, but Morris abandoned that direction for his present introverted style, where coils of melody and pockets of riffs are cycled over a head-nodding pulse.

Pulse doesn't mean countable time. One of the most engaging qualities of Morris's music is its evasion of four. Sometimes the trio gives the illusion of extended rubato, but the pulse is almost always there, constant and methodic. His alluring piece, "Lowell's House," introduced on *Symbolic Gesture* (1993, Soul Note) but greatly expanded in performance, centers on an eight-measure theme with an understated backbeat and legato pull—Morris subtly tips the rhythmic feeling of his music by accenting a note the instant before or after you expect. At the Knit, the theme emerged tenuously from a muted, minor-key, and vaguely Spanish setting and faded into a realm of free-time variations, reappearing often enough to stabilize the work's melodic spell. Yet while the backbeat slid in and out, the pulse remained staunch. Here and elsewhere, the trio plays rhythmically free while sustaining a kind of perpetual one/one beat.

In several of his liner notes, Morris mentions Cecil Taylor and musicians in Taylor's orbit as primary influences, a fairly provocative notion. For the most part, the connection is obscured by the limitations of the guitar and by Morris's sense of order, which is a lot less providential and dynamic than Taylor's. Charlie Parker and Charles Mingus both named Art Tatum as a formative influence, but they transmuted his harmonic ingenuity into something radically different—from Tatum and from each other. Morris's connection to Taylor is most evident when he plays alone, as in his solo disc, *No Vertigo* (1995, Leo), where he is heard on acoustic guitar, mandolin, and banjouke. In addition to increased density, compensating for the absence of bass and drums, he explores plucky aharmonic figures of short duration that are not unlike Taylor's flurries. On "Equilibrium," Morris flits from mood to mood, busy here, spare there. If you've ever wondered what Taylor would sound like if he were Bill Monroe (something that I've pondered for years myself), the answer is "Found in the Ground": Cecilian fragments adapted to the keening pitch of mandolin.

Still, Morris is most at home with the electric guitar, on which his notes are invariably personal, polished, controlled, and lived in. He can get a cold knifelike edge or a warm buzzy center, but the sound is always his, private and deliberate. At times, his playing is almost reclusive, confidently reticent, as though he were quietly typing his phrases, or nibbling them off the cob. But he tends to avoid the pitfall of noodling by the improvisational design of his solos, an alteration of knotty melodic figures and vigorous riffs that crop up like punctuations. In this, he is less beholden to Taylor than to Ornette Coleman—those riffs often alight with Coleman's particular buoyancy, but without the wail. Morris works high on the frets. His left hand will remain in one position for the better part of a solo, finding—with whopping speed and infallible accuracy— an uncanny number of places to go in the space of three or four frets. He assiduously avoids high-note effects, melodramatic slides, and other blues/rock conventions. In the bottom octaves, he uses such techniques as the low-E drone (hello Duane Eddy) to blend with the bass, creating a 10-string hybrid.

The challenge for Downtown improvisers in the aftermath of emotionalist outpourings is melody. Harmony and rhythm, however much they function as structural absolutes, must ultimately support a sequence of notes that is either persuasive or dull. Morris belongs to a generation that strives to avoid comfort melodies, preferring blues locutions and riffs and dynamics, as well as coming up with fresh tunes that compel attention even if you can't sing them in the shower. One such player, Matthew Shipp, drives and is driven by Morris in their mutual pursuit of novel combinations of notes. If Shipp often resorts to two-fisted chords, his linear phrases are the nub of his art, and in Morris he has a like-minded explorer. On Morris's *Elsewhere* (1996, Homestead), with bassist William Parker and drummer Whit Dickey, and Shipp's *Thesis* (1997, hatOLOGY), the interaction is tenacious enough to suggest an illusory orthodoxy, swinging and stately. For an ideal example of the post-ballad ballad, consult *Thesis*'s "Broader Orders," where the forest is familiar and the trees alien.

Morris works from an even closer bond in his trio, heard at the Knit and on *Antennae*, which burns with a perverse intentionality, as if even the ad-lib episodes were ordained. It begins with the bouncy intervals of "Synapse" and pushes into deeper waters with the title selection, played in proximate unison by guitar, bowed bass, and drums. Morris's solo has a nearly verbal explicitness, chatty but focused. Drummer Jerome Deupree is obviously well acquainted with the intensity Morris can generate, and he lays out with as much élan as he digs in. He could be more decisive at times, but he is nimbly alert, effecting split-second change-ups on a good riffs-run-amok tune, "Stare into a Lightbulb for Three Years." Nate McBride is a gifted bassist, a one-time student of Cecil McBee, who has some of William Parker's teeming audacity. His solo on "Virtual Whatever" is the performance's flashpoint, a strenuously strummed midrange cascade of notes. He yanks the strings horizontally instead of vertically from the wood, and gets a surprisingly warm and pitch-accurate result that he tweaks with twangy asides from

the Delta. He and Morris have an uncommonly sensitive rapport, and
the nerviness of the music is heightened in their entwined skills. Morris's
playing can be airless, a rest-free maze of configurations refueled by
cunning riffs, but once you enter it's easy to find your way.

[*Village Voice*, 11 November 1997]

45 ❖ Lit at Both Ends (D. D. Jackson)

For their last set in the short-lived Minetta Lane Theater series some
weeks ago, D. D. Jackson and James Carter elected to make the most of
their capacity for bravura exuberance. Carter's gleaming metallic sound
on reeds and Jackson's heavy-lifting keyboard attack resonated in episodes that were by turns sensational and showy, even ersatz, and you
wished they would cool down, dim down the ecstasy a little, find an
amenable backbeat, groove on the changes. Yet in the end alienation was
allayed during a modishly anarchistic "I Got Rhythm," which com-
menced with expansive allusions to "Battle Hymn of the Republic" (Red
Nichols would have passed out if not away), "The Marine's Hymn," and
other lockstep ditties. Grooving primarily on themselves, they made
technique for its own sake its own reward, and you found yourself
laughing encouragingly at the pleasure—the old homo ludens—they
took in exchanging phrases, solitary pitches, squeaks and clusters, staccato bullets, rattling eruptions, and copious digressions, not least a sort
of *Crime Doesn't Pay* police show anthem.

Admittedly, much free jazz, in its happy mood as opposed to its
throes of emotional disgorgement, is little more than chronic back-and-
forth, reflexive echoes in place of meditative conversation. But rarely is
it ventilated with the confidence of musicians who can, on the dime,
finesse chaos, their solutions no less elegant than those of musicians
likely to scowl at the commotion. Jackson and Carter belong to a growing
generation of players who have gone past the ability to work inside and
outside, a double-gatedness that not too long ago practically defined
pomo jazz virtuosity. Apparently, they don't even think in those terms.
Everything is grist for the mill—they are the best possible repudiation
of those who want to divide jazz against itself with loyalty oaths to the
proprieties. You may not like what they play, but you'd be hard-pressed
to argue that they can't play.

Indeed, on some levels they are throwbacks. When Carter microwaves his sound on a ballad, he can invoke Don Byas, a classic rococo tenor saxophonist long neglected and as unexpected a resource as Paul Gonsalves proved for David Murray. Jackson filters his melodic sense through gospel chords and mines the 19th-century vestiges of his classical education. His two-volume project of duets, *Paired Down* (Justin Time) begins with their "I Got Rhythm" variation (they call it "Rhythm and Things"), and the first splash of ice water is Carter's use of the archaic C-melody saxophone, usually the province of antiquarians who have memorized Frank Trumbauer solos. The second is that they signal the changes at the release more obviously than, say, Teddy Wilson would have done 60 years ago. These guys are candles lit at both ends, reexamining the rudiments of harmonic improvisation even as they light the way to a post-schismatic future. At the end of the performance, Carter heads toward a "good evening fri-e-ends" kicker with popping and double-tonguing that would have warmed the bones of the old vaudevillian Rudy Wiedoft, whom one had thought Coleman Hawkins laid to rest at the dawn of time. Everything is grist.

Jackson is one of the most stimulating of the many gifted young pianists to come along since Geri Allen opened the floodgates. Unlike Jacky Terrasson, who contains his equally ebullient technique in formalistic mazes, Jackson can hardly keep the stopper on. Like his mentor Don Pullen, he inclines to dense gestures encompassing the entire keyboard, which he smashes with remarkable accuracy. Born Robert Cleanth Kainien Jackson, in Canada, of black and Chinese parentage ("di-di" is Chinese for "little brother"), he studied classical music at Indiana University, where he played in the ensembles of jazz educator David Baker, and earned his master's at the Manhattan School of Music under the tutelage of Jaki Byard. His postgraduate studies with Pullen led to his first important tour, with Jane Bunnett, and subsequent work with, among others, Carlos Garnett, Andrew Cyrille, Vincent Herring, Hamiet Bluiett, and David Murray, who in a *Village Voice* wrap-up on young artists called him "the most innovative musician of his generation." His most impressive collaboration with Murray is *Long Goodbye: A Tribute to Don Pullen*—on DIW, if you can find it.

Paired Down suggests one measure of his authority as a performer in his selflessness as an accompanist, and in the overall design: encounters with Carter, Murray, Bluiett, Bunnett, Billy Bang, Hugh Ragin, Ray Anderson, Santi Debriano, and Don Byron. But it also underscores his weaknesses. His balladic originals are soft and indistinct, relying overmuch on Keith Jarrett–style gospel grace notes to the point of sentimentality (Pullen deflected such clichés with his punishing attack and rangy harmonies). This is especially true of his laments. "One of the Sweetest" is sticky with blues notes, displaying the affect but not the substance of a reflective song. The threnody for Pullen, "For Don," is even sappier, though redeemed in his increasingly poignant improvisation, heightened at the dramatic finish by Bluiett's pitch-perfect cries and the whisper of air rushing through his baritone sax.

Unmitigated delights are plentiful, however. One compositional angle Jackson has mastered is the vamp, and he is full of good ones, reflecting a close look at the champions, notably Horace Silver ("African Dreams" has more than a glancing acquaintance with "Song for My Father") and Abdullah Ibrahim (notably "Peace of Mind," a rolling, pounding surf supporting the indefatigable Murray). The undervalued trumpet player Hugh Ragin should get a particular boost from his contributions; he reveals a gift for thoughtful pastiche in two memorable pieces (all others are by Jackson)—"Ballad for Miles" aptly borrows "Motherless Child," and the marvelous "Fanfare and Fiesta" (the vamp of which suggests *A Love Supreme*) is just that, a parade of alarums that delivers on its mariachi promise. Ragin combines tremolos, growls, blasts, and a broadly expressive timbre, and Jackson is prodigious, working thunderous bass rumbles against skittering frills. Ragin is also heard on one of Jackson's best tunes, "Subliminal Messages," weaving a full tapestry of lightly tongued and staccato phrases and diverse vocalisms. Perhaps Jackson's most confident showcase is "Chick-isms," a nod to the Corea of "Spain," in which he solos with a succinct and focused clarity, indulging his unmistakably ringing sound, and bluffing Debriano as playfully as he does Carter.

Billy Bang is featured in his merry Stuff Smith mode on "Bang's Dream," an exercise in swinging abandon with a fine a cappella episode, and the highly dramatic "Pleasure and Pain," which offers very little pain, building darkly on a deft six-note piano vamp that anchors him in a carefully constructed rhapsody that spins outward in a widening yet staunchly disciplined orbit. Ray Anderson rocks with buoyant aplomb on "Catch It," skimming Jackson's melody and chords, and Don Byron exhibits his prettiest tone on "Time," one of Jackson's prettiest melodies, cast in a subtly Middle Eastern vein that acknowledges the clarinetist's trips down klezmer lane. Murray is Murray, essaying his munificent sound in gospel-tinged numbers that imply a benediction in "Easy" and near Ayler-esque lunar-lyricism in "Love Song." Jackson emerges from these discs as protégé and advocate, and you feel he has scarcely begun to show all he can do.

[*Village Voice*, 9 December 1997]

46 ❖ They're Bo-o-o-o-xed!
(The Best Reissues of 1997)

The most vivid memory of live jazz '97 that I take with me into the New Year was sown at the Vanguard a few weeks back, when Jackie McLean fronted the incomparable Cedar Walton Trio (David Williams, Billy Higgins). With nary a pause following a stoic "Never Let Me Go," McLean stomped a breakneck "Lover," and before he was 16-bars out of the starting gate, something unusual happened, a flashback to a wilder time: The audience got into the act. First, just an isolated shout and whoop, then a mass low-level rumbling, with more shouts and applause for a particularly nimble turnback or long-legged phrase or spiral conceit. It sounded like a Jazz at the Philharmonic album, the congregation mid-rashing the soloist, who at one point spun out the most befitting quotation in an evening of quotations: "He flies through the air with the greatest of ease . . ."—speaking for himself and Walton, who backed him with pulsing, vital chords and mixed in "Melancholy Baby" and "Comin' Through the Rye." When McLean initiated eights with Higgins, neither man could contain himself for long and the exchanges became a duet, until the drummer took over with customary savoir-faire.

It may have sounded like JATP, but it wasn't the kind of performance that would work on an album. Some of the very passages that kept one leaning ever closer to the bandstand were those that would sound faltering or clumsy on a record: the hesitation before choosing an entrance point, the suspense as the rhythm turned this way and that, the breath-catching moments of rumination: the exhilarating, rumpled cool of making it up on the spot. Quel difference from the jazz records now edited and dubbed to a shine, creating a studio reality that makes the tradition of real-time recording seem astonishing—no retakes for Armstrong to get that "West End Blues" cadenza to line up right, and imagine Holiday singing in the studio right there with the band, not in a glass booth with earphones. Yet when it comes to reissuing classic jazz albums, the opposite fallacy takes over. The ongoing excavation of studio archives continues to undermine model albums with bum takes, false starts, and flat chatter (what is so bloody enthralling about hearing someone say, "Let's try it again, fellas, okay, untitled blues take seven"?) in a posthumous revenge on the gloried past. It is box time.

Last year, even those of us who worship at the shrine of Miles and Gil learned more about their labors than we wanted to know—and it's a relief to have the superbly remastered classics available singly, with the better alternates packed off at the end. The current box of choice is *Coltrane: The Complete 1961 Village Vanguard Recordings* (Impulse), not because it offered many surprises (only three previously unissued performances), but because in recreating the context for such landmarks as "Chasin' the Trane" and "Impressions," it underscores the drama of Coltrane's evolution and provides a more realistic look at his ensemble as it was shaped. No excesses here.

Verve initiated a series of 20-bit Master Editions that in many cases rank with audiophile discs. For one example, Kenny Burrell's and Gil Evans's *Guitar Forms* segregates the loser takes at the end and has as much depth as and greater radiance than the original vinyl. On the other hand, *The Complete Gerry Mulligan Meets Ben Webster*, one of the most exquisitely realized of LPs, is now two discs, with original and alternate takes integrated in an attempt to recreate a day in the studio—a document of men at work, proving that music's labors are marginally more entertaining than watching an actor memorize lines or a writer revise a paragraph. The three-volume *Complete Ella Fitzgerald and Louis Armstrong* isn't 20-bit, but the sound is excellent, and despite awkward packaging (an accordion photo-album that barely opens) is an irresistible set—no alternates, just splendid music.

Blue Note had one of the best mid-year boxes with *Dexter Gordon: The Complete Blue Note Sixties Sessions*, which exudes that labor-of-love thing. Four of six discs close with Gordon's monologues and the booklet is peppered with a fascinating correspondence between Gordon and his producers. I wish they had retained the original sequencing, but this is an indispensable set, the master at his peak and beautifully recorded. More recently, *Hot Jazz on Blue Note* explores the label's pre-Monk past with Ed Hall, Art Hodes, George Lewis, and especially Sidney Bechet, who generally fared better in concert halls on the occasion of his centenary than on discs. *Herbie Nichols: The Complete Blue Note Recordings* was indifferently mastered, but recycles a captivating music that has outgrown the precincts of culthood. Do not miss *Stan Getz: The Complete Roost Recordings*, which has famously dim sound (apparently Roost destroyed original tapes), but who cares? The second of three discs collects the 1951 Storyville sides, fraught with the kind of drama Jackie McLean triggered at the Vanguard. They are often noted for the alloy of Getz and Jimmy Raney (and Al Haig's lyricism), but the real chemistry is between Getz and the great drummer Tiny Kahn, who jumps on the saxophonist's Lestorian riffs, driving him mercilessly from one peak to another. Getz had not yet evolved his mature ballad approach, but he was never more gazelle-like than on "Parker 51" and Gigi Gryce's honeysuckle-variation, "Mosquito Knees."

Rhino, which evenhandedly boxes the ridiculous and the sublime, made a strong showing with *Charles Mingus: Passions of a Man*, collecting his work during five years at Atlantic (1956–61), plus the subsequently released 1960 Antibes concert and a long interview conducted by Nesuhi Ertegun, though once again the original sequencing is sacrificed to the great god Chronology. It's a strange and frequently electrifying trip, from "Pithecanthropus Erectus," which was way ahead of the jazz curve, to "Eat That Chicken," which was way behind it. Mingus generously featured his bass in those days, and he surrounded himself with the best saxophonists. I hear people argue that Jean Shepherd's shtick on "The Clown" has dated badly. Unfair: It was just as preciously hip when recorded. Rhino's five-volume *Ray Charles: Genius & Soul* is also a stellar survey, with a couple of minor missteps, reaching a predictable apex in the 1959–66 period, when his voice peaked in warmth and versatility. Another singer also celebrating a golden anniversary gets similar treatment from Mercury: Patti Page's *A Golden Celebration* tracks the nightmarish descent of the epitome of blonde soul into a morass of questionably priced doggies, mockin' bird hills, and boogieing Santas. I shy away from absolutes, but "Go On with the Wedding" represents a pop nadir with few if any equals. Yet what a richly expressive singer she could be with good material, her southern twang more decorous than Kay Starr's and almost as resonant. Mercury's sister company, Verve, ought to collect her big band recordings, which are sampled on the last of four discs.

The mail-order company Mosaic is in the business of rediscovery and offers a major excavation in *Classic Capitol Jazz Sessions,* a 12-disc set of mostly forgotten singles, some of them pretty dire. But in this context even the dross has a certain fascination: The grab bag is so capacious that I find myself blindly dipping into it, marveling at the mixture of excellence, corn, and sheer desperation that went into Capitol's peculiarly regressive West Coast attempt to market jazz as metadixieland. Except for sessions by the fine clarinetist Stan Hasselgard and Red Norvo (who co-leads the Blues Band with Jesse Price and has a reed section of Dexter Gordon and Jimmy Giuffre, thus breaking the anomaly bank), this is a survey of the 1940s as they might have evolved if Charlie Parker had never been born. A few selections really are classic (e.g., Billie Holiday's "Trav'lin' Light" with Paul Whiteman) and some ought to be (e.g., Bobby Hackett's "Pennies from Heaven" from a 1945 session on Melrose, half of which was never issued). For the most part, we get performances by Benny Carter, Kay Starr, Mel Powell, Cootie Williams, Wingy Manone, and others that fell through the cracks, uncovering not a few gems— among them a sound stage recording of the title song from *A Song Is*

Born, with Armstrong, Dorsey, Goodman, the Golden Gate Quartet, et al.

Hard to know what to make of RCA, which celebrated the 80th anniversary of the first jazz recording (the Original Dixieland Jazz Band, waxed by the Victor Talking Machine Company) with the half-measures of a conglomerate that can't quite believe it has a history worth commemorating. The eight-volume *RCA Victor 80th Anniversary Collector's Edition* can be had boxed or in separate volumes, depending on whether you require a few enchanting anthologies—the first five, to be exact—or a lesson in entropy. Actually, volume eight is so much better than six and seven that you might assume that the company is turning around, but there isn't much supporting evidence. Nor is there any quality control. In recent months, RCA released its *Complete Sonny Rollins*, six discs of exceptionally well recorded music now made brazen and artificial, and *The Complete Paul Desmond*, five discs of music that wasn't recorded as well, but is now expertly remastered and surpasses previous editions. Still, Desmond (with strings and Jim Hall) is as dry as the martini he always wanted to be, and Rollins (with rhythm and Jim Hall) achieves a borderline satori.

The outstanding boxed vinyl was issued with a nearly obsessive perfectionism and a high ticket by Acoustic Sounds. *The Great Prestige Recordings* by the Miles Davis Quintet reshapes the marathon session albums with ambience and imaging to rival the original issues. The mistitled *Riverside Tenor Sessions by Thelonious Monk* (the European concerts with Rouse are missing, as is a Coltrane selection) is even more impressive—"Jackieing" sucks the air out of the room, as it should, and "Brilliant Corners" is so unequivocal one can practically hear the splices. The point here is to recreate original albums as finished and sequenced by the artists, without newly found scraps of studiospeak, flawed takes, and other desiderata of the anally compulsive. Not to say that digitalization hasn't made strides, for example, two Nat King Cole ballad LPs engineered for DCC, *Love Is the Thing* and *The Very Thought of You*. Gordon Jenkins's arrangements may cause toothache, but when the singer emerges from the strings on "When I Fall in Love," one gets the eerie feeling that Nat hasn't left the building. Soundman Steve Hoffman found a way to set the strings back and bring the voice closer to the mike. It's hard not to participate, if only with a grateful sigh.

[*Village Voice*, 6 January 1998]

47 ❖ Piano Men
(Teddy Wilson / Lennie Tristano / Bill Evans)

Teddy Wilson abides as a benchmark figure in the development of jazz; his historical role is secure. Yet he is chiefly remembered for associations with more perennially celebrated musicians. As a member of Benny Goodman's trio and quartet, Wilson helped to create and sustain chamber jazz, while breaching segregation (in his later years, he was often referred to as music's Jackie Robinson). As the director and frequent leader of Billie Holiday's early recordings, he piloted the most inspired small-band sessions of the 1930s, which helped to establish the jukebox market. His immense influence as a pianist with an exceptionally lilting conception, nearly Mozartian in its blending of formality and irreverence, is less frequently honored. Wilson's Columbia prewar sessions without Holiday, including his vital solo piano work, have been unavailable for decades, and a generation has grown up with little awareness of his music.

In a 1956 poll of 100 musicians, conducted by Leonard Feather, 68 named Art Tatum as the greatest jazz pianist of all time. Only two other pianists scored double digits—Bud Powell (21) and Teddy Wilson (10). In those years, he was a household name, working the ritzier supper clubs and recording regularly for Verve and Columbia. Those records have also disappeared, except for all-star sessions or reunions with Lester Young. As Wilson's playing grew increasingly staid and conventional—he hewed to a routine of intro-and-two-choruses on tunes he had been playing for decades—he began to appear more retrograde than, say, Earl Hines, whose playing retained a sometimes illusory volatility, and by the time of his death, in 1986, he had lost the attention of young listeners. All of which make *The Complete Verve Recordings of the Teddy Wilson Trio* (Mosaic) one of the more significant, revelatory, and pleasurable releases of recent years. Most of these performances are new to me, and I am astonished at their robustness—and that they have been forgotten for so long.

Wilson was an original, which is to say he assimilated his influences (Hines, Fats Waller, Tatum) into an unmistakable approach of his own—one of fluid contradictions. Headily percussive, he refined the stride approach into patterns of free-ranging tenths, producing an unmistakable, belling attack of great beauty and sophistication; harmonically progressive, he alternated exquisite melodic inversions with delirious flights of reclusive abandon. Wilson's music has immense dignity, while incarnating the aggressive embodiment of swing. His arpeggios can be as colorful and sleek as Tatum's, but he eschews rhythmic change-ups or rubato, preferring a coolly unstoppable propulsion. Snapping the beat in the company of Buddy Rich and especially Jo Jones, who achieved some of his finest later work with Wilson in 1955 and 1956, he sounds almost impatient to fire up his classy repertoire.

On "Darn That Dream," he barely embarks on the theme before skittering off in an improvisational venture, and his "Lady Be Good," from the same inspired 1952 session, is a transfixing example of his ability to maintain delicacy at top speed while twisting the screw with altered keys. His sprinting 1957 "Tea for Two" is comparable to Bud Powell's version and his 1956 "It Don't Mean a Thing" has the rhythmic assurance and harmonic wit that impressed Thelonious Monk, whose earliest records demonstrate his debt to Wilson. Yet the most miraculous moments are the ad-lib figures that follow his theme statements, melodic ideas of genuine compositional authority. Among more than 50 examples, consider "It Had to Be You," where he sustains bold invention chorus to chorus, or "On the Sunny Side of the Street," with his alert left-hand pattern, or "Basin Street Blues," though here he shortchanges himself for a bass solo. For the most part, Wilson's is a melodious, sweet-tempered music, which of course is one reason it fell out of favor.

Simultaneously released cartons of music by Lennie Tristano and Bill Evans underscore Wilson's pandemic influence on pianists who came of age before and during the war. Simplified jazz histories often locate Wilson between Hines/Waller and Powell/Monk, yet his rhythmic constancy, flowing phrases, and harmonic poise were no less important to Tristano and Evans, both of whom suggested something of a modernist alternative. Tristano attempted to reduce rhythmic accompaniment to the faceless steadiness of a metronome, so as not to interfere with his improvisation. Evans, himself influenced by Tristano, settled on an antithetical approach, encouraging audacious interplay with bass and drums. One surprise of Wilson's later Verve sessions is his responsiveness to bass playing that, despite an excess of bass solos, supports the pianist with an inventive free-flowing stream of ideas—something you expect from Evans, not from a player of Wilson's vintage. Like Wilson, Evans developed an instantly recognizable touch and a gift for melodic paraphrase and harmonic enhancement.

The Complete Atlantic Recordings of Lennie Tristano, Lee Konitz & Warne Marsh (Mosaic) should prompt a reassessment of the exclusionary Tristano school. Alto saxophonist Lee Konitz is most heavily featured, and he is in great form, shunning in his improvs the over-reliance on triplets and long static phrases that make some of the heads tiresome. His "You

Go to My Head," from a 1955 gig in a Chinese restaurant, is an exceptional example of his playing in that period, fervent and heady; it's a tonic to hear him and tenor saxophonist Warne Marsh—a union far more interactive in Tristano's absence than when the pianist calls the shots—perform with top-shelf drummers and bassists like Kenny Clarke, Shelly Manne, Philly Joe Jones, Paul Motian, Oscar Pettiford, and Paul Chambers. Yet the prize of this haul is disc three: Tristano's piano solos with and without prerecorded rhythm—an oracular music of profound individuality and, as annotator Larry Kart writes, "the summit of Tristano's art." In addition to using prerecorded rhythm tracks, Tristano altered his phrasing electronically so that certain passages have a brittle, grainy quality. "Becoming" and "Line Up" are especially riveting—airless, linear, pumping, rhythmic sieges of notes. Comparisons with Bach are inescapable (the Chaconne for sheer density), but this music is an unambiguous expression of jazz and isn't easily forgotten.

In the 160-page booklet that accompanies *The Complete Bill Evans on Verve*, an annotator insistently draws a connection between Tristano and early Evans, but this odd reissue calls more attention to itself than to the music it enfolds. No label has done better CD reissues than Verve, from comprehensive boxes to flawless restorations. Yet this 18-disc Evans box is a debacle, its container a hideous metal vault disfigured by designer rust, the metaphorical meaning of which is beyond my imagination. Nor is it complete, as one discovers trying to find the Tristano-influenced Evans solos (from a Lee Konitz date) referred to in the booklet. The decision not to include Verve and Emarcy sessions on which Evans served as a sideman is fair enough, if the idea was to present only his records as a leader. But also missing is his rarest and admittedly poorest Verve album, the 1963 *Theme from the VIPs and Other Great Songs*, which few Evans fans have had the opportunity to hear. Isn't one purpose of an overpriced catchall box the inclusion of material that doesn't warrant release on its own?

The defensive, uninformative, excessively art-directed 160-page booklet fails to answer one question that has puzzled Evans fans for 30 years: Why was Volume Two of the 1966 Town Hall concert never released, and why is it not released here? The relevant (parenthetical) comment reads: "an unissued big band segment with arrangements by Al Cohn has never been in Verve's holdings." Oh? Then why did Verve release *Bill Evans at Town Hall, Volume One,* and in whose holdings is it? Elsewhere, an unattributed teaser states, "MGM, the producer, and myself" decided against releasing Volume Two. "Myself" is unidentified, but why did it matter what MGM (Verve's parent company at the time) decided if the music wasn't in its "holdings"? Worse, the integrity of the original LPs is savaged in favor of the chronological recording-sessions approach, with tedious alternate takes crowding the masters, turning what should be a pleasurable experience into a kind of graduate study.

For all the newly discovered music, most notably five-dozen concert selections, not a great deal of new information emerges. The Verve years were difficult ones for Evans. He began well: The box opens with Irving Berlin's adaptation of "Frankie and Johnny" (he called it "The Washington Twist"), an example of Evans's sly humor from a lively album with an over-miked Shelly Manne, and continues optimistically with Gary McFarland concertos and the thrice-dubbed *Conversations with Myself*. But then he begins to falter with the uneven *Trio '64*, going on automatic pilot for *Trio '65*, before indulging in unsuccessful if often intriguing collaborations with Claus Ogerman and replications of earlier triumphs, this time with mostly detached results—another meeting with Manne, a second encounter with Jim Hall, additional conversations with himself. Eddie Gomez became his too constant and predictable bassist and a couple of his drummers were rhythmically challenged. Yet there were magical moments—the superb Town Hall concert and the equally beguiling 1968 set at Montreux with Jack DeJohnette; plus dozens of previously unreleased Village Vanguard numbers from 1967, with Philly Joe Jones, many of them superior to the selections culled for the album, *California, Here I Come*—these will surely be issued on their own at a later date. If you think you know the kind of fellow Evans was from, say, his six-handed version of "Spartacus," you'll want to hear him sing "Santa Claus Is Coming to Town," madly giggling between takes.

[*Fi*, February 1998]

48 ❖ *The Arranger's Monk* (Bill Holman / T. S. Monk / Fred Hersch)

Bill Holman, who may be the premiere living jazz orchestrator and is surely a contender, is back, at 70, in rare form. One of the best records of 1997 was *A View from the Side*, and whatever 1998 brings, few albums can top *Brilliant Corners: The Music of Thelonious Monk*. Holman always keeps busy in Los Angeles and Europe, but records released under his name are so infrequent that they support a long-standing cult without confirming his reputation as a major figure in the development of big band music. *Brilliant Corners* may not change that, but it provides standards for an idiom that too often waffles in amateurish unoriginality and is sure to keep you searching for more of the same.

The work of all great arrangers raises the question of where the line is drawn between composition and orchestration. Several of the best, from Gil Evans to Nelson Riddle, were insignificant melodists who brought organizational genius to the melodies of others. Holman has composed several effective pieces—"Invention for Guitar and Trumpet," "The Big Street," "Far Down Below," "Concerto for Herd"—but he is never as inspired as when recasting a familiar tune. He is at bottom a variations man and a good theme frees his imagination, which exults in diverse effects, tempos, humor, melodic juxtapositions, and vigorous rhythms. The wonder of his *Contemporary Concepts*, written for Stan Kenton in 1955, is that he simultaneously reconfigured the big band for a world bereft of ballrooms while stressing the Count Basie dictum to pat your foot, in addition to transfiguring melodies like "Stompin' at the Savoy" and "What's New" and turning the intransigent "Stella by Starlight" into a concerto for Charlie Mariano that would have earned the alto saxophonist a footnote in jazz history all by itself.

Yet the concerto style is not Holman's forte, except in the Bartók sense of a concerto for orchestra. A Holman arrangement is distinguished by several hallmarks, chief among them his ability to keep several balls in the air at the same time. Something is always happening. It is a cliché to say that a bandleader makes a small group sound like a big band or a big band sound like a combo. Holman makes a big band sound enormous—given the luxury of 16 musicians, he seems to imply, "use them, all of them, all the time." Another hallmark is his distinctive use of counterpoint, which he never launches in a Bach-like fantasy, one melody bouncing off another, but in a kind of unison responsiveness, as though the melody under discussion suggested one or two related melodies that fit when played together. Why settle for a single tune when you have enough musicians to play several? Another hallmark is that the result is never cluttered and the secondary melodies often have a linear integrity to match the originals.

A typical Holman moment is an epiphany of sorts, as if contemplation of the melody at hand spurred an unexpected juxtaposition, idea, or joke. *Brilliant Corners* bubbles over with them. Indeed, Monk's title isn't a bad description of Holman's method. He keeps the big, colorful balls floating in front of your eyes, but you don't want to miss the action at the edges. A few Holman moments: Toward the close of "Thelonious," he harmonizes Monk's insistent one-note theme (actually, three notes, not that you'd notice) for unison flute and piano and you realize that the tune is Morse code—in any case, Monk code; in the middle of "'Round

Midnight," he inserts a four-note riff from an introduction popularized by Miles Davis, but gives the first three staccato notes to the trumpets and the fourth to a wry trombone, conveying conversational whimsy even in this fleeting transition; "Rhythm-a-ning," a chart from 20 years ago and inspired by Basie's "Little Pony," begins with Monk's theme—how conventional!—but at the second eight bars is joined by a parallel figure and, after the chorus, the tempo crashes and the reeds invoke five seconds of Tadd Dameron's "Hot House." Holman is a fiend for Rorshach-test allusions. Elaborate variations on "Ruby, My Dear" include a bar of "Groovin' High," "Brilliant Corners" is spelled by a Charles Ives interlude, and a fleeting reference to "Nardis" wafts by during one of the transitions in "'Round Midnight."

The endings of all 10 selections are pure Holman and utterly savory, none more so than the gearing up of drums to launch three thunderous blasts of brass in "Straight, No Chaser." On a few occasions he uses bent or sliding notes. The ultimate slurp is a tailgate trombone lick some six minutes into "Friday the 13th." Before you can wonder what it's doing there, the band is off on a full-throttle shout chorus, but the performance closes with solo soprano saxophone, which just happens to finish with a left-field slur. "Misterioso" is nothing but Holman moments. A bright two-note riff is immediately countered by a deep-blues bass figure to remind you what kind of piece this is. Then the melody hits and you have all three in the air—the riff, the bass line, the tune. Profligate with invention, Holman writes a completely different variation after each solo, though they all counter ominous blues voicings with unexpectedly cheerful riffs, including one that has the reed section competing with itself and another that amounts to a four-bar swing era interlude, right before a deep-blues bass solo. The other great blues, "Straight, No Chaser," is deconstructed from the top down, so that in the first few minutes the band plays not Monk's theme but a Holman variation based on the same rhythm; when a canonical transition two-thirds through finally triggers Monk's tune you feel you have earned its comfort, but before long Holman—whose chords are now waxing in heft and dissonance—can't resist pointing out that it reminds him of *Til Eulenspiegel*.

I haven't mentioned the soloists, and there are good ones—especially the saxophonists Lanny Morgan, Bill Perkins, and Pete Christlieb (whose "Rhythm-a-ning" cadenza pays homage to Wardell Gray). Solos in work like this invariably seem somewhat generic. Like a film or theater director, a bandleader exercises control over the performances when he chooses his cast. When big band soloists were innovators, they were as important as arrangements and sometimes more so. But as Basie pointed out when he regrouped in the early '50s, the writing lingers on after the soloists have gone. Holman has a crew of solid professionals up to every task he assigns, but the play is the thing and during the best of solos it is the orchestral backing, rhythmic change-ups, and Monk allusions (often fanciful or abstract) that excite your attention. Although "'Round Midnight" was originally recorded by Cootie Williams's big band and Hall Overton successfully adapted Monk's own harmonies for an ensemble with seven winds, Monk is not often heard in orchestral arrangements (a notable exception is Ellington's 1962 "Monk's Dream"). The trick is to love Monk's music without attempting to replicate his style, which is matchless. Only Holman's "Bemsha Swing" disappoints, because his dated boogaloo beat pales next to Monk's geometric rhythms, and even here the secondary themes punch up the action to the point of near-euphoria. Elsewhere, the euphoria is fully realized—enhanced by JVC's audiophile mastering.

Other recent forays into a world once characterized as impenetrable have taken increasingly personal and satisfying turns. Last year's *Monk on Monk* (N2K) is by T. S. Monk, the great man's son, a drummer who aptly reconfigures Monk's rhythms with his own rock-influenced attack. Don Sickler has written dense, power-packed arrangements for seven winds and rhythm (they are not variations on Overton, except for the instrumentation). The mighty heads—"Little Rootie Tootie," "Jackieing," and a gnawingly infectious newly discovered piece called "Two Timer" are especially good—feature a roster of guest stars, including trumpeter Arturo Sandoval, who soars on "Bright Mississippi." Less pleasing is a Nnenna Frelon and Dianne Reeves regatta on "In Walked Bud." A no less personal and far more ruminative meditation is *Thelonious: Fred Hersch Plays Monk* (Nonesuch), a triumph of assimilation. Hersch knows Monk well enough to echo him (the first pass at "Light Blue," for example), but he is moved by the beauty and playfulness of the music to pursue feelings that, though hardly foreign to Monk, are not ordinarily emphasized. Hersch has the requisite vigor for "I Mean You" and the wit to parse "Let's Cool One" over a very cool stride bass, but he's at his best on the ballads, which he addresses with a deceptively angelic simplicity that locates them somewhere between the nursery and the after-hours saloon, as on "Ask Me Now," "Reflections," and "'Round Midnight." He plays not only with Monk's melodies, but also his clusters and rich use of dynamics (as on a mischievous "Think of One")—at times his sotto voce touch and abrupt transition recall the contemplative Cecil Taylor. For the reflective radiance of Monk, hear Hersch; for the storming bravado of Monk, hear T. S. For dancing in your head, go with Holman.

[*Village Voice*, 17 February 1998]

49 ❖ Reviving the It Girls (The Boswell Sisters)

Later it would be called *hip* or *cool*. Before the war, the word was simply *it*, not as defined by flapper sexuality, but by a musical savvy that acknowledged America's panracial music with that rhythmic grace it don't mean a thing without. In a 1930 radio broadcast of "Does My Baby Love?" the Boswell Sisters interpolate the question: "Has he got it?" And 10 years later, when only Connie was hitting the boards, she and Bing Crosby introduced Sy Oliver's "Yes Indeed!" with characteristic Southern-fried badinage:

> BING: Now has you got it, sister Constance, tell me, has you got it?
> CONNIE: Whoayeah, I got it, brother Bingstons, now you knows I got it.

Connie, Vet, and Martha Boswell, the subjects of a stirring new revue, had it from an early age, growing up in middle-class propriety in New Orleans in a musical family, hanging with neighborhood kids like Louis Prima and Leon Roppolo, while playing chamber trio classics—Martha on piano, Vet on violin, and Connie on cello. According to Chica Minerly, Vet's daughter, that changed when Connie got hold of a saxophone and Vet picked up a banjo. Soon they had a vaudeville act good enough to take them to Chicago and then Hollywood, where they scored on radio. Chica suggests that they thought more like instrumentalists than as singers. As they realized that their singing went over best with audiences, they dropped other aspects of the act, which involved dancing and about a dozen instruments (including spoons), retaining only Martha's piano.

By 1931, they had developed the best sister act in an era rife with sister acts and put most of the rest out of business; the others didn't have it—they simped while the Boswells swung. When they joined Crosby as regulars on his Woodbury radio show, he called them "three girls with but a single fellow—harmony." He subsequently changed *fellow* to *thought*, but either way they had two fellows or thoughts. One, undoubtedly, was harmony, which they approached with an intuitive ease that allowed them to shift ground phrase after phrase, serendipitously tweaking their voicings. The arrangements were carefully worked out, though never transcribed, but that didn't mean the girls had to stay in place. When the Boswells came along, small vocal groups had not greatly evolved from barbershop quartets; to sing sweetly and in tune was what counted. Crosby and the Rhythm Boys changed that by emphasizing an improvisational camaraderie and jazzy spirit, but their unison harmonies were at best routine. The Boswells and Mills Brothers brought the genre to a level never equaled, though '50s groups like the Hi-Los made a big deal of showing off their flashy progressive harmonies. The Hi-Los now sound corny—the Boswells and early Mills do not. While the Brothers imitated instruments, simulating Ellington arrangements, the Sisters sang as though they were instruments.

That other "fellow," of course, was rhythm; because the Mills Brothers were inclined to luxuriate in their more beautiful voices, not even they swung as consistently as the Boswells. Consider "It's the Girl," which opens with the usual all-star band in full throttle, Joe Venuti's violin swirling in time, before the singers make their entrance, sustaining the rhythm with total assurance, then going into their trademark half-time tempo change, breaks, and unison waddah-daddah fills. Their most bizarre routine was a nonsense language they invented as girls. In his superb account in *Jazz Singing*, Will Friedwald describes their method as "a more complicated form of pig Latin. By this process the word 'boy' becomes 'boggledoy,' 'swing' becomes 'swingleding.'" The best example is "Everybody Loves My Baby," in which they zip through an interpolated chorus sounding very much like banjos. That recording is also notable for Connie's Armstrong-inspired rhythmic slurs, Martha's steady piano backing, and a vocal chorus of written variations complete with scat, breaks, melodic inversions, and walloping swing.

Connie and Vet worked out the arrangements, sometimes dictating them to Glenn Miller to translate for the ensemble. They are so inventive that at times a three-minute record seems more like a suite, something Ellington and Bill Challis, among others, had already achieved in big bands. The difficulty for singers is that if you keep changing the groove you have to instantly be at one with the new groove, or else you lose the listener. "Roll On Mississippi" begins with the sisters scatting phrases from Hoagy Carmichael's "Riverboat Shuffle," before Connie enters with the song proper, soon joined by Vet and Martha and a flurry of tempo changes. But every groove is nailed deep in the pocket. On the rejected first take of "Was That the Human Thing to Do," Connie sings *thing* as written, low and sullen, but on the next take, she jumps it an octave, hitting it like a trumpet. Their instrumental instincts extend, in the same number, to unison tremolos that accent and extend certain words, building via breaks to a peak that gives way to a bluesy half-time finish.

Like Artie Shaw, the Boswell Sisters left music at their peak, in 1936, with only Connie continuing (as Connee) for the next 25 years. The Andrews Sisters were their putative successors, but they were a commercial act buoyed by Vic Schoen's smart arrangements, with little of the Boswells' vocal edge, subtlety, or dazzling surprise. In some respects, I think a truer heir is the Beatles, whose open harmonies suggest something of the Boswells' synchronous originality and swing (in the larger sense of the word that subsumes rock). In this regard, it may be noted that the Boswells' hipness extended beyond reviving Armstrong's "Heebie Jeebies"—in two versions, one using his scat chorus, the other his coda— and recording the first vocal versions of several Ellington tunes (among them "Sophisticated Lady" and "Mood Indigo"), to introducing in 1934 (with an exclamatory "Yeah!") the first song employing the title phrase "Rock and Roll." It was created for them by composer Richard Whiting and forgotten lyricist Sidney Clare ("Rock and roll like a rockin' chair / Laugh and smile while we drown each care / In the tide / As we glide / To the rollin' rockin' rhythm of the sea"), whose output ranged from "Please Don't Talk About Me When I'm Gone" to "On the Good Ship Lollipop."

The Boswells made only about 80 records, a quarter of them major hits, most of which can be heard on such CD collections as *The Boswell Sisters Collection, Vol. 1, 1931–32* (Collector's Classics, an import), *That's How Rhythm Was Born* (Columbia/Legacy), and *Airshots and Rarities 1930–1935* (Retrieval, an import). The records have fueled generations of loyal admirers, among the most persistent of them Mark Hampton and Stuart Ross, who created an off-Broadway revue, *The Heebie Jeebies*, in 1981, and have now launched *Rhythm on the Rainbow: The Hot Harmonies of the Boswell Sisters*, for a month at Rainbow & Stars. They had a good trio then and a better one now, in Dee Hoty, Sally Mayes, and Nancy Opel, and they have learned from past mistakes, jettisoning a dreadful book. This is cabaret, not theater, so the music has to carry the weight of the hour, which it does with vivacious authenticity. The current threesome is more animated than the Boswells, while lacking their quirky edge, twangy nasality, and Southern diction, which pronounces s's as z's, as in their name or the phrase, "what's been done muz be." But records can't do what live music can, and from the first measures of "Let Yourself Go," the new show is alive with a close enough approximation to forestall doubts and comparisons. The women are most effective in the unison work, which shimmers in numbers like "Crazy People," "Shout Sister Shout," "Everybody Loves My Baby," and "Going Home." They are also effective in alternating the leads, forgoing all Broadway affectations and giving themselves to the Boswells, until a misguided segment in which each is featured with a solo.

At that point they choose appropriate songs but inexplicably undermine them with au courant Broadway vocal overkill. My theory is that the end of Broadway singing as a palatable art began with that little girl who sang "Tomorrow" in *Annie*; it is a short, slippery slope from there to Mandy Patinken or "Memories." The worst offender is Dee Hoty, who shows impeccable taste in the trio numbers, but elects to do "You Ought to Be in Pictures" with a histrionic vibrato more suitable to Stephen Sondheim or Andrew Lloyd Webber. Nancy Opel begins "That Old Feeling" in the right era, but climaxes 60 years later—especially distracting because she expertly captures Connie's deep contralto on "When I Take My Sugar to Tea." Sally Mayes, the least affected, is stuck with the interminable "Until the Real Thing Comes Along."

Despite that lapse—and a stiff and barely adequate supporting trio, too—when the singers are piping together on "Heebie Jeebies" or "It's the Girl," it is not difficult to imagine you are in a 1930s nightclub hearing this music for the first time, rendered with energy, skill, and charm. Attending opening night were Chica Minnerly and the Boswell historian David McCain, who have been working on a book and a Boswell Museum in East Springfield, New York, which presents concerts and workshops as well as displaying mementos. Chica conveyed two theories as to why Connie became Connee: In one, she fell under the influence of numerology; in another, she made the switch during the war so as not to have to dot all those *i*'s signing autographs.

[*Village Voice*, 17 March 1998]

50 ❖ *Turner Classic Moves*
(Mark Turner)

Mark Turner is now playing his first gig as a leader in a major New York club—a split-week at Sweet Basil—to celebrate his first album as a leader for Warner Bros. Yet the album, *Mark Turner*, was actually recorded in 1995 for the Criss Cross label, which had released his true debut earlier that year. The new CD is thus two years older than the very weird jam session album he made for Warners last year, *Warner Jams Vol. 2: The Two Tenors*, which was lost in the shuffle of 1997 releases. In retrospect, that's hardly surprising: Turner, then virtually unknown, was billed equally with the legendary James Moody, prompting a confused cry of Mark *Who?*—as in, shouldn't we know who he is and is it wise to admit we don't? Worse, a note in the useless booklet identifies

Moody as on the left channel and Turner on the right, when the reverse is true. In any case, the new disc demands reconsideration of the old one, which has the virtue of relative contemporaneity.

Turner, who was born in Ohio in 1965 and lives in New Haven, routinely commuting to the big city's various jam havens, has named Bach, Coltrane, and Warne Marsh as primary influences. Marsh, of course, is the ringer, and helps explain how Turner escaped the penumbra of Coltrane. As a key interpreter of Lennie Tristano, who favored dual saxophones, Marsh may have helped generate Turner's comparable bias. On his Criss Cross debut (*Yam Yam*), he shares the front line with two tenors, Seamus Blake and Terence Dean, and on *Mark Turner* he uses saxophonist Joshua Redman on three tracks.

At 32, Turner has an anomalously cool sound, and is in the process of working out a style that favors a sober midrange, lithe phrases, and a penchant for prettily sustained ballads. Yet because the album is poorly sequenced—front-loaded with the Redman duets and two consecutive pieces in triple-time—his identity is slow to emerge. The first track, and his only original in a time when most young players eagerly parade their mediocre heads, is "Mr. Brown," a blues in six with a theme that suggests more complications than the soloists are obliged to heed: a 16-bar melody by the tenors (nice triplet figure in the middle), in and out of synch, followed by a tenor coda in five four-bar units that suggest the ubiquitous influence of Wayne Shorter in the sustained notes, descending cast, and repetition. The solos, though, are 12-bar grids, and Turner, playing five choruses, defers to his guest, who plays nine, beginning with a Wayne-like shrug (note Edward Simon's Hancockian arpeggio and brisk chords), before building a head of steam, howling against the rhythm until the two players resume the unison theme and coda.

Turner comes more into focus on Tristano's piece, "327 East 32nd Street," which begins straightaway with only a preliminary beat for orientation. Turner riffs eight bars with unhurried ease and then plays economically in the high midrange—he clearly likes the feeling of the notes just above the octave key. He sets up phrases here and elsewhere by barreling through low notes, but in his third and fourth choruses he is relaxed, mixing melody, triplets, and rests with an almost Lestorian shapeliness, finishing with a smooth if lick-heavy finish. Marsh notwithstanding, Turner's light, dry sound recalls Hank Mobley, who stood out from the pack nearly four decades ago for the same reason Turner does now—a relatively cool tone in a hot idiom. The two tenors handsomely intone Ornette Coleman's exquisite "Kathelin Gray," but might well have bid her adieu after the theme; Simon's piano tries too hard to extend the mood and the twin tenor variations produce a keening whininess (cf.

Coltrane in his "Welcome" period) that can't compete with Coleman's ragged edge or the perfect circle of the piece itself. Not every theme requires variations.

With Redman gone, Turner emerges full force on "Hey, It's Me You're Talking To," a 16-bar Victor Lewis tune with a neat two-note closing punctuation. After the head is played twice, Turner whirls around in what amounts to a transitional runway and then kicks out the jams for a dozen choruses, rolling through the turnbacks and closing with Marshian finesse. His individuality is in part his determination to resist the Coltrane line in favor of a fluid regularity, reedy and occasionally chromatic, mostly logical and controlled. (The performance is marred only by a hapless fade, undermining the finality of Lewis's theme.) He is never more independent of Coltrane than when treading his turf, as on "26-2," Coltrane's obscure take on "Confirmation" with "Giant Steps" harmonic alterations. And the Coltrane influence disappears entirely on his slow ballads. The only one on the CD, unfortunately, is "Autumn in New York," which exemplifies his willingness to rely on the tune itself and his ability to craft spare variations out of a handful of notes, like the three (think the first phrase of "Stormy Weather") with which he begins his improvisation.

Turner's ballad feature on *The Two Tenors* is in the same vein. He plays "We'll Be Together Again" in the tenor's alto range, and though his phrases sometimes meander with a slight imbalance, they indicate a searching quality and ultimately float confidently to ground. If you missed this album—just about everyone did—it is worth searching out. Turner holds his own fairly well, but he is clearly unnerved at times, and there is no disgrace in that: Moody is imperial throughout. A veteran of tenor conclaves (with Sonny Stitt and Gene Ammons, among others), Moody is of a generation that values friendly competition. He has been bested only once, by Dexter Gordon, who unnerved Moody much as Moody does Turner (a telltale sign is the profusion of pet licks that keep cropping up like *ums* and *you knows* in a conversation), and sounds even more acerbic and voluble than usual up against Turner's more modest timbre. Inspired, the younger man stretches out in search of more elaborate and varied conceits, but his steadiness is crippling as he perambulates across the range of the saxophone, while Moody easily varies his attack with long and short phrases, smooth and woolly timbre.

The disc concludes with a telling lesson from the master. W. C. Handy's "Hesitation Blues" opens with Larry Goldings's pellucid piano (far more decisive than his organ), and Turner follows, exploring au courant changes and ambling vocal inflections, leaning on his licks but growing stronger as he continues. Yet he determinedly eschews raw blues phrases, which is precisely what Moody uses to make his entrance, wailing from the first bar in an utterly centered performance that hits a few outré notes en passant, but cleaves to the heart of the matter and produces a model tenor blues. Turner is especially winning on "Satellite," presumably his idea—a Coltrane tune ideal for Moody, as it is based on "How High the Moon." Once again, Coltrane's theme prompts him to depart from Coltrane's methods; his spiral phrases are handsomely balanced, and though he resorts to a few stock figures, he is at ease rolling over the changes and building clouds of momentum with evenly paced phrases. Moody eventually trumps him, telling a more varied and urgent story, but he begins his solo by echoing the younger player's approach, a generous tip of the hat that speaks volumes about the distinctiveness of Turner as a work in progress.

That Turner is moving forward is also attested by his sole contribution, "Pure Imagination," to the largely vapid 1997 *Warner Bros. Jazz Christmas Party*, and his consistently thoughtful work on Reid Anderson's *Dirty Show Tunes* (FSNT), where the often laborious originals focus and inspire him to the kind of eloquent understatement that is at once a signal gift and a distinct restraint, as on "Think of Mingus." As a sideman, Turner is a confirmed classicist, yet without the sense of regurgitated greatness you get from his younger competitors. It's impossible to tell where he is headed. But it would be nice if his next album were recorded in 1998.

[*Village Voice*, 14 April 1998]

51 ❖ Fusions
(Wayne Shorter / Odyssey)

Wayne is coming to Lincoln Center. What will Wayne do? What will Wayne, who like Miles needs no last name (no more than Herbie, Ron, or Tony), *ever* do? The only thing certain is that he won't do whatever we expect. No, that isn't quite right. He has trained us not to bring expectation to his performances, but rather anticipation—though he cannot quell our vain hope that he will parcel us into a time machine and do do that voodoo that he once did so well. Dream on, or better still, go back to the recordings, which have grown in stature as few from that era have.

The Lincoln Center program promised a new work for chamber orchestra and jazz musicians, an adaptation from Sibelius, and a retrospective running the gamut from the Blue Note pinnacle, *Juju* and *Speak No Evil*, to the recent Verve enigmas, *High Life* and *1 + 1*. It did not promise nor deliver the saxophone virtuoso of yore. Indeed, as the orchestra set progressed, with Wayne alternating constantly between tenor and soprano—phrasing with the strings, overlaying a few fragments, launching blood-rushing solos that quickly ran aground in the clogged arteries of the composition—one couldn't help suspecting that the musician who never wanted to be a leader, or at least postponed the obligation until he had no choice, was no longer interested in playing the saxophone either. Fair enough: focus on the composition.

Easier said than done. If Franz Liszt announces a new work, follows the conductor onto the stage, and seats himself at the piano, you figure he's going to play the damn thing. If the piece does not require his keyboard pyrotechnics, then Franz should either conduct from the podium or retire offstage. When Wayne holds a tenor saxophone in front of an open microphone, it is impossible to listen to the strings sawing a characteristically repetitive theme over funky rhythms without expecting him to mount a vigorous assault. And when he repeatedly teases you with startling introductory figures only to quickly put the instrument down, lift another, and stand peering at the score, you find yourself focusing not on the piece but on the absence it underscores. Where is Wayne? He's there but he isn't there.

The chimera of fusion obscures Wayne Shorter's accomplishment and dilemma. Fusion isn't the issue—he turns in his boldest playing in years on *High Life*. My guess is that, like Sonny Rollins, he is one of those painfully honest musicians who can't happily fake an orgasm or traverse old ground. And if the commercial advantages of fusion kindle suspicions of compromise, the complexity of the work ought to defuse them. Jazz is in the business of fusing musics. In a radio interview a few years ago, Shorter offered a commendable riposte to those who would isolate jazz from the rest of music. I paraphrase loosely from memory: If all the outlets and inlets of a great lake are closed, it will become fetid and die. More often than not fusion is meretricious and deserving of contempt. But that can hardly be said of Shorter or of James Blood Ulmer, who regrouped the Odyssey band at the Knitting Factory the same week Shorter mines the instrumentation and techniques of Europe and pop. Odyssey subsumes Hendrixian guitar colorations and the indigenous values of native fiddling and trap drumming in a trio that, for all the intimated borrowings (they are legion), stands quite alone.

Jimi Hendrix, like the early Ornette Coleman, embodied total freedom as a soloist, indulging in long phrases and feedback wailing that couldn't be contained in structural grids, supported by bass and drums. Ulmer, like the later (harmolodic) Coleman, plots his moves in tandem with his musicians, elaborating the illusion of freedom through compositional devices. The obvious lineaments of Ulmer's style as a singer and guitarist savor of Hendrix, but the distinctions are far more obvious. Hendrix did not play jazz—or at least not as well as rock: check his Wes Montgomery–inspired post–"Star-Spangled Banner" blues at Woodstock—and Ulmer will never be mistaken for a rock guitarist. *Odyssey* earns its star-spangled crescendos by a studied, incremental buildup of elemental blues riffs enveloped in the sweet burly dissonance of guitar and the siren wail of Charles Burnham's electric violin. Their intertwining, abetted by Warren Benbow's drums, is so quenching that the addition of bass, let alone keyboard or wind instruments, might seem irrelevant at best and intrusive at worst.

Ulmer's 1983 *Odyssey* (Columbia/Legacy) remains a singular album, a funhouse of reflections that change shapes depending on who's in front of the mirrors. Pointedly excluded from the framework, despite Burnham's academic training, is Europe. Instead we get a native American stew of jazz, blues, country, rock, pop, gospel, an extended riff on "Pop Goes the Weasel"—a solid-state mosaic, never a pastiche, in which musicianly conductivity is amplified by compositional finesse. After 15 years, the band that made *Odyssey* has adopted the name, with Ulmer so absorbed in the group aesthetic that he is second-billed to Burnham on the new record, *Reunion* (Knitting Factory Works). The violinist takes more expansive solos than he did 15 years ago, but they are tethered to Ulmer's guitar-generated themes, and when they twirl in patterns with the drums, as on "Love Dance," they produce something akin to a sophisticated reel. Many of the solos are embellishments on a centered thematic figure, which, when configured in a perpetual downward cast, can hardly fail to recall trademark compositions of Shorter.

Although he had already contributed to Art Blakey's Jazz Messengers such noteworthy themes as "Lester Left Town" and "El Toro," the true Wayne, as opposed to the hard-bopping apprentice, made his debut with the 1961 "Contemplation" (*Buhania's Delight*), a markedly colorful progression of chords wedded to a moody, memorable melody. Never widely performed, it established the m.o. of the composer who soon remade the Miles Davis Quintet with his naggingly original, gloomily unforgettable themes. Differences between his methods as player and composer were unmistakable: In the first role, he could not bear to repeat himself—even riffs were avoided; in the second, he made repetition a sine qua non that reached its apogee in the melodically static "Nefertiti"—and appeared in several guises at the Lincoln Center concert, especially in a vamp-till-ready encore with a booming emphasis on first beats.

As his association with Davis ended and he looked around for another leader (enter Joe Zawinul), Shorter found a second voice on soprano, taming that recalcitrant instrument with his dreamy, pitch-perfect articulation, generating an expressively melancholy sound that retained its abrasive edge in the upper register but avoided the Middle Eastern wail. His own albums, not as widely recognized in the '60s as later, included *Juju*, which is so comprehensive a display of his tenor that you can begin to intuit from it his need to move on, and the more thematic works— from the folkloric *Speak No Evil* (with its homage to his daughter) to the cosmological *Super Nova* (with its homage to Billy Strayhorn), plus his intervening attempt to explore God's own purview in *The All-Seeing Eye*. I often got the feeling, perhaps unfairly, that he was hiding out in Weather Report, but I hear little in those years to rival the pictorial intensity of his writing since then, especially on the *1 + 1* duets with Herbie Hancock—an insidiously programmed collection of unwavering pensiveness that can only be appreciated or endured a few tracks at a time. Two pieces from that album provided the highlights at Lincoln Center. For while there was a mild charge in hearing tight Blakey-era harmonies on "Speak No Evil," his vocalized skittery arpeggios on "JuJu," and an inexplicable four-beat treatment of Sibelius's "Valse Triste," there was true beauty in "Meridianne—A Wood Sylph," for which pianist Eric Reed outdid himself laying out changes behind Shorter's written statements and then embroidering them in his solos, and "Aung San Suu Kyi," perhaps Shorter's most enchanting ballad to date. He hardly improvised on those pieces, and didn't need to. They filled the room in a way the chamber orchestra could not. The fusion process was—as it should be, as it is in Odyssey—invisible.

[*Village Voice*, 12 May 1998]

52 ❖ *Is Everybody Happy?*
(Texaco–New York Jazz Festival)

Why complain if a jazz festival is no more than a highly publicized, highly congested confluence of concerts? It provides work, a little excitement, an occasional surprise, and focuses attention on jazz, New York, the impresario, and the sponsor. Is everybody happy? You bet.

Happy, but perhaps not entirely festive. The Texaco–New York Jazz Festival stomped into town June 1 for a two-week party, offering something for everyone. Produced by Michael Dorf and centered at his Knitting Factory and other points south of Canal Street, it was not the rowdy "What Is Jazz?" thumbsucker of years past, but rather a big, big tent, assimilating mainstream jazz (Joe Henderson, Kevin Eubanks) and pop (Bela Fleck, George Clinton) along with the avant-garde and Downtown genrefication.

Texaco is no longer a challenge to the musical status quo, but rather a would-be challenger to the entrepreneurial powers that be. Its jaws are primed to sink into the throat of JVC, which recently considered and rejected a collusion with BET, a most uninspiring prospect: JVC's conservatism is earned, a reflection of George Wein's taste as well as the demands of expensive concert halls; BET's conservatism is institutional—it requires fodder for TV. Texaco hasn't abandoned its roots, but in true arriviste fashion, it wants establishment respect and will do anything to get it, even to the extent of generating the phony baloney New York Jazz Awards, handed out at Lincoln Center before an audience drawn largely from "the industry" and willing to pay benefit-priced tickets ($150, half for civilians). The awards are administered by Dorf's KnitMedia, which selected the voters and counted votes. You won't be surprised to learn that virtually every nominee is signed to a major record label. The Jazz Journalists Association also handed out awards at the same ceremony—a clever bid on Dorf's part to find a credible beard; JJA president Howard Mandel committed his organization without a formal referendum.

The hunger for respect failed to alleviate a pervasive flatness, or maybe I was just hanging with the wrong people. San Francisco glows with civic pride during its jazz festival, which, like Texaco, is all over town, as do cities with jazz spectacles as varied as those in New Orleans, Pori, Cork, and the Hague. But those events take producing seriously, which was not the case here. With few exceptions, we got to hear working bands and not the one-time-only blow-your-mind extravaganzas that only festivals can mount. The most exciting jazz event I attended wasn't part of Texaco and had no vocals and only ancillary instrumental solos. But later on that.

I went out in pursuit of pianists, and began with Sephardic Tinge (Spanish Jews, Spanish tinge—get it?), a trio created by Anthony Coleman, who has the rhythmic subtlety and anvil touch of Dave Brubeck, another pianist who tried to make a case for swinging the Middle East. Coleman opened for Muhal Richard Abrams, who proceeded to open for himself, devoting nearly half of his long (90 minutes) and continuous set to a throat-clearing study of the relationship between slablike soprano saxophone tones, played by Patience Higgins, and heavily pedaled rumbling piano. Bass and drums entered and there were pinprick moments of light, including passages of drumlike piano (hammered a la Gershwin) and brazen saxophone chords, but it was all foreplay, without melody or focus. Then, after a mallets solo by Reggie Nicholson, Abrams struck up a vamp, Higgins took up his tenor, and great godamighty they were free at last, finding midpage what should have been their lead.

At one point Abrams laid out, leaving the field to Higgins, who affirmed his growing reputation as a well-kept secret. Adapting his timbre with a powdery grit, he played undulating phrases with patches of melody (a line from Glenn Miller wafted by too quickly to catch), balancing a mid-range attack with bottom-note blasts, sustaining two-note chords, and demonstrating the durability of a resolute free jazz. That pushed Abrams's button, and he bounded in with splayed chords in leaping rhythmic patterns that evolved into a swinging, flashing linearity. He made the piano ring and played all of it, settling into a serpentine figure that Nicholson capered against. After a bass solo by Greg Jones, the quartet fired up again, fourth-quarter full-court press, percussive and coherent, if overlong. At the wind-down, I wondered if the first part, which no longer seemed so laborious (pain has no memory), was a kind of ploy to make desert more rewarding.

Every time I see Cecil Taylor I forget, until the first grunt in the dark, that he is going to begin with a vocal warm-up (pain has no memory). Then, having no choice, I submit. A small price to pay, because you know that any minute he is going to sit down and do what no one else on earth can do, notwithstanding his many imitators. And so it was. His current quartet mines a surprisingly conventional pulse, and the soprano saxophonist adds little, but Taylor likes the option of receding into the mix every once in a while. Still, the others are not in Taylor's class and you can't help but wait on his brilliance—the onslaught of trilling, caroling runs; bass-chord punctuations; an occasional forearm for emphasis. He did it all—the cascades and dynamics and sudden change-ups. And then he slowed, the caesuras turning into stabiles, and the others incapable of picking up the slack. I thought for a tremulous moment: Is age (he is three seasons away from 70 and playing with uncompromising bravado) beginning to tell? The performance whimpered away, as he rose, stood for a moment, then quickly left the stage. But he just as quickly raced back for a splashy three-minute encore that said yes in thunder and lightning. Fuck age.

Eric Reed can't blame age for a midnight set so innocuous you wondered where you were. Is this really the Knit? No, the Blue Note? Jeez, I am tired. I used to trace Reed to Hampton Hawes, because he has so much technique and savvy that I didn't want to mention Ramsey Lewis. Reed had played responsively and with imagination at the Wayne Shorter Lincoln Center concert and I wanted to hear more in that vein. But he chose to plug his Broadway songs album ("Send in the Clowns," "Maria," oy). He also played two long blues and a fastidious "'Round Midnight," he and his trio executing everything with the éclat of Oscar Peterson—the relentlessly busy phrases modified by Lewis's gospel blues tropes and superficiality. The audience loved it—one couple in the balcony danced. Earlier that day, I had listened to the new Nicholas Payton album (*Payton's Place*) and only the heavy mix on the bass told me I wasn't listening to the start of an old Blue Mitchell album that was also in the carousel. Jazz always finds strength and renewal in the anxiety of influence; but now we are too often getting the influence without the anxiety. Which is one reason I was blown away by the show at the Variety Theater.

Savion Glover Downtown was a largely improvised program created by Glover, featuring him and six other dancers. Prospects looked especially good when Eli Fountain's quartet took its place and in the center was Patience Higgins. I admired Glover in 1989 in *Black and Blue*, but never footed the bill for *Bring in Da Noise, Bring in Da Funk*, so forgive a latecomer for shouting: Glover, who is 24, is one of the most inventive, stimulating jazz players in years. True, his instrument is his feet, but I heard no Texaco solo more riveting or intricately musical than his extended variations on a medley of "Billie's Bounce" and "Now's the Time," or wittier than his rendition of "Cheek to Cheek"—wearing a tuxedo T-shirt in a pas de deux with Ayodele Casal, whose birthday that evening prompted a jam session with more fire than the staged jams you hear at most jazz festivals.

Glover has invented a stamping style that is already widely imitated, and he can pounce on a theme like "Milestones" or "Caravan" and work it with the same nonstop intensity as Cecil Taylor, until your head is spinning. But he can also be sweet and slow, as in an intoxicating version of "In a Sentimental Mood," introduced with a rapturous tenor solo, replete with Higgins's trademark grit and two-note chords. Higgins has recorded memorably (Abrams's *Think All, Focus One*, David Murray's *South of the Border*), but in the era of cloned jazz he remains conspicuously neglected. Glover's music, however, isn't as easily packaged: He taps a splendid, sandy obbligato to Abbey Lincoln on "Who Used to Dance," but an album?—Baby Laurence tried that. Movie musicals are dead, yet a 21st-century Comden and Green could surely fashion something worthy of him, because whether or not he can sing (I guess not, since he doesn't), he can apparently express anything with his feet. A highlight of *Black and Blue* was Bunny Briggs's double- and triple-time tapping to a very slow "In a Sentimental Mood." The lesson was not lost on Glover, who, refraining from all upper-body acrobatics, zeroed in on the melody with his feet and softly and expressively played the music. He would kill at a jazz club or a jazz festival.

[*Village Voice*, 23 June 1998]

53 ❖ *Requiem for a Flag-Waver (JVC 1998)*

As I was saying: Why complain if a jazz festival is no more than a congested confluence of concerts? JVC followed on the heels of Texaco (discussion of jazz is fated forevermore to sound like adspeak) and lay over the city like a shroud. People were still asking me when it would open as it was closing. Critics made the rounds glassy-eyed, somnambulant, shoulders set in permanent shrugs, as if to say don't ask before anyone could. Buzz? There was no buzz—no I-can't-wait-to-hear-that or good-idea-for-a-concert or wasn't-that-amazing. As always, there were moments: I won't soon forget Al Grey's "Black and Blue" or Clark Terry reviving his duets with himself, or Joao Gilberto, who isn't a jazz musician except by association, or . . . I've run out of things I won't soon forget. Better consult notes.

The festival began with six concerts at the Kaye Playhouse, a pleasingly petite theater that fosters specialty programs that would barely make a dent in Carnegie, Avery Fisher, or Symphony Space, unlike the Brazilians and Cubans who accounted for at least five major events in the halls that used to present Duke Ellington, Sarah Vaughan, Miles Davis, Stan Getz—you know, jazz stars. Last year's Kaye series was an imaginative mixture of mainstream and jazz rep, so they did it again, only without the imagination. The almost exclusive focus on prewar (as in WWII) styles had, inevitably, a valedictory effect, combining memory and desire with the morbid fear that some venerated players might not be around much longer, which is one reason I felt grateful to be there. Still, when a tribute to Fats Waller got underway with Al Grey in a wheelchair and Clark Terry on the arm of an aide, the desire to pay homage was undercut by the assumption that these great men would be working at a fraction of their capacities. Yet whatever was ailing them did not affect their lungs, embouchure, or brains; along with 82-year-old guitarist Al Casey, who recorded with Waller, and 75-year-old pianist Ralph Sutton, who imbibed Waller's records until they were part of his motor memory, they salvaged an inaugural concert that was more requiem than flag-waver.

For the first set, the accent was on Waller the songwriter and singer. That became evident as soon as impresario George Wein sat himself at the piano and warned that he would do the singing. Wein is an amiable Teddy Wilson–inspired pianist who has led some fine all-star ensembles without doing damage, but if he were forced to eat with his left hand he'd soon shrink to the size of Michael Dorf. Waller without a left hand isn't Waller, no matter how many choruses you lay down of "Honeysuckle Rose" or how desperately Clark Terry mugs "Your Feet's Too Big." And "Black and Blue" is no song for a vocal dilettante, not after an Al Grey solo that left nothing to add. His tone and pitch steady as you go, Grey used the slide and mute to inflect every note with the befitting *mwahhh* or *grrrr*. On "Crazy 'Bout My Baby," Terry, his sound improbably restored and buffed, did a routine he made famous in the '60s, trading phrases and then pitches between flugelhorn and muted trumpet, and it was as funny and smoothly done as ever. The unassuming Al Casey played sliding chords and swinging fillips with a quietly rocking outlook that made you wonder if he knows it isn't 1939 any more.

The cast changed for the second half (Kenny Davern, Warren Vaché, Howard Alden), but belonged to Ralph Sutton, if not the finest living stride pianist then certainly the most individual. Most of the form's practitioners play with braggadocio, chatting away or puffing on a cigar as though their hands were independent contractors—wind them up and off they go. Sutton's signature is an almost conservatory seriousness as he plots every lateral sweep of the left hand and dancing conceit of the right with meticulous care, his sound solid and his rhythm unshakable. Much of his appeal lies in his infallibility. Untouched by modernity, Sutton's music freshens the paper doily elegance and flourishes of another world, yet he's a bear for abstracting melody and hallelujah finishes. He played Willie the Lion Smith's "Echoes of Spring" with driving rapture. On Waller's "Viper's Drag," he stressed the contrast between the ominous prowl of the opening and the elated striding that follows, much as he emphasized the disparity between boogie tension and melodic release in Waller's "Alligator Crawl."

At the other Kaye shows predictability ruled. Herb Ellis deserved his tribute, but did it have to be played—as Barney Kessel's was last year—only by guitarists, with bass and drums for ballast? At least open the gates to some fresh faces and maybe even a couple of mavericks like

Ulmer, Ribot, or Morris. Pleasurable though it is to hear Mundell Lowe's moonlit melodies or Ellis's twangy blues, the quantity of notes eventually rocks you into indifference, like a long religious ceremony where the vestments are guitar straps. An evening that thriftily combined homages to Jimmy McPartland and the team of Mildred Bailey and Red Norvo was too thrifty by half. Warren Vaché played the trumpet part in a pro forma set of Chicago-style Dixieland with only a few standouts: Marian McPartland's delicate "Singin' the Blues," handsomely harmonized and paced with a chiming finish; trombonist Bobby Pratt making hay on "Louisiana"; Howard Alden's "Davenport Blues," arranged for solo guitar with a bass line in the manner of George Van Eps. Alden played well all week, resisting the temptation to answer showy technique with showy technique, though at the Harold Arlen tribute he offered a dense introductory cadenza on "If I Only Had a Brain" that inspired his accommodating partner, Ken Peplowski, to observe, "If I only had a brain I'd know what he was playing." Carol Sloane was in good voice, and people who play Arlen well played well.

Twenty years ago, George Wein would not have reduced Mildred and Red to one set featuring singer and pianist Daryl Sherman. He'd have brought in an orchestra to play the Eddie Sauter arrangements, the best vibes players around, and the kind of musicians who could make "Dance of the Octopus" shimmer all over again, so that you'd leave the hall knowing why a salute was in order. That said, Sherman has locked into something in exploring her affinity for Mildred, whose supple phrasing, lilting tones, and eloquent time she captures with feeling and charm. Unfortunately, she was backed by an ensemble that would have been more appropriate for Lee Wiley—more Chicago Dixieland than forward-looking swing; it all but drowned her out on "Arthur Murray Taught Me Dancing in a Hurry," though she recovered on "Lover Come Back to Me," until the band charged her on the out-chorus.

The tribute to Dick Gibson, who died earlier that week, was another missed opportunity. No one remarked onstage who Gibson was or why he was worth saluting; at the very least, one expected a few dozen anecdotes—Gibson was an anecdotal man, as teller and subject. Wein's remark that he was important for starting a party circuit that provided musicians with work was spectacularly short of the mark. Putting aside the careers revived or spurred and the bands created during the 30 annual Colorado jazz parties lavishly thrown by Gibson and his wife Maddie (who was in attendance), they had an incalculable influence on the international revival of the mainstream jazz that fuels JVC's festival. If Gibson proved less than brilliant in keeping track of his finances, he never stinted on jazz—I can't imagine Wein (or anyone else) flying

Trummy Young from Hawaii for annual duets with Vic Dickenson, matching Joe Venuti with Zoot Sims, delivering Carl Fontana from pit band hell or John Collins from studio obscurity, or arraying the stage with 11 trombonists (OK, that last one was a little iffy). "The First Ever New York Jazz Party," as it was billed, offered several players who I doubt would have made the Gibson cut, and failed entirely to capture the mix-and-match madness he mischievously forced on beboppers and Dixielanders alike. A few musicians, however, seized the day: trombonists Urbie Green and Slide Hampton on "Blue Monk"; guitarists Bucky Pizzarelli and Howard Alden on "Three Little Words"; clarinetist Kenny Davern on "Moonglow"; trumpeter Joe Wilder on "Squeeze Me"; Jerry Jerome with his old-time tenor saxophone timbre on "Pennies from Heaven." Yet the evening never caught fire.

You couldn't say that Joao Gilberto caught fire either. As Jon Pareles wrote in the *New York Times*, he "may well be the coolest man alive." Without fanfare (no blathering DJs for him), he walked onstage with his guitar, acknowledging the standing ovation with a nearly imperceptible bow, and then played 90 minutes of bossa nova, never once availing himself of the bottled water by his chair on an otherwise bare stage, and never responding to the crowd, which after the first hour or so was beginning to levitate. Pareles reported that "once, just once, he smiled." I must have been scribbling—missed it completely. For the final number, he introduced singer Bebel Gilberto, who said, "Good evening." A ripple of laughter rolled over the audience; except for Joao's mumbled introduction for his daughter, they were the first (and last) words spoken all night.

At 67, Gilberto is, if possible, even more economical than when he made those groundbreaking albums with Stan Getz. Thus his every gesture is magnified. Only late in the evening did he play an instrumental chorus, otherwise declining even pickups and breaks. Each piece was an intimate communion of voice and guitar, understated yet glistening, his rhythms enameled in their certainty, his embellishments supple but contained. He expended no apparent energy, though the music requires great energy—the lyrics are wordier than in American songs and the melodies subtly insular, with a heavy reliance on seventh chords. At the 1964 Carnegie Hall concert recorded for *Getz Gilberto #2*, the saxophonist rather haplessly tried to explain the secret of his partner, at first suggesting that he refrains from injecting his personality into songs, then backtracking at the absurdity of that idea. Getz was right: He's there and not there, singing as though he didn't need to breathe, the voice a barely vibrating string-instrument drone—a reminder that Carnegie Hall will pick up every whisper of musicians who treat it right.

The place was back to normal for the Roy Haynes and Chick Corea concert. Haynes's new trio with pianist Danilo Perez played a powerhouse set, beginning with Monk's "Bright Mississippi" and continuing with such standards as "I Hear a Rhapsody" and "It's Easy to Remember," a lesson in the value to be found in the harmonic steeplechases of good songs. The great drummer, in a chartreuse suit and exhibiting his usual cockiness, exerted a geometrical control over the arrangements, but the trio waxed and waned as a unit and left me wanting more. Whereas I was sated by Chick Corea's Origin, which is peppery and inventive and mines several moods, from Spanish-tinges ("Hand Me Down") to outright sentimentality ("Bewitched, Bothered and Bewildered"). The problem is that, as a soloist, Corea greatly outdistances his three wind players (only altoist Steve Wilson stood out), so that their lengthy perorations become dead air. Other new bands were also shaky: The violinist Regina Carter, turning away from funk pabulum, exhibited energy, humor, and a vocalized timbre, but her show-off pianist banked all momentum with an opaque and incoherent cadenza on "Don't Explain," and Rodney Jones is too good a guitarist to be recycling Wes Montgomery charts. Alto saxophonist Kenny Garrett, who shared a Symphony Space bill with her, was similarly bent on recycling John Coltrane, less so in a version of "Giant Steps" than in a couple of originals; his amiable chanting ("as we travel through space"), gospel and blues licks, and handclapping cadenza didn't help.

On the other hand, Celia Cruz—in great form, her vibrato rolling *r*s like a drill—and Tito Puente couldn't be anyone else if they tried. Arturo Sandoval, opening for them, did an exciting if overlong meditation on Dizzy Gillespie, with triple-tongue scat singing, but couldn't resist synthesized strings on numbers only a record label would encourage. The Cubans, as usual, played to a packed, exuberant house at Carnegie Hall, underscoring the problem that JVC and Festival Productions face. Since not many gringos do nearly as well, Latin musicians have taken over Mel Tormé's old job of shoring up the big halls, albeit for a different audience. The mainstream is in twilight, having been pushed aside in the 1965–75 period, when jazz struggled against the rock hegemony with avant-garde and fusion. The only solution is creative producing, Wein's strong suit back when the festival represented or tried to represent a world series of the art. Other than Sonny Rollins, who won't participate, you had to wonder at the absence of Tommy Flanagan, Geri Allen, the Heath Brothers, David Murray, and two-dozen others. JVC is looking yellow around the gills—another year like this one, and it will be a miracle if anyone takes note.

[*Village Voice*, 14 July 1998]

54 ❖ The Original Dixieland One-Step (New Orleans Jazz)

The train hurtled from Texas to New Orleans through the steamiest night I'd ever experienced. The windows were sealed for some reason and nothing would alleviate the heat, not even stepping out on the platform and getting whipped by muggy breezes. The view, a few cabins and cows and horses on a flat expanse, was bleak and dull and fearsome. It was July 1963, and all that I and the other kids—a dozen 15-year-old New Yorkers touring the perimeters of the United States—knew of the deep South was fire hoses, attack dogs, and politicians who spoke, as Louis Armstrong said of Orval Faubus, like uneducated ploughboys. Sometime before morning I finally slept and was groggy when we pulled into New Orleans and were transferred to the bus that took us to our motel. Half-dozing as we pulled into the motel court, I peered out the window and saw a wall with three doors designated Men, Women, and Colored Men. On the train, I had read John Steinbeck's *Travels with Charlie*, which described Southern racism, and in New York I had watched news reports, but still—seeing this manifestation in person was chilling. I poked a friend, waking him to see the three doors, and we stared in disbelief.

That was my introduction to New Orleans. Later in our room, we decided that Colored Women must have been around the corner, though for a while we debated if segregation was different for women. In truth, we felt angry and superior: I didn't know until many years later that Duke Ellington couldn't dine in certain New York establishments and that when she tried to enter, Josephine Baker had been famously humiliated at the Stork Club. All of us on the tour were white and few if any had black friends or classmates, but we found our "cause" in civil rights. During the next couple of days, other incidents fueled our outrage and astonishment. Yet they contributed nothing to my determination to hear jazz; a music-lover who had grown bored with Top-40 radio, I was simply curious, and, besides, that's what tourists were supposed to do in New Orleans. A newspaper ad promoted a Sunday afternoon concert at a hotel. Pushing through swinging doors into a small ballroom illuminated by fancy crimson wallpaper, I thought I had stumbled into an alternate universe. If most shop windows were festooned with Confederate flags and pickaninny dolls, the sight before me was a profound and surprising solace: white and black men and women chatting and waving smokes and cocktail glasses at each other as though they were all members of the same country club. I had never seen that in New York or in movies or on TV. Even before we took our seats and the music began, I knew I'd found a new home. The band—billed as Emanuel Sayles's Silverleaf Ragtimers featuring George Lewis—and its music shot me sky high. During intermission, I stood by the bandstand—the only kid in the room—and the pianist, Joe Robichaux, beckoned me over and asked about school and how I liked the music, and then called some of the others over to say hello and sign my program. I left after two sets and my feet didn't touch the ground for half a mile.

That afternoon was vividly brought to mind while I listened to the new Mosaic set, *Atlantic New Orleans Sessions*. Its four discs, recorded between 1955 and 1962, mostly at Preservation Hall in July 1962, contain essentially the same music I heard a year later. My memories are offered as a mea culpa for any lack of objectivity. Listening to this stuff has for me the effect attributed to drowning—my life passes before my eyes. I later learned that the concert I attended was significant: a farewell party for George Lewis before his famous tour of Japan. (In 1977, I ran into Emanuel Sayles in Nice, of all places, and we talked about it.) The jazz society sponsoring the party had recently been founded to support the city's jazz musicians. Preservation Hall was only two years old. The musicians who worked with Lewis and Sayles were born at the turn of the century and many had worked outside music for most of their lives. They represented the last generation that knew jazz as a folklike functional music, a balm at picnics, parties, and funerals as well as in honky tonks—the last who knew first-hand the world of Oliver, Morton, and Armstrong. By 1970, most would be gone.

The music they played is often characterized as Dixieland, which isn't quite on the mark, not only because the sociology of semantics mandates a less-loaded term, but because the most popular Dixieland bands, from Turk Murphy to Pete Fountain, have been slick semi-virtuoso ensembles with large repertoires and addictions to hefty euphoric out-choruses. The music of Lewis and company is, by contrast, primitive, insular, local. Lewis, born in 1900, was a clarinetist who first came to prominence during the New Orleans revival of the 1940s, as partner to the regenerated Bunk Johnson. Not least because of ludicrous overstatements made then and occasionally now on behalf of just about every elderly black jazz musician who remained in New Orleans, younger fans and musicians often ridiculed their music. In 1963, when Pete Fountain and Al Hirt were at their commercial peak, many of the best records by New Orleans players could be had only through mail-order from local labels like GHB and Southland—this despite Lewis's fame, which resulted in albums for key modernist labels, including Blue Note, Riverside, and Verve.

Atlantic's Nesuhi Ertegun, a lifelong fan of traditional jazz, arrived in New Orleans a year after Preservation Hall opened and directed sessions over six days (the label took its time releasing the albums). The results are uneven, representative, and fascinating. The key argument made against these musicians by Northern critics is that they had minimal instrumental technique and remained in New Orleans because they weren't good enough to make it anywhere else. That seems a pretty fair assessment to me; of course, the same can be said of numerous country, Creole, gospel, blues, and folk musicians who represent provincial styles. The New Orleans aesthetic, as embodied by the workaday locals, is less concerned with prodigious individuality than with a collective vision that has its own rhythm, intonation, and repertoire. If most of Lewis's associates weren't good enough to make the northward trek initiated by Morton and Oliver, they demonstrated the value of an antiquarianism that boasted plenty of sincerity and authenticity. Put another way, what Lewis lacked in technical aplomb, he made up in feeling. The claim that he represented an Edenic jazz before commercialism gussied it up was foolish, but by the time Lewis died, in 1968, he was as decisive a figure in the '60s revival as Bunk had been 20 years earlier. He conjured a piquant world in which jazz could be re-imagined as community music, untouched by ambition or genius.

That said, most modernists coming to these records for the first time will be bemused by their resemblance to the avant-garde, in which short, stabbing, tenuous individual contributions combine to construct an assured, commodious, fixed canvas. In that regard, New Orleans traditionalism is kin to the Art Ensemble of Chicago or, for that matter, Sex Mob (Steven Bernstein's slide trumpet has a passing resemblance to the playing of Kid Howard or Punch Miller). When, in 1983, I reviewed the Young Tuxedo Brass Band album that leads off this collection, I mentioned blindfold tests I had conducted with friends on "Lead Me Savior," which produced guesses ranging from David Murray's Octet to Henry Threadgill's Sextet, maybe because it was assumed that only the avant-gardists pitch notes as precariously as clarinetist John Casimir does in funeral dirges that play fast and loose with quarter-tones. Yet as New Orleans parade music is overwhelmingly diatonic, it soothes even as it disturbs, at least it does in reasonable doses. These numbers—recorded outdoors in 1958—might be considered field recordings. Professor Longhair fans will find the Young Tuxedos quoting his most famous lick in "Lord, Lord, Lord."

Drummer Paul Barbarin's session was recorded in New York in 1955, and as the rhythm section is filled out by bassist Milt Hinton and guitarist Danny Barker, it has a smoothness in its thumping quite unlike the

Preservation Hall sides made seven years later, which sound relatively Arcadian. On those numbers, when drummer Joe Watkins (a marvelous singer, though he didn't get to sing at these sessions), bassist Alcide "Slow Drag" Pavageau (the pipe smoker on the Mosaic box cover), and banjoist Manny Sayles attack the four/four beat, their rhythm has the tenacity of a pneumatic drill—four thumps to every measure. Lewis liked that kind of backing, but on slower pieces (for example, "Corrine Corrina") it can have the effect of relentless stop-time. Lewis offers an excellent rendition of his signature tune, "Burgundy Street Blues," and a pretty good "Winin' Boy," though not as good as the one he made with Sayles six months later for GHB.

Two splendid vocals suggest the bizarre range of material: Punch Miller growling "Sugar Blues" and Billie Pierce lamenting "Love Songs of the Nile." The latter is rendered so personally that it sounds like generic New Orleans music, but, in fact, it is from a 1933 movie, *The Barbarian* (best remembered for Myrna Loy's bathing scene), and I'd love to know where she learned it—I don't know anyone else who did. On more familiar ground, you can hear Miller stomp the 1909 pop-tune-turned-campfire-anthem, "Casey Jones," and De De Pierce (trumpet playing husband of Billie) give a rollicking account of "Caribiribin," also from 1909, but usually associated with Harry James. Other items range from charming to acceptably excruciating. The sound is fine and so are the notes by Bruce Boyd Raeburn, though I wish Mosaic had reproduced original album jackets. There will always be Dixieland, but not bands like these. They evoke a particular time and place, and a domain of expression unlike anything else in the jazz canon.

[*Fi*, October 1998]

55 ❖ *Rousing Rabble* (*JATP*)

As Illinois Jacquet chomps down on his reed and squeals for the fifth or sixth time, you may feel a tad self-conscious about listening to *The Complete Jazz at the Philharmonic on Verve 1944–1949* (Verve) at home alone. No, the way you want to experience a good portion of these 10 CDs is to rent a hall and invite fifteen hundred or so rowdy friends to shout encouragement as the music unfolds. You might also consider recruiting someone who can leap from a balcony to add mythic resonance, and actors in pinstripes to pretend to play on stage. Of course, having gone that far you may as well junk the discs and hire real musicians. Gosh, why hasn't anyone thought of that?

JATP, so-named because the first concerts were staged at the Los Angeles Philharmonic, began in the early '40s, the brainchild of Norman Granz. The hugely successful series toured the United States until 1957, and continued in Europe for another decade. It popularized staged jam sessions and concert recordings and furthered the cause of integration in theaters (discussed in Nat Hentoff's welcome liner-note interview with the normally reclusive Granz) as well as the careers of Illinois Jacquet, Charlie Parker, Flip Phillips, Oscar Peterson, and Ella Fitzgerald, among others. Critics loathed JATP and its audience; in a 1946 piece reprinted in the 224-page CD booklet (which includes everything but the track descriptions you'd expect), the reviewer observes, "Every hydrocephalic and congenital idiot in Chicago was on hand," and declares Jacquet "the lousiest tenor in the country making over $50 a week." Musicians, too, balked at JATP excesses. Asked to appear in a finale, the majestic Coleman Hawkins, the MVP of this collection, told Granz, "I don't play numbers like that."

For 50 years, JATP has been synonymous with showboating and vulgarity in jazz, a case amply made in several performances—I had to fast-forward through some of trumpeter Shorty Sherrock's exertions. But there is much fine, even historic music here, recorded at a nexus of swing and bop and r&b that suggests a stylistic rapprochement rare in any era. JATP had something going for it beyond great music. Lots of concerts produce great music. JATP produced great audiences, hydrocephalic or not. They generated the mayhem, and their roar was the prize for which musicians like Jacquet battled. One of many previously unissued performances is an excerpt, the last two minutes of a Coleman Hawkins ballad, "The Talk of the Town," too brief to be of musical value, but worth including for the fans' rapturous yes—and for a ballad, yet.

JATP did infect the staged jam with tastelessness by no means indigenous to the form. Legendary jams of the 1930s were, by all reports, as highly musical as the Battles of the Bands at the Savoy. During the last 30 years, the numerous jams staged by George Wein (especially Radio City blowouts in the early '70s) or Dick Gibson (at his Colorado Jazz Parties) boosted musical competition in a context that honored humor, melody, and resourcefulness as much as or more than yeoman straining. Why was JATP different? In part because in those years swing was fading, bop was impending, and r&b was making trouble on the sidelines. At JATP those styles found common ground on the solid rock of 4/4, the changes hammered out without subtlety (you can't fail to hear every bridge a soloist crosses), the aggression offering a raucous alternative to dance as a way of participating.

The r&b is strongest at the beginning, in 1944, on "Lester Leaps In," as Les Paul's slashing rhythm guitar sets the stage for the good West Coast honker Jack McVea, who two years later successfully invaded Louis Jordan's territory with "Open the Door, Richard." He's far more poised than his fellow Lionel Hampton alum, Jacquet, who squeals and whistles and stomps and bellows. Call it a temper tantrum or youthful indiscretion; his solo on an unissued excerpt from "Oh, Lady Be Good" may be the tawdriest performance of his career. Other musicians keep their heads, including J. J. Johnson, laying down slablike riffs rather than twirling bebop triplets. Yet it's the pianist who consistently steals the show: Nat King Cole is the savviest soloist, and you look forward to his rhythmic aplomb, comic juxtapositions, and sly asides, just as you look away from Jacquet's tormenting variations on the same hell-raising solo.

By contrast, the infamous 1947 "Perdido" is almost well tempered. Flip Phillips begins with an avuncular jauntiness, then grates his sound as he challenges Jacquet, who has to wait his turn as Howard McGhee, bebop's answer to Roy Eldridge and at his peak in those years, builds his own drama. Jacquet snorts a few Lester Youngish choruses before charging, and avoids the gimmicks, retiring from the field without causing alarm, as though Phillips had sobered him up. Hank Jones and the underrated Woody Herman trombonist Bill Harris cajole the piece to a finish. On "Mordido," Jacquet strikes first with a genuinely exciting solo before remembering the stakes and then squealing till the crowd signals catharsis. Phillips gets the ransom, however, with a solo of monstrous tackiness—live by the rabble, die by the rabble—that agitates Jacquet to go ballistic on "Endido."

The January 28, 1946, concert with Charlie Parker and Lester Young represents JATP at its most profound and uneven. Drummer Lee Young, Lester's brother, keeps the session swinging like mad, but the overwrought altoist Willie Smith and high-note trumpeter Al Killian are out of their depths. Parker's solo on "Oh, Lady Be Good," a triumph of the blues imagination, is one of his most celebrated and influential, and, after a clubfooted bass solo that goes on for a day and a half, Young stays in the game with a solo that is phenomenal in its own right—so melodic it inspired a song, King Pleasure's "Golden Days." In the absence of jousting pugnacity, the more refined jams do not cohere. You succumb to the good parts and suffer or skip the bad ones. Parker was billed below Hawkins and Young (their promised Battle of the Tenors is thoroughly noncombative), but if you think bop was too sophisticated for the clamoring throng, listen to the thunder the first time Granz introduces Bird.

In addition to numerous non-jam sets, ranging from Billie Holiday, in gorgeous voice, to the hilarious Slim Gaillard, who brings down the house every time he announces "Groove Juice Special," the boxed set—which looks like a cross between a highway billboard and a Japanese house and demands an altar rather than a CD shelf—has many surprises. Hawk, Young, and Buck Clayton are magnificent on "I Surrender Dear." The two tenor mandarins have de facto dueling seconds on "Bugle Call Rag," in Corky Corcoran (a Hawkins man) and Babe Russin (in his Lester period). Even Jacquet calms down in their presence, demonstrating his own mastery with a forthright sprint on "Philharmonic Blues" (he can't resist that *Martha* lick, though, which on another selection Bill Harris mimics). Dizzy Gillespie is spellbinding on "Crazy Rhythm," as is Mel Powell's virtuoso extension of Teddy Wilson, whose approach shapes every pianist on hand except Meade Lux Lewis and Nat Cole, much as Charlie Christian animates all the guitarists, especially Les Paul and Dave Barbour. A 1945 set combines Hawkins, big band sidemen, and an unknown bassist named Charlie Mingus—"a recording man around town." "I do hope that we dig you rightously," an announcer says. Hawkins, superb in every appearance, can rouse rabble as well as anyone, but he does it with the tough-guy incisiveness of, say, Bogart. After a weird Buddy Cole intro on "Body and Soul," he spins variations on his variations.

Volume Six is special, despite poor sound and dated spoken commentary. It salvages surviving scraps from a 1946 Carnegie Hall program, including an exceptional Lester Young quartet set. The brightest jewel is a reading of "D.B. Blues" on which he plays two choruses for an even deeper performance than the Aladdin recording. An excerpt from "I Got Rhythm" fades in on Lester playing a superfast interpolation of the usually languid "Blue Lester." Billie Holiday sings "Fine and Mellow"—a yawp of recognition follows the first notes—with beautiful obbligato by Buck Clayton. Backed by pianist Bobby Tucker, she tosses off a beguiling 90-second Ethel Waters–styled "You're Driving Me Crazy." Another savory discovery is buried in an otherwise discursive B-flat blues: a dynamic 11-chorus solo by Roy Eldridge that may have been too breakneck and intricate to engender a riot, yet is one of the meatiest solos in the whole box.

Still, the biggest payoff of all is a re-creation of the September 1949 Carnegie Hall Concert, two-and-a-half hours of music spread over the last three discs, with Parker, Young, Eldridge, an entire set by Hawkins, Oscar Peterson's U.S. debut (backed by Ray Brown), and solo after solo by an ebullient Ella Fitzgerald, whose joy-of-bop scat and spot-on Louis Armstrong impersonation were still new to the general public. Her radiance is amplified by the crowd's astonished delight. By then, the audience ought to have suspected that the musical anarchy of the '40s was fading in favor of the precious and the cool, to be reborn half a decade later in a form it could never dig. Yet it may also have gleaned in that intoxicatingly girlish yet assured lady some continuity toward a merrily swinging future.

[*Village Voice*, 8 December 1998]

56 ❖ Old Guys Yes, Retro Never (The Best Jazz Records of 1998)

The retro vogue muddied the water a bit. Some jazz enthusiasts thought they had to proffer at least qualified support, as in: Isn't this what we fantasized—a popular revival of swing, big bands, touch dancing, and, let's just say it flat-out, an antidote to that damn rock? Indeed, if we can impeach the '60s, why not go whole hog and eradicate the '50s, where the trouble began? I call on every young person reading this to forage in granpappy's and granmammy's closets, keeping an eye peeled for round cardboard boxes—they may contain wartime fedoras and pleated skirts. Free passes to *Saving Private Ryan* and *The Thin Red Line* to the first person to locate a snood, dead or alive.

On the other hand, don't bother with old vinyl recordings, even if you can figure out how to play them, because a taste for retro will not necessarily translate into a taste for '30s and '40s jazz. Retro is exclusively dance music, like acid jazz, like second-rate orchestras of the Swing Era. It's about generation, costume, and perhaps rebellion, all fine and dandy. But a cursory examination of records by such bands as Royal Crown Revue, the Flying Neutrinos, or Indigo Swing reveal little to interest listeners. Every tempo is jitterbuggy, every riff an homage to "In the Mood," every beat laden with bass; arrangements and solos are generic, which is to say in opposition to the imperial individuality that sparked competition among the great players and bandleaders of the swing era. And the vocals are shameful. Who would have imagined that the worst vocals of 50 years ago would one day be considered forerunners? Merv Griffin and Harry Babbitt, your day has come.

"Tradition," wrote Engels, "is a great retarding force, the *vis inertiae* of history." Originality curbs production! Diana Krall excelsior! By my calculations, retro swing should lead to retro r&b in about 2003, followed by retro bop in 2007, retro r&r in 2017, retro folk in 2021, retro rock in 2029, and retro retro in 2056, which will start up the cycle all over again. Plan your wardrobe accordingly and beware the likelihood of retro disco, retro new age, and retro smooth jazz.

Having said that, it was a '70s sort of year, and not half bad at that. That period was notable not only for a generation of musicians of instantly identifiable originality, but also for the return of masters who had taken five during the years of peace and love. Among the latter were Tommy Flanagan, who made one of the best instrumental CDs of the year, and Andy Bey, who made one of the best vocal CDs. A theatrical epiphany came late in Warren Leight's *Sideman*, a superior hybrid of *The Glass Menagerie* and *Really the Blues*, when three sidemen, relaxing during a break at a Lester Lanin gig, play a tape of "A Night in Tunisia," from Clifford Brown's last recorded gig, discovered and released in 1973. They just sit there and listen to the entire tape, quiet but for appreciative nudges, and at the performance I caught, the audience gave Clifford a major ovation. Joao Gilberto, whose last stateside hit was *Amoroso/Brasil* 20 years ago, offered the year's most memorable recital, anomalously at JVC, which was also notable for stirring returns to form by Clark Terry and Al Grey, the latter playing from a wheelchair but laying down a gauntlet on the merits of authentic plunger-mute incantation as opposed to the ersatz kind. Back in 1977, Grey left Basie—one year before Flanagan left Ella—to spur the mainstream revival, which was the obverse of retro though you could certainly dance to it (full disclosure: he played at my wedding). Capping the year was the dedication of the Louis Armstrong House and Archives at Queens College, an exuberant, moving, and long-awaited triumph for the inventor of American music, who died in 1971, less honored then than he is today.

Similarly, the year's best concert, and a moving event in its own right, was David Murray's big band investigation of "The Obscure Works of Duke Ellington and Billy Strayhorn," at Aaron Davis Hall on December 5, drawing an early bead on the coming centennial brouhaha, which may get as repetitious as last year's Gershwin party, though I don't expect to complain. Murray's all-star big band, augmented by a full-bodied and rhythmically adept string section, was arranged mostly by James Newton and conducted seriatim by Newton, Murray, Craig Harris, and John Purcell. With smashing solos by those four as well as Hugh Ragin, Hilton Ruiz, Gary Valente, Joe Bowie, and Alex Harding, the performances radiated the unmistakable fruits of adequate rehearsal time, casting an anteretro spell of individual empowerment as everyone knuckled down for the greater cause of kaleidoscopic charts based on the piano trio *Money Jungle* and revised gems like "Northern Lights," "Praise God," and "Blue Pepper." As Murray declaimed "Chelsea Bridge" with strings, one could hardly resist pretty thoughts of Ben Webster. Carmen Bradford, whose excessive melisma with Basie was irksome, found her own voice on "African Flower." It's been far too long since we heard a Newton flute cadenza—the lavish harmonics, staccato mischief, and virtuoso sheen, as on his ravishing adaptation of "Blood Count."

Still, the surprise solos of the evening were by two utility players, John Stubblefield, one of the first AACM guys to arrive here, in 1971, and James Spaulding, who'd been playing sharp for a decade. Spaulding's alto saxophone obbligato and heated cadenza on "Warm Valley" were imbued with a glowing confidence heightened by his uncharacteristically centered pitch. "Such Sweet Thunder" opened with the expressive trumpet of Hugh Ragin, who lately seems incapable of playing a dull note, but Stubblefield's tenor took the piece into JATP realm with a foot-stomping peroration that had people whooping. Trombonist Gary Valente—with his grittier, blaring Trummy Young sound—followed with a fitting reference to *Martha*, which is to say "Flying Home." The evening was suffused with old-home-week qualities, as was Sam Rivers's big band reunion at Sweet Basil. Still, the nostalgia had less to do with remembrance than with longing for players who can announce who they are the minute they stand up.

For it wasn't only retro that cast an assembly-line pall over much that passed for jazz. The record companies continued to sign the young and innocent, musicians schooled in classic records and imported directly from the classroom into the studio—a generation that thinks the point is to mimic the titans rather than find their own wings on the tarmac. So on disc after disc, we have musicians doing a little Sonny or Trane or Wes or Cannonball or Miles, or worse, succumbing to producer themes, reclamations of music that the producers grew up with. How else to explain the weirdness of Nicholas Payton following *Gumbo Nouveau*, the duets with Doc Cheatham, and a superb 1997 JVC turn with *Payton's Place*, which sounds like a 1962 Blue Note album released by Verve in 1998. Blue Note's Bob Belden showed how to imaginatively revisit the past in the "Blue Note Now as Then" volume in the 14-disc 60th-celebration, *The Blue Note Years*, but no label seems to recall the importance of apprenticeship recording, even though it was Alfred Lion who showed that in a post–touring-band world, one brought leaders along by training them as sidemen. Sherman Irby made a striking return with *Big Mama's Biscuits* after his disastrous debut, while the gifted young vibist Stefon Harris inadvertently proved that knowing one's way around a recording studio is not an inborn talent, as did Marcus Printup and Gregory Tardy before him. As for Impulse, revived only to fold into a new merger, it continued to make a mockery of its old credo, "the new wave of jazz," and won't be missed.

Still, some good, possibly great, records were issued last year. Here are a baker's dozen, in no particular order:

1–2. Tommy Flanagan, *Sunset and the Mocking Bird* (Blue Note). It was foolish not to banner the Village Vanguard, because this is one of those magical albums that live up to the live-at-the-Vanguard legend. The pianist's solos are spare and sculpted, hammered like fine silver, and Peter Washington and Lewis Nash have the kind of motor nerve responsiveness of Billy Higgins. The tunes include two each by Dizzy Gillespie, Tom MacIntosh, and Thad Jones, whose "Let's" is a riot, but the subtext is Monk, signified on the side. Martial Solal's *Just Friends* (Dreyfus), with Gary Peacock and Paul Motian, is an overdue opportunity to wallow in the razzle-dazzle of the genre-proof pianist who won this year's Jazzpar Award.

3–4. David S. Ware, *Go See the World* (Columbia). Maybe his best record, in any case endlessly bracing, yet rife with serpentine details, not least in the reflexively witty rhythm section—Matthew Shipp, William Parker, Susie Ibarra—which recalls the way Jaki Byard, Richard Davis, and Alan Dawson once covered the waterfront (as on Prestige's recently reissued *The Jaki Byard Experience*). The Ware threesome is out front on Matthew Shipp's *The Multiplication Table* (hatOLOGY), including a thinking-out-loud breakdown of "Take the A Train."

5. Gustav Mahler / Uri Caine, *Primal Light* (Winter & Winter). Far more than an exercise in jazzing the classics, this is an idiosyncratic attempt to reclaim Mahler as a suppressed Jewish klez, whose charmingly woebegone minor-key melodies—wrested from aggressively confident major-theme opuses—engender swinging improvisations by a crew that includes Dave Douglas, Don Byron, Joey Baron, and a hand-drumming cantor.

6–8. B. B. King, *Blues on the Bayou* (MCA). Self-produced by King at 73, this is an ur-B.B. disc, recommendable as a starter or refresher course, with no apologies to *Live at the Regal* or *Blues Is King*. With neat Phil Marshall string arrangements amplifying the band and James Sells Toney's rude keyboards, King's guitar is serenely cushioned and no one is singing better than he does on "Blues Man" or "If I Lost You." Mary Cleere Haran isn't a jazz singer, but *Pennies from Heaven* (Angel), her best record to date, splits the difference, suggesting how a retro attitude can be redeemed by respect for authenticity. Maybe he was just ahead of his time, but Andy Bey is on a roll with *Shades of Bey* (Evidence), his voice dark and grudging and mysterious.

9. Sonny Rollins, *Global Warming* (Milestone). I know and at first I agreed, but I couldn't keep away, until finally I realized that there is

nothing seeming about those seemingly anarchic solos in which every phrase begins and ends somewhere other than where you expect, grinding through detours along the way. The facade may be neat—as is the gracefully adroit Stephen Scott—but the spine trembles with the thrill of anarchy.

10. Cecil Taylor, *Qu'a* (Cadence). Until I heard this performance, recorded at Sweet Basil in March, I underestimated how organic this quartet is. Taylor moves in and out of the lead in close accord with Harri Sjostrum, Dominic Duval, and Jackson Krall, insistently reflective, as though he were undergoing a personal passage surprising even to him.

11–12. Joe Lovano, *Trio Fascination* (Blue Note) and Randy Weston, *Khepera* (Verve). It may be tiresome to list them year after year, each time with a warranty that the latest is the best, but if these aren't, they're close. Lovano, with Elvin Jones and Dave Holland, has rarely sounded happier—those who thought Chu Berry had a lock on "Ghost of a Chance" will have to think again. Much as I admired Weston's *Saga*, the ferocity of the latest African Rhythms foray goes another step, especially "Niger Mystery" and "Mystery of Love."

13. Ruby Braff, *You Can Depend on Me* (Arbors). Nat Hentoff long ago observed that as trumpet players grow older they sound more like Louis Armstrong. Braff began as an Armstrong man, developing a prim, glimmering, nuanced take of his own, yet he has never sounded more maturely in his thrall than here, backed by a quartet (including the late Bob Haggart) that knows better than to get in his way.

Betty Carter and Frank Sinatra, rest in peace.

[*Village Voice*, 12 January 1999]

57 ❖ *A Bottomless Well (Duke Ellington)*

Duke Ellington liked to claim he won his job at the Cotton Club in December 1927 because he showed up three hours late for the audition, as did the owner, who heard only Ellington and none of his rivals. After five years of touring or working in arson-prone saloons, it was the luckiest of breaks. Radio broadcasts transmitted from the gangster-owned, segregated (blacks on stage, whites at the tables) Harlem nightclub were relayed across the country and ultimately the world, bringing him instant recognition. The long engagement enabled Ellington to double the size of his orchestra, encouraged a daring prolificacy, and provided him with a daunting apprenticeship working with top-flight choreographers, songwriters, dancers, singers, comics, set designers, and other professionals involved in developing the Cotton Club's slick and sexy revues.

Ellington responded with a wry, insinuating music—erotic, exotic, and, at once, ironic and ingenious. He invented his own instrumental voicings and found uncanny soloists whose virtuoso embellishments seemed to burble from the ravishing brew like the nighttime chatter of an urban jungle. Some considered Ellington's music as salacious as the serpentine dancing it accompanied, but music lovers in and out of the academy heard in it a fresh, audacious musical language and a genius for sultry melodies and startling harmonies. Ellington tapped into something recondite, almost occult, yet accessible—unshackling characters as shadowy as "The Mooche" and as seductive as "Black Beauty," while issuing injunctions on the order of "Rockin' in Rhythm" and "It Don't Mean a Thing If It Ain't Got That Swing."

By the time I discovered Ellington's music, in 1963, he had been leading his orchestra for 40 years, few of which found him just marking time. That became evident to me when I bought my first Ellington albums and realized that immersion in his music generated a mystery that could be solved only through obsession; the variety was overwhelming. Knowing nothing about him except that he was a key figure in a music with which I was newly fascinated, I began with the gorgeously expansive arrangements of 1950's *Ellington Masterpieces*, thinking "masterpieces" was an advisable place to start in anyone's education. Wanting to hear more, I picked up RCA Vintage compilations that covered the '20s and '40s, Columbia LPs from the '50s, collaborations with modernists John Coltrane and Charles Mingus in the '60s, suites, symphonies, dance records, collections drawn from his pop standards (from "Mood Indigo" to "Satin Doll"), and the then-new monuments, like *Far East Suite, And His Mother Called Him Bill*, and the Sacred Concerts. Here's the punch line: Even after accumulating a hundred Ellington LPs, it seemed to me that each revealed something the others did not.

Yet none conveyed the adventure of hearing the band live. In addition to the extraordinary charm and practiced wit of Ellington himself, his concerts revealed intricacies in his music that the highest of hi-fidelity recreations failed to capture. The Ellington band appeared in the mid-60s one summer afternoon in New York's Central Park, on a provisional stage in the unceremonious setting of a few hundred folding chairs. No one seemed to mind that a few of us wandered right up to the raised apron. Standing there, a few feet from the reed section, I heard something I've never experienced with any other orchestra—something that gets to the heart of the Ellington mystique. While all five saxophones performed in perfect unison, I could hear each distinct voice. They blended and yet did not blend. I heard perfect organ-like chords and, at the same time, the distinct virile edge of Harry Carney's baritone saxophone, the piping wiles of Johnny Hodges's alto, and the foggy burr of Paul Gonsalves's tenor, among the others. It was magic, a unified front that honored the individual—an Ellington epiphany.

That same year, coincidentally, the Pulitzer Committee rejected the unanimous recommendation of its music jury to present Ellington with a special prize honoring his life's work. Ellington's much-quoted comeback was, "Fate is being kind. Fate doesn't want me to be too famous too young." One of the singular ironies of his career is that his immense celebrity never compromised his tenaciously protected privacy. He was omnipresent, playing one-nighters in every conceivable venue, from the waystations of the fine arts to 4-H clubs to palaces, but when he died, in 1974, at 75, newspaper obituary writers did not know if he was married or to whom. He was as unknowable as Salinger or Pynchon, but without making a fuss. Perhaps he maintained the veil so successfully because his music was so elegantly illuminating of himself, of the rest of us lost in its glistening rhythms, and of the country it vigorously honored.

Late in life, Ellington wrote, "I live in the realm of art and have no monetary interests," yet there was nothing monastic about his art. He eschewed ivy tower experiments and inside curves, yet innovated ceaselessly, attempting every idiom, including opera and musical theater. He wrote for and about people, shrewdly assessing their responses on dance floors and in concert halls, yet he was also the first to break the three-minute tyranny of the 78-rpm record; the first to compose specifically for the LP; one of the first to create a television oratorio. He belonged to no particular fashion or epoch—the Swing Era was a mere 10-year blip in his 50-year road trip. During a few months in 1959, Ellington wrote the gentle *Queen's Suite* and the crisp score to Otto Preminger's *Anatomy of a Murder*. The film score revved up a popular film and was heard by millions. The suite, a gift to Elizabeth II, was for her ears only; Ellington privately pressed two copies, delivering one to the Queen, and no one outside his inner circle knew of its existence until two years after his death, when it was finally released and acclaimed a masterwork. Imagine being that certain the tap would never run dry. Ellington was that certain. And it never did.

[*American Greats*, edited by Robert A. Wilson
and Stanley Marcus, Public Affairs, 1999]

58 ❖ *Jaki Byard, 1922–1999*

Lea was two months old the first time we took her to a concert—Jaki Byard's 1989 recital at Weill Hall. He sat at the piano and played a 10-note discord. She whimpered and looked distressed. But he followed instantly with a lambent stride passage. She raised her head, smiled, then fell into an hour's sleep. I knew the feeling. Jaki never put me to sleep, but he always made me smile and frequently knocked me out. Listening to him was like turning on a tap in which all the strains of modern piano, from James P. Johnson to Cecil Taylor, flowed in one luscious rush. Yet having described the most obvious aspect of his playing, I feel obliged to backpedal from the old saw that his music stood for no more than a promethean eclecticism. His style was his own and unmistakable, by turns hard, percussive, witty, sentimental, sardonic, whimsical, subversive, ebullient, anguished. Like Sonny Rollins, he could fake you out—making you think, for example, that those corny arpeggios were a joke, so that you didn't know whether to feel embarrassed or grateful at the emotions he extracted from them.

Jaki died February 11, at 76, of a gunshot wound, in his home in Hollis, Queens, and rumors abound—an intruder, someone personally close, suicide. I don't believe the last, though he was hit hard by the death a few years back of his wife, Louise, his devoted and amusingly acerbic companion of some four decades. He left two daughters, Denise and Diane, whose names and occasional singing are known to admirers of his compositions and recordings; a son, Gerald; and a passel of grandsons and great-grandsons. He also left an enormous number of students past and present, both institutional—he taught eight years at the New England Conservatory of Music, four at the Hart School of Music, three at Harvard, among other affiliations—and private, including Marty Ehrlich, D. D. Jackson, Jason Moran, and a young musical therapist named Vanessa Kaster, who came to learn improvisation and recalled last week, "Every particle of him was music. Sometimes the lessons would last three hours. His clock wasn't set to real time, only to music."

I studied with him in 1974, when he was part of the faculty at Martin Williams's critics colloquium at the Smithsonian; but I'd been studying his music long before that. In the mid-'60s, he was one of the pianists who regularly played the Village Gate mezzanine. If you were short on cash, you could sit at the bar and nurse a beer through several sets and no one bothered you. I loved trying to follow his stream-of-consciousness forays, medleys of songs and techniques—never dull, never indifferent.

He was a master of stride, r&b, ballads, and free improvisation. He was a great Garner, Tatum, and Hines player; these were not affectations, but integral to what he knew and believed about piano. When Vanessa asked him about stride, he said it was no big deal, that you could find it in classical music, that it was all part of the piano repertoire. Still, what I liked best was what I came to think of as Jaki's core style, a driven bebop linearity that ranged over the whole keyboard with a fierce purposefulness, every note struck like a hammer. He could make a piano thunder. But soon as you thought you knew the song, he turned the corner and you were in another country.

One night at the Gate, a little juiced-up Billy Eckstine wannabe who sang as "Junior Parker" (his real name was Arthur Daniels) and had no fixed address, just an oversized overcoat, walked in and asked to sing. Jaki shrugged, and soon Junior was there every night, arriving in the middle of the set to wail "Getting to Know You" in an impossibly slow, cello-like arrangement. Jaki included him and it on his next album, the irresistible *Freedom Together!*, after which Junior disappeared. On a college break, I went to the Gate to find Jaki no longer in residence, and asked if he was playing anywhere. "Oh, Jaki's at the 82 Club," someone said, giving me directions to the East Village. When I finally found the joint I was greeted by a midget transvestite who said he'd never heard of Jaki Byard but that I was certainly welcome; I stomped out, annoyed at the joke played on me. Years later, I told Jaki. He said, "Man, you should've come in. Those were nice people. Actually, that was one of my better gigs."

Which was probably true. He was briefly in the rotation at the Village Vanguard, but after 1970 I mostly heard him in restaurants or one-shot concerts—among them, encounters with David Murray, Greg Osby, and Archie Shepp. In later years, he was inconsistent, sometimes noodling in introspective meditation, waiting—Rollins-like—for the muse to jump-start him. He looked increasingly like a bemused bear, his hair a straightened thatch sprouting around his head, his face round and line-free, his expression quizzical. He loved big bands more than anything—he had come up with Herb Pomeroy in Boston (despite more than three decades in Queens, he never lost an iota of his accent), toured the country as pianist and arranger with Maynard Ferguson, and worked closely with Charles Mingus (he arranged much of the 1964 Monterey concert). Occasionally, he subbed for an ailing Duke Ellington. Incredibly for a guy who struggled to get trio work, he organized an orchestra, the Apollo Stompers—named, he was quick to point out, for the Greek god, not the theater. His final recording, made last spring and as yet unreleased, was his third with the big band.

Jaki will be best remembered, however, for the astonishing records he cut between 1961 and 1972, mostly for Prestige, though he insisted his personal favorite was a solo date for Futura in Paris (1971, never released here); and for piloting Richard Davis and Alan Dawson in one of the best rhythm sections ever assembled. If he never acquired a commensurate following, he was long a critical favorite and he had a loyal and imaginative producer in Don Schlitten, who assembled that rhythm section, in 1963, for the first of the Booker Ervin "Book" LPs. Like Armstrong's Hot 5 or Morton's Red Hot Peppers, it existed only in the studio, but over the next decade it proved a telling alternative to HerbieRonTony as a combustible, cohesive, swinging unit that never tempered the individuals involved—you couldn't believe what was going on in that cauldron.

Many of the albums were out of print, some for more than 15 years. But the Prestiges are slowly returning, one by one, and they merit reassessment. Jaki was the kind of musician who played "Giant Steps" slow (*Here's Jaki*) and "Lush Life" fast (*Out Front*). On *Hi-Fly*, he disguises the title tune with a full-bore rhythmic build-up and makes James P. Johnson's "Yamekraw" sound modern. He was an exceptionally versatile and deep blues player, as you can glean by comparing "Searchlight," "Out Front," and "Freedom Together." The out-of-tune piano at a place called Lennie's on the Turnpike inspired him (as did saxophonist Joe Farrell) to one bashing climax after another on the two volumes called *Live!* (a third volume was never released, but the complete tapes would make a helluva memorial). For the full Byard effect, though, you must follow him into the twilight zone of *Freedom Together!* (Schlitten liked exclamation points); *On the Spot!* (the title track is brutal hard bop while "Alexander's Ragtime Band" is r&b); the dazzling *Jaki Byard Experience* (with Rahsaan, a friskier companion to Kirk's own *Rip, Rig, and Panic*); and the staggering *Sunshine of My Soul*, where his assimilation of Taylor is given free reign on "Sunshine" and "Trendsition Zildjian," his fluent Tatum chops sweep through "Chandra," and his own bopping proclivities erupt on "Diane's Melody." *Jaki Byard with Strings!* has "Cat's Cradle Conference Rag," in which the leader plays "Take the A Train," Ray Nance plays "Jersey Bounce," George Benson plays "Darktown Strutters Ball," Richard Davis plays "Intermission Riff," Ron Carter plays "Desifinado," and Alan Dawson plays "Ring Dem Bells"—at the same time. A few complicated arrangements notwithstanding, that album is mostly an upbeat jam. His most resonant work is to be found on the lavishly varied recitals, *Solo Piano, There'll Be Some Changes Made, Duet!* (an ardent pairing with Earl Hines), *To Them—To Us, At Maybeck*. Perhaps, someday, even that Futura album he loved will cross the Atlantic. Jaki gave up waiting long ago; me, never.

[*Village Voice*, 16 March 1999]

59 ❖ *Out of the Vinyl Deeps (Record Rarities)*

All music lovers become record lovers and many record lovers become collectors. Records approximate Malraux's museum without walls, offering an inexpensive way to pursue not only masterworks and favorites, but also oddities that fill the side galleries where dilettantes rarely venture. Before the late 1930s, old records were relegated to bargain labels; there was little call for the technocracy to cede a part of its holdings to nostalgia—even movie studios assumed that yesterday's productions had no future. Now there is a respectable market that buys only old, supporting an endless stream of reissues. Yet the vaults remain jam-packed, timed to burst open on that increasingly distant day when the vintage stuff goes public domain (as it already has in Europe), a day, sadly, that Congress is determined to forestall as long as "special interest" lobbies grease its wheels.

In the interim, record companies go about their business with the cryptic motives that have long made them so beloved of music lovers—numerous jazz masterpieces remain unavailable, while relative obscurities bob to the surface. Fortunately, some of those obscurities really do deserve a second chance. They may not be masterpieces, but they're at least as good as and more revealing than the bottom-drawer output of many socially condoned savants.

I revel in them—albums I once bypassed by artists I had not heard of or did not like; albums that disappeared so quickly I never caught up; albums I coveted but couldn't afford. With mono LPs going for $2.49 in the mid-'60s (a buck more for stereo), and no chance to audition them in stores or on radio, one made choices. So until Koch began leasing LPs from their indifferent owners, I never heard, for example, *These Are My Roots: Clifford Jordan Plays Leadbelly*, a 1966 Atlantic that remained sub-rosa even after Jordan became prominent a few years later. Unlike anything in his oeuvre or in jazz, it's a shrewd, authoritative take on a hero of the '60s folk boom that never sounds patronizing or touristy.

Deploying a septet for diverse effects (the great rhythm section of Cedar Walton, Richard Davis, and Tootie Heath is augmented by Chuck Wayne's banjo), the ensemble can sound dense or stark, dark and brooding or big and bright, and Jordan's tenor saxophone has rarely been better framed. Even the unknown woman singer on two tracks, Sandra Douglass, is first-rate.

A more recondite Koch reclamation is *The Most Happy Fella*, by the Jazz Modes, a 1957 Atlantic session I'd never heard of. The Jazz Modes lasted on and off for four years, a collaboration between Julius Watkins, who could make a French horn roar and sputter like the usual jazz brasses, and Charlie Rouse, a cult figure despite all those years with Monk and Sphere; people dig him or shrug their shoulders. I love his soft-shoe sound and jittery phrasing; his solos here are frustratingly short, but enough to warrant attention. Thanks to Shelly Manne's *My Fair Lady* bonanza, everyone was jazzing Broadway back then. Some chose well (Oscar Peterson's *Fiorello* or Cannonball's *Fiddler on the Roof*), while others were saddled with notorious flops (Ellington obliged to deal with *All-American*, which did produce a great song in "Once upon a Time," or Roland Hanna trying to build a career on *Destry Rides Again*). The Jazz Modes chose a hit, but didn't record until after it closed. The album is very low-key (East Coast cool), but the charts are clever (notably "Standing on the Corner" and "Like a Woman"), and the quintet swings with pithy solos; an unknown singer mucks up only one track.

Although a few prominent film scorers were permitted to go into the studio and record de facto suites, most original movie soundtracks, even good ones, consist of a tuneful theme or two and lots of truncated cues. That problem is alleviated on MGM's reissue of Johnny Mandel's *I Want to Live* by the inclusion of the Gerry Mulligan septet recordings that were excerpted in the film and issued separately. (The two albums combined run just short of an hour.) In his later scores, Mandel recycled variations on a single popular theme (e.g., "The Shadow of Your Smile" in *The Sandpiper*), but for his first try, Mandel marshaled his vast orchestrating chops to keep *I Want to Live* edgy and unpredictable. Brief solos by Joe Maini, Bill Holman, and Jack Sheldon enliven a few extended cues, but the stunner is "Stakeout"—a four-minute percussion quartet that anticipates Ellington's "Maletoba Spank," not to mention M'Boom. Mulligan appeared in the film but not on the track proper; the pieces Mandel arranged for Mulligan's small group with Art Farmer, prefiguring the ensuing edition of his quartet and the Concert Jazz Band, are a significant, long neglected part of his canon.

One major jazz figure who was long a mystery to me is violinist, singer, and composer Stuff Smith. I liked just about everything I heard by him, but never found much to hear. Although he began recording in 1928 with Alphonse Trent (terrific vocal on "After You've Gone"), wrote a popular hit for Louis Armstrong ("It's Wonderful") and a novelty for himself that made him a 52nd Street star ("I'se A-Muggin' "), and died in 1967, after relocating to Europe, available records were few: the lightning exchanges with Nat Cole on *After Midnight*, the pairing with Ben Webster on Ella's *Ellington Songbook*, uneven albums made in Europe— I recall a Violin Summit performance of "It Don't Mean a Thing" on which he was cut pretty badly by Grappelli, Asmussen, and Ponty. The celebrated Verve albums were impossible to find until a few years ago, when Verve reissued the sessions with Dizzy Gillespie and Oscar Peterson. Mosaic's *The Complete Verve Stuff Smith Sessions* should trigger a reevaluation. Nearly half the material on four CDs was never previously released.

Midway through the second cut, "The Blues I Knew," I was a goner. Smith named Joe Venuti and Louis Armstrong as influences, and his blend of violin agility and sweep with brusque trumpetlike linearity, propped by a truckload of riffs, sets him apart, as do his nuanced blues sound and relentless—at times dizzying—swing. He crackles with melody, his own (the first 13 selections, all previously unissued, are originals) and everyone else's. His one failing is an eagerness to quote—even the theme of "Live and You'll Learn" is a succession of borrowings. As the first to amplify his violin, Smith might be considered kin to Charlie Christian, a parallel underscored by his harmonic daring, including octaves that prefigure Wes Montgomery and tritones beyond bop, let alone swing. The material with Gillespie is an apogee of mutual inspiration. On the 11-minute "Rio Pakistan," taken at a loping tempo, the complicity in style and mood is uncanny. More surprising is a restored 1959 session, from which all tracks with an unknown woman singer were originally excised; the singer was Shirley Horn, at 25 and quite wonderful.

While Mosaic specializes in completist editions of postwar musicians, TOM, another mail-order operation (in San Mateo, CA), patrols the outer limits of prewar arcana—dance bands, radio singers, studio orchestras. The latest discovery of TOM's George Morrow, who did the archival restoration for minstrel Emmett Miller's Columbia sides and a definitive three-volume edition of Frank Trumbauer, is Charlie Palloy (possibly a pseudonym), a singer and guitarist who disappeared after recording for Crown in 1932 and 1933. Those were years when the record industry almost collapsed, when labels merged and dissolved so frantically that by 1934, only two were standing—Victor, protected by the RCA network, and ARC, a holding company that picked up Columbia, Brunswick, and others at fire-sale prices. The business turned around after Decca reduced discs from 75 to 35 cents, forcing its rivals to do likewise. Before that, bargain labels offered knockoffs of pop tunes by unknown performers using stock arrangements and cheap pressings, sold in chain stores like Woolworth's for a quarter. Crown, however, was pressed by Victor, so the sound was excellent. And Palloy was a hack with a difference. Though hired to cover Bing Crosby, he was the sort of singer Crosby ran out of town, yet he had a snarky charm and a savvy taste in songs (he covered "It Don't Mean a Thing" before Ellington's ink was dry). Still, it's his guitar that makes him worthwhile; annotator Allan Dodge calls him a "cut-rate Crosby with a built-in Eddie Lang." At a time when guitar improvisers were rarer than good baritones, how did a member of the tribe that included Lang, Lonnie Johnson, and Bobby Sherwood avoid history's radar? He croons, he scats, he swings, he winks—beating Bill Murray to his lounge act by 45 years. And he makes you wonder what else Woolworth's was selling for 25 cents.

[*Village Voice*, 20 April 1999]

60 ❖ *Prisoners of the Past (JVC 1999)*

Midway through the week, the JVC Jazz Festival kicked into life at a sedate homage to Charlie Parker's romance with strings, when the featured soloist, James Moody, bounded into an exultant "Cherokee," shaking off the ensemble like a great swan beating the wet from its wings. He soared, dove, and crested. The rhythm section floated him on the song's hammered harmonies, inspiring him on his tear while the resting chamber players looked slightly glazed with wonder. When he finally looped the last loop into a mocking shave-and-a-haircut finish, the crowd levitated. We talk about bop as though every postwar jazzman who plays changes with a beat enjoys equal access to its mysteries, but in fact few can essay the music's curvy melodic purity and drive of 50 years ago, when it was mint, daring, and not a little unbelievable. Though Moody was one of the first to augment and even parody the style, he never lost the knack—he just doesn't go for broke that often.

Moody was also one of the first to record with strings, two years after Parker; the subject in 1951 was "Cherokee" and he didn't do much with the piece that Parker had made his personal anthem. When Moody finally put his mark on the song in the 1960s, he adapted it as a virtuoso flute vehicle. So those who heard his "Cherokee" on alto last week will likely remember it, as there is no equivalent on records. And if you plodded through the whole festival, which was consumed with the past, you could not help but mark the distinction between art under glass and art under the gun. Stringing along with the Classical Heritage Ensemble, Moody was a choirboy; under-rehearsed, tentative, and polite to a fault. Marking his own time—on quartet spin-offs of "Lover Man" and "Parker's Mood," too—he was a 74-year-old terror.

The Parker-with-strings concert embodied everything about JVC that is worthy and everything that ought to be a lot better. On the surface, it was quixotically generous, an attempt to revisit Parker's most controversial venture. The execution, however, was fatally halfhearted. The Ensemble, directed by Kermit Moore and bolstered by an enthusiastic Mike LeDonne rhythm section and James Fiorello's oboe, knew the notes better than the tempos, which were lackluster, while the unprepared soloist was inhibited by the complicated entrances and exits, missing a cue on "April in Paris" (LeDonne smartly filled the vacuum). Worse, the numbers were poorly chosen; four were genteel Jimmy Carroll arrangements from the first Parker strings session, the fifth an overwritten "I'll Remember April" by Joe Lippman, whose work Parker preferred. Not that more Lippman would have improved things. The opportunity lost here was to do something far more innovative: resurrect the superior pieces for strings that Parker commissioned from George Russell, Jimmy Mundy, and Gerry Mulligan, but never formally recorded, and secure the proper rehearsal time. A record company might have—should have, I mean—assumed the additional costs.

Jazz lovers have long since grown inured to close-enough approximations of ideas that look good on paper and falter in performance. But how much collective shrugging is permissible when jazz repertory assumes almost total dominance, as if it were no longer an option, but an oppressive movement: from swing to bop to post-historical reclamations? Everyone from Cassandra Wilson and Ken Peplowski to Geri Allen and Branford Marsalis had history on the brain, some of it fairly recent, and so did audiences who like nothing better than to hear what they've heard before. The 1999 JVC Jazz Festival was George Wein's 45th as a producer and my 31st as an attendee, and I can't recall a stranger one. It was not awful (as some were)—just gray, overcast, nostalgic yet unreflective.

There were moments. There are always moments. But for reasons I suspect not even Wein can explain, a festival assumes a character, a sum total of its parts, and this one—at least the part that was played out in the major halls—struck a tired note of surrender, to what I'm not sure. Between Bell Atlantic and JVC, between new music and old, a gaping hole opened that was once filled by the mainstream, the jazz lingua franca that everyone used to know. I should have caught the Joshua Redman and Diana Krall concert, which by all reports answered that need for twentysomethings (as the competing Dave Holland and Brad Mehldau didn't quite manage for me). Mired in the past, the festival made me feel like a frequent visitor to a museum that never changes its paintings.

Miles Davis is dead eight years, and he figured, directly or not, in three concerts. Cassandra Wilson performed selections from her Miles Davis tribute album with a sextet directed by her bassist, Lonnie Plaxico. In a welcome change of attitude, she played to the audience, which responded gratefully, but moments of genuine intensity—a compelling "Blue in Green"—were few. The ensemble's soft rhythmic scrim was one palm tree too many. An absence of edgy four-beat swing and colorful harmonies enervated pieces in which her throbbing chants provided the sole signs of emotion. A steady diet of scalar improvisations in eight, tarted up with atmospheric percussion, will definitely take off weight. Shirley Horn, who was also scheduled to muse over Miles, elected not to, except maybe for "I Fall in Love too Easily," and she was elegantly poised in vignettes she made of signature Billie and Peggy songs— "Foolin' Myself," "How Am I to Know?," "Fever." But she, too, was resolute about avoiding an adrenalin rush or even a wakeup call.

A steadier intensity pervaded "Kind of Blue at 40." It began anxiously if fittingly with "Milestones" and "On Green Dolphin Street," which offered little justification for another retread of Miles beyond Vincent Herring's boisterous alto and Geri Allen's robust chords. Yet the set devoted to *Kind of Blue* itself managed, at its best, to produce something like suspense. We know the record so well we forget the original challenges imposed by the pithy choruses of "Blue in Green" or the amorphous form of "Flamenco Sketches." Instead of blindly following decisions made by Davis and company, Allen, Herring, Wallace Roney, and Ravi Coltrane tiptoed through those minefields, focused by brevity, and recovered a measure of spontaneity. Roney inevitably suggested Miles (he stuck with that D-minor scale on "So What"), Herring attacked with an openness redolent of Cannonball Adderley, and Allen nodded toward Wynton Kelly on "Freddie Freeloader." Yet the immediacy of the task kept them on point. Ravi Coltrane scrupulously avoided his father's ghost and jubilantly waltzed through "All Blues," the one piece with a real sextet head on it. Jimmy Cobb, who played on the original, interlocked with Buster Williams, who took liberties with "So What" but firmly grounded "Blue in Green." The six players fulfilled a primary tenet of jazz rep, making a sacred text human without diminishing it.

Wayne Shorter and Herbie Hancock recalled Miles only because they cannot avoid doing so. Those who knew their duet album, *1 + 1*, were less disappointed than those who expected the Miles Davis Quintet of 1965 minus three. And even they were given the unexpected bonus of a closing "Footprints"—just the melody, not the blues grid. Shorter produced the most apposite quote of the festival when he interpolated a reference to "Rockabye Baby," though it was appreciated only by those not already asleep. Actually, he played quite well, his flat broadsword of a sound on soprano rolling over Hancock's progressive—le mot juste—chords, particularly on his haunting "Aung San Suu Kyi." But like Horn, the twosome knew but one tempo, which like Wilson didn't exactly canter. Still, it was preferable to a closing set by Roy Hargrove's quintet that sounded like a rejected 1958 hard bop album. Only pianist Larry Willis seemed attentive—maybe "Rockabye Baby" did more damage than we thought.

And so it went. Ken Peplowski had taken his Benny Goodman band on tour, so lack of rehearsal could not explain its by-the-numbers approach to 1930s arrangements, mostly by Fletcher Henderson. Randy Sandke and Loren Schoenberg were the liveliest soloists—they are rare among swing revivalists in sounding comfortable in their own skins— along with Peplowski, especially in a duet with Dick Hyman, who stepped out of the audience to press him on "Tiger Rag." But the rhythm section was plodding and the introverted precision of the winds gave no inkling of what made people whoop when this music was new. The newest repertory was heard at a tribute to the much missed pianist Kenny Kirkland, feted in an ambitious evening by Branford Marsalis, with cameos by Sting and Harry Connick, Jr., and redundant filmed interviews that recalled him as a likable and gifted musician. Yet the audience was given little incentive to follow up, as none of his compositions were identified—and the film editor would have done Marsalis a favor by clipping his remark about Dizzy Gillespie, unlike Kirkland, not being "literate" in Afro-Cuban rhythms. In jazz repertory begin responsibilities. But then, even James Brown appeared uncertain of what he was conserving as he preached more than he sang, introduced Al Sharpton while praising Giuliani, and gave a third of his set to one Tommie Raye, whose intonation would have been ambiguous even if she hadn't been trying to sing while shaking her blond tresses from side to side.

I close with another near miss. After playing routinely (except for an unaccompanied revival of "Thank You") with his longstanding quartet, the indefatigable Dave Brubeck began his second set with James Moody, who opened on tenor with a "Polka Dots and Moonbeams" that shimmered with warmth and seemed to shave 30 years off Brubeck, most of whose best music was achieved in company with saxophonists of Moody's stature. The next number, however, was given to Moody's admittedly funny yodeling vocal on the World War II parody, "Benny's from Heaven." Then the usual Brubeckians returned. Moody salvaged "Blue Rondo" and "Take Five," yet, more important, he intimated a genuine chemistry with old Dave, and you couldn't help but wonder how far they might have traveled in the course of an entire burlesque-free hour. Maybe they can do that on a record. But how far have we come when we look to records to fulfill the promise of dashed concerts?

[*Village Voice*, 6 July 1999]

61 ❖ *Rapprochement* (*Cecil Taylor / Elvin Jones / Dewey Redman*)

Momentum Space (Verve) by Dewey Redman, Cecil Taylor, and Elvin Jones—yes, the billing order is strange—was recorded last year and released several months ago with no fanfare and little serious response, pro or con. I have heard it denounced as disappointing, which makes me wonder how lofty are the prayers that haven't been answered and reminds me of reviews of the 1961 collaboration between Armstrong and Ellington. Critics then were disgruntled because Ellington didn't compose a concerto to mark the occasion; critics now embrace their meeting as a hitherto neglected jewel. I have also heard *Momentum Space* dissed as a rip-off because the full trio appears on only two selections, which is tantamount to spurning a great Monk solo because Coltrane laid out. The two selections, incidentally, total 30 minutes, more than half the CD's playing time, though that's beside the point. This is a considered, committed album—not an autumnal all-star caucus like the Giants of Jazz in the '70s, but a unique and artful collaboration.

Even if the music and conceptual organization were less remarkable, this disc would be one for the books, as a detente deferred much longer than the Armstrong-Ellington sessions. The avant-garde movement that took shape in the late 1950s and 1960s was unparalleled not least for the distance maintained by the three principals: Cecil Taylor, Ornette Coleman, and John Coltrane. That breach was only partly mandated by their discrete apprenticeships—respectively, in the conservatory, r&b, and jazz itself—and the routes they took in fomenting a new jazz. Parker,

Gillespie, and Monk went separate ways, but that didn't stop them from partnering each other; if they weren't less competitive they were surely less adamant about guarding their turfs. Coltrane recorded once with Taylor and once with Coleman's band, but never with Coleman, who has never recorded with Taylor.

It may sound slighting to think of Elvin Jones, the most influential drummer of his generation, and Dewey Redman, a masterly and versatile tenor saxophonist, as proxies for Coltrane and Coleman, but *Momentum Space* doesn't merely imply a convergence of these three academies. It delivers. In case anyone misses the point, Redman quotes "Lonely Woman" a minute or so into the climactic selection. The interpenetrating echoes of the original troika are heightened by the absence of bass or any other instrument. Indeed, those echoes were underscored after the fact by the stunning duets Taylor and Jones recently performed at the Blue Note, as 11:30 add-ons to sets by Jones's regular band.

There were lines east and west of the door for the September 9 set, a historic evening less for what it said about the past than for the electric immediacy of the event. With theater kept to a minimum—Taylor wore all white but for a red scarf and Jones wore all black but for a few red salmon on his T-shirt—and the host limiting himself to the low-frequency rumble of mallets, the encounter was peaceably fervent, the music rising and falling like mountains and plains seen from a train, the peaks in density giving way to hushed parabolas of melody, much of it expansively romantic and yet exacting.

The album is something else. For one thing, it *is* an album, the seven parts organized to suggest a de facto suite. At just under an hour, it possesses the happy semblance of an LP. Tracks one through three might be considered side one and the remaining four side two. How fitting that the innovators of a music famous for solos of unequalled length should buck the CD edict of more-is-more with a work of overall restraint.

It opens with a bang. Redman launches his own "Nine" with one raucous ascending arpeggio, followed by an interlude in which an aggressive Jones and quizzical Taylor feel each other out until Redman's return. Despite his warmer sound and centered pitch, Redman embodies the Coleman style, and as he guns his motor we hear for the first time ever a congruence of the avant-garde's key schools—the Coleman cry amid rugged polyrhythms of the sort that shadowed Coltrane, plus the keyboard-splashing Taylor conceived to evade or negotiate every kind of harmonic radar. Taylor is consistently fascinating, playing step passages in accompaniment and glisses to set up his own solo, which erupts with trinkling chords (a Theloneologism, as in "Trinkle Tinkle") and storming bass marches that counter treble cataracts, all contained with a blues-shaded repetitiveness—hardly atonal (that deathless canard), though the key darts around like a gazelle.

Jones's "Bekei" is a playful mallets solo that could serve as a bare-bones demonstration of his trademark approach to time. Other drummers found their way to metrical freedom by de-emphasizing the one in favor of changeable patterns that trampled the bar lines. Jones has always relied on the one to impose order, but in superimposing three over four and adding rhythmic crosscurrents, he implies—in a harmolodic sort of way—many rhythms at once. His affinity for triple-meter sets him apart; Jones is the true waltz king. In "Bekei," he maneuvers a deceptively simple three-beat figure (two on the bass drum, the third on cymbals) through variations that imply multiple time-signatures. On "Spoonin'," a duet with Redman that follows, he holds the rhythm in suspension as he drives the time, finally breaking out in a typically charged onslaught. Except during a parallel burst of heady harmonics, Redman mines his most soulful timbre, spinning a tale on the borderline of customary swing.

If this were an LP, you would flip it for the suite within the suite, Taylor's triptych: "Life As," "It," "Is." The opener, for solo piano, is a marvel of concision and control. He begins impassively with two tones over 15 seconds, then probes melody without conventional form or resolution—melody that exists more in the alternations of single pitches and chords and of bass and treble than in linear design, but melody all the same. The opening gambit and the sudden dynamic buildup of crisp chords and utopian tremolos are reminiscent of Liszt's Sonata in B Minor, but without the gothic melodrama. Thoughts of Liszt disappear as chord flurries curl up at the edges with blue notes and Taylor's distinct motifs abound, patterned with eighth-note rests, before the symmetrical wind-down, which includes a great climactic vortex that returns to silence with one long sustained note.

Contrastingly, "It" begins with springing dancelike figures—Taylor in a chipper mood and Jones following his every step with polyrhythmic chatter on snares and cymbal. This is a freer and more kinetic number; about two-thirds through Taylor tickles the keys until the piano rocks with laughter, then sighs as the drums take it out. Redman returns for the balladic opening of the oddly structured 21-minute piece de resistance, "Is." The surprising reference to "Lonely Woman" is made especially notable by the response: the spreading ripples of the cymbal, the swirling keyboard arpeggio that cradles the melody. Other memory-chords are struck as well: Redman's long yearning notes recalling Coltrane in his "Alabama" period, or the brittler Archie Shepp sonority he invokes in a later passage; Jones chasing a mercurial Taylor with the

Blakey-style press rolls he employed to keep Coltrane on track while "Chasin' the Trane." In this context, they become waves for Taylor to surf. The intensifying trio consummates the euphoric madness of '60s free jazz, and even after Redman drops out, Taylor's simultaneous bass lines and flashing chords create the illusion of a trio—Elvin and two Cecils.

After a midway recap, Redman disappears from the piece and is conspicuously absent from the closing recapitulation. Maybe he shied away from reentering because of the intensity of the duet that ensues, with Taylor rocking and riffing and slowing down for contemplative respites. Jones, too, takes a break during the most fanciful of the piano meditations, complete with a shimmering glissando that suggested a supersonic harp, until Taylor brings him back with a two-note call and they fade off, two septuagenarians who remain constitutionally incapable of making background music. Redman returns for a 40-second sign-off of split-tones and a holler. What else is there to add except amen? Don't wait 40 years to join the congregation.

[*Village Voice*, 12 October 1999]

62 ❖ *Good Vibrations* *(Stefon Harris)*

Before this year, music lovers were known to remark on the odd statistic that all of the most eminent players of the vibraphone (and its acoustic forbears, the xylophone and marimba) were alive, defying the normal mortality rate while encompassing most of jazz's history. True, vibraphonists constitute a small crowd—so small that jazz polls usually consign them to the same miscellany as French horn, bassoon, and didgeridoo. Like passengers on the Ark, they have arrived in pairs and at generational intervals: Lionel Hampton and Red Norvo (both born in 1908); Milt Jackson and Terry Gibbs (1923, 1924); Bobby Hutcherson and Gary Burton (1941, 1943); Jay Hoggard and Steve Nelson (both 1954). Their ranks have now ebbed by a fourth with the passing of Norvo in April and Jackson a few weeks ago, a loss partly relieved by the arrival of Stefon Harris (born 1973).

No one starts out on vibes—musicians generally get there via the two instruments it fuses, piano and drums. Yet if for no other reason than that the vibes are quintessentially African, you might expect a lot more players, particularly in this world music epoch. Even the tube resonators beneath the wood bars of the xylophone and the rotary ones beneath the metal bars of the vibraphone have precedence in the African balafon, which attaches calabashes to the planks for the same purpose. The chief distinction of the American variations is that the bars replicate a piano keyboard, creating a hybrid. The keys say piano, but the thumping of those keys with mallets says drums. And this design determines its character.

You can get a sense of the difference by sitting or standing at a piano: When you sit, the keyboard stretches away at left and right and you focus on sections of it; when you stand, you dominate it, more inclined to tackle it whole. Mallets increase the musician's command of the keys, as each hand is reduced to one or two fingers with a reach that can hardly fail to transgress octaves, inspiring riffs that span 30 notes when other instrumentalists are likely to work within a dozen. While dense piano harmonies elude the vibist, he can usually adapt the linearity of piano solos. Yet it's almost impossible to imagine a great vibes solo played on piano—not the plinking melodies of Norvo nor the blues-drenched drama of Jackson nor the quicksilver whoosh of Hutcherson. The vibraphone can electrically raise, lower, or flatten vibrato in the blink of an eye, allowing for colors not made of harmony but of quivering air.

Stefon Harris, who was born in Albany and educated at Eastman and the Manhattan School of Music, was a low-profile presence until last year, when Blue Note issued his first album, *A Cloud of Red Dust*. He had worked with Max Roach and Bobby Watson and recorded with Terrell Stafford, Steve Turre, Russell Gunn, Joe Henderson, and others before his album and tour pushed him into the kind of prominence that can be heady and damning for a young musician, as signings of fresh-faced players in the '90s have often balefully demonstrated. In the '60s, Blue Note routinely promoted rookies to sidemen and, after substantial apprenticeships, gave them their own sessions. Who has time for apprenticeships with the millennium breathing down everyone's neck? Still, Blue Note has been canny with Harris, grooming him with Greg Osby and Charlie Hunter and bringing him along with another talented newcomer, pianist Jason Moran. The payoff came last week at the Village Vanguard, where he led a quartet with one of the label's piano stars, Jacky Terrasson, and with the release of his new CD, *Black Action Figure*.

Vibes players tend to be either cool or frantic—Norvo staring straight ahead with a stoned grin as though he had no idea what his hands were doing, or Hampton, a stick of dynamite with a fast fuse; Hutcherson, a statue with blurred wrists, or Gibbs, a gum-chewing nervous affliction. Milt Jackson may have been the coolest musician of all, dispassionately examining the middle distance, yet hitting every cue on the dime with a percussive force that made one's heart jump. Harris belongs to the cool school. He has a charming stage manner and likes to talk to the audience, but he reigns over his instrument with casual authority. At the Vanguard, his solo on "Feline Blues" began with swift, jumpy phrases that shot off into the air, avoiding the resolutions of bop cadences, and employed long rests to set up crackling riffs that crested and dilated into another and then another—you can hear a good instance of this on his first album's "Sophistry." His sound mutated from the staccato of a marimba to the billowing tremulousness of fully whirring vibes. He relied too heavily on tremolos, a corny pitfall for the instrument, especially during Terrasson's appealing "Baby Plum," but sustained interest with his command of dynamics and the pedals, his diverse timbres, his wit (on one number, he and Terrasson exchanged famous quotations from Ellington, Monk, and Ornette), and his ability to change direction. Just when you think you've got him pegged, he breaks into something different—a fierce tap dance in the treble, a cascade in the middle, a dull-edged jaunt in an echoey cavern of the bass clef.

Black Action Figure (great title) is a more involving album than *A Cloud of Red Dust*, though it partakes of some of the earlier disc's strengths and shortcomings. "Feline Blues" is one of his better originals, a welding of two blues choruses, the second modifying the changes of the first, and is handsomely arranged for the ensemble with unison winds and a vibes countermelody. Harris begins his solo by tracking a two-note blip through 12 bars, and taking his time, accelerating and retarding the rhythm. He likes to play with the organization of his discs, and on the new one expands on his penchant for interpolating one-minute transitions or send-ups between main selections. For example, he edited out the pause between "Feline Blues" and a stunning trio version of "There Is No Greater Love," which recalls Bud Powell in its intensity, speed, and catchy profusion. That standard, however, and a riveting 90-second solo on "You Stepped Out of a Dream" point up his weakness as a melodist, clever though his compositions can be. Crafty interludes do not mitigate the sameness of his writing, underscored by his predilection for high-register instruments, notably a flute-vibes combination—reminiscent of Hutcherson's "Little B's Poem." But then, Harris and just about everyone else in his generation stand slightly right of their left-of-center Blue Note antecedents of 35 years ago. Think of Hutcherson's *Components* and *Dialogue*.

Yet as *Black Action Figure* also makes clear, Harris, bassist Tarus Mateen, drummer Eric Harland, and pianist Jason Moran, with guests Steve Turre, Greg Osby, and Gary Thomas, are moving upward and outward.

Harris's new ballads, "After the Day Is Done" and "Faded Beauty," are more fetching and less derivative than those on *A Cloud of Red Dust*. "Of Things to Come" is a solid 32-bar invention, with a modulated one-bar riff for its first half and an expansive melody for its second. Writing, though, will never be the primary attribute of a gifted jazz player, which Harris surely is. A musician who can individualize standards with such brio and wit cheats himself and his audience by not exploiting the great melodies at his disposal. His stylistic clout makes you want to hear his take on the repertory.

The jazz-is-dead crowd, never absent for long and an especially tempting club in a month that witnesses the loss of Harry Edison, Art Farmer, and Milt Jackson, is too busy mourning its own lost youth and enthusiasm to open its ears and arms to new players who embody both. But a musician like Harris focuses attention with the promise of a future worth watching and chronicling. May he be suitably nurtured and challenged. The identity of his doppelganger remains to be determined.

[*Village Voice*, 9 November 1999]

63 ❖ *Lester Bowie, 1941–1999*

When an e-mail informed me of Lester Bowie's death—at 58, on November 8, of cancer—I was reading Marshall Berman's *All That Is Solid Melts into Air*, and suddenly everything he wrote about Goethe and Marx seemed to be about Lester. "Why should modern men, who have seen what man's activity can bring about, passively accept the structure of their society as it is given?" A pretext for avant-garde jazz if I ever heard one. A subsequent idea, that revolutionary activity undercuts bourgeois rule by expressing energies "the bourgeoisie itself has set free," is pure Lester: Lester in his long white lab coat, with not one but two Mephistophelean goatees waxed into points, his hair a flattop, his eyes smiling and luminous, his trumpet knifing the air with jerky parabolas of sputtering fragments, like a machine in need of oil.

Lester was the most bourgeois of underminers, the wiliest jazz provocateur of his generation. He earned the glint in his eye honestly, along with the six children and 10 grandchildren, the Brooklyn brownstone, the Lexus, and the cigar that accentuated his preternatural calm; when he removed it, he was seriously intelligent, expansive, and funny, but when it was in his mouth you half expected to hear the heh-heh-hehs that occasionally marked his records. He was raised in St. Louis, where his father played trumpet, but he was formed by carnivals, the Air Force, a flock or r&b and soul bands, the liberating wonders of Muhal Richard Abrams's Experimental Band, and the pop culture surrounding him, especially that of the 1950s, which he tweaked as only a fan can. Maybe you have to know that era to be moved by the 40 seconds of "When the Moon Comes over the Mountain," intoned with his plump creamy timbre on *The Great Pretender* (ECM, 1981), climaxing a side with the relentless title number, a peanut gallery's "It's Howdy Doody Time," and a cataclysmic snapshot called "Doom?"—the '50s tied up with Kate Smith's bow.

Another formative influence on Lester was his idol, Louis Armstrong, whom he celebrated when the great man was still alive. You can't imagine how refreshing it was to encounter a young avant-gardist in the early '70s who understood and loved all of Armstrong, not just the '20s classics. When Lester recorded "Hello, Dolly" on *Fast Last!* (Muse, 1974), everyone assumed it was a send-up. But you only have to listen to realize how urgently personal and affectionate it is, a eulogy from one who knows, right through to the chortling sneeze of a coda, one of the essential tracks of that decade. "Hello, Dolly!" began Lester's ardent 25-year pursuit of what he recently titled *The Odyssey of Funk & Popular Music* (Atlantic, 1998), the only record, I'm confident, with tunes by Puccini, Cole Porter, the Spice Girls, Andrew Lloyd Webber, Teddy Pendergrass, Notorious B.I.G., and Marilyn Manson.

In that period, Lester devoted most of his energy to the punctilious Brass Fantasy and the grievously undervalued New York Organ Ensemble (with James Carter and Amina Claudine Myers never better), which made two albums in 1991 for DIW that will make my short list for the decade. Some of his pop excavations fell flat. *Avant Pop* (ECM, 1986) was all pop and no avant, though it boasts Lester's memorable solos on "Blueberry Hill" and "Crazy," an oddly moving, comic fantasia. But he ultimately brought the two poles together. If the initial "Great Pretender" achieves some of its levity by comin' atcha and atcha and atcha, the tight Steve Turre arrangement on Brass Fantasy's *The Fire This Time* (In + Out, 1992) gives it the satisfying feel of a hard-won theme song, climaxing another essential disc, one that also includes Turre's version of Jimmie Lunceford's "Siesta at the Fiesta," E. J. Allen's best writing and playing, and the affecting "For Louis," composed by and dedicated to the memory of drummer Phillip Wilson. Turre also arranged (and plays a wicked solo on) the title cut from *My Way* (DIW, 1990), a reminder that Lester at his best isn't a satirist. His dirty secret was the same as Armstrong's and Fats Waller's—the stuff they play is the stuff they love, animated by a considered sense of irony.

But all this was part of Lester's later phases, and it's the earlier period I most relish, because I can't imagine the 1970s without him. Berman writes that 1960s attempts at modernism failed, but "sprang from a largeness of vision and imagination, and from an ardent desire to seize the day." True: Coleman, Taylor, Coltrane, Mingus, Ayler—only they did not fail, Marshall. "It was the absence of these generous visions and initiatives that made the 1970s such a bleak decade." Right again, or so it appeared until we New York provincials began to hear of a generation of musicians in Chicago who went national after a mostly triumphant tour of Europe. They were nothing like the preceding avant-gardists, though they could not have existed without them. They played everything and they played nothing (the longest rests on records ever); they revealed technical aplomb while developing a methodology that put their skill in question. They almost always went out swinging, but before that—this was the Art Ensemble of Chicago's m.o.—they put you through an anthropological hour of bells, chimes, chants, beeps, blats, honks, and squalls. Man, you *earned* your catharsis.

When I learned of Lester's death, I needed to hear his first album, *Numbers 1 & 2* (Nessa, 1967), which I hadn't played in at least 15 years. It holds up, truly, and so do its mates—Roscoe Mitchell's *Congliptious* and *Old/Quartet* and all the early Art Ensemble of Chicago LPs, just to mention a few Lester landmarks. These albums pass the time with an almost arrogant indifference to the clocks of the world. The music suns itself on the porch and if it gets too hot for you, stick around because the weather changes every minute or so. In assessing the influence of Lester and his comrades, consider Terry Martin's parenthetical liner comment on the instrumentation: "three horns and a bassist!!" That sort of lineup wouldn't merit a single explanation point today. Lester's best-known band had four trumpets, two trombones, tuba, French horn, and two drummers!!!

About a quarter into "Number 1," Lester plays a lovely, lyrical passage of sustained notes, before kneading his timbre into more expressive and eccentric tones, ending in the tuba's range. Much has been made of his flutters and growls, his ascending rips that fade off into high, whinnying slurs or his guffawing half-valve effects, but he was a commanding, skilled trumpet player—here and in the startling unison episodes of "Number 2," the limning of the melody in part two of the Art Ensemble's epochal *People in Sorrow* (Nessa, 1969), and many other instances. He showed how much he could play one night in 1977, sitting in with Roy

Eldridge at Jimmy Ryan's, an encounter still talked about. Eddie Locke, Roy's drummer, recently recalled that Roy arrived three hours early he was so nervous, and though, as usual, he kept his crown, Lester acquitted himself admirably and the older guys were impressed—they didn't like the avant-garde, but they knew whatever he played must have been deliberate, because he had the chops and knew the changes.

Listening to the discs today, it's hard to believe anyone questioned his ability, but the same doubts were registered about Ornette and Cecil. Lester's importance as a trumpeter can hardly be overstated. Except for Don Cherry, the instrument was all but moribund in the new music. Don Ellis's antics had become academic, Freddie Hubbard couldn't make the leap, and players like Bill Dixon, Mike Mantler, Donald Ayler, and Eddie Gale lacked either the technical or intellectual resources to carry through. In restoring the panoply of jazz trumpet effects, Lester brought it back to life and inspired a generation of brass players.

The Chicagoans' national impact was first felt in the mid-'70s and helped to overcome the direst malaise in jazz history. But they began recording in the 1960s—Lester's debut came out a year after *Unit Structures*, two after *Ascension*. Yet it divines a different world, far removed from the buoyant swing of Coleman, the steamrolling ardor of Coltrane, the virtuoso exhilaration of Taylor. Berman quotes Octavio Paz's observation that modernity is "cut off from the past and continually hurtling forward at such a dizzy pace that it cannot take root [or] recover its powers of renewal." That's just what Bowie and company were attempting to do, with their bells and harmonica, their irreverent reverence for blues and swing and pop tunes, their humor and ceremony, their music that only made sense if you listened, because you wouldn't get too far patting your feet.

Inevitably, perhaps, Lester renewed himself by returning to gospel and pop, the world of his past and the world around him, all bourgeois grist to seize a new day. Perhaps the symbolic moment of transition between the Art Ensemble Lester and the Brass Fantasy Lester took place in February 1979 at Symphony Space, when he conducted the 59-piece Sho' Nuff Orchestra, with a cast that amazed then and seems incredible now; the reed section included Roscoe Mitchell, Anthony Braxton, Henry Threadgill, Julius Hemphill, Oliver Lake, David Murray, Arthur Blythe, John Stubblefield, Frank Lowe, Frank Wright, and Charles Tyler. The evening began when *Jism Magazine*'s Dave Flexingbergstein ran out, press card in hat, and popped the question first heard on Bowie's 1968 record, "Jazz Death?": "Isn't jazz, as we know it, dead yet?" Lester stepped out of character, rolled his eyes, and replied, "Well, that all depends on what you know." The evening ended with a churchy hymn,

the band whooping in time, which showman Lester interrupted to inquire if we were having a good time. We absolutely were.

[*Village Voice*, 14 December 1999]

64 ❖ The Masters Have It
(The Best Jazz Records of 1999)

The arbitrariness of annual top-10s always becomes clearer the week
after, when you look at other lists and think, damn, how did I forget
that album and why haven't I heard this other one? Then again, maybe
the most honest list you can come up with eschews research and second-
guessing in favor of albums that instantly come to mind because you've
returned to them time after time and filed them in that corner of your
skull reserved for potential classics, or at least music you expect to live
with more fully in the future. Every generation of critics is obliged to
make cases for works neglected the first time around and puncture those
that get a free ride on the wings of received wisdom. I don't know how
1999 will stack up, but my 10-bests usually run to about 17 albums, and
this year I wasn't certain of reaching 10.

    The fact that it was a grand year for reissues (a subject for later dis-
cussion, though in the interim do pick up Vanguard's restoration of *From
Spirituals to Swing*) and that most of the new albums that pleasured me
were by musicians over 70, puts me in mind of the early and middle
1970s, when posthumous Ellington or Clifford Brown routinely aced out
the living as we waited for Godot. Godot and friends finally arrived from
the heartland (R.I.P. Lester Bowie, Julius Hemphill, Phillip Wilson, Fred
Hopkins, Steve McCall, et al.), and something similar will break up the
academic malaise of the present. For now, there are the old masters,
though fewer than last year (R.I.P. Harry Edison, Red Norvo, Milt Jackson, Art Farmer, et al.). Of 10 CDs that made the cut, the top three stand
out, but one dominates, the CD of the year:

    1. John Lewis's *Evolution* (Atlantic). Only a pianist as mature, canny,
and knowing as Lewis would have the nerve to play as few notes as he
does in the 11 selections of this recital. Having winnowed his technique
to an expressive core, he belongs to the wasteless tradition of Basie and
Monk—inimitable touch, rhythmic infallibility. *Evolution* crosses the line

between sonata and sonnet, its stray phrases and suspenseful caesuras ringing with images as specific as metaphors and luminous as reflection. Although a 19th-century sensibility is apparent, everything Lewis plays suggests the imaginative rigors of a purebred jazz musician—in the harmonies, the ratio between composition and improvisation, in a swing that is vital even at the slowest tempos, and in an attack that encompasses much of the American keyboard tradition from rags and blues to boogie and bop and beyond.

In *Moby Dick*, Ishmael remarks of Queequeg's table manners, "But *that* was certainly very coolly done by him, and every one knows that in most people's estimation to do anything coolly is to do it genteelly." No one has ever questioned Lewis's gentility; indeed, it has been held against him. But his fastidiousness is so cool in the '90s sense of the word, which comports with Melville's, that he conveys an emotional authority rare in any art. Was there a wittier performance all year than the arrangement here of "Sweet Georgia Brown"? Or a more generously moving one than "For Ellington"? Or a more inventively re-imagined one than his total rethinking of "Django"?

For all the improvisational electricity he generates, these pieces, so concisely arranged and played, have the lacquered finish of composition; you can imagine a classical pianist transcribing and interpreting them, though he would have to have awfully good time—Jean-Yves Thibaudet won't do. Their real strength, however, and the thing that sets them apart, lies elsewhere. In an age short on melody, a true melody-man like Lewis seems to have almost shamanistic powers. We are accustomed to calling anyone who can cobble together a hummable phrase lyrical. But Lewis is the real thing. He thinks tunefully, and whether he plays his own pieces ("Afternoon in Paris" and "Two Degrees East, Three Degrees West") or standards ("September Song" and "Don't Blame Me" get surprising facelifts), Lewis builds them from the ground up with winning airs, often riveted with boldly considered rests. Also, every note peals like a chime: You don't often see an audio engineer billed in the same font as the artist and his producers, but E. Alan Silver has created a state-of-the-art disc.

2. Lee Konitz, *Another Shade of Blue* (Blue Note). How many contemporary musicians play solos that can withstand the scrutiny applied to those single-chorus jewels of the 78 era? At his best, Konitz can and does. What distinguishes this performance—a concert with pianist Brad Mehldau (more engaging here than on his own recent disc) and bassist Charlie Haden—is how long the great alto saxophonist can sustain his high-wire act. He offers a glossary of unhackneyed blues licks on the title track

and flies in from Mars to open "What's New." If you're put off by his tart tone, get over it. And don't tell me about *Motion*; this disc is every bit as entrancing.

3. Cecil Taylor, Elvin Jones, Dewey Redman, *Momentum Space* (Verve). A long-delayed reunion of sorts that lives up to its billing, especially Taylor's gripping triptych.

4–6. Sam Rivers, *Inspiration* (RCA Victor); Chico O'Farrill, *Heart of a Legend* (Milestone); The Vanguard Jazz Orchestra, *Thad Jones Legacy* (New World). Each of these big-band projects brims with the exhilaration exclusive to the form. Rivers had a week at Sweet Basil before making his, and it shows. The music is wonderfully schizoid; the dense voicings are dissonant, but the riffs and pithy solos are downright toasty. O'Farrill's overdue sequel to the 1995 *Pure Emotion* is less ambitious but more entertaining, with guest soloists and the elation of an ensemble that has had a long spell at Birdland to get it right. Which makes the veteran Vanguard Jazz Orchestra what—perfect? Just about. In making a case for its co-founder, it reclaims "Central Park North" from the banalities of funk, and goes ape on "Fingers."

7–8. Teri Thornton, *I'll Be Easy to Find* (Verve); Abbey Lincoln, *Wholly Earth* (Verve). I also liked new vocal records by Carla Cook (Maxjazz), Denise Jannah (Blue Note), Laverne Butler (Maxjazz), Paula West (Noir), Tony Bennett (Columbia), and Diana Krall (Verve). But these two startle. Thornton was one of many Dinah Washington clones 40 years ago, yet she has evolved a style entirely her own—sustaining tension with top notes you think will veer out of tune, but never do. Good tunes, good arrangements. Lincoln puts me off with the harmonizing on "And It's Supposed to Be Love," but overall she is as penetrating as usual—the Billie Holiday of the fin de seicle. Bobby Hutcherson is enthused, too.

9. Joe Lovano and Greg Osby, *Friendly Fire* (Blue Note). No battle, just a meeting of minds. The two saxophonists seem bent on pleasing each other, working with clever originals as well as way hip standards by Dolphy, Monk, and Coleman.

10. Uri Caine, *The Sidewalks of New York: Tin Pan Alley* (Winter & Winter). Okay, it's not a jazz record, though jazz musicians are involved, including Caine (whose director credit is in teeny print inside the booklet), Don Byron, and Dave Douglas. A collage about the turn of the last century, it has sound effects, murmuring crowds, horse snorts, singing, monologues, a seven-minute rehearsal for a four-minute "Some of These Days" (by a red-hot mama named Barbara Walker), "Take Me Out to the Ball Game" in Yiddish—it's a stew of ethnicities. Put aside 77 minutes to hear it whole, and it's like a time capsule, rich in sentiment,

never sentimental. Come to think of it, that's even truer of John Lewis's
Evolution.

[*Village Voice*, 29 December 1999]

65 ❖ *Hammond's Best and Brightest (From Spirituals to Swing)*

Some 20 years ago, Columbia Records, then operating under the benevolent jazzcentric hand of Bruce Lundvall, threw a party at Broadway and
52nd Street, the site of the original Birdland. Many great musicians from
the bop era performed in a jam session, but the music usually had to vie
with conversation. At the end of the night, though, a few swing musicians took the stage, fronted by Helen Humes and Buddy Tate, and they
wrapped the room in a sling and twirled it above their heads. Humes's
piping, girlish voice and Tate's stark riffs locked into a beat so rigorous
it silenced everyone. The place went crazy; no one wanted to follow them
on the bandstand. I turned to the veteran critic Stanley Dance, the last
of the Charlie Parker haters, and said something brilliant like, "Jesus-
fuckingchristalmighty." With characteristic noblesse oblige, Stanley replied, "Well, you know, I always thought bebop was rather corny."

Corny? I had never heard that one before. But for those few minutes
I was willing to raise the white flag. We had just heard something unlikely to be repeated, no matter how many times we would see Buddy
and Helen or musicians like them. Rhythm is a mysterious thing, and
the most mysterious rhythm is the one for which the Swing Era was
named. Compared to the jazz rhythms that followed, it is elemental, a
ready thumping of all four beats. Compared to what came before in jazz
and followed in r&b or r&r, it is plush and elegant. It was made for
dancing, of course, but when it goes into overdrive you realize it was
also made for over-the-top, death-defying exhilaration.

Don't take my word. Vanguard has restored *From Spirituals to Swing*,
the classic 1959 album compiled from the two concerts that John Hammond produced at Carnegie Hall in the late 1930s. Nearly two-dozen
previously unreleased selections—about an hour of new music—have
been added, including the opening number at the 1938 concert, Count
Basie's "Swingin' the Blues." Basie's original Decca record is a killer, but
it is staid compared to this version.

You can hear Basie stomp the tempo—a tempo so fast that in a ball-room it would have cleared the floor of all but professional jitterbuggers. The big climaxes are tossed off with a kind of knowing hilarity, because the whole thing is a climax. Hammond probably rejected this performance because the soloists were off-mike. Yet that turns out to be a good thing; you get to hear the workings of the ensemble like never before. Forget Lester Young for a moment, and listen to the audacity of the punctuating brasses, attacking as one, as if the sections had a mind of their own. The reeds introduce a new swirling, kibitzing riff that rolls under and over Buck Clayton. The studio version builds, closing with a Jo Jones drum solo. This performance, a minute longer, is a Jo Jones concerto. He is omnipresent, stoking the engine, the sections, the soloists, messing with the minds and metabolisms of the audience.

This "Swingin' the Blues" reminds us that before swing became an idiom, it was the music of the young competitive guys who invented it, hailing themselves and vanquishing all comers. It underscores as well the diversity of swing. No one ever swung harder than Louis Armstrong, and the swing era has been called orchestrated Armstrong. But he did not swing in the precise manner of Basie, anymore than did Charlie Parker or Miles Davis or Ornette Coleman or David Murray. Moreover, the Basie of 1960 did not swing like the Basie of 1938. What makes *From Spiritual to Swing* enthralling is its arrogant freshness. "Swingin' the Blues" pushes one style of swing as far as it can go, into the realm of head music, because at this velocity few people's feet will do their stuff. It's a fairly short hop, at least in retrospect, from Basie in extremis to the full-bore head rhythms of Charlie Parker's "Koko."

There are other examples. Joe Turner and Pete Johnson had never sounded more euphoric, and now, in addition to "It's All Right Baby," we get a second world-beating number in "Low Down Dog." Meade Lux Lewis and Albert Ammons were always on a tear, but you may need a Valium after the former's "Honky Tonk Train Blues" and the latter's "Boogie Woogie," both previously unreleased. Among softer, no less riveting discoveries are Lester Young's clarinet on "I Never Knew," James P. Johnson's savory "Blueberry Rhyme," and Helen Humes's future signature song (written by James P.) "If I Could Be with You One Hour Tonight." Standouts among unearthed blues and gospel numbers are two by Sister Rosetta Tharpe, and Big Bill Broonzy's "It Was Just a Dream," accompanied by Ammons and the fully involved laughter of the audience, for whom the topical words were brand-new.

The Vanguard CDs resolve John Hammond's titillating comment in the notes to the 1959 release: "And there is still enough good material left for another three sides." They also illuminate his 1971 admission that not all the music on the records was really recorded at Carnegie; he added a few selections—among them Humes's "Blues for Helen" and Hot Lips Page's "Blues with Lips"—that were made in a studio six months before the first concert, and recorded his spoken introductions in 1958 (the tape was sped up and drenched in echo to make him sound younger). By 1959, no one recalled the concerts well enough to dispute him.

The new production is exemplary in every way. Producer Steve Buckingham sequenced the material, for the first time, so that we can hear what the 1938 and 1939 concerts were really like. Doug Pomeroy worked with tapes of Hammond's discs that were made before the 1950s Vanguard engineers began splicing out pops, and he has superbly enhanced the sound. The three-disc box comes with two booklets, one with commentaries old and new (one error: Spencer Williams's "I Ain't Got Nobody" is attributed to Bert Williams), the other a facsimile of the concert program, "The New Masses Presents an Evening of American Negro Music." It includes a plea for the children of Loyalist Spain, fascinating advertisements, and the single paragraph of Hammond's that propelled the legend of Robert Johnson, who had been booked but died before the concert.

The reason Vanguard, the folk label, received the rights to *From Spirituals to Swing* is that the company saved Hammond in the darkest days of his career, hiring him to record jazz sessions in the mid-'50s. Those albums are among his least remembered, but shouldn't be and perhaps won't be now that Vanguard is putting them out again. Buckingham, presumably for contrast and to muddy the business of which sessions were best, has edited anthologies from the original albums, which is fine with me, as long as all the material finally gets out. The discs—decently mastered and well annotated by Sam Charters—capture several swing epiphanies. The two Jimmy Rushings, *Oh Love* and *Every Day* (the latter has an amazing "Evenin'"), are splendid. The best of the Basie Bunch CDs is *Cool Two*. The two volumes of *Duets* by Ruby Braff and Ellis Larkins are neglected classics of an Armstrongian jazz romanticism. The arranged ensembles on the Mel Powell discs, *The Best Things in Life* and *It's Been So Long*, are commonplace, but the piano pieces are cunning and stately. Sir Charles Thompson, a much-underrated pianist, shares honors with the leader on Vic Dickenson's *Nice Work,* and with Coleman Hawkins (check Hawk's entrance on the aptly titled "Fore!") on his own *For the Ears.*

When Hammond left Vanguard to return to Columbia, his long exile at an end, he signed artists who added to his 1930s legend as talent scout and producer—Aretha Franklin, Bob Dylan, Bruce Springsteen, Stevie

Ray Vaughan. But he recorded only Aretha and Dylan, briefly, before they were "taken away from me," as he used to complain. He was involved in many memorable projects, including the 1967 *Spirituals to Swing* concert and album; he launched George Benson and relaunched Helen Humes. But looking over his discography, I wonder if he had a happier or more sustained burst of postwar creativity than in the years 1953 to 1956, reunited with his old swing pals at Vanguard. He didn't, after all, call the 1967 concert *Spirituals to Jazz* or *Spirituals to Rock*. The last time I saw him, a few weeks before he died in 1987, he was in a wheelchair, chain-smoking (his left side was partly paralyzed and he asked me to hold his ashtray) and reminiscing about Bessie Smith, Basie, and the '30s. His heart belonged to swing, and it surprised and infuriated him when the magic got older and turned into something else.

[*Village Voice*, 9 May 2000]

66 ❖ Hipper Than Thou (Bob Dorough)

I was having a high old time listening to Bob Dorough's new record, *Too Much Coffee Man* (Blue Note), which may be his best, when my assistant Elora walked in and exclaimed with a slight interrogatory, "*Schoolhouse Rock*!?" She had never heard of Dorough, but she recognized the voice. I had never heard of *Schoolhouse Rock*, so she brought in her four-disc Rhino set and played her favorites, including a masterpiece, "My Hero, Zero," noting "You will not find anyone of my generation who does not know the words to 'Electricity Electricity' and 'Conjunction Junction.'" She proved the point with a recitation augmented by a description of the animation that accompanied the songs when the short instructive cartoons appeared on television. Dorough was music director for the series and wrote most of the songs. "I learned the multiplication tables from him," Elora marveled. "We had great TV then."

Well, every generation thinks it had great TV. But it occurred to me that many people over the past 50 years have heard Bob Dorough without knowing it. He has cast a pretty long zigzag shadow since he left Cherry Hill, Arkansas, got a degree in composition at North Texas State, moved to New York to be part of the jazz scene, and served two years as music director for—no kidding—Sugar Ray Robinson. In the '60s, for example, he pulled strings for Spanky & Our Gang and Chad Mitchell, wrote arrangements for the Fugs, and helped create Allen Ginsberg's wheezing album of William Blake's poetry.

I can tell you exactly how a few thousand young jazz fans first heard him in 1967. For some reason, producer Teo Macero was putting out jazz records without personnel listings. This had its comical side: After I loaned a friend *Monk*, he called excitedly to tell me how wonderful Monk was, adding, "I like the piano player, too." With Miles, however, who was recording erratically with his new quintet, the absence of info lent an air of mystery. You had no idea what to expect of *Sorcerer*, with its drop-dead cover profile of the then little-known Cicely Tyson and a Ralph J. Gleason, um, poem on the back. Not much longer than half an hour, the album was a strangely sleepy collection of originals, and Miles didn't even play on one of them. Then, just as you were nodding out to "Vonetta," you heard a high-pitched nerdy male voice singing a 115-second panegyric, "Nothing Like You" (a Fran Landesmann lyric), backed by winds and bongos. I like to think of Miles fans in dens and bedrooms across the country saying in perfect unison, "Hunh?"

We later learned that the singer was Bob Dorough and that the track was left over from a 1962 Davis session arranged by Gil Evans; it required 45 takes. Davis had admired Dorough's debut album on Bethlehem, the 1956 *Devil May Care*, and when Columbia insisted he participate in a Christmas album, he tracked Dorough down in California and asked him to write a Christmas song ("Blue Xmas"). Dorough flew to New York and they recorded three tunes. Listening to *Sorcerer* now, I see that Dorough's use of diminished chords sort of fits with the pieces by Wayne Shorter, who, coincidentally, had played on the "Nothing Like You" date, two years before joining Miles's band. Gil Evans liked the tune enough to record an orchestral version for a 1964 album, *The Individualism of Gil Evans*, though no one knew about it until it turned up on a 1988 Verve reissue.

Shortly after *Sorcerer*, I came across the 1966 *Just About Everything*, on Focus—Dorough's first album (except for a Music Minus One project) since *Devil May Care*, and the last until his self-produced *Beginning to See the Light* in 1976. That was his recording schedule for the first 30 years of his career—one album per decade, like clockwork. *Just About Everything* is irresistible. Jazz musicians usually come a cropper when they try to get down with rock tunes. Yet Dorough begins with "Don't Think Twice, It's All Right" in a version I prefer to Bob Dylan's. The rhythm is exactly right, but what locks it down for me is the way he phrases "Don't think twice, baby, it's all right"—the last three words emitted in a rapid bullfrog croak. Dorough is every bit as eccentric a singer as Dylan; one comes from Woody Guthrie and the other from Charlie Parker, but they strike me as fraternal small-town outsiders. Indeed, Dylan's ensuing *Self-Portrait* reminded me of *Just About Everything*, which has four distinct originals (including the weirdly echoing "The Message," written with bassist Ben Tucker), as well as "The Crawdad Song," the best rendition ever of "Baltimore Oriole" (although the Tangipahoa is in Louisiana, not Baltimore, as Dorough interpolates), and "Tis Autumn," all of which he makes sound like eccentric originals.

I suppose it's the eccentricity that inclines me to approach Dorough in an autobiographical mode. The trouble with eccentrics is that you can never be sure if they know how strange they seem, and for a time I was uneasy about whether I was always laughing with him. When, near the end of what turned out to be his *Schoolhouse Rock* days (1973–85), he made a few appearances in New York, I got really uneasy. He is now 76 but hasn't changed appreciably in the past 20 years and maybe a lot longer—witness the cover of the 1976 reissue of *Devil May Care*, retitled *Yardbird Suite* (he sings Parker's theme and solo delightfully), on which he poses with the original jacket. He has always been rail thin, his face an open, eager, goofily boyish circle, occasionally split by an Alfred E. Newmanish grin. I assume he didn't have the ponytail in the 1950s, but he's had it whenever I've seen him. Backed by the late Bill Takas, his longtime bassist, he revealed laudable bop piano chops, confirming my impression that he was at home with diverse rhythms, and sang with creaky disregard for conventional musical protocol.

But after giggling at Dorough's craggy swoops and idiosyncratic melodies, which have Escher-like loops, I was invariably brought up short by "Winter Moon" or "Lazy Afternoon," both mined for much unexpected emotion. He can interpret a lyric as though it were an anecdote. When he goes into bopping swingers, he seems almost indifferent to how much energy he can generate. The whole effect has freaked many, and he has endured some of the most scathing reviews I've ever read. It's not just because he spent so much time writing songs explaining multiplication that Dorough is only infrequently booked in the nightclubs he once hoped to make his habitat. In his notes to his 1997 Blue Note album, *Right on My Way Home*, he gives as one of his ambitions, "to sing you a song and have you not walk out on me."

Had I known *Schoolhouse Rock*, I'd have been hipper sooner. But what finally convinced me he was totally in on the joke was his indispensable self-produced 1990 album entitled *This Is a Recording of Pop Art Songs by Bob Dorough and friends produced and copyright by Scharf/Dorough for distribution on their label, Laissez-Faire Records*. The songs combine classical, jazz, and pop settings with found lyrics: He sings, verbatim and with no embellishments, a weather report, a collection letter, a recipe for apple pie, a draft card notice, a social security card, Webster's definitions of love, and my three particular favorites—a laundry ticket ("Not Responsible for Shrink"), air passenger instructions ("Should the Need Arise"), and an upholstery label ("Do Not Remove This Tag"). At no time does he even hint that any of this is funny.

Dorough's new album, which he is promoting this week in a rare appearance at Deanna's (an attractive room on Rivington), opens like a house afire with "The Coffee Song." His jumping recitation is as serious as, say, "A Plea of Guilty" (his traffic ticket song), complete with the aside "thought I told you," when the lyric is repeated. One big reason the record roars is the presence of alto saxophonist Phil Woods. Too bad he's only on four tracks, but he is inspired on all, not least a new version of "I've Got Just About Everything." Dorough's more recent pieces include a dedication to his wife, "Wake Up Sally, It's Saturday," constructed to resolve on a froggy two-note *ribit* phrase; a solo meditation, "Yesterday, I Made Your Breakfast"; and the heavily caffeinated title number, "Too Much Coffee Man." Best of all is a performance of "Fish for Supper," by Cootie Williams, though I don't think he ever recorded it, with Woods, bassist Ray Drummond, and drummer Billy Hart. The lyric goes, "We got fish for suppah, first one thing then anothah," a very Dorough-like rhyme. After a smooth piano solo, he and Woods interject Tadd Dameron's "Good Bait," as if to prove that the nerd of yesteryear is one of the last hipsters standing.

[*Village Voice*, 16 May 2000]

67 ❖ *Freed Jazz: Bell One (Ornette Coleman)*

On a recent Thursday morning, I visited the recording studio and rehearsal space Ornette Coleman has created in a building at 125th Street and Park. Fifteen mostly young musicians were coming to grips with Coleman's "La Statue," subtitled "The Country that Gave the FREEDOM Symbol to America." Commissioned in 1989 for Bastille Day and performed several times in Europe by Ensemble Moderne, it will receive its American debut Thursday night, June 1, at the Battery Park kickoff to the New York Bell Atlantic Jazz Festival. On the same program, Coleman will perform in and present new work composed for the Global Expressions Project—with Charnett Moffett, Denardo Coleman, and Asian musicians, including Badal Roy—and the immortal trio with Charlie Haden and Billy Higgins.

The last time Coleman presented a triptych in New York was four years ago at Lincoln Center and that was spread over as many nights. His erratic performing schedule over the past 40 years has had the benefit of keeping the ardor of his fans at a constant low flame. When a fix is in the offing, the flame erupts, and if the fix includes a reunion with Haden and Higgins, time stops. You will never get to see Oliver and Armstrong at Lincoln Gardens, or Ellington at the Cotton Club, or Parker and Gillespie on 52nd Street, or Brown and Roach in concert; Coleman, Haden, and Higgins, however, live and breathe. Did I mention that this concert is an Event? Michael Dorf must be praying everything will go off without a hitch, despite the broken toe Ornette recently suffered, in which case we can happily concede that he is a true showman—the Florenz Zeigfeld of jazz.

But up on 125th Street, the rehearsal was moving forward in fits and starts, mostly fits. All the musicians present, excepting trumpeter Lew Soloff and percussionist Greg Bendian, had been recruited from the classical world by violinist and conductor Tom Chiu, and they needed to talk the piece through. "La Statue" belongs to that part of Coleman's oeuvre you might call classical but I call notated. As with his woodwind octet and symphony, every note is written—complete with bowing markings for the strings. Yet the 20-piece orchestra (five members were absent), which includes a double string quartet, will appear as the Harmolodic Chamber Ensemble, and you know what that means. Well, actually you probably don't, and neither did most of the musicians, which is why they were talking so much. One violinist asked, "What style do we play?" Tom Chiu answered, "Pretty much your own style. You have to bring yourself to it."

Coleman, the philosopher king of American music, could not attend the rehearsal because of his toe. A harmolodic pep talk would have been something to hear. The main challenge posed by the piece is this: It consists mostly of solos that, while notated, do not have to be—and, preferably, ought not to be—played literally. That does not mean a musician can ignore a passage and substitute a B-flat blues. But it does mean walking an adventurous line between discipline and freedom. The conundrum is not, from a jazz perspective, as radical as it may seem. The beauty of Coleman's music has always been that it honors instinct before theory. In conventional jazz, where harmony, movement, and melody are not fused into a single term, the player has to walk a similar line— it's called chord changes.

Coleman is not opposed to musical conventions and has used a lot of them since the days of *Free Jazz*. For one noteworthy example, "La Statue" has time signatures; it begins in 12/8 and all the passages I heard were pretty comfortably parsed in multiples of four. But he draws the line at predetermined chord changes—he would rather musicians rely on his score than hazard the clichés lurking in a standard progression. Although if he wrote it the progression wouldn't be standard. At least I assume he feels that way. Thinking through harmolodics is a bit like playing them; you have to bring yourself to it. Coleman will presently finish his book on the subject, which will make everything crystal, but for now we can say with some confidence that no one has more original and interesting ways to break down the barriers between written and improvised music. His soloists, in "La Statue," can change a note, reconfigure a phrase, alter rhythm, range, even the key—or not.

It occurs to me that maybe we have misread the phrase "free jazz," and that "free" isn't an adjective, after all, but a verb—as in Free Mandela or Free the *Voice* of E-mail Spies. Coleman has certainly helped to do that, freeing it to be minimally or maximally governed by compositional dicta. There was not one passage during the rehearsal that did not suggest his particular jazz pedigree, with its high voicings, tympani rhythms, and melding of keys into a harmonic palette as broad as the skies of America. Whether it was clarinetist Dave Morgan practicing an eight-note phrase or the entire ensemble falling into an episode welded to a tympani bounce, the result was pure Coleman. At one point, he scores the winds in fourths and fifths and the strings in seconds and minor seconds; he uses harmonic grinds throughout and the tonal centers are almost invariably ambiguous. Yet what power they convey. The climax is astounding, a harmolodic jig built entirely on quadruplets—a spare, mostly quarter-note figure propelled furiously into rapid-fire eighth and sixteenth notes, all built on a four-note foundation, and finally lifting off like a rocket. After the group played the final section, it cheered itself. The statue that inspired the piece will be visible behind the musicians at Battery Park.

Coincidentally, three albums from 1971 to 1975 that plot the emergence of Coleman's harmolodic revelation have just been reissued, though the third was kept under wraps until 1982. He was under contract to Columbia for a year before the company chose to prune the roster (this was the era of Jive Clive Davis, himself recently pruned); out went Coleman, Mingus, Bill Evans, and Keith Jarrett. *Science Fiction* and the fugitive tracks later released on *Broken Shadows* (which, I am chagrined to realize, are new to me) have been collected as a two-disc set, *The*

Complete Science Fiction Sessions. Most of the material comes from September 1971, and notwithstanding a few charmless vocals, it positively glimmers: in numbers by the great quartet, of course, but also in the quintet with Bobby Bradford and Dewey Redman, and especially in a fantastically supple septet—a kind of *Free Jazz* double-quartet with just one bassist. I am too overwhelmed by my belated discovery of the four septet numbers ("Written Word" is unreleased) to suggest a comparison with the octet, except to note that Bradford is more in sync with Don Cherry and the music than Freddie Hubbard was and Dewey Redman is every bit as persuasive, maybe more so, as Eric Dolphy: His solo on the exhilarating "Happy House" is classic.

The symphony *Skies of America*, recorded by Coleman with the London Symphony Orchestra conducted by David Measham, is the work that introduced the harmolodic theory. But these two albums combined with the third, *Dancing in Your Head* (Verve), recorded in 1973 and 1975, offer an inadvertent guide to the theory in the guise of one recurring melody. In *Science Fiction*, it is called "School Work," though an element of the theme also appears in "Happy House." It's the third movement in *Skies*, "The Good Life," which lets you know in a minute or so that the lowering skies will be periodically brightened by Coleman candles, most of them in the second half, ignited by his own alto (especially an extended cadenza in "The Men Who Live in the White House" that resurrects the rhythm of "The Good Life")—the only improvising instrument on the recording.

Then the tune charges into harmolodic heaven—worked up by repetition from a quasi-blues to a fervid chant and improved by a hot closing cadence—as *Dancing in Your Head*'s "Theme from a Symphony" (variations one and two), which excepting two brief tracks with the Master Musicians of Jajouka (one previously unissued) constitutes the short—by watch-time only—disc. A quarter of a century later, *Dancing* is more remarkable than ever, perhaps because back then we assumed it would open a floodgate of like performances, if only by Coleman and his harmolodic passengers. Yet it remains entirely sui generis, an extended saxophone romp and rant that for sheer creative volatility is rivaled in that period only by Sonny Rollins's "G-Man." At the time of its release, many were troubled by the plugged-in guitars and bass, but far more interesting was its structural similarity to the symphony—once again Coleman was free in a tableau largely notated.

Coleman has said that his written-improvised works, unlike the heads-and-solos numbers, require frequent performance so that players can adjust to their possibilities and audiences can appreciate the variety of performing options. At Battery Park, the harmolodic strain will connect the extremes of his achievement and master musicians and new-comers will have the opportunity to find out who they are.

[*Village Voice*, 6 June 2000]

68 ❖ *Comeback Number Six*
(Lonnie Johnson)

Lonnie Johnson is back, sort of. It's only fitting: He's been coming back every decade or so since the 1920s, casting big shadows and then receding into them, as though he were nothing more than a footnote to his own text. Had he died in 1930, he would be remembered as a legend twice over: in blues, as one of the two men—along with Scrapper Blackwell (whom he preceded on records by three years)—responsible for the single-line guitar style that supplanted the denser, scruffier Delta attack; in jazz, as one of the two men—along with Eddie Lang (who preceded him on records by one year)—present at the birth of jazz guitar, consigning the banjo to riverboat oblivion. He is the only player claimed as an influence by T-Bone Walker and B. B. King as well as by Django Reinhardt and Charlie Christian.

But he died in 1970, filling in time between rediscoveries by working in steel mills and at other nonmusical jobs, all the while learning and writing more songs, so that by the time of his last corporeal go-round, he baffled at least as many listeners as he pleased. The blues and folk audience looked away in embarrassment when he sang "How Deep Is the Ocean," "My Mother's Eyes," or "Red Sails in the Sunset." The jazz crowd dismissed him as a relic. According to notes for the just-released *The Unsung Blues Legend*, Duke Ellington, with whom Johnson recorded so memorably in 1928, declined to appear with this "old blues guy," when he guest-starred with Ellington's band at Town Hall in 1961. No evidence is given, but it could be true; the *New York Herald Tribune* caught the flavor of the moment with the headline "The Duke and the Janitor Hold a Jazz Reunion." There was no reunion; Ellington, who introduced Lena Horne, didn't even introduce Lonnie.

Johnson, New Orleans–born and city-bred, once complained of folk-lorists who tried "to stick a crutch under my ass." Given his druthers, he was perfectly capable of modulating from a guitar arrangement of "Danny Boy" to a vocal wail on "Backwater Blues," which is, in fact, one of the medley transitions on the remarkable new CD that resurrects

Johnson with an intimacy new to records. *The Unsung Blues Legend*—an unhappily restrictive title, considering the contents—was recorded in 1965, in the Forest Hills home of his friend and benefactor, Bernie Strassberg, who turned on his Wollensack as Johnson performed for friends and family—at one point, a small voice cries out, "Daddy!" Several years later, Strassberg gave the tape to Jim Eigo, who recently conceded that he had to mature 20 years before he realized how special it was and prepared to issue it on his new label, Blues Magnet.

Johnson's whole career bounded between worlds that were not nearly as conflicting in the 1920s as they later became. His records with Louis Armstrong crest the highest peaks of the Hot Five/Seven series (on that occasion, he practically invented rock and roll triplets). He once described his dapper duets with Eddie Lang, who recorded as Blind Willie Dunn as a nod to the color bar, as "my greatest experience." But he recorded hundreds of traditional blues in the same period (1925–32), many self-composed. Briefly the worlds collided, when he was rediscovered in the 1940s, and scored the number one rhythm and blues hit of 1948 with "Tomorrow Night," a song by Sam Coslow, who was more commonly associated with Bing Crosby. Relaxing in a Queens home, in 1965, he keeps all those ghosts at bay, beginning with a nod to Frank Sinatra, "This Love of Mine." He bends it easily to his style, accepts applause, and continues with "September Song." Then, after a chorus of "Don't Cry Baby," he segues to "Solitude," and from that point he is on a stream-of-consciousness bender, running the gamut from George Jessel ("My Mother's Eyes") and Russ Columbo ("Prisoner of Love") to "Careless Love," "St. Louis Blues," and a rueful blues of his own ("There's Been Some Changes Made") before finishing with "Rockin' Chair." He is riveting.

Except for "Danny Boy," his guitar work is mostly confined to honeyed obbligato breaks, bass lines and chords, and introductory figures that often partake of a signature phrase made famous in "Tomorrow Night." Johnson's guitar is at once repetitive and inventive; just when you think you know his limitations, he comes up with a zinger. One of the great unknown guitar solos is his spot on "West End Blues," from the 1965 *Stompin' at the Penny*, recorded with a Canadian Dixieland outfit, Jim McHarg's Metro Stompers. (It was briefly available from Columbia Legacy, until McHarg launched a justifiable suit; the CD had been issued under Johnson's name, though he appears on less than half of it, and the players were unidentified.) Considering his classic jazz work, it is amazing how rarely Johnson got to work with bands in his many comebacks. But necessity and his own blues background mothered the inventiveness that allowed him to recreate himself as a free-standing troubadour with

a huge book and a guitar that followed him like a second voice. You
could not ask for a better demonstration than *The Unsung Blues Legend*.

[*Village Voice*, 13 June 2000]

69 ❖ Mrs. Swing
(Mildred Bailey)

Poor Mildred Bailey. Her life was short and difficult and the neglect of
her art has been long and impervious. During the height of her career,
she was accounted one of the most important singers in jazz or popular
music, universally admired by critics and peers. Yet she enjoyed fewer
than a dozen hits, most of them in the years 1937 to 1939, when Bailey
and her husband Red Norvo were optimistically promoted as "Mr. and
Mrs. Swing." Norvo's band, with its plush Eddie Sauter arrangements,
was no less prized, but it also eluded popularity. Mildred's deceptively
girlish voice and Red's nuanced polish had to fight for a place at a banquet dominated by lusty swing and mooning nostalgia, when the only
kind of fighting they knew was to remain stubbornly independent. After
they split up, Red brought his xylophone and (as of 1943) vibes to Benny
Goodman, bebop, and Woody Herman, and established himself as a
maverick jazz star. Mildred recorded for small labels while fighting debilitating illnesses for nearly a decade, before dying, in 1951, at 48.

Every so often, someone mounts a tribute or mourns her lack of recognition or releases a CD, but attempts to restore Bailey to the pantheon
never take hold. Part of the blame must go to Columbia Legacy, which
controls most of her best records and has declined to reissue them. In
1962, John Hammond edited a three-volume LP set, *Mildred Bailey: Her
Greatest Performances 1929–1946*, doing for her what Columbia had done
for his other favorite singers, Bessie Smith and Billie Holiday. Musically,
the collection was superb, but Hammond, who favored singers and records he produced, had a self-serving agenda and ignored dozens of sides
that have remained unavailable since the era of 78s. Neither that set nor
the better one Bailey merits has made it to CD. Her second act is long
overdue.

She was born Mildred Rinker, in 1903, on a large wheat farm 12 miles
from Tekoa, Washington, across the border on the Idaho side. Her
mother, Josephine, was part Coeur d'Alene Indian, and as the farm was
on the reservation, the land had been deeded to her tax-free. Mildred

was the oldest of four children and their home was filled with music. On occasion, neighbors from miles around would arrive in buggies for socials at which Mr. Rinker played fiddle and his wife piano. Every evening after supper, Mrs. Rinker, who had studied music with the nuns at the Catholic Academy in Tekoa, ventured selections from opera to ragtime. She spent hours at the piano with Mildred, teaching her to play and sing. Mildred was a skillful bareback rider who rode a buckskin pony five miles to school every morning with her brother Miles clinging to her waist. Her brother Alton—who would became Bing Crosby's vaudeville partner and later a member of the Rhythm Boys and a radio producer and composer—remembered those early years as idyllic.

In 1912, Mr. Rinker bought one of the first automobiles in the area to transport equipment from the city. Realizing he preferred the city, he leased the farm and moved the family 60 miles west to Spokane, where he opened an auto supply shop. Mildred was enrolled at St. Joseph's Academy, where she studied piano and became an able player. Tragedy struck in 1916, when Josephine contracted tuberculosis and died. Faced with raising four children, Charles Rinker hired a string of housekeepers and married one—an abusive grasping woman, who moved in with her daughter while insisting he send his kids to boarding school. Rinker resisted her threats, trying to keep the family together, but Mildred despised her. Al remembered her at the piano singing songs of longing and faraway places: "Siren of the Southern Seas," "Just a Baby's Prayer at Twilight," "Araby." In 1920, at 17, Mildred packed a bag and ran off to Seattle.

For a while she lived with an aunt and supported herself by demonstrating sheet music at Woolworth's. Within a year, however, she married a merchant named Ted Bailey; the marriage was brief, but she decided to keep his name because she thought it sounded more American than the Swiss-derived Rinker. With the advent of Prohibition, the government's gift to jazz, Mildred began to sing in speakeasies on the coast and in Canada. While working in Vancouver and Calgary, she met and married a bootlegger named Benny Stafford. In those days, she looked nothing like the overweight "Rockin' Chair Lady" of 1930s radio fame. She was barely five feet and weighed under a hundred pounds. When her father finally shed himself of the wicked stepmother, Mildred visited Spokane to sing at Charlie Dale's speakeasy.

Her brother Al, four years younger, was unable to see her perform, though she shared with him records she collected by Bessie Smith and Ethel Waters. But Al's friend Bing apparently did see Mildred at Dale's, even if his recollection of her as "the area's outstanding singing star" was a substantial exaggeration; she appeared locally only once and was little noted—speakeasies weren't reviewed. "She specialized in sultry, throaty renditions with a high concentrate of Southern accent, such as 'Louisville Lou' and 'Hard-Hearted Hannah,'" Bing recalled.

Mildred and Benny moved to Los Angeles, where they bought a house at 1307 Coronado, a few blocks off Sunset Boulevard. He was prospering with his bootlegging and she was earning a reputation singing sad songs in local dives. In 1925, she was working for tips at a speakeasy in the Hollywood Hills run by a friend, Jane Jones. The place was a converted private house set back from the road and surrounded by a fence. A lookout vetted customers and ushered them into a large crowded room with tables, a bar, and a small platform for the piano and singer. The regulars, many of them movie stars, could avail themselves of prostitutes as well as booze. When the spirit moved her, Jane Jones, a big woman with a brassy style (Crosby later featured her in his movie *East Side of Heaven*), would sing a song or two, but her customers preferred the cooing subtlety of Mildred, whose melodramatic warhorses, such as "Ships That Never Came In," generated a river of generous tips.

Mildred was working at Jane's when Al and Bing arrived, unannounced, on her doorstep, hoping she could help start them in show business. She took them in, encouraged them, advised them of auditions, played records she thought they ought to hear, and boarded them until they were on their feet, which did not take long. By then, she had become an obsessive cook and Al was shocked to see how heavy she had become. She instantly hit it off with Bing, who called her Millie. They both liked a good time and shared advanced and expansive tastes in music. Al found her "a little too barrelhouse for me," but to Bing she was "*mucho mujer*, a genuine artist, with a heart as big as the Yankee Stadium, and a gal who really loved to laugh it up." Within a year, Paul Whiteman hired the boys, who resolved someday to help her attain the break she deserved. Nearly three years later, they had their chance.

The Whiteman band returned to Los Angeles in 1929, to make *King of Jazz*, but everything went wrong and after weeks of waiting for the studio to come up with a script, the frustrated bandleader prepared to pull out. Whiteman made it clear he was not hiring anyone, least of all another singer (he had turned down Hoagy Carmichael that week), but Bing and Al were certain that if they could just get him to hear Mildred he would fall under her spell. Millie had become friendly with several guys in the band that summer. She took them horseback riding, cooked up a storm, and served her home brew, which created a sensation, as good beer was hard to find. Bing and Al persuaded her to throw the band a farewell party. Whiteman, a prodigious beer drinker, happily accepted the invitation. As Bing recalled, "Paul didn't know it at the time, but he was a goner when he walked into the house."

Hoagy Carmichael, Roy Bargy, and Lennie Hayton took turns at her Steinway. Rinker described what happened next: "Bing turned to Mildred and said, 'Hey, Millie, why don't you sing a song?' No one had ever heard her sing but they all joined in, 'Yeah, c'mon, Millie, let's have a song.' At first, Mildred acted reluctant, but I knew it wouldn't last long." She asked Al to accompany her on "(What Can I Say) After I Say I'm Sorry," and "she sang the hell out of the song." After a brief silence, everyone started to cheer and Whiteman, who had been in the kitchen, asked who was singing. Bing barked, "That was Millie, Al's sister." Whiteman walked over, kissed her, and asked for an encore. "All her past experience singing in speakeasies and night spots came out as she sang. Her small, pure voice gave the songs feeling and meaning, and you knew you were hearing a singer who was very special," Al wrote. That night Paul hired her to sing "Moanin' Low" on his Old Gold radio show. Weeks later she was on a train to New York, a contract in her purse—the first "girl singer" to tour with an orchestra. A year later she was the highest-salaried performer on Whiteman's payroll.

She made her first record in 1929, with Eddie Lang, and became an instant favorite of the jazz elite—the one white woman (she preceded Lee Wiley and Connie Boswell by a couple of years) with an identifiable style who could hold her own in a field dominated by black singers. She had been one of the first to assimilate the styles of Bessie Smith (whose blues she sang in an audition for Hammond), Ethel Waters (whose lighter voice was closer to home), and Louis Armstrong (whose time and invention liberated everyone). She would emerge as a transitional figure between them and the band singers that followed, including Billie Holiday and Ella Fitzgerald, though Bailey had a style all her own. Her high light voice inclined to a whirring in the top notes while packing plenty of power; her time and enunciation were exemplary. After a couple of years as a sidewoman, indulging in excessive vibrato, she rid herself of affect and ornamentation. She focused on the language of a song, the meaning, the special story it had to tell. She was funny, cool, smooth, and always in a groove.

In 1933, she married Whiteman's xylophonist Red Norvo, and during the next couple of years, before he organized his own orchestra, she became famous for her radio appearances, billed as the "Rockin' Chair Lady," after her 1932 success with the Hoagy Carmichael song. For a while, she and Red lived with violinist Joe Venuti and his wife Sally on 55th Street. Along with Bing, himself a radio star, and his wife Dixie, living at the nearby Essex House, the two couples often socialized, anticipating few hardships in riding out the Depression. But Mildred was bedeviled by a fierce temper, enormous pride, and a lonely soul that she attempted to soothe with food. Al thought she used the dishes she prepared and her pets—a fleet of dachshunds—as a substitute for children. As sentimental as she was high-strung, she was an easy touch and a formidable enemy. Trombonist Milt Bernhart related a story he learned from Norvo, years after her death, when he mentioned that the first time he heard the classic records she made with Teddy Wilson, he—like many others—assumed she was black. Red chuckled and told him a story that he thought summed her up.

After Mildred became a star in the early 1930s, headlining on radio and in theaters with Whiteman's orchestra, a rival singer spread rumors that she was black and a Hearst columnist began publishing hints to that effect. Whiteman didn't care in the least—he would have hired black musicians if his management hadn't talked him out of it. But Mildred was incensed. One day she asked Whiteman if he was still friendly with William Randolph Hearst, whom he had known during his salad days in San Francisco. Whiteman said he was. She demanded he phone Hearst and have the columnist fired. Whiteman complied, as did Hearst. A couple of years later, she and Red emerged from a theater when a man in a threadbare overcoat walked over and asked, "Miss Bailey?" The former columnist apologized for what he had written and turned to go, by which time Mildred was convulsed with tears. She asked his name and address, then went to Whiteman and got him rehired.

Her marriage to Red lasted until 1945, but by then the war and changing tastes had challenged them in a way the Depression could not. Bailey adapted to a modern context with an even more robust yet austere attack, but was relegated to a fading era. Unlike Billie and Ella, whose producers recorded them in pop contexts saturated with strings, she pressed on with small-group sessions devoted to mostly good but little-known songs. She recorded some of her finest work in her later years, while suffering from diabetes and heart disease. Yet attention was no longer paid.

Several excellent CDs track her progress while skirting the period owned by Columbia; unfortunately, they duplicate each other. The best introductory discs are *The Rockin' Chair Lady* (Decca) and the British import, *That Rockin' Chair Lady* (Topaz), both of which have the Teddy Wilson date with Johnny Hodges and Bunny Berigan. The Decca includes her 1941 session with the Delta Rhythm Boys, stunning versions of "Lover Come Back to Me" and "It's So Peaceful in the Country," and her last studio records, from 1950, which reveal how vital she remained. The

Topaz is a 1930s greatest-hits anthology, including sessions with the Dorsey Brothers, Benny Goodman, and an all-star band with Teddy Wilson and Chu Berry ("When Day Is Done" and "Someday Sweetheart"), and a few of her and Norvo's Columbias, notably "Thanks for the Memory," "Don't Be That Way," and the incomparably spooky "Smoke Dreams."

For a closer look at how she developed, two volumes on TOM track her from 1929 to 1934; they repeat all the Dorsey and Goodman tracks from Topaz and the Casa Loma date from Decca, but offer much more. Volume one, *Sweet Beginnings*, shows how labored her Ethel Waters–influenced vibrato was in the early years—to the point of a Jolson-esque theatricality that is oddly effective on "Travlin' All Alone," one of two tracks heightened by Jimmie Noone's stirring blend of clarinet and alto sax. She jettisoned a trademark *hanh-h'-hanh-h'-hanh* humming bit, thankfully, heard on the Casa Loma "When It's Sleepy Time Down South," which is not nearly as good as the Whiteman version, recorded months later and also included. By November 1931 ("Too Late"), she is entirely in her element, and remains there for volume two, *Band Vocalist*, which is marred only by a few "darkie" songs—but that's history. *Red Norvo—Featuring Mildred Bailey* is an enchanting selection of Columbias, including the very swinging "I've Got My Love to Keep Me Warm," but most of her benchmark performances from that period are unvailable—the sublime 1938–39 dates with "Ghost of a Chance," featuring Mary Lou Williams, "Bob White," the hilarious "Weekend of a Private Secretary," and many more.

The later period is spottily covered by *The Legendary V-Disc Sessions* (VJC) and *The Blue Angel Years* (Baldwin), which duplicate some of the same V-Discs. But the former, though impaired by the most unctuous radio voice ever heard, includes four duets with Teddy Wilson, among them an achingly slow "Rockin' Chair," and a few intriguing breakdown takes with Norvo, as well as a definitive reading of the song that should have been her second signature tune, "I'll Close My Eyes." That little-remembered gem is also included on the Baldwin CD, which focuses on the sessions she made for Crown and—far better—Majestic, with pianist Ellis Larkins. The best known of the Majestics (produced by Hammond in 1946), however, are found on the unreasonably short *Me and the Blues* (Savoy), though a more comprehensive edition has been issued in Europe. Among the highlights are the studio version of "I'll Close My Eyes"; the best song written by her brother Al, "You Started Something"; the first date-rape anthem, "It's a Woman's Prerogative"; and her heavenly "Lover Come Back to Me." Once you get Bailey's light liquid voice in your head, you want more and more.

[*Village Voice*, 13 June 2000]

70 ❖ Saved by the Classics: Bell Two (Bell Atlantic 2000)

Okay, so Michael Dorf is not the Flo Ziegfeld of jazz, not yet. Forgive the pre-festival enthusiasm, but the pain of festivals past, like the pain of pregnancy, has no shelf life. Last year at this time I was vowing to be in another country this year at this time, but then I looked at the schedule—Ornette! Max and Cecil! the Art Ensemble!—and capitulated to a heedless optimism. Where else would you want to be and how could anything go wrong? Such a simple concept: You exchange a ticket for a specific seat, the lights go down at a prearranged time, great musicians emerge to play great music.

But that's not exactly the way the Bell Atlantic Jazz Festival works. In its second year and with tentacles in D.C., Boston, and Philadelphia, the heir to the long-running Knitting Factory What Is Jazz? Festival and a fleeting season of Texaco sponsorship wants to be at once inclusive, legit, and Bohemian.* So the great music that *was* played cost more than the price of a ticket. Consider the following triptych of big events. All were imperfect. But unlike many of the lesser shows, at least they weren't predictable.

You may have heard about the blinding yellow lights, emanating from the stage and into the eyes of the audience, that went on a half-hour into Ornette Coleman's final set—the one with Charlie Haden and Billy Higgins—at his opening night Battery Park concert. The Parks Department chose to impose a curfew, subjecting patrons (who paid as much as $65) to an indignity it would never think of implementing at a free Central Park concert with Diana Ross or the New York Philharmonic, where the audience is many times larger. The lights were commissioner Henry Stern's way of saying, "Coleman, you've got five minutes to finish your piece." The lights did not merely blink a warning, but remained on, while generators in the rear roared into clattering motion, until it was no longer possible to play or be heard. There were no assaults, no fights, no disturbances of any kind to warrant such treatment, though the crowd might have considered tarring and feathering Stern and the imbecile who hit the switch.

Except for jazz reviews, the incident didn't make the evening news;

---

*It turned out Bell Atlantic wanted mostly to be legit. This was its last collaboration with the Knitting Factory; Dorf, reeling from financial difficulties, did not present a festival in 2001 or after.

we have become a city willing to accept arbitrarily imposed curfews. Incidentally, the lights went on not at midnight or 1 A.M., but at 10:10. The concert began at 7. Unless the Statue of Liberty wanted to take a nap, the likelihood of residential complaints was nil. The whole business was pure thumb-in-your-eye bureaucratic idiocy. But it didn't begin there. From the late start, there were occasional jackhammers, as if the city and Bell were unaware of each other's existence. The sound, Bell's problem, was dismal for the opening set—the debut of Coleman's Global Expression Project, in which the backup musicians were amped at the same level as Coleman. Audio was especially cloudy in the press section, a holding pen populated mostly by suits who were louder than the jack-hammers. George Wein figured out how to amplify an outdoor space and handle ruly crowds at Newport 45 years ago. At Battery Park, you'd have thought open-air concerts were a novelty.

For the second set, I escaped the pen and had no trouble hearing the American debut of the chamber piece alternately known as "La Statue" and "Freedom Symbol," a marvelous 40-minute paradox that begins and ends with notated ensemble sections and has a long middle part in which each player solos—improvising or embellishing a notated episode. Drawing on diverse influences from Renaissance music to 19th-century romanticism to jazz, the players generally acquitted themselves well, though Lew Soloff's startlingly rangy trumpet episode, accompanied by guitar and suggesting an exalted Coleman ballad, so outdistanced the rest you couldn't help but wonder what the piece would sound like if most of the players had been drawn from jazz rather than classical. The speedy, mounting closing section, bouncing off Greg Bendian's tympanis, is a roller-coaster thrillride.

The hastily interrupted trio should have sent everyone away drifting on a cloud. Against Haden's buoyant rumble and Higgins's pneumatic suspension of time, Coleman's gorgeously ragged riffs swan-dived and jackknifed, ageless and serene, instantly echoing a distant foghorn, dropping momentary references to "La Marseillaise," "Autumn Leaves," and "The Good Life," and freely reveling until our guardians stepped in, for our own good.

Little attempt at crowd control was necessary at Columbia University, where Max Roach and Cecil Taylor revisited the site of their original 1979 duets. The city could not interfere and the music went on for hours, though most of those hours were prelude to the main event, including one by Bob Stewart's La Guardia High School jazz orchestra, with guest soloists (Warren Vaché, James Spaulding, Wessel Anderson). Does any other music promote amateurism—from school bands to weekend dilettantes—the way jazz presently does? I was reminded of a story Ira

Gitler tells about standing backstage with Gerry Mulligan at a concert in Europe while students played. A woman enthused, "Aren't they cute?" Gerry retorted, "Madame, jazz is not cute."

Happily, part of the evening was given to David S. Ware's quartet, with Matthew Shipp, William Parker, and Guillermo E. Brown, a tremendous ensemble of virtuoso excess. Ware is a true believer who, combining Ayler's tonal grit, Coltrane's volubility, and Rollins's muscular drive, is an avant-gardist by design. He has not only taken the flash-fire music of the '60s another step, but also constructed an inspired rhythmic foundation. Despite one piece with a triple-meter vamp, the quartet never let up and never lost the audience, which leaped to its feet at the end. Free jazz has always had a communal appeal, breeding a concert excitement that doesn't necessarily carry over to records—the kind of intensity that can be oppressive at home can be liberating when diffused through a crowd of thousands.

A few years back, I dreamed I detected a mellowing in Cecil Taylor's playing. If his recent work with Elvin Jones had not disabused me of such heresy, his reunion with Max Roach would have. From the git (no recitation, no song), he was titanic, pushing great parabolic blocks of sound as though brushing aside gnats. As he wound up, throwing in an occasional elbow, he suggested a high-wire athleticism—headstands, somersaults, leaving the wire altogether to fly! fly! fly! fly! Roach, who leaned heavily on a tuned-tom that suggested a tenor tympani, never flinched. Au contraire: After 50 minutes, Taylor began what seemed a negotiation for closure; he looked up at the drummer and offered a possible clearing space, to which Roach responded with a furious fuselage that brought the pianist back to the front line. That happened several times—Taylor working toward an exit and Roach slamming all the doors. Finally, at the hour mark, they agreed to desist, or at least ventured enough of a pause for Taylor to walk away from the piano, at which point Roach embarked on a drum solo. These guys, 71 and 76, would have known how to handle that punk Henry Stern.

For much of the week, I felt like I was in the hall of mirrors in Chaplin's *The Circus*—or maybe the party of ghosts in Kubrick's *The Shining*. One night I accepted an invitation from pianist Bill Savory to attend a memorial gathering for his late wife, singer Helen Ward, at the Hotel Pennsylvania. He had rented the penthouse ballroom, provided food, erected huge speakers to play his wife's records with Benny Goodman and others, and set up a bandstand for musicians who chose to sit in. Maybe a dozen people arrived. Staring out the window at neighboring gargoyles, with Helen and Benny swinging behind me, I imagined eternal ballrooms, sparsely attended by those who wish to recall a dusty era, and asked a few of those present how it felt when their particular world ended, but no one could remember.

Helen was still singing when I left for the Jazz Standard, where Uri Caine had different gargoyles on the brain, wrestling with Bach's Goldberg Variations. I like his Mahler, not so much his Schubert, and now it's time for Caine to come back to the blues. This was a novel montage-music that changed course often enough to avoid boredom, but without making a point. When Caine or his violinist played it straight, they didn't do it as well as Gould or Schiff; when his saxophonist (Greg Tardy) or trumpeter (Ralph Alessi) issued jazzy variations they punctured any illusion of continuity. A tango variation was slick and amusing, but Barbara Walker's gospel and DJ Olive's turntables added little beyond the suspension of belief. At least they got a few laughs. "As Long as You're Living Yours: The Music of Keith Jarrett," with Tom Harrell, Mike Manieri, and George Garzone, took the same stage later in the week to reflect reflections of pieces that do not exactly cry out for reinvestigation. When I could no longer feel a pulse, mine or the music's, I left. A few days later the same bandstand would be resurrecting Hank Mobley. Help!

I arrived early at the Knitting Factory for the Art Ensemble of Chicago's tribute to Lester Bowie and heard a terrific soundcheck, as Roscoe Mitchell, Malachi Favors Maghostut, and Famoudou Don Moye bopped with great insouciance and charm, Mitchell testing his flute (he practiced a strain from Bach), tenor, alto, and soprano, producing vital and distinctive timbres on each. The stage was packed like a winter closet with racks of drums, cymbals, gourds, xylophones, shakers, blowers—a complete store of "little instruments." The doors opened at 8 for an 8:00 concert, guaranteeing a late start—8:30 to be precise.

The trio finally arrived and began to explore the little instruments, which took another half hour. Longuers are part of the Art Ensemble's bag of tricks, but in all the times I've seen them I've never experienced an interlude this tedious, not even when the point was provocation (as if you could provoke an audience at the Knitting Factory). When, at long last, Mitchell rose from the floor, where he had been crawling through the bric-a-brac, and played an extended, breathless, unwavering note on tenor, it was like rain in the desert. As Favors and Moye closed in, he configured a slow, familiar theme and followed with a relatively brief (maybe seven minutes) but enticing solo, flush with vestigial touches of Sonny Rollins. Changing to soprano, which he plays with hot-house ardor, Mitchell let loose a hurricane of overtones, at times spinning parallel phrases as if playing two instruments, and swinging with candid exhilaration over an arching four-beat. On alto, he swaggered boppishly over an appealing eight-bar theme. The Art Ensemble, a quintet until

Joseph Jarman left, is now a trio since the death of Lester Bowie, but it remains nonpareil, one of the finest bands we have. Maybe it's time to park some of the little instruments in the attic.

[Village Voice, 27 June 2000]

71 ❖ *Touring the Jazz Museum (JVC 2000)*

Is jazz a dead historic thing or is it simply homesick for another era, any other era? The first concert hall ever built to house jazz is about to go up at Columbus Circle; the academy is rapt with attention, building new departments, endowing chairs; statues will follow. But what exactly is being honored: a music of unceasing innovation and achievement, or an archive parsed into its historical components? If jazz in the 21st century is to become what classical music became in the 20th century, an art of reconnaissance and interpretation, then this year's 2000 JVC Jazz Festival may be remembered as a key transitional event. For the first time in its history, JVC looked backward every night. Two concerts by modern players, Don Byron and Dave Douglas, were canceled for lack of audience interest. But, then, Byron was scheduled to play his score for a silent picture and Douglas has been exploring Mary Lou Williams. It's as though we were strapped into a time machine without the lever that moves it forward or back: Time marches on, but we are stuck—with our memories.

So let me blur the matter by adding that this was the most satisfying JVC in several years. It was especially eventful for singers—Joao Gilberto, Cesaria Evora, and Cassandra Wilson (no real surprises there); Dianne Reeves, Diana Krall, and Joan Osborne (many surprises there). It raised the question from night to night, even from set to set, of whether you can go home again. The resounding final answer was: Some can, some can't. It also raised questions about racial authority, as James Williams and Don Byron essayed Bill Evans and Benny Goodman, and Mike Halby and Joan Osborne attempted Big Bill Broonzy and Sister Rosetta Tharpe.

Perhaps the most characteristic evening was the supremely peculiar "From Spirituals to Swing," an attempt to replicate the 1938 and 1939 Carnegie Hall concerts produced by John Hammond. I think the way to be true to Hammond's vision is to violate it: honoring his gift for recognizing innovation and genius, while acknowledging his limitations.

Hammond's goal was not didactic. He wanted to make a case for music he loved by presenting its finest exponents. Associate JVC producer Danny Kapilian showed courage in going beyond the usual jazz rep suspects, but was unwilling to dispense with the original instrumentation and repertory.

Nor could he let go of a bewildering self-consciousness about race, telling the audience that color blindness is a good thing as though he expected an argument. He did, in fact, get a lot of mumbled arguments when he claimed that the original "From Spirituals to Swing" was Carnegie Hall's first integrated concert, forgetting Benny Goodman's milestone (produced by Sol Hurok with help from Hammond) almost a year before. Besides, assertions of color blindness often raise embarrassing questions. Like: Was the evening's emcee, Danny Glover, who bungled every introduction, hired because of his love of music?

The concert began well enough with transplanted African Anjelique Kidjo, accompanied by ace studio percussionist Danny Sadownick, singing and strutting and getting the audience to clap in time. She was followed by Dr. John, paying homage to "Boogie-Woogie Masters," who the host said had something to do with New Orleans, and stride pianist and songwriter James P. Johnson—yet more creative history. No matter: Dr. John didn't quite raise the head of steam pumped out by Albert Ammons, Meade Lux Lewis, and Pete Johnson, but he held his own, interpolating "Sheik of Araby" into a blues. Don Byron and Steve Wilson joined with him for a trio that was supposed to suggest Sidney Bechet, but probably would have made him reach for his pistol.

Then came David Hidalgo and Mike Halby to confirm every possible prejudice against white guys singing the blues. Their dull-edged electric guitars turned the sound system to fog, and their interpretations were humorless and inept. Big Bill Broonzy had gotten big laughs with every punch line of "It Was Just a Dream"; Halby never got a chuckle, except when he conceded that he and his partner felt "like a couple of midgets." Race aside, you cannot sing blues without Authority. Glover returned to ask, "Do you feel Robert Johnson at the crossroads?" A witty rejoinder would have been too easy. So while I was thinking, "Stevie Ray notwithstanding, color blindness is not always a virtue, especially when so many good, authentic, black blues guys are around," out came Joan Osborne, who sexily cocked her hip and—backed by Wendell Holmes, a genuinely rocking guitarist—did two Sister Rosetta Tharpe numbers so effectively that, being color-blind, I figured Osborne was light-skinned. Later, I learned she is a Caucasian from Kentucky who apprenticed on the blues circuit and scored a rock hit. Her contralto rang true and clean, without affectation or fake humility, and seemed no less at home when she joined with the 11 singers of the SRC All-City Chorale for Tharpe's "Can't No Grave Hold My Body Down," the choir shadowing her like an orchestra.

Color was less the point than attitude when Don Byron allegedly played tribute to Benny Goodman's sextet; Byron's band, like Goodman's, was integrated. Now if Kapilian had recruited someone like Ken Peplowski, we might have heard Benny through the looking glass, but in hiring Byron he was aiming for a more interesting take and got it, though I did not get the point of the unswinging "Flying Home" or the "Memories of You" with a Latin vamp that ignored the melody until the last chorus. Drummer Joey Baron smashed his cymbal on every beat, as though packing bricks; his lack of elegance was reflected in inchoate solos by everyone but vibist Stefon Harris, who played with a direct, relaxed, melodic sparkle. By the third number, though, "Tuskegee Strutter's Ball" (Byron's "I Got Rhythm" variation), the group came into its own. Baron calmed down, and the leader delivered a good, chancy solo, quoting Monk and others, that wiped away the last vestiges of homage in favor of his own brave new world.

Another sextet followed, this one modeled after the Kansas City Six, with Geri Allen and with Steve Wilson's alto instead of Lester Young's (or Buddy Tate's) tenor. Twenty-year-old Bilal Oliver tried to get a rise out of "Going to Chicago"—a departure from the original program—but was too eccentric and whimsical (e.g., falsetto scat) to make his case. What came next, however, was the week's unexpected triumph. Dianne Reeves joined the band to do two Ida Cox blues, and while I would like a tape for confirmation, it seemed to me she was more enchanting than Ida herself. I reviewed Reeves in the '70s, when she was in her teens, and raved—thinking I was in the presence of a young Sarah. Every performance and record since has knifed my expectations. I have invariably found her mannered, showy, superficial, overproduced, whatever. I am now smitten once again.

She counted off a dangerously slow tempo on "Low Down Dirty Shame," coolly limned by Geri Allen, and attacked the song as though she'd just come in from a TOBA vaudeville tour, mining the lascivious wit in every line and getting all the laughs. She commanded attention with her nuances and unfailing time, inspiring Steve Wilson to his best solo and Randy Sandke to a sympathetic Shad Collins–style obbligato. "Four Day Creep" was even better. Without suggesting mimicry or overt homage, she captured the old blues diva aesthetic: natural, funny, and sure, incarnating the blues as short stories with coquettish punch lines. In a duet with Dr. John, she zeroed in on "Come Rain or Come Shine," dramatizing it to the hilt.

By contrast the Basie band, directed by Grover Mitchell, merely sounded great (the dynamics, the tuttis), when the Basie band should be more than that. It was nice to hear Kenny Hing and Doug Miller trade choruses on "9:20 Special," but no sooner did they start than they had to sit—each number was expeditious and short, except "One O'Clock Jump," which featured nine or 10 choruses by Don Byron, his most adventurous outing of the night, particularly when the band riffed at him like a hot poker. The finale consisted of the McCollough Sons of Thunder from Harlem—a tailgate trombone brass band, led by Elder Edward Babb—that marched down the aisles to the stage for an exhilarating close.

If "From Spirituals to Swing" was peaks and valleys, "Porgy and Bess & Sketches of Spain" was level and emphatic—maybe the best case made for jazz rep since Maurice Peress and the Carnegie Hall Jazz Band revived *Black, Brown and Beige*. The names Miles Davis and Gil Evans appeared nowhere in the playbill and were not mentioned on stage. Small point, but a program would have been nice. Last year, JVC presented a performance of *Kind of Blue*, so Miles continues to be a major draw. Yet conductor Maria Schneider and soloist Jon Faddis did more than offer a robust and faithful rendering of two classic albums; they argued by example that here are two of the great concerti of our time. It would be a shame to put them back in mothballs.

The presentation was immaculate—no emcees, no talk of any kind. Just bam! right into the roaring, weirdly Asiatic chords of "The Buzzard Song," and no rest for the weary. Schneider produced a hugely persuasive orchestral sound. Only the recollection of Paul Chambers's magnificent bass was shortchanged, especially on "My Man's Gone Now," which tends to flaccidity even on the original; fidelity to the text does not mean you can't kick the tempo a little if warranted. Still, for the most part I was happy to forget the records. Jon Faddis remains one of jazz's enigmas—an outstanding trumpet player and guaranteed crowd pleaser who is rarely cogent on records, partly because he cannot resist the Faddispheric climaxes that are his signature. He generally dodged high notes and did not attempt to imitate Miles. Playing flugelhorn and trumpet, he finessed each piece on its merits, delighting in the sliding two-pitch blasts that identify "Solea." It will be interesting to see if he can translate such Milesian caution into something more personal.

The audience was wonderful. At first, it refrained from applause between movements, as though paying respect to the rituals of classical music. But after "Gone" (excellent drumming by Dana Hall and a pointed Faddis solo), it said the hell with protocol: no obligatory applause, but no restraint when something merited an ovation. Faddis was almost too understated at times—I missed Miles's sobs and cries—but, working closely with Schneider, he kept both works on target, and may have surprised even himself with his hard-bitten eloquence on "Saeta" and Rodrigo's adagio. Carnegie, too, responded in kind; every instrument, from tuba to harp, rang clear, as did the shimmering woodwinds on "I Loves You Porgy," the building riff of "Prayer," and the Tchaikovsky-like colors on "Pan Piper."

Other moments during the week were no less memorable. Even the dreadful Bill Evans tribute at the Kaye Playhouse, which attempted to honor him as a composer and produced an arid, fat, and comfortable music, had two privileged moments: Renee Rosnes captured none of his drive or touch, except on "Epilogue" (from the 1966 Town Hall concert), a fleeting glimmer of his genius; and James Williams brought artful voicings to Evans's arrangement of "My Man's Gone Now." The first of the Carnegie Hall concerts, a Cliff's Notes history of tango called "Passion and Swing!" whetted the appetite for more of Pablo Ziegler's piano and Julia Zenko's voice—she sang a startling passage from a 1968 Astor Piazzola opera that consisted of constantly rising phrases, allowing few discernible rests. No less appealing, in collaboration with Ziegler, was Gary Burton, whose playing burbled with melody and whose lightning four-mallet technique remains wizardly. Another nice touch: dancers.

Cesaria Evora's band, with its Djangological guitarists and meticulous arrangements, was as enchanting as her slow, subtle, mid-register Cape Verdean blues. Cassandra Wilson was as shoeless as Evora, whose encores she followed with a smaller and more cohesive band than usual. A highlight of Wilson's engaging set was a duet with Cyndi Lauper, bearing a dulcimer; Lauper sang "Blue in Green" (*Kind of Blue*) while Wilson sang "Blue Skies" (Irving Berlin) and it worked just fine. Joao Gilberto had an attack of nerves and arrived at Carnegie an hour late to sing a 95-minute set that was like listening to a waterfall. Warren Vaché's big band at Kaye Playhouse was practiced, and offered the chance to see Jake Hanna, one of the swingingest drummers alive. Diana Krall at the Supper Club pretty near made me a believer, but I'll save her for next year when I'm more confident.

I can't do justice to the concert that was the most fun—the tribute to 90-year-old Milt Hinton at Kaye—because it was an uncontained and unembarrassed lovefest; reviewing it would be like evaluating a family reunion. Still, a few things: John Clayton managed an intricate program with incomparable savoir faire and everyone played well; Byron Stripling's vocal on "Minnie the Moocher" was a riot and so was Jay Leonhart's song-memoir about knowing Milt Hinton; Ron Carter's unaccompanied "Willow Weep for Me" reminded one why he is revered.

On "Jumpin' at the Woodside," Jimmy Heath reached back into his bag of riffs and, even amid the hustle, made the place sit up a little more. It was the kind of dyed-in-the-wool moment that obviates, for the time being, questions of jazz's vitality and relocates the music where it lives best—in the spontaneous exertion of a great soloist touched by the spirit.

[*Village Voice*, 18 July 2000]

72 ❖ *Carterology*
(James Carter)

Atlantic's simultaneous release of James Carter's *Chasin' the Gypsy*, a tribute to Django Reinhardt, and *Layin' in the Cut*, an exercise in jazz funk, reminds me of a moment from my childhood when the same label released two LPs by Bobby Darin, *At the Copa* and *For Teenagers Only*. Darin was trying to cross over to a grown-up, moneyed audience while keeping the allowanced one in line. Carter, as he notes in a press release, wants, "in light of the millennium thing, to have one foot in the past, in a musical sense, and another moving forward in time." So which is which? The way I hear it, the noisily diverting *Layin' in the Cut* takes the limited idea of virtuoso noodling over an electric backbeat as far as it can go, while the creamy homage opens new vistas in the realm of reinterpretation.

Admittedly, this realm is no longer a princely one. The jazz landscape is littered with pointless tributes and reinterpretations. What a relief to hack through all the Monk and Ellington salutes to get back to Monk and Ellington. Still, I don't think *Chasin' the Gypsy* will fade so quickly. It will make you want to hear the great Django—the better you know the originals, the more you can savor Carter's heady adaptations. But loving the Romany legend, many of whose best sides have now been issued by Mosaic as *The Complete Django Reinhardt and Quintet of the Hot Club of France Swing/HMV Sessions 1936–1948*, will not satisfy the anticipation Carter creates for his own faithfully intense, high-calorie vision. Carter's approach to the past, demonstrated less pointedly on earlier records, is not to turn backward on bended knee, but to go after it like a benevolent Ahab. He makes Django a 21st-century man.

Carter has always been a bear for ear-pinning entrances, beginning with the 1993 *JC on the Set*, and remains true to form in *Chasin' the Gypsy*, opening with the 1940 theme, "Nuages," which established Reinhardt as a French idol during the occupation. He begins with a thumping bass-drum-and-castanet vamp and then introduces the melody on bass saxophone, a sleepy-eyed brontosaurus in the hands of most players that here turns deep-chested and remarkably limber. Reinhardt himself began his recording with a weirdly minacious intro that seemed to augur a train piece, not the nostalgically Debussyan melody that became his calling card; he employed two clarinets to beef up the climax and a cowbell to ruffle the rhythm. Carter permits an unnecessary touch of cowbell (little more than an in-joke), but the beef is all his own. The bass sax alone would rumble the china, while Charlie Giordano's accordion obbligato captures a world of French lyricism—it might have served a Tati film score. Guitarists Jay Berliner and Romero Lubambo are usually heard in tandem, as they are here, doubling the time and avoiding Djangoisms. Carter's barreling solo lacks the poignancy and detail of the Gypsy's, but it is vindicated by a romantic fury and total commitment to the chords and their ambient demands. He closes with the first of the album's several cadenzas, gliding to a lovely high note to bring in the ensemble.

If "Nuages" is anthemic, the follow-up is the album's most obscure and charming touch, the childlike melody of "La Derniere Bergere," which Django recorded once, in 1935, as accompanist to singer Jean Sablon, whose concerts at Theater Daunou a couple of years earlier had helped establish the guitarist's career. Sablon performed the unusually constructed piece with rubato elasticity, slowing and rushing the time, as Carter does in the first chorus, before a transitional guitar episode charges the rhythm. Here the details count for a great deal. Carter is never more at home than on tenor—the rippled low notes at the first turnback, the crafty tonguing, the increasing ripeness of his timbre, and the shrieking full-bore climax, wasting the song's gentility, then returning to it for a protracted coda.

The English composer and critic Constant Lambert described Reinhardt as "without doubt, the most interesting figure in the world of jazz since Duke Ellington, and like him he is not so much an arranger as a composer." Carter makes a persuasive case for Django's tunes with his own luminous arrangements. He treats "Manoir de Mes Reves," his most Ellingtonian theme (especially in a 1945 big-band version), with alternating toughness and tenderness over a sturdy four-beat, kicking off his solo with a bluesy "Black Coffee" lick. Django, who soaked up the melodies heard in music halls and cabarets, had an infallible ability to cauterize sentimentality in devising his own, something Carter achieves with his extravagant virtuosity.

His technique abides relatively quietly in "Manoir," which ends with one of his patented two-note chords, and leads to an all-out assault on two coronary attacks, "Chasin' the Gypsy," an original based on "I Got Rhythm" changes, and the 1920s standard "Avalon." The first opens coolly enough with soprano and Joey Baron drum breaks, but after the head, the rhythm section stiffens into an automaton to keep up; the joke is that the second choruses of Carter's and violinist Regina Carter's solos rush the tempo into a brittle no-man's-land where you can't help but be dazzled by the very conceit of the thing. Regina, in her most impressive recorded outing, easily holds her own, quoting Django's trademark Bach—the D minor concerto for two violins. She and James also dominate the more frantic "Avalon," which begins with a guitar solo that enters on the downbeat with no intro at all, and then skirts the tune. Carter's first tenor chorus is swinging joy, the second screechy grit. Eight-bar and four-bar exchanges between the Carters (no relation) whoosh forward like a roller coaster; don't miss James's balancing of top and low notes in bars 9–12 of their second chorus. The closing supersonic ensemble ends on a dime, except that someone dropped gear and they decided to keep the noise on the record—sort of like the clop cymbal at the end of "West End Blues."

Perhaps the finest arrangements, however, are "Artillerie Lourde," a Reinhardt swing riff that recalls "Tuxedo Junction" and anticipates "Such Sweet Thunder" in its brassy bravado, and "Oriental Shuffle," which has an illusory slowing-down in the second half of the A sections and features Carter on F mezzo saxophone, which suggests a serpentine alto. Carter plays bass sax with tremendous bite on the former, while the accordion plugs in the theme's offbeats. The latter opens with a cymbal wash and exotic scene setting, before Carter states the theme with a surging, humorous-happy lyricism reminiscent of Benny Carter (no relation). Baron, who occasionally sounds busy on the potboilers, is mostly plush here.

The album has two lullabies, Carter's "Imari's Lullaby," a brief rubato tenor and guitars meditation, and a stunningly slow, almost dirgelike "I'll Never Be the Same" that is all texture—violin states theme, counterpunched by bass sax, with accordion filling in the middle—and rich as pastry. I don't think I've ever heard a bass sax sound as supple, melodic, and personable; the bubbling bass line he plays in counterpoint as the violin takes the lead is a champagne highlight in a champagne album.

Because the material is so varied and, by the standards of au courant jazz, unusual, *Chasin' the Gypsy* is a near perfect distillation of Carter's technique. Virtuosity is every bit as central to *Layin' in the Cut*, but here it seems more studied and I find myself often admiring the gee-whiz tricks more than I like them. The record is not dull, except in a few ponderous codas, and the aggressive daring is amusing almost by default, but the brittleness and constancy of his attack wear me down after a couple of tracks. When he brought his state-of-the-art electric band—Jamaaladeen Tacuma, Jef Lee Johnson, and G. Calvin Weston (Marc Ribot didn't make it)—into the Blue Note recently, I was dazzled by two pieces and anaesthetized by the other two. Listening to the album, I continue to prefer the same two tracks, not least because they surmount hidebound funkiness: Johnson's ebullient "Terminal B" and Carter's engaging "G.P.," a Horace Silver-inspired piece complete with suspenseful two-bar breaks. Carter needs melody to balance his steely precision. In funk terrain, the popped keys and tongued reeds, the harmonics and circular breathing, the whole retinue of saxophonics seems slightly robotic. Put another way, *Layin' in the Cut* is mostly muscle. *Chasin' the Gypsy* is heart and soul—the future, I hope.

[*Village Voice*, 8 August 2000]

73 ❖ *Zooids New and Old (Henry Threadgill / Roswell Rudd and Archie Shepp)*

Schoenberg warned a century ago, during that twilight zone between Wagner and Stravinsky, that the tempered scale was used up—its melodies worn out, its thematic variations a close-order drill going nowhere. Jazz proved him dead wrong by revitalizing the verities with blue harmonies, rhythmic force, and melodies of expressive and exuberant originality. Still, he was right about European classicism, a not insignificant field at the time, and his solution, serialism, forced his adherents to disavow habits and conventions. This produced a whole new musical world, though not many hits. Meanwhile, jazz snubbed its nose at the worrywarts and had a high old time for 50-plus years, until it, too, began to ruminate about habits and conventions, opening the gates to rock 'n' roll, which took up the hit-making gap. Now at the dawn of a hip-hopping new century, one cannot help but notice that the tempered scale once again seems used up—its melodies worn out, its thematic variations a close-order drill going nowhere.

Jazz's Schoenberg, Ornette Coleman, devised three solutions. The first was the chimera of free jazz, which ventilated spontaneity with a blank grid, producing a montage of ebullient melodies, 1/1 rhythms, and providential harmonies—though Freddie Hubbard's bebop habits, as displayed on the 1960 *Free Jazz*, revealed that freedom might be at least as hard to negotiate as the steeplechase progressions of not-free jazz. Wary of spontaneity's limitations, Coleman issued solutions two and three in 1976, on *Dancing in Your Head*. At the time it was released, in the twilight zone between fusion and neoclassicism, many thought the big story was Coleman's use of electric instruments and backbeats, but it became luminously clear that the key innovation was scrupulous notation that forced the rhythm section to abandon predictable patterns. By including a brief collaboration with the Master Musicians of Joujouka, Coleman cracked the door open to a third source of rejuvenation, patronizingly known to the West as world music.

Coleman wasn't out there alone—others were working along the same lines before and during. But where other innovators release albums, Coleman has a way of producing manifestos. The fact remains that most modern jazz that isn't mainstream-conservative combines free improvisation, heady notation, and, not to put too fine a point on it, exotica. You could not ask for a better example than the new band Henry Threadgill recently debuted at the Knitting Factory, a sextet he calls Zooid (1. *Biology*. An organic cell or organized body that has independent movement within a living organism; especially a motile gamete such as a spermatozoon. 2. *Zoology*. One of the usually microscopic animals forming an aggregate or colony, as of bryozoans or hydrozoans. *American Heritage Dictionary*).

Threadgill's been collating the free, written, and world options since the mid-'70s, beginning at least as far back as Air and pieces like "Untitled Tango." But Zooid, even in its sometimes tentative premiere, boldly stepped beyond Air and such later Threadgill ensembles as Very Very Circus and the ongoing Make a Move in combining a raucously exuberant familiarity with fastidious notation that forces both the chamber unit and its members to think fast and fresh. The group's internationalism is literal. Only Threadgill and acoustic guitarist Liberty Ellman are American-born; Tarik Benbrahim, who plays oud, is Moroccan; Jose Davila, who plays tuba, is Puerto Rican; drummer Dafnis Prieto is Cuban; and accordionist Tony Cedras, a holdover from Make a Move in a guest appearance, is South African. Much emphasis is placed on the strings, but the band's peculiarly erratic heartbeat is, naturally, rhythmic. The meter changes, at times from measure to measure, keeping the players' eyes on the lead sheets and their minds on the moment.

Zooid was conceived as a stopgap for a gig that was booked before Threadgill realized that not all of his Make a Move musicians would be available. He might have taken it easy, jamming with friends for a few nights, but instead configured an ensemble that required new music and much rehearsal. He composed eight new pieces, four featuring his flute and four his alto saxophone, and readapted Very Very Circus's "Hope A Hope A," a perfect, dessert-like set-closer. The evening began with two flute pieces. "Tickle Pink," an undulating six-note riff and tremolo, emerged carefully with the ensemble hewing to written harmonies and meters as the leader navigated a solo. The piece cohered best when Ellman eased his way into an invention with knifelike articulation (he plucked at or near the bridge), sustaining long phrases that crested the changing rhythm. The arranged time and harmonies made a relaxed swing impossible—Threadgill had stacked the deck against habit and convention—but did inspire novel improvisational figures. Even Cedras, who plays expansively on *Where's the Cup?* (a Columbia CD quietly released a year after the label bumped Threadgill), sounded wary.

As the set continued, a mutual authority kicked in, and a negative print developed into a vividly colored picture. Threadgill's alto helped. His sound is always a tonic, combining two standard fruit metaphors—pear-shaped pitch and peach-fuzz timbre. Parts of "Do the Needful" suggested a clattering mechanical toy slowly winding down, only to get a sudden burst of life. The leader's grainy solo, a storm of ferocious, arpeggiated dives and swoops, steadied the center, even when simultaneous meters vied for attention; where do you look?—the drummer says one thing, the tuba another. Then, with a stunner called "Around My Goose," the issue of forced originality disappeared, as the ensemble bonded into a practiced chamber sextet, capering through the soft melody with the push-me-pull-you suppleness of an accordion and providing a pneumatic cushion to float the solos. The meter, too, was compelling; you couldn't tap four, but you wanted to tap something.

On "Hope A Hope A," first heard on *Spirit of Nuff . . . Nuff*, you could tap all the fours you wanted. Familiarity bred fluency and, after a charismatic drum solo that established the second-line beat, and a full-bore Threadgill alto attack, Cedras found his balance, and bounded mightily on fat resilient chords. Then the gifted Ellman introduced a thoughtful lyricism with suave touches of Django. This is a guitarist quick on his feet; he examines the rhythmic turf, thinks his phrases, and within a few bars finds a groove. Prieto also made a strong impression, feeling his way through the metrical skipping and hopping and, at times, generating slam-bang audacity. Oud and tuba were used almost exclusively within the ensemble—making it a thumping, reedy, herky-jerky contraption of surprising elegance. Zooid will be back.

If you owned a record label and had the pick of musicians, you would sign Threadgill for the innovative richness of his imagination. But you would also want the kind of funky, pop-jazz band that can be counted on to pay the bills—a crowd-pleasing group that packs bars and clubs, gets big jukebox action, and sells a zillion records. Who would have thought in the 1960s that this means you would want the Archie Shepp–Roswell Rudd Quintet, which returned last week, after a 34-year layoff, at the Jazz Standard? Opening night may have been something of an open rehearsal, but, never mind: club life hasn't been so much fun since repeal. From the evening's first selection, an expanded version of Rudd's "Keep Your Heart Right" (the first track on Shepp's 1966 Impulse classic, *Live in San Francisco*, which become a true classic only after the 33-minute masterwork, "Three for a Quarter, One for a Dime" was added to the CD), you knew all was right with the world.

It may be tempting to note that aging avant-gardists always return to the blues, that spontaneous inventions end up seeking tonics and sub-dominants and bar lines and so forth, but you have only to search out Rudd's *Everywhere* and Shepp's *Four for Trane*, *Live in San Francisco*, and, if you can find it, *Live at Donaueschingen* (all with Rudd), to know that they were never as scary as they thought we thought they were. It's been a long time since Shepp's rueful, dark baritone voice told us about Rufus's snapped neck, semper Malcolm, and the Attica blues. But even then a bluesy bemusement and balladic tenderness infused his music, just as a Dixieland blowziness has always abided in Rudd's. In the intervening years, each disappeared from the front lines for long stretches. Whatever was ailing them has been cured. With and without plunger, Rudd was electric, a workman come to work. And Shepp, in his black fedora and double-breasted, was equally compelling whether tinkling an insouciant piano waltz or letting rip with patented long and gritty tenor saxophone loop-the-loops.

The upholstery was strictly Rolls Royce: bassist Reggie Workman and drummer Andrew Cyrille shimmered and thumped, staying mostly in the background, keeping the funk palpable, then disappearing during a couple of duets—including Herbie Nichols's "Change of Season." It was good to see the fifth wheel, trombonist Grachan Moncur III (who chimed in with Rudd on Shepp's *Mama Too Tight*), but his elliptical solos were less commanding than his ability to beef up the ensemble. Rudd suggests the old man of the mountain, while Shepp with his dimpled grin suggests a keeper of secret ironies. They are wonderful together. Even "Steam," Shepp's 1976 portrait of a cousin who was killed in a street fight at 15, became a comic turn as the players mused on what a cool nickname Steam is ("His real name was Robert," Shepp said quietly). This is in no way a reactionary band; sometimes, as Edward Albee wrote

around the time of *Free Jazz*, you have to go a long way out of the way
to come back a short distance correctly. I'll leave it to you to figure out
a connection between *The Zoo Story* and Zooid. I'm just relieved to find
so much hot jazz in town.

[*Village Voice*, 3 October 2000]

74 ❖ *Saturnal Sorcery*
(Sun Ra)

Early one morning, listening to Sun Ra's recently restored *Pathways to
Unknown Worlds*, I became preoccupied with the grainy glissandi that
bassist Ronnie Boykins was bowing, rifflike, against a cluttered rhythm
and pointillistic wind-playing. Then the phone rang and I hit pause; the
music stopped, but Boykins kept at it. What Saturnal sorcery was this?
Turned out it wasn't Boykins at all, but a carpenter on the roof laboring
with some kind of drill. In fact, a lot of effects that I had been admiring
came from him and other workmen who fused so beautifully with Sun
Ra's Arkestra that I had to turn the volume up to sort out who was
doing what.

A Cageian moment, and long live indeterminacy. Nearly two minutes
into "Cosmo-Media," the fourth track on the same album, Sun Ra uses
his Moog to sound more like a drill than the drill. Long live serendipity,
too. The 1986 Coney Island concert by Sun Ra and John Cage failed
utterly, musically and even symbolically, because Ra, a conservative in
this regard, thought art was the process of making something out of
nothing, and Cage, a composer turned philosopher turned confidence
man, could no longer think of anything worthwhile to fill the silence he
had so famously introduced into the concert arena. Ra, often characterized as a trickster for his extraterrestrial, occultist, costumed, show-
business blarney, which he believed in no less sincerely than did Cage
in the musical uses of the I Ching, never permitted himself to be seduced
by the sound of silence. His notion of chance extended to record sessions
that declined to distinguish between performance and rehearsal and audio engineering that embraced feedback, footsteps, a ringing phone, a
pneumatic drill.

In the '60s, when he first made his national mark as a 50-something
avant-garde visionary (*The Heliocentric Worlds of Sun Ra* on ESP-Disk, a
label initially founded to spread the universal language of Esperanto,

was a breakthrough) with an inscrutable past, Ra blended right in with the general state of confusion. He was something of a musical parallel to *The Morning of the Magicians,* and anyone who had ever seen Porter Waggoner knew that his space suits were no weirder than the shit they wore in Nashville. No, the cynicism that arose had less to do with the interplanetary stuff than the sheer diversity and profusion of music, live and on records, that often made him seem bigger than life and smaller than his intentions.

Over the past decade, Ra, who died, or "left the planet," in 1993, at 79, has been made more human and impressive through the efforts of biographer John Szwed, whose *Space Is the Place* is illuminating and convincing, and Jerry Gordon, who once sold Ra's white-cover or hand-painted Saturn albums at a Philadelphia record store and now restores many of them for his label, Evidence. An indication of just how enigmatic Ra's story remained was the widespread astonishment, in 1996, when Evidence released the two-disc set, *The Singles.* Sun Ra singles?— nearly 50 of them, many doo-wop?? But then, *Jazz in Silhouette,* recorded in 1958, is almost certainly the only consensus jazz classic that was unheard—as opposed to ignored, underrated, attacked—by the generation for which it was created.

Evidence continues its mission with five new releases of material that was long unavailable or, in the case of the double-volume *The Great Lost Sun Ra Albums,* never previously released. According to liner notes by Ed Michel, the Impulse producer who contracted with Ra to reissue albums from Saturn's catalog, *Cymbals* and *Crystal Spears* were part of the mess of tapes Ra turned over to him; he issued 10 LPs (among them, *Jazz in Silhouette, Angels and Demons at Play, Supersonic Jazz,* and *The Magic City*—all now among the highlights of the Evidence catalog), and then the deal fell through. This does not make sense. If I read Michel correctly, Impulse refused to sign Ra because he wanted to control his copyrights, so it agreed to license previously released albums. But the deal was made in 1972 while the two lost albums were recorded in 1973, and only three tracks were ever released on Saturn. It would appear that Ra and his partner Alton Abraham simply made the albums they wanted to make in the first place, sold them as old material, and retained the copyrights— a poetic con if there ever was one.

In the end it worked and didn't work; by releasing too much too soon, Impulse glutted the market and gave up on Sun Ra before it had released more than half of the 22 masters it acquired, adding to the impression that his oeuvre was cosmic (in truth, it's not as large as Ellington's or Kenton's). On the other hand, it did give Sun Ra a platform that smaller labels like ESP-Disk and Delmark, let alone Saturn, could not have matched.

The lost albums will be chiefly of interest to completists, though they have many pleasing moments. Sun Ra was much ridiculed for his pitch-challenged musicians and ensembles, but a cursory sampling of his work (including 21 titles on Evidence) reveals that he could be as in-tune as he wanted. He uses dissonance to get your attention; if you play along, even moments that seem aimless at first blush take on depth and interest. Which is not to say that he was never slipshod, especially in the '80s, when he revisited his swing-era roots and played Fletcher Henderson arrangements with spotty accuracy; like Dr. Johnson's dog, Sun Ra was given a critical pass because he could do it at all—a lofty view of an artist whose best bands were vigorously on target. But for those who wish to be overwhelmed by a masterly avant-garde anomaly, the 20-minute closer to the lost albums, "Sunrise in the Western Sky," is not to be missed. John Gilmore's tenor saxophone solo may strike you as chaotic and ugly or (as I prefer) elliptically anguished, but it is unlike any other solo that comes to mind. Instead of a sustained burst of energy, it cries out in bellowing spurts interrupted by long caesuras, building not so much in intensity as in stubbornness. The rhythm section sustains an Africanate swingless tableau while Gilmore wails, disappears, returns and aches, wanders off, returns again and shrieks, rages, wags his finger, then finally leaves while the rhythm follows an imperviously cool eight-beat into infinity or at least until cymbal crashes bring it to ground.

Lanquidity is the only title I knew on LP, and I find it marginally more interesting now. Recorded in 1978, this is Ra's acknowledgment of Miles Davis's dark magus period, boring (if you prefer, lanquid) in a witty sort of way, very repetitive, with riffs and piano noodling that create a mood and sustain interest if you make the leap of faith—think of a jaunty "He Loved Him Madly" and you're on your way to "Twin Stars of Thence." The music mostly sits there, the rhythm designed not to push it forward, but to situate it in the present. Most of the selections might have been half or twice as long and it would make no difference. *Lanquidity* is mood music, but so is most of Sun Ra's music—mood, not background. If you are not in the mood for *When Angels Speak of Love*, the most striking of the five new releases, don't even try it.

Had this astonishing album been widely released the year it was recorded, 1966, it would have been reviewed alongside Cecil Taylor's *Unit Structures* and would have a reputation today, not least because, without the slightest hint of nostalgia, it faces down aspects of what Francis Davis once tellingly referred to as Ra's "race memory," where swing, rhythm and blues, bebop, hard bop, doo wop, Tadd Dameron voicings, and the rest converge. With a few glass-shattering disharmonious blasts, it announces his intention to join the avant-garde ferment of the 1960s—which in some respects he anticipated, but, in others, adapted. For examples of the latter, his assimilation of Taylor's piano playing, chapter and verse, on "The Idea of It All" and the title ballad, itself a throwback to the serene melodies Ra occasionally wrote in the 1950s, are delightful surprises. Ra was an uneven but effective pianist (hear the solo *St. Louis Blues* on IAI), and he had his own way of breaking conventions—e.g., his solo on the 1960 "Rocket Number Nine Take Off for the Planet Venus"—so his reference to Taylor is shrewdly deliberate. Like Jaki Byard, another veteran of big bands and one of the few pianists listening to Taylor no less carefully in 1966, he also allows bop memories to come into play. Another pleasure is the rare opportunity to hear trumpeter Walter Miller at length. Miller apparently started out with Ra in Alabama in the late 1930s, but by the time of *When Angels Speak of Love*, had absorbed Don Cherry and found his own flight paths—his solos are consistently personal and inventive.

Sun Ra, who tended to go normal with a big band, was at his best with the kind of 10-piece group heard on *When Angels Speak of Love* and on the '50s records included on *Greatest Hits*, a fine compilation, though the absence of Julian Priester's "Soft-talk" and a personnel listing is annoying. Conceived as a sampler of the galaxy's lighter side, it includes "When Angels Speak"; the delectable "Enlightenment," featuring elusive trumpet player Hobart Dotson; "'Round Midnight," with one of Ra's more agreeable vocalists, Hatty Randolph; the aforementioned "Rocket Number Nine," which has everything—a loopy chant, oddball piano intro, Boykins's buzzing arco bass, and a Gilmore solo that begins with a Coltrane quote and proceeds to push the envelope into the area Coltrane explored a year later at the Village Vanguard. The set gets underway with Ra's theme, "Saturn," which combines a six-beat piano intro; a contrapuntal 7/4 seven-bar melody (14 bars on the *Jazz in Silhouette* version); the main theme, a memorable unison "I Got Rhythm" variation with substitutions, in four; and lively solos by Gilmore and trumpeter Art Hoyle—with lively electric bass by Wilburn Green. It's a three-minute prophecy of what was to come. You cannot help but wonder what its impact might have been had it been released in 1956 by a real record company.

[*Village Voice*, 17 October 2000]

75 ❖ The One You've Been Waiting For (Sonny Rollins)

Last August, at Lincoln Center Plaza, 70-year-old Sonny Rollins gave one of the most exhilarating, inspired, go-for-broke, don't-look-back performances I have ever seen. Okay, I've probably written something like that before, but having missed maybe three of his New York engagements over the last 35 years, I rate this one very high—in the top five, anyway. For one thing, he played two hours and fifteen minutes without a break. You can tell right off when Rollins is feeling cramped because he can't get out of the heads; on this night, he could scarcely wait to eject himself into improvisational flight. His infallible time reflected a wary, boplike sagacity, a witting agility; as the rhythm section hammered down the beats like pickets in a fence, he alternately stepped back to launch parabolas and charged forward hugging the ground—Calypso Joe roaring and guffawing. For another thing, he introduced more new music than usual: tributes to Harold Vick and Charles Mingus and two forgotten trade-winds ballads so unlikely that no one else would have dared. As the huge mob stood waving like wheat stalks, a woman asked no one in particular, "Did you ever think you would be grooving to 'Sweet Leilani'?" Not like this.

All of that material is on Rollins's splendid new album, *This Is What I Do* (Milestone). In 1972, when he resumed recording after a six-year sabbatical during which he was constantly asked when he would make his next album, he issued *Sonny Rollins' Next Album*. The next 15 years were a slough of searching but spotty records. Cries went out for *The Sonny Rollins Album You've Been Waiting For*, a fantasy construct released in excerpts, as demonstrated by the 1996 anthology, *Silver City*.

Long before the anthology, however, it was evident that the new Sonny was making peace with the old Sonny in what now seems like a CD quintet, bookended by a full-bore Rollins rampage, *G-Man* (1987), and a pinnacle of poetic paraphrase, *+3* (1995), and enclosing three increasingly powerful steps toward detente: *Dancing in the Dark, Falling in Love with Jazz,* and *Old Flames*. Still, a viral cynicism had come to infect old-time Rollins fans, the complaints often focusing on the bow-taut electric bass lines of Bob Cranshaw. *This Is What I Do* may serve, not only for those who came of age with the '60s RCAs and Impulses, but even for those who refused to let Rollins age beyond 1958, as, well, the Sonny Rollins album they've been waiting for. Cranshaw is still electric, but superior engineering mixes him down to where the bass ought to be, making it easier to appreciate what an ironman he is and why, for nearly three decades, he has played a role with Rollins not unlike that of Freddie Greene with Count Basie.

Rollins's 1998 *Global Warming* alienated many by putting a pop veneer on some of his most avant-garde playing in years—"Clear Cut Boogie" harks back to the days of *East Broadway Rundown*. It is marked by an ironic tentativeness, a stretching out of notes past the border of conventional pitch, a dry sound, and a discursive attack. Even on "Mother Nature's Blues," he puts himself through woolly locutions to get to the more comfortable blues-bop payoffs. On his ballad, "Echo-Side Blue," he appears yoked to the theme's wryly nostalgic yearning, as though stuck in an uneasy mode between past and present. Most themes are short, as though he can't wait to play, yet his solos feel truncated; he plays five superb choruses on "Global Warming," but leaves off just as he's kicking into overdrive.

This Is What I Do is *Global Warming*'s reverse counterpart. Rollins's sound is warmer and fuller and focused in the midrange, less grainy than on *+3*. He makes much use of grit and grain and shouts and cries, but always for accent, to italicize specific notes in a phrase. His virtuoso aim in this regard is stunning, even for Rollins—for example, his second solo on "Salvador," where inflections underscore the rhythmic muscle of his overall conception. The result is a return to supernal authority, touched with nostalgia validated by on-the-beat assurance and producing a melodic joy and humor that—though removed from the euphoric Rollins who whips ballads until the cream runs over and stomps calypsos until you feel foolish for sitting—comes closer to the Rollins concert experience than most of his studio albums.

Take "Salvador," as richly songful a calypso as he has recorded, not just the theme, but the whole performance, the almost indivisible logic between head and solo, underscored by buoyantly thematic phrases that parse his improvisation. The 40-bar theme (the bridge is 16) has built-in hesitations that spur Rollins's turnbacks through three solo choruses rife with lush embellishments, charged riffs, and a climactic final bridge. Stephen Scott, Rollins's most distinctive pianist since Stanley Cowell if not Ray Bryant, follows with three of his own, which also massage the theme and build to a heated bridge; his second chorus, fixed on a single chord, includes a turnback that recycles the piccolo obbligato from "High Society," a conscious nod, I presume, to New Orleans second-line ecstasy, which Rollins sustains in his follow-up.

Split between originals and standards, the album also includes "Did You See Harold Vick?" and "Charles M." The former, dedicated to the tenor saxophonist who died young in 1987 and was primarily associated with soul and organ groups (including nearly five years with Aretha), is a typical Rollins diptych of a piece (actually AABBA), with the second section a stop-time gambit. It's more than nine minutes long and it is all Rollins, most of it a trio improv backed by Cranshaw and drummer Perry Wilson. Scott strolls with them for about 16 bars, then lays out as Rollins deliberates his way through six choruses, submitting the album's le quote juste, "I'm Just Wild About Harry" (twice). Other melodies are also jimmied in, yet this is his most outré invention on the date, a vigilant, lucid saunter—the old Sonny, making it up as he goes along. The Mingus tribute is also vintage Sonny, a dilatory, back-in-the-pocket blues, nailed at every step by Cranshaw, and the only track with a round-robin of solos, by Rollins, Cranshaw, Scott, and trombonist Clifton Anderson, who picks up nicely Scott's insistent closing riff and uses a mute for understated plunger effects. Rollins finishes it off with a straight-bourbon reprise.

No jazz instrumentalist has a broader appreciation of classic songs and obscurities than Rollins. His '90s albums have offered surprises— "Tennessee Waltz," "Delia" (Lehar's "Vilja, O Vilja"), "Cabin in the Sky"—amid the more familiar standards. Two of the three on the new CD restore memories of the man who adapted "Shadow Waltz," "Toot Toot Tootsie," "Wagon Wheels," and "To a Wild Rose." All three— "Sweet Leilani," "The Moon of Manakoora," and "A Nightingale Sang in Berkeley Square"—were introduced between 1937 and 1940, when Rollins was a boy, and each of them made an impression on his parents' generation. Playing them with tremendous feeling, he puts them back in contention.

"Sweet Leilani," though taken at a snail's pace, is played with a back-beat and tracked with great finesse by Cranshaw and drummer Jack DeJohnette, who appears on all the ballads. For the theme, Anderson's trombone recapitulates Lani McIntyre's obbligato from the original Bing Crosby record, and Rollins colors the melody with a full palette of cries, sighs, sputters, and rumbles, turning his phrases precisely on the beat. The second chorus of his improvisation is especially imaginative, but the song is always there no matter how elaborate a trellis he constructs around it. Ultimately, he makes it a blues—a conceit extended by Scott and then redoubled by Rollins. "A Nightingale Sang in Berkeley Square" was the musical equivalent of lend-lease in 1940, an English stage hit adapted by American performers in a display of anti-isolationist sympathies. Rollins attacks the first phrase with bluff command (you can hear a hint of "Rockin' Chair" in his paraphrase) and limns the tune with an eloquent modesty. The tune was written as 38 bars, with each of the 10-measure A sections ending on a bar of instrumental filler.

Rollins strips the second 10 of one bar, moving it along that much faster. Scott inserts Monk's "Friday the 13" and DeJohnette keeps the time loose enough to let him get away with it.

"The Moon of Manakoora" is, for me, the prize of the lot. One of the first successful songs with a Frank Loesser lyric, Alfred Newman composed it (his only major song hit) for the score of John Ford's *The Hurricane*. Rollins plays the theme as a laid-back waltz, crooning the 16-bar theme twice before embarking on a five-chorus solo that opens with short fragmented phrases drawn into a melody. He phrases with utter ease, gliding over the rhythm, employing canny riffs and creative embellishments, all so casual it seems effortless—exuding a reserved magnificence, like Ben Webster in his later years. We are witnessing something new in jazz: the triumph of the AARP musician. Through most of jazz history, elder statesmen were valued for continuing to play well, while the main focus was on younger players whose energy opened new channels. But who today plays with more energy, originality, and purpose than Cecil Taylor, Max Roach, Ornette Coleman, John Lewis, Roy Haynes, Lee Konitz, Sam Rivers, and Sonny Rollins? And which young tenor terror will make an album as strong as *This Is What I Do*?

[*Village Voice*, 21 November 2000]

76 ❖ *All the Things He Was (Carnegie Hall Jazz Band)*

While visiting Hollywood in 1946, a few months after Jerome Kern's passing, Dizzy Gillespie collaborated with arranger Johnny Richards on a Kern memorial album. They recorded four of his most famous songs— "Who?" "The Way You Look Tonight," "Why Do I Love You?" "All the Things You Are"—in a novel setting of more than a dozen strings plus woodwinds, French horn, harp, and a state-of-the-art rhythm section (Al Haig, Ray Brown, and Roy Haynes), nearly three years before Charlie Parker's first aborted attempt to record with strings. Gillespie was in superb form, playing with exhilarating finesse on "The Way You Look Tonight." Yet those records were largely lost to history. One 78 was issued by Paramount and promptly withdrawn because of complaints from the Kern estate that Gillespie's approach was insufficiently respectful. The remaining tracks were buried until all four turned up on an underground label 30 years later. Kern's estate had no legal standing, only powers of suasion, and as a result Kern has often been presumed to be anti jazz.

Putting aside the fact that Gillespie's treatments are far from irreverent (something else must have been going on behind the scenes), Kern's estate had to learn to love jazz and quick, because in succeeding years the songwriter's sumptuous harmonies and cagey key changes become a measure of jazz invention, some of it fairly radical. Kern's songs had always been popular with jazz musicians and singers because of his expressive melodies, but it took the headier precincts of modern jazz to appreciate all the harmonic possibilities, which became so much a part of bebop thinking that musicians often abandoned the melodies, superimposing what Max Roach once called "parody" tunes that they could copyright. One way or another, jazz kept much of Kern alive long after the pop world skittered away from him.

All that is remembered of Kern's 1939 flop musical, *Very Warm for May*, for example, is the imperishable "All the Things You Are," first recorded by Artie Shaw (vocal, Helen Forrest), Mildred Bailey, and Tommy Dorsey (vocal, Jack Leonard), and then abandoned until Gillespie and Charlie Parker tackled it in 1945. Two years later, Parker secured its place as a jazz perennial with his magnificent knockoff, "Bird of Paradise"; from the moment he intoned the dramatic intro, his vamp and Kern's harmonic plateau were mated forever. Parker loved the tune and Oscar Hammerstein II's lyric—he used to call it "YATAG," an acronym for the line, "You are the angel glow." But his recording showed that a harmonic sequence can so vividly support a melody that the mind's ear registers the theme even when the musician spins nothing but variations. Kern worried that his indulgence in enharmonic changes (e.g., around the bridges of "All the Things You Are" and "The Way You Look Tonight") would alienate the public, but they were and are turnback heaven for jazz musicians.

So the November 16 concert by Jon Faddis and the Carnegie Hall Jazz Band devoted to Kern's music (no singers, no lyrics) suggested a worthy collaboration, if not a rapprochement, between jazz and a composer who—whether or not he or his heirs approved—has long since become part of jazz's DNA. As usual, the CHJB assigned songs to its team of arrangers, leaving a few to feature the guest soloist, Gary Bartz (a last-minute replacement for the ailing Jackie McLean). From the first, it was evident that the subtext of the evening was the old issue of how much deference is due a venerated songwriter. The heirs who balked at Gillespie's embellishments would have hemorrhaged in horror at some liberties taken by Faddis's writers, especially the senior scribe, Manny Albam. Yet it was also apparent that the writers had done their homework.

Whatever Kern may have thought about jazz (is he on record anywhere with an opinion?), he deeply loved traditional forms of African American music, specifically spirituals: "Look for the Silver Lining" is indebted to "My Lord, What a Morning" and "Dearly Beloved" suggests a hymn refracted by harmonic sorcery. The evening began with Michael Philip Mossman's transfiguration of "Yesterdays" into a brass and woodwinds psalm, the melody arrayed in choirlike layers—no rhythm section, no solos. Another Mossman arrangement, "Smoke Gets in Your Eyes," took the opposite tack, one especially suited to the dynamic strengths of the CHJB. Engineered with foursquare swing and plush reeds, the chart flamed with Basie-style brass tuttis, spare piano interjections, and the occasional drum fusillade. Faddis began a compelling solo with Dizzy half-valves and focused on his midrange, allowing his sound to spread at the release and indulging too many quotations ("As Time Goes By," "There's a Small Hotel," a Harry Edison lick) before rising to a heroic but controlled climax of the sort no one else can pull off. This was one chart the CHJB can file away for its greatest-hits retrospective.

Oddly, or not, Mossman, the youngest of the arrangers (born 1959) was also the most conservative. Michael Abene (born 1942) turned "Why Do I Love You?" into a clipped canter as played by Faddis, trombonist Steve Turre, and altoist Dick Oatts before settling into a modernist groove for their solos, handsomely supported by the band (nice unison trombone accents) and closing smartly with ensemble variations. But Kern was accessed for his harmonies only, the tune cropping up chiefly in Turre's solo—a quote, as it were. The breach between song and arrangement was less pleasing in Abene's "Look for the Silver Lining," which opened with a brass choir hymn and devolved into head and solos in which the latter failed to sustain the feeling or tempo of the former.

Albam (born 1922) has developed a liking for high voicings, and his "Dearly Beloved" was typical, opening with a netting of flutes, soprano saxophone, and muted brasses (a bass clarinet served as ballast) that emphasized the song's hymnal qualities and subtly parted to reveal bassist Todd Coolman bowing the tune. Coolman has a cello-bright arco tone, but too much depended on him and the high-register brew, and the result was dilatory and flat. His version of "Old Man River" was, by contrast, almost obstreperously clever, with speedy dueling trombones, a locomotive (okay, steamboat) vamp, clamorous fours, and a Cat Anderson overlay from the leader. It was hip enough and swinging and maybe the song is too much a cliché to play straight, but Kern was left at the dock and the point of the adaptation lost.

The second half began with arguably Kern's greatest songs, "The Way You Look Tonight" and "All the Things You Are," but this time the band, excepting the rhythm section, was nowhere to be seen. Just as well: These numbers featured Gary Bartz, who was burning with pitched lyricism. One of the things that has always distinguished jazz musicians is their determination to find signature sounds or timbres—instantly recognizable calling cards that let you know right off if Coleman Hawkins or Ben Webster is playing. Yet certain timbres are now so much at the heart of jazz that other musicians, no matter how individual, eventually gravitate to them as platonic ideals. Louis Armstrong's trumpet is one and Charlie Parker's alto is another. Bartz, always an imposing technician, who began his career in the 1960s with a ragged, edgy attack and later adapted a Coltrane-indebted effusiveness, can now summon Parker's burnished voice without sacrificing his own. It's a fluent, opulent, blues-driven approach that contains multitudes of jazz history and speaks with complete authority.

On both pieces, Bartz balanced shadow and light, taking his time, mining the changes, employing the melodies. He served Kern as he served himself, using the enharmonic riff the songwriter inserted in "The Way You Look Tonight" as a refueling station, slowing it down before revving himself up, and turning "All the Things You Are" into a homage to Parker, beginning with his vamp and interpolating "Now's the Time." It would have been gratifying to hear more of Bartz, say in a quintet with Faddis. It would be more gratifying still to see him recording for a major label, documenting what may well prove to be the apogee of his career. Evidently due to a lack of rehearsal time, he performed only once with the band, on Mossman's spacy, Milesian "The Song Is You," and struggled with the arrangement though his solo shot off like a bullet.

But there were other bright moments. Mossman's sparkling arrangement of "I've Told Ev'ry Little Star" began with a cool staccato intro and moved into an unexpectedly fitting Latin rhythm—the melody lazing over the "Manteca" beat as naturally as if it had been born on the islands. Several soloists were allowed to shine, especially the much underrated tenor saxophonist Ralph Lalama, who leaped in with a series of breaks and pushed forward with his spacious sound, relaxed swing, and storytelling logic. Like Bartz, he suggests the history of an instrument in his knowing timbre and attack, and is another gifted player who, though not yet fifty, operates beyond the radar of the record business for reasons that have nothing to do with music. Faddis, who has never quite made his high-note blasts fit the confines of a recording studio, showed how evenhanded he can play on Abene's discretely arranged "Sure Thing" (from *Cover Girl*). Pianist Renee Rosnes, who was excessively featured, revealed her ample technique without quite making a point on Albam's best piece of the night, a concerto version of "Can't Help Lovin' Dat Man," with a diffuse voicing of the theme. If you're going to pay tribute, you gotta play the tune. Even Gillespie, back in those not so innocent days of 1946, knew that.

[*Village Voice*, 5 December 2000]

77 ❖ *Signposts of Post-history (The Best Jazz Records of 2000)*

So the year 2000 in jazz, which was supposed to be the year of Louis Armstrong, turned out to be the year of *Kind of Blue*. True, Pops has a year to go—he gets a double centennial, one for his presumed birth in 1900 and one for the actual one in 1901. And if Ken Burns's *Jazz* achieves nothing else, it will reposition him in cultural history. Meanwhile, *Kind of Blue* appears to have achieved a Valhalla of its own. Sony, which caused nary a ripple of news when it dismantled its jazz department, reports that Miles Davis's 1959 classic sells 5,000 copies a month, more than all the company's recent jazz discs combined, while Ashley Kahn's illuminating book of the same name (subtitled *The Making of the Miles Davis Masterpiece*) is breaking sales records in jazz lit: some 25,000 copies in five months. Sony, or one of its vestigial Columbia appendages, also released the most significant of the numerous Armstrong reissues, an imperfect but hard-to-resist *Complete Hot Five and Hot Seven Recordings*, and collaborated with Verve on a five-disc boxed companion to Burns and 22 Burns-selected individual-artist discs.

So you'd think that Sony, of all companies, would be madly waving the red-white-and-blue of jazz, instead of breaking the staff over its knee. But, in fairness, none of the record companies have a clue anymore. Blue Note hires Rudy Van Gelder to remix its inviolable catalog and people who already own the LPs and CDs buy them again. The newer stuff is harder to sell. Young people aren't coming to jazz because a cool cat like Miles or Coltrane or Rollins or even Corea draws them in; they come to hear the cool sounds that Miles, Coltrane, Rollins, and even Corea left some time back—much as you came to classical music to hear Bach or

Stravinsky, not Elliott Carter. That's why Sony's ax didn't make *60 Minutes*, didn't raise an uproar like the one that followed the abandonment by other labels of domestic symphony orchestras, didn't engender the outrage that ensued when New York lost its last commercial jazz station. These are the post-historical doldrums: What's past is prologue, text, and epilogue.

Much of the anticipatory anguish over Burns's *Jazz*, about which, as a consultant, I will reserve comment, revolves around whether it will be interpreted as the celebration of a living art or a valedictory for a dead one. Similarly, Jazz at Lincoln Center, which, with its customary secretive brusqueness, recently rendered its suddenly reticent leader Rob Gibson a nonperson like Aline Bloomgarden (who got the thing started with the Classic Jazz Orchestra and has scarcely been heard from since), is about to launch the first major concert hall ever built to the specifications of jazz, and the question is, Will it spur new music or memorialize the gloried past? More to the point, since—let's be real—it will undoubtedly try on some level to do both, will the new music be worth memorializing?

Another non-story big story was the almost total lack of interest in comprehensively assessing the tonnage of CDs released in the previous season by Wynton Marsalis—the most issued by a single musician since Cecil Taylor's Berlin cataract of 1989. Perhaps our smarter heirs will rap the dust of our knuckles for failing to recognize the lineaments of genius in an act of vanity that is said to have contributed directly to the tanking of Sony jazz. But right now the reception—indifferent silence—to an outpouring by the most famous living jazz player seems more noteworthy than the work itself, perhaps because a consensus of disregard is better than no consensus at all.

Kind of Blue, on the other hand, forged a consensus from the time it was released and has never wandered very far from center stage, even though, until 1997, Sony did not produce an acceptable CD version (a frantic collector once offered me $200 for my LP). It's not the best jazz record ever made—there isn't one—and its universal appeal is not beyond suspicion. The music, after all, is superficially easy listening, however radical its underpinnings; even Coltrane goes down like mother's milk. Yet it summed up the immediate past, defined the present, augured the future, and left a wellspring of indelible melodies, written and improvised. No jazz record in recent years has done anything remotely like that. Nor has any forged more than a fleeting (at best) consensus. In compiling my own best-of-year list, I perused others and found one topped by a CD I rejected as cliché-ridden (clichés always have appeal) and a second topped by a winner that seemed to me ersatz and overproduced. The point is that in the absence of anything suggesting a movement, we are less united than ever before. A reviewer in an Oakland-based journal described Sonny Rollins as "the worst tenor player on the scene today. He is a honker, his tone is very, very flat, in the sense that it is not rounded or full"; what's more, his "execution is that of an amateur." So it's not surprising that when you leave the big cities, you meet—I speak with anecdotal evidence—jazz lovers who tell you how great jazz is for aerobics or speak glowingly of Boney James. "I don't know his work," I lied. "But I thought you were a jazz critic," she said. "Well, I'm just beginning," I apologized.

And I am. Because the post-historical era, the existence of which I have been resisting and denying for a decade, is new and requires new guidelines for listening and evaluating. Originality is nice to find but is no longer the grail. Interpretation has trumped it. "Can you play?" has supplanted "Can you play something I've not heard before?"—something that comes only from you, and not from your favorite records. We will see more homages, derivations, counterfeits, and re-creations before we see fewer. We have been so spoiled by the overflow of genius that we simply expect it as our due: to every generation its Armstrong, Ellington, Tatum, Parker, Gillespie, Monk, Davis, Rollins, Coltrane. Give it up! I have. That way I'll be surprised when genius comes along. In the interim, I can guiltlessly enjoy the only period in jazz history when the most resourceful, energetic, and irreverent musicians are over 65, and the best-selling jazz album of the year was recorded 41 years ago. I can treasure well-made recordings, infrequent though they are, without worrying about consensus. That said, here are some CDs I like, a baker's dozen in no particular order except #1.

1. Sonny Rollins, *This Is What I Do* (Milestone). Nothing else this year fills my speakers with as much ebullience, humor, and humanity. A plus is the LP-ballpark length. You can take it in in one sitting. How many 75-minute epics, excellent in sections, become wallpaper by the eighth nine-minute track? Small wonder people exercise to them. This one is a succession of ocean waves and the surfing is spectacular.

2. *The Roy Haynes Trio* (Verve). Beautifully recorded high-octane music and a template for drummers. Haynes is doing something ear-catching *all the time*, yet is never intrusive or overbearing. John Patitucci's linear bass phrases pick up where Scott LaFaro's left off. Danilo Perez has never recorded a better set; he is far more commanding here than on his own overwritten album—vitally engaging Monk and Powell (the tune selection is unbeatable) on his own terms.

3. James Carter, *Chasin' the Gypsy* (Atlantic). Have reeds, will travel. Carter is the Paladin of his day: faster, warier, and guaranteed to come

out on top. But sometimes he needs restraint, and Django channeled his powers into a provocative tribute that explores and embraces the music, accepting its challenge rather than lying dead before it—as most homages do.

4. Dee Dee Bridgewater, *Live at Yoshi's* (Verve). Throw a banana peel out the window and you are sure to slip up a jazz singer in her/his twenties or thirties. But the huge boomer generation that is about to bankrupt social security has contributed only one ready for the pantheon, and this is her best album. For one thing, it's live, so you get the shtick, which is worth getting; for another, she takes her time on the ballads, rather than winking them into more shtick. You know she's going to whack "Cherokee" out of the park, but you don't expect her to take over "Love for Sale." Runner-up: Abbey Lincoln, *Over the Years* (Verve), another splendid addition to her series, with Joe Lovano and a neat guitar prelude by Kendra Shank. Am I missing somebody, or is Lincoln the first great singer-songwriter in jazz since Fats Waller? Second runner-up: Bob Dorough, *Too Much Coffee Man*, a funny, offbeat hipster hoedown with Phil Woods, by the man who just might be the somebody I was missing.

5. Matthew Shipp, *New Orbit* (Thirsty Ear). This is his second trumpet quartet record of the year, after the more conventional but worthy *Pastoral Composure* (Thirsty Ear), which tackled hard bop ("Visions"—good blindfold test material) and Ellington. It represents a major breakthrough for him as a composer and is a knockout forum for Wadada Leo Smith, whose trumpet never sounded more compelling. William Parker is, as ever, an orchestra unto himself, and, with drummer Gerald Cleaver, the quartet moves in block formation. It's not a toe-tapper, but the music is filled with hooks and counterpoints and witty asides, not to mention the joy of freshness—you haven't heard this before. Is it jazz? Damn right. Runner-up: William Parker, *Painter's Spring* (Thirsty Ear), which has a startling opening minute; saxophonist Daniel Carter sustains interest, as some of Parker's trio mates have not, and Parker remains the most teeming bassist since Mingus. Second runner-up: David S. Ware, *Surrendered* (Columbia), a prophetic title considering it may be the last Columbia gem for a while. Not as righteous as last year's *Go See the World*, though easier to get a handle on: hard to believe Shipp is the minimalist bopper on "Sweet Georgia Bright," or that "African Drums" begins with a vamp out of Brubeck.

6. Joe Lovano, *52nd Street Themes* (Blue Note). Gunther Schuller and Manny Albam were logical choices for orchestral albums, but Willie "Face" Smith? A jazz veteran from Cleveland, Lovano's hometown, Smith was around for the birth of bop and his nonet arrangements of

Tadd Dameron have a quietly sublime authenticity. The band is improbably tight, with everyone taking solo spots as though making 78s and wanting each bar to count. Runner-up: *Grand Slam* (Telarc), with Lovano, Lewis Nash, George Mraz, and Jim Hall, who unaccountably steals it with elliptical solos and gentle strumming you can't turn away from.

7. David Murray, *Octet Plays Trane* (Justin Time). The Iridium performances were so startling, you wondered if a record would measure up. It does, though you may need a breather after the opener, a room-filling assault on "Giant Steps," complete with a polyphonic transcription of Coltrane's solo. There was a time when a Murray octet was news; this one—easily a match for its predecessors—glided in mostly undetected. D. D. Jackson makes up for his slick RCA albums, and who can explain how Murray manages to keep lighting fires under James Spaulding?

8. Clark Terry, *One on One* (Chesky). An unexpected stunner that doubles as a primer on jazz piano. Terry and 14 pianists, from John Lewis to Tommy Flanagan to Kenny Barron to Geri Allen to Eric Lewis, engage in duets dedicated to 14 great dead jazz pianists (Hoagy Carmichael is in on a pass—any excuse to play "Skylark"). Yet it's not just another repertory tribute, because Terry plays with a wry magnificence that belies his 80 years (as of December 14). In sweeping in so many important players, it creates an ipso facto lingua franca. Good liner notes by the musicians.

9. Keith Jarrett, *Whisper Not* (ECM). A similarity in tempo and attitude; recurring bass solos, which, even when played by Gary Peacock, are recurring bass solos; and the pianist's mouselike squeals are overcome by sheer elation as he delights himself (and a Paris audience) with bravura variations on familiar but well-chosen standards: eight jazz, four pop, and one in between—"Wrap Your Troubles in Dreams," which he begins with lambent stride. The ballads succumb to slow motion, but the meditative longuers and facile bluesisms are gone. When Jarrett, Peacock, and Jack DeJohnette lift off at medium-up tempos, they create their own orbit. "Bouncing with Bud," "Groovin' High," and "What Is This Thing Called Love?" are spectacular, as are the encores.

10. Marty Ehrlich's Travelers Tales, *Malinke's Dance* (Omnitone). He's everywhere, but this may be the most completely pleasurable album Ehrlich has made. The quartet is taut as a wire, with Jerome Harris and Bobby Previte laying down the rhythm, and tenor saxophonist Tony Malaby bringing more bite to this session than to his own *Sabino* (Arabesque). But it's the leader's centered alto saxophone that shines hottest, galloping through "Pigskin" and jauntily essaying a cadenza on an "I Remember You" variation aptly named "Bright Remembered."

11. Jason Moran, *Facing Left* (Blue Note). This grew on me slowly, but

it's a good sign when you keep coming back. Moran may be the least linear, chord-stringing pianist since Ahmad Jamal. He subordinates melody and harmony to rhythmic configurations, mesmerizing himself with vamps. It's delightful to hear a revival of Jaki Byard's "Twelve" or Ellington's "Wig Wise," and even his own compositions seem to have been born of *Money Jungle*, the Ellington-Mingus-Roach trio disparaged four decades ago, now a classic text. For originality this rivals Shipp's *New Orbit*. Sensible length, too.

12. Andrew Hill, *Dusk* (Palmetto). His most appealing album since the 1968 *Grass Roots*. Ehrlich, Ron Horton, and Greg Tardy man the front line, rolling with the punches of his knotty originals, but the pianist is the heart of the matter. Hill's solos step forward with the determination of a man unwilling to play anything that anyone might anticipate; he bypasses familiar cadences and resolutions as though they were land mines, and he generates suspense if you're stepping close behind him, wondering if he'll make it. He always does.

13. Benny Golson, *Remembering Clifford* (Milestone). This is one CD I knew would make my list months ago, though when I examined the small print, I realized it came out in 1998 and got lost in the recesses of my office. I include it anyway, because I discovered it in 2000, just as I expect I will discover or rediscover CDs that came out this year and did not get the attention from me they merit. Golson shares the tenor spot with Ron Blake, and Mike LeDonne chairs the rhythm section, and the nothing-new of it is accomplished with charm and maturity.

[*Village Voice*, 9 January 2001]

78 ❖ Bedside Jazz
(More Best Jazz Records of 2000)

The other day, tunneling through boxes of books stored for lack of space, I came across a 1945 anthology, *The Bedside Tales*, subtitled "A Gay Collection with an Introduction by Peter Arno." The unidentified editor merged golden oldies by Hemingway, Faulkner, and Perelman; forgotten efforts by Hammett, Cain, and Joseph Mitchell; once famous tales now known for the movies they inspired ("The Most Dangerous Game," "The Sobbin Women"—*Seven Brides for Seven Brothers*); neglected writers like Bemelmans, Hecht, and Asbury; humor and journalism—a large compilation of found treasure. So it never occurred to me to question the compiler or complain about the inclusion of so-and-so at the expense of what's-her-name. The delight of anthologies is that of giving oneself up to someone else's taste. It was precisely that delight that chaperoned many of us through historic jazz during the LP era.

If you bought the Columbia Golden Era Series or RCA-Vintage compilations or Decca Heritage collections, you got a short-order survey of flash points, one masterpiece after another. In the 78 era, reissues meant pricey, bulky photo-albums, rarely with more than six or eight sides. The LP greased the process of salvaging history. A jazz expert like George Avakian, Mike Lipskin, or Stanley Dance would select 12 or 14 or 16 tracks that best represented a given artist, and a generation was weaned on the old even as it pursued the new. Then a strange thing happened. After you had committed to memory every measure of the 12 classics on *Lady Day*, you wanted more. So the label released a boxed set (48 tracks), which did well enough to justify a second box. By now you had heard a helluva lot of Billie Holiday and you wanted to get beyond the anthologist's subjectivity: You wanted everything. You bought imports and bootlegs, traded tapes, focused on chronology and the sessions themselves, and railed against the capitalist pigs who were keeping all this stuff in their corporate vaults.

Ultimately, some of you went to the trough yourselves and began producing reissues, offering the public what you had once hungered for: completeness—every track, in order, with every alternate take, short take, false take, plus studio chatter and even (cf. the CD version of Benny Goodman's 1938 Carnegie Hall concert) the sound of furniture removal. By 1990, our shelves sloped under gravemarker boxes—historical documents that tried to reveal what *really* happened at those once secret conferences laughingly known as recording sessions. We listened and we marveled. Once. And then we went back to the anthologies—though few of them made the transition from vinyl. Many young producers, stamp collectors at heart, were too modest or inept to pick and choose. When they did choose, they often relied not on musical taste but on ancient chart rankings.

As an occasional teacher during the first decade of the CD, my hardest job was recommending records. Students did not want and could not afford the complete works. They wanted 12 Holiday masterpieces, or maybe 25. What's more, digitalized sound was so offensive (particularly on the early Columbias and RCA CDs) that those of us who didn't know our high end from our rear end suddenly discovered that it was possible to filter all the joy out of records that had sounded just fine for 50 years.

The pendulum has swung back. It may be cold comfort or none at all to acknowledge an upturn in reissues at a time when major labels are turning thumbs down on living jazz musicians, but at the moment jazz classics are a better investment than Microsoft. The outstanding reissues of recent months include admirable examples of long-sought completeness and the best anthology series since the advent of the CD. Ideally, they ought to work together. But such is the topsy-turvy world of jazz that instead of getting a crème de la crème disc of Mildred Bailey that leads to a complete works, we begin with the latter—and hope it will generate enough attention and sales to spur the interest of the copyright owner, Sony Columbia. Meanwhile, *The Complete Columbia Recordings of Mildred Bailey*, a limited edition (5,000) from the mail-order company, Mosaic, in Stamford, Connecticut, does what a serious survey ought to. It isn't just a handy storage box, but an argument on behalf of an important but long neglected artist—an overdue assessment (voluminous notes by Will Friedwald) and an opportunity to follow her career from 1929 to 1942 (she recorded for other labels during the same period and through 1951) with an exactness never previously possible.

The key years here are the mid-'30s, when Bailey rarely took a false step. During that period, following the decline of Ethel Waters and Bessie Smith and before the rise of Ella Fitzgerald and Frank Sinatra, Mildred— along with Holiday and their male counterparts, Louis Armstrong and Bing Crosby—was a dominant force in jazz and pop singing. If her high girlish voice seems to date her, her impeccable time and phrasing and extraordinary subtlety keep her current. Having written at length about Bailey not long ago, I defer to a singer-friend who succinctly explained why she remains so compelling: "You always believe her." More than half the 214 tracks, including 36 alternates, are new to me and I'm only beginning to glean the details. When I first played the 10 discs, I grumbled that the alternate versions had not been collected at the end. I've changed my mind: After a perfect take of, say, "Rockin' Chair," you wonder why she would take another. Discreet tweaking is the invariably rewarding answer. In this regard, the great January 10, 1938, session ("Thanks for the Memory," "Lover Come Back to Me") is most illuminating.

In addition to Red Norvo's skillfully baronial big band, her accompanists included Eddie Lang, the Dorseys, Bunny Berigan, the Casa Loma band, Benny Goodman, Coleman Hawkins, Teddy Wilson, Chu Berry, Ben Webster, Ed Hall, Buck Clayton, Artie Shaw, Mary Lou Williams, Roy Eldridge, and the Charioteers—a serious chunk of jazz history. One caveat: Bailey, although partly Native American, unaccountably sang several numbers of the little-colored-boy-who's-so-cute-he's-practically-human variety; prepare yourself for a handful of gwines and a Larry Hart line about a Harlem songwriter in the woodpile. An anthropologist needs to acknowledge them; the anthologist who, in time, edits a more manageable selection doesn't.

Just how much of a boost jazz gets from Ken Burns's *Jazz* remains to be seen, but even his most venomous detractors will have to credit him for using his clout in getting Columbia and Verve to participate in a remarkable series of 22 retrospective discs that lease material from RCA, Blue Note, Fantasy, and anywhere else the compilers' eyes wandered. Producer Sarah Botstein choreographed this considerable sleight of hand and savvy anthologists (Michael Brooks, Bob Belden, Ben Young, Michael Cuscuna, others) selected the material. If asked, I can now, for the first time in 20 years, comfortably recommend a lone Armstrong disc— in fact, this is the best Armstrong starter ever, covering the waterfront from "Chimes Blues" to "What a Wonderful World." The other subjects (each CD bears the artist's name and the *Ken Burns Jazz* logo) are Ellington, Bechet, Goodman, Vaughan, Rollins, Davis, Monk, Henderson, Brubeck, Coleman, Mingus, Hancock, Parker, Gillespie, Basie, Coltrane, Blakey, Fitzgerald, Holiday, Hawkins, and Young. You can quibble over the selections, if you like; I am mostly content to surrender my speakers to the editors.

Some collections cover entire careers, others focus on peak periods. Some are surprising—*Miles Davis* ignores his greatest quintet, yet offers a heady and persuasive joy ride from "Donna Lee" to "Tutu." The Bechet falters a bit, with too much Noble Sissle and none of his later work, and you may want to skip two fusion epics on the Hancock, which is otherwise a Blue Note special. Yet the Hawkins outdistances the superb RCA Vintage LP of the '60s; the Young is without peer; the Holiday rivals *Lady Day* and may make just as many converts; the Henderson is a far more inviting introduction than the multi-volume *A Study in Frustration*; the Vaughan is luscious, the Monk cagily impeccable, and so on. Even if you have the complete works, the pleasure of hitting the high spots is not to be denied—and if you don't know the first names of those mentioned above, this is the way to find out. I hope the labels keep it up with or without the Burns imprimatur.

Other recent reissues are worth seeking out. Volume One of Duke Ellington's *The Treasury Shows* (D.E.T.S.) has been imported from Denmark and consists of complete 1945 broadcasts, including a moving memorial tribute to FDR (passages from "New World A-Comin'" and *Black, Brown and Beige* are woven into it), marred only by a sentimental announcer. Sarah Vaughan's *Linger Awhile* (Milestone) is not, strictly speaking, a reissue as it combines previously unreleased performances from 1957 through 1982, but it offers the opportunity to follow the blooming of her voice, and "All of Me" is a miracle of concision. JVC has been releasing an excellent series of audiophile editions of classic (and obscure) albums, and *Thelonious Himself* has never sounded so good; it includes a 25-minute running tape as he nails down "'Round Midnight." The five-disc Sonny Rollins carton, *The Freelance Years* (Riverside), doesn't make a lot of sense, since most of his freelancing is absent, but it is a convenient catch-all for his Riverside, Contemporary, and Period sides, and an opportunity to discover or rediscover Abbey Lincoln's *That's Him!*, one of the great neglected vocal LPs of the 1950s. The three-disc *Thelonious Monk: Complete Prestige Recordings* is weighed down by a surprisingly laborious 1953 date with Rollins, but contains his 1944 session with Hawkins, the superior 1954 Rollins date, the entire 1954 Miles Davis encounter, and "These Foolish Things," perhaps the most rollicking piano solo he ever recorded. Armstrong's *The Complete Hot Five and Hot Seven Recordings* has a scratched-up "Willie the Weeper" and an awful lot of vaudeville shading the sunbursts (anyone who thinks vocalizing and comedy entered his music in the '30s might count the ratio of vocals to instrumentals, not to mention the percentage of novelties)—but it's complete and in this instance more is more.

Sadly, an important year for jazz classics was followed almost immediately by the death of one of the idiom's chief commercial archivists: Charlie Lourie, who created Mosaic Records with Michael Cuscuna. No company has done more to slake the thirst for completeness: Instead of bedside companions, Mosaic produced living-room monuments. But beyond memorializing the great, it has—as with Mildred Bailey—triggered second thoughts about a wide range of music, from the Nat Cole trio and Ike Quebec to Gerald Wilson's big band and Capitol's obscurities. Charlie will be missed.

[*Village Voice*, 23 January 2001]

79 ❖ *Parajazz*
(The Avant-garde)

1.

For many jazz lovers, the avant-garde is an inferno that derogates them and the orthodoxies that make jazz appealing. Feeling personally reproached, they respond with anger or contempt. Although the avant-garde's audience is international, its achievement vast, its influence sweeping, and its history fully half as long as that of jazz proper, it is often regarded as a thing apart—a separateness sanctioned by those enthusiasts who listen to nothing else. Like much of jazz history, this schism has a precedent in European classical music: the divisive reaction—augured by Shavian critics who championed radical Wagner at the expense of reserved Brahms—to serialism, which begat converts and antagonists, but few neutrals.

The avant-garde has been treated as a metaphor rather than as music by proponents and enemies alike. The former have adapted it to suit social and political movements as various as Marxism, mysticism, pacifism, internationalism, black nationalism, and integration, implying at times a revolutionary-cause-du-jour applicability. Not surprisingly, the avant-garde is often characterized as music of the left. But so is jazz itself—"a people's music," in Sidney Finkelstein's 1940s phrase. Detractors revile avant-gardists as both elitist and barbarous: on the one hand, as insulated academics who hijacked jazz and turned it into a nearly occult pursuit only they can comprehend; on the other, as charlatans who clothe their ineptness in fashionable rhetoric. Either way, naysayers invariably insist, the avant-garde alienated the very "people" it hoped to liberate.

I offer two anecdotes to confirm and muddle prejudices in each camp. At a Finnish jazz festival in the early 1980s, two saxophonists from East Berlin, performing outside the wall for the first time, spoke poignantly of jazz's liberating power and then embarked on a fusillade of shrieking high-note blasts. After several minutes of this, a notable American avant-gardist turned to me and said, "Let's go. This stuff is a lot more fun to play than to listen to." At a rehearsal by a New York jazz orchestra a few years later, musicians bitterly groused when it was announced they would be conducted by a famous avant-gardist in a program of his music: "he can't play," "it's a mockery," etc. When the guest conductor arrived and the musicians read his scores, they marveled at his craftsmanship and, having assured themselves of his skill, earnestly embraced the rigors of his music. After the concert, the most outspoken of the early skeptics conceded to me, "He's a brilliant guy. I wish we played more music like that."

If we are to rescue avant-garde jazz from parochialism of any kind, we need to define the term. The dictionary is the place to begin: "n. 1. A group, as of artists and writers, regarded as pre-eminent in the invention and application of new techniques in a given field. 2. The admirers of such a group and critics acting as its spokesmen. adj. 1. Of or relating to the vanguard, as in the arts. 2. Ahead of the times." These definitions are useful, but quite obviously too general. A distinction must be made between a universal avant-gardism and the school of jazz known as the avant-garde. I emphasize "known," because most innovators resist the pigeonhole; indeed, they vigorously resent a characterization of their music that presumes complexity and mayhem, virtually warning their potential audience to exercise caution.

Jazz has always had a vanguard, performers who propelled the music in new directions, dismaying generations of fans content with what they already knew. Louis Armstrong, Jelly Roll Morton, Duke Ellington, Bix Beiderbecke, Earl Hines, and Coleman Hawkins were among the jazz pioneers of the 1920s, each in his way an avant-garde musician who helped relegate customary jazz, rag, and blues styles to the dead ends of the past. Their innovations were perceived not as assaults on convention, but as the kind of ingenuity that enhances traditions without undermining them. Yet in raising jazz to a new plateau of emotional and technical expression, they precipitated the greatest schism of all, delivering art music from folk music and dividing artists from journeymen. Since we venerate them much more than we do their dimly remembered predecessors, we do not burden them with the stigma of otherness often associated with the avant-garde, but rather honor them as forebears.

Nor do we think of the swing era as avant-garde. The Basies, Goodmans, Shaws, and Luncefords were undeniably "pre-eminent in the invention and application of new techniques," and conservative critics predictably assailed them for enfeebling and commercializing classic jazz, but you can hardly call them "ahead of the times"; they *were* the times. Lester Young may have been considered too far out for New York in 1934, yet two years later countless musicians, and not just tenor saxophonists, were trying to play like him. Staunch anomalies such as Red Norvo's "Dance of the Octopus," Coleman Hawkins's "Queer Notions," or Duke Ellington's "Reminiscing in Tempo," though avant-garde for the day, were too singular to suggest a movement or even a style.

Bebop created a greater divide, splitting the jazz world in two and engendering as much contumely, ridicule, and recrimination as the avant-garde school born in its wake. The methods of Charlie Parker, Dizzy Gillespie, Bud Powell, Thelonious Monk, and dozens of others—a peer group in thrall to a new music and a new way of thinking about music—were quintessentially avant-garde, except for one thing. Even as contemptuous pundits poked fun at alleged bebop manners, the music supplanted its predecessors almost as completely as Armstrong's generation superseded the raggy beats and polyphony of Dixieland. Yet Armstrong and swing didn't disappear with the advent of bebop, but were pressed into a historical frame. Like Bach leading to Mozart leading to Beethoven, jazz had now established a history of unceasing revision;

it was an expanding and developing art that continued to infuriate the musically complaisant while keeping the adventurous if not on the dance floor then certainly on their toes.

2.

Aspects of the avant-garde jazz movement can be traced back to every other kind of jazz. Consider its reintroduction of polyphony—one of the avant-garde's dominant facets. Bebop evolved from the past with an attitude of determined modernism, setting itself in opposition to the clichés and styles of the past; the avant-garde opposed clichés but not styles, accepting the entire canvas of jazz history as its platform. Still, its direct roots lie in bebop, which raised issues about harmony, melody, rhythm, and instrumentation that succeeding generations could scarcely fail to explore. Charlie Parker said he came alive when he realized he could improvise on the higher intervals of chords. His successors expanded that quest, exploring the limits of chords and then dispensing with them altogether. Even as bop introduced a categorical, tight-knit virtuoso style, it encouraged innovations that challenged its own precepts. Was bop an obstacle course of refined chord changes? George Russell composed a piece for Dizzy Gillespie's orchestra ("Cubana Be/Cubana Bop") that eschewed chords in favor of modes or scales. Were bop's rhythms of such velocity that only cymbals could mark the beat? Gillespie and Parker introduced Afro-Cuban rhythms and Latin percussion instruments. Was bop hot? Miles Davis gave birth to the cool. Were bop variations so cunning they obscured the themes? Monk stressed thematic variations.

Monk was branded a charlatan for his unconventional style as pianist and composer. Russell's "A Bird in Igor's Yard," which meshed jazz and classical techniques, and Lennie Tristano's "Digression," a "free" group improvisation (without pre-stated melody, harmonic structure, or tempo), were considered so avant-garde in 1949 that Capitol Records refused to release them. Yet, again, these were isolated performances, and though they heralded jazz schools (third-stream, the Tristano cult), they were not the stuff of a movement. That came later, triggered by musicians who came of age during the bop era, but were regarded as outcasts by their contemporaries. Considering the number of directions jazz took in the '50s—cool, hard bop, third-stream, soul, modal—and the remarkable range of personalities that flourished, a player would have to be fearsome indeed to earn a nearly unanimous disrespect. Happily, a few were.

After three years at the New England Conservatory, Cecil Taylor relocated to New York and was laughed off bandstands until he began to attract like-minded musicians, even disciples. In 1956, at age 27, he recorded his first album, *Jazz Advance*. Not exactly a salvo, it introduced a startling new voice, that of a pianist who played at and around chords while sidestepping the assortment of linear melodies that were the foundation of practically all modern jazz improvisation. His touch was so brisk and percussive, he seemed to be beating drum patterns on the keyboard. On "Rick Kick Shaw," he offered a template for a piano style redolent of diverse jazz and classical influences without quite deferring to any of them. The album was largely ignored or ridiculed.

At the same time, John Coltrane, an apparently insignificant tenor saxophonist who had worked with Gillespie and Johnny Hodges but was not above playing low-rent bar gigs, experienced a musical and personal rebirth and dedicated himself to the compulsive study of scales. At 30, he was hired by Miles Davis and revealed a keening high-register sound and a prolix style that crammed so many notes into a chord he left little for his accompanists to play. With his scorching rhythm section—McCoy Tyner, Jimmy Garrison, Elvin Jones—Coltrane developed his music in astonishing leaps, winning and losing audiences along the way. One initially admiring critic described his approach as "sheets of sound," only to dismiss "Chasin' the Train"—an apocalyptic sheets of sound performance—as an "airleak" a few years later.

At the same time, in Los Angeles, Ornette Coleman—who, to hear him tell it, was run out of his native Fort Worth for playing alto saxophone in a way that made usually peaceable musicians resort to violence—was attracting followers willing to put their preconceptions on hold, notably Don Cherry, Charlie Haden, and Billy Higgins. Desperate for work, he offered his compositions, singular melodic inventions that could be immensely moving and wittily tumultuous, to Contemporary Records. The label surprised him by signing him to play them. His first album, recorded at age 28, proffered the exclamatory but reasonable title, *Something Else!!!* Its successors were more insurgent: *Tomorrow Is the Question, The Shape of Jazz to Come, Change of the Century*. Coleman's ebullient, raw quartertone pitch conveyed the primitivism of rural blues and, at the same time, a shocking modernist mockery.

If Taylor, Coltrane, and Coleman represented the beginnings of a new jazz movement, it was unparalleled on several levels. For one, they were making an impact at relatively advanced ages; Louis Armstrong and Charlie Parker effected revolutions at 25. For another, they tended to eye each other cautiously, from a distance. Unlike the progenitors of swing or bop, who frequently performed and recorded together, these three offered widely disparate approaches to a new kind of jazz. Coltrane recorded once with Taylor and once with Coleman's band, but never with Coleman, who in turn never recorded with Taylor. Each man was a school unto himself, their divergent musics reflecting uncommonly diverse backgrounds. Parker, Gillespie, and Powell came from different points on the map, but all were spawned by jazz. By contrast, Taylor was classically trained and Coleman apprenticed himself in rhythm and blues; only Coltrane issued directly from jazz.

That they signaled the beginnings of a musical movement did not become clear until the early 1960s, when the attention they garnered encouraged numerous other musicians to join them on the jazz fringe. Unlike musical uprisings of the past, this one did not admit of a generational divide. Eric Dolphy, a late bloomer from California and an accomplished technician by any standard, moved to New York to play with the Charles Mingus Quartet and instantly attached himself to Coltrane and Coleman. Mingus himself, the superb bop bassist who now publicly criticized musicians in his own band for relying on bop's clichés, cast a wary eye at the newcomers but was himself liberated by the spirit of radical adventurism. Jimmy Giuffre, the tenor saxophonist who wrote Woody Herman's "Four Brothers," organized a free-form trio with bassist Steve Swallow and the influential pianist Paul Bley, who had worked with Coleman and was developing his own approach to free improvisation. Sun Ra, born in 1914 and an alumnus of jazz's first great orchestra leader, Fletcher Henderson, moved his much recorded but neglected Arkestra to New York in 1960, and emerged as a dynamic mobilizer of the new music.

In 1960, Coleman recorded his double-quartet, *Free Jazz*, and gave the movement a name, though ultimately one of limited utility. Freeform improvisations unquestionably accounted for much of the new jazz; they marked an inevitable response to the highly structured patterns of bop. The year before, Miles Davis enjoyed immense success with *Kind of Blue*, one of the most iconic of jazz LPs, popularizing a modal approach to improvisation. "So What" is commonplace in form (AABA, 32 bars), but instead of a system of chord changes, the harmony consists of one scale (D-minor) for 24 bars and another (a half-step higher) for the release. A few weeks later, Coltrane, who played on that session, took the opposite tack on "Giant Steps," which has two chords to each measure. Davis winnowed bop's harmonies to encourage original improvisations, and Coltrane maximized them for the same reason. Coleman took the next step: complete freedom from fixed harmonic and, for that matter, rhythmic patterns. He focused on melody, allowing harmonies to emerge serendipitously. His music had a buoyantly swinging rhythmic pulse but abrogated the steady demarcations of a four/four beat. You couldn't listen with half a mind because there were no familiar resolutions; you had to concentrate on the escapade of Coleman's solo and the way the ensemble accompanied it.

The new music took a major leap in 1962, when Cecil Taylor's trio—altoist Jimmy Lyons, drummer Sunny Murray—performed and recorded at Club Montmartre in Copenhagen. In addition to abandoning fixed harmonies once and for all, Taylor pushed farther than Coleman had in liberating rhythm. Coleman's beat was rootless, but the pulse was regular. Taylor, with Murray's support, allowed the rhythmic pulse to permutate, moment by moment, as a consequence of whatever he played; the energy of his attack governed the time. Swing was no longer a downbeat you could follow with your foot, but a percussive wailing you followed as closely as you might a melodic variation. Taylor also shared the Club Montmartre bandstand with Albert Ayler, a young tenor and soprano saxophonist, recently discharged from the army, whose ballistic harmonics, singsong themes, and otherworldly solos were so startling some thought he had to be kidding.

Meanwhile, Coltrane continued to speed into the stratosphere of musical expressionism. Cynics could deride Ayler and Coleman as fakes, and Taylor and Dolphy as virtuoso aesthetes. Coltrane, however, had come through the ranks. Though one critic branded him "anti-jazz," no one questioned his technical command of jazz harmony and rhythm, the exquisite pitch-perfect beauty of his sound, the emotional resolve of his ballads and blues, or his sincerity. If he chose to play free, committing himself to a new music that alienated so many, he had to be taken seriously.

By 1963, the avant-garde had the verve and brawn of a genuine crusade. A year later, a series of six concerts produced by 39-year-old trumpeter, composer, and educator Bill Dixon at New York's Cellar Cafe brazenly proclaimed the new order as nothing less than "The October Revolution in Jazz." A whole generation of players was ready to storm the gates, among them Archie Shepp, Milford Graves, Roswell Rudd, John Tchicai, Marion Brown, and Pharoah Sanders. Two record labels announced their commitment to the new music. The independent ESP-Disk, originally created to promote Esperanto, got off to an invigorating start with Albert Ayler's *Spiritual Unity*, and introduced new musicians on an almost monthly basis, including a few who considered the avant-garde a musical option, not a religion: pianist Don Pullen, who would create one of the major ensembles of the '80s, linking avant-garde and mainstream techniques; bassist Eddie Gomez, who enjoyed a long association with Bill Evans; and Bob James, the godfather of "jazz lite." The most widely distributed avant-garde label was Impulse, then a subsidiary of ABC-Paramount, which signed Coltrane and bannered its gate-fold covers with the slogan "The new wave of jazz is on Impulse!"

The movement had a profusion of competing names—free jazz, the new wave, the new music, the New Thing, black music, revolutionary music, fire music, out music. That the term "avant-garde" remained after the rest had faded into a miasma of 1960s oratory may be attributed in part to its prevailing, inoffensive meaning. But it also came into play because of the strange circumstances that followed the music's ostensible acceptance, when in spite of its expanding influence, the avant-garde showed signs of corruption and a general languishing.

3.

Avant-garde jazz reflected the turmoil of the 1960s. It was a minority music, expressing euphoria and sadness and daring and resentment and anger and other feelings through styles so extreme as to utterly alienate most of the traditional jazz following—itself a withering minority in the age of rock. The rhetoric for and against was often ugly, as it had been during bop, though now you also heard accusations of racism, tomming, and worse. Most of that passed quickly enough, though a lingering distrust continued to rend the jazz audience. Veteran musicians felt that their art had been fatally subverted, and some tried to make common cause with rock, while others accepted private students or joined school faculties, and still others sought studio or pit-band work until the storm abated. The avant-garde players, as always, had an even rougher time. After the novelty value waned, not even the innovators sold enough records to maintain a vivid presence. Many of the most critically lauded avant-garde works sold a few thousand copies at best.

And yet the influence of the avant-garde was everywhere. Established musicians were responding to its musical challenges and emotional immediacy. They adapted, in their different ways, what they found viable, even if it was nothing more than license to go overboard. I recall musicians, in the mid-'60s, expressing astonishment at how "inside" Coleman sounded, when only a few years earlier he had seemed impenetrably "outside." Small wonder. In the interim, the avant-garde rubbed off on almost everyone who didn't bolt from jazz entirely. A new genre appeared: the ultra-modern album by mainstream-modern musicians to the right of the avant-garde, who could not resist testing its turf. Consider Sonny Rollins's *Our Man in Jazz*, Jackie McLean's *Destination Out!*, Charles Mingus's *Black Saint and the Sinner Lady*, Andrew Hill's *Point of Departure*, Stan Getz's *Sweet Rain*, Tony Williams's *Lifetime*, Sam Rivers's *Fuscia Swing Song*, Wayne Shorter's *The All-Seeing Eye*, Roland Kirk's *Rip,*

Rig and Panic, Bobby Hutcherson's *Components*, Modern Jazz Quartet's *Space*, Jaki Byard's *Sunshine of My Soul*, Miles Davis's *Miles in the Sky*, and Gil Evans's *Blues in Orbit*, among many others, all of which partake of the avant-gardism rife in the 1960s. Rock groups also borrowed licks from the new jazz; by the mid-'70s, the studios were rampant with Coltrane imitators—heard on pop records, in TV bands, and in film scores.

Still, with all this going on, the avant-garde appeared to curl up in hibernation. Coleman's label, Atlantic, dropped him in 1961, and he recorded erratically in the years to come, often traveling in the opposite direction of free jazz, with notated works for string quartet, symphony orchestra, rock band, and other ensembles. His unique sound and attack, however, abided. Inexplicably, Ayler, whose finest work was lavishly flamboyant in the best sense, began to record hippie fusion anthems before his tragic death in 1970. Of the major avant-garde figures, Taylor—like Monk before him—had to wait the longest for acceptance. Between 1962, when he recorded at the Montmartre, and 1973, his only records were two stunning 1966 Blue Note LPs, *Unit Structures* and *Conquistador!*, a concerto written for him in 1968 by 24-year-old Mike Mantler (recorded by his Jazz Composer's Orchestra), and a taped concert from Europe in 1969. Taylor spent a few of those years teaching at colleges in the Midwest.

Coltrane's death in the summer of 1967 had a baleful impact on all of jazz, but it marked the beginning of the Coltrane legend. A church was consecrated in his name in San Francisco, and his record sales—mostly modest during his life—began to soar. His passing symbolized jazz's capitulation to rock in the late '60s, though there was really nothing symbolic about it. ESP-Disk became a reissue operation, as did Impulse, despite a series of ambitious recordings by Archie Shepp and Sam Rivers. Record labels folded and clubs went dark. The next few years were a rough patch in jazz history.

But jazz came roaring back in the mid-'70s. This was a period in which a slew of not-very-old masters—among them Rollins, Mingus, Dexter Gordon, Sarah Vaughan, Gerry Mulligan, the Modern Jazz Quartet, James Moody, Hank Jones, Red Rodney, and Phil Woods—tired of their sabbaticals and side trips and returned to action with new energy, helping to refuel the mainstream audience. It was also the period in which a new coterie of avant-garde musicians took much of the jazz world by surprise, thoroughly overturning some of the assumptions generated by their predecessors. They had a broader agenda, and they interpreted the idea of freedom as the capacity to choose between all the realms of jazz, mixing and matching them not only with each other, but with old and new pop, r&b and rock, classical music and world music.

These musicians ambushed the national press because they had been honing their music not in New York, where much of the press and the record industry resides, but in points west, especially Chicago, Los Angeles, and St. Louis. Some had toured Europe, and several had recorded for small labels, little more than vanities for the most part, with the noted exception of Chicago's Delmark Records. On that label, one began to hear of a cooperative called the AACM (Association for the Advancement of Creative Music) and to hear the music of its guru, Muhal Richard Abrams, an erstwhile bop pianist, and its younger members including Bowie, Roscoe Mitchell, Joseph Jarman, Leroy Jenkins, Henry Threadgill, Anthony Braxton, Chico Freeman, Steve McCall, George Lewis, and Leo Smith. Before long, many of them relocated to New York, where seemingly overnight new venues—in many instances, apartments or lofts (hence the phrase "loft jazz")—opened shop to present their wares.

This was all pretty astounding, sociologically and musically. Instead of lone paladins arriving from different cities, hoping to sit in, win recognition, and make a name, here came gangs of accomplished players, some just getting started, others past 40. In addition to the AACM musicians, there was the Black Artists Group from St. Louis, including Julius Hemphill, Oliver Lake, Hamiet Bluiett, and Baikida Carroll. A kind of offshoot of the AACM developed in New Haven, where Yalies Anthony Davis and George Lewis worked with Leo Smith and Fred Anderson. From Los Angeles came a network of players without an acronym but with a history of working together, ranging from John Carter and Bobby Bradford—associates of Coleman long before he came to New York and now in their forties—to Arthur Blythe, a veteran of Horace Tapscott's Los Angeles orchestra, to college students James Newton, Mark Dresser, and David Murray.

It is impossible to overstate the degree to which all these players countered the most meretricious effects of fusion and sparked a renewed hunger for creative jazz, setting the stage for the return of many of the aforementioned mainstream jazz stars. They were a new breed of musician, often doubling as painters and poets and entrepreneurs. They formed small bands that lasted for years, decades, including the trios Revolutionary Ensemble and Air, and the ongoing Art Ensemble of Chicago. They defied expectations; Threadgill's Air played free and used hubcaps for percussion but also cannily interpreted tangos and Scott Joplin. Many musicians harbored big-band ambitions and eventually realized them, energizing orchestral jazz for the first time in a decade. Yet they also performed in any way that was economically feasible, pioneering solo wind concerts and duets. They made it a point of honor to write original music but were not averse to playing standards and jazz

classics. Though contentious rhetoric was occasionally heard, it was usually a benign expression of black pride; the music was more often satir-
ical than angry. When Arthur Blythe arrived in New York with a
nickname given him by friends as a young man, Black Arthur, one critic
attacked him for the moniker alone, assuming him to be a crazed mili-
tant. When Blythe played his alto, though, he produced a dynamic, brittle, pear-shaped sound, sweet and sour, that hadn't been heard in jazz
since Benny Carter, and that perfectly reflected the man.

Free jazz to these musicians was not a specific, aharmonic way of
approaching improvisation, but one style among many. Even when they
played free solos, they often couched them in contexts that were scrupulously notated. The main point here is that they were not limited by
the artificial boundaries of idiom. Sun Ra, long a Midwesterner, understood this from the start, and at his concerts in the 1980s, he typically
combined impetuous blowouts with complex arrangements, visual spectacle, blues and tap-dance rhythms, a sermon, a Fletcher Henderson arrangement, and "Hello Dolly!" It was not uncharacteristic for a pianist
like Anthony Davis to play Ellington one season and compose an opera
the next; or for Muhal Richard Abrams to orchestrate an Ellington piano
piece at one concert and employ ripped newspapers as voicings at the
next, or for Julius Hemphill to record aggressive unaccompanied saxophone solos one year and devise a theatrical pageant the next.

Perhaps the most resourceful of the younger players was tenor saxophonist, bass clarinetist, composer, and bandleader David Murray, who
at 20 paid homage to Albert Ayler, identifying himself with the avant-
garde tradition, and before he was 30 added homages to Hawkins,
Young, and Paul Gonsalves. Murray never had one band when he could
have several, so you could hear him with a quartet, his widely celebrated
octet, his big band, as well as solo and in duos and trios. With Hemphill,
Bluiett, and Lake, he created the World Saxophone Quartet, which at
first played free because they had nothing written, but soon built up an
outstanding book of original pieces. In the late '90s, Murray played with
jazz musicians from every generation, as well as rock, hip-hop, gospel,
European, Guadalupian, and African musicians.

4.

Wave after wave of avant-garde musicians continue to show up, bringing
to bear the influences of whatever musics they know and adapting them
into the broadest possible jazz context. In New York, they now appear
regularly at places like the Knitting Factory and Tonic. Dozens of labels—the most prominent include the pioneering Black Saint and Soul

Note in Italy, DIW in Japan, and the expanding Knitting Factory Records in New York—record them. The names and faces change, but they continue to explore avant-garde traditions. Joe Morris plays Ornette Coleman on guitar and John Zorn's Masada explores Jewish themes in a context directly related to Coleman's '60s quartet. There is hardly a pianist, no matter how traditionally trained, whose attack hasn't been affected by the belling cascades of Cecil Taylor. David S. Ware's quartet, one of the most highly regarded ensembles of the decade, is made up of two Taylor alumni (Ware and the omnipresent bassist William Parker) and a pianist, Matthew Shipp, who extends Taylor's methods in an entirely personal direction. The Rova Saxophone Quartet transcribed and recorded, note for note, Coltrane's *Ascension*, which 30 years ago was considered the most exhilarating or appalling assault on musical conventions ever created. Several avant-garde players routinely join with mainstream musicians; competence is rarely an issue.

The avant-garde is no longer a jazz school, like swing or bop, and cannot be supplanted. It is rather a kind of parajazz, which has evolved in various directions over the past 40 years, blending with every other kind of jazz and every other kind of music, including r&b, klezmer, electronica, country, Bulgarian folk songs, koto, gamelan, Mahler—you name it, you can find it. Though the avant-garde enjoys a predictably narrow following, the audience is constant in the United States and even more so in Europe, where fusions between jazz and classics are more readily assimilated. Most avant-garde jazz is clearly anchored in jazz, and some of it is just as clearly anchored alongside. Though no longer an exclusive territory of innovators, gadflies, and prophets, it remains a loose confederation of individualists who take nothing—not even swing or blues—for granted. Like jazz, parajazz offers something for everyone.

[*Jazz*, by Geoffrey C. Ward and Ken Burns, Knopf, 2000]

PART TWO

❖

The Second Century, 2001–2003

80 ❖ The Neglected King of Song (Bing Crosby)

For the last decade, whenever I mentioned to anyone that I was working on a life of Bing Crosby, the usual response was, "Why?" I can't say I was surprised. For 30 years, between 1927 and 1956, Crosby was a looming presence in America's cultural landscape. At the peak of his career, in the 1930s and 1940s, he was thought by many to be the most famous American alive. For much of that period, he was undoubtedly the most beloved. The cycle of "Road" pictures with Bob Hope established Crosby as an accomplished comic actor. Yet by the 1960s, the ocean began to roll over Der Bingle, and though he continued to sell millions of records—chiefly holiday songs—he had morphed into a grand old man while retaining little of the bite of his contemporary, Louis Armstrong, or his offspring, Frank Sinatra. When he made his unexpected return to the stage in 1976, at New York's Uris Theater (his first live appearance before a paying audience in more than 40 years), I attended a rehearsal as well as the show, and spoke with him briefly. My review (included in *Riding on a Blue Note*) was appreciative but skeptical. I found him at once irresistible and detached, a fascinating vestige from another age.

Crosby's personal reputation faltered along with his music after his death, in 1977. When his eldest son, Gary Crosby, published a bitter memoir describing the unflappable Bing administering vigorous corporal punishment, his halo tilted and crashed. Soon the afterlife of his career imploded. Jazz lovers kept Crosby's memory alive, mainly because of his early records and the later collaborations with Armstrong, Louis Jordan, Les Paul, and others. But jazz lovers are by nature classicists, and Crosby had spent most of his life on the other side of the divide: the pop world, where success is measured in numbers—a world remade by rock, in which even the oldest of oldies postdate "Heartbreak Hotel."

Yet consider this: In 1946, three of the year's five top-grossing Hollywood pictures (*The Bells of St. Mary's*, *Blue Skies*, *Road to Utopia*) were Crosby vehicles; for five years running (1944 to 1948), he was number one at the box office; his radio programs (1931 to 1962) attracted at their wartime peak as many as 50 million listeners; he recorded nearly 400 hit singles, an achievement no one—not Sinatra, Elvis, or the Beatles—has come close to matching. Could a man who spoke so deeply to so many for so long have nothing to say to us now? For a biographer, Crosby's career offers far more incentive than mere statistics. He is the ideal figure for tracking the rise of American popular culture. He played a pivotal role in the development of the recording, radio, and film industries, while virtually defining the microphone as a singer's instrument. His influence on other singers—including Sinatra, Elvis, and John Lennon, avowed fans all—would be hard to overstate, and he managed to maintain his popularity through several major cultural upheavals in 20th-century American history: Prohibition, Depression, World War II, the cold war, and the affluent society.

The deeper I went, the more I began to think of Crosby as a Fritz Lang movie in which nothing is what it seems. (Even Gary Crosby praised and defended him during the many hours I interviewed him.) A few years before Bing appeared at the Uris, Louis Armstrong remarked on the David Frost show that in all the years he had known Bing, he had never been invited to his home. I mischievously asked Crosby about it. Completely unperturbed, he answered, "I heard Pops said that. But you know Louis and Lucille never invited me to their home." A witty riposte, I thought, cool as a cucumber. He did not bother to say what it took me years to discover: that Armstrong had been Crosby's idol from the moment he heard him; that they had been friends, influencing each other at the dawn of jazz; that Crosby, more than anyone else, including Armstrong's manager, brought him out of the jazz world and into the full glare of mainstream pop, upturning Hollywood racial conventions in the bargain; that he wrote the check that allowed completion of the posthumous Armstrong statue in New Orleans. Close inspection also toppled my assumptions about his singing.

Like many in my generation, I was drawn to the enunciated clarity, effortless swing, and insouciant scat-singing of Crosby in his jazz years while ignoring his later work as meretricious. After listening to his exhaustive discography, more than 2,000 recordings (including radio broadcasts), it became apparent that his voice and style peaked not in the 1920s, when he joined Paul Whiteman's orchestra as the first-ever full-time band singer, but a decade later, in Hollywood. Jazz-born prejudices are often inadequate in evaluating a popular idol. Irving Berlin once said he wrote music for the "mob" and that as far as he was concerned, the mob was always right.

Crosby's Dickensian appetite for every kind of song obliges us to savor the validity and verve of music created not by or for the elect, but for the delectation of millions. The mob is not always right. Its infinite longing for rote repetition and screwy novelties ("Three Little Fishies" anyone?) is matched by its impatience with music that demands concentration. Yet the ability of the millions to discriminate is hardly negligible. Examine the pop records released between 1934 and 1954, and compare the major hits to the numberless misses: You cannot help admiring the mob's batting average.

The public had little trouble distinguishing between Crosby and his rivals in the 1920s. His first solo record, though not a hit, showed those who were paying attention that the times were changing. A year after Armstrong recorded "Heebie Jeebies," the explosive scat-driven number that put his vocal style on the map, and three months after Crosby had begun touring with Whiteman, he was allotted a chorus on "Muddy Water." The session took place on March 7, 1927, at Liederkranz Hall in New York. Crosby's record, unlike Armstrong's, no longer seems as radical as it once did—unless you listen to it in tandem with the other white pop records of the time, in which case his debut seems absolutely astonishing. The song itself is a conventional idyll about life "down Dixie way," created by an integrated team, the white composer Peter DeRose and the black lyricist Jo Trent.

In Matty Malneck's arrangement, "Muddy Water" opens with a trombone and a bold unison ensemble chorus, promising a jazz performance; yet only the vocal, backed by viola and rhythm, makes good on that promise. Compared to his mature work, Bing's chorus is stilted, almost formal. But his rhythm and articulation are sure, especially on the bridge, in which he emphasizes "there" and "care" with a trilling vibrato that displays his innate affinity for swing. Giving each word its due, his winged phrasing banishes sentimentality. The sound of his voice is unlike that of any of his contemporaries: a vibrant, virile baritone, completely at odds with the effete tenors and semifalsetto warblers who dominated male popular singing in that era. After hearing him, Duke Ellington vowed not to hire a male vocalist until he found one who sounded like Crosby.

Four performers, each to some degree rooted in jazz and blues, originated the modern style of American popular singing, as distinct from the theatrical emoting of the minstrel and vaudeville eras. All but one were African American: Bessie Smith, Ethel Waters, Armstrong, and Crosby. In their day, Smith, who was born in 1894, in Chattanooga, Tennessee, was the least widely known. Yet as the finest heavy-voiced blues singing (some said shouting) contralto of the era, she established vocal techniques intrinsic to the American style, most notably an undulating attack in which notes are stretched, bent, curved, moaned, and hollered. She perfected and popularized an old style of melisma that had been described by the writer Jeannette Robinson Murphy in an 1899 issue of *Popular Science Monthly*. Trying to instruct white singers in the art of "genuine Negro melodies," Murphy insisted it was necessary "that around every prominent note [the singer] place a variety of small notes, called 'trimmings.' " She said the singer "must sing tones not found in our scale . . . careful to divide many of his monosyllabic words in two syllables." Smith had a limited range, but she proved that emotional power does not depend on traditional vocal abilities.

Ethel Waters, born in Chester, Pennsylvania, in 1896, was another story. Though initially characterized as a blues singer, she came to embody the aspirations of black performers determined to make it on "white time." With her higher range and light supple voice, she lacked the weighty sonority of Smith, but her superb enunciation, gift for mimicry, and versatility allowed her to switch between irrepressible eroticism (she was the queen of double entendre) and high-toned eloquence. Smith and Waters dazzled the young white jazz acolytes of the 1920s, and Crosby was exposed to their records early on by another exceptionally influential singer, Mildred Bailey, the benefactress of his apprentice years. What's more, Bailey told Bing that if he was really serious about singing, he would have to find out about Louis Armstrong, a young trumpet player and singer in Chicago; the grapevine was buzzing about him, though he had made few records—none of them vocals.

Armstrong, born in New Orleans in 1901, was the most extreme force American music had ever known. Having absorbed every valuable tradition in the 19th-century vernacular, sacred or secular, he offered a new vision that liberated American music vocally and instrumentally. Armstrong transformed everyone who heard him; musicians who came under his spell felt freer, more optimistic and ambitious, willing to take risks. He anchored, as Bessie Smith could not, the blues as the foundation for a new American music; and he revealed, as Ethel Waters could not, that swing, a seductive canter as natural and personal as a heartbeat, would be its irreducible rhythmic framework.

Harry Lillis Crosby—nicknamed Bing at the age of seven because of his fondness for a syndicated newspaper parody, "The Bingville Bugle"—was born in Tacoma, Washington, in 1903, the fourth of seven children in a working-class family governed by a strict Irish Catholic mother. It was their easygoing Protestant father, however, who brought home the appliance that changed Bing's life: an Edison phonograph, purchased to commemorate the family's move to Spokane, in 1906. Bing listened to every record he could get his hands on, especially those by Al Jolson, who began to record in 1911; when he got to watch Jolson in action six years later, he began to contemplate the life of an entertainer. He eventually dropped out of law school to play drums and sing with a local band, before leaving Spokane with his partner Al Rinker (Bailey's brother) to try for the big time.

When he encountered Armstrong in Chicago, in 1926, Crosby had barely a year of vaudeville under his belt, and he was utterly transfixed. Crosby was the first and, for a while, the only singer who fully assimilated the shock of Armstrong's impact; he would later call Armstrong "the beginning and the end of music in America." One of the most important things Crosby learned from him was that the contagious pulse known as swing did not have to be exclusive to jazz. It was a universally applicable technique that deepened the interpretation of any popular song in any setting. Crosby's uncanny ability to hear "the one"—the downbeat of each measure—was unheard of among white singers in the 1920s, and it never left him. Jake Hanna, Crosby's drummer in the 1970s, observed: "Bing had the best time, the absolute best time. And I played with Count Basie, and that's great time." Most singers who imitated Crosby in the 1920s and 1930s—Russ Columbo, Perry Como, Dick Todd—took the superficial aspects of his style without the jazz foundation, which is why much of their work is antiquated.

To the mix as developed by Smith, Waters, and Armstrong, Crosby added three elements that were crucial to the fulfillment of pop singing: his expansive repertory, expressive intimacy, and spotless timbre. He grew up in a time and place when young music lovers were not concerned with the snobberies of high versus low, hip versus square, in versus out. The phonograph was a new invention, and each record was a mystery until it was played. Every record collection was a canon unto itself. Crosby saw no contradiction in his love for the great Irish tenor John McCormack, the Broadway minstrel Al Jolson, and the jazz and blues groups that excited his contemporaries. Yet he offered something different from them.

Crosby had begun his career just as the condenser microphone was perfected, replacing the silly looking megaphones he had used in his school band. He realized that the mike was an instrument. He understood instinctively the modernist paradox: Electrical appliances made singing more human, more expressive, more personal. They also enriched his unique style: rich, strong, intimate, and smart. Listeners who were put off by vernacular growls and moans could enjoy his relatively immaculate approach. His focus on the meaning of lyrics helped reshape the popular song. With his combination of intelligence and rhythmic acuity, Crosby could transfigure trite songs tritely arranged ("I Found a Million Dollar Baby"), but also underscore the banality of June/moon bromides, hymns to a mother's tears, and "darktown" caricatures. A new generation of lyricists—Larry Hart, Cole Porter, Leo Robin, Al Dubin, Mitchell Parish, Yip Harburg, and the self-renewing Irving Berlin— found in Crosby an interpreter who brought their subtlest verbal conceits to life.

Everything came together during the Depression, when Crosby proved you could be all things to all men and all women. At the same time that he reached jazz peaks in his flights on "Sweet Georgia Brown" and "Some of These Days," he transformed other songs into Depression anthems, including the vivid protest number "Brother Can You Spare a Dime?" and "Home on the Range," a then little-known saddle song that he turned into the most renowned of western ballads. As the most popular singer in the world, he recorded an unparalleled variety of songs: from hymns and minstrel arias to jazz, country, and rhythm and blues. Not even Sinatra, who would deepen the interpretation of lyrics, could handle such a spectrum.

On a 1943 edition of *Command Performance*, a radio series recorded on transcription discs for shipment to overseas forces, the emcee, Dinah Shore, remarked, "You know, Bing, a singer like Frank Sinatra comes along only once in a lifetime." Bing's famous response: "Yeah, and he has to come along in my lifetime." From 1931, when Crosby first triumphed on network radio and his rivals faded, through 1940, when Tommy Dorsey took the country by storm with "I'll Never Smile Again" and other records featuring vocals by Sinatra, Crosby ruled mainstream pop. Armstrong, Bailey, Billie Holiday, and Jimmy Rushing prospered in jazz, just as diverse singers succeeded in country, blues, or gospel. But Crosby was king of the mountain—the national voice, America's troubadour. In Sinatra, he had at long last a contender and a worthy heir. By the end of 1943, Sinatra beat him in the *Down Beat* poll of popular singers. High school and college clubs and newspaper pundits routinely debated their respective merits.

Yet, contrary to the Sinatra myth, at no time in the 1940s did Sinatra seriously crimp Crosby's popularity. This was the period when Bing was twice nominated for best-actor Oscars (he won in 1944 for *Going My Way*), when he recorded the most successful record of all time, "White Christmas," and when he was named in a poll of servicemen as the man who had done most for army morale. (Enlisted men initially had little use for Sinatra, who was disparaged as a draft dodger and seducer.) When the troops came home, Crosby enjoyed a new crest in popularity, while Sinatra's career dimmed and almost faded to black. It was Crosby who best captured the tenor of the times in recordings like "It's Been a Long, Long Time," a definitive home-from-war anthem, which never mentions the war.

By 1955, things began to change. The previous year had been a glorious one for Crosby. He had starred in the top-grossing picture of the year, *White Christmas*, and scored his third Oscar nomination for his stunning portrayal of an alcoholic has-been in *The Country Girl*. Yet what a difference a year made. Sinatra revived himself, retooled as a jet-age hipster balladeer, with a deepened voice and style and a poise fine-tuned by tribulation. Elvis Presley was knocking them dead in the South and about to break nationally. Crosby's vocal style had remained cool, almost automatic. He could still sing with swinging élan, as revealed on his 1957 album, *Bing with a Beat,* and he continued to enjoy other triumphs. He joined with Sinatra, Armstrong, and Grace Kelly for *High Society,* in 1956, and was widely thought to have outshone his rival; perhaps for that reason, he later chose his duet with Sinatra ("Well, Did You Evah?") as his favorite movie scene. And Crosby's television specials, through the mid-1960s, were highly musical and invariably successful, as were his many subsequent appearances on the variety show *Hollywood Palace.* Yet in the new climate, his greatest strength was a liability. Sinatra rang the rafters, Tony Bennett poured out his heart, Presley rocked. But Crosby's preternatural calm, his canny gentleness, was too laid back, too easy for the nuclear age.

By then he had begun to retreat from the stage. He now had a young wife, Kathryn Grant, and three small children, and he was determined not to repeat the mistakes of his first marriage to Dixie Lee, when his work kept him away for long stretches and he tried to compensate by imposing strict disciplinary measures on his four sons. He continued to tape Christmas specials, which led to a much-publicized duet with David Bowie ("The Little Drummer Boy"), and displayed more daring in tandem with Armstrong, Ella Fitzgerald, Johnny Mercer, and many others on *Hollywood Palace.* Yet his film career came to an end with *Stagecoach,* in 1966, and American record companies no longer wanted to record him; his 1970s comeback was fueled with albums made and released in England, including a savory 1975 album with Fred Astaire, *A Couple of Song and Dance Men.* When Crosby died two years later, his contemporaries mourned him, but to a younger generation he had become a Norman Rockwell poster, an irrelevant holdover from another world.

His art, however, retains its power in unexpected ways. His key performances of the great pop songs and jazz classics have lost none of their charm. Yet his versions of late-19th-century and early-20th-century songs are also compelling, and it is difficult to imagine another singer (Sinatra, for example) attempting them; I once saw an opera expert reduced to tears by Crosby's "Sweetheart of Sigma Chi." His superb Depression waltzes ("The One Rose," "Mexicali Rose") recapture the dark side of that era as nothing else does. Crosby's early collaborations with Ellington and Bix Beiderbecke and later ones with Armstrong, Mercer, Eddie Condon, Connie Boswell, Woody Herman, Bob Crosby (his kid brother), Eddie Heywood, Bob Scobey, Rosemary Clooney, and many others

sparkle with ingenuity and rhythmic zest. No matter how popular he became, his prowess and his jazz beat kept him honest. For that reason, he
continues to speak to us, and in that sense, he remains our contemporary.

[*New York Times Arts & Leisure*, 28 January 2001]

81 ❖ Here's the Melody (John Lewis)

Melody is the rarest of musical talents and the most treasured, which is
one reason only a handful of 19th-century composers continue to speak
to us. Those who do are true melodists as opposed to generic ones:
preachers who hear a kind of songfulness no one else has heard rather
than parishioners who elaborate on that approach, reducing inspiration
to style. True melodists may be few, yet they seem to arrive in groups,
carrying the ball for a paternal titan, as though waiting for a properly
melodious climate—thus Mozart kicked off for Schubert, Mendelssohn,
and Schumann; Verdi for Bizet, Tchaikovsky, and Puccini; Berlin for
Kern, Rodgers, and Porter. This schema is simplistic but helps pass the
time as we wait and wait and wait for melody's return. In the hip-hop
era, its stock has fallen in direct proportion to rhythm's rise.

Jazz has been abundant in melody, or should I say improvisational
lyricism. It produces far fewer Jelly Roll Mortons, Duke Ellingtons, and
Thelonious Monks than Louis Armstrongs, Lester Youngs, and Charlie
Parkers. A more melodious musician than Young never lived, but his
genius is to be found in ad-lib solos, not in his handful of copywrited
tunes. Stan Getz was immensely lyrical, yet never wrote a single important tune. On the other hand, some players are more adept at melodious
themes than at sustaining them in variations, most notably John Coltrane
and Ornette Coleman. At the present time, jazz is, inevitably, caught up
in the same antimelodic vice as the rest of the musical landscape. So
when we hear the real thing, it can be overwhelming.

Which leads me, as discussions of melody invariably do, to our
greatest living melodist: John Lewis. Jazz at Lincoln Center presented
him in a retrospective on January 18 and 21, 2001, called "Evolution: The
Music of John Lewis," a title that positioned the concert as part of a
project that launched his lustrous Atlantic CDs, *Evolution* and *Evolution
II*. I considered the former the best record of 1999, and still do, and will
rate the latter among this year's best. The concert was just about perfect,

an evening no one present is likely to forget; my inclination toward hyperbole is tempered only by the report of a reliable witness who says the second performance was even better.

Lewis, who practically reinvented jazz presentation in the postwar era, in and out of concert halls, is by nature decorous and formal. His manners are such that, though he is 80 and has been ailing, he insisted on standing after alternate selections to discuss the genesis of the preceding piece and the one he was about to play. The formality extended to the program, which included four piano solos, four duets with Wynton Marsalis, four trios with Percy Heath and Herlin Riley, and a full set of big band works, as Lewis conducted the Lincoln Center Jazz Band with Eric Reed on piano. The great paradox about Lewis, however, is that his moderation masks a ruefully blues-driven vivacity that proceeds inexorably from the strategies of his compositions. More than anyone else, he has combined jazz and classical techniques into an insoluble whole, and yet they often bring him to a terrain (cf. "Cain and Abel" or "Come Rain or Come Shine" on *Evolution II*) one is more likely to associate with Ray Charles.

The first piece was startling, though it was by far the most familiar. "Django" established Lewis as a composer and the Modern Jazz Quartet as a going concern and he has rewired it repeatedly, each time underscoring different elements. On the *Evolution* CDs, he offers two versions so dissimilar a casual listener might not realize they were developed from the same piece. He played the version from the first CD at the concert and articulated it in such a way that, until I went back to the disc, I thought it was yet another recomposition. The chief conceit is a repeated four-note bass clef arpeggio capped with ringing single notes in the treble that state the melody. By underscoring the arpeggio in concert, he heightened the arrangement's drama. Lewis's ease with rests and uncanny ability to speed or retard time so that it is ever so slightly askew until he sets it right again turns drama into a mode of suspense—which he sustained through the jauntily evolved "That! Afternoon in Paris" ("La Marseillaise" leads to "The Old Folks at Home"), "Trieste" (no longer a tango), and the haltingly comical "The Festivals."

The duets with Marsalis began exuberantly with Lewis's ingenious variation on "Sailor's Hornpipe," a piece fraught with fast turns and loops that both men navigated with aplomb, Marsalis employing only a few of his often overworked half-valve gambits to color a bright and consistently inventive solo. The more customary "DeLaunay's Dilemma," with its "I Got Rhythm" changes, was similarly empathic. Lewis and Marsalis have clearly spent many hours working together, and for some reason the bebop veteran, especially on this piece, brought out the young neoclassicist's swing—as opposed to bop—bias, evident in phrases more reminiscent of the generation of Roy Eldridge or Charlie Shavers than of Dizzy Gillespie or Miles Davis. On the sumptuous waltz, "Skating in Central Park," however, the trumpet player faltered on the last eight measures, as if striving for the composer's understated lyricism but achieving only the guise of his gentility; he got his own back with an open-horn solo that at times recalled Ruby Braff, and on "Two Degrees East, Three Degrees West," wrestled between polite hesitancy and episodic bent-note wailing.

Gentility is a hard line to walk without falling into the straight and narrow, but the trio was too buoyant to worry about walking. From the first measures of "Blues in A Minor," introduced by Percy Heath's pizzicato and sparked into time by Herlin Riley's brushes, it locked into the most jubilant groove of the evening, and continued to negotiate between parlor and porch on the exquisite, heartbreaking "December, Remember," which adapts a theme from Lewis's "In Memoriam." That piece and the ever-changing, ever-radiant "For Ellington," a piece with history and memory in its bones, were the evening's flash points, underscoring why this performance was different from any other in all the world's jazz clubs: an unfettered genius for the melodic phrase, poignant and robust, forthright and shameless. Between those pieces, Lewis played his splendid transcription of Charlie Parker's 1948 "Parker's Mood," on which Lewis made an early mark. The piano arrangement includes Parker's intro, Lewis's transition, Parker's solo, Lewis's solo, and then a new solo, and it's a highlight of *Evolution II*.

The big band segment was filled with surprises, as pieces formerly conceived for brass or voice were amplified to accommodate reeds, which were so richly phrased one could not escape the feeling that orchestration was an aspect of Lewis's gift that had been much underexploited. The orchestra began with "Animal Dance," an excerpt from the ballet, *Original Sin*, but came alive in four episodes from the once maligned suite, *The Comedy*. Lewis compared the improvising traveling troupes of commedia dell'arte to jazz's early territory bands, specifically the Young Family Band (as in Lester), and described each section vividly, priming the audience for the expressive aria—with its dissonant note of dismay—of "La Cantatrice" or the gorgeous wide-open harmonies of "Piazza Novana." Eric Reed was a curious choice as pianist, since his busy Petersonian attack is the antithesis of Lewis's, but he acquitted himself with panache, interpolating a neat Erroll Garner passage into "La Cantatrice." The other soloist was Marsalis, who got to shout a bit, a prelude to his more memorable escapades on a stunning revision of "Three Little Feelings," a triptych written to fill out Gunther Schuller's

Music for Brass that stole the LP. With Warren Smith and Wycliffe Gordon bouncing the first movement on tympani and tuba, respectively, Marsalis began his solo with a few decaying stabs of sound before going to town, more brazen than Miles Davis was on the original, and more broadly romantic in the second movement, his dark growls entirely suitable to the ominous cast of the piece.

A standing ovation brought an encore, and the enthusiasm mirrored not only Lewis's achievement but that of Jazz at Lincoln Center, which this time got it exactly right. Even the acoustics behaved. And if you wanted more, as I did, there was *Evolution II*, which closes with an ur-Lewis transfiguration: the old standard "What Is This Thing Called Love?" turned into a forceful sprint that builds to a passage of stalwart block chords, every chorus filled with melodic gems the equal of the tune to which they invariably allude—melody on top of melody; melody, melody, and more melody.*

[*Village Voice*, 6 February 2001]

*John Lewis died two months later, on March 29, 2001.

82 ❖ Over the Transom (Arnie Carruthers / Larry Vuckovich / Nicholas Hoffman / Gold Sparkle)

The first time I met John Hammond he regaled me by playing reel-to-reel tapes of unissued Artie Shaw and Joe Turner. This was back in 1969, and much of his desk, the top of the radiator, and just about every other flat surface in his office was stacked with white reel-to-reel boxes. Did they all contain such gems? Oh, God, no, he explained with a shudder; they were mostly over-the-transom or under-the-table offerings from unknown musicians and managers hoping to grab the attention of American music's most fabled talent scout. He claimed he listened to them all and he probably did (Springsteen and Stevie Ray were in his future), but he seemed perfectly content if not transported as Joe Turner rumbled through "Roll 'Em, Pete" for the millionth rip-roaring time.

I am reminded of those stacks whenever someone slips me, as though it were contraband, a homegrown cassette or CD. A certain amount of mutual embarrassment invariably colors the transaction, which is instigated with a remark like, "I'm sure you get these all the time, but . . ." or "Do you mind if . . ." or the increasingly popular "A friend asked me to . . ." Critics are not talent scouts, nor do they wish to be; we come later in the process, evaluating professionals, not amateurs looking for help or a kind word. I never know what to do with these gifts, though my silent response is usually, "Damn, now I've got to carry this stuff around all night," because I am too cowardly to throw it out. An angel sits on my right shoulder, warning, "It could be the next Bird," while the devil on my left mocks, "Don't be a chump." The devil's been around.

The hypocrisy is palpable. After all, one is delighted to discover talent attending a concert or auditioning a record on the smallest of vanity labels or even encountering an artist on a street corner. Maybe it's the difference between asking someone out and being asked out: an outmoded male thing. Yet the material inconvenience is also real. One will blithely attend 20 concerts in search of the next Bird; but a stack of 20 cassettes and discs by guys with day jobs is onerous. Cassettes, of course, can be erased—waste not, want not. CDs are hairier. Someone actually went through the trouble not only to set up a microphone, but also to hire a liner note writer and an art director to make the liner notes unreadable, just like the pros. So I do give them a once-over; occasionally, I am rewarded, never more than on a recent book tour that focused on the Northwest.

In Spokane, someone handed me, on behalf of "a friend," *I'm Still Swingin'* by Arnie Carruthers, a 1999 disc on MNOP—a label, I subsequently learned, that no longer exists. I looked at the picture of the older fellow on the jacket, noted the tunes ("Satin Doll," "Body and Soul") and gloomily said, "Thank you." By now, I was toting several discs from city to city, but the hotel clock-radios played CDs and I began spinning them, thinking I could leave a few to keep company with the Gideons. Carruthers, a pianist, begins his disc with "Dearly Beloved." Right off I was struck by his trio's zest, a sparkling arpeggio leading into the second part of the tune, passing chords, and a rhythmic acuity that had him lean one way and then another without faltering. His technique is full-bodied, alternating block chords and steely 16th-note passages; he renovates a familiar theme like "Lush Life" with a thumbed bass line and romps with Peterson-Newborn dispatch. I listened to the album half a dozen times.

Then I looked at the liner notes and discovered the guy has one arm. His left side has been paralyzed since a stroke in 1974. I didn't want to make too much of this, because the music is not gimmicky and, besides, I figured he overdubbed some of the bass lines and chords, though I needed to make sure. Unable to find listings for the label, producer, or his usual jazz club venue (also defunct as of last year), I located him through a booker for Montana's Glacier Jazz Stampede, and got an emphatic "No" to the dubbing question. That might incline anyone toward a close listening for the wrong reason: not for what he does, but for how he does it.

As best I can tell, he's developed a variety of voicings and tremendous speed in his right hand, allowing him a mobility that gives the illusion of a broad-range attack and makes possible his engaging interaction between single notes and chords, which would be no less engaging if accomplished with two hands. Consider the lovely substitute chords on "S'Wonderful." He uses the pedals to keep tones in one register ringing while his hand shoots off to another octave. How he pilots the concurrent bass lines or the rolling entrance into his solo on "Satin Doll" is something I would like to see, but probably won't.

During our brief phone conversation, Carruthers said, "I feel like after 40 years in Spokane I finally have a connection with the outside world." Actually, he is well known to musicians in the Northwest, and those from the outside world who have used him when passing through include Dizzy Gillespie, Joe Venuti, and Barney Kessel. Spokane did produce Jimmy Rowles, Don Sickler, and a couple of singers named Bing Crosby and Mildred Bailey. But Carruthers is nearing 70 and I don't see any impresario bringing him east in the near future. He is, however, sitting on the last hundred copies of the one thousand CDs pressed in 1999, and you can buy one by writing him in Spokane.

If Arnie Carruthers is unknown here, many fondly remember Larry Vuckovich, a big-cheese pianist and bandleader in San Francisco, from his relocation here in the 1980s, when he entered the piano bar rotation for several years before heading home. Vuckovich, who was Vince Guaraldi's protégé in the 1950s when the latter was getting started, records infrequently and never treads the same ground twice. *City Sounds, Village Voice* (1983) brought the lineaments of modern jazz to the traditional music of Yugoslavia; *Tres Palabras* (1990) did as much for Brazil. *Young at Heart* (Robbins-Tetrachord; try lvuckovich@usa.net) does the same for Lester Young. Except for the superb drummer Harold Jones, the members of the sextet are unknown to me, but the twin tenors of Noel Jewkes and Jules Broussard give the album the urbane flush of an abbreviated Basie reed section.

Broussard has the heavier attack and persuasively captures Herschel Evans on "Blue and Sentimental," though he's a little rhapsodic playing Young's famous Keynote solo on "Sometimes I'm Happy." Jewkes is a genuine find, a fluent Youngian on tenor and clarinet whose solos are long, sure, twisty phrases with surprising turns and knowing resolutions—dig his get-off and chorus on "Jumpin' at the Woodside." The album hits the doldrums with an uneventful—except for Jewkes—"She's Just My Size" and an unnecessary vocal (by the bassist) on "Sweet Lorraine," but is otherwise dapper, smart, and swinging, with Vuckovich displaying nearly selfless regard for the economy of Basie piano. He has arranged "Young at Heart" as a lyrical three-note riff with the tenors spreading like butter on the release.

Two more undercover discs I admire are Nicholas Hoffman's *Jazzy's Dance* (Jazz Friends, Bellingham, WA; jazzkoo@memes.com) and *Nu Soul Zodiac* by Gold Sparkle Band (Squealer, Blacksburg, VA; contactus@squealermusic.com). Hoffman may be an unknown guitarist, but his sidemen include the alternating organs of Dave Mathews and Joey DeFrancesco and long-time-no-see saxophonist Hadley Caliman, who himself led a couple of obscure sessions in the '80s. The quartet is occasionally cluttered, though the leader is shrewd enough to take his time and build orderly solos; the backbeat cuts—Willie Dixon's "My Babe," Larry Young's "Backup"—are most effective. "This Can't Be Love" has steady guitar, but could have used a second take to lose the corny tag ending, which undermines Caliman's hip reference, just prior, to "Chasin' the Train."

The four members of Gold Sparkle Band—altoist/clarinetist Charles Waters, trumpeter Roger V. Ruzow, bassist Adam Roberts, and drummer Andrew D. Barker—also know their Coltrane and their Ayler and Hill and Shepp and Zorn. And all those avant shadows tend to mitigate the overwhelming influence of Ornette Coleman, giving the ensemble a sound of its own, with centered pitch and buoyant rhythms (they know Eddie Blackwell, too) and a touch of klezmer. Only five of eleven selections are over four minutes, and all the pieces are focused, some to produce a single effect—the kinetic drum riff of "Double Bump," the planned chaos of "Splintered Synapse"—while others are rendered dirgelike with arco bass and the addition of cellist Kim Lemonde. Ruzow growls and whinnies but has a fat broad sound when he wants and the musicianship is high all around.

The big question about outatown jazz is, How would it stand up in cities with heavyweight jazz populations, which presently appear to be New York, Boston, Chicago, and Los Angeles? When you are starved for good jazz on the road, you listen less for individuality than competence, and even fair players can sound great lording it over their own villages. Then when you get home, the thrill is gone. These discs sounded good on the road and they still sound good.

[*Village Voice*, 27 March 2001]

83 ❖ Memorophiliac
(Vijay Iyer)

The long fingers of pianist Vijay Iyer, who appeared with his quartet in the Jazz Gallery series, "Pianobility," look like tarantula legs as they scamper across the keys, arched high and slightly bent at the knuckles. In liner notes and promotional materials, he has aligned himself with the percussive school of jazz piano—Ellington, Hines, Monk, Powell, Taylor, Nichols, Weston, Tyner, and the rest—and you can hear the influences at work, but he doesn't sound like any of them. His touch is firm and dramatic, in accord with his penchant for vamps (put Ibrahim on the list) and architectonic structures and ringing overtones (Jamal, too); yet its very deliberation suggests more of a pressing than a striking of the keys (also Pullen and Walton). In an era of homages, Iyer is no slouch: His notes to his first CD, the nicely titled *Memorophilia*, include his pantheon of more than 80 musicians "and many others, of course." Still, his sound is his own and you would recognize it in a blindfold test.

That alone is impressive, particularly for an academic—degrees from Yale and Berkeley and a dissertation, "Microstructures of Feel, Macrostructures of Sound: Embodied Cognition in West African and African-American Musics." (Academics have to write like that; it's a law.) Iyer is full of words and himself: His music, he says in the notes to *Architextures*, is about "what I have learned as a member of the post-colonial, multicultural South Asian diaspora, as a person of color peering in critically from the margins of American mainstream culture, and as a human being with a body, a mind, memories, emotions, and spiritual aspirations." That may be true, but, happily, his music lacks any whiff of homework. Like his touch, it is spry and darting—very smart and without a need to show off or push a point. South Asian tropes are handily reconciled. Programmatic titles aside, his music is all music.

Iyer, not yet 30, has recorded three discs as a leader for Asian Improv. Each is significantly better than its predecessor, and his Jazz Gallery appearance suggested advances since he recorded the soon-to-be-released third, *Panoptic Modes* (Red Giant). The first two were recorded in 1995 and 1997, and released in 1998. For *Memorophilia*, he borrowed credibility by using a few established players, including Steve Coleman and George Lewis. Iyer's affection for bedrock vamps is evident, as is his inclination to begin improvisations behind the beat with exploratory figures—the tarantula feeling its way before it charges into a rhythmic dance, bounded by pulsing chords and riffs. Although the bass and drum solos are integrated into rhythm section passages, they do not always sustain interest; some of the pieces are more focused than others. "March & Epilogue" gets life from a march beat conjoined with inventive piano responses, before George Lewis's stormy trombone takes it way outside. "Peripatetics," with Liberty Ellman's guitar, an electric bass ostinato, and a whimsical theme, is more satisfying. Iyer's solo grows in assurance and dynamics, as if looking for a home and then finding it and then receding from it as bass or drums garner strength and take the spotlight—practically an idée fixe.

Sometimes, as in the unaccompanied "Algebra," he shifts focus from nuance-and-overtone to dissonance, repetition, block chords, and a driving percussive prance of a solo; but always, he is an avant-garde acolyte who insists on structure. When his fingers seem to drag him into the realm of step exercises, he saves himself with overt swing rhythms; an algebraic stiffness crops up throughout, creating trade-offs between his need for order and the suppleness of his best playing. *Architextures*, for trio and octet, is a vast improvement, continuing his association with Ellman and adding two saxophonists, Aaron Stewart (who leans toward Shorter) and Eric Crystal (who leans toward Coltrane). He opens with an unaccompanied "Prelude," showing keen understanding of Cecil Taylor's softer side (and the caprice of Jaki Byard, also in the pantheon), and continues with "Meeting of Rivers," which begins with reference to Ellington's ballet *The River* before the saxophones kick up a unison riff. This is a far tighter group than on the first album and Iyer's playing has taken on a cultivated lilt. "Three Peas" has a touch of the snake charmer, probably with deeper roots in Ellington and Coltrane than in South Asia, but there's a sustaining authenticity to the solos, especially that by altoist Rudresh Mahanthappa. Both discs are too long, of course—"always leave 'em wanting more" is not an avant-garde maxim—but they document an artist sidestepping eclecticism even as he shifts from one base to another.

Iyer strides a lot closer to home on *Panoptic Modes*, which features the same quartet that appeared at the Jazz Gallery—Mahanthappa, bassist Stephan Crump, drummer Derrek Phillips. The pieces are brighter and inventively voiced and the group is more than just tight. It's a unit that avoids head-and-solos routines and integrates the ensemble almost to the point of doing away with soloist-and-accompaniment. On "Atlanean Tropes" and "One Thousand and One," for example, Iyer micromanages the performances with vamps, simultaneously playing a bass clef unison with the bassist and a treble unison with the altoist. The most Eastern-sounding piece is "Invariants," which alternates piano and alto phrases with a unison alto-piano high note serving as a punctuation mark. Iyer's

solo is illustrative—his trademark approach, pacing himself with hesitations before revving up aggressive spidery phrases that charge ahead
with imposing conviction. Influences are apparent. "Configurations"
suggests Tyner and "Circular Argument" is Iyer's take on bop, complete
with flatted fifth—but the defining touches are distinct: the unison voicing on the former, the large intervals in his solo on the latter. He seems
to strum the chords on "Mountains," which is airy and restive enough
to tranquilize Hans Castorp.

Vamps are Iyer's strength and weakness, animating some of his pieces
and stultifying others. More to the point, they are devices he uses to
excess, as he does passages in which the bass comes to the fore. The idea
is sound, but the bass solos are neither varied not distinctive enough to
justify the space they get. These quibbles remained unaddressed at the
Jazz Gallery, though most of the performances were even livelier than
on the album. Mahanthappa, a gifted player with precise intonation and
a propensity for the middle register, played with tremendous exuberance, as did Iyer, who loves the foot pedals and occasionally plucks the
strings. Vamps, ostinatos, bass lines, and punctuating chords focus the
solos so that improvised figures zoom into full stops—periods. A wri-
terly analogy becomes still more pronounced when Iyer and Mahanthappa exchange phrases of varying length, as on "One Thousand and
One"—they aren't trading fours, but whole sentences, seemingly free
and yet bound by an ostinato. When Iyer really digs in, you know you
are in the presence of an accomplished musician, but you also get the
sense that he is keeping something in reserve. He is a work in progress
and his third album whets the appetite for his fourth.

[*Village Voice*, 17 April 2001]

84 ❖ *Weird and Forgotten Dreams (Charles Mingus / Helen Carr / Herb Jeffries / LH&R / Sarah Vaughan)*

Reissues usually get their due at year's end, when they come gift-
wrapped in cloth or steel boxes with fancy prices and hyped-up art direction, but record companies stay alive and keep their distributors
happy by recycling old records all year long. Many classic LPs remain
unissued after 20 years of digitalization and a trunkful of 78s that never

even made it to LP waste away like Edmond Dantés in the vaults, awaiting their second acts. Yet now that most of the better-known product
has returned in two, three, and more CD incarnations, labels are burrow-
ing deeper, proving that wondrous unearthings are still possible.

The year's most remarkable recovery has produced *Charles 'Baron'
Mingus, West Coast, 1945–49* (Uptown), 23 sides made under Mingus's
leadership for five fly-by-night labels that couldn't distribute farther than
their car trunks. The names alone smack of Central Avenue postwar
optimism and desperation: Excelsior, Four Star, Dolphins of Hollywood,
Fentone, Rex Hollywood. Some of these platters were so hard to come
by that the Smithsonian abandoned an attempt to create such a collection
in the 1980s; they are cited with errors or not at all in Mingus discographies and biographies. Research by co-producers Robert E. Sunenblick,
whose blindingly detailed notes make up the bulk of a 96-page booklet,
and Chuck Nessa correct a number of long-held assumptions. For one
thing, Mingus is not the cellist on "He's Gone"; it's Jean McGuire, one
of many people Uptown interviewed. For another, the long-sought mystery record, "God's Portrait," made for Fentone, was never issued. Ralph
J. Gleason either pretended to review it in 1949—on Mingus's say-so,
the producers suggest—or heard a long-lost test. In any case, Gleason's
comments sent a generation of collectors on a wild goose chase for a
record that does not exist, when, in fact, Mingus did record the piece a
few weeks later, for Rex Hollywood, as "Inspiration," which turns out
to be an early version of his trademark melody, "Portrait." (As a work
of scholarship, *Charles 'Baron' Mingus* is marred only by the inexplicable
absence of Gene Santoro's Mingus biography, *Myself When I Am Real*,
from the bibliography.)

The music will fascinate Mingus buffs, Central Avenue buffs, and
1940s buffs, and some of it is actually very good. A cursory examination
suggests a parallel to Sun Ra's *The Singles*. The range is surely comparable, from r&b and jump to Ellington and Kenton to bebop and ballads
to classicism and an ur-Mingusian mess, "The Story of Love," which
prefigures *Tijuana Moods*, complete with tambourine and "Night in Tunisia" derivation. Indeed, much of this work is derivative. Mingus's r&b
ballad, "Baby, Take a Chance with Me," recorded three times, is so generic one is startled to find his name on it and realize that it wasn't a
hit. Vocalist Charles Trenier is a brazen chameleon who affects Eddie
Cleanhead Vinson's high glissandi on one number and Herb Jeffries's
froggy croon on another, while tenor saxophonist William Woodman
blusters with the rote authority of Bumps Meyer. But there are also versions of "Weird Nightmare," a blueprint for "Boogie Stop Shuffle," attempts at vastness (played by a 22-piece orchestra), and glimmerings of

Lucky Thompson, Willie Smith, Britt Woodmann, Buddy Collette, Art Pepper, and an awkward 20-year-old Eric Dolphy. And there is far more bass playing than you might expect from anyone in this period, outside the Ellington fold. Mingus is always instantly recognizable—game, dauntless, and stirring.

One doesn't expect a two-and-a-half-minute ballad recording from 1949 to begin with a 16-bar bass solo, yet that's the agenda on Irving Berlin's "Say It Isn't So." Mingus's prelude introduces Helen Carr, a Billie Holiday-influenced singer with a smile in her voice, a ticklish melisma, and personality to spare. Dead at 38 and soon forgotten, she would be no less obscure than Mingus's other vocalists except that she recorded two 1955 albums, which have just been reissued as *Helen Carr: The Bethlehem Collection* (Avenue Jazz). Even so, she is not mentioned in any jazz or pop reference book, proof that there were more golden-voiced warblers in that era than we know. She had a knack for finding overlooked songs—"Not Mine," "Summer Night," or "Moments Like This"—by the usual gang of golden-age writers, and also put her own stamp on moldy hits from the past, such as "Got a Date with an Angel" and "Do I Worry." She could swing when she had to, but that was not her métier. In her ballads, you may glimpse Mildred Bailey and Anita O'Day, an unlikely couple. But they reside in the shadows of her own distinctive élan.

Another long forgotten Bethlehem album features the former Ellington vocalist Herb Jeffries, who is approaching 90 and still singing. (He did a memorable week at the Village Vanguard a few years ago, singing cowboy music with jazz backing.) *Say It Isn't So*, from 1957, begins with his mannered bass-baritone drawl, located somewhere between Crosby and Eckstein, and before long you find yourself getting lost in the lyrics, which he patiently interprets with an oddly vivid result. You can't escape their meanings, their relentless woe. While it's hard to imagine the strapping Bronze Buckeroo, as he was billed on movie marquees, pining for jilting women, as opposed to fighting them off with his six-shooters, he convinces you over the course of his 12 thematically constant standards that Sinatra had it reasonably easy, crying in his beer to barkeeps. Jeffries, afraid to leave his room, asks one lover to return to save him the embarrassment of everyone knowing she dropped him: hey, "It's the Talk of the Town." They're laughing at him in "Angel Eyes." He orders "Dinner for One, Please James," though he's "Glad to Be Unhappy," and "If You Could See Me Now," you'd know "I Only Have Eyes for You." His "Ghost of a Chance" is almost as good as Eckstine's, his "It's Easy to Remember" almost as good as Crosby's, yet as often as I have heard them sing those and the other songs, I have never been quite so conscious of what they are about. Russ Garcia's attentive strings nod in commiseration.

Two better-known but long unavailable vocal benchmarks have also been reissued. *Sing a Song of Basie* (Verve) was the first and best of the albums by Lambert, Hendricks & Ross. The trio did not yet exist as an act during the year it took to conceive and execute their unique debut, a triumph of multi-tracking in which three singers become the Count Basie Orchestra (aside from the rhythm section) and capture more of its dynamics and swing than anyone would have thought possible. With Annie Ross hitting the trumpet tuttis, Dave Lambert providing the trombone range, and Jon Hendricks wailing the saxophone solos and, in one of the most prodigious verbal feats in jazz history, writing all the lyrics, they replicate the band while infusing it with an exhilaration that only the voice can impart. On their sensational "Everyday," they increase the drama of Ernie Wilkins's instrumental prelude and capture the subsequent orchestration as Hendricks sings the Joe Williams vocal. They make Neal Hefti's "Little Pony" a horserace, as Hendricks turns Wardell Gray's tenor solo into a stream-of-consciousness rant and concludes with comic cheek. (Brasses: "Don't be quittin' just when you're hittin' the peak." Gray: "Get a record that will play a week.") After you've heard Ross sing the piano solo on "One O'Clock Jump," you can never again hear Basie's record the same way.

After living with this album for years or decades, you begin to hear the original instrumentals as though they had all been planned, composed, inevitable. If I haven't made it clear, there is no scat singing on *Sing a Song of Basie*. Every note of the original orchestrations and improvisations has a word fitted to it and becomes part of an overall story. As on the original LP, all lyrics except "One O'Clock Jump" are provided, but one of the startling things about this venture is that you don't need them; they are all clearly enunciated, despite bruising tempos. Three negligible tracks have been added, including choir-besotted versions of "Four Brothers" and the Hendricks whirlwind, "Cloudburst," presumably because the label didn't want to issue a 30-minute CD. The 30 minutes, however, are magic and quite enough.

Viva! Vaughan (Verve) was last issued as part of the multi-box *Complete Sarah Vaughan on Mercury*, but has not been seen on its own in 35 years. Recorded in 1964, it fell between the cracks of her jazz following, which at that time felt sorely tested by the meretriciousness of her record companies, and the pop world, which could not be seduced by yet another attempt to board the bossa nova bandwagon. Too bad for everyone, especially arranger Frank Foster, some of whose finest post-Basie writing is heard here. Vaughan's wit is evident with "The Boy from Ipanema"'s very first note, a spooky dissonance that slides into pitch, before she embellishes and seduces the shopworn melody into a new place. Foster's wit was equal to the task, and he makes the most of a big band augmented by strings and bongos, thrusting blatting trombones at her at one point, sighing flutes at another, or rocking the percussion crew beyond the usual restraints of faux-Brazilian writing, as on the backbeat drive of "Tea for Two" or the cunning opening of "Stompin' at the Savoy." Vaughan embellishes everything, practically recomposing "Quiet Nights" to a degree that might have confused the listeners this album never reached. She and Foster have but two or three minutes to make their points, so they do what they can. "Fascinatin' Rhythm" is not yet the virtuoso extravaganza she later developed, but—like Mingus working his way through weird nightmares—she already owns it.

[*Village Voice*, 24 April 2001]

85 ❖ A Quartet of Five (Dave Brubeck)

No postwar jazz musician has cultivated his audience like Dave Brubeck. His success has Pavlovian dimensions. The simultaneous release of *Double Live from the USA and UK* (Telarc), a lively two-CD set drawn from 1995 and 1998 concerts, and the long-delayed reissue of *The Dave Brubeck Quartet at Carnegie Hall* (Columbia/Legacy), a two-CD set recorded in 1963, suggests that time, which he has calibrated and deconstructed for five decades, may have stopped for him, his music, and his audience. As soon as he leaps into the clanging 9/4 head of "Blue Rondo a la Turk" or the "Take Five" vamp, he elicits a bellowing roar rarely heard at concerts anymore. The response is less feverish now, the stomps and whistles replaced by falsetto *whoos*, but these are still true believers. Brubeck has called the audience the fifth member of his quartet. Before intermission at the 1963 concert, he thanks it for "helping us along." In a time of rampant jazz politesse, the bursts of applause when a solo peaks and elated cries when it finishes are intoxicating.

By 1963, Brubeck's career had gone awry. From his earliest years in music, he presented himself as an avant-gardist. He had studied with Darius Milhaud and began his recording life with a stuffy Third Stream octet. After forming a quartet with Paul Desmond in 1951, he became known for all the avant-garde stuff that keep crowds at bay: long performances, spontaneous improvisation, original pieces, counterpoint, world fusions, and polymeters, polytones, and anything else that can be polyed. Cecil Taylor once said, "I learned a lot from him. When he's most interesting, he sounds like me." But while Taylor effortlessly achieved penury and culthood, Brubeck was subjected to fame, riches, and the indignity of a *Time* cover, convincing many critics and fans that he no longer merited serious consideration.

It may be difficult to imagine the popularity Brubeck enjoyed in the 1950s, even before *Time Out* skyrocketed him to the fringes of mega-pop. His hornrims, square-faced smile, and stubbornly articulate defense of jazz and himself were ubiquitous. Even his name seemed emblematic: like Miles, the informal Dave was appellation enough. The two were connected in other ways. When Dave was wrestling with the octet, which with typical bravado he described as "a major contributor to jazz," Miles was working with a nonet that really was. Modern jazz's two most famous vamps originated in 1959—the other one is Davis's "All Blues," in 6/8. Miles recorded Dave's "The Duke" and "In Your Own Sweet Way," and other pieces Dave made jazz-friendly, like "Someday My Prince Will Come," and pursued polymeters, though he didn't talk about it. Each man made a fateful mid-'50s switch from an independent label to Columbia, which is now reissuing everything it can find by them. But Miles has become a god and Dave, still active at 80, is more respected in classical circles than in jazz, where his clamorous audience is as isolated from the jazz mainstream as the Dixieland troops.

Brubeck and Desmond were always controversial. Eddie Condon once said Desmond sounded like a "female alcoholic"; for years you were not allowed to publish a review of Brubeck without using the word "bombastic" twice. But in the beginning critics and musicians admired the quartet. Brubeck came up with a brilliant idea: touring colleges, creating a long-term audience while giving his bookings a veneer of hipster prestige, and then releasing records of the concerts. Those LPs established Fantasy as a thriving label; one of them, *Jazz at Oberlin* (1953), would make many short lists of the decade's outstanding albums. On that session, Desmond abandons the ground melodies before he has time to establish them, and builds riff-laden cathedrals with fire and perhaps a slightly facetious intensity; he may be famous for being the altoist who didn't play like Charlie Parker, but on "Perdido," Bird hovers impressively, though it's the Desmond wit—twirling into a turnback with "The Music Goes 'Round and 'Round"—that elicits the audience's first cheers. Brubeck is wonderfully, stubbornly quirky, increasing the tension before springing the release. His block chords had not yet taken over, and his novel style engendered surprise.

In 1954, Columbia continued the pattern with *Jazz Goes to College*. Two minutes into "Balcony Rock," Desmond converses with himself, balancing phrases between two octaves. Elsewhere he converses with Brubeck, affirming a weirdly fetching contrast between his own ethereal musings and Brubeck's splayed 10-note chords—jazz goes to Valhalla. After graduation, Columbia recorded the quartet at New York's Basin Street, releasing tracks on *Brubeck Time*, including the eerily haunting blues, "Audrey," a Desmond meditation triggered by a suggestion that he imagine Hepburn walking though the woods; and the long unavailable *Red Hot and Cool*, the earliest of Columbia/Legacy's four recently reissued Brubeck titles (including the *Vocal Encounters* sampler, which is entertaining, though you would do better to get the complete *Real Ambassadors* and his albums with Jimmy Rushing and Carmen McRae). This admirable series is an antidote to the blue-rimmed "Columbia Jazz Masterpieces": good sound, original cover art and notes, addenda from Brubeck.

The title of *Red Hot and Cool* refers to a line of lipsticks Columbia was cross-promoting, though the cover simply seemed routinely cheesy—a red-mouthed model draping herself over the piano while Dave giddily smiles. The album serves as a fascinating transition to the time-code Brubeck. Dave shows off his interest in fractions on the opening "Lover," phrasing in waltz time as drummer Joe Dodge guns an insistent four-beat. The a&r man George Avakian wants us to note "something very new" here and predicts it will create a "sensation." But there was nothing new about superimposing three over four—for example, Louis Armstrong's 1927 scat vocal on "Hotter Than That." The nearly 11-minute "Little Girl Blue," however, shows where Brubeck is heading. The Rodgers and Hart song is unusual, with a 36-bar AAB chorus divided as 12/12/8+4. The four bars coming off the bridge may have seemed too abrupt to Brubeck, because after playing the theme as written, he extends it by another eight for the solos, ending up with a 44-bar chorus. Desmond bites off two choruses with blues locutions and a hint of "You Must Have Been a Beautiful Baby" before Brubeck puts the blues aside for a solo that is twice as long and compels attention with harmony, dynamics, and daunting cross-rhythms. Melodic content is almost nil. This is Brubeck as energizer bunny, forging his way through the brambles until he finds a clearing, then forging some more. In the second chorus, you wonder how the drummer can keep track—probably by focusing on bassist Bob Bates, whose occasionally corny phrasing holds to an ironclad four-beat. Brubeck finishes the chorus with drumlike rhythms and goes into the third with figures that evade the changes as tenaciously as they do the downbeat. His last chorus is even more rhythmically abstract and you feel relief when the quartet reasserts swing.

Red Hot and Cool also introduces "The Duke," which emerges with a shining melodic intensity while hitting every key as it traverses its two or three chords per measure. You could say it foreshadows "Giant Steps" as a harmonic labyrinth, except that Coltrane conceived his steeplechase for improvisation while "The Duke" is a set piece. "Indiana" has a splendid Brubeck solo, intense and prolix yet linear and swinging—if he had quit right then, he might now have a place in the pantheon with Herbie Nichols. But he was just getting started and fast becoming an issue. You couldn't ignore him, but you could try. The 1955 Newport Jazz Festival souvenir booklet, hardly a critical treatise, opines Desmond is "officially a sideman with the Dave Brubeck quartet" but is "to some of his admirers the most important feature in that organization." His boss is merely the leader of "the most commercially successful small combo in the history of jazz."

It became a Lennon and McCartney thing. Desmond was the hip Beatle and Brubeck was the nice guy who finished first. While it is good to know genuine niceness exists, as Martin Williams memorably observed of Dave, niceness is not the purpose of art. Joe Goldberg and Whitney Balliett included profiles of Desmond only in, respectively, *Jazz Masters of the 50's* and *American Musicians II*. Both San Franciscans, Dave was the brash son of a rancher who wanted to write cantatas and masses and pop songs and played as though he were bringing Jericho to its knees, while Paul was a quietly witty intellectual who spurned leadership offers and said he wanted to sound like a dry martini. Dave married, produced many children, built elaborate homes; Paul remained single, dreaming of Audrey in a New York apartment. Dave appealed to the masses, which tolerated Paul; Paul appealed to the elite, which didn't tolerate Dave.

After the classic quartet came into being, with Gene Wright on bass and Joe Morello on drums, and *Time Out* hit the charts, it became hip to like everything about Brubeck except Brubeck. As John Ford said when *The Informer* won Oscars for score, screenplay, actor, and director while the biggest prize went to *Mutiny on the Bounty*: "I guess they liked everything about it except the picture." Desmond insisted that Brubeck was a superb accompanist, but insiders figured he was being tactful. Musicians covered his hooky tunes, but insiders dismissed them as cute or pretentious. Jazz players as diverse as Armstrong, Rushing, McRae, Mulligan, Alan Dawson, and Anthony Braxton wanted to play with him, but insiders assumed it was a personal thing. Yet Desmond, who made six RCA albums with Jim Hall, never played as passionately under his own steam as he did with Brubeck, a self-effacing accompanist however blunt his solo attack.

The Brubeck-Desmond quartet lasted 17 years, until 1967, followed by reunions, and its pleasures derive directly from the contrast between the two men and the context the leader created. The original themes are rigorously arranged so that you are always aware of the contributions of all four men. This is not to say that Brubeck the pianist can't be a thudding bore. But not to acknowledge his authorship of some of the most diverting and original albums of the period is snobbish. Brubeck is a gifted composer of melodies that settle in the brain like fleas (this is true of some of his long-form work, too, including the neglected "Elementals" on the long unavailable *Time Changes*), but melody abandons him as soon as he starts to improvise, giving way to rhythm and harmony. Yet he has lyric moments, including the just reissued *Jazz Impressions of Japan* (1964).

Here the solos are more evocative than the tunes, which unconsciously parody Asian music. "Tokyo Traffic" is typically fleshed out on the head, and if the gong is a bit ripe, the solos are occidentally cool: Desmond interpolates "God Rest Ye Merry Gentlemen" and Dave quotes and re-quotes, almost as motifs, "High Society" and "How Dry I Am." When he plays this well, you fear Wagnerian thunder, but on this album it never comes. It's bombast free. Some of the selections are supposed to convey deeper feelings than they do—Brubeck's variation on "The City Is Crying" is more affecting than the theme. When he returns to the blues ("Osaka Blues," "Koto Song") he's on firmer ground. Yet by 1964, his studio tracks were getting shorter. One of his cleverest blues from the period, "Mr. Broadway" (written for a short-lived TV series with a press agent hero) is treated like a potential single on *Jazz Impressions of New York*. Better versions of that theme and "Koto Blues" can be heard on *Buried Treasures* (1967), first released in 1998. That's a concert recording, and Brubeck is at his best with the fifth member in attendance.

The 1963 Carnegie Hall album is exemplary. The opening "St. Louis Blues" begins with a spare Desmond solo, followed by Wright, who finishes his solo with an E natural, which Brubeck makes a big deal of in the liner notes. For a man steeped in learned harmonies, Brubeck derives much pleasure from the basics, like playing naturals where the key demands flats. He repeats the E natural while trying to figure out what the hell to do next. Soon, he begins pounding the beat, four to the bar. When Errol Garner does that, he sounds like he's strumming a guitar; Dave is moving furniture. When he plays against the time, though, Morello and the underrated Wright, who has his own way of superimposing meters, are right there. Still, Brubeck keeps pounding. He and his audience don't mind patches of thinking aloud because they know this is foreplay.

Orgasm is Brubeck's true signature—all the fancy fractions in the world cannot disguise that. He gets there by stockpiling thicker and

thicker chords in drummed patterns, before blurting into a world of ecstatic consonance. Sure enough, he soon finds his wings and you don't
know if the audience is applauding in joy or relief. Just in case it wants
more, a Morello solo follows. You don't hear many marathon drum solos
today, but in 1963 they were unavoidable: Tony Williams recorded his
"Walkin'" solo that year and every Monk concert had a Frankie Dunlop
extravaganza. Stars like Blakey, Roach, Candido, Rich, and Krupa were
expected to stretch out. So toward the end of the concert Morello does
10 minutes, and while these things do not usually travel well, his playing
is so epic it will hold your attention at least once.

Whether due to temporary exhaustion or deliberate teasing, however,
orgasm is not automatic. "For All We Know" showcases the Brubeck
who drives nonbelievers nuts. Desmond spurns the melody five bars into
the head and doesn't cite it again until the end of the theme chorus,
when he restores the song's prettiest phrase ("tomorrow was made for
some"). He continues, lyrical and sure. Now comes Dave on a journey
of his own, playing variations on a theme composer J. Fred Coots would
hardly recognize. His first chorus is conventional enough, with stabbing
riffs and curt headlong arpeggios played against time and gliding niftily
over the turnbacks until he hits a two-note figure (think "Cabin in the
Sky") and a bright spot of melody, ending ominously with a couple of
jabs to the bass clef. Those low notes, one every two bars, dominate the
second chorus, until he mows down the changes and effects a clean slate
on which to compile blockbuster chords for chorus three. He reverts to
single-note phrases and seems about through, slowing down for dramatic emphasis, but it's a fakeout. He goes for a fourth chorus, by which
time you wish he had put a lid on it, though you keep listening because
you don't know what he's doing and suspect he doesn't either—a little
romantic bravura, some swinging interplay with Morello, back to romance, straight time, three against four, and then—can it be?—a fifth
chorus.

He is reenergized for "Pennies from Heaven," starting off with a Garneresque name-that-tune intro. Desmond is so hot by now he allows
himself to squeak—a very good sign. Brubeck is at his best in his first
two choruses, recomposing the material with a riff he develops before
essaying a ferocious flurry. Then the chords start, but this time he generates a big band largesse and his daredevil persistence convinces;
he comes out of the chorus playing the closing riffs from "Four Brothers."
He keeps it up for two more choruses, disarming the audience with
passages on the beat, then behind the beat, and ultimately in an exciting new lockstep beat of his own that finally gets folks whistling and
stomping.

And so it goes—surging again and again with "It's a Raggy Waltz" (programmed in its proper place, not possible on the LP), the Morello feature ("Castillian Drums"), and "Blue Rondo a la Turk," which hits the audience's G-spot big time. You no longer hear such roars at jazz concerts. Dave makes a little joke about playing in nine, but the solos are in four, which is why the piece works—the contrast between the frantic Middle Eastern one-two one-two one-two one-two-three and Desmond's descending octave into bluesville. Desmond is so up he recycles the same climactic piping riffs on "Raggy Waltz" and "Blue Rondo." When they finish the latter the crowd is pretty well freaked. It truly does want more. Do me all night, Daverino. When he responds with the "Take Five" vamp, you can hear people shouting "Yaaaaayyyy."

Dave is still playing concerts. But even he may never see an audience like that again.

[*Village Voice*, 15 May 2001]

86 ❖ *Billy Higgins, 1936–2001*

Is it spring or the waning days of autumn? The festivals are getting underway, so it must be spring. Yet it feels like a shivery October in the realm of jazz mortality, as every passing week brings news of another loss, beginning late last year with Milt Hinton and continuing with Jack McDuff, Norris Turney, Lou Levy, George T. Simon, Les Brown, Buddy Tate, Ike Cole, Billy Mitchell, and two radiant beacons of the modern jazz movement and all of American music, as players and composers, J. J. Johnson and John Lewis, who spoke for them all when he remarked, "Everybody wants to be in the image of God. That's why I play jazz." Unlike many of their predecessors, they at least made it past 70. Billy Higgins, who died May 3 of liver and kidney failure, did not, which is one reason his passing hurts, even though he had been ill for years and was awaiting his third liver transplant. The main reason, of course, is that he gave so much pleasure. When you walked into a club where he was playing drums, you knew you were going to hear good time and have a good time.

Drums do not present time as simple four-to-a-bar tapping, which you can do with your foot. They clothe the elementals of tempo and meter in an elaboration of sound and pulse. At their best, they are richly colored and intensely musical, and can generate an emotional gravity to equal any other component in the performance. If in 1934, Sonny Greer and Jo Jones had traded jobs, the music of Ellington and Basie would have evolved much differently. Even when we are fixed on the soloist, seemingly oblivious to the drums, we are in their thrall, which is why bad drummers are so insidious—they do not allow us to ignore them. Great drummers don't either, of course, except when they want us to forget they are there, at which time they become merely the walls, the floor, the ceiling, the very air we breathe.

Shortly after I left college, I experienced a drums epiphany at a place called Boomer's, where Cedar Walton and Clifford Jordan had a quartet. I was given a seat hugging the right-hand side of the stage; the drummer's left ride cymbal hung over my head. I figured I would try a number, and leave if necessary. I knew Higgins's work from records— Ornette Coleman, Thelonious Monk, Sonny Rollins, Dexter Gordon, Lee Morgan, Jackie McLean—but had never seen him and did not think any drummer could be inconspicuous or quiet enough to make that kind of proximity endurable. An hour later, I left in a state of elation, and the thing is, at no time was Higgins inconspicuous or quiet. He was—no other word will do—beautiful. He didn't get in the way of my hearing Walton, soloing on the other side of the stage, yet I was always aware of the glowing sound of the cymbals and snares, the way he made them mesh in cross-rhythms, as though they were made not of metal and canvas but of something pneumatic and plush.

A few weeks after my first *Voice* piece appeared, in 1973, I was asked to write liner notes for a Jimmy Heath album, *Love and Understanding*, and was pleased to see Higgins at the date. Later, Jimmy told me about the new pieces written for the session; one was called "Smilin' Billy," composed, he explained, "for the love of the way Billy Higgins plays and for his love of music and of playing." Now this was at a time when, for many people, the title was less likely to recall an old comic strip (Smilin' Jack lost his wings that very year) than a type of behavior (smiling) considered unbecoming for an African American male. I mentioned that Louis Armstrong, two years dead, was still getting pilloried for it, but Jimmy laughed and the nickname stuck. Higgins *always* looked kinetic behind the traps, smiling, almost laughing, eyes sparkling, flashing his hands like a quick-change artist having the time of his life. This was true up to the end, at reunions with Coleman and at the annual two-week December gig at the Village Vanguard with Walton and McLean.

Back at the Heath date, though, I was still coming to grips with my evening at Boomer's, because I wrote, "He has developed a clean and personal sound on cymbals and snare that rivals Kenny Clarke's and is one of the few drummers of any generation who plays with the taste and restraint that allows a listener to sit right by his traps and not be deafened." Clarke was an obvious forebear, though Higgins had also studied with Ed Blackwell, an earthier player whose contrapuntal patterns influenced him, as did his melodic tuning, which in turn suggested Roy Haynes, who brought a virtuoso shine and bass drum anchor to the modernist techniques devised by Clarke. But Haynes and Blackwell are about syntax; they bring an original language to trap drums. Clarke and Higgins, for all their influence (Clarke's was decisive for a generation), make themselves known through their shimmering sound and immense poise, no matter how hard they drive.

Higgins is on one of the 1960s' key jazz hits, Lee Morgan's "The Sidewinder," and yet no one associates him with its hit-making beat, partly because he didn't latch on to it, hoping for some kind of commercial crutch. Even when you listen to the record, Higgins is easily the freest spirit of the three rhythm players, swinging the vamp without chaining himself to it. He plays alternately on and against the backbeat, always with a liquid freshness that enlivens the beat when it would have been so easy to cheapen it. Maybe that's why he is often overlooked in discussions of the great drummers of that period. When you hear Tony Williams or Elvin Jones, you feel you are in the presence of genius. With Higgins, you feel you are hearing perfection, which is neither as sexy nor as easy to talk about. In his book *Different Drummers* (1975), Billy Mintz transcribes and analyzes the playing of 19 percussionists, Higgins not among them. Yet the last sentence of his text, after a paragraph in which he recommends his favorite jazz and rock artists, reads: "Listen to everything with Billy Higgins playing drums because his time is so swinging that it just floats along."

The nature of his swing is panstylistic. Of course he didn't change horses to ride "The Sidewinder"—this is an artist who initially became famous playing free jazz with Coleman (he recorded with Cecil Taylor in the same period), who aided Rollins in navigating the straits dividing free and not-free, buoyed Dexter Gordon to crests of invention, and in every instance sounded exactly right and exactly like himself. He could play a written part as well as anyone—McLean's brilliantly cornered "Melody for Melonae," for example; or cross the T's on a rumble crafted especially for him—Morgan's "One for Higgins," for example; or fashion cool breezes—Charlie Haden's *Silence*, for example. His brief solo on the latter's "Conception," built on a basic march pattern, is riveting yet wittily self-effacing. But he was also a relentlessly driving accompanist and perhaps the greatest miracle of his playing is how beautifully and calmly swinging he sounds even when he's playing to beat the band. The flip side of *The Sidewinder* LP offers the blues waltz "Boy, What a Night," in 12, a meter that can easily generate inflexible triplets. Higgins is loose and infectiously zealous. Joe Henderson, Morgan, and Barry Harris turn in vivid solos, as the Cheshire Cat hovers over them all.

Higgins, who was born in Los Angeles in 1936, started on the drums at five. Still in his teens, he worked with Don Cherry in the Jazz Messiahs, a band led by James Clay that was inspired by the Davis-Rollins sessions, and sat in with the area's leading beboppers (Sonny Criss, Teddy Edwards) and r&b bands (Bo Diddley, Amos Milburn). In 1956, he met Coleman, who astonished everyone, one way or another; Clay took his tenor to Ray Charles's orchestra for a quarter century, while Cherry, Higgins, and Blackwell, who had known Coleman for several years, were drawn to the altoist's ragged cry and glancing tunes. With Blackwell ensconced in an r&b band, Higgins made the Hillcrest engagement, recorded with Coleman (*The Shape of Jazz to Come, Change of the Century*), and took the historic leap to New York. Even those who scoffed at Ornette recognized Higgins as an extraordinary drummer after seeing him at the Five Spot or hearing him on "Ramblin'," "Una Muy Bonita," or "Focus on Sanity." But things went badly. Higgins was busted for drugs and lost his cabaret card; Blackwell, who had skipped bail with his wife after they had been imprisoned in New Orleans on a charge of interracial marriage, took his place.

Higgins would reunite often with Coleman over the next 40 years, turning in one of the most memorable performances of his life at the 1997 Coleman triptych at Lincoln Center, with Haden and Kenny Barron. But by then he had also morphed into something unexpected—the much coveted, unofficial house drummer for Blue Note records, and one of the most recorded musicians of the era. In later years, he worked with David Murray, Charles Lloyd, Hamiet Bluiett, Harold Land, Art Pepper, and many others, in addition to countless engagements with Walton, and, last year, the most unexpected gig of all, one under his own name, dedicated to the Blue Note songbook. Pepper, before he and Higgins fell out over a bassist, called him the greatest drummer who ever lived. He wasn't really. It just seemed that way whenever you listened to him.

[*Village Voice*, 22 May 2001]

87 ❖ Boom!
(Louis Armstrong)

Amid the crush of CD releases timed to accompany Louis Armstrong's centennial celebration, a two-year event that acknowledges his avowed birth date in 1900 as well as his true one in 1901, a remarkable curio has glided in under the radar of many fans. It's an appendage to a collection of 1950s records by Lotte Lenya, the Viennese-born singer and actress whose own centennial in 2000 was strangely neglected. *Lotte Lenya Sings Kurt Weill / The American Theater Songs* includes her robust duet with Armstrong on "Mack the Knife," an uncommon but hardly unknown performance. The curio is a funny eight-and-a-half minute rehearsal tape that allows us to be flies on the wall as Armstrong teaches her to syncopate.

The excerpt begins with a complete run-through of the song, which is persuasive until the very end, when Lenya is supposed to sing, "Now that Mackie's [quarter note rest for rhythmic accent] back in town." She ignores the rest and drags out the last three words for a mile and a half. Armstrong good-naturedly explains to her the jazzy cadence, growling a "boom" to indicate the rest. She laughs and tells him, "That's easy for you." Taking charge, Armstrong informs the producer that there is no need to re-record more than a closing insert, and encourages Lenya ("That's it," "There you go") until she gets it almost right. The irony is delicious: Armstrong coolly coaching Lenya, a near-legendary figure in her own right, on a song her late husband had conceived expressly for her—and she displaying not one iota of prima donna resentment as he spots her take after take. Also amusing is the precise and unchanging pitch with which he repeatedly cues the "boom." The episode reminds us how alien jazz rhythms could be as recently as midcentury. Today, few 10-year-olds would have any difficulty mastering that rest. Thanks largely to Armstrong, we live in a syncopated world.

Armstrong was the most influential, popular, and celebrated jazz musician who ever lived. No one disputes that. But he was also the most bitterly criticized. The Armstrong schism began as early as 1929, before his fame reached anything resembling national dimensions, and it was triggered by his willingness to record and perform Tin Pan Alley songs with—this is what really bugged many of his early antagonists—large bands, which embodied the heresy of the imminent swing era. The argument made no sense, yet stuck around for many years, having been made gospel by Rudi Blesh in his 1946 jazz history *Shining Trumpets*.

"Louis Armstrong could conceivably return to jazz tomorrow," he assured his readers. "He did it once before, from 1925 to 1928, when he left [Fletcher] Henderson and returned to Chicago." But then, after Earl Hines and Don Redman joined his band, the "quality deteriorate[d] into a sort of sweetness foreign to Louis' nature, one belonging to sweet-swing." "West End Blues," he wrote, though a "record of great beauty," "narrowly misses banality" because of Hines, and signals Armstrong's descent into "a dark romanticism foreign to jazz."

Reading Blesh, you get the feeling he was determined to protect jazz from the unwashed as well as from swing bands, and that he might have been happy on an island populated by professorial Dixieland addicts and noble savages to satisfy their jones. Perhaps I am unfair. Yet he also wrote that Duke Ellington composed a "*tea dansant* music trapped out with his borrowed effects from jazz, the Impressionists, and the French Romantics." To those who lamented that Ellington had forsaken jazz, Blesh advised, "The Duke has never played it." He could see little difference between "Daybreak Express" and the "theatrical corn" of Ted Lewis. So the hell with unfair.

Armstrong and Ellington were the first major jazz figures subjected to judges who knew better than they what they were supposed to be doing (an arrogance that might appear quaintly eccentric today had it not been embraced so vigorously by the Lincoln Center crowd in the 1990s). Ellington was lambasted for reaching too high, Armstrong for stooping too low. Those who were touched by the latter's genius were offended by his clowning, risqué humor, and acceptance of all the habiliments of pop—never mind that he tailored them to his own tastes. In *Early Jazz* (1969), Gunther Schuller, one of the most perceptive and influential critics of early Armstrong, wrote that "West End Blues" proved "jazz had the potential capacity to compete with the highest order of previously known musical expression." In *The Swing Era* (1989), however, he reported, "our memories are beclouded by recordings of a sixty-three-year-old Louis singing, 'Hello, Dolly!' against a cheap brassy Dixieland sextet."

To which one might shrug: Not my memories, pal. But musical memories are now governed by technology, specifically the accessibility of records, which leads to a kind of critical historicism. Consider the Armstrong myth that dates an overall decline to his wholesale acceptance by the public and his inability to resist commercial blandishments. In the past, even critics sympathetic to late Armstrong were likely to conclude that only when he stepped into the mainstream, in the mid-1930s, did he begin to rely on vocals, beyond his patented scat volleys, and pop songs. The LP generation accepted that because when it came along, the

Hot Fives and Sevens were represented on records solely by 36 prime tracks collected on the first three discs of Columbia's four-album series, *The Louis Armstrong Story*, issued in 1951 on LPs and 45s, and kept in catalog for more than 20 years. The only way you could hear the complete works was on European collections.

The story that emerged and hardened into received wisdom is known to every jazz lover and goes like this. Between 1925 and 1928, Armstrong made several dozen records by small studio units known as the Hot Five, Hot Seven, and Savoy Ballroom Five. They are the foundation for jazz's ascension as an art—indeed, for much of what we value highest in jazz and popular music. At those sessions, Armstrong supplanted the march-like two-beat of the New Orleans style with a steady and occasionally throbbing four/four; established the imperative of blues tonality; replaced the polyphonic or group approach to improvisation with solo inventions of, in his case anyway, uncanny radiance; and freed the vernacular voice that remains at the center stage of American song. All this is true. The greatness of those records exceeds their influence. We do not pay passive homage to Armstrong's genius, but, rather, lose ourselves in its emotional grandeur, stately tone, earthy comedy, and discriminating rigor.

In 1929, he brought all these strengths to bear on a popular song by Jimmy McHugh and Dorothy Fields, "I Can't Give You Anything but Love." This number was no more compromised by Tin Pan Alley expediency than the songs he had already recorded by such successful songwriters as Spencer Williams ("Basin Street Blues") and Fats Waller ("Squeeze Me"). But their songs were the product of the close-knit world of young African American musicians making headway in jazz and on Broadway. "I Can't Give You Anything but Love" was blues-free white pop. It was also superior to much of the material Armstrong had recorded to that time, and his superb interpretation, in effect, provided a jazz pedigree for a song that would live on as a standard. Still, it generated a simmering pique among the most hidebound of his admirers, who may have astutely surmised that he would no longer belong exclusively to them.

In truth, he never did. Here is where received wisdom was skewed by the vagaries of Columbia Records. Blesh complains that he had abandoned jazz *before* 1925, working with Henderson and an assortment of vaudevillians, including a very mixed bag of blues divas, but ignores the pop records he made between 1925 and 1928, as though they never existed. Until the late 1980s, you could not easily find a complete edition of the Hot Fives and Sevens. But Columbia finally issued a poorly mastered set (a better edition, simultaneously released in England on JSP, can still be ordered online), followed last year by the improved but troublesome *The Complete Hot Five and Hot Seven Recordings*. Today, listeners have no choice but to take them all in—the gold, silver, and lead. In this context, we are no longer blinded by an exhibition of mostly instrumental masterpieces, from "Struttin' with Some Barbecue" and "Potato Head Blues" to "Tight Like This" and "Muggles." Instead, we are treated to a more complicated panorama in which those works alternate with lighter yet almost always earthier, if not downright vulgar, pieces intended to entertain.

If you include the spoken raps on "Gut Bucket Blues" and "King of the Zulus," 14 of the first 24 Hot Fives have vocals. On "He Likes It Slow," the Hot Five appears in support of vaudevillians Butterbeans and Susie, and on "Sunset Cafe Stomp" and "Big Butter and Egg Man," Armstrong's guest vocalist is May Alix, a nightclub performer known for her splits (a routine later incorporated into Armstrong's shows when he hired singer-dancer Velma Middleton) and for being so light-skinned that Ellington balked at taking her on tour. Four numbers, including those with Alix, were created by Percy Venable, who staged floorshows at the Sunset Cafe. One of them, "Irish Black Bottom," begins as "When Irish Eyes Are Smiling," interpolates "Black Bottom" (also a white tune, incidentally) and finds Armstrong singing, "I was born in Ireland—ha ha!—so imagine how I feel." As it is intended to make you laugh, it will never appear on a serious best-of Louis anthology, nor should it. Neither does it becloud one's memories of "Potato Head Blues."

In short, at no time in Armstrong's career—which began with him singing for pennies on New Orleans street corners and progressed to social functions like picnics and funerals that were not covered by the press (alas)—did he devote himself exclusively to a fancied shrine of jazz; at no time was he disinclined to entertain; at no time did he forswear popular material. All the songs he sang were pop or would-be pop. No one wrote tunes, least of all Armstrong, in hope of achieving a cult status. The songs he recorded are jazz classics because he did them. In jazz, the singer makes the song, never the reverse. The most famous of his early vocals is "Heebie Jeebies," for popularizing scat; "West End Blues" and "Basin Street Blues," for his soft wordless crooning; and "Hotter Than That," for his virtuoso scat romp. Less talked about is the 1928 "St. James Infirmary," another essential performance, because here for the first time we hear what Armstrong could do with a good song, perfectly gauging the high notes and propelling the chorus with rhythmic emotion—three months before the more inventive breakthrough on "I Can't Give You Anything but Love."

Luis Russell played piano on the McHugh-Fields song, and it was Russell's band that Armstrong would front—after he returned from his European sojourn—between 1935 and 1943. Those were the Decca years, which, for me, mark his greatest period as a singer. His voice had a smooth, lustrous, supple quality, richer than in the preceding decade and not as gravelly as in the one to follow, though by the early 60s, it attained another crest—deeper and richer and more authoritative than ever. Perhaps never before or after did his trumpet produce so many gleaming, acrobatic flourishes as in this period—most notably the dazzling and superior remake of "Struttin' with Some Barbecue." The Deccas are still not as widely known as they should be, because they have yet to be properly issued, though with Verve now in possession of the catalog there is hope.

Meanwhile, a company in Andorra, where I suspect copyright laws are more flexible than here (or nonexistent), has done the job splendidly on six CDs in two volumes, *The Complete Decca Studio Master Takes 1935–1939* and *The Complete Decca Studio Master Takes 1940–1949* (they are available through the mail-order company, Collectors' Choice). With trumpet and voice each at a distinctive peak, Armstrong's creative consistency is amazing. Nobody was singing or playing anything to match his "Love Walked In," "Jubilee," "Thanks a Million," "Swing That Music," "Lyin' to Myself," "My Darling Nellie Gray," "Pennies from Heaven," "Among My Souvenirs," "The Skeleton in the Closet," "Shoe Shine Boy," and dozens more, not least the modern spirituals he put on the map: "When the Saints Go Marching In" and "Shadrach." Some 60 years after they were made, these records sound as fresh and surprising as anything in American music and seem to contain seeds for everything that followed, including hip hop. Consider his rhythmic recitation at an anomalous March 14, 1940, session, which produced "Hep Cats Ball" and the marvelous "You Got Me Voodoo'd." The latter begins with jungly thumping—by Sid Catlett, no less—and a spooky vamp, before Armstrong declaims:

> Just like some magic potion,
> You fill me with emotion.
> You control my very soul.
> You've Got Me Voodoo'd.
> You knew the goddess Venus
> Would start this love between us.
> You inspired me with desire.
> You've Got Me Voodoo'd.

You knew you had the power
And even picked the hour,
When the full moon was up above.
I was hypnotized when I looked into your eyes:
My heart was filled with love.
Just like the siren Circe,
You've got me at your mercy.
Always yours to have and hold,
Mama, you've Got Me Voodoo'd.

The number is credited to Armstrong, Russell, and Cornelius C. Lawrence, an obscure playwright, actor, and lyricist who also wrote songs with the intriguing titles, "Curfew Time in Harlem" and "Ink Spink Spidely Spoo." Each line of the lyric is the equivalent of two measures, which makes for an AABA song, only without a melody. Louis's trumpet chorus, unlike the proper Prince Robinson clarinet solo that precedes it, uses the rapped rhythm as a starting point before juicing it with melody and taking off on the bridge—a model for what can be done with an intrinsically unmelodic form.

Armstrong always trusted the sound of his own voice, even when no one else did, and often used it with comic authority—on several of his earliest records, the tunes allow him to boast of his sexual prowess. On the first session as a leader, in November 1925, he used "Gut Bucket Blues" to introduce the men in the band (a much imitated gambit, e.g., Jimmie Lunceford's "Rhythm Is Our Business," Andy Kirk's "Git," Slim Gaillard's "Slim's Jam"), letting us know that he was in charge and knew exactly what he was about. Of banjoist Johnny St. Cyr, he chortles, "Everybody in New Orleans can really do that thing." But, truly, no one in those days could do that thing like Armstrong, and it is entirely possible that had he not come along, jazz would never have become a full-fledged art of universal appeal. After the Dixieland fad faded, it might have remained a lively regional folk music. Even Ellington might have gone a different route, composing theater and dance band music, had Armstrong not awakened his respect for the blues. The confidence we hear in Louis's barking in "Gut Bucket Blues" is not much different from the helpful "boom" he offered Lotte Lenya 30 years later. It wasn't Louis Armstrong who changed. It was us, the people.

[*Village Voice*, 12 June 2001]

88 ❖ *Found and Lost*
(Terence Blanchard)

Terence Blanchard's reach and tone have broadened just about equally in the 15 years since he graduated from Art Blakey's Jazz Messengers. He has tested his skills as trumpeter, composer, and bandleader in a variety of overlapping projects: the quintet with Donald Harrison, formalized during a sabbatical from Blakey and continued through 1989; several film scores, most for Spike Lee; on-and-off-again groups, in recent years framed around his collaboration with pianist Edward Simon; and 11 Columbia or Sony Classical discs, each a defined project, lending a meticulous drama to his recordings. His latest, *Let's Get Lost*, differs from the rest yet remains true to a cycle that alternates originals (as on its predecessor, *Wandering Moon*) with classic songs—this time a salute to Jimmy McHugh, abetted by the three most fashionable under-50 jazz singers (Cassandra Wilson, Dianne Reeves, and Diana Krall) and one who wants to join them (Jane Monheit). It should be more fun than it is.

McHugh is an ideal choice for a jazz survey. A prolific composer for stage and screen, he wrote sundry jazz standards, including trademark numbers associated with players as diverse as Louis Armstrong, Fats Waller, Billie Holiday, Jimmy Rushing, Nat King Cole, Johnny Hodges, Chet Baker, Thelonious Monk, and James Moody, who turned "I'm in the Mood for Love" into bebop's only jukebox perennial. McHugh jazzed up stages with *Blackbirds of 1928* ("I Can't Give You Anything but Love," "I Must Have That Man," "Digga Digga Doo") and the Cotton Club reviews; he was instrumental in getting Ellington his Cotton Club audition and wrote several pieces for him, like "Harlem River Quiver" and "Harlemania." He was said to have purchased "I Can't Give You Anything but Love" and "On the Sunny Side of the Street" from Fats Waller, whom his son claimed was so upset they became hits he would not allow them to be played in the house. This seems unlikely, since Waller's record of the former helped make it a hit. Ellington claimed, somewhat cryptically, to be pleased that a rhythmic figure he introduced in "Birmingham Breakdown" was popularized by McHugh in "The New Low Down." But McHugh did not have to steal; he wrote hundreds of songs and dozens of hits over three decades, from "When My Sugar Walks Down the Street," in 1924, to "Too Young to Go Steady," in 1955. And Blanchard has soundly chosen 11.

Blanchard is one of the most distinctive trumpet players of his generation, but his trademark, a purring glissando, has become fussy and predictable. It marked the first notes of his unaccompanied "Motherless Child," on his eponymous first album, became more pronounced by the first notes of "Unconditional," on *Romantic Defiance*, and is now an intrusive tick that, far from underscoring the very real lyricism of which he is capable, disables his solos, compromising invention with a mannered self-consciousness. *Let's Get Lost* is pocked with these squeezed notes, which cross Rex Stewart's half-cocked whimsy with Ruby Braff's meditative irony but are too overworked to serve either purpose. During a recent set at the Village Vanguard, he put aside the glisses and whimpers during a driving "I'm in the Mood for Love," and his vigorous playing suggested a happy repose that is increasingly hard to find on his records, however handsomely programmed or arranged.

That same tune is a highlight of the album. The mannerisms are more apparent than at the Vanguard, but he controls them and crafts a pleasant solo. Tenor saxophonist Brice Winston follows with the headiest blowing of the session; when Blanchard returns, they play in tandem, producing the first head of steam on an album halfway to the finish line. Blanchard's best solo is on "Exactly Like You," where he eschews stylistic habit in favor of the higher altitudes of improvisation. If only the whole album was as smartly played as these pieces, both arranged by Simon, who combines a simple unison voicing with tempo changes and canny harmonic substitutions that provide a contemporary tang. Simon also wrote endings, which are especially welcome on an album that often runs to ground with 40-second fadeouts. Seven tracks are given to the singers.

This is Blanchard's third homage with voice, after *The Billie Holiday Songbook*, with Jeanie Bryson, and *The Heart Speaks*, with Ivan Lins singing his own songbook. They are all strangely subdued, sometimes to great effect, as in Bryson's poised "What a Little Moonlight Can Do," her phrasing dispassionately removed from the driving background as she places her notes in all the right places. Singing McHugh, Cassandra Wilson and Diana Krall are most effective, especially when they mine the similar veiled low notes of their contraltos, the latter suggesting the influence of the former. Both have come a long way. Krall, whose Nat Cole repertory portended a callow gimmick, now sounds aged in the wood, and her "Let's Get Lost" is intimate and sexy, keyed to a vamp and backed by her own piano, which capers suavely with Blanchard's trumpet, before the long, long fade.

Wilson is more playful and rhythmic, phrasing "Don't Blame Me" on the beat, steered by a strong bass line, and suggesting a depth that evades the other singers. She tends to recompose every song she sings, curving all the edges until they fit her mold—you could say the same of Holiday or Abbey Lincoln. As a result, she generates a degree of tension as to how she will shape a tune, which notes will get pressed in what direction. Blanchard's obbligati are less precious than elsewhere, but Wilson introduces her own mannerism, hollowing out her voice, like a trombone, to accent an occasional note. She takes more risks, in her dour way, with "On the Sunny Side of the Street," pitched so low she has to speak a few phrases, and altering her vocal mask a few times. At the Vanguard, the surprising thing about Wilson (who, along with Monheit, appeared for two nights of Blanchard's gig) was how much star power she packs. Not too many years ago, she all but hid behind the band, barely acknowledging the audience. Stage presence isn't something you are born with—even Sarah Vaughan, awkward at the outset, had to learn it. So has Wilson.

So has Dianne Reeves, but she's more self-conscious about it. With Wilson, it isn't about the dress or the hair, though she attends to both, but rather the way she takes the microphone and moves in on the material. With Reeves, sometimes you get the feeling she thinks she's Judy Garland. On her new album, a tribute to Vaughan entitled *The Calling* (Blue Note), she poses as a grande dame on the cover, the foreground littered with roses, and sings amid an ocean of strings and woodwinds. At her best ("Embraceable You," "Lullaby of Birdland," "I Hadn't Anyone Till You," "Send in the Clowns"), she is thoroughly persuasive, but too often she lacks the personality to keep the orchestra in its place. The same is true in the confined straits of the Blanchard album. On "I Can't Believe That You're in Love with Me," she nails Vaughan's cello range, but her improvisational gambits are hapless as she loses sight of the song and the beat. She is in much better form on "Can't Get Out of This Mood," a McHugh peak (with a Frank Loesser lyric), swinging comfortably for her first chorus and with abandon on her second.

Jane Monheit's two entries place her in the Russ Columbo tradition: Apparently she can sing nothing that isn't set at a very slow tempo, and even then is too conscious of vocal production to give the song much due. Her pedestrian new CD, *Come Dream with Me* (Warlock), raises the question of what she is doing in a jazz context at all. She has the sort of large glowing voice, particularly bright in its upper reaches, that 30 years ago would have drawn her to "Michael, Row the Boat Ashore" and 10 years ago to *Cats*. It is neither expressive nor appealing enough to justify her crawling pace, and her idea of jazz filigree is melismatic phrase endings, occasionally suggesting the moaning excesses of Morgana King.

At the Blanchard gig, she looked, at 23, appealing and sure, but out of her element. On "Too Young to Go Steady," she sold the melody with dynamics and feeling while overdramatizing the banal lyric. The absence of wit was more problematic on the very witty "I Can't Give You Any-thing but Love," where the modestly cantering rhythm unmoored her, as it does on the record. Monheit has a reserve of evident talent but is being pushed into an area obviously unsuitable for her. The implication is that the jazz bar is low enough for a newcomer to find an immediate niche; judging from the hype, that may be true for now. The marketing of her CD is disingenuous to say the least. An all-star sextet is promised on the jacket, but never actually appears. The soloists play on only se-lected tracks, never together, on what turns out to be a pop session with strings. The booklet features strange upscale photos of Monheit wearing Rebecca of Sunnybrook Farm ringlets, lurking around a corner and humping a wall, along with notes by hack producer Joel Dorn that are almost entirely about hack producer Joel Dorn, while noting that the selections by Joni Mitchell and Bread prove she is not "just a jazz singer." She is better on Blanchard's album, but considering the vocalists he might have signed instead, he could have done better. So could Jimmy McHugh.

[*Village Voice*, 12 June 2001]

89 ❖ *Ladies Day*
(Billie Holiday)

How many Billie Holidays are there and which do you prefer? Elated or dour, funny or truculent, sweet or sour, our Lady of Sorrows or 52nd Street's Queen, early Billie or late, Billie of hope or heartache, Billie with Pres or with strings, Lady Day or Lady Nightmare or Lady in Ermine, Lady Be Good, Lady in Red, Lady Luck, Lady Blue, Lady Divine, the Lady who Swings the Band, Lady Mine—crank up the record machine, listen closely, and take your choice. For Billie Holiday is one of those exceptional artists whose work is a perfect tuning fork for our own in-clinations. She echoes our emotions, rehabilitates our innocence, cauter-izes our nerves.

How she managed so capacious a vision with her slim vocal range and infinite capacity for nurturing demons is a miracle to which gener-ations of interpreters have been and will continue to be drawn. The greatest art never loses its mystery. The better we know hers, the more dreamlike and sensational it seems.

I am inclined to connect her with the equally inscrutable Edgar A. Poe, perhaps because I became mesmerized by both at the same age. What can she and the 19th-century writer have in common, beyond sharing an association with the South; spending critical years in Baltimore and New York; taking to drink and drugs; and dying, derelict, in their forties? For one thing, their power to haunt the soul. Consider that flawless short fiction, "The Fall of the House of Usher," a story peculiarly remade by the imagination of each reader who, obliged to identify with a deliberately vague narrator, must examine feelings and maladies the narrator discounts as beyond analysis. Holiday, whether singing a stalwart lyric like "I'll Get By" or an insipid one like "What a Little Moonlight Can Do," requires no less rapport. The songs cannot account for the passion she engenders; it's a matter of alchemy. We transform such artists into romantic figures and bring our baggage to them, expecting them to lighten it. And they do!

Asked to choose one visual image to suggest the character of Holiday's sublime Columbia recordings, made between 1933 and 1942 (and in most cases originally issued by Brunswick, Vocalion, and OKeh), I would turn to the casual photography of Denmark's Timme Rosenkrantz. A jazz diehard and scion to a family that left him a title—baron—but little funds, Rosenkrantz crossed the Atlantic whenever possible, exploring Harlem from the ground up, or down, drinking his way through bars visited by few whites. He was 24 in the late summer of 1935, armed with a camera in the Apollo's back alley, shooting a singer that few people had ever heard of. Only a month earlier, Billie had recorded her first important session, as vocalist with Teddy Wilson, and one selection, "What a Little Moonlight Can Do," was about to break as a jukebox hit. The Dane was clearly enchanted by her: The most famous of the pictures he took captures a radiantly lovely young woman, 20 years old, flashing a direct and perfectly symmetrical smile, arms entwined with those of two musicians, while another kneels before her and a fourth stands behind.

This picture has been reproduced many times, though never as dramatically as in the booklet to Columbia's 1962 three-LP box, *Billie Holiday: The Golden Years*, where it bleeds over a full two pages, including a wall of lovelorn graffiti. (A Rosenkrantz shot of Billie alone was used on the cover.) It offers us a very different Holiday than the star—gowned in scarlet with a white orchid in her hair—she would quickly become.

In 1935, with her hair brushed back and skin glowing, she is a country girl in a short-sleeve, open-neck, gingham dress with pockets on the skirt. Her figure is, to use a favorite press adjective, buxom. Pigmeat Markham, a comedian who shared an Apollo bill with her the same year, remembered her as "a simple lookin' girl" who didn't know how to do "the things that girls do to pretty up." Yet she appears sexy and sure, happy to be one with the musicians: saxophonists Ben Webster (who played on the Wilson date), to her right, looking off, distracted, and Johnny Russell, to her left; pianist Ram Ramirez, an erstwhile prodigy who would later co-write her signature hit, "Lover Man," in front; and, behind, a man with a guitar who turns out not to be a musician at all, but a stagehand known as Shoebrush.

The camaraderie Rosenkrantz caught characterizes the best of Holiday's early records, made when she was just another musician, waiting her turn and often singing no more than a chorus. Yet her contributions never indicate an obligatory vocal refrain of the sort bandleaders included to sell a lyric. Holiday's choruses are genuine solos. Working in fast company with the greatest players in New York, which is to say the world (Wilson, Webster, Benny Goodman, Roy Eldridge, Bunny Berigan, Artie Shaw, Lester Young, Buck Clayton, Chu Berry, Johnny Hodges, and on), she always holds her own, singing confidently behind the beat with an improvisational bravura that frequently bests them all. By that time, she had endured a childhood of fear and privation far worse than anything Dickens contrived for Little Nell. But unlike Nell, Billie lived to tell her own tale.

Her 1956 memoir, *Lady Sings the Blues*, opens with one of the most widely quoted passages of its time: "Mom and pop were just a couple of kids when they got married. He was eighteen, she was sixteen, and I was three." In truth, Billie was no writer; the ironic style is the work of "ghost" William Dufty, a journalist and one of her most loyal friends. (Two years later, he wrote the autobiography of Edward G. Robinson, Jr., whose only accomplishments were drunk driving and an attempted suicide, but whose tale starts off with a similar wallop.) In any case, like much of the book—which is well worth reading—it was only slightly true. Mom and Pop were kids when Billie was born, on April 7, 1915, but did not marry. Sadie, at 18, had two years on Clarence Holiday, who abandoned her and the child. As biographer Donald Clarke has shown, Billie was born Eleanora Harris (Sadie's family name), but her mother, whose own parents did not marry, assumed her father's name, Fagan, and Billie grew up in Baltimore as Eleanora Fagan.

Clarence, who went on to play banjo and guitar in prominent bands, played no role in Eleanora's upbringing, except perhaps to draw her, by example, to jazz and to capricious and abusive men. Sadie, with whom she developed a close relationship, was rumored to have run a whorehouse, and often sent her to board with relatives. Eleanora spent her tenth year in charge to the nuns at the House of the Good Shepherd for

Colored Girls, where she may have been molested. A year later, she was raped by a neighbor and sent back to the nuns. At 12, she worked in a waterfront brothel, picking up extra change by singing to records. She later claimed her favorites were Bessie Smith and Louis Armstrong. If she never picked up Bessie's devotion to 12-bar blues, she did learn to infuse everything she sang with a blues feeling and tonality. From Louis, she learned style, swing, improvisation. Above all, she recalled, "I wanted Louis Armstrong's *feeling*."

After moving with her mother to New York, she worked in a whore-house, did time on Blackwell's Island, and began singing for tips at small Harlem clubs like the Nest, Pod's and Jerry's, the Yeah Man, and Monette's. This was before microphones were common in high-class nightclubs (Bing Crosby had begun popularizing them in 1930, at Hollywood's Coconut Grove), let alone after-hours joints where the performers sashayed from one table to the next, often collecting tips with body parts other than their fingers. Eleanora, who scorned such indignities, learned to project at the same time she learned how to communicate intimately. She changed her name—borrowing Holiday from her father and Billie from actress Billie Dove and, possibly, Clarke suggests, a friend and fellow singer named Billie Haywood.

In 1933, entertainer Monette Moore opened Monette's Supper Club. With her hands full as hostess, she hired Billie to do the singing. In that late-night environment, Billie met a great many musicians and person-alities, not least the talent scout, critic, and jazz lover, John Hammond, who had come to see Moore and left raving about Holiday. He, at 22, was a wealthy prude with powerful connections; she, at 18, was a hellion, eking out a living the best she could. Hammond introduced her to Benny Goodman, who briefly dated her, and arranged for her to sing one number at a record session on November 17, 1933. The featured performer that day was the great and imperious Ethel Waters, backed by a Goodman ensemble. The irony was Poe-etic.

Waters had been a Columbia recording star for eight years. This session would end her affiliation with the company and, except for a dozen Decca sides and a superb but little-noted comeback for Bluebird in the late-'30s, wrap up the recording career of one of the most influential singers in American music. After she completed her numbers, the highly competitive Waters listened to Billie make her debut, romping through "Your Mother's Son-in-Law" in an uncharacteristically high key. She was not impressed, and later commented that Holiday sang as though her shoes were too tight. Billie had been unnerved by her until pianist Joe Sullivan advised her to just close her eyes and sing. For years, I wondered about a seemingly incomprehensible line in the lyric—"You don't have to sing like fatso"—until the producer Michael Brooks pointed out that she is actually singing "Bledsoe," as in Jules Bledsoe, who played Joe in the original production of *Showboat*. Fatso or Bledsoe, her record went nowhere.

Still, on the same day that Ethel—whose great triumphs on the stage and in film were still ahead of her—departed Columbia, Billie's career was inauspiciously launched, at \$35. And if the rivalry between those two women led the younger to omit the older from all discussions of her musical influences, we are obliged to stand outside the ropes and credit Waters's unmistakable impact. The 1923 "Ethel Sings 'Em" includes a stanza ("love is like a faucet . . .") that Billie would make famous in "Fine and Mellow," and the 1928 "My Baby Sure Knows How to Love" bodes Billie's way of inflecting vowels with a waver. Waters's style also anticipates the elocutionary precision with which Billie attacks consonants—for example, the dentalized t's in songs like "Getting Some Fun Out of Life," "Back in Your Own Backyard," and "Swing, Brother, Swing!" ("stop this dit-tle dat-tle")—an articulation that Dinah Washington, in turn, picked up from Billie. One could argue that Waters's influence on Holiday exceeded Bessie Smith's. Her most decisive model, however, remained Louis Armstrong.

Hammond, who contrived to get Billie on another Goodman side in 1933 ("Riffin' the Scotch," with a Johnny Mercer lyric that has nothing to do with the title), did not find the right formula for her until the summer of 1935, when she recorded with a seven-piece pick-up band fronted by Teddy Wilson. Several months earlier, she had sung, without credit, "Saddest Tale," in the Duke Ellington film short, "Symphony in Black," in a scene in which she is knocked down by a lover. Ellington did not, however, hire her for his band. When Wilson first heard her, he was no more impressed than Ellington. Near the end of his life, Wilson conceded that he initially thought of Billie as a gimmick: a girl who sang like Louis—a cute idea, but so what? He soon changed his mind.

The Wilson sessions are among the preeminent glories of recorded jazz, brisk and pointed and incredibly swinging. They were made largely for the jukebox trade, which in the ghastly years of the Depression emerged as the largest single market for records. Yet as brief and spontaneous as they are, these exemplary tracks overflow with detail and invention, rarely wasting a second, with each player obliged to make a personal, identifiable statement in just a few measures. Benny Carter once noted, "It's a pleasure to hear a guy like Ben Webster. He blows a note and you know he's there—and who he is." The great players could do that; they developed individual styles that told you right off who they were and what they were like. Fans did not need an announcer to inform them that a soloist was Webster or Young or Coleman Hawkins. Wilson's sides offered a de facto guide to the era's giants, because Hammond raided the big bands that happened to be playing New York when a session was scheduled, recruiting key players from Basie, Ellington, Goodman, Calloway, and the rest. These sessions remain an unbeatable primer on the leading soloists and rhythm players of the swing era.

They also offer an unusually rounded thesaurus of American songwriting in the golden age, juxtaposing the gold and the tin. Except for "I Wished on the Moon," the songs at the first session were decidedly second-rate, and they did not get much better over the ensuing year. Yet Holiday, Wilson, and friends readily turned Tin Pan Alley dross into bullion. Of the first 15 songs, three—"I Wished on the Moon," "What a Little Moonlight Can Do," and to a lesser extent, "Miss Brown to You"— became a permanent part of Billie's repertoire. Others endured as classic records. The quality of her material took a dramatic turn for the better in the summer of 1936. At the June 30 date, Billie helped to establish "These Foolish Things" as a standard and revived the 1920s hit, "I Cried for You." She also performed magic with the utterly forgotten "It's Like Reaching for the Moon," confirming the jazz axiom: 'Taint what you do, it's the way that you do it.

The songs got even better in late-summer, after John Scott Trotter—a former arranger for Hal Kemp who would become famous as Bing Crosby's music director on *Kraft Music Hall*—was hired as chief of recording for the American Record Corporation, the holding company that controlled Brunswick, Vocalion, Columbia, and other labels through most of the 1930s. Hammond considered Trotter merely a busybody executive. But the fact that Billie immediately recorded the three main songs from *Pennies from Heaven*, a film Trotter had just finished orchestrating, and was backed at the first session by Bunny Berigan, Trotter's buddy in the Kemp days, suggests that Hammond understated his contribution, perhaps because he resented Trotter's authority. Trotter was undoubtedly a square. Yet during his tenure, Holiday recorded new songs by Porter, Kern, and Berlin, as well as older tunes, like "I Must Have That Man," which, with Berlin's "This Year's Kisses," inaugurated the uncanny bond between Billie and Lester Young, whose tenor saxophone—borrowed from Hammond's favorite orchestra, the Basie band— invariably complements, echoes, spurs, and inspires her in one of the most gratifying, unusual, and far too brief musical collaborations of the past century.

My favorite of the records they made together was generated not by a classic of the songwriter's art, but by one of the dimmest numbers Holiday ever sang, "A Sailboat in the Moonlight," written by Carmen Lombardo and John Jacob Loeb ("Boo-Hoo!" was another of their creations) for the former's brother, Guy. When I first got to know the record, playing it endlessly, I thought it a fine melody, with pretty chord changes, and words that might be corny but didn't seem so bad when Lady Day delivered them. Then I chanced to find the sheet music at a midwestern bazaar; at home, I picked out the melody with one finger and was astonished at how different it was from what Holiday sang. Until that moment, I had not fully gauged how freely imaginative her embellishments could be. By ironing out a phrase here, retarding another there, raising this note, slurring that, she transformed a hopelessly banal and predictable melody into something personal, real, meaningful. When she and Lester "sail away/to Sweetheart Bay," riding the waves side by side, you've got to clamber on board.

Another profound example of her transformative powers comes from her last wartime Columbia session, on February 10, 1942, and an impossible song called, "It's a Sin to Tell a Lie," the subject six years earlier of one of Fats Waller's most extravagant burlesques. "I love you, I love you, I love you," he intoned contemptuously. And here comes Billie, declaiming, "I love you, yes I do, I love you," rhythmically pinning every syllable to its post and employing a Lestorian slur on the last "love." Do you believe her? How can you not?

By then, she had become a very different performer, a jazz star of high rank, proudly bearing the nickname, Lady Day, conferred upon her by Young (he called her mother Duchess). She in turn dubbed him Pres: Lester, she said, was to the saxophone what President Roosevelt was to the nation. Their musical association, however, was largely in the past. The very nature of her records had changed. Between 1937 and 1939, she recorded as often under her own name as under Wilson's; after the January 30, 1939, Wilson session, she recorded almost exclusively under her own name. The level of musicianship remained high and her own singing grew increasingly nuanced, but she was no longer one of the guys, waiting her turn. She was every inch a star.

When Lester had appeared on the "I Must Have That Man" session, he was 27, six years older than Billie, yet it was only his third time in a recording studio. His accompaniment was tenderly amorous, sometimes exuberantly so ("Me, Myself and I," "When You're Smiling"), but usually gentle and more delicate than the ardent honking and high-flying fancies he offered followers of Count Basie. The platonic tenderness that sheltered Lester and Billie could not, however, be sustained for long. In all, he appeared on five sessions with her in 1937, not including a couple of Basie broadcasts, five more in 1938, and only one per year between 1939 and 1941. Over time, his alcoholism and her addiction to heroin tore them apart, and though they occasionally shared the stage at Jazz at the Philharmonic concerts, producer Milt Gabler never used him on her Decca sides and producer Norman Granz, who had Lester under contract, never used him on her Clef and Verve records. They were reunited on one serene number in an unforgettable television broadcast, in 1957, and died two years later—Lester on March 15 (his widow prohibited her from singing at the funeral), and Billie on July 17, after nearly two months in a hospital, much of that time with a police guard at her door. She was, as Faulkner famously wrote of one of his own characters, "Doomed and knew it; accepted the doom without either seeking or fleeing it."

Tough as nails yet prone to abuse, Lady had long since become America's Little Sparrow (she and Edith Piaf were born in the same year), perhaps even better known for her woes than her music. And yet she had come a long way on her own terms. In the beginning, she played the Famous Door on 52nd Street for four days, having walked out when the owner told her not to socialize with white customers. At that time she had to contend with stage managers who complained that she sang too slow and with song publishers who griped that she took too many liberties. Her standing took a turn in 1939, working at Barney Josephson's Cafe Society and closing her sets with Abel Meeropol's vivid threnody about a lynching, "Strange Fruit." She returned to the Famous Door as a major draw—treated accordingly—and, ironically, something of an earth mother to white servicemen who spent shore leave listening to her. After recording "Strange Fruit" for Milt Gabler's Commodore, because Hammond wouldn't touch it, Holiday was taken up by some with political agendas. But she had her own reasons for sticking with that song for 20 years, making it her personal anthem, thrusting it in the teeth of people who thought they had come to be amused.

She had toured briefly with Basie and Artie Shaw, leaving the former, she claimed, because Hammond wanted her to sing more blues like Bessie Smith (maybe, maybe not, though Hammond told me a few weeks before his death that he much preferred Bessie), and the latter because of racism. Forget the South: New York's Hotel Lincoln insisted she use the freight elevator and the Old Gold cigarette company would not allow her to broadcast with Shaw's band. She retained her independence and spirit, living the life she chose, singing the music she loved in a style she invented. She did not suffer slights quietly: In 1946, she was signed to appear in her only feature film, with her idol Louis Armstrong, but, cast as a maid, she stormed off the set of *New Orleans* before it was completed. Melancholy themes had begun to loom over her repertoire, and they increased over time. No longer sailing in the moonlight in a sunbonnet blue and laughing at life, she sang of despair, longing, betrayal: "Gloomy Sunday," "Lover Man," "Travelin' Light," "Good Morning, Heartache," "Detour Ahead," "Don't Explain," "God Bless the Child."

She suffered for love, evidently indulging a masochism that sometimes got out of hand. It also bound her to drugs. In 1941, Holiday married a handsome hustler named Jimmy Monroe and began smoking opium. Then she moved in with trumpet player Joe Guy, who used heroin. She capitulated to an addiction that could not be tempered by a voluntary six-week hospital cure or a judge's 1947 decision to incarcerate her for a year and a day at the Federal Reformatory for Women in Alderson, West Virginia—the result of Billie's decision to plead guilty and not to testify against Guy, with whom she was busted. Guy, a musician of limited abilities, walked. Billie served her time and lost her cabaret card. That meant she could not work anyplace in New York where alcohol was sold, undermining her career and guaranteeing her return to narcotics. There were subsequent arrests and countless tabloid articles that almost always referred to her as "blues singer Billie Holiday."

She took up with a vicious pimp named John Levy (not to be confused with the bassist of that name who often performed with her), and then fulfilled the prophetic lyric of "Riffin' the Scotch": "Swapped the old one for a new one / Now the new one's breaking my heart / I jumped out of the fryin' pan / And right into the fire." Louis McKay was a low-level hoodlum whose one saving grace was that he lacked Levy's unreasoning violence. But he was a relentless exploiter, who squandered her money and used drugs to keep her under control. In 1956, Billie and McKay were busted in Philadelphia, and he convinced her to marry him to prevent her from testifying. That she could see through him, but loved him, is apparent from her desperately scribbled letters, almost always written on hotel stationery and occasionally quoting song lyrics (I have not attempted to replicate Holiday's quirky use of capitals, and have ventured a few guesses about punctuation):

Mr. McKay,
Let's face it you're not my husband. Not even my boyfriend. You have no time for me. Everything is your kids, Mildred or just anything comes before me so I am not important to you in any way. You have even made cracks about [some?] dirty bitches that meant

more to you than me. So why don't we come to some kind of understanding. Well you know. Just be my manager until after the Phila story. No I have no one else and don't want anyone. But Louie how much can I take. You're in New York two days and I, your wife, see you five minutes. So just lets be friends and forget it.

Lady

Louis when you left this morning I know you had no more feeling for me so lets get together, lets call this whole thing off. Your not happy with me and I am very unhappy. Thank you for everything you have done for me.

Lady Day

This is It
I've had it goodbye
Waited hoped and prayed but nothing goes my way. This is it, so long. Tried not to see but I am not blind to all the tricks you played on me. This is it. Oh well you say that I am dumb but how dumb can you get. This is it This is it This is it This is it. You can't be mine and someone else's too. What are you trying to do. This is it. Good bye.

On one occasion Billie had McKay tailed, and what she saw made her "feel sort of cheap and dirty." Had she lived, she undoubtedly would have sent him packing. Instead, he assumed control of her estate, making sure he was portrayed—by Billy Dee Williams, no less—as the romantic and devoted sole love of her life in the appalling movie *Lady Sings the Blues,* which didn't even use her voice, never mind her story. But then her voice *is* her story, the only one that counts, the one that can't be distorted by lovers or haters, exploiters or philanthropists, critics or fans. Her enchanted records tell the truth and nothing but the truth—indeed, more truth than most of us knew, if you pay attention to the alternate takes and ponder the risks she took, gliding too high for her range or, touchingly, casting for the right note on which to end. Lady Day at the summit of her art is as glorious now as 60 years ago, an imperishable fixture in the cultural life of America and the world.

[*Lady Day: The Complete Billie Holiday on Columbia 1933–1944,*
Columbia/Legacy, July 2001]

90 ❖ Mood Swings
(Tom Harrell)

Tom Harrell's unevenness as an improviser and composer has generated one of jazz's most consistent dramas over the past 25 years. When the planets come into alignment in a Harrell solo; when all is focused and driven and he knows where he is headed but takes his time getting there, diverting himself with melodic fragments and oddly accented color notes; when his tone is warm, moist, supple, and sure, despite an attack that can be downright fierce, it is tempting to throw caution to the winds and proclaim him the finest trumpet player of his generation. But then there are those other moments, when he struggles to find the target, when his influences predominate or he succumbs to a drab, almost sentimental lilt, underscored by his affection for samba and other placating Latin beats. Both Harrells are on display on his new album, *Paradise* (RCA Victor), and they vied for attention last week at the Village Vanguard.

The drama finds at least a partial exposition in his much-discussed lifelong battle with schizophrenia and the medication it requires—a subject treated with remarkable lightness in the punning titles of several Harrell pieces, including "Upswing," "Mood Swing," "Bear That in Mind," "Wishing Well," "Blue News," "Viable Blues," "Rapture," and "Glass Mystery," which recalls Bud Powell's "Glass Enclosure." And it finds a corollary in his bandstand presence, stock still, never even tapping a toe, then raising horn to lips, and BAM!—off to the races. Harrell's intensity, musically and personally, may be one reason so many musicians play with daring and concentration in his bands. Joe Lovano, Danilo Perez, Billy Hart, Kenny Werner, Don Braden, Dewey Redman, Greg Tardy, and others, obviously do not need Harrell to play well, but they have all recorded some of their finest work on his watch.

After a big band apprenticeship with Woody Herman and Stan Kenton, Harrell made his name during long stays with Horace Silver in the 1970s and Phil Woods in the 1980s. The Silver period was formative. After Blue Mitchell left the Silver quintet in 1964, the pianist spent a decade trying out trumpeters (Woody Shaw, Charles Tolliver, Randy Brecker, Cecil Bridgewater) before settling on Harrell and featuring him on the *Silver 'N* series—five LPs recorded between 1975 and 1979, which climaxed his tenure with Blue Note and, coincidentally, brought the label itself to a four-year hiatus. (*Silver 'N Strings* was the last Blue Note session until 1983, when the company was brought under the EMI umbrella and reawakened with George Russell's *The African Game*, a factoid I gleaned from Michael Cuscuna and Michel Ruppli's *The Blue Note Label*, published by Greenwood for a sobering $135; notify your library.) Though marred by heavy-handed didacticism in song titles and lyrics, these long neglected albums—all out of print—offer shrewd writing and playing while tracing Harrell's progress from a melodic but tentative solo on *Silver 'N Brass*'s "Kissin' Cousins" (he was 28) to a breakout statement on "The Soul and Its Expression" (*Silver 'N Strings*): He follows a ferocious Larry Schneider tenor solo with an intricate figure, cannily developed, and leaves his several influences in the dust.

Harrell has himself spoken of multiple personalities, and at least two dominate the early period: the cheerfully rounded lyrical exuberance of Clifford Brown and Blue Mitchell ("The Mohican and the Great Spirit" on *Silver 'N Percussion* is a good example) and the vehement fury of Freddie Hubbard and Woody Shaw ("Assimilation" on *Silver 'N Wood*). Sometimes, both approaches merge, lighting a fire on "Togetherness" (*Silver 'N Voices*; Bob Berg's tenor is also inflamed) and running to wry and moody complexity on the same album's "Mood for Maude." When he joined Woods, Harrell's stylistic confidence peaked, yet two or three Milesian personalities emerged in his own records—the skittery Miles of the charged arpeggios, melodic shards, and rhythmic displacement ("Eons," *Sail Away*); the unearthly, balladic Miles of the careful aphorisms and fat sound ("Shapes," *Time's Mirror*); the anarchic Miles of the drone chords, dynamic change-ups, and eight-beat rocking ("Story," *Stories*). Harrell assimilated each approach—you rarely think Miles when listening to him. On the exceptional 1990 *Form*, where he is exuberantly backed by Lovano, Perez, Charlie Haden, and Paul Motian, his trumpet ghosts are, at best, sampled—I mean to imply something more like current electronic appropriation than traditional jazz borrowing—never indulged.

Yet Harrell doesn't come alive as a rounded figure until the RCA Victor series that began with *Labyrinth*, in 1996, and has continued with *The Art of Rhythm*, *Time's Mirror*, and the current *Paradise*. RCA does not do much with jazz but has given Harrell his head—permitting him guest soloists, a big band, a string quartet and harp, allowing him to boldly advance as a composer. Despite a too-frequent reliance on Latin rhythms, a lot of ground is covered and his penchant for sampling is exponentially increased as his tunes employ fragments that he promptly transmutes. This is not an instance of eclecticism—a little this, a little that—but rather a freely associative drawing upon whatever melodies, riffs, and vamps float around in his memory bank.

Like many of his themes, *Labyrinth*'s "Samba Mate" has a vague familiarity—hard to pin down, almost generic, yet rendered distinct; it evidently has Kenny Werner thinking of other tunes, because he hardly starts his solo before flashing a measure from the *Nutcracker*. "Majesty," an overtly classical piece, could pass as the love child of Grieg and Villa Lobos. A particularly poignant Harrell solo is heard on "Blue in One," a slow blues with substitute changes that begins with solemn ensemble chords over a lonely cymbal beat, which soon fills out into plush drums as the nonet heads into an undulating, boppish, big band theme of a kind Woody Herman took to the bank 30 years ago. After Gary Smulyan's excellent baritone sax solo, the drums retreat into a brief rest before Harrell makes his entrance with a melodic paraphrase of his theme—a five-note motive that typifies the direction of his four ensuing choruses, each designed with cautionary elegance. If the easy pacing, rich mid-register, and occasional phrase or two recall Miles, the poetic effect suggests, as Ira Gitler once observed, the snug introvert ruminations of the overlooked Tony Fruscella.

The Art of Rhythm is not as consistent but is perhaps more personal. Harrell plays only with the ensemble on "Caribe," a de facto concerto for Dewey Redman that suggests Ellingtonian precision; for all I know, Harrell wrote it 30 years ago, but it sounds as though it were conceived for Redman and that's the point. It goes from a throat-clearing Coltrane setting to a groggy steel drum theme that is, in turn, opposed by ominous ensemble chords, before Redman's yearning tenor takes off on its pitch-stretching trip. The big band album, *Time's Mirror*, is not as expressively imagined; half the arrangements date from the 1960s and often reflect Stan Kenton's influence, albeit with a leavening wit. "Autumn Leaves" incorporates an appealing counter melody and a strong Alex Foster tenor solo, and "Chasin' the Bird" fills out the harmonies, intensifying the contrapuntal theme. Some of the writing, though, feels dated and oppressive.

With the release of *Paradise*, Harrell's RCAs suddenly seem to parallel the *Silver 'N* cycle—happily lacking lyrics, singers, and advice to young people. It isn't just the changing instrumentation or project-like productions. Harrell's strings echo Silver's, as do his several ostinatos. The opening sections of Silver's "Empathy" or "Optimism," before the vocals, would blend right in with Harrell's work, as would the strings/harp interplay on "Progress Through Dedication and Discipline." Yet while Silver also wrote pieces called "The Tranquilizer Suite" and "The Mental Sphere," his work rarely looks into corners the trumpeter regularly examines. So it is disappointing when Harrell lightens the material, as he did during a Vanguard set, giving way to the samba and letting saxophonist Jimmy Greene provide the heat. Harrell was merely polite on "Baroque Steps," one of the album's headiest tracks. His one aggressive solo of the set, on flugelhorn, forced the drummer to abandon what had become a tranquilizing Latin foundation.

The album has its longueurs, too, but overcomes them with a suitelike design, as vaguely similar melodies and scoring echo each other over the long haul. "Daybreak" is the first but not the last theme that suggests Silver's long-stepping melodies that wind around like a carousel. It also suggests the steel drum theme of Harrell's "Caribe." After a rest, the band takes up the head in roaring hard-bop fashion and Harrell plays with cool wrath. "Baroque Steps" is startling: The ostinato, combining an eight-beat figure for cello and three-note counter vamp by the other strings, precedes a darker theme with two parts, one sorta Asian, the other sorta Middle Eastern, before coming home with a howdy from the bridge of Monk's "Epistrophe." Early Silver is also recalled: The ostinato and theme, for example, are reminiscent of the piano comping and theme of "Sayonara Blues." Harrell's meditative improv is perfectly matched to the material.

"Nighttime" is a bit too sumptuous, almost genteel; Harrell offers occasional high-calorie notes that suggest Bobby Hackett, which is fine, but not here. Xavier Davis's piano is cocktailish and the strings reprise would have served beautifully for a Douglas Sirk movie. At 11 minutes, it lumbers. Toward the end, a passage for flugel and rhythm restores candor, and Harrell plays a few notes that hurt the way Miles hurts on *Sketches of Spain* before the movie music returns. The last third of the piece wrestles between his fever and the strings' damp cloth. Wah-wah guitar undermines "Wind Chant," though the head (a vague nod to Silver's "Tokyo Blues") sustains a feeling of unity that becomes more pronounced in the terrifically foreboding strings ostinato at the start of "Paradise Spring." This passage too quickly dissolves into a 6/8 clave beat, but, dark unto himself, Harrell revokes its feeling in his questing, softly motific solo. The two-part "Morning Prayer" is somber yet funny. The first section, written entirely for the strings, has a forlorn and shivery theme ending in mustache-twirling tremolos. The idea, according to Harrell, is to contrast "despair and hope," as for example Don Ellis did in "Despair to Hope" and Weather Report did in "Orange Lady"—comedians file jokes by subject and Harrell references melodies by programmatic ideas. Naturally, Part Two is an upbeat samba, charming and almost serene. But you know that isn't the end of the story. You just don't know what the next chapter will be.

[*Village Voice*, 3 July 2001]

91 ❖ Nashville
(Ted Nash)

Eclecticism has been so much the norm in jazz during the past 30 years that you expect just about every player who comes along to have one foot in jazz proper and the other tapping elsewhere: Cuba or the Balkans or Argentina, or if not a geographical locale then a time period, like that of ragtime or swing or r&b, or another idiom entirely, classical or hip hop or gospel. Not to overstate, but has any other work proved more philosophically on the money than Ellington's posthumously released *Afro-Eurasian Eclipse*, the suite he said was inspired by McLuhan's prediction that no culture would be able to retain its identity, and that no individual, in Ellington's words, will "know exactly who is enjoying the shadow of whom?"

Carla Bley deserves credit as an early brewer of musical influences for her work on Gary Burton's *A Genuine Tong Funeral* and Charlie Haden's heartfelt frolic, *Liberation Music Orchestra*, not to mention her magnum magnum, *Escalator over the Hill*, which someday I plan on hearing in its entirely, though not yet, Lord, not yet. Bley colonized styles—from Weimar Germany to Spain and Asia—that became standard sources for those who followed, not least Holland's deft, daft jester, Willem Breuker, who pursued them seriously but also parodied them to expose the eclectic habit as little more than a fad for a disoriented generation. The phrase "world music" had not yet been coined and jazz players, like the peripatetic Zusaan Kali Fasteau, had yet to acquire vast collections of flutes and bells. In those days, you were playing world music if you hired an "extra" percussionist, and world musicians paid homage to every American improviser.

These days, world music is fully domesticated and, according to a recent *Times* article, Europeans—and maybe South Americans, Asians, Australians, Eskimos—think American jazz musicians suck. Of course, they do not suck. They are simply lonely and looking for love, even if they have to turn to travel in time or space to find it. Having exhausted the chords and the modes, they want something new: a tango circa 1913, a freilach circa 1924, a Platters hit circa 1955—anything but "How High the Moon," unless, like Abbey Lincoln, they can do it in French. At the same time, none of these gambits are likely to make for lifetime commitments, so we get a lot of projects and movements, bands conceived to try this or that. John Coltrane had only one band at a time. Today, he might have as many as Dave Douglas.

One promising new project is Ted Nash's band Odeon, a name absent from the cover of his CD, *Sidewalk Meeting* (Arabesque), but featured prominently in its May 31, 2001, performance in the Jazz Composers Collective series at the New School. The music could serve as a Rorschach: tango, klezmer, second-line rhythms, impressionism, Ellington voicings, marches, the Near East, the Middle East, the Far East, and, representing the West, country music and jazz itself. Sometimes it sounds as predictably unpredictable as you would expect, but its best work is as smoothly blended as overpriced Scotch.

Odeon should dramatically raise the profile of one of New York's eternal sidemen. Nash is a first-class saxophonist, whose infallible technique is most often found melding with kindred reeds in big bands, for which he has also composed. An erstwhile prodigy (and the son of trombonist Dick Nash), he was touring in his mid-teens, paternally displayed by Lionel Hampton, Louie Bellson, and Don Ellis before nailing a chair in Mel Lewis's Vanguard Orchestra for 10 years and then moving to the Lincoln Center Jazz Orchestra. Seated, he serves the band; standing, the audience—he's a solid and dependable player. In 1991, he and the three musicians with whom he soon helped found the Jazz Collective made a quartet album, *Out of This World*, which proved that he knew his Coltrane. His 1999 Double Quartet album, *Rhyme & Reason*, combines the Jazz Collective with a string quartet and is more affecting and individual, and exceedingly well written, yet lacks the kind of urgency or risks that incite more than passive admiration.

Odeon opens the windows, airing out the place, its very instrumentation forcing a reconsideration of its eclectic assets. Nash plays clarinets and saxophones, combining the sensibilities of modern jazz and chamber music; Wycliffe Gordon plays tuba and plunger-mute trombone, which invokes a jazz world so prehistoric it didn't have access to a bass; Miri Ben-Ari plays violin with a romanticism verging on the rhapsodic; Bill Schimmel plays accordion with a shine that evades the nostalgia clichés with which—even in a world of Zydeco, avant-gardists Guy Klucevsek and Andrea Parkins, and the Piazzolla craze—it is often associated; and Matt Wilson and (on the record only) Jeff Ballard play drums that establish bearings and connect the parts. The band had one problem in concert that is mitigated on the album, a matter of sound mixing: Tuba vamps were so loud that their repetitions sucked the air out of the arrangements and the room. Even the record has passages that make you realize how relieved the bandleaders of 1926 must have been to discover the quietly elegant bass.

The most successful tracks are those that Nash arranged but did not compose. Indeed, "Premiere Rhapsodie" and "Amad" are too good to miss. Debussy wrote the former in 1910 as a conservatory exam for clarinet and piano, and later orchestrated it as a clarinet concerto. Sue me, but at pretty near the same length as Debussy's, Nash's version is less redundant and more eventful. His resourceful voicings are ever-changing, and the instrumentation itself evokes all kinds of tangents: for example, Gordon's *ya-ya* (as opposed to *wa-wa*) trombone calls to mind Tyree Glenn's brief but memorable stay with Ellington; and Nash's phrasing of the key motif creates an accord between Debussy and Kurt Weill that would probably have pissed them both off. The arrangement assigns equal parts to all five players—a neat trick for a clarinet concerto. Nash's tenor sax has an elated bite, rumbling within the confines of chords that sustain the original harmonic plane while pushing at the borders of free jazz—a neat trick for Debussy. The secondary motif, the one that was lifted for "Some Day My Prince Will Come" ("how thrilling that moment will be") has never sounded so, well, Snow White.

"Amad," the climactic punch in Ellington's *Far East Suite*, is wittily faithful but tosses off its own allusions with shrewd blends that go further east. The accordion introduction fuses an Ellington figure with Liszt's Sonata in B minor. Wilson's drums are perfectly in synch, driving the constantly shifting Ellington melodies. Unlike the original, which is almost entirely composed until the closing trombone solo, Nash's version opens quickly for a vivaciously bowed violin invention, bouncing over the thematic vamp, followed by equally effective solos on bass clarinet and accordion. Gordon's tuba—no trombone here—maintains the gait in a dialogue with drums, and ends it with two harrumphs.

The most appealing of Nash's five originals is the title piece, "Sidewalk Meeting," which is so generically country or gospel—in any case, Southern—it may remind you of any number of tunes; one listener asked me if it was Patsy Cline's "Why Can't He Be You," and damned if there isn't a resemblance. It opens with a super trombone cadenza—virtuoso plunger stuff with trilling growls and chortles, funny and brazen—that would have gotten Gordon a job with Ellington, who loved novelty bits. He comes out of it to visit *wa-wa* (as opposed to *ya-ya*) Nashville, backed by bass clarinet. In concert, Odeon climaxed in New Orleans with a Dixieland reprise, but on the record the Dixie segment is heard in a separate track. "Tango Sierra" is also attractive, more so in performance, merging gypsy violin with klezmer clarinet and ending with what could pass for a French apache dance.

The rest is less effective. "Summer Night in the Deep South" was fired up in concert by Ben-Ari's violin; it's a slow march, a dirge, prone to nostalgia and intriguing mostly for a breathlike accordion vamp, which inhales and exhales as only a squeezebox can. Monk's "Bemsha Swing" has moments, most of them in Gordon's responses to Nash's tenor, but his tuba underscores a second-line beat and cadences that are banal compared to those Monk had in mind. "Reverie" is a handsomely played duet for clarinet and accordion, and finishes with Ellingtonian tremolos, but feels more like an exercise than the Debussy exam. "Jump Line" spends too much time marching in place to a tuba vamp, yet comes alive with a dancelike jollity in passages when it breaks free. At its best, *Sidewalk Meeting* does more than break free. It makes you think of the possibilities Odeon has yet to explore. It recharges the eclectic impulse and mandates a follow-up.

[*Village Voice*, 11 July 2001]

92 ❖ *Minnie the Moocher's Revenge (JVC 2001)*

Say this of JVC: the plot changes annually. It may look the same on paper, may list toward the same artists, suffer the same limitations, and capitulate to the same distractions, but George Wein's flagship festival manages to take different turns each summer. If I am especially conscious of past vagaries, triumphs, subplots, and themes, contrived or otherwise, it is because midway through this edition, I realized that I had been reporting on the behemoth variously known as Newport–New York, Kool, and JVC for 30 years, and perused a few of my old reviews. Two seem most relevant: In 1991, the cast focused on under-40s and over-60s, leaving the boomers out in the cold, not for the last time; in 2000, every event paid its respects to the past. The current edition reversed both trends.

Identifying bona fide boomer jazz heroes requires some precision. I refer to those who came into their own when we first started to listen, as opposed to those who, though slightly older or even younger, were already established parts of our inheritance. Dewey Redman, who turned 70 in May but had no national reputation until 1967, makes the cut; Phil Woods, who turns 70 in November but was a star long before 1960, does not. Boomer heroes (notably Redman, Wayne Shorter, Keith Jarrett, Jack DeJohnette, Chick Corea, Wayne Shorter, Michael Brecker, and did I mention Wayne Shorter?) accounted for most of the expectations and red meat at JVC 2001. Jazz's past was evoked, but not fetishized. At a tribute to Coltrane keyed to the 75th anniversary of his birth, for example, no one ever mentioned John Coltrane or played any of his music in his style.

A very boomeresque motif developed. Never in my experience at a jazz festival was so much audience participation encouraged. Credit it to the unacknowledged influence of either Minnie the Moocher or Pete Seeger. I counted no fewer than four singalongs and four clap-fests, not to mention practiced routines in which the audience was obliged to stand and whoop for five minutes in order to get encores already scheduled. We received no payment for our efforts.

The major concerts got under way at Kaye Playhouse, with "Who's on First?" Repeating (sometimes verbatim, down to the patter) the Los Angeles engagement that Blue Note issued last year, Bob Dorough and Dave Frishberg alternated individual sets and duets. Entertaining as the album is, the two must be seen to be fully appreciated: Frishberg, the short Brooks-blazer Midwestern Jew who honed his neuroses during long stays on both coasts, writing and singing songs to fend off rude times and highfalutin clichés; and Dorough, the grinning, ponytail-wearing Arkansan beanpole, writing and singing songs to celebrate the dawn of a new day, invulnerable to absurdity. They have been friends for four decades, co-composed "I'm Hip," and worked on *Schoolhouse Rock*. Each began as an accomplished bop pianist and celebrates jazz heroes in the language of jazz fans. Frishberg is knowingly funny, if occasionally saccharine; Dorough is accidentally funny, if occasionally overbearing.

On his own, Frishberg rambled from an understated piano medley of Harold Arlen to several of his best known portraits—"My Attorney Bernie," "Quality Time," meditations on Zoot and Bix, the brilliantly arch yet nostalgic "I Want to Be a Sideman," and a new song, "The Hopi Way," which derives much of its humor from the melodic/verbal surprise of the tagline, countering a list of temptations and woes with the singer's improbable allegiance to the Hopi creed. Dorough, for his part, patrolled the stage waving branchlike arms, switching between pianos, milking the audience, and having the time of his life, croaking and twanging benchmark numbers: "Devil May Care," "Nothing Like You," musical settings to official prose (parking summons, laundry ticket), tributes to Bird, Billie, and Bechet (Don Nelson's affecting "Something for Sidney"), and homages to Hoagy Carmichael—"Hong Kong Blues" and "Baltimore Oriole." They wrapped up with a duet on "Conjunction Junction," Dorough conducting the audience on the refrain. The crowd, apparently suffering from stage fright, was eerily high-pitched.

On the second night, instead of one of the usual swing or guitar evenings, Wein allowed Joshua Redman and Eric Reed to bring to Kaye a touch of Gen-X modernism, which amounts to the modernism of mid-career Coltrane and Oscar Peterson. The event was borderline disastrous. Redman's quartet, with the splendid drummer Gregory Hutchinson, spent 80 minutes playing his new CD, *Passage of Time*, which itself clocks in at under an hour. Dazzling cadenzas, unison tenor/piano themes, and the accretion of drones, fragmented figures, several meters (I think one long passage was in seven) provided moments of tension and variety. But such attractions were undermined by the increasingly evident pre-planning of the thing—each passage fussily worked out until the life was leached out and the climaxes, accented with heroic body English, producing more false endings than *Gone with the Wind*. Reed's septet played much of the same material from a recent Lincoln Center concert and his new CD, *Happiness*, when he wasn't indulging in lengthy introductions. He is a facile pianist who can approach profundity, as on "Three Dances," but his compositions are banal, sometimes patronizingly so, as in tributes to African American women, especially "Black Beauty" (the name of one of Ellington's early masterpieces). I didn't last the set.

The third night, inexplicably titled "Cabaret Jazz Hall of Fame," offered a suave set by Freddie Cole, his combo, and his royal timbre; followed by Blossom Dearie and her trio, mining more laughs from "My Attorney Bernie" than its composer with her faux-innocent phrasing and high-pitched voice. She fared best overall. Act two was more of a provocation: Ronny Whyte, who wore a white dinner jacket but chose to scat "Buttons and Bows" for the occasion, sent me racing to the lobby; it was my understanding that JVC provides a safe haven from lounge acts. Then it was time for 85-year-old Joe Bushkin. Jack Kleinsinger, our voluble host, uncharacteristically announced that he would turn over the introduction to Judy Garland, who led off an entertaining 10-minute film in which Bushkin spoke of his life amid clips with her, Tommy Dorsey, Sinatra, Crosby, Armstrong, and others. At a normal program, the lights would then have risen to reveal the man himself; instead they revealed Kleinsinger for another introduction. Bushkin had had enough. He walked out and later made a rude remark about the majordomo that induced more gasps than laughs. Yet he played splendidly in his pop 1950s Teddy Wilson-at-cocktail-hour style, lush and spry; sang his two hit songs; told anecdotes mostly of the war; and started a medley from *High Society* that ignored "True Love" in favor of "Love for Sale" and "The Lady Is a Tramp."

"A Love Supreme: Remembering John Coltrane," at Carnegie, offered another kind of drama—waiting for some acknowledgment of Coltrane, which never came. A totally silent Roy Hargrove led his sterling quintet through the festival's single worst morass of acoustic madness. The sound was so boxy you had to strain just to penetrate the echoes and hear the notes. The first piece, which may actually have been by Coltrane, defeated me completely. But switching to flugelhorn for a few exceedingly laid-back ballads—two that Coltrane recorded ("I Wish I Knew," "Nature Boy") and one he didn't ("I'm Glad There Is You")—Hargrove penetrated the mist. Few musicians, Gen-X or other, can embrace standards with Hargrove's polish; at JVC, only Keith Jarrett matched him. I have no doubt that he could pull off, Clifford-like or, better still, Coltrane-like, an entire album of ballads. Altoist Jesse Davis played ferociously, though most of his efforts disappeared into the ceiling, and pianist Larry Willis offered acute comping and a lithe, Tatumesque touch. (He was exceptional later in the festival, as a member of Jerry Gonzalez and Fort Apache.)

JVC's most ambitious debut, the oddest in some time, was Slide Hampton's arrangement of *A Love Supreme*, performed by Jon Faddis and the Carnegie Hall Jazz Band with guest soloist Michael Brecker. The very idea was daunting, but Hampton pulled it off by ignoring religious connotations, focusing on the eight- and 12-bar themes from parts two and three, and permitting Brecker free reign in a cadenza that acknowledged only the gods of ravenous virtuosity. It was impossible, on one hearing, to grasp all the intricacies; I'm not sure how the first section—a 10-minute episode beginning with a choir of winds, a vamp, a percussion transition, and piping Faddis top-notes—relates to the original. The delayed arrival of Coltrane's first-movement ostinato introduced Brecker, who played with the rhythm section. "Resolution" was almost shocking, with baritone saxophone fronting stark voicings topped with pitched brasses, the eight-bar figure played in unison with as many different endings as Coltrane indicated and possibly more. The long Brecker cadenza replaced penitential passion with razzle-dazzle showmanship, complete with double-note ripples that reminded me of the old Varitone electric sax, except Brecker gets his effects without help. Considered religiously, if we must, the approach was less Coltrane than Ellington, who put virtuoso display, including an elaborate drum solo, at the center of "In the Beginning God." Brecker had the audience on its feet cheering as the ensemble went into "Miles' Mode," featuring short solos by CHJB saxophonists (none of whom invoked the once ubiquitous Coltrane style) and another powerhouse display from Brecker. Indeed, the concert resembled a religious service in the number of times the congregation took to its feet. Still, it was not a good idea for Faddis to ask the audience to sing "A Love Supreme" with the band, which I swear he did.

The boomers got to worship at greater length a few nights later, as

Keith Jarrett, Gary Peacock, and Jack DeJohnette filled Carnegie—something I suspect no other piano trio could pull off. I had not seen Jarrett, never a favorite of mine, in more than 20 years, since the days of the grumpy hour-long meditations replete with blues clichés that you found either transporting or numbing. But last year's *Whisper Not* made me regret my assumptions and dig through many other albums of standards he recorded in the '90s; I can still live without the earlier records, including the quartet with Dewey Redman, but I will never again underestimate an artist who can make me listen to "Love Is a Many-Splendored Thing." So I awaited this performance eagerly and, though there were none of the triple somersaults heard on, for example "Groovin' High," I was not disappointed. The trio is spectacular. Records, however, have an advantage: You don't have to watch him levitate from the bench like beer foam, gyrating his hips and swiveling toward the audience with a grimace indistinguishable from a grin or vice versa. Alas, live and on records, you have to put up with his vocal accompaniment—a keening *eeeeehhhhhh* that is no more pleasing than Glenn Gould's—and a constant regimen of Peacock solos that reminded me of Ellington's comparison of bass solos to TV commercials.

But from the opening "Green Dolphin Street" on, the music paid its way. The sound was acceptable, too, thanks in part to DeJohnette's ingenious restraint. Jarrett may not be the only pianist of his era who can embrace "I'm Getting Sentimental over You" at a relaxed medium tempo, indulging the melody while avoiding cocktailisms or Bill Evans devices, but is anyone else as convincing? The energy, poise, flow of ideas, and determination to mine the changes in a thoroughly modern context suffused that song and the others—"What's New?," "Lover," "Honeysuckle Rose," "Last Night When We Were Young"—with a heady mixture of discipline and originality. He played "Yesterdays" slowly and then jauntily, dramatizing the piece twice over, and closing with a quietly elegant finish. On "Honeysuckle Rose," arranged to begin with quasi-stride (as on the *Whisper Not* version of "Wrap Your Troubles in Dreams"), DeJohnette used brushes and took off on a rocking march-like solo perfectly appropriate for the piece. Only an untitled free improvisation got away from them. A medium blues caused the Brubeckian audience to explode with naked adoration, acceding to the ritualized routine of encores—for which time was permitted by limiting the second set to half an hour.

As the audience cheered for more, members of the trio hugged each other, which was sort of cute. Members of Chick Corea's and Wayne Shorter's bands did the same; it's a boomer thing. Corea's New Trio, as he calls it, refers to the fact that although he has been working with bassist Avishai Cohen and drummer Jeff Ballard for four years, he conjoined them as a trio eight months ago. The acoustics at Avery Fisher promised to serve the band pretty well, but Cohen had a faulty pickup that, incredibly, the players could not hear. Even after the audience protested the distortion—every bass note was accompanied by a loud blat—the musicians expressed surprise. Corea got off a good line, though: "You want to listen with headphones?" After a couple of numbers, the bass mike was turned off, an improvement if you preferred piano-drums duets. Not until the last piece did someone arrive on stage with a mike. Maybe he had to go to Carnegie to borrow it.

The set had moments, but no passion. You never wonder why Jarrett is playing a particular song—the performance tells you. But Corea turned "I Hear a Rhapsody" into an exercise: rubato theme, much dialoguing with Cohen, who was all over the bass (an occasional four-beat walk would be a relief), tempo changes—all of it light, bright, and slightly preening. Even at his best, Corea is rarely emotional. The pleasure he affords is basically that of exceptional musicianship. "Life Line," the final piece, ended with Corea and Cohen picking up cowbells and sticks to join in Ballard's drum solo, and it was fun, truly, more so than the sing-along on "Spain," with Corea playing phrases on piano and the audience la-di-dahing responses. Hi-de-hi-de-hi-de-ho!

There is no more beautiful or pined-for sight in jazz than Wayne Shorter holding a tenor saxophone, especially if he means to play it. Following Corea and receiving a standing ovation just for showing up, he did. Surrounded by the uncannily supportive piano, bass, and drums of Danilo Perez, John Patitucci, and Brian Blade, he created a spellbinding hour, brimming with feeling and pleasurable apprehension. Although the rhythm team never sounded remotely like Herbie Hancock, Ron Carter, and Tony Williams, it re-created the kind of suspense that made the second Miles Davis Quintet a revelation—not merely backing the soloist but collaborating fully on every measure. The result was true quartet music, driven by spontaneity, impulse, and a shared commitment. Shorter achieved what Joshua Redman attempted, an organic whole.

They opened with Shorter's adaptation of a Sibelius theme, "Valse Triste," and although his tenor lacked the power of his epochal '60s work, it found its way with the wasteless grace that is the hallmark of his mature style. After the debacle at Lincoln Center a few years ago and the sometimes narcoleptic duets with Hancock, his recommitment to the tenor and acoustic jazz would be reason enough to pat him on the back, but excuses were not necessary. The key responsibility of a musician is to keep it interesting, and Shorter knows how. His shy, tentative, gingerly designed phrases, occasionally interrupted by a roar or a siren arpeggio banking into the clouds, were etched with sure narrative logic. The piece itself accelerated and decelerated, with Perez following his lead, sidling into a solo with equal deliberation, and then relaying the spotlight to bass and drums. Shorter once remarked that composing is the same as improvising, only slower. "Valse Triste," melding the two, ran about 15 minutes without a false step. Even the hall's sound was bright and clear.

Although Shorter's compositional style is easily recognized, his titles, like Monk's, tend to blur. Interestingly, the one piece everyone recognized was his most recent, "Aung San Suu Kyi," introduced on the Hancock duets CD, and the only piece he played on soprano; the audience erupted when Perez played the introductory chords. Shorter performed it with more vitality and rhythmic definition than on the record, expanding on the theme with stop-and-go concentration. Like Bill Evans used to do with bassists, he relayed the lead to Perez so deftly that he denied himself applause. Thirty-five years ago, his solos seemed like a respite after Davis's soul-baring candor. Now Shorter's the soul-barer, mining the material with repeated notes, limpid asides, and sudden flurries. He has recast "Masquelero," sustaining the third note of the opening phrase, but the piece seemed stillborn, taking its time being born in a de facto dialogue between Shorter and Blade, and never quite delivering on the promise. Even here, however, the cohesion of the quartet sustained interest, intuiting directions. It was like walking through a dark room, feeling your way to the light, then slipping into the dark for good.

Blade kept time with hand patterns on "Atlantis," which began with arco bass and had Perez citing "Aung San." Played at a yawningly slow tempo, it did not induce yawns because after wondering where it was going, you realized it was already there. Like "Nefertiti," it was a vehicle for the rhythm players. Shorter stood out front, but in repeating the theme he was really the background, until the last note, resolved with a lovely consonance. After ritual hugs and standing cheers, he reached back to the Blue Note womb—from which so many jazz boomers were yanked into life—for "Juju." As Perez pummeled the keys with crossed hands and Blade, who may be at the forefront of Gen-X drummers, set off assorted fireworks, Shorter played his busiest solo of the evening, only without dynamics—reclusive, enigmatic, alluring. Imagine the old "Juju" phrased like the old "Infant Eyes," and you get an idea not only of this number but of the entire set.

Last year, I demurred on Diana Krall because I was on the fence; I've now got my feet on the ground but am demurring again until her new CD is released. The concert was very retro and very lush, with orchestrations for strings by Johnny Mandel (stately) and Claus Ogerman (predictable), and Krall was often compelling, not least in her piano solos. Gladys Knight arrived half an hour late, but once she got going all was forgiven; except for an unnecessary guest saxophonist, her 90-minute set—which included a vaudeville routine with her sole remaining Pip—was show business heaven. Yes, she could probably sing jazz, but her old material is so good she doesn't need to.

One of the festival's best new ideas was to run parallel evenings at Birdland, enabling players who can't fill the major halls to sell out a club that enshrines bebop and its derivations. A Phil Woods quintet plus guest Johnny Griffin and a Dewey Redman quartet plus guest Sonny Fortune delivered as expected. Woods revived a couple of pieces you don't often hear anymore ("Bohemia after Dark," "Little Niles"), eliciting from pianist Bill Charlap an inventive sparkle intermittently apparent on his own recent CD. After Fortune deconstructed "What's New?" Redman went from an Ornette stop-and-go piece—inadvertently demonstrating how close the Coleman and Adderley legacies really are, at least from this vantage—to a backbeat rocker worthy of your neighborhood bar, during which he wandered around tables getting everyone to clap. It was that kind of night, that kind of festival. A boomer thing.

[*Village Voice*, 17 July 2001]

93 ❖ *Go Tell It on the Mountain (David S. Ware)*

Let's be bold: The David S. Ware Quartet is the best small band in jazz today. I realize that I'll almost certainly hear another quartet, or trio or quintet or octet, this week or next, that will make me want to backpedal. But every time I see Ware's group or return to the records, it flushes the competition from memory. Besides, hyperbole is so much fun and I do it so rarely, no? Thus, with the first set of last week's two-night Blue Note gig resounding in my ears, along with a new CD, *Corridors & Parallels* (Aum Fidelity), I effortlessly banish from consciousness every other bandleader who might inspire a like-minded leap of faith and stoke the experience of listening to Ware and wanting—in that interval at least—to hear nobody else.

His sound alone is enough to clear the room of contenders. It is huge, big enough to house a large family, a parrot, and half the holdings of the Metropolitan Museum of Art. Size is not and has never been a sine qua non for tenor saxophonists; Coleman Hawkins had an extrovert sound and Lester Young an introvert sound, and yet they are equals in God's view. Nor is size per se of much value if it isn't unique, personal, inviolable. Ware's sound is virtually unrelated to the roomy traditions of soul tenors, honking tenors, or deep-chested boudoir ballad tenors. It derives from the classic, free, often vociferous tradition of Ben Webster as filtered through the 1960s trinity of Rollins, Coltrane, and Ayler, all of whose shadows can be traced—Rollins in Ware's capacious low register, Coltrane in his high overblowing, Ayler and Webster in the grit that coats his every note with a sandstone finish, all four in the euphoric tenacity he calls bliss.

Shadows, however, are only shadows. Ware's distinct sound and Holy Roller fervor were evident when he was 25, performing in Cecil Taylor's 1974 Carnegie Hall big band. He became more assured touring with Taylor's working unit and Andrew Cyrille's Maono, promising a formidable career that suddenly petered out. For several years, he drove a cab and worked out his next move, which took shape in the late 1980s, when he organized a quartet for a record date. He chose pianist Matthew Shipp, who was completely unknown; bassist William Parker, with whom he had worked in Taylor's band; and drummer Marc Edwards, whose chair was subsequently taken over by Whit Dickey, Susie Ibarra, and, at present, Guillermo E. Brown, the quartet's most aggressive percussionist. A series of astonishing albums followed, among them *Flight of I*, *Third-Ear Recitation*, *Godspellized*, and *Go See the World*.

Although his style combines high-energy free improvisation, brazenly distended ballads, and "godspellized" bliss pieces, Ware communicates easily and readily, his improvisations suggesting a nearly vocalized urgency intensified by a virtuoso attack. Too much downtown time got him pegged as a shocker, but he has always had broader appeal; it simply hasn't been exploited. Rollins praised him in interviews, and after Columbia distributed two of his DIW CDs, Branford Marsalis signed him—Ware is the only artist he brought to the label during his tenure as an executive. Two superb albums followed: *Go See the World* and *Surrendered*. Neither was publicized in any way. Then Ware was jettisoned, though what will you bet that both CDs are issued a few years from now as classics with alternate takes and acerbic liner comments about Columbia's stewards of the early 2000s?

Meanwhile, the Ware Quartet became home base for a small jazz industry, as Shipp and Parker pursued diverse recording and performance projects. Like the extracurricular activities of Miles Davis's second quintet, their outside work differs greatly from what they play with Ware.

Take for example their current CDs. *Piercing the Veil, Volume 1* (Aum Fidelity), by Parker and Chicago's spellbinding percussionist Hamid Drake, is a rollicking entertainment—not what you'd expect from a bass-drums duo. Yet they double on so many winds, flutes, and bells that the variety is almost as relentless as the wit and high spirits. According to Steven Joerg, the brains behind Aum Fidelity, the second volume, due next year, will be volume one remixed in a "DJ/club style."

Shipp's String Trio album, *Expansion, Power, Release* (hatOLOGY), with Parker and violinist Mat Maneri, is an enticing work that should make many of the year's best-of lists. It was recorded in late 1999, before last year's stunning *New Orbit*, but completes his cycle of six Hat Art CDs. Call it his Bernard Herrmann project, although all the music is original. The 14 brief selections are held together by a mesmerizing ostinato figure in the Herrmann style that might have served *Vertigo* perfectly. In this it carries on from Shipp's preceding Hat disc, *Gravitational Systems*, a duet with Maneri—specifically "Forcefield," with its six-note ostinato, similarly reprised here in "Waltz," and "Speech of Form." The principal vamp this time is an eight-note variation, heard on the opening "Organs" and, later, "Functional Form." These recurring, repeated, appealing figures lend unity to an album that achieves a rare level of emotional satisfaction. It offers anomalous delights as well: Shipp's candid nod to early Cecil at the top of "Combinational Entity," Maneri's unaccompanied solo on "Pulse Form," and the closing groove track, "One More," which might have been called "One More Time," given Parker's bluesy bass walk, Shipp's rocking and rumbling chords, and Maneri's solid elaboration, which includes a few glisses that sound more like swipes.

Ware's *Corridors & Parallels* should prove controversial, as it omits one of the quartet's central pleasures—Shipp's piano, sacrificed to the introduction of Ware's Korg synthesizer played by Shipp with settings devised by himself and Ware that range from organ tonalities to hurricane winds to Sun Ra tinkering to funk, Afro-Cuban, and Afro-Afro rhythms. Consisting of eight main selections and three short untitled transitional pieces on which Ware does not appear, the paradoxical net result is a first-rate Ware showcase—even though he makes his first entrance five minutes into the disc. At that point Shipp—in his organ mode—mostly lays out, and tenor, bass, and drums lock down for the relatively conventional and aptly titled "Straight Track," an exuberant instance of Ware's capacity to avoid cliché while upholding passion and clarity. Parker snaps the strings so hard you can almost feel them slap the wood. Shipp returns toward the end, piling on the rhythm and joining in a nicely abrupt finish.

"Jazz Fi-Sci" is less successful, a disjointed back-and-forth dialogue between tenor and synth that offers a certain gimmicky pleasure but smacks too much of foreplay interruptus—just when you think Ware will finally take off, he halts for a synth interlude. "Superimposed" is a mini Ware festival, boasting an elaborately hooting solo, played (without dubbing) against synth rhythms that suggest a tribe of percussionists. The euphoric edge is fully extended until the humorous wind-down— Ware sounds as if he's running out of fuel. No less pleasing is "Sound-a-Bye," in which he creates barely mobile melody out of what is essentially a three-minute drone, continuing after the others fade away and then fading himself. It's completely convincing and like nothing else I can think of. More ambitious is "Corridors & Parallels," with its synth-whistling, funk, zooming arco bass, and a bristling Ware, who enters like an electric jolt and essays an upbeat holler of a solo that produces an oddly liturgical feeling—sort of "Ascension" meets "He Loved Him Madly." After its mere eight minutes, you may feel washed in the blood of the lamb. Even the layered fade, with Brown's backbeat lingering the longest, works.

"Somewhere" and "Spaces Embraces" are three-minute toss-offs—the first all creaky synth, arco bass, and swirling snares, and the second a vain attempt by Ware to salvage the disc's one meretricious misfire and losing to old-hat sci-fi synth banality. He comes roaring back for a masterly performance in his best fire-and-brimstone manner. "Mother May You Rest in Bliss" is both fresh and familiar, built on foundations laid by Rollins and Coltrane, erected anew on Parker's buttressing bowed bass. It is raucous pop gospel, brimming over with melody, harmony, and wind chimes. As is often the case, Ware becomes more ardent the longer he goes and the more agitated he becomes. Only the brief rhythm transition disappoints—what you want here is a cannonading Shipp piano solo—but Ware returns for the amen chorus.

At the Blue Note, the quartet was its old captivating self, everyone stretching out, each solo a short novel. Working from his usual book, he began with a 30-minute "Surrendered," which opened and closed with Ware's incantatory song and found Shipp kneading the piano in a chordal solo, leading in turn to display-work on bass and drums, including a high-hat fantasia. They continued with a fast, intense, and unified "Lexicon" (*Go See the World*); the very blissed-out "Sentient Compassion" (*Third-Ear Recitation*), complete with almighty cadenza; and the less blissful but more punctilious set closer, "Bliss Theme" (*Great Bliss*). Best small band in jazz today.

[*Village Voice*, 7 August 2001]

94 ❖ Looking for Better Than That (Diana Krall / Jeanie Bryson / Vanessa Rubin / Etta James / Rosemary Clooney)

Early Tuesday, September 11, conniving for a lead to begin this column, I fancied myself Diogenes in search of an honest singer, squinting through the light of my lamp and defeated by darkness time and again. A meager joke, but at 8:30 A.M., having spent days listening to dozens of new recordings by women vocalists (saving the men for later), jokes were still easy to come by. Those who began the day with the *Times* were treated to a sidesplitter, as the paper of record inexplicably devoted an arts lead to the book-plugging of two unrepentant Weathermen bombers who said, from their prosperous academic perches, that they would do it again. The punch line was yet to come, of course. I suddenly recalled a promise to an editor friend to write 300 words about Harry Belafonte's *The Long Road to Freedom*, so I turned to do that—the easy stuff. Then I discovered a voice-mail message from my assistant Elora, who said she would be late because, apparently, a plane had crashed into the World Trade Center and subways were stalled. I had finished Belafonte and returned to Diogenes when a thumping on the door revealed my wife Deborah, aghast and breathless, having just been evacuated from her office in the Empire State Building. Had I heard? Yeah, some kind of accident. The Pentagon was also hit, she said, and I, still in Diogenetic mode, said, "That's not necessarily a bad thing." Then we turned on the TV, and the jokes went out of me like bad food. Hours later, when I listlessly tried to return to the job, I felt ludicrous solemnizing over whether this singer was in pitch or that arrangement suitable. Had I chosen something to rave about, like the Belafonte, maybe I could have continued, certain in my faith that art conquers all. But the task of equivocating, of giving these women a hard time, seemed if not, to use a favorite word of talking heads, heinous (long *a* or long *e*, take your pick), certainly inappropriate. Never had I felt so utterly feckless as a writer.

If warfare waged by monsters who count life worthless could make my job insupportable on Tuesday, why should it seem less so on Wednesday or Thursday? Because—I reasoned, reduced to clichés—art is a balm, a reason for living, a hallowed calling, a religion that, unlike others, kills no one; at its best, it wounds pride and shocks complacency, but it always leaves body parts intact. The only value of politicians is to keep political trouble at bay so that we can safely savor family, friends, and art—that's my mantra; at the risk of sounding Dorian Gray ("Was it not Gautier who used to write about *la consolation des arts*?"), I believe it. Critical attacks that get personal are unwarranted, but rooting out meretriciousness is always necessary. By late Wednesday I could begin again, buoyed by little incidents of the day. Crossing 14th Street on my way to the *Voice*, I had been stopped by a state trooper who was manning a barricade. He asked for ID and destination and explained that as he wasn't from New York I would have to tell him where 36 Cooper Square is. When I did, he said, "Have a good one," which you don't expect at Checkpoint Charlie. At the editorial meeting I was moved by how moved everyone else was; journalistic cynicism was in smithereens and Diogenes off sunning himself. Later I stood 10 minutes in line at Astor Place to buy a *Times*, just missing the last one. When I pointed to the copy where the vendor was sorting his change, he handed it to me, refusing my money! Since he had refused no one else's, I took this for an omen: Give Diana Krall a break. Or some such, oracles being so oracular.

Most of the problems with these singers—that they begin well but cannot sustain the length of a CD, that they repeat the same songs, that they are poorly served by arrangers looking for a moneyed sound—are secondary to an issue echoed by events on TV: an insufficient attention to the meaning of words. Following his AWOL afternoon, the president proved why the job should require respect for the English language. Pundits parroted FDR from 60 years ago, but all one could recall of Bush two minutes later was his nervous clasping of hands and an over-wrought metaphor about steel girders and steel resolve that will live only in infamy. Similarly, Krall, who was so imaginative and even lively in her recent concert appearances and on last year's *When I Look in Your Eyes*, has knuckled to flat mannerisms on *The Look of Love* (Verve), an intermittently pleasing lite-jazz set orchestrated by veteran menace Claus Ogerman, who, lacking the honest schmaltz of a Gordon Jenkins, resorts instead to drawn-out endings and showy classical lifts. Deprived of her cheery trio, Krall is reduced to decorative piano solos ("Love Letters"), Joao Gilberto and Julie London imitations, half-spoken phrases, and practiced groans. She is better than this, better than lite, better than Oger-man, better than the booklet's cheesecake.

Jeanie Bryson's first album in six years, *Deja Blue* (Koch), on the other hand, is treasurable—though hardly the unalloyed delight it ought to be. Bryson and arranger Ted Brancato have revived the indefensible Fender Rhodes, which is going around like flu; combined with vibes and guitar it insinuates an arid 1970s sound at odds with Bryson's gift for economical heat. Still, it boasts a masterpiece, "Am I Blue," a slow and steady composite of vulnerability, mockery, and assurance in an elegant arrangement that begins with Christian McBride bowing "Con Alma." Ethel Waters's version has had no peers for three-quarters of a century, but it does now. Having paid homage to Peggy Lee on the memorable *Some Cats Know*, Bryson shows how deeply she has absorbed Lee's lessons of directness and thrift. Here and on other tracks, including two solid vehicles by her mother, Connie Bryson, "Deja Blue" and "Do You Sometimes Think of Us" (a third, "Sadness," is trite and doesn't sit well with her voice), her lightly smoky contralto gives each tale its due. She gives the players room—Steve Nelson has a pointed vibes solo on the title cut—and effortlessly holds her own in a duet with Etta Jones. But beginning with Phoebe Snow's "Poetry Man," she is distracted and the listener deadened by Fender-bent charts that may evoke nostalgia for her but mean root canal to me. She is better than that. "Am I Blue" is legions better than that.

Etta Jones also pops up on Vanessa Rubin's *Girl Talk* (Telarc), which peaks early with a confidently swung "Comes Love," and—notwithstanding Jones shaking it up on "But Not for Me"; hearty solos by Cedar Walton, Javon Jackson, Larry Willis, and others; and a battle-of-the-sexes concept—succumbs to good manners, supper club conventions, and intransigent songs. Cannonball Adderley could make something of "Matchmaker, Matchmaker," but not even he could have salvaged "Loving You"—singers are better than that. The other Etta, however, knows no restraints in her conceptually similar CD, *Blue Gardenia*. Etta James, whose influence on young white women singers may have finally displaced that of Aretha, has sung jazz standards since the beginning but has usually shied away from jazz settings—maybe because Dinah Washington once cleared a nightclub table of glasses and chased her off the stage for singing "Unforgettable." Her voice is heavier now, at times strained, but her phlegmatic phrasing and imperious melisma give the familiar material (including Dinah homages "This Bitter Earth" and "Blue Gardenia") a backbeat tang that is nothing if not genuine—no forced metaphors or compromises.

For honesty without melisma and with an evenly dispatched beat, the new release by the FDR of lyrics-readers, my pal Rosemary Clooney, is exemplary. Backed by a vigorous neo-swing big band, Matt Catingup's Big Kahuna and the Copa Cat Pack, her *Sentimental Journey* (Concord Jazz) might be distributed as a textbook in meaning what you sing. Much of the charm redounds to her equipment, which has sacrificed range and purity but not personality or distinction. Yet the voice alone cannot explain why when she sings "I'll Be Around," you feel comforted; or why when she intones a line like "I got my bag, got my reservation," you think bags and reservations; or how she manages to invest "I Got a Right to Sing the Blues" with unmistakable pride; or, following a canny 1950s block-chord piano solo, how she uncovers a world of irony in "You Go to My Head." Clooney made many compromised records in her heyday. What a shame if Bryson, Krall, and others wait as long to assert their own best instincts. Listening to her, an honest singer, the weight of the day begins to lift.

[*Village Voice*, 25 September 2001]

95 ❖ Strictly Solalian
(Martial Solal)

Probably the worst label one can stick on a jazz musician is Intellectual, a nebulous term that almost always serves as a warning: You may be expected to work—if you consider close listening work. The second most insidious label is Virtuoso, which is invariably smudged with special pleading. Combine the two and you are very likely left with an artist who requires rapt attention while compensating for emotional reserve with technical flair. You might well call it spinach and say the hell with it. But then your roughage may be Jack Daniel's to me. At one time, Ahmad Jamal and Bill Evans were characterized as skillfully complex, usually to hold them at bay, yet each man attracted passionate followings that fermented into substantial popularity. Jamal usually keeps me at arm's length, while Evans usually invites me in; it may be the opposite with you. Lennie Tristano is routinely described as cerebral, which once seemed tenable to me, yet now I find his Atlantic sessions flat-out thrilling. We could make this a parlor game, identifying undoubtedly brilliant musicians—Benny Carter, Lee Konitz, Herbie Nichols, Henry Threadgill—who remain alien to a broad audience.

It may seem inconceivable today that Parker, Gillespie, and Monk were initially derided as spinach, and yet they did contribute to the dismantling of the audience that embraced jazz in the 1930s, much as Coleman, Taylor, and Coltrane wore out many who had come aboard in the 1950s. But they've long since been enshrined in the pantheon. I'm concerned here with those who keep circling Olympus without quite getting a footing, of whom the patron saint is Art Tatum—the virtuoso's virtuoso, the pianist's pianist, the musician's musician, and undoubtedly a god, but one who to this day, because he rejected a standard approach to linear improvisation, preferring juxtapositions that demand attention, becalms many listeners into hapless indifference. One of his primary heirs is the brilliant French pianist and composer Martial Solal, whose appearance at the Village Vanguard during the week of September 18 began with a half-filled house only partly attributable to the attack on the World Trade Center the preceding Tuesday.

Around the time Solal first visited America, in 1963, the forever staid Martin Williams got so heated that he closed his review alarmed that he might have written a "panegyric." "I do not mean that," he apologized, then cast about for a caveat—something about Solal not being a natural blues player. He closed with reference to "Solalian lyricism," coining an adjective that has become so widespread in European jazzcrit that it sometimes gets a small *s*, though it refers less to lyricism than to a time-less fluency that transcends genre and idiom. Williams subsequently interviewed Solal for the *Saturday Review*. The pianist affirmed the influence of the bright, orchestral keyboard stylists—Tatum, Waller, Garner—before he absorbed Powell, from whom, he conceded, he took more than from anyone else save Tatum. He said he knew little of classical music after Debussy, putting to rest assumptions of an au courant academicism; in fact, like Monk, another influence, he found his method largely through the grammar of jazz. He also noted that he had not heard Bill Evans's records with Scott LaFaro and Paul Motian (a frequent Solal drummer) until arriving in New York, underscoring what his 1960 trio sessions with Guy Pedersen and Daniel Humair prove—that he was striving for a triangular, equal-participation approach to the piano trio at the same time as Evans and Jamal.

Solal had been around. He was born in Algiers in 1927, and according to an old liner note was expelled from school in 1942 because of race laws (his father was Jewish). He turned to jazz after hearing Goodman, Waller, and Reinhardt, among others, and played piano, saxophone, and clarinet professionally, eventually realizing he would have to relocate to Paris to have a career. He made the move in 1950, and soon earned a reputation, appearing on Reinhardt's last session in 1953, working with visiting American players, writing orchestra charts, and scoring New Wave films by Melville and Godard. The 1960 trio made a tremendous impression, as did his ability to spontaneously recompose familiar themes. Solal's unaccompanied 1960 version of Tadd Dameron's "The Squirrel," for example, is a rigorous paradigm of virtuoso exultation kept in check by his thorough control of form—just when you think the fingers will fly away, the gravity of the piece and his sense of proportion bring them home.

As of 1963, Solal was known here, if at all, for the movie *Breathless* and two durable if little-remembered albums. In 1957, he had recorded with the New Orleans guru Sidney Bechet, at the older man's request; their mutual give-and-take, shown to advantage in robust exchanges on "These Foolish Things," proved that the generations could meet profitably in a period when they barely glanced at each other. Throughout, Solal shows individuality, empathy, clarity, and a whetted cleverness, as in the reharmonization of "It Don't Mean a Thing" or a "Rose Room" solo that extends his accompaniment for an uncharacteristically overwrought Bechet. The other album documented a 1962 concert at Paris's Salle Gaveau, opening with a rhythmic deconstruction of "Jordu" and increasing tension through six knotty originals, including a dreamy ballad, "Aigue Marine" (revived with greater radiance and polish in the 1979 version included in his invaluable out-of-print Radio France anthology, *Live 1959/85*), and "Nos Smoking," which commences as a crazy-quilt exposition of quick tempo adjustments and fleeting references to silent comedy whims and bebop changes before caroming into an extraordinarily fast blues episode. The album, which is unlike anything else in that era, was released here by Liberty (now owned by EMI, so a Blue Note reissue is in order), and it should have become a classic and established his stateside presence.

That didn't happen. Over the past 38 years, Solal has performed at festivals in Chicago and Monterey, but has rarely appeared in New York. The Vanguard gig represented his first visit in two decades and his first club date since he hit the Hickory House in 1963. Most of his records are impossible to find here, though a few have crossed the Atlantic, including the 1983 Soul Note, *Bluesine*, and the current series on Dreyfus: *In & Out* with Johnny Griffin; the stunning *Just Friends* with Motian and Gary Peacock, an ideal introduction; and the new *Dodecaband Plays Ellington*, which shows off his arranging skills at the helm of a band he has led since 1980. Solal's writing, like his playing, never stands still. They are alike in others ways—the saxophone that skitters away from the theme might be a right-hand arpeggio; the high voicing of two soprano saxes might be a dissonant thumping in the treble and the trombone slur a bass clef response. Occasional episodes are too intricate for their own good, but like they say about the weather in the plains, if you don't like it, wait eight bars. Solal shows no interest in aping Ellington. He is attracted to tunes we know so well that they can flit in and out of view (along with odd quotes, like "Reveille" in "Satin Doll"), always centered in his broad variational dramas: How timely are those impending storm clouds at the start of "Caravan," a 15-minute stream-of-consciousness desert song with who knows how many references to Solal's years in Africa.

Still, the Dodecaband lacks the romping joy and surprise of his trio, which, with drummer Bill Stewart and bassist Francois Moutin, gave the Vanguard a palpable lift. Sticking to standards, he played a vivacious shell game with the themes, sometimes keeping them hidden until well into the piece, yet filling out the changes so comprehensively that the melody, when it did appear, seemed to be the only natural conclusion. Solal's authoritative technique is inescapable. Yet his virtuosity is nothing like Tatum's—he avoids adverbial flourishes, preferring the kind of two-finger hammering that Gershwin wrote into the piano arsenal in *Rhapsody in Blue*. His grounded harmonies and impetuous rhythms result in an idiosyncratic attack: I once played a Solal album of Parker compositions for two colleagues—one guessed it was Tatum, the other Cecil Taylor. Ellington's phrase, "beyond category," comes to mind.

I think the intellectual aspect that either draws your attention like steel filings to a magnet or leaves you unmoored is his devotion to good old theme-and-variations. Most jazz performances follow that dictate, but so often the improvisation abandons the theme that we tend to think of the result as head-and-solo, which is very different. Solal, like Tatum or Monk or Rollins, is constantly playing with the piece under scrutiny. Obviously, you don't have to know the song to find his inventions spellbinding: His original pieces are just as compelling. But you do need to know "The Song Is You," "I Can't Get Started," and "Tea for Two" to fully enjoy the wit, caprice, mystery, and implacable sense of structure that informs each selection.

Even then, he will throw a wrench into the mix, usually to leaven the set, for example, a brief, faithful rendering of "La Vie en Rose," in which the real variations were assigned Moutin, who has a neat trick of rapidly sliding a fretting finger down a string while plucking melody notes that seem to sparkle like a percussive piano arpeggio; or opening a number with Stewart playing buoyant triplets as prelude to "'Round Midnight" (the source of several Solal triumphs, all strikingly different), treated as a waltz—a fast waltz at that. "What Is This Thing Called Love" and its shadow melody "Hot House" became a world of fragments while sustaining, measure for measure, the logic of a theorem. Using chords as a grounding point, he is as free in his movements as free jazz can be. His influences were assimilated so long ago that you would be hard-pressed to hear a touch of Tatum or Powell or Garner or Monk. What you do hear of them, beautifully transmuted, is a lineage—the whimsy, spark, and bemused craft of the inspired quick-change artist. Everyone around me was smiling.

[*Village Voice*, 9 October 2001]

Blue Note Records is turning out to be, of all things, the Blue Note Records of our time—in an unexpected way. Hard bop is not on the agenda. And the label has not yet found a jukebox favorite like Jimmy Smith, Horace Silver, or, briefly-but-big-time, Lee Morgan, though it has come close with Cassandra Wilson, Charlie Hunter, and, briefly-but-medium-time, US3. Instead, it is flourishing, musically if not commercially, by extending what I've come to think of as jazz's Secret History, that school of resolute, autonomous wizards who swim right of the avant-garde and left of the mainstream, and usually have to wait, as Monk warned, for the public to "pick up on what you are doing—even if it does take them 15, 20 years." Alfred Lion's devotion to Monk established Blue Note's alternative vision; later signings, beginning with Herbie Nichols in 1955, endorsed an ongoing new wave that never quite rolled into shore though it endures as incredibly clairvoyant.

When was the last time you listened to Sam Rivers's brilliant 1964 *Fuscia Swing Song*, which should be heard as presented by Mosaic (*The Complete Blue Note Sam Rivers Sessions*), including three utterly dissimilar alternate takes of "Downstairs Blues Upstairs"? In 2001 terms, the only element that betrays the recording date is the rhythm section of Ron Carter and Tony Williams, cutting edge then and in every way exemplary, but clearly of its time. The playing of Rivers and Jaki Byard, however, is 30 years ahead of its time. *Fuscia Swing Song* was one of several 1960s Blue Notes that epitomize the struggle to remake jazz structure, employing free spirits unleashed by the avant-garde without embracing the potential chaos of unstructured improvisation. Consider also Jackie McLean's *Destination Out!*, Eric Dolphy's *Out to Lunch*, Tony Williams's *Lifetime*, Wayne Shorter's *The All-Seeing Eye*, Andrew Hill's *Point of Departure*, and Bobby Hutcherson's *Components*.

Bruce Lundvall's gamble on a new generation of well-schooled musicians, apprenticed for the most part to the often stirring if unpredictable Greg Osby and then promptly given their head as bandleaders, is now paying off. The release last year of *New Directions*, organized by Osby, seems like a quiet manifesto, and more rewarding than the label's earlier attempts to refurbish its catalog of '60s classics and semi-classics. This isn't your father's "Song for My Father" or "The Sidewinder," and it isn't as good, but the revision is fanciful enough to indicate a polite coup. I'm assuming I'm not the only listener who needed help to figure out the four/four of the former, since the beats in the three-measure ostinato are fixed irregularly (four, five, three, I'm told). Mark Shim, whose performance is confident and shrewd, has yet to make a fully representative album of his own, but Stefon Harris already had and Jason Moran soon would, with his second CD, *Facing Left*. And Tarus Mateen and Nasheet Waits may be the most dynamic rhythm section since William Parker and whoever.

How significant a development is this? The new Moran album, *Black Stars*, is an encouraging payoff—possibly a Blue Note benchmark, definitely one of the year's outstanding discs. Its genius stroke is the presence of Sam Rivers. Conversin' with the elders, as James Carter termed his Atlantic sessions with Buddy Tate and Harry Edison, is no longer unusual; at Blue Note, Osby has recruited Andrew Hill and Jim Hall, and Joe Lovano has commissioned new work from Gunther Schuller and Manny Albam. Still, Rivers, who may close a circle for Moran, a four-year student of Byard's, stimulates the trio as perhaps no one else could. He earns respect as a 78-year-old (as of last week) monument while thinking on their wavelengths, so the deference is never unwarranted or coddling. Rivers forges and Moran, Mateen, and Waits follow, each understanding that the goal is not to stay abreast but to share in the risks. This is an album brimming with wonder, urgency, and here's-mud-in-your-eye elation. All three players sound as if they're working at something so cool they'd pay Blue Note for the pleasure.

Moran is a crisply distinct pianist, sometimes gnomic, never precious. Though his models—Byard, Nichols, Hill, Muhal Richard Abrams—and his attack place him squarely among the new generation of percussive pianists, including D. D. Jackson, Marc Cary, and Vijay Iyer, his resonant attack has no soft edges and expresses little interest in harmonic variation. In this he recalls Ahmad Jamal and Ellington, several of whose rhythm pieces are integral parts of his repertoire. His improvisations are dynamic, abrupt, eruptive, keyed to the composition at hand, and, even when hewing to the changes, more drumlike than melodic. If Art Tatum could suggest the saturated hues of Technicolor in an arpeggiated sweep, Moran operates in the world of black and white. Yet his technique is no less mesmerizing. The moment I knew I'd be spending a lot of time with this disc occurred on a train, when I tightened my headphones to blot out the cacophony of cellphoners and found myself replaying a splintering arpeggio four-and-a-half-minutes into "Foot Under Foot"—a palpably impulsive gesture of a sort that occurs throughout the album and never fails to startle. Note, for example, the ringing double-barreled glissando triggering the theme on "Kinda Dukish." Like Ellington, he articulates with the brash certainty of someone who never expects to miss hitting the right keys, and he does not miss many (none on the CD, one during a set at Iridium).

What he achieves is inseparable from the intensity of the trio, which he calls the Bandwagon. Tarus Mateen's solos are so well integrated into the performances that sometimes you don't know he is soloing until the trio dynamics bring him to the fore, and even then his variations have a compositional integrity (for example, "Draw the Night Out") that avoids showboating. Nasheet Waits is the son of Freddie Waits, a versatile and forceful drummer who worked with everyone from Johnny Hodges to Al Green to Cecil Taylor. He has his father's rugged aggression and clarity, combined with Tony Williams's finesse on the snares ("Earth Song," for example), and reflexes that allow him to close the sale on any conceit Moran comes up with. With Rivers added to the mix, each man is at once responsive and audacious, so that your attention is always pulled but not really diverted—they achieve an updated version of the rhythm-as-foreground flexibility heard in Miles Davis's '60s band. That tremendous sense of unity and drive animates "Skitter In" with a diligent abandon, and transforms "Summit," on which Rivers plays flute and soprano, from Asian reflection into a venture in supple lockstep empathy. Their playing is instinctive—they follow each other instead of chorus-and-chord graphs—and the pieces are too tight to permit the occasional waywardness that occurs in concert, where thinking aloud is part of the fun.

Moran's first CD, *Soundtrack to Human Motion*, suffers from melodies like "Gangsterism on Canvas" and "Still Moving" that recall the forced lyricism of middle-period Keith Jarrett. If there is nothing simpering about the riveting *Facing Left*, neither does it extend the romantic generosity glimpsed in the Ravel selection on the first album or his own "Commentary on Electrical Switches," a telling dedication to Byard, on *New Directions*. On *Black Stars*, however, Rivers cuts the sweetness like lemon peel in a Coke, helping to serve up lyricism without sentiment on "Gangsterism on a River" or the duet "Say Peace," or especially "The Sun at Midnight," an excursion into found melody where Moran sustains the mood established by Rivers's flute with a staunch and spiky solo. Consider the piano crescendo that signals Rivers's return or, for that matter, the waltz-time passage that similarly triggers the returning theme on "Foot Under Foot." A trio piece, "Draw the Night Out," builds on a swirling ostinato that suggests Monk's "Misterioso" at supersonic speed. Three surprises: Moran attaches the funeral march from Ellington's "Black and Tan Fantasy" to "Kinda Dukish"; he goes solo on "Out Front," the quirky blues Byard wrote in memory of Herbie Nichols, dressing it up with Byard's distinct approach to stride; and on the closing duet, "Sound It Out," he turns the piano over to Rivers, whose own keyboard attack has proved prescient, then subtly takes over as Sam turns to flute.

Iridium has moved to a large basement at Broadway and 51st Street, doing away with uptown chi-chi and gaining better sound and sight-lines. With Rivers at home in Orlando, Moran's trio opened last week and the first set was a sparkling display of stream-of-consciousness accord, as one piece turned into another and then another and the hub shifted from one player to the next in the course of a very fast hour. Unexpected was Ellington's "A Single Petal of a Rose," more melodic than Moran's usual choices, though the bass clef figure evidently appeals to his mathematical rectitude; taking his time, he shape-shifted that piece into Ellington's "Wig Wise" (a highlight of *Facing Left*) and Monk's "Monk's Dream," then closed with his restructured "The Sidewinder." The more Moran looks backward the more certain he is in moving forward. At 26, he is good news for jazz's future.

[*Village Voice*, 17 October 2001]

97 ❖ *Master Class*
(Jimmy Heath)

The October 19 and 20 Jazz at Lincoln Center tribute to Jimmy Heath, commemorating his 75th birthday, was called "He Walked with Giants"—a title typical of that series, and also of its unduly modest guest, whose superlative Riverside LPs were once anthologized as *Fast Company* and who himself titled a later album *Peer Pleasure*. Still, the implication that Heath is great by association riles me. I don't want to overstate his claims—merely allow them to stand on their own. Miles Davis and John Coltrane, born the same year as Heath, are giants in a way that he is not, though they both benefited from his skills as bandleader, composer, and player. Heath's achievement is of a different kind. He is primarily a craftsman, one of the most distinctive of his generation. If he remains undervalued even in his autumnal years, when he is routinely accorded living-legend status, it is because craftsmanship has limited charisma, especially when married to understatement, his stock in trade.

In Heath's case, craft is inseparable from melody, which, like comedy, is a favor of the angels—harder to play than drama or rhythm. If you've got the gift, you'd be a fool to sacrifice it. Yet Hollywood is littered with the corpses of comedians who coveted the tragedian's prestige, and jazz saw a generation of lyrical players bite the bullet of rhythms on top of rhythms combined with expressionist howls. Davis and Coltrane, once supreme melodists, could make the journey outward, fired by the force of genius and innovation. When Heath acknowledged the antimelodic fashions of the '70s—overblowing, extra percussion, vocalisms, Afrocentrism—he applied them as painterly touch-ups to an already centered approach steeped in his distinctive bebop lyricism.

Why distinctive? It became clear during the big band half of the Lincoln Center concert that Heath, a product of bop, was a child of the swing era whose love of big band bravura gives his tunes a peculiarly robust shine. Except for Heath Brothers albums, where he has usually worked with brothers Percy and Albert on bass and drums and a guitarist or pianist, he rarely records in the typical saxophone-plus-rhythm format, preferring to add at least a couple of brass instruments—French horn and tuba as well as trumpet and trombone. That instrumentation suggests an ear for subtle hues and dynamics, but disguises the unfeigned generosity of his melodies, which give off an orchestral charge no matter how small the ensemble. The tunes themselves make small groups, his and others that have covered them, sound larger. Despite his affection for minor chords, Heath's writing has an extrovert openness and rhythmic finesse that recalls orchestrations from the swing era, when the best and smartest music in the land courted inclusiveness.

I'm not certain precisely what makes some pieces, say Charlie Parker's "Ornithology," which was developed from a lick Bird played on a big band record, sound like combo music, and others, say Bud Powell's "Bouncing with Bud," which was written for a quintet, convey the valorous attack of an orchestra. Part of it has to do with the fact that some heads sound like extensions of what a musician might improvise in a solo, while others bespeak the interactive detail of composition. Of the great jazz tunesmiths whose work was often performed in the 1950s— Monk, Silver, Lewis, Mulligan, Weston, Mingus, and Heath among them—none has a more consistent feeling for orchestral attack than Heath, which is especially remarkable if you consider that most of his best known pieces are blues. Though elemental in structure, they are enlivened by substitute chords, rhythmic vamps, rests, and imaginative voicings, as well as Heath's alert and knowing melodic command.

A good example is "Big P," introduced on *Really Big*, his second of six Riverside discs (one a year between 1959 and 1964, all presently in print), featuring seven winds plus rhythm. The piece is basically a 12-bar blues, but the head is 24 bars, the second 12 a variation on the first with slightly altered chords and a different voicing. The tune, which begins with minor chords and erupts into major ones, is a stately band riff with almost as many rests as notes, at first divided between reeds and brasses, which unite for the climax of each chorus like Ellington in full flower. Cannonball Adderley adapted "Big P," which suited his own inclination for ensemble might, but the Heath piece that ignited Adderley's sextet was the blues waltz, "Gemini," with its six-note mock-classical call to arms and a written transitional passage that excitingly spells the soloists. Adderley uses bass for the call and flute for the head, while Heath's sextet versions assign both parts to French horn (*Triple Threat*, 1962) or cello (*Love and Understanding*, 1973), underscoring a broader and warmer palette. In all cases, the ensemble mines the give-and-take tradition of orchestral section work.

These pieces not only cast each member of the group in an essential role; they also stimulate improvisation—Freddie Hubbard, Wynton Kelly, and Cedar Walton, among others, recorded some of their best work of the era on Heath's watch. During a four-year sabbatical from playing in the 1950s, he wrote many durable tunes, including four for the 1956 Chet Baker and Art Pepper sextet LP, *Playboys*. The difference between the way that band plays them and an earlier Heath anthem, "C.T.A.," and two cooler numbers by Pepper, which are decidedly of their time, is startling. In 1953, with Heath on tenor, "C.T.A." had given Miles Davis's band a notable thrust, and in 1966, "Gingerbread Boy"—perhaps his signature piece, with a funky vamp that seems to presage Tony Williams and a memorable blues line—sparked unison playing by Davis and Wayne Shorter on *Miles Smiles*, famous for its otherwise discursive heads.

Heath's records never sold as well as those that covered his pieces, but they abide. The Riversides prevail as boldly gentle reminders of a creative period in jazz when the rules of bop were stretched to breaking, including *Swamp Seed*, with its stirring brass quartet, and the more conventional *On the Trail*, an apparent blowing session (with Kenny Burrell's guitar) that is nonetheless orderly, polished, and varied. Variety was never an issue: *The Quota* opens with two blues that are nothing alike—the title tune, another twice-played (and arranged) theme that leads to four Heath tenor choruses, with trumpet and French horn kicking in at the climax so that you can hardly believe it's just a sextet; and "Lowland Lullaby," which begins with a waltzing 24-bar intro based entirely on a yawning two-note riff that kicks into four for a melodic theme in which the earlier riff signals rhythmic changeups in each improvised chorus. No less impressive are the even less well-known albums from the early 1970s, a relatively uncreative period in jazz, from which *The Gap Sealer*, *Love and Understanding*, *The Time and the Place*, and the lone quartet session *Picture of Heath* stand out as gently independent, fully realized projects. Significantly, at this time he also wrote his *Afro-American Suite of Evolution*, each movement dedicated to jazz idols of the past and thus way ahead of the curve for jazz repertory and reverence.

With the Lincoln Center Jazz Orchestra's performances of "Gemini," "Like a Son," "Gingerbread Boy," "The Voice of the Saxophone," and Parker's "Yardbird Suite" ringing in my ears, I've focused on Heath's writing at the expense of his playing, and yet nothing was more evident than the degree to which Heath, usually limiting himself to two-chorus solos while cheerleading the younger players as well as a few peers (Slide Hampton, his brothers), outclassed everyone. Initially influenced by Parker (when he played alto he was known as Little Bird), and later by Dexter Gordon and still later by Coltrane, who had played in Heath's legendarily unrecorded Philadelphia big band in the late 1940s, he has long since developed a natural, dry, aged-in-the-wood style and timbre of his own. Like his writing, his playing has a candid, sage authority that never calls undue attention to itself. Its meaning stems from feeling, not technique.

Compare his two recorded versions of "The Voice of the Saxophone," playing a borrowed alto (for the first time in 24 years) with a 1974 quintet (*The Time and the Place*), and tenor with the 1992 *Little Man Big Band* (sadly his only big band album, savory despite harsh engineering that favors the rhythm section to no one's advantage). On tenor, he is the soul of authority, brimming with confidence, vigor, and the dark, knowing sound of an old master—appropriate for a homage to Coleman Hawkins. On the alto, though, he recapitulates the poise of untrammeled bop, a yearning back-of-beat sound that Parker invented—it's almost as though the instrument brought him back to another era. He communicates two very discrete moods simply in the way he intones the melody. With Heath's 1972 recording of "Invitation" (*The Gap Sealer*), he proved himself one of the few saxophonists who could play the soprano in tune, focusing on melody notes rather than a shrill wail, more in the line of Zoot Sims than Coltrane. At the concert, the very containment of his solos on tenor and soprano made the more angular assertions of his former student Antonio Hart and members of the orchestra, including Wynton Marsalis, seem overwrought by comparison. They played well enough, but the only solo that matched Heath's savoir-faire was by the band's veteran baritone saxophonist, Joe Temperley.

During the first half, Heath actually danced to his solos and others', reveling in a good time he was eager to share, playing Strayhorn's "Day Dream" at a provocatively fast tempo, raising the barometer with a Lestorian one-note ride on his marvelous "Indiana" variation, "Nice

People." For the big band half, he chose mostly to conduct and was just as buoyant, because his arrangements never stand still: every solo at some point gets orchestral commentary, every section of the band fully deployed and on alert. For most of the past three decades, Heath has buttered his bread as an educator, heading the Jazz Masters program at Queens University (he stepped down in 1998). But he teaches whenever he unfurls a score or plays a saxophone solo. He has quietly, without fanfare, become the soul of jazz, and if you don't pay attention, you will miss something.

[*Village Voice*, 31 October 2001]

98 ❖ *Fearless*
(Tony Bennett)

Frank Sinatra, who later called him the best singer in the business, pegged Tony Bennett at the start of his career when he observed, with apparent astonishment, that Bennett had "four sets of balls." He was probably thinking of Bennett's dynamic, nervy, over-the-top attack and vocal range, but he proved more discerning than he knew. Two decades later, the remark might have also referred to Bennett's challenging repertory, heart-on-sleeve emotionalism, actorly inflection of lyrics, or stubborn idealism, which motivated him to leave Columbia Records and go independent when he felt corporate powers cared more about the marketplace than his musicianship. Indeed, it's impossible to survey Bennett's 51 years of recordings—capped this month with the almost absurdly demanding *Playin' with My Friends: Bennett Sings the Blues*—and not marvel at the guy's sheer moxie.

His daring was apparent from the beginning, when Bennett made the big leap from Astoria, Queens, to the Village Inn in Manhattan, where Pearl Bailey championed him and Bob Hope invited him to sing in his show at the Paramount Theater. After Bennett finished his number, Hope joked, "Well, I was getting tired of Crosby anyhow!"—another remark with more significance than intended. For two decades, Bing Crosby had ruled the mainstream of pop singing, engendering countless imitators and a genuine rival in Sinatra, all of them casual baritones. Bennett was a tenor and "casual" was not in his makeup. He was more of a shouter, albeit less in the tradition of Big Joe Turner and Jimmy Rushing (though you can hear an inkling of Rushing's effulgent tenor in his approach) than in that of Leoncavallo and Puccini. Lacking operatic chops and timbre, he nonetheless sang ballads Pagliacci-style, as if his life depended on it. But he also had more than a touch of Manhattan bop in his soul, and his jazz-infused swingers paraded raw emotions with a hipsterish élan—even the high notes radiated a husky, hustling, local-boy temperament.

Bennett's first important record, strictly a local hit (initially made as a demo and then polished for Columbia in 1950), was an odd selection for an ambitious 23-year-old Italian-American, whom Hope had renamed because he didn't fancy Anthony Benedetto on a marquee. The team of Harry Warren and Al Dubin wrote "Boulevard of Broken Dreams" for a 1934 movie, *Moulin Rouge*, in the faux-tango fashion just recently popularized by Crosby's "Temptation." It had produced one hit, by the Lombardo-influenced bandleader Jan Garber, whose forgotten vocalist, oddly enough, was named Lee Bennett. For some reason, the song had stayed in Tony Bennett's memory, and it served as a fitting audition for the young man's purple passion. He followed it with "Because of You," the nation's number one record in the early summer of 1951.

At a time when Italo-pop meant the lean, homey Sinatra of wartime (the brassy hipster was yet to come), the good-natured lassitude of Perry Como, or the light ballads of Bennett's contemporary, Vic Damone, Bennett's zealous, sometimes melodramatic assault on the pop charts had the effrontery of an alarm clock in church. In a way, he had more in common with two utterly different but equally dynamic contemporaries: the opera singer manqué Mario Lanza, whose "Be My Love" preceded him by a few months in the number one slot, and Johnny Ray, the white r&b phenomenon whose "Cry" followed a few months later. All three were unafraid of broaching vulgarity in the cause of making an emotional connection, taking listeners by the lapels and shaking them up.

Of course, Bennett had the requisite taste and versatility to go farther than they did. His voice has a gruff persuasive edge, friendly and conversational in the midrange where he does his best work. He earns those magnanimous climaxes in the upper reaches. Like Rosemary Clooney, who supplanted him at the top of the charts in the late summer of 1951 with "Come On-a My House," Bennett emerged from the Columbia Records hit factory as a stellar interpreter of the classic American songbook. Over the next decade, he would fearlessly take on the Count Basie Orchestra or record an album of voice-piano duets with his longtime musical director Ralph Sharon. When it looked like the pop charts were beyond him, in 1962, he tried to bounce back with "Once upon a Time," from a failed Broadway show, *All American*, plugging it at every appearance until a Columbia executive told him the label was getting more response for the flip side, "I Left My Heart in San Francisco"—the kind of record that can float an entire career, covering for musical sins as well as outbursts of integrity. "I Left My Heart" did not crown the charts; it just hung around forever.

He sang it at Carnegie Hall on June 9, 1962, a career milestone that produced one of his most characteristic albums, *Tony Bennett at Carnegie Hall*, and the audience went wild—two months before the single really took off. "Judging by the reception," Sharon forecast in his liner notes, "the song will go on to become a standard and a 'must' in Tony's repertoire." Still, "I Left My Heart in San Francisco" was not golden enough to secure Bennett the independence he needed from Columbia. Significantly, the only other number that received an equally huge Carnegie ovation was Ellington's "Solitude," the kind of art song with which Bennett could rattle an audience, but had no currency on the hit parade. So he left Columbia, started a boutique label, Improv, recorded two acclaimed albums with pianist Bill Evans, played concerts, clubs, and benefits, and then, after a dozen years, returned to Columbia on his own terms.

In 1994, now approaching living-legend status, he was reborn as an MTV poster boy. During the past decade, he has made a remarkable series of thematic albums, including tributes to Sinatra, Astaire, Ellington, Holiday, and Berlin. The 1996 *Bennett/Berlin*, in particular, adumbrates the current album as an example of playing with friends, in this instance three jazz soloists. Though very short, barely half an hour, Bennett takes the chances of a singer exulting in reclaimed or newly discovered capabilities, while giving Sharon's trio more space than usual. The intimacy underscores his focus on lyrics, his use of parlando to heighten meaning, while sacrificing nothing in the way of aggressive rhythms, which he brings to such unlikely material as "They Say It's Wonderful" and "Isn't This a Lovely Day." Dexter Gordon adds a glowing obbligato on "All of My Life" and "White Christmas" and Dizzy Gillespie provides one of his finest recorded solos of the period on "Russian Lullaby." George Benson plays and scats on "Cheek to Cheek," "Let Yourself Go" is turned into a bass feature for Paul Langosch with vocal interjections, and "When I Lost You," once considered too dated for a contemporary singer, is an a cappella lament.

On the new album, his friends consist of three generations of singers from the worlds of pop, rock, and blues, with supplementary ties to jazz and country. The subtitle, "Bennett Sings the Blues," is another indication of the singer's moxie, and may make you cringe if you recall the days of, say, *Eydie Gormé Sings the Blues*. The blues have never been a core part of Bennett's repertory, but as the song says, he has a right to sing them. He is so comfortable with who he is that he brings to them his usual equanimity, with no need to growl, groan, or posture: a song is a song, even when it's just 12-bars long. *Playin' with My Friends* is half-split between bona fide blues—"Everyday (I Have the Blues)," "Eve-nin'," "Old Count Basie Is Gone," a reworking of Joe Turner's "Old Piney Brown Is Gone"—and blues-inspired pop—"Blues in the Night," "I Got a Right to Sing the Blues," "Stormy Weather." Bennett tackles each one with characteristic authority and not a little of the old bravura.

The trouble with duets is that they require at least the pretense of a musical reason, something beyond the commercial gimmick of bringing a lot of famous names under one roof. Crosby, who recorded more duets than anyone else, always made them sound as unaffected as two friends enjoying an impromptu visit. Sinatra closed his career with two discs of ponderous duets, his guests phoning in their parts while listening to prerecorded tracks. The results were mechanical and indifferent—only Bennett projected respect for the older man, turning a futile exercise into a near-homage. At 75, Bennett has adapted Crosby's attitude to Sinatra's template, engaging each of 10 singers in the studio, determined to have fun. He has also added four solo tracks and one editing extravaganza, the title cut, for which each guest dubbed a part. The arrangements are breezily minimal—the Ralph Sharon Quartet, with the expert guitarist Gray Sargeant, plus, on a few numbers, organist Mike Melvoin and saxophonist Harry Allen.

The results are predictably mixed: either you have two singers communicating or merely performing their lines. Bennett was in rare form, however, and the gems beam with pleasure. He is wholly in tune with Stevie Wonder, who plays a terrific mouth harp improvisation on "Everyday (I Have the Blues)," B. B. King, and Ray Charles, sharing similar inclinations and commiserating with humor. He is very good with Diana Krall on "Alright, Okay, You Win," who begins a bit too poised, but snaps out of it after Bennett bellows the release; when he tells her "That's more like it," he might be referring to the lyric or her sudden bounce—a lesson from the master. Bonnie Raitt acquits herself well on "I Got a Right to Sing the Blues," yet there is no rapport between her and Bennett. On the other hand, "Keep the Faith, Baby," offers diverting give-and-take between him and k. d. lang, but she's a bit more histrionic than the lyric demands.

Billy Joel matches Bennett's dynamics and timbre on his "New York State of Mind," reflecting the older man's influence as they exchange phrases, though Joel dilutes the effect with unnecessary and unconvincing melisma. Sad to say, the great Kay Starr's voice is shot (she's 79), though Bennett gallantly carries her on the too infrequently sung Count

Basie ballad "Blue and Sentimental." Natalie Cole's work on "Stormy Weather" is merely nondescript. It was a mistake to open "Good Morning, Heartache" with Sheryl Crow, who treads water, her waifish enunciation indicating little understanding of the lyric. Yet after the Bennett boost, even she sounds more assured. This track has a lovely moment, when Bennett sings the phrase "got those Monday blues," putting a neat turn on "Monday"—an emphatic homage to Billie Holiday. Bennett, swinging with easy assurance, mines every lyric for meaning, and when he really lets loose, as he does on almost every track, you can still hear the nerviness that impressed Sinatra 50 years ago.

[*New York Times Arts & Leisure*, 18 November 2001]

99 ❖ *All Around the Town* *(Uri Caine)*

With irony now rotting in the grave, Uri Caine demonstrated a prescient sobriety two years ago when he recorded *The Sidewalks of New York*, which—adapted and abridged—received its New York debut November 3 at the Center for Jewish History. The disc is an audio kaleidoscope, convening singers, spielers, musicians, and sound effects to create a moving sense of the city in all its ethnic motley as the 19th century gave way to the 20th. I know of no other album quite like it—a couple of 1950s recreations of minstrel shows approximate its ambition, but not its reach or achievement. The absence of irony was especially notable at the time of its 1999 release. Caine made his name with Don Byron and Dave Douglas, frequent indulgers in musical caricature, and through adaptations of Mahler, Wagner, Schumann, and Bach that go as far afield as gospel singing and turntabling and serve even at their most honestly affecting (the Mahler works, *Primal Light* and *Mahler in Toblach*) as discerning provocations.

Yet *Sidewalks* emerges as a heartfelt period piece that betrays hardly any interest in modernizing the material. Dedicated to Caine's father, who had died shortly before the recording was made, its musical modesty is underscored by the absence of Caine's name on the cover—he is listed inside among the performers and as music director. The epoch he examines begins in the wonder year of 1892 ("Daisy Bell," better known as "A Bicycle Built for Two," "After the Ball," "The Bowery") and ends in the seminal era of 1914 and 1915, when the influences of minstrelsy, jazz, ragtime, and operetta produced a new hybrid in dance music (James Reese Europe's "Castle Walk"), the first modern ballad (Jerome Kern's "They Didn't Believe Me"), and the wit and wisdom of Irving Berlin ("Cohen Owes Me Ninety-Seven Dollars" and "When I Leave the World Behind" are two versions of the same theme). The only conspicuous omissions are Berlin's "Alexander's Ragtime Band" and songs pertaining to the First World War—the 1915 cutoff precedes America's intervention.

If Caine and company were willing to fade into the mosaic of another age, they understood that reverence and humor are no less compatible than sentiment and technology. *Sidewalks of New York* is a powerfully funny record on several counts. First, there is the material itself: Berlin's delightful preemptive strike about money and Jews, in which an exceedingly long verse about the dying Old Man Rosenthal tumbles into the brisk punch-line chorus, "Cohen owes me ninety-seven dollars/And it's up to you to see that Cohen pays"; Bert Williams's more celebrated preemptive strike about blacks and victimhood, "Nobody" ("Who soothes my thumping, bumping brain? Nobody!"); a recitative of Charles Hoyt's lyric to "The Bowery" ("I'll never go there anymore"), a song so chillingly popular in its day it was blamed for the decline in Bowery realty; and Norworth and Van Tilzer's "Take Me Out to the Ballgame" in Yiddish. The one chink in the fourth-wall is an amusing rehearsal for Shelton Brooks's "Some of These Days," followed by the finished performance; but, of course, rehearsals were necessary in 1910, too, so this one does nothing to destroy the work's bubble of illusion.

The most comical element is also the most dramatic, and one that lends cohesion, visual cues, and a raptly claustrophobic feeling to the whole work: the taped effects—the whinnying horses with their hooves echoing off cobblestones, crowd noises, kids playing in the streets, clinking barroom steins, storming rain, Coney Island in July, some of which I'm freely extrapolating from the constant obbligato of sounds, a singularly emotional use of musique concrete. During one seemingly pointless anecdote, "Sidewalk Story," you hear in the background someone whistling "My Wild Irish Rose," then a piano tinkling a couple of Joplin rags, then as the story reaches its point—how its teller came to play the accordion—a squeezebox player commiserating with "My Gal Sal." Was there ever really a Manhattan neighborhood or vaudeville bill that encompassed an Irish mezzo wailing "Has Anyone Here Seen Kelly?", a blues diva shimmying through "Some of These Days," a band marching to "You're a Grand Old Flag," and one soubrette insisting "Everybody's Doin' It" while a trio of soubrettes ask, "How'd You Like to Spoon with Me?" Probably not, but as a melting pot fantasy—"Boys and girls together/Me and Mamie O'Rourke/Tripped the light fantastic/ On the sidewalks of New York"—you could scarcely hope for a finer hallucination.

So how does all this play live? Very well. The record works because Caine came up with an ideal cast and he was able to bring most of it together at the Center for Jewish History—a superior new theater on West 16th Street with good acoustics and much potential for concerts that draw in the low hundreds. He excised and added a few numbers, rearranged the order, and focused on four vocalists, supported by his septet and the "sound design" (tapes) of Kyle Hartigan. In the blessed absence of costumes and stage props, the performers—wearing street clothes and climbing on and off stage, stepping over wires and around mike stands—had to create the old specters with voice and attitude. Nancy Opel, a radiant mezzo and something of a vocal chameleon, was from time to time briny Irish, Ziegfeld warbler, and sashaying advocate of doin' something other than the turkey trot. Barbara Walker, the piece's red hot mama, occasionally threatened to overdo the climaxes, but generally caught herself in time and controlled her inclination toward melisma. Saul Galperin, an elderly gent who I suspect is not a professional singer (Caine's or his label Winter & Winter's disdain of program notes does his cast and his work a disservice), handled the Yiddish with dry humor—and regularly announced the score of the sixth World Series game, eliciting many groans. Sadiq Bey walked onstage with what appeared to be three unfurled condoms hanging from his breast pocket; they turned out to be white gloves, which he wore for "The Bowery," the best of his three quirkily dour recitations.

The first-rate band included trumpeter Ralph Alessi, who played a dynamic lead, and Greg Tardy, who demonstrated an unexpected panache in his raggy clarinet wailing. Violinist Joyce Hammann filled out the front line, supported by banjoist David Gilmore, bassist Steve Beskrone, drummer Ben Perowsky, and Caine, with occasional accordion respites by Ted Reichman. The new numbers added to the album's mix included "A Hot Time in the Old Town Tonight," a whopping "Ballin' the Jack," and one unhappy ringer, "I'm Gonna Move on the Outskirts of Town," which was written more than 20 years after the others and didn't belong, even if Walker's growls and Tardy's heavy metal clarinet seared it nicely. By contrast, Walker's "Some of These Days" exulted in blues diva authenticity even more splendidly than on the record. More disillusioning was Caine's decision to modernize his solo numbers; he played a decent "Charleston Rag" on the CD, but in concert elected to upend "Maple Leaf Rag" with dissonant chords and bass-clef clusters, sacrificing period feeling for anarchic spontaneity, not a good trade.

The taped street sounds were effective and helped tie the numbers together. Less successful were the tuning-up interludes, which suggested an abrupt switch from one genre to the next, as though we were being whisked from studio to studio as a succession of bands prepared for the ensuing songs. Some of those passages went on too long; I shudder to think that I've misread the intention and that they were supposed to represent an avant-garde commentary on the last century. A more insistent attempt to spike the sentiment occurred during a closing singalong of "Sidewalks of New York" that devolved into a kind of Art Ensemble of Chicago discursiveness before returning to the world of Delancy Street Dixieland. Most of the audience was too shy to sing, which was just as well. Still, one had to wonder if Caine's distancing effects didn't vitiate a powerful feeling of longing and community that subsisted just below the surface of the concert and proudly skims the waves on the album. This is a work that merits more live performances. Its possibilities are limitless. But when in doubt, Caine might revisit the 1999 disc and go with his feelings.

[*Village Voice*, 20 November 2001]

100 ❖ *Bad Haircut, Good Ragtime (Brun Campbell)*

In westerns, the saloon pianist never gets any respect. Always a foil and never once a hero, he's there in a thousand movies, utterly nondescript in his bowler and gartered sleeve—a professional dweeb who plays "Hot Time in the Old Town Tonight" too fast and if he's lucky gets to back Ann Sheridan or Angela Lansbury, but whose primary job is to look nervous when trouble brews and duck as soon as the fists or bullets start flying. Who is this guy? Was he schooled, did he have a wife and kids, did he audition for the gig, could he read music, did he have a day job, was he paid tips or salary, was he a solid citizen or a drifter, where did he find material, did he ever get applause, did he have to supply his own garter? In real life, the job was not without allure. The adolescent Irving Berlin, for one, could think of no grander position.

Chicago-based Delmark, which, now in its fifth decade, documents blues, traditional jazz, the avant-garde, and anything else its founder and owner Bob Koester admires, has just issued a surpassingly strange disc that restores to posterity a barroom piano player who worked turn-of-the-century saloons as the Ragtime Kid. Brunson Campbell is well known to ragtime experts, because in addition to privately making a handful of records in the 1940s, one side only ("If they want to hear two tunes," he told writer Floyd Levin, "let them buy two records"), he was an influential propagandist for the postwar ragtime revival. If Campbell and his compatriots remain unknown to the rest of us, blame the lingering paranoia, snobbery, and ignorance that segregates jazz from its predecessors. Eubie Blake spent decades in the wilderness before his amazing comeback in 1969. Grove's new three-volume *Dictionary of Jazz* doesn't even have an entry for Scott Joplin. Compared to them, Campbell is a footnote's footnote, but one worth savoring.

Campbell's modest fame rests on his standing as Joplin's first and possibly lone white pupil. Though only 14 when he ran away from his Kansas home to pound the keys, Brun, who was born in 1884, would stroll into saloons and play a few rags or accompany barbershop quartets to "pick up easy money" from customers, who, during his 10 years on the road, included the outlaws Cole Younger, Henry Starr, and Emmet Dalton, as well as Pawnee Bill, Buffalo Bill, Lew Dockstader, Bat Masterson, and Teddy Roosevelt. "In those days," he wrote in Art Hodes's magazine, *The Jazz Record*, "pianists played on old battered square pianos. Some were inlaid with mother-of-pearl, and none I ever played on were in tune." He witnessed his share of fights and shoot-outs, but his eureka moment came early, in an Oklahoma City music store, in 1898, when ragtime pianist and composer Otis Saunders showed him a handwritten manuscript of "Maple Leaf Rag," and told him he was on his way to join its composer in Sedalia. Campbell headed that way too, and Joplin taught him how to play his first four rags.

In 1908, when ragtime was at its height, Brun abandoned professional music and married. Twenty years later, he established himself as a barber in Venice, California, where he quietly plied his trade until the 1940s, when young enthusiasts discovered him; with a little encouragement, he would close shop and regale them with stories. Turk Murphy told pianist and historian Terry Waldo, "You could always tell the guys who were going to see him, because of their haircuts. He wasn't really that good of a barber—but he played good ragtime." He was also, by all accounts, a good man. His early encounter with St. Louis's black ragtime elite washed away any taint of racial prejudice the South might otherwise have instilled. He argued passionately for recognition of the superior black players, recorded for the sole purpose of sending royalties to Joplin's ailing widow ("Of all Scott's old friends, you are the only one who has ever offered to do anything for him," she wrote him), and helped establish the Joplin memorial at Fisk University.

After Campbell's death in 1953, Paul Affeldt released some of his recordings on his label, Euphonic, a catalog that Delmark has been reissuing over the past year. The Campbell collection, *Joplin's Disciple*, includes about 20 numbers and fragments—most of them under two minutes, previously unissued, and presented in master and alternate versions. The sound is primitive, but the raw spunk of the playing is amplified by spoken comments, Campbell's homage to Joplin, and Joplin's piano roll of "Maple Leaf Rag," pumped by Campbell. Is he any good? Yes and no. His chops are limited, he makes mistakes, his rhythms are as pumped up and automated as a pianola in overdrive. His "Maple Leaf Rag," for example, is almost as studied as Joplin's roll, though he makes the key melody sing as few interpreters do. Yet he plays like no one else and he makes ragtime sound more plebeian, in a good way, than those who stick to the scores. If the sedate Joplin promoted in the 1970s by Joshua Rifkin and Marvin Hamlisch put you in a coma, consider Campbell's ur–rock and roll approach an antidote.

The album illustrates two musical theories. In *This Is Ragtime*, Waldo describes ragtime as an "expression of the mechanical age . . . its haunting quality (arising) from the juxtaposition of the older, lively Negro folk tunes within a hollow, metronomic framework." If you can accept a metronome that rushes, Campbell is q.e.d. In *Rags and Ragtime*, pianists and historians David A. Jasen and Trebor Jay Tichenor put forth a case for the folk rag, a generic kind of ragtime based not on specific scores but on a pool of melodies and rhythms mixed and matched at the performer's will; Campbell is cited as one of the first proponents. The new CD has many examples, though the piece they consider his masterpiece, "Chestnut Street in the '90s," is the only one not included, presumably because it never appeared on Euphonic.

The pianist enters like a moose on "Essay in Ragtime." Had Brun encountered any tuned pianos in his Midwestern travels, his left hand would have undone them. The force is so startling that you may not notice the modest embellishments or blues strain inserted at the trio. Campbell likes to combine two formats—the traditional 16-bar (or 8+8) ragtime strain and the 12-bar blues—and sometimes he doesn't seem to know which way he's headed until he gets there. Whenever he opts for the blues, it's either "Frankie and Johnny" or a variation on "Frankie and Johnny." For the rag of that name, he begins with blues choruses, switches to a 16-bar B strain, and then alternates the two, rushing the blues sections. "Lulu White" reverses the process, beginning with a 16-bar strain, played twice, followed by an F&J variation, then alternating them. On the second take of "Frankie and Johnny," he gets lost in the third chorus, as the left hand goes one way and the right another until he settles on the blues; he cuts the last chorus short by about seven beats.

That surely sounds like a mistake, but with Campbell you can't be too sure. On "Campbell Cakewalk," which he seems to be making up on the spot, he begins with a 28-bar strain: 8+12—though the 12 is not a blues—+8. The B strain (touch of "Who's Sorry Now?") is 16 and so is the C (touch of "Twelfth Street Rag"). About seven bars into the D strain, he suddenly turns the rhythm around, gaining two beats (or losing six) in the process and continuing with the new rhythm for another seven, thereby ending up with a strain of 14 and a half bars. If you think that must also be a mistake, consider "Barber Shop Rag," which hints at "Twelfth Street Rag" and "Muskrat Ramble" before arriving at a C strain that loses two beats in the 10th bar, ending up with an episode of 15 and a half bars. It sounds like a mistake, except there are two takes and it comes out that way every time.

Sometimes, as on "Ginger Snap Rag," he winds himself up into a state of near euphoria, but more often he gives sway to a blustery contrariness, as in three distinct takes of "Twelfth Street Rag," the first ending with a phrasing of the melody that unmistakably presages the theme from *The Third Man*, the second accentuating the counterpoint between melody and bass line, and the third additionally embellishing accents. For sheer asymmetrical pulsing jollity, nothing beats "Rendezvous," which begins with a five-bar intro, followed by blues choruses and a 16-bar strain that in its second and final incarnation winds up 17 and a half bars, as though he were about to extend the last eight into a blues but thought better of it.

On the B strain of "Rendezvous," Campbell flashes a treble gliss, recalling a segment from "Lily Rag," the best-known rag by Charles Thompson, whom Campbell says on his album was "the best of all of 'em." Recordings culled from two parties Thompson played shortly before his death in 1964, were released last year as *Neglected Professor*, one of Delmark's first Euphonic releases. Just as Campbell's life was transformed by Joplin, Thompson's was turned upside down by James P. Johnson, the Broadway composer and piano god whom he had met between 1912 and 1917, when Johnson was first getting started. The encounter encouraged Thompson to expand the ragtime idiom to include a wider range of rhythmic attacks, including boogie woogie and stride. He recorded little and few people heard him outside of St. Louis, where he operated a club. Thompson lacked Johnson's inventiveness, virtuosity, and spirit but had enough technique to evolve his own intimidatingly flashy style. Except for a couple of ponderous standards ("How Deep Is the Ocean," "Tennessee Waltz"), the Delmark disc is an impressive showcase for a pianist who replaces Campbell's brute force with razzle-dazzle syncopations and flourishes—he employs Johnson's Charleston beat on "Dicty's on 7th Avenue." Thompson, who became legendary for besting Tom Turpin in a much celebrated contest, could play and write rings around Campbell ("Lily Rag" is a peach). But he was also more conventional and there are passages when his chops cannot hide the wind-up aspect of a mechanical music. Through Thompson's polish and Campbell's primitivism, however, we can experience part of the foundation from which jazz and swing arose, and credit the rowdy world of cardsharps and wild women who paid the bills.

[*Village Voice*, 28 November 2001]

101 ❖ Laureate
(Irving Berlin)

In the aftermath of September 11, the whole country seemed to be singing "God Bless America," underscoring Irving Berlin's unimpeachable place in American song. (Berlin wrote the piece toward the end of World War I, but suppressed it until the outbreak of World War II, fearing that it might be too broad or corny.) No other songwriter has written as many anthems, including "White Christmas," "Easter Parade," and "There's No Business Like Show Business." No one else has written as many pop songs, period. Yet although Berlin was lauded as a tunesmith of genius as far back as 1911, when he debuted "Alexander's Ragtime Band," he is often undervalued as a lyricist and said to lack Porter's erudition, Hart's interior rhymes, and Mercer's homespun wisdom. *The Complete Lyrics of Irving Berlin*, edited by Robert Kimball and Linda Emmet, spans 81 of the composer's 101 years (1888–1989) and implicitly asks us to reconsider his achievement. In addition to highlighting his gift for economy, directness, and slang, it presents Berlin as an obsessive, often despairing commentator on the passing scene.

Berlin and just about everyone else in the Broadway and Hollywood songwriting factories of the early 20th century would have been surprised at the scholarship and fuss. Back then, their song lyrics were published in popular monthly magazines like *Hit Parader* and *Song Hits*, crib sheets for keeping up with radio—pop fodder, not to be taken seriously at a time when light verse as practiced by Ogden Nash, Dorothy Parker, and Phyllis McGinley was a staple of best-seller lists. By 1969, when many rock songs were valued for their topical relevance and Eric Sackheim offered the blues as poetry in his anthology, *The Blues Line*, the old Tin Pan Alley style had come to be seen mostly as hack work. Robert Kimball helped to redress that view with a series of oversized compilations of great lyricists. He began in 1971 with *Cole*, a shrewd choice as Porter's wit suited the printed page especially well. He moved forward with complete editions of the equally intricate work of Hart and Gershwin. Last year, with his longtime editor, Robert Gottlieb, he compiled an indispensable anthology, *Reading Lyrics*, which focuses exclusively on classic pop (blues, jazz, folk, rock, gospel, and country lyrics demand a companion volume). Surprisingly, it contains more songs by Berlin than anyone else. Now, in collaboration with one of Berlin's daughters, Kimball has broken the locks off Berlin's fabled archive, giving us the oeuvre, a third of which—nearly four hundred songs—was unknown.

Berlin wrote about everything: the wars, of course, and most aspects of show business, all the national holidays, and every kind of cooing and wooing; but also economics, Roosevelt, Capone, nudist colonies, censors, Bolsheviks, lynching, Prohibition, New York's finest, sex, loneliness, isolation, insomnia. On balance, Berlin was sadder and funnier than we knew. As a parodist, he took on Porter ("I'm a eunuch who / Has just been through an op—/ But if, baby, I'm the bottom, / You're the top") and himself ("God bless America, / Land I enjoy, / No discussions with Russians / Till they stop sending arms to Hanoi"). A swarm of puns on the word "step" in "Everybody Step" is worthy of the Marx Brothers, and "I've Got My Captain Working for Me Now" remains a rare comic response to the aftermath of war. Some of his lines might have passed muster with Dorothy Parker: "Someday I'm going to murder the bugler; / Someday they're going to find him dead—/ I'll amputate his reveille, / And step upon it heavily, / And spend the rest of my life in bed."

Berlin's lyrics are often crude, though never cruel, and many more are pure swill. Yet from the beginning he had an ear for the telling phrase, employing dialects to freshen familiar tropes: "I just couldn't stop her, for dinner and supper / Some kisses and hugs was the food; / When she wasn't nice it was more better twice, / When she's bad she was better than good." Still, his greatest work is that which instantly entered the public imagination, and if it is impossible to read "Isn't This a Lovely Day," "How Deep Is the Ocean," "Let's Face the Music and Dance," "White Christmas," "All By Myself," "I've Got My Love to Keep Me Warm," "How About Me?" and many more without hearing the melody in the mind's ear, that's the way it's supposed to be. The trick was to find the right words for the right tune, and no one did it better than Berlin.

[*The Atlantic*, December 2001]

102 ❖ Heroes at Work ("*Made in America*")

A new organization called Jazz Alliance International produced "Made in America," a jazz concert to benefit "the heroes and victims of September 11," on December 5 at Town Hall. No financial details were supplied about the poorly publicized and sparsely attended evening, except that it raised—obviously not from ticket sales—$260,000, which was given to the Robin Hood Foundation to aid "lower income victims." Save one mercifully brief speech by the JAI's president and an equally brief intermission, the program provided three hours of music, as each performer or band appeared for one number and then disappeared or remained on stage to play with the next configuration. None of the music was shabby, which is pretty impressive for an event of this kind; more amazing was the presentation's overall smoothness. However successful JAI may or may not be at raising money, it already knows how to organize a show; the only failing was the overmiked sound. Rhetoric was reserved for a playbill with musician bios, lists of board members (some 40) and absentee politicians, and a statement of purpose. The musical numbers were permitted to turn like pages in a novel, breezily unmolested, and it was impossible to reenter the night without thinking that jazz is a lot healthier than it's usually made out to be.

Despite minimal press coverage and no commercial broadcast presence at all; despite records that don't sell and clubs that depend on tourists who don't know the exchange rates; despite stars whose cumulative luster can validate festivals but who individually cannot be depended on to pack major halls; and despite desperate crossovers and the slander of jazz lite, mainstream jazz seemed on this night to be rock solid—knowing, optimistic, spirited. There were no blow-your-mind, never-to-be-forgotten moments, and though that might be deadly at the usual jazz festival, in this admittedly poignant context it redounded to the event's credit. What we got instead was a steady outpouring of insouciant inspiration. Not even inept sound (Town Hall's jazz-friendly acoustics were buried in amplification), which made the upper reaches of the piano sound like clattering silverware and sucked any group larger than two into fog, could dim the general eloquence. Dullness had few chances to wax.

Mainstream jazz is always a vexed concept, as the mainstream is thoroughly reconstituted every decade or so. Still, the boomer unity showed off the richness and diversity of what some might consider a narrow boomer perspective—one that draws most of its fuel from bebop as reconceived by Davis, Monk, and Coltrane. Of prebop swing (forget earlier idioms) not a note was heard; postbop approaches were accessed in digested and polished form. The 1940s avant-garde is roots to this sensibility, the 1960s avant-garde pretty much standard fare. The bona fide avant-garde of 2001 was entirely absent, as was downtown's mix-and-match eclecticism, midtown's neoclassicism, and uptown's blues-and-ballads earthiness. Also in conspicuous short supply was the living-legend generation; the only musician over 70 was Benny Golson and the only other ones over 60 were Wayne Shorter and Ron Carter. Except for Jane Monheit, callow youth stayed away, and she came off less callow than usual.

Songwriter choices were notable: No Ellington or Strayhorn, no Kern or Gershwin or Berlin, though Hoagy Carmichael, Woody Guthrie, and Peter Gabriel were sung. Thelonious Monk and Ornette Coleman received nods, but the favored jazzsmith of the night, surprisingly, was Charlie Parker—"Ah-Leu-Cha," "Confirmation," and by association, "Cherokee." I do not cite these limitations critically. The jazz audience has been so balkanized for so long, it was intoxicating to hear clamorous approval for a program that was at once various and like-minded. A few ringers would have sustained interest. But jazz is a language with several dialects, and "Made in America" showcased the lingo most likely to restore JATP enthusiasm to the broad base the JAI would like to reach. We are, sadly, better behaved than JATP fans—no catcalls and only one rising to the feet, at the end—yet the audience was unmistakably absorbed.

Partly because of the sound soup, duos came off particularly well, and the show began with a strong one: Greg Osby and Jason Moran. Moran's swinging arpeggiated sweep of the keyboard and in-and-out-of-sync phrasing with Osby kicked up the adrenalin and mandated another number that didn't come. No time to complain, though, because Moran was then joined by Christian McBride, Lewis Nash, and Joe Lovano in a brisk and bustling deconstruction of Coleman's "Broadway Blues," almost comically aggressive as it hurtled along on its sturdy bass vamp. Terence Blanchard, Kenny Barron, and Ron Carter joined with Nash to back Monheit, who caused a few moans by opening with the bridge to "Over the Rainbow," but, floated by exceptionally precise comping from

Barron and an ardent Blanchard trumpet solo (a bit heavy on the whimpering during his obbligato, though), made good on her choice, demonstrating greater rhythmic control and fewer mannerisms than on her record; the band hit a serious groove, which she did not disable. The groove intensified as Nicholas Payton, Benny Golson, and Paquito D'Rivera joined the rhythm for "Confirmation," taking two sage choruses each, trading fours, and playing the ensemble variation with drum breaks.

Banjoist Bela Fleck came out alone to play the first of the evening's several anthems, turning the national one into a kind of chaconne, with a reference to the Minuet in G amid the Bach, an impressive feat that stretched the jazz boundary, and what's wrong with that? His million-note solo on a quartet version of "Ah-Leu-Cha" was more a stunt than a variation, but the matchless team of Carter and Nash, the former hugging the ground with loping double stops, reaped another whirlwind and Blanchard rode it with the kind of burning panache you rarely hear on his CDs. It was followed by an even more engrossing duet by Barron and Regina Carter, whose work together (notably *Freefall*) has developed into something telepathic. They exchanged notes—she plucking one, he staccato-chording the next—on "Misterioso," then settled into it for an astutely elemental blues, deep and abiding, with terrific interplay, expected Barron elegance, and perhaps less expected rhythmic vivacity from Carter, who combined energetic riffs, sustained high-note bowing, and violin vocalisms that recalled Clark Terry's Mumbles.

And so it went: Kenny Werner entered to a smattering of applause to play a medley of "America the Beautiful" and "God Bless America," and left to cheers, not for patriotism, but because he turned them into coherent blues, sustaining rare feeling and closing with lightly tapped piano keys that sounded like whistling. Ruben Blades lent his big voice to (I think) a Panamanian ballad, backed by Danilo Perez, who stayed on stage as Brian Blade and John Patitucci came out to back the ineffable Wayne Shorter, whose elliptical soprano saxophone phrasing maintained an almost constantly understated suspense on "Masquelero." The trio responded with depth charges, locking into the fiercest rhythmic storm of the evening, powered by the patented Tony Williams funk-march and focusing the leader's epigrammatic story. Cassandra Wilson and her trio followed with the exceedingly prolix "Waters of March," and, joined by Fleck and Regina, "This Land Is Your Land," which had more vamp than dynamics, though the poor sound sabotaged the risky arrangement, if not Regina's rhapsodic solo.

A Michael Brecker–John Scofield quartet armed itself with Coltrane ecstasy, but also had to fight audio mud and, after a solid showing by

Brecker and a clouded one by Scofield, collapsed into a teeming Patitucci bass solo. Brad Mehldau, with the mood and restraint of a slow-blues player, soloed on "New York State of Mind," but couldn't escape the head, which he repeated relentlessly; he did better reuniting with Mc-Bride and Blade in Joshua Redman's old quartet ("Rejoice"), a controlled virtuoso display for which Blade unleashed none of the explosions that riveted Shorter. k.d. lang joined them on "Skylark," opening her considerable pipes to mine the great release, but holding on to certain notes a tad longer than necessary, compromising swing and never quite settling in as she does when she works with country bands. The finale found Dianne Reeves in stunning voice, lending her vivid, clinched melisma to "In Your Eyes," giving more than she received from that negligible song; she is primed for a greatness she keeps eluding.

Better to close with the trio that preceded her: McBride, Gregory Hutchinson, and Kenny Garrett frying "Cherokee" to a crisp, in a long-meter venture at racehorse tempo, with Garrett's slightly acrid timbre essaying the tune as written, then laying it into the flames, his alto phrases burbling a millisecond behind McBride's staunch beat, before challenging Hutchinson to a contest of raging eights—the kind of thing that loses steam on records, but can make a concert hall hiss with satisfaction. Too bad it took a national tragedy to bring together so many heroes of one of the nation's great prides. But the best jazz events these days are usually benefits or memorials—paradoxical evidences of its undaunted life.

[*Village Voice*, 18 December 2001]

103 ❖ *Brutality and Revival (The Best Jazz Records of 2001)*

Last year at this time I sermonized about the lack of consensus reflected in best-of-year record lists and tried to pep myself up for the long haul of a jazz post-history in which no one had the stomach for—let alone expectations of—genius or innovation. *Kind of Blue* was the year's best-selling jazz album; Louis Armstrong's centenary was off to a shaky start; and Ken Burns's *Jazz* was poised to change everything.

What a difference a year makes. Not that anything revolutionary took place, short of a dismantled Taliban and a vanished surplus, yet jazz optimism grew throughout the year, triggered by responses to the PBS documentary (even vitriolic criticism helped keep small-j jazz in the news) and underscored by the sparsely attended but inspiring "Made in America" 9/11 benefit. *Kind of Blue* continued its box office rule; Armstrong's centenary was disgracefully neglected by mass media; and the incredible rise in record sales following the *Jazz* broadcast could not be sustained, especially in a Bush economy, though the show's long-term effect won't be known for years—dozens of anecdotes have been reported like the one I heard from a man in a midwestern bookstore, whose 14-year-old came home from Tower with two CDs: Britney and Satchmo.

The jazz business is more than ever an oxymoron, so where are the signs of revival? Chiefly in the return of consensus. For the first time in several years, a handful of recordings roused general admiration—many of the same faces make the best-of lists every year, but I discerned a fresh excitement, a shared have-you-heard-so-and-so enthusiasm regarding live performances as well as records. Admittedly, this was mostly a critics' thing, but agreement of any sort is useful, even if it doesn't affect profit margin. Not a seat could be found as Cecil Taylor reunited with Elvin Jones at the Blue Note, too many seats went begging at Lincoln Center's Jimmy Heath tribute—neither event translated into record sales. Still, the first year of the new century effectively replaced wails of despair with many satisfactions, even as it cleared the decks with a relentless barrage of deaths.

Necrologically, 2001 was brutal: Al Hibbler, Billy Higgins, Billy Mitchell, Brother Jack McDuff, Buddy Tate, Cal Collins, Joe Henderson, Harold Land, Chico O'Farrill, Etta Jones, Flip Phillips, Jack Elliot, Jerry Jerome, J. J. Johnson, John Collins, John Lewis, Larry Adler, Les Brown, Lorez Alexandria, Lou Levy, Makanda Ken McIntyre, Manny Albam, Moe Koffman, Norris Turney, Panama Francis, Ralph Burns, Ralph Sutton, Spike Robinson, Susannah McCorkle, Tommy Flanagan. Also Anita Moore, Charles Ables, Frank Parker, Harold McKinney, Ike Cole, Janusz Zabieglinski, Jay Migliori, Nico Assumpcao, Paul Hume, Peter Schmidli. Plus tangential figures, including Charles Trenet, Chet Atkins, Ernie K-Doe, Francis Bebey, George Harrison, John Lee Hooker. And writers and producers: George T. Simon, Helen Oakley Dance, Jack Sohmer, Milt Gabler, Norman Granz.

One spot of good news on the mortality front: The new edition of the *Grove Dictionary of Jazz* includes a complete list of death dates as well as birth dates, and it appears that no one in jazz has ever died on March 14. True, many people are not listed in *Grove*, including anyone who played ragtime; but the inclusiveness is sufficient to warrant the belief that March 14 is Passover for jazz people.

There was much good news on the recording front, despite the reported death of Atlantic and the AWOL status of Columbia. Too bad Wayne Shorter didn't release anything—a CD companion to his two showings in New York would have clinched his jazzman-of-the-year status. Jazz CDs may not sell, but tireless artists, incurably enthusiastic indies, and a few stalwart majors continue to turn them out, and this year was fat with discs that will, in time, very likely join the more remunerative world of reissues. In no particular order, excepting numbers one and two, these are the ones I return to with increasing faith.

1. John Lewis, *Evolution II* (Atlantic). This time with a rhythm section and every bit the match of its 1999 predecessor. We will never again hear a keyboard touch like this, or as gloriously introverted a feeling for deep blues and saturated melody.

2. Jason Moran, *Black Stars* (Blue Note). Moran, at 26, has, like Lewis, that rarest of qualities—an unmistakable touch. His trio with Nasheet Waits and Tarus Mateen invents its future at every turn, here stimulated by crafty Sam Rivers, who is himself roused by a production that keeps the tracks short. The solo Jaki Byard homage, "Out Front," is a cognac interlude.

3. Louis Sclavis, *L'affrontement des prétendants* (ECM). ECM also released the 1996 *Les Violences De Rameau*, focusing on Rameau's last, long-buried opera, *Les Boréades,* and featuring the trombone of Yves Roberts; but while the nervous jump-cuts and amusing interpolations of the Baroque and the hysterical produce a compelling smorgasbord, the even more violent aggression of Sclavis's latest makes it something of a jazz-qua-jazz breakthrough. Excepting Bruno Chevillon's bass, he introduces a new quintet including a daunting if underused trumpeter, Jean-Luc Cappozzo, but Sclavis's high-calorie tone—the richest bass clarinet since Dolphy—and diverse voicings keep every track humming, especially the cortege, "Hommage à Lounés Matoub," written for the Algerian singer who was cut down a few years ago by a dozen assassins; it builds to an improbably affirmative whirling-dervish dance.

4. David S. Ware, *Corridors & Parallels* (Aum Fidelity). I disliked the movie *Lord of the Rings* (never read the book), but since seeing it, I find that Matthew Shipp's electronic interludes here remind me of the dark caves, and when Ware's tenor arrives, finally, and rises to its full height, it's like Gandalf knocking Christopher Lee on his ass. In other words, after five months, this album still seems pretty grand.

5. Matthew Shipp, *Expansion Power Release* (hatOLOGY). A series of appealing, mesmerizing ostinatos lift this final string trio project into the realm of ominous lyricism conjured by Bernard Herrmann—there is plenty of rock and rumble and blues, but the melodic gambits accomplish the come-hither thing.

6. Ted Nash, *Sidewalk Meeting* (Arabesque). Placing his reeds in the unlikely setting of violin, accordion, and tuba produced a ripping new sound that avoids pastiche even when reexamining Ellington and Debussy; in fact, those are the high points, and more fun than you'd think possible, with Wycliffe Gordon doing the vocalized plunger work. Also, the year's best album cover.

7. Ballin' the Jack, *The Big Head* (Knitting Factory). In mostly short takes of 16 pieces by Ellington, Django, Hawkins, Ammons, and Leadbelly via Clifford Jordan, Matt Darriau—who wrote many of the charts and co-produced with George Schuller—zeroes in on melodies and riffs. This is the second go for a band that derives from Schuller's Orange Than Blue, but with the mordancy turned up and everyone pledged to les tout ensemble.

8. Trio 3, *Encounter* (Passin' Thru). Oliver Lake, Andrew Cyrille, and Reggie Workman unite with a kind of loft-era thrift, and everything works—the energy level high, the affect sparkling yet controlled, and never a tossed-off moment. Lake's timbre is a saw with inch-long teeth and thoroughly fetching; I'd love to hear him commune with Lee Konitz.

9. Lee Konitz, *Parallels* (Chesky). Speak of the devil. The ageless improviser, splendidly recorded at Saint Patrick's, cuts deep swaths through two ballads and two originals, then explores the Tristano-era book with Mark Turner in the Warne Marsh role. During spontaneous "Star Eyes" variations and a smooth-as-satin "Subconscious-Lee," they achieve peace on earth.

10. Henry Threadgill, *Up Popped the Two Lips* (Pi). He simultaneously put out the modestly electric Make a Move's *Everybody's Mouth's a Book* on the same label (the titles are phrases from a Threadgill poem), but I slightly prefer the debut of the acoustic Zooid, with galumphing tuba and oud, sinuous cello, and spacey Liberty Ellman guitar—by all means, "Do the Needful."

11. Fred Anderson, *On the Run* (Delmark). Live at his own club, Anderson sustains interest with fragmented figures that wax and wax, spurred by bass vamps and electrifying percussionist Hamid Drake for what may be the best album ever by the smoothest and most elusive of the AACM saxophonists.

12. Bob Belden, *Black Dahlia* (Blue Note). Sentimentalizing a 22-year-old casting-couch hooker and murder victim would seem to be a senseless cause, but the result is so era-specific you can forget the backstory and dream up another; Belden and a cast of 65—winds, strings, rhythm, Joe Lovano, Kevin Hays, a powerfully expressive Tim Hagans, and himself in the final elegy—meld Miles and Jerry Goldsmith to make an enveloping noir soundtrack.

13. Roni Ben-Hur, *Anna's Dance* (Reservoir). Eloquent as a cool breeze, this understated exercise in bebop equilibrium wafts by so easy you might underestimate the magic—something only Barry Harris can effect. Ben-Hur, a guitarist with a low flame burning in each note, and Charles Davis, trading in his Sun Ra baritone for a suave tenor, speak Harris's lingo like natives.

14. Ahmad Jamal, *Olympia 2000* (Dreyfus Jazz). Saxophonist George Coleman and Jamal were psyched at this concert, within the borders of the leader's punctilious trio arrangements—which seem all the more impressive for having to support a guest. After four fast-moving, expansive quartet ballads, the trio returns for two lessons in Jamalian dynamics.

15. David Murray, *Like a Kiss That Never Ends* (Justin Time). This is a bringin'-it-all-back-home quartet (Hicks, Drummond, Cyrille) that opens with a jaunty bebopping "Blues for Felix," one of Murray's best pieces in years, and proceeds with the title tango, his only extravagant blowout; a gospel number; and a debonair bass clarinet version of Monk's "Let's Cool One," complete with witty tongue-popping intro and asides—all pleasure, no regrets.

16. Kenny Barron & Regina Carter, *Freefall* (Verve). More pleasure with Barron at his empathic best as Carter matures into a soloist of depth. The material—Romberg to Hodges to Sting, plus originals—was cannily chosen, but the freeform stuff closes the sale—the title cut and a rumination that serendipitously turns into Shorter's "Footprints."

17. Matt Wilson, *Arts and Crafts* (Palmetto) The exceptional young trumpet player Terrell Stafford continues to score as a sideman—he lets you know instantly that Wilson's trenchant "Lester" is not about Young, then rises to the challenge of Bud Powell's "Webb City." Larry Goldings plays piano (only he thinks he does better on organ), as the fastidious drummer-leader and bassist Dennis Irwin sustains a we're-swinging-and-it-ain't-no-big-deal merriment. Extra points for reviving Ornette Coleman's "Old Gospel."

18. Marc Ribot, *Saints* (Atlantic). I understand why his band, Los Cubanos Postizos, is a bigger draw, but I'll take the idiosyncratic solo recitals, of which this is Ribot's first on records since *Don't Blame Me*; every taut and quivering string is beautifully recorded as he connects Charley Patton to Duane Eddy in the name of Albert Ayler, burlesques Les Paul, and impersonates sitar, koto, dobro, and Monk.

19. Vijay Iyer, *Panoptic Modes* (Red Giant). A gifted pianist with his own distinctive nail-hammering attack, Iyer makes an equally strong impression in the way he regroups his quartet, micromanaging each piece with ostinatos and unison phrasing, especially in tandem with the sanguine saxophonist Rudresh Mahanthappa, creating an open, playful music.

20. John Hollenbeck, *No Images* (Blueshift). This maddening CD makes Martin Luther King's 25-minute sermon on the "drum-major instinct," backed by three blustery trombones and Hollenbeck's drumming, unreasonably emotive. Tenor blowouts by Dave Liebman and Ellery Eskelin provide more conventional ballast.

21. Archie Shepp and Roswell Rudd, *Live in New York* (Verve). Not quite the party it was in person, but the equation of boisterous Rudd, a restored and plaintive Shepp, and Cyrille-Workman interplay is so poetically involving even Baraka sounds good.

[*Village Voice*, 8 January 2002]

104 ❖ Reissues by the Box, Singers by the Cut (More Best Jazz Records of 2001)

Reissues and reclamation projects (vintage recordings that never previously saw the light of day) are the oxygen in which jazz, as a living art, breathes. They are the classics, benchmarks, standards, soul, and history of the music. They are proof that an improvised art can defy time; an excuse or demand for re-evaluation; a prize for the curious, the nostalgic, the acquisitive; and an economic security blanket for record companies that can't count on the sales of contemporary artists to satisfy their distributors or stockholders. Skeptics bewail the constant recycling of the old and reliable, rightly so when the only excuse is pointless tampering— like some of those microgroove remixes by Rudy Van Gelder (his recent work with 78s like Miles Davis's *Birth of the Cool* is another story entirely) that are sabotaging his reputation as well as the music he so brilliantly documented. Novices complain at the number of reissues, yet 20 years after the CD juggernaut many important performances have never been digitalized—try to find Teddy Wilson's "Blues in C-Sharp Minor," Stan Getz's "Diaper Pin," *The Jazz Odyssey of James Rushing, Esq., Miles Davis in Europe*, Sam Rivers's *Crystals*, Pee Wee Russell's *Ask Me Now*, Archie Shepp's *Live at Donaueschingen*.

Proof of how much remains to be done is demonstrated by how much *was* done in 2001, a year so rich in spelunking expeditions that a mere list won't do—better to swim amid the currents of newfound, rediscovered, and restored jewels. My liner notes notwithstanding, I cannot not identify the choice classic-jazz box as *Lady Day* (Columbia), because it nails one of the preeminent achievements in the canon, including rejected takes that really mean something, and because its expert mastering wipes away the taste of the label's abysmal-sounding 1980s Holiday CDs. It's obviously not the place to begin with Holiday, but it's the only way to wind up. Two other elaborate boxes merit no less attention. *Screamin' and Hollerin' the Blues: The Worlds of Charley Patton* (Revenant), includes a complete transcription of his lyrics, providing a new dimension to the most incomprehensible of seminal blues mumblers, and is packaged— like Holiday, only much more elaborately—in a 78-style album. It also features superior liner notes, not to mention a facsimile reprint of John Fahey's 1970 Patton book.

Still, the revelatory release of the year is *The Long Road to Freedom* (Buddha/BMG), an investigation into African American music from the middle passage to the pre-jazz beginnings of the 20th century, created by Harry Belafonte at several recording sessions between 1961 and 1971, and then, for reasons never explored in the unsatisfying booklet, abandoned for three decades. Belafonte recruited choirmaster Leonard de Paur to arrange songs—some famous, many unknown and marvelous, especially the lost Civil War anthems—with historical authenticity in concert versions that mine the tradition of the Fisk Jubilee Singers. Superbly engineered and performed by voices both raw and slick, from Joe Williams and Gloria Lynne to the Georgia Sea Island Singers and an unforgettable yet forgotten little girl named Sharon G. Williams, this immensely entertaining and thoroughly original voyage rewrites and expands exponentially what we think we know about black America's music, which is to say America's music.

The leading purveyor of jazz boxes is the mail-order company Mosaic, which enjoyed a discerning year with, among others, *The Complete Vee Jay Paul Chambers-Wynton Kelly Session, 1959–61* and *Classic Columbia Condon Mob Sessions*. No less appreciated is the oddly edited *The Complete OKeh and Brunswick Bix Beiderbecke, Frank Trumbauer and Jack Teagarden Sessions (1924–36)*, which includes Bing Crosby's jazz masterpiece, "Some of These Days," which Columbia keeps out of print. But the two sets I most value, and will discuss next time, are probably the most uneven— *The Complete Roost Sonny Stitt Sessions*, partly because it's almost entirely new to me, beginning with a wild date arranged by Johnny Richards, and serves as an object lesson in the vagaries of a too prolific paladin, heard here at his best and near worst; and *The Complete Capitol Bobby Hackett Solo Sessions*, which to my great surprise, having spent several years and much money hunting down the original LPs, is more impressive in aggregate than the single albums ever seemed.

The least expected and most revealing recovery of lost or forgotten discs was *Charles 'Baron' Mingus, West Coast, 1945–49*. Other discoveries include John Coltrane's *Live Trane* (Pablo), the quartet in Europe from 1961 to 1963, most of it previously unissued; Art Pepper's *The Hollywood All-Star Sessions* (Galaxy), small bands in L.A. from 1979 to 1982, previously issued only in Japan and including encounters with Stitt and Lee Konitz; and Miles Davis's *The Complete In a Silent Way Sessions* (Columbia), a gorgeous little monument that made me reconsider what I had long regarded as a mildly involving transitional album. The majority of reissues, however, simply revive long-deleted LPs. Verve's excellent Master Editions restored Louis Armstrong's rare and controversial late Decca LPs, offering the pop joys of *Satchmo Serenades*, *I Like Jazz*, the "angels" and "Good Book" concept albums, and the often incandescent *Satchmo: A Musical Autobiography*, which should have created more of a stir than it did, and might have with better packaging.

One Verve curiosity, easily overlooked yet worthy of its second chance at life, captures Bill Evans in 1958, when he was still a work in progress. His name never makes the roster of hard-driving pianists, because he is so closely associated with elaborate chord substitutions and an introverted approach. But back before *Kind of Blue*, Evans's music was defined by his Riverside debut and his fancifully percussive work with George Russell. His linear phrasing had an electric immediacy that strengthened his distinctive lyricism. A case in point is Eddie Costa's *Guys and Dolls Like Vibes*, an exceedingly rare 1958 Coral LP with Evans, bassist Wendell Marshall, and drummer Paul Motian. Costa, who died at 31, was an exceptional pianist, known for his rigorous solos centered at and below middle C, but he was also a distinctive vibes player, with an eerily muffled sound and an ear for close harmonies. For the six shining Frank Loesser songs on this album, Costa stuck with the vibes, allowing Evans to caper freely through his lively arrangements. Together, they turn "Adelaide" into a near blues—Evans interpolates a hunting call.

Delmark discovered a lovely, unissued, 1970s mostly blues recital by Art Hodes, *Tribute to the Greats*, and rediscovered the most obscure of ragtimers, Brun Campbell, who took off from barbering in 1947 to relive his heady youth on *Joplin's Disciple*. Yet Fantasy's OJC wins the obscurity sweepstakes for Don Sleet's *All Members*, an all-star-except-for-the-leader 1961 date (Jimmy Heath, Wynton Kelly, Ron Carter), led by a 22-year-old trumpeter about whom little is known, except that he died 25 years later, having made one impressive album. OJC also finally got around to Jaki Byard's *Sunshine of My Soul*, one of the great 1960s trio sessions (David Izenson, Elvin Jones), even if hardly anyone knew it: Discover and marvel.

BMG Bluebird offered the positively last word on Charles Mingus's immortal *Tijuana Moods* and Coleman Hawkins's neglected *The Hawk in Hi-Fi*, arranged by Billy Byers, one of the better jazz-and-strings dates, the great man bristling with invention. The finest and most comprehensive reissue program of the 1960s was RCA Vintage, an 85-LP series that erased the boundaries between Jelly Roll Morton and Woody Guthrie, and was crassly dropped. Now Koch has issued one—count 'em, one— Vintage entry, *Things Ain't What They Used to Be*, the 1940 Ellington small-group dates nominally led by Johnny Hodges (truly luminous) and Rex Stewart (darkly witty). Koch is also issuing the complete Ralph J. Gleason Jazz Casual broadcasts; the famously taciturn Count Basie is surprisingly talkative throughout his entry.

The interviews aren't always as easy to hear on the big-band-bebop-meets-tango-and-bossa-nova State Department concert captured on *Dizzy in South America, Vol. 3* (CAP), but you have never heard a trumpet-break like the one Gillespie plays on this stunning "A Night in Tunisia," which inspires Benny Golson to heights of his own. Another exuberant if more recent big band find is *Traveling Somewhere* (Cuneiform), a 1974 concert by Brotherhood of Breath, the irreverent UK avant-garde group led by the transplanted South African pianist, Chris McGregor. Jazz Unlimited has collected key Jubilee Armed Forces broadcast numbers on *A Jumpin' Jubilee*, complete with archaic Ernie Whitman intros—it's the only place to hear Hawkins and Lester Young side by side, or Charlie Parker, Benny Carter, and Willie Smith side by side by side with Nat Cole. Forgotten works by forgotten but engaging singers were also disinterred, notably the lamented Teri Thornton's *Open Highway* (Koch), with its inspired selection of obscure songs, arranged by the utterly obscure Larry Wilcox; *This Is Lucy Reed* (OJC), who turned down a spot with Ellington to stay home with her family, but managed to get Gil Evans *and* George Russell to arrange her album; and *Miss Helen Carr* (Avenue), a Holiday-influenced skylark who died at 38 in a car accident.

Okay, singers. My God, there are a lot of them, often displaying more cheesecake than early issues of *Nugget*. Generally I found myself less disposed toward whole albums than to particular cuts. Rene Marie, on *Vertigo* (Maxjazz), does not always know when to give a riff a rest and scats with more abandon than is strictly necessary, but her nervy medley of "Dixie" and "Strange Fruit" is chilling, perfectly executed, and not to be missed. Jeanie Bryson's *Deja Blue* (Koch) is fairly consistent, except for her "Am I Blue," interpolating "Con Alma," which is so masterly I end up cutting to the chase. While Tony Bennett's *Playin' with My Friends* (RPM/Columbia) offers almost as many gems as guests, the piece de resistance is "Everyday," with a wailing Stevie Wonder. You won't find a bad cut on Shirley Horn's *You're My Thrill* (Verve), yet there is an epiphanic moment, "My Heart Stood Still," as there is on Rosemary Clooney's elegiac *Sentimental Journey* (Concord), its title number.

Several tracks reverberate on Bob Dylan's *Love and Theft*, including "Bye and Bye," with its partial steal from "Blue Moon," complete with "sugarcoated words"; or "Floater," with its melodic bridge and touch of "The Whiffenpoof Song"—Dylan singing changes, Dylan coming as close to jazz as he ever has, when he isn't singing blues like "Summer Day," which may be his best Louis Jordan–type jump tune since "Maggie's Farm," and "High Water," which begins in Joe Turner's Kansas City and travels to Charley Patton's Mississippi. I wish he had let the players solo, especially guitarist Charlie Sexton, but then, the words are important too.

The big surprise for me was Karrin Allyson's *Ballads* (Concord), because though she's been around, I'd been unaware. A singer who has the moxie to cover John Coltrane's smoldering 1962 classic of the same name, however, is going to get noticed. Supported by a James Williams rhythm team and saxophonists James Carter (who sounds a bit stir-crazy in his entrance on "Say It [Over and Over Again]" but makes a shifty comeback), Bob Berg, and Steve Coleman, Allyson coolly stakes her claim on almost every number (only "It's Easy to Remember" gets by her), reminding us that not the least part of Coltrane's genius was his ability to choose good tunes. She brings a timbre that is part ice, part grain, and lilting high notes for which she drops her vocal mask in favor of a near-falsetto liberation, always well pitched. Her versions of "I Wish I Knew," "What's New" (stellar Berg solo), and an unexpectedly expressive "Nancy" are incisive, original, and emotionally convincing. And by cheesecake standards, she provides a photo that is actually sexier than it is silly: vocalist in bed in pink sweater, left nipple pointing at camera. Did Coltrane ever pose like that? Oh, right, forgot about that phallic soprano saxophone.

[Village Voice, 22 January 2002]

105 ❖ *Long Roads*
(Harry Belafonte)

You won't find Harry Belafonte's name on the cover of the handsome, oversized box that houses *The Long Road to Freedom*, or on the title page of the 140-page book that accompanies its five CDs. Take that as an

example of the modesty and restraint that led him to create this astonishing treasure in the first place. In the late 1950s, when he first proposed
documenting a history of African American music from the early days
of slavery to the close of the 19th century, only Elvis Presley rivaled
Belafonte as RCA's top seller. The company president, George Marek, a
genuinely musical executive (they existed in those days) who later wrote
several accomplished biographies, committed the label to the project.
Many recording sessions took place, beginning in 1961 and continuing
over the next decade. Yet after Marek died, the work died as well, abandoned and apparently forgotten for nearly 30 years. Its belated release
now by the RCA/BMG affiliate Buddha Records is a major event, perhaps the most important of several major releases in the fall of 2001, for
it will influence the way we hear, understand, and write about African
American music.

Still, although it hit shops in early September, you very likely have
not heard about it. The tragedy of 9/11 undoubtedly derailed some press
coverage but does not explain Buddha's less than stellar promotion of
an achievement that, though it concerns one of this country's most vile
transgressions, has the power to make one feel perversely patriotic and
proud—proud of what the enslaved segment of the population produced
in music as a joyous, subversive, spiritual counterpoint to unimaginable
hardships and unreasoning hatred. To the degree that all of us share that
heritage, *The Long Road to Freedom* represents a national birthright, reminding us that white America is culturally more than a little black, and
hallelujah for that.

I know of no other work like it. Most anthologies of this kind simply
collate old records. Belafonte, however, insisted on researching three
hundred years of black America's folk music and recording new performances that highlight the music's aesthetic durability while emphasizing historic authenticity. Although he was often dismissed as a slick
entertainer by the coffee house folkies of the 1950s, Belafonte seriously
devoted himself to exploring the folk roots of this and other countries.
If his blues performances sometimes suffered from a theatricality that
muffled the sheer pleasure he imparted to calypsos, he looked more
deeply into his material than most performers and played an important
role in introducing African (remember Miriam Makeba?) and other musicians to the American palate—long before the phrase "world music"
was coined.

His approach for *The Long Road to Freedom* was firmly rooted in the
neglected and misunderstood tradition of the Fisk Jubilee Singers, who
presented spirituals in concert arrangements in the 1870s—a conflation
of reality and art directly at odds with the faux-nativism marketed by

'60s pedants, who wanted their rediscovered blues heroes in overalls and straw hats. Bluesman Lonnie Johnson once said, in effect, "Someone is always trying to put a crutch under my ass." Belafonte, who sings on several selections with a patented histrionic emotionalism that was as effective at these 1960s sessions as it was in his "Day-O" years, corralled a handful of recording stars (including Joe Williams, heard at a magnificent vocal peak, Brownie McGhee and Sonny Terry, the much underrated Gloria Lynne, and the matchless Bessie Jones and the Georgia Sea Island Singers). But his most important decision was to seek out choral director Leonard de Paur, whose arrangements bring a chilling, provocative, and, in many instances, unknown repertoire to new life. De Paur assembled the choir in the course of nationwide auditions, hiring only those singers with distinctive timbres.

The entire project is abetted by stunning audio engineering and remastering that belies the age of the recordings. From the opening assault of African percussion and an array of voices from the Congo, Nigeria, and Ghana, representing the middle passage, through the blues performances that presage the 20th century, one can scarcely believe these vibrant performances have been sitting in a vault for so long. The music unfolds in movements, or chapters, documenting the development of the 19th-century style in town and country—Civil War anthems, Christmas songs, children's songs, prison and chain gang songs, minstrel songs, spirituals, hollers, hoedowns, early blues. The material is often revelatory. Did you ever wonder precisely what kind of music was performed in New Orleans's Congo Square in the early 1800s? De Paur and company demonstrate three possibilities. The Civil War threnodies created by black troops add something genuinely new to our knowledge of the conflict—how, one wonders, did songs as powerful as "The Colored Volunteer" and "We Look Like Men of War" disappear from the country's ongoing folk tradition? Even pieces that are very well known—"Betty and Dupree," "Stagger Lee," "Pick a Bale o' Cotton"—sound revitalized by context and performance.

Sadly, some documentation from the original sessions was lost; a few of the soloists are unidentified, and we learn nothing about those who are known. Who, for example, was Sharon G. Williams, the little girl with the steely voice heard on the ring game, "Oh, Johnny Brown," and what became of her? The book, attractive and informative though it is (with black and white drawings by Charles White, photographs by Roy DeCarava, a good interview with Belafonte, and a long essay by Mari Evans), fails to investigate the origins of much of the material or explain why the project was discontinued. The primary essay draws on familiar sources—most conspicuously Alan Lomax's New World Records album,

Georgia Sea Island Songs—but breaks no ground, leaving too many questions unanswered and unaddressed. A bonus DVD is included, with a Belafonte interview that repeats some of the material in the book while underscoring a sense of the excitement involved in producing the original recordings and the elation at rediscovering the masters decades later. Folklorists and musicologists will have their hands full pinning down the selections, authenticating or refuting the choices that were made. The music makes its own case. Bright as if it had been recorded yesterday and so potent it is best savored in sections, it's like a secret opera, drawn from one century to unfold in another.

[*The Absolute Sound*, January 2002]

106 ❖ Gypsy State of Mind (Bireli Lagrene)

Bireli Lagrene, whose electrifying new album, *Gypsy Project* (Dreyfus Jazz), represents his best work in several years, must have days when he feels like Michael Corleone: Every time he gets away from the Django Nostra, they drag him back in. I'm not sure who "they" is, except for admirers like me, who—though startled by the intensive authenticity of his homage to Sinatra (*Blue Eyes*, 1998), his reclamation of unlikely standards such as "C'est Si Bon" (*Standards*, 1992), and the ostentatious bebopping excesses of what is perhaps his best previous album, *Live in Marciac* (1994)—long to hear him mine his Sinti roots, especially since no one else can do the Django thing with his fortitude or aplomb. To be sure, he has always revisited parts of Reinhardt's repertory: "Nuages," "Body and Soul," "I Got Rhythm" and its ubiquitous changes. But summoning Reinhardt means more than replicating a guitar style or a set of tunes or a special instrumentation (guitar, violin, bass, rhythm guitars). It means a state of mind.

It's the last part, the state of mind, that is and ought to be most elusive. With Reinhardt, it involves the innocence of prewar swing, the nose-thumbing subversions of occupied France, the cool arrogance of bebop, and, tying them together, a uniquely Gallic combination of jazz and sentiment. Lagrene captures much of that, because his understanding of Reinhardt is deep and abiding, but he doesn't belong to that world, and probably doesn't give much thought to it. The best and worst thing you can do to his *Gypsy Project* is compare each track to the Reinhardt models: best because the correlation underscores his originality; worst, because it reveals the limitations of devotion and virtuosity. He lacks Django's patience, dark moods, expressive feeling, and constructivist logic.

Lagrene is all fireworks and jubilation, the possessor of 10 magical fingers (Django could count on only eight) that sometimes seem to have their own minds. He needs all his wits just to control them. Right off, with the first notes of the first track, "Blues Claire," he blazes his own turf. This was a tour de force for Django in 1943—a 13-chorus blues solo that he paced by strumming the sixth chorus and changing the game in the ninth, as the rhythm section briefly dropped out, returning to catch him in a new key. As is the case with almost every track, Lagrene's version is faster and brighter. He gets you by the short hairs with his knowing, percussive attack, tossing in lightning tremolos; he goes on to combine melodic comets with delirious runs, clarifying the schema with eight-bar riffs and fancy four-bar resolutions, and, after six choruses (he strums the sixth for those keeping track), turning it over to Florin Niculescu, an extraordinary violinist who reads Bireli's mind the way Stephane Grappelli read Django's. No key change, no steady buildup—just canny exhilaration, glowing tenacity, churning rhythm.

In every instance but one, Lagrene's versions are shorter than Reinhardt's. Often, I wish they weren't—that he would let himself go on, if not quite as relentlessly as at Marciac then at least as much as Reinhardt. Yet by sticking to 78-rpm length performances, Lagrene focuses his statements, compressing them into jewel-like effusions, which is one reason this album never wears out its welcome. It's also one way for Lagrene to channel an aspect of the Reinhardt state of mind available to him. At Marciac, playing electric guitar (as Django sometimes did after the war, beginning with his only American tour, in 1946), he did what you'd expect to "Donna Lee" and went over the top on "Autumn Leaves," maybe the fastest interpretation of that tune since Miles Davis played Antibes, although the brilliance itself can be wearying. The Django mind frame not only encourages him to make every note count, but also increases a respect for feeling and mood, for site-specific improvisation, for melody. The very sound of the acoustic guitar induces a greater sensitivity to the moment.

Lagrene is the only musician I've ever spent an afternoon watching cartoons with. In 1980, he released his first album, *Routes to Django*, at age 13—one of the most dazzling debuts in jazz. A couple of years later, I convinced a magazine to send me to Salzburg to interview him and see for myself the young man whom Joseph Reinhardt claimed had inherited his brother's right (flat-picking) hand. He was not yet 16, and spoke no more English than I did Sinti (a Gypsy patois), German, or French, languages in which he was fluent. So through an interpreter, he explained that he began playing at four, began teaching himself Django records at eight, and, after learning that the fourth and fifth digits of his master's fretting hand had been paralyzed, spent the next three years teaching himself to play Django's runs with two fingers. He listened to everyone from Charlie Christian to B. B. King to Pat Martino, but stayed away from electric guitar, which he said did not afford him the sound he wanted. And then his favorite cartoon shows came on, the interpreter put a finger to his lips, and that's how we spent the rest of the day.

At that time, I wrote that he was not as comfortable with ballads as supersonic tempos. That still appears to be true. But there were changes in the interim. After he made his American debut in 1984, and was discovered by other guitarists while he in turn discovered fusion and found the electric sound he liked, he seemed unmoored. Teenage years are hard on everyone. Even after he returned to more conventional jazz settings, learning English well enough to sing "The Lady Is a Tramp" without an accent, a portion of his individuality still seemed sacrificed to his teeming virtuosity. *Gypsy Project* suggests a return to form. It's a buoyant exercise in recycling classic records through a generational warp. The upshot is he seems most himself, most inspired, when frankly steeped in the Reinhardt legacy.

His selection of tunes is noteworthy. The album has a couple of standards from the early Quintette du Hot Club, "Limehouse Blues," "Viper's Dream," and two takes of "Daphne," patterned after the 1940 version, with Richard Galliano added on accordion; and several from the war, among them "Blues Claire," "Swing 42," and "Vous et Mai." From the latter period comes the most unlikely number, perhaps the album's highlight: "Je Suis Seul ce Soir," which Django recorded as the guest of a big band in Brussels, in 1942. The sentimental melody was assigned to the orchestra, which opened with a cornball intro, and the record was salvaged by Reinhardt's jaunty improvisation. Lagrene's interpretation, the only track to exceed five minutes, is an improvement in its deliberate intro, medium-tempo bounce, and affecting Niculescu theme statement, with pointed guitar obbligati, strummed and picked. Lagrene begins his improvisation with melodic embellishments, sustaining them with poise and feeling, notwithstanding his aggressive attack, impromptu rhythms, flashy harmonics (high semi-articulated ghost notes achieved by lightly plucking the string an octave above the stopped note). Even here, as soloist and bolstering accompanist, Lagrene trots where Django strolled, pushing the beat, but effectively and with rare equilibrium. He improves the theme statement of "Belleville," too, replacing its dated, foursquare phrasing with "Nagasaki"–like drive; yet while Lagrene's solo, with its varied accents and strummed turnback, is just fine, a comparison with Django's superb bridge and concluding harmonics helps keep a sense of proportion.

Most selections, however, are from Reinhardt's neglected later years— including the standards "Coquette" and "Embraceable You." On the first, Lagrene retains the bowed bass and basic arrangement of Django's original, except for a brighter tempo and shorter solos that bring it in at just over two minutes; it's enough—Lagrene's confidence is stunning (he opens with a paraphrase of "Exactly Like You"), as though he can hardly wait to get out of the starting gate. Django's original "Embraceable You" is a benchmark performance, for Grappelli's double-time solo as well as the guitarist's fantastic, logical profusion of ideas, right through to the strange ending, combining a bop lick with a violin cadenza. Still, Lagrene has his own ideas—he delivers a walloping chorus before opting for an abrupt finish.

He retains the boppish finish to "Festival 48," and turns the rhythm around in his solo, Django-style, primed for speed, chugging up a sand-storm behind Niculescu, who manages not to get lost in the dust. By contrast, he misses the ominous quality of "Si Tu Savais," playing an exposition that is lovely in itself yet lacks Reinhardt's lyrical foreboding. Jaw-dropping pyrotechnics emphasized by brevity are the order of "Limehouse Blues" (all 110 seconds of it), "What Is This Thing Called Love?" (with "Hot House" interpolated), and "Vous et Mai" (with a disarming opener of swirling harmonics), but the most bravura episode comes in the "version longue" (2:56), as opposed to "version courte" (2: 25), of "Daphne." The extra 30 seconds allow Lagrene and Galliano to play a chase chorus of four-bar exchanges—the kind of thing you want to hear again immediately. If Lagrene loves life as much as his footloose fingers suggest, you might as well enjoy it with him. Plenty of people can tug at your heart. Lagrene can make it beat faster.

[*Village Voice*, 30 January 2002]

107 ❖ *Surviving the Marketplace (Sonny Stitt / Bobby Hackett)*

All artists who have to work for a living are coaxed into adjusting the aspirations of their talent to the fashions of the marketplace. Recent compilations on Mosaic, the mail-order company in Stamford, Connecticut, indicate how two freelancers handled this dilemma. Although only nine years separate Bobby Hackett from Sonny Stitt, that's a generational leap in jazz—it's the difference between coming of age with Armstrong's big bang and to maturity in an era of Dixieland and swing, and coming of age with swing's big bands and to maturity with bebop and r&b. Yet from the purview of a new century, the symmetries overwhelm the distinctions. *The Complete Capitol Bobby Hackett Solo Sessions* and *The Complete Roost Sonny Stitt Studio Sessions* capture both men at personal peaks while muddling through compromised or indifferent settings. Mosaic, it should be noted, does not edit best-of sets. If the constituent albums were available separately (they aren't at present), one or two from each box might satisfy most listeners. On display here are warts-and-all biographical portraits of two pros making their way.

One obvious parallel involves questions of influence, which caused greater anxiety among critics than these particular musicians. Stitt (1924–82) idolized Charlie Parker and had begun to master his music by 1943, before Parker was known to the public. He adapted Parker's light, bright sound, speed, and a lexicon of his riffs that he never stopped using. Stitt's alto had its own fire (e.g., 1949's "All God's Chillun Got Rhythm"), but he underscored his emerging style by taking up tenor, allowing the classic swing legato of Lester Young more parity in his work (1950's "Mean to Me"). No matter how thrillingly or distinctly he played, though, Stitt was bedeviled by the comparison. Hackett (1915–76) initially made his name in 1938, playing a one-minute Bix Beiderbecke solo at Benny Goodman's Carnegie Hall debut, and had to withstand decades of assumptions that made no sense, because Hackett's approach to trumpet and cornet is thoroughly individual on every level, from timbre to phrasing. His Beiderbecke readings on a 1955 session (see Mosaic's *The Complete CBS Recordings of Eddie Condon and His All Stars*) are conspicuous for the absence of Bix licks.

Homages to Bix and Bird were the least of it. Pigeonholing bound them to generic conventions—polyphonic revels for Hackett, harmonic steeplechases for Stitt. This was natural enough, on the surface, yet one can't help but feel that their promise was stifled by the comforts of routine. Thus Hackett flitted predictably between Condon-style Dixieland and mood music, for which he apprenticed during a brief but momentous stay with Glenn Miller and a blockbuster success as the soloist on Jackie Gleason's seduction LPs. Thus Stitt flitted predictably between small bop ensembles, including frequent jousts with other saxophonists, and the humbler mood music of organ bands—a love child of bop and r&b that got radio play. Hackett, who liked to perform modern pieces live, often recorded great tunes in corny settings; Stitt, who had a taste for Tin Pan Alley detritus, often recorded corny tunes in hip settings.

For a while, each had to overcome the bad habits of a generation: the bottle for Hackett, the needle for Stitt. That didn't make them any more independent. Yet the ways they acceded to commercial dictates could hardly have been more different. Stitt, who would record anytime, anywhere, usually with a pick-up band, had an invulnerable sense of noblesse oblige. If the session was uninspiring, say an organ group or electric saxophone venture or a rent-paying session with a dull producer, he just connected the dots, letting arpeggios unreel while his brain vacationed, assuming that his serious fans could tell his committed music from his work for hire. I'm speculating, but not without experience, having, in 1975, produced Stitt's worst album. He arrived at the studio, took one look at the all-star band I assembled, the lead sheets I dared to propose, and my own callow but eager face, and demanded, consumed, and regurgitated a quart of scotch, before mentally leaving the building—yet how his fingers flew!

The Mosaic set has plenty of both Stitts. "Cherokee" (naturally) is pure exhilaration—incisive bebop acrobatics, spry and sly, pushed forward by a heroic rhythm section (Hank Jones, Wendell Marshall, Shadow Wilson), with Stitt so adroitly commanding that even his Bird quote has a kind of stubborn brio. Many of the Roosts are this good, including the rare use of large ensembles arranged by Johnny Richards, whose modernist harmonies are close and almost cuddly, yet juiced by occasional dissonances, and Quincy Jones, who employs a Basie-alum rhythm section—Stitt draws energy from Freddie Green's guitar on "My Funny Valentine"; on "Lover," when he feels a cliché coming on, he bats it away like a gnat.

Stitt has his cornball side—tag endings and those little pick-me-up turnbacks with which he wheels from one episode into another, not to mention a predilection for ditties like "My Blue Heaven" and "(Keep Your) Sunny Side Up" (mistakenly described as a Stitt original!), both heard on the excellent 1959 *Sonny Side Up*; here, on tenor, he is his own man, even when insinuating Parker in his double-timing or channeling Young in his yearning introspection, as in the neat eight-bar units with which he poses variations on "My Mother's Eyes." But then there's "Sposin'," from one of the many sides he made with organist Don Patterson, where mellowness is a consequence of distraction and the turnbacks are covered in moss. It's almost laughably predictable and flat as the plains. Nor does he perk up for a session with Thad Jones and Chick Corea that verges on jazz lite—a producer's idea, no doubt. He goes out on a high note, however, stimulated at his final Roost session by Harold Mabern and Roy Haynes.

Hackett had a lot worse to contend with than Stitt, but his response was to play every solo as though it might be his last. The same silvery brilliance he brought to sessions with his own bands is heard amid arrangements of breathtaking awfulness. Mosaic uncharacteristically presents the albums as originally sequenced, reserving two infelicitous concept LPs for the last disc: on *Blues with a Kick*, which has little in the way of blues, he delivers on those rare occasions when he is permitted to poke his horn through the charts (his break on "Sugar Blues" goes off like an alarm clock—it failed to wake up the producer, but did amend the shuffle rhythm); on *Hawaii Swings*, a good little band is restrained by cuteness.

Don't Take Your Love from Me, however, could be the most schizoid album every made; the utterly appalling charts by one David Terry present Hackett with the obstacle of a three-women choir from the banshee school of wordless shrieking (they suggest a theremin at times), plus such condiments as tambourine, tympani, and harpsichord. And yet, and yet: Hackett plays with the infallible tact and expressive determination of a man who doesn't know or care that he's surrounded by philistines. On songs like "Autumn Serenade," "Street of Dreams," and the obscure "Wonderful One," there are passages of ludicrously alien yet genuine drama, a meeting of the mind and the mindless. So much for apologies. The other seven albums wreath Hackett in clover.

When I was younger, I used to resent the short playing time of, say, *The Bobby Hackett Quartet*. But in this context, as gorgeous details proliferate in one number after another, I'm more inclined to appreciate how complete and realized his every solo is. Only one number, "My Monday Date," from *At the Embers*, comes to an ungainly or abrupt end; elsewhere, a daring grace dominates, a combination of animated arrangements and Hackett's alacrity in attacking the melodies. Most of this music is supposed to be not jazz lite but light jazz, '50s style—supper-club fare. So the depths he achieves romping through "Spring, Beautiful Spring," of all things, is a reassuring surprise, as though he were aiming every note in defiance of the dollar sign Capitol was trying to stamp on his brow. This isn't mood music: You could do aerobics to "C'est Magnifique." One marvels at the energy of the opening notes on "It's Been So Long" or the swinging élan of "If I Had My Way," the stuff of barbershop quartets, wondering how he got away with playing as hard as he does. Of course, he didn't score the big hits. But then, I don't imagine Mosaic will be collecting the Capitol quartets of Jonah Jones, who did.

From the first bars of *Soft Lights and Bobby Hackett*, for which he is backed by rhythm and an efficient string quartet that never becomes oppressive, Hackett embellishes tunes more boldly than he is generally thought to do (Jon Hendricks could write a lyric to his choruses on "Old Black Magic"), hitting key melody notes while kneading harmonies to bring out every lovely curve, invariably maintaining the equilibrium of a dance—for example, his breaks on "I Cried for You." Something else brought into sharp focus by this box (and Dan Morgenstern's superb notes) is the variety of sounds he effects through mutes without sacrificing his impeccably controlled timbre—for example, the Harmon-mute buzzing on "You Turned the Tables on Me."

Still, I prefer his open horn, as on the exceptional April 3, 1956, session, when Hackett recorded four masterpieces, including an almost embarrassingly sexy "Moonlight Becomes You." His timelessness is underscored by a session that borrowed the style of George Shearing's Quintet (the label, which had him under contract, might better have borrowed Shearing); its calculated modernism now sounds cloying in a way Hackett's variations do not. Hackett kept growing: his "Embraceable You" from 1959's *Easy Beat* rivals his classic 1939 version, and trumps it in harmonic complexity. Sonny Stitt has always benefited from the imprimatur of the modern, which sees him and us through a lot of journeyman work. Maybe Mosaic, which previously released Hackett records on *The Complete Capitol Fifties Jack Teagarden Sessions* (including the ebullient *Jazz Ultimate*), *Classic Capitol Jazz Sessions*, *Classic Columbia Condon Mob Sessions*, and the aforementioned *The Complete CBS Recordings of Eddie Condon and His All Stars*, has earned for Hackett an overdue reevaluation beyond the stereotypes of Dixieland and Muzak.

[*Village Voice*, 29 January 2002]

108 ❖ *The Microtonal Man (Joe Maneri)*

One of the infrequent pleasures of ethnic weddings and bar or bat mitzvahs in the era before DJs began contributing to musical unemployment was the chance encounter with jazz players working anonymously in the bands. I can recall coming across sidemen once associated with Fats Navarro, Woody Herman, Thad and Mel, and Cecil Taylor. Musicians call those gigs socials, and often play them for the same reason many critics write liner notes and press releases: It's a living. As a rule, they bring their jazz expertise to the gig and take little if anything away. Joe Maneri suspended that rule. The saxophonist and clarinetist, who celebrated his 75th birthday with a full house at Tonic on February 9, took to heart the pitch variations in Greek, Israeli, Middle Eastern, and other party musics he mastered in the line of duty, noting their affinity with scalar particularities in the music of West Africa and India as well as jazz, and made his way into the alternate universe of microtonality.

Having flirted with instrumental vaudeville (two instruments at the same time), Dixieland, swing, and Tristano-style modernism, Maneri studied dodecaphony with Josef Schmid, a student of Alban Berg; supported himself with gigs at ethnic clubs, where he learned uncommon time signatures as well as sliding scales; and landed, in 1970, a professorship at the New England Conservatory, where he evolved a concept of microtonality that identifies five distinct pitches between two notes of the tempered scale, or 72 pitches per octave. As all this happened away from the international stages of jazz, his sudden arrival as an avant-garde star and ECM recording artist (he had earlier recorded for Hatology) in the mid '90s, when he was in his late sixties, added up to one of the oddest overnight success stories since Grandma Moses. He was acclaimed a prophet, and his first—and, in my judgment, best—ECM album, *Three Men Walking*, a 1995 performance with violinist Mat Maneri (his son) and guitarist Joe Morris, did not disappoint. It is original and deeply compelling. While the two Maneris tend to blend, Morris counterposes a different yet complementary key, suggesting harmolodic spatiality. He is at once apart and in synch.

The comparison with Ornette Coleman doesn't end there. If Coleman plays off-pitch from the tempered scale, he is always in tune with himself, producing a deliciously raw and ragged sound; his use of microtones is a natural, unforced consequence of his effulgent style, also reflected in his whoops and glissandi. Maneri begins with conventional tuning, but probes for the notes between notes. I don't know if a listener can detect them all, or even what a 72-note scale sounds like. But the effect is of a music in which virtually every note is virtual, a moaning glissando that swims one way and then another. On *Three Men Walking*, Maneri is a communicative player: his sound on tenor, alto, and especially clarinet is impressively distinct, his phrases logical and meaningful. Nowhere is this more evident than on his version of "What's New," which begins disarmingly with the standard's first two notes and continues to limn the melody while veering deeper into it, so that instead of theme-and-variations you experience something akin to an inspired dissection.

Maneri's achievement was underscored by the 1998 release of *Panoits Nine* (Avan), which combines a demo made for Atlantic Records at precisely the wrong time, 1963, when Coleman had disappeared from the label, selling far fewer albums than his blizzard of press notices or the splendor of his music promised, with a live klezmer performance from 1981. The album is great fun, demonstrating his ease with tricky time signatures and search for authenticity. Yet little attempt is made at bringing the ethnic styles to a jazz template, and some of that is derivative. The title piece, in 9/8, is unmistakably Brubeckian; the whimsical "Why Don't You Go Far Away" is a pitch-challenged combination of Monk and the Pink Panther. I suspect that other numbers are the kind of thing one might have picked up on albums bought in the Middle East during the same period. On *Three Men Walking*, however, such influences are so thoroughly assimilated into what appears to be an instinctive microtonality that they might not come to mind at all if the listener wasn't primed to seek them out.

Subsequent albums are less enticing, though they all have moments. *In Full Cry* features the quartet heard at Tonic—the Maneris, bassist John Lockwood, drummer Randy Peterson—and shows off the saxophonist's control of harmonics, producing brazen chords and notes that swell in the middle as on a string instrument. He suggests Artie Shaw's silvery technique and Pee Wee Russell's microtones (who knew?) on "Shaw Was a Good Mann, Pee Wee." But what's with "Tenderly," a cloying tune that other avant-gardists have also resuscitated? Two spirituals are less than emphatic and an original called "Outside the Dance Hall" emphasizes the absence of music from inside, where the pulse is bound to be more assertive. The search for microtones here and on *Blessed* (consisting mostly of duets with Mat) is no substitute for, say, Coleman's melodic and rhythmic exhilaration, which may seem apples-and-oranges except that a few numbers at Tonic and passages on the superior *Tales of Rohnlief* ("Bonewith," "Hold the Tiger") show that Maneri can light a fire beneath his weeping glissandi when he chooses to.

A highlight of the Tonic set was a brief, laid-back violin passage by Mat Maneri, who chain-smoked throughout the hour while affecting a smug insouciance, yet achieved a rhythmic suppleness and communicative ease of his own. In recordings with Matthew Shipp and in a version of "Body and Soul" that is perhaps the expressive acme of *Blessed*, he has suggested growing maturity. The promise is realized on his recently released ECM debut, *Trinity*, a solo recital of unexpected depth and variety. His adaptation of "Sun Ship," a stark and rather insubstantial Coltrane fragment, begins with barely a hint of the source material, then proceeds to locate it in the course of deliberate microtonal stages, building to a vigorous peak as if the Coltrane figure had to be earned. He seems to have assimilated his father's assimilations to the point where he may be able to achieve his own rapprochement between microtonality and jazz qua jazz.

[*Village Voice*, 26 February 2002]

109 ❖ Singing Cool and Hot (Cassandra Wilson / Dee Dee Bridgewater)

Can it be that little more than a decade ago, jazz singing was widely written off as a dead art? No one had come along to take the stages abandoned by Sarah Vaughan, Ella Fitzgerald, and Carmen McRae, though Betty Carter and Abbey Lincoln had survived the wilderness years to reassert their own claims as supreme individualists in an un-crowded field. They in turn influenced many young singers, which was a great relief from that strange period in the '70s when all black woman singers tried to sound like Aretha and all white woman singers tried to sound like Annie Ross—a trite landscape of unholy melisma and run-away hipsterism. Yet the most gifted singer of the boomer generation, who might have changed all that, Dee Dee Bridgewater, relocated to Paris after a fleeting try at disco and was rarely heard here while the most promising singer of the next generation, Cassandra Wilson, was mired in M-Base science fiction and seemed to consider it a matter of artistic integrity not to connect with her audience.

The subsequent return of Shirley Horn, who'd been away longer than Lincoln and Carter combined, testified to a hunger for words as well as music. Soon we were engulfed in singers, mostly indifferent, and some-times promising or damned promising. The '50s influences predomi-nated, but they had been absorbed and transfigured, mitigated by the acknowledgment that rock and its tributaries have been flowing for nearly half a century. Now people are actually arguing about singers again—their affect, hair, and cheesecake as well as repertory, pitch, and style. (I'm focusing on women, because the men mostly disappoint and I don't get Kurt Elling.) Say what you will of Diana Krall, but she is about to open at Radio City Music Hall, reminding us that jazz has long depended on singers to popularize it. Abbey Lincoln continues to reign as queen bee, as her forthcoming triptych of concerts at Lincoln Center attests, but center stage is now dominated by Bridgewater and Wilson, who, at long last, have planted themselves squarely at the crossroads. They are matchless performers who sound like nobody else even when paying homage—pantheon singers at a time when many had assumed the pantheon was closed for good.

Significantly, the latter three have played major roles in solving the dilemma usually blamed for the demise of jazz singing: a dearth of new material and a wearing out of the old. No one writes the kinds of songs that fueled the great singers of the pre-rock era, and contemporary pop doesn't lend itself to balladic or swinging treatments. So Lincoln and Wilson have written their own songs, and Wilson and Bridgewater have additionally added to the repertoire—the former by drawing on blues, rock, and country, the latter by examining jazz itself and reinvigorating golden-age standards. Last week, both were in town—Wilson at the Blue Note and Bridgewater at Iridium—and hearing them back-to-back suggested the cornucopia of old New York, when a maze of high-priced saloons competed in offering Sarah Vaughan, Billie Holiday (till the cabaret law cut her down), Peggy Lee, Ella Fitzgerald, Dinah Washington, Anita O'Day, June Christie, Della Reese, Kay Starr, Nancy Wilson, and the rest. I mean to say that these two beautiful, exquisitely authoritative women, who could not be more different had they hailed from Jackson and Memphis, which in fact they do, made the skyline glow like Fat City.

Wilson previewed her CD *Belly of the Sun* (Blue Note), which was mostly recorded in Mississippi with various guests. At the Blue Note, she had the band used on most of its tracks—two guitarists, two percussionists, a bassist—and from the first notes of "The Weight," she radiated pleasure and faith, mining her cello range, enunciating the words, her voice mixed way in front of the ensemble, the better to crest its steady and untroubled waves. But then, at some point, perhaps when "Waters of March" suddenly switched, with nary a second for applause, to "Wichita Lineman," the set morphed into something like an open rehearsal or party, possibly a reflection of first-night jitters, or of an insouciance bordering on the impulsive.

Navigating from Caetano Veloso ("Little Lion," recorded for but cut from the album) to original songs ("Cooter Brown," "Show Me a Love") to James Taylor ("Only a Dream in Rio"), she stamped them all with her smoked timbre and unfeigned embellishments. Yet the sameness of the ensemble arrangements—despite an incredible array of guitar-family instruments, including mandolin, dobro, and banjo, played by Kevin Breit, and a small forest of percussion instruments played by Cyro Baptiste— undermined the drama. At times, one pined for a real soloist to spell or interact with her. "Corcovado," however, which will be on the Japanese edition of the album only, picked up the tempo; and her voice and phrasing were glistening on a medley encore of Robert Johnson's "Hellhound on My Trail" (from her *Blue Light 'Til Dawn*) and B. B. King's "Rock Me Baby" (originally slated for but cut from *Belly of the Sun*), accompanied by guitarist Marvin Sewell for the kind of slow-drag recitation she has made her calling card, rocking way back on her heels and coasting on the resolute backbeat.

The new album assimilates diverse material with disarming ease. The usually dour "Wichita Lineman" is perhaps the ultimate representation here of the old axiom "It ain't what you do, it's the way that you do it." She slows it down to a mid-afternoon glide, puts the lyric in the third person, and unfolds the story as if it were blues. For "Darkness on the Delta," a 1930s standard initially popularized by Mildred Bailey and later adopted by New Orleans revivalists and Thelonious Monk, she is backed solely by the unremarkable pianist, Boogaloo Ames; a choir of children accompany her on "Waters of March"; India.Arie shares the vocal on her original, "Just Another Parade"; an old friend of Wilson's, Rhonda Richmond, wrote and plays piano on "Road So Clear," with Olu Dara on trumpet. She gives a particularly shrewd reading of Bob Dylan's "Shelter from the Storm" and closes with the most upbeat and unlikely of Johnson's delta visions, "Hot Tamales." Indeed, not unlike *Love and Theft*, *Belly of the Sun* suggests a compendium of American music, specifically that of someone who came of age in the early '70s, and wasn't afraid to turn the dial on her radio. Yet almost every piece is made to reflect the singer's Mississippi roots. It should be a big hit.

Dee Dee Bridgewater is something else again: a consummate entertainer of the old school—funny, ribald, unpredictable, frequently outrageous. No other jazz singer has ever played so unremittingly with her sexuality. Someday one of those ringside patrons she fondles and bats her eyes at is going to keel over dead. She is also one of the hardest-swinging musicians alive, almost relentless in her energy. Accompanied by a trio led by her longtime pianist and organist, Thierry Eliez, she walked out onto the Iridium stage singing the vamp to "All Blues," and was soon scatting through three or so octaves of her glistening voice, aggressive and gritty, demonstrating full-frontal id, holding nothing back, her body advancing from gentle body English to dance to borderline calisthenics. It was the kind of number the old pros put at the end of a set, because what could follow it? For Bridgewater, it was an hors d'oeuvre.

If Wilson is laid-back and cool in the belly of the Mississippi sun, Bridgewater, who was born in Memphis but raised in Michigan, is almost always scorching. Having paid wicked homage to Horace Silver and crafty respects to Ella Fitzgerald on previous albums (though a better place to start is *Live at Yoshi's*), she will devote her next album to Kurt Weill (typical Dee Dee one-liner: "It's coming . . . and so am I"), and most of her set served as a preview: "September Song," "Speak Low," "My Ship," "This Is New." She drew on her powerful vibrato to accent the beat in the slow-motion verses, then opened up on the choruses—rising to the top of her range with improvisational crescents that recalled the Dinah Washington who matched high notes with a trinity of trumpet players on *Dinah Jams*. "We're a little timid with these songs," she said, "because we just rehearsed them." Actually, she was exhausting, and the superbly modulated "My Ship"—a ballad qua ballad—was a gratefully received respite.

Silver's "Cookin' at the Continental," a Bridgewater specialty that didn't make her all-Silver *Love and Peace* album, was more characteristic, taken way up, spotted by a healthy organ solo, but never more vigorous than in the singer's emphatic drive. Happily, a fan asked her for "Come Sunday," and, cradled by Ira Coleman's bowed bass, she perched herself on a stool and burnished every note, every syllable; I've never heard a more stark and persuasive version, and cannot imagine why she doesn't settle down more often. From Ellington's "God of Love," she snapped into familiar territory ("let's talk about sex, baby") with what has become a signature closer that she would be truly hard-pressed to follow. Her near literal interpretation of "Love for Sale" is an extended fantasia with autoerotic gestures, dancing, and caressing of men at ringside, and it had half the audience shimmying in its seats. When the lights went up on her 75-minute set, she continued to scat one last chorus. Call it a defiant gesture to prove that jazz singing is still potent and still in flower.

[*Village Voice*, 5 March 2002]

110 ❖ *Our Chopin (Cecil Taylor)*

Some people decry Cecil Taylor as a composer because he rarely revisits pieces and doesn't provide song-form themes for others to play, just as some people decry Thelonious Monk as a composer because he was constantly revisiting pieces and worked almost exclusively with song-form themes that are played to distraction. Consistency is the hobgoblin of jazzcrit. What can be said with certainty is that Taylor, like Monk, has invented his own compositional method and his own approach to the keyboard and that they are indivisible. In the 45 years since he recorded *Jazz Advance*, he has shaped an original vocabulary, a thesaurus of leaps, runs, skitters, eruptions, pauses, rhythms, melodies, thrusts, and counter-thrusts. In this, he is nothing unique, merely a member in a very exclusive club of self-invented pianist-composers. You want Chopin melodies, there's only one place to go. Same with Taylor, though melody probably isn't what you're seeking from him.

I have no interest in whether Taylor's music will survive the next century as handsomely as Chopin's did the last, but I do suggest that in the realm of uncontained piano ecstasy, he is the modern analogue—fittingly, one more likely to nuke romance than dwell upon it. Consequently, his every appearance is a gift, especially those rare American forays into concert halls, where the formality virtually guarantees as much attention to solo piano as to whatever unit he is leading. His February 28 performance at Lincoln Center's Alice Tully Hall, presented by the World Music Institute and Thomas Buckner, was typical, which is to say stunning. After only a minute or so of off-stage guttural yowls and, I think, maracas, he hastened (black skullcap and pants; white, black, and gold blouse; rainbow socks) to the keyboard and began a characteristic buildup with blocked chords—some consonant, others dissonant, but all richly foursquare and spelled by sly rests. "Measurement of sound is its silences," he wrote a long time ago.

Taylor usually begins his extended piano works with poised motifs, building variations stolidly in a kind of foreplay before letting loose the climaxes of pianistic frenzy, the cascades and avalanches that sate the gallery and torment the disaffected. But the compositional authority with which he launches pieces has increased dramatically—from his first great period of piano recitals in the 1970s, through the miniatures and encore-length samplings of the '80s, to recent pieces that are at once mellower and more vigorous, possibly more composed, certainly bespeaking a greater composure. A superb example is Taylor's new CD, *The Willisau Concert* (Intakt), recorded in September 2000. Three of its five movements are under two minutes, providing easy entry for the wary, but it is the opening episode of the 50-minute first movement that overwhelms with impeccably plotted drama, wit, and command—the narrative skill of a vital composer.

So it was at Lincoln Center, where his sense of proportion and moment equaled his digital precision and amazing energy. The measured chords were followed by two-note tremolos parked in various keys, as though looking for the right room; rhythm figures that pirouetted in the air and landed in splat chords; and his fast-tumbling arpeggios, dispersed so that there was no time to take them for granted. Most remarkable about the first piece was an absence of repetition; one expected, even desired, repeats of the more daredevil conceits, but Taylor, drawing on an apparently bottomless well, insistently moved forward. Only the ending was tenuous; in fact, one couldn't be certain that he wasn't just pausing to peer at the music. As the moment for applause was missed, the recital took on the ipso facto temper of a sonata—only in reverse form, with a sort-of allegro following a sort-of adagio. The more aggressive second piece, or movement, unfolded with cursory melodic fragments, a brief passage that actually swung in a conventional way (he did it again, too, later in the set), a mass of overtones achieved without pedal, and his equivalent of riffs—worked-out figures played twice—before Taylor unleashed an orgasmic, foot-pedaled onslaught, if only for a tantalizing minute or two.

This time, the audience threw caution to the winds and applauded. The third piece, picking up from the second, was teeming and dense, but no less worked out. He used fists and the heels of his hands. One figure required the right heel to bound, quicksilver, over half a dozen clusters; in case anyone thought the passage was entirely serendipitous, he repeated it exactly. Then he began moving big climactic chords from the outer rim to the center, interpolating blues notes and a soupcon of swing, before increasing the tumult and suddenly relinquishing it to stake out a seven-note melody that recalled the theme to *The Honeymooners*. Overtones were still ringing as he took his bows.

The trio half, with bassist Dominic Duval and drummer Jackson Krall, was an altogether woollier affair, beginning with an interlude of Taylor declaiming words and affecting poses while Krall played on the floor and every other available surface besides the drums and Duval warmed up with double and triple stops. In these episodes, I assume that the words (most of them inaudible) are of less significance than the exercise of voice and body that Taylor conceives as part of the total process of performing. I've come to accept it, patronizingly, as a playful eccentricity, at least on stage, and sometimes on records: I like his baritone recitations on *Chinampas*, but cannot abide *In Florescence*. Soon enough, he sat down and grounded the piece in bass chords, before applying both hands to contrapuntal figures that had the openness and clarity of ragtime. Really. And then: the deluge.

Taylor, who turns 73 on Friday (March 15), is ageless, and the image of him immersing himself in a no-holds-barred three-way rocket-launching extravaganza of the sort he has been doing for almost as long as I have been sentient is one of modern music's tonic wonders. Yet unit music represents another side of Taylor. The logical variations

and overall symmetry of his solo piano work has a classicist's sensibility—compositional finesse and beguiling virtuosity is hard to resist. I
recall a classical musician in the late '60s comparing Taylor's recitals to
Mozart (I still don't get that) and Ravel (sure), but balking after a few
minutes of his quartet. No matter how you slice it or what you call it, a
Cecil Taylor unit of any size plays unequivocal avant-garde jazz. That
means that the whole concept of structure changes from that of motific
development to group interaction. Whenever I felt my attention bludg-
eoned into insensibility, as I concede it was, I worked my way back in
by focusing less on Taylor's exertions than on how Duval and (especially) Krall responded to them. At which point, the monolithic blitz
broke down into component parts and, soon, such virtues of the solo set
as variety and contrast reasserted themselves.

But let's face it, details aren't as important in this context; it's partly
the experience of being washed in blood that makes a Taylor juggernaut
invigorating. He dropped out after the climax, allowing bass and drums
to bring the piece to ground. The follow-up was a brief, ancillary, and
understated example of controlled mutuality. The first of two sweetness-
and-light encores began with a minute of solo piano, joined in lockstep
by Krall and Duval, who used a stick to stop the strings—quadruple
stops. The second was Taylor alone, practically whispering the notes and
finishing with a rumble in the bass. The standing audience continued to
cheer, but Taylor—I swear I never thought I would get to write this—
knew when enough was enough and disappeared with one final bow.

The encore is always a special moment at a Taylor concert, because
its very brevity has the effect of raising the wizard's curtain and letting
you glimpse, in relative isolation, a few of his tricks. They have been
highlights of his records since *Silent Tongues*, in 1974, and may have
inspired—along with his 1978 triumph at the White House, when he
stunned his detractors with a seven-minute performance—the shorter
pieces that figure in several of his best solo albums, including *Fly! Fly!
Fly! Fly! Fly!* in 1980, *For Olim* in 1986, and the "Stone"/"Old Canal"
sequence (five pieces, each under two minutes) on *In East Berlin* in 1988.
A dozen years later, *The Willisau Concert* is on a par with them, and a
major statement of Taylor's maturity. You hear nothing of the halting
melody of, say *Air Above Mountains* (no matter if it does recall "The Very
Thought of You"), or the waspish anger of, say, *In Florescence*. From the
first notes, you know you are in the hands of an absolutely confident
composer. The piece works its way through short, self-contained units,
set off by inhalation-like pauses, maintaining a cohesive integrity that
keeps the work focused, its routines less like riffs than the repeats in a

sonata. He even tosses in a Jerry Lee Lewis gliss. If you think listening to a piano piece for 50 minutes is daunting, consider the concentration required to keep it moving and coherent. Of course, you can always work your way backward from the encores. In either direction, this is a recital to hear.

[*Village Voice*, 19 March 2002]

111 ❖ She Writes the Songs (Abbey Lincoln)

The result of Abbey Lincoln's decision to make her concert triptych at Alice Tully Hall (March 7 through 9) a referendum on her songwriting can only be described as triumphant. If the performances were occasionally uneasy, her ipso facto argument left little doubt that her oeuvre is compelling, distinctive, and, oddly enough, given her recurring melodic tropes and dilatory tempos, varied. Boring she never was. Two questions heard ringing in response were: Who will be first to record an Abbey Lincoln songbook album, and why hasn't it been done before? The second question, though hardly new, may be answered in part by the fact that her book seems older than it is. Many of the 30-plus songs she presented were composed or recorded in the 1990s. A few that dated back to the 1970s—"Throw It Away," "Playmate," "Caged Bird"—weren't much heard then. Plus there is the intimidation factor, the seeming inextricability between songs and performer.

Perhaps more important, pop singers aren't in the market for the jazz hymns that are Lincoln's specialty, and cabaret singers (Baby Jane Dexter is an exception) and jazz singers (Kendra Shank is another) are a timid and conservative lot. In pre-Depression days, when jazz singers were mostly blues singers, it was not uncommon for them to add to their material, contributing a lyric and even a melody. But as jazz relied more on the Broadway and Hollywood songwriting factories, singers became interpreters. Rare exceptions (Billie Holiday wasn't really a songwriter, Bob Dorough and Dave Frishberg obviously are) simply prove the rule of Ella, Sarah, Carmen, and the rest. A good number of jazz standards and semi-standards arose when lyric writers claimed tunes by musicians (Billy Strayhorn, Thelonious Monk, Ralph Burns, Benny Golson, Horace Silver, Randy Weston, and Bill Evans, among many others), but none of those composers could offer three evenings worth of songs conceived as songs. You would have to go back to the prewar era of Ellington and Waller for that.

So Lincoln's accomplishment, historically, has little precedent, especially considering its late flowering. Though she began recording in 1956, her career veered in so many directions with long detours from music, that she was a peripheral figure before Polydor France initiated a series of Verve CDs in 1990, when she was 60. *The World Is Falling Down* reestablished her as a force, not least because she was memorably cogent on its two originals, the great title tune and "I Got Thunder (and It Rings)." The magnificent *You Gotta Pay the Band* clinched the case, and six smartly produced subsequent releases—faltering only with the children's choirs on *Devil's Got Your Tongue*—uncovered the range and poetic intensity of her repertory while occasioning reassessment of her previous work. Long before Jazz at Lincoln Center's triptych, she had taken on diva stature, her unmistakable vocal attack complemented by her signature appearance: a tall, lean, mature beauty in a long black dress, with a broad-brimmed black hat, cornrows, and a cool stately manner that italicized every phrase. As her voice became huskier, she retained her breath control, exemplified in whole notes, high notes, shouts, and climactic finishes. Her increasing strength as an artist was no illusion. The records prove it.

All of her attributes were on display at the concerts, along with her familiar acerbity in getting the rhythm section to follow her lead or provide a decisive lead of its own. Several times she asked for a meatier introduction or a tightening of the beat; yet if those stop-and-go moments suggested inadequate rehearsal time, they also provided serendipitous diversions, as when she admired the pizzicato solo of cellist Jennifer Warren and asked for similar accompaniment to her vocal reprise, or asked for the band to lay out, or pressed the beat, or turned it around. She also fooled around with her repertory, which each evening began in accordance with the *Stagebill* program, but soon veered away. Even so, she focused on songs for which she wrote words and music with only two last-minute exceptions, and she wrote words for one of them as well. If the first night was shakiest—she had trouble getting what she wanted from pianist James Weidman, who played on her '80s Holiday-tribute CDs—it benefited from yeoman solos by Joe Lovano, who, like Warren, had appeared on Lincoln's *Over the Years*. In a couple of instances, he didn't seem to know the tunes, so he'd begin by playing eight bars straight, then double-time stirring improvisations.

On a few pieces each night, she augmented the ensemble with two strong-voiced backup singers, Bemshi Shearer and the very impressive

Stacie Precia, sometimes for birdlike effects, but more often to sing refrains, usually in out-of-synch arrangements that turned them into can-
ons. Her erstwhile pianists Rodney Kendrick and Marc Cary brought,
respectively, a Monkish percussiveness to the second concert and flush
empathy to the third—Cary was right on point. The key saxophone soloist at those concerts was Steve Coleman, dressed in his hip-hop gear,
who got hung up on whole notes for much of concert two, loosening up
on "Being Me," but gave freer rein to his pearly timbre and fleet phrasing
at concert three, particularly on "Another World." Of the other guests,
the dynamic Savion Glover improvised a thunderous, intricate, but always accessible obbligato and solo on "Who Used to Dance," and Freddy
Cole sang Lincoln's "Circle of Love," backed by Cary, and impeccably
finessed his baritone to her alto on "Should've Been," alternating phrases
on the chorus tag and clearly relishing the blend.

Lincoln's performances, notwithstanding a few forgotten lyrics (she
got a laugh announcing of her first night's encore, "everybody knows
this song," and singing Hoagy Carmichael and Ned Washington's "The
Nearness of You"), were impassioned and even chilling—specifically her
top-note cries and surprising slabs of sustained pitch, the a cappella passages, the growls, the rising glissandi—and her intonation was controlled and sure, though she appeared weaker at the middle concert,
which she cut short. Her songs never failed her; at no time did one wish
she would abandon them in favor of the standard repertory. It is a measure of how prolific she is that she never got to sing—in some cases,
didn't even program—some of her best and best-known pieces, including "Turtle Dream" and "I Got Thunder."

Many of Lincoln's songs proudly—even jauntily—ride on a slow-drag
rhythm that she has made her own. She implies a powerful backbeat,
but lays so far back on the time that the pieces seem freer than they are.
And, in fact, they are pretty free in the best sense, exemplifying her
craftsmanship as a composer and lyric writer in songs made up of stan-
zas of different length, though usually 16- or 8-bars. Even when she uses
the same stanza or a conventional 32-bar format, she writes more than
a single verse; the beguiling "Conversations with a Baby" has four 16-
bar verses, with a characteristic rhyme scheme: ABCBDEFE. Several of
her tunes sound alike, yet under scrutiny reveal defining differences.
When she uses a hymn format or feeling, she often underscores the melody with chords that recall the diminished and augmented substitutions
of bebop. The disparate constructions allow her to stay moored in a
similar tempo—as in an opening segue from "The World Is Falling
Down" to "Bird Alone," two of her finest—without flagging in interest
or intensity. If some hymnlike pieces (the vividly eloquent "Down Here

Below") suggest a kind of American chanson, others (the incantatory "Music Is the Magic," done twice) have a gospel-flavored innocence.

"Playmate" and "You Gotta Pay the Band" have uncannily nostalgic themes. The former, heard in a fine duet with Weidman, is a characteristic Abbey-tune yet redolent of "Red River Valley." Lincoln likes long declarative statements and has written verses that consist of well-parsed, conversational sentences. "When I'm Called Home," a highlight of the third concert that began as a duet with Cary, has three 10-bar verses, each made up of two or three sentences and, though it's about dying, begins with a disarmingly witty first phrase: "When I'm called home I will bring a book." But that's just the beginning; after a rest, it continues, "that tells of strange and funny turns and of the heart it took to keep on living in a world that never was my own, a world of haunted memories of other worlds unknown." On "I Could Sing It for a Song," she shakes up the hymnlike construction with broken rhythms, not to mention unhymnlike chord changes. Perhaps due to limited rehearsal time, she programmed but didn't perform it; the rhythmic conceit with its retards and pauses has to be perfect, as on the record (*Over the Years*). But she tackled others that were no less challenging, including the fast "Storywise," which Lovano rescued when she lapsed on the words, and the ebullient "Story of My Father," with its rocking eight-bar gospel verses, and "Being Me," the best of her self-reflective ballads, and the brazenly cyclic "Love What You Doin' Down There," sung twice and achieving undulating rhythms in its relentless refrain. By the time she wrapped up the last evening with the 24-bar blues taunt, "Hey Lawdy Mama" (her words, music by Nina Simone), the Abbey Lincoln songbook had positioned itself as an admirable inducement to singers in every idiom.

[*Village Voice*, 2 April 2002]

112 ❖ *Black Arthur's Return* (*Arthur Blythe*)

Arthur Blythe's story may not make a movie, but it certainly works as jazz allegory. He came to New York from San Diego in the magical mid-'70s, and on his second night out sat in with Elvin Jones. Although he had been critically neglected at home, at 34 he was hardly inexperienced—having studied with, among others, the 1940s Lunceford saxophonist Kirtland Bradford and bandleader Horace Tapscott, in whose groups he had played for a decade—and he came East complete with the attention-grabbing sobriquet Black Arthur Blythe. Far more impressive was his wholly original approach to timbre. He made the saxophone sound uniquely fat and pungent: round as Benny Carter, ardent as John Coltrane. Along with Julius Hemphill and Oliver Lake, he put the alto back into contention. His hard-riffing, economical phrases were girded by a fast, edgy vibrato that at its best cut like a Ginzu and at its not-best vibrated with the whining nasality of Al Jolson. The phrases, too, were original, punchy with a fastidious lyricism. When in 1975 he performed at a loft concert with the no less distinctive 20-year-old David Murray, it seemed as though western winds were, at last, blasting jazz out of its long night in the doldrums.

Relocating his family to New York and supporting himself at times as a security guard, Blythe quickly emerged as a key mover of the loft era, when living-room performance spaces, art galleries, converted warehouses, and other venues welcomed a fresh, nervy new jazz. Neither avant-garde nor mainstream, it embodied a pragmatic rapprochement between the two—one that spurned meretricious fusion while pursuing the merger potential of harmolodic rock. Blythe typified the moment: he concurrently led bands with unconventional instrumentation (Bob Stewart's tuba, Abdul Wadud's cello), standard rhythm sections (a John Hicks piano trio), and electricity (James Blood Ulmer's guitar). His presentations were far from typical. A meticulous man, he started his 8 P.M. sets at 8 P.M., and they were impeccably ordered—the selections succinct and pointed, the solos logically coherent, emotional but never self-indulgent. During the next few years, he joined Chico Hamilton's band, worked often with Gil Evans, recorded with Lester Bowie, and cut his own LPs on the new indies, India Navigation and Adelphi.

By 1978, Columbia Records, which a few years before had jettisoned its jazz roster, began paying attention. Bruce Lundvall was at the helm, and Dexter Gordon's "homecoming" proved a huge success. Blythe was signed as a token representative of the new generation. *Lenox Avenue Breakdown*, a triumphant disc with dance rhythms and radiant colors, has grown in stature. Yet back then, an over-the-top press campaign that compared Blythe with Charlie Parker guaranteed instant backlash. Tell the world you've signed a brilliant new saxophonist, and the world will say, "Good, let's hear him." Tell the world you've signed the Messiah, and it sharpens its knives. No one doubted that he could play, but for some the ripe, quavering tone was too much. Meanwhile, Blythe's follow-up albums revealed increasing scope: jazz standards on *In the*

Tradition; poignant originals and aggressively edgy funk on *Illusions* (Stewart, Wadud, and Ulmer in one band); the gamut from free improv to basic gospel on *Blythe Spirit*; the perfection of a novel septet on *Elaborations*; the homage to Monk on *Light Blue*. They sold the way jazz records sell, and the diversity probably didn't help; for example, everyone likes one track on *Blythe Spirit*, few like them all.

So, in 1984, the Lundvall regime gone, Columbia prevailed on Blythe to do a couple of frankly commercial albums—which failed to generate a new audience but succeeded in disillusioning the old one—before showing Charlie Parker's heir the door. (According to his discography, a final and more characteristic Columbia album, *Basic Blythe*, with strings, came out in 1988, but I've never seen it and was unaware until now of its existence.) During the next few years, his visibility sharply decreased, despite appearances with World Saxophone Quartet, the Leaders, and an underemployed quintet he co-led with Chico Freeman. Returning to San Diego, he did not issue an album of his own until the attractive if sorrowful 1991 *Hipmotism* (Enja), which extended his collaboration with Stewart, guitarist Kelvin Bell, and a significant new partner, vibist Gust William Tsilis, on whose 1987 *Pale Fire* Blythe had been featured.

Though uneven, the sporadic Blythe albums issued since 1993 suggest a maturing in tone, style, and rhythm, especially evident in new versions of signature pieces. His blistering yet tempered duet with bassist Wilber Morris on "Jitterbug Waltz" (*Live at the Bim*, 1996, a round-robin trio effort with pianist John Fisher) obliterates the 1979 Columbia reading; his retarding and doubling of the beat brims with a masterly, almost offhand confidence. His slightly drier sound and easy wit are evident in a 1997 duet album with cellist David Eyges, *Today's Blues* (CIMP)—the serene coherence of the unaccompanied "My Sun Ra," the easy swing of "Warne Waltz." If the live recordings, *Retroflection* (piano quartet, Enja) and the superior *Spirits in the Field* (tuba trio, Savant) fail to capture the concentration of his best playing, they do have moments of the boisterous resolve that also breaks through the overdetermined lyricism and awkwardness (an oddball "Blood Count") of the calypso-influenced *Night Song* (Clarity). None of those albums makes a concerted statement.

The new one, aptly titled *Focus* (Savant), does. This album is so utterly and persuasively sui generis that it should spark a reassessment of Blythe, much of whose work for Columbia isn't even in print. Martin Williams once wrote of a Sonny Rollins classic that it was the kind of jazz you could play for your uncle, which made sense in the 1950s. This is one you could play for your nephew. At 62, Blythe has found an ideal setting for his lusty, swelling, sometimes caustic music: a quartet that bounces on the beat of Bob Stewart's tuba, nourished by the harmonies of Tsilis's concert grand marimba. No less remarkable is the drumming of producer Cecil Brooks III, which eschews detached timekeeping in favor of rigorous patterns that delineate the tunes in unison with the saxophone. Blythe deploys the quartet intelligently, spelling it with duos and trios, and there isn't a dull or wasted moment.

For all the concision and variety, the album's most affecting attribute is the leader's sound, still plump, still bolstered with vibrato in the middle and lower registers. Yet the bright-eyed glow is dimmed, seasoned with a greater sense of life lived. His strongest work—and there is no indifferent playing here—is imbued with a paternal warmth that strengthens his rhythmic assurance. Every remake is triumphant. A new version of "In a Sentimental Mood" has enormous integrity and personal impact, where the original now appears relatively forced and showy. The engaging "Night Song" is rendered here with a sexy candor that redefines it. And while it's difficult to choose between treatments of "My Sun Ra" (though the one on *Illusions* is an instance of Jolson-esque excesses), this one derives unique opulence from the way the quartet is maneuvered.

The album begins with its most dilatory jaunt, "Opus," in 12/8, a meter that, as drawn by Stewart's vamp, waddles through its eight-bar phrases—Blythe's solo is particularly spare compared to the percussion choir created by marimba, tuba, and drums. Pleasant but emotionally reticent, it's a warm-up for what follows. Blythe assigns the composer credit for "Children's Song" to Monk, who recorded it in 1964 as "That Old Man." It's really the p.d. ditty "This Old Man," which Monk essayed with dashing humor. Blythe turns it into a boldly expressive memory piece, with Stewart's tuba evoking arco bass and Blythe's solo resourcefully elaborating theme and mood. By contrast, he growls on the backbeat blues, "C. C. Rider," clearly relishing the fun. At the close of Blythe's solo, Brooks extends his turnback into a drum solo with tuba support, scrupulously maintaining the vigor and feeling. On another blues, "Night Creeper," Blythe airs his affection for Johnny Hodges and Earl Bostic. This is irresistible stuff, but even the freer pieces benefit from a pellucid attack—notably a meditative duet with Tsilis on "Once Again." A more extensive duet with Stewart, "Hip Toe," is extraordinary— Blythe's rippling solo begins as a lexicon of his patented phrases, but in the second half he takes a favorite Parker lick (it's the first figure in his second ad lib chorus on the 1945 "Now's the Time") and treats it as a motif, swinging blissfully. Throughout *Focus*, Blythe plays as though he means every note, his unspotted timbre conveying the same buoyant individuality that powered his initial volley on New York. Blow, western wind, blow.

[*Village Voice*, 2 April 2002]

113 ❖ Enchantment
(*Johnny Hodges / Rex Stewart*)

A masterpiece, by definition, ought to be singular, or at least uncommon as regards an artist's accumulated work. Yet during his 50 years in recording studios, Duke Ellington often produced two or more classics at a clip, particularly in the early 1940s: "Ko-Ko" and "Jack the Bear" one day, "Concerto for Cootie" and "Conga Brava" another. And yet even by his standards, the sessions of November 2, 1940, and July 3, 1941, were astounding. On each of those enchanted afternoons, Ellington directed two seven-piece ensembles, respectively starring and nominally led by saxophonist Johnny Hodges and trumpeter Rex Stewart—creating no fewer than four masterworks by each group on each occasion: eight per date, 16 in all, like falling off a log.

When RCA-Victor began transferring its '40s Ellington trove to LP in the 1950s, it focused on his big band, and the small-group achievements faded into memory for two decades. Not until 1966 were the Hodges and Stewart recordings finally reclaimed in RCA's two-year-old Vintage series. *Things Ain't What They Used to Be* was greeted with much fanfare, in part for Don Miller's subtly faithful mastering. Vintage had renounced artificial stereo, which at that time had become the bane of every jazz lover's existence; it actually respected RCA's superb prewar engineering, cleaning and enhancing the originals without sacrificing warmth and intimacy. This was essential because the Hodges and Stewart sides are deceptive: They are painstakingly scripted, but sound casual, even conspiratorial, as though made up on the spot.

Koch's reissue replicates the original LP in more ways than one. The charm of these records resides in the image they project of musicians grouped around a simple recording device, blending their timbres like voices in a choir. My rig fails to register a significant audio difference between LP and CD. Koch's cozy sound rebuts by example RCA's botched 24-volume *Duke Ellington: The Centennial Edition*, where digitalized brittleness highlights only static. Moreover, Koch is restoring masterworks that—excepting that tombstone of a box—have been largely unavailable for well over two decades. It's time, once again, for a new generation to break out a magnum and discover the moonlit genius of this music.

But first, a cheer for Vintage, a unique series that record collectors of the '60s will surely remember. Brad McCuen created it in 1964, to mine Victor's 78-rpm mother lode. This was before an anal obsession with chronology, alternate takes, and studio chatter turned jazz reissues into academic theses. The point was simple: to reintroduce a crate of music that had been lost in the shuffle, without worrying about idiomatic boundaries. Although the liners to each album recommended a few others in the same genre, the series itself crossed borders—the first five titles focused on Coleman Hawkins, Woody Guthrie, Kurt Weill, Isham Jones, and Leadbelly. Experts were invited to program and annotate particular entries—for example, Martin Williams on King Oliver and Mike Lipskin (who took over the entire series in 1966) on Fats Waller. Audio engineering was accurate and unobtrusive.

The imprint was hardly perfect. A ban on using sides already in print forced the producers to choose second best in some instances and to ignore many of RCA's major figures. But imaginative sequencing made up for shortcomings, especially in a few biographical portraits that traced the careers of artists (Hawkins, Jack Teagarden, Henry Allen) over four decades. One learned to trust Vintage's logo: the famous cover graphic employing a wine rack was enough to get one to try several artists—the blues and country compilations were real eye-openers for a suburbanite like me. The Vintage catalog began with number 501 and ended, in 1972, with 584 (by which time producer Don Schlitten had revived the series after a hiatus, introducing bold gatefold covers), but I can account for only 78 titles. Do we have a numerical pun here, or can a more rigorous collector fill in my missing entries (509, 527, 539, 571, 572, 575)? In any case, I dwell on Vintage in the hope that Koch will find a way to lease the entire catalog; RCA, naturally, has no interest.

Things Ain't What They Used to Be sensibly separates the Hodges and Stewart tracks, sequencing them within each group by tempo, mood, and key. I am relieved to say that several alternate takes, which may be found in *The Centennial Edition*, have not been added to the LP configuration. Sixteen masterworks are enough for any disc, particularly when they are plotted as densely as these; averaging three minutes each, they do not waste a single measure. Indeed, in his 1990 exegesis, *Duke Ellington, Jazz Composer*, Ken Rattenbury devotes 70 pages to a note-by-note analysis of just two of them, "Junior Hop" and "Subtle Slough," a statistic that may seem incomprehensible to those who experience the elegance of these apparently guileless works.

God, however, is in the details and even the transparently obvious may turn out to be something other than what it seems. Consider, for example, the way Ellington juggles blues and song forms. "Things Ain't What They Used to Be," which, incidentally, begins bang-off with the theme (no intro beyond a pickup-note by the bassist), is a blues, yet the melody goes directly into an eight-bar B-theme, played just once as a transition during which Hodges and the ensemble split up and come together—Hodges venturing a solo in the third bar of the episode and the ensemble closing in for a chord on the first beat of the fifth bar, a wonderfully warming moment. The ensemble is small, but behaves large, rarely failing to escort the soloist with proportionate economy. Ellington plays a chorus almost as spare as Count Basie, followed by Ray Nance's discreetly vocalized trumpet, after which Hodges returns with one of his waxing siren notes—he never indulged verbosity when a sustain, glissando, or tremolo would do. With typical Ellington symmetry, the performance ends with the theme, followed by a bass note.

These are flawless ensembles. Ellington's piano flits in and out of view with striking drama; bassist Jimmy Blanton, who invents the future of his instrument on these sides, constantly repays close attention; and drummer Sonny Greer slaps the beat a bit heavily at times (as on "Things"), but is mostly inspired, finding different percussive tonalities for each soloist. Those three support Hodges and a wind section made up of baritone saxophonist Harry Carney, trombonist Lawrence Brown, and trumpet players Cootie Williams (1940) or Ray Nance (1941). The Stewart band is the same except that he takes over on trumpet and tenor Ben Webster spells Hodges. Yet the ensembles are markedly different. The Hodges group is serene, smooth, sublime; Stewart's is dark, boisterous, mischievous. For decades, commentators—forgetting Ellington's history of hermetic voicings—assumed that there had to be more than three winds in the supporting ensemble, so full and diverse are its effects.

Two of Billy Strayhorn's supreme works are here, decked out in a nearly violet raiment by Hodges, "Passion Flower" and "Day Dream." The former is total bliss—listen to Blanton behind the soloist from the first note, and marvel at those eerie ensemble harmonies that track the song's chords and melody. Hodges modulates notes and range dynamically, as though recomposing the work as he plays it. If his 1967 version of "Day Dream" (*And His Mother Called Him Bill*) has the advantage of high fidelity and a prolonged running time, the original wins the day for forthrightness and concision, beginning with an eloquent Ellington piano intro and Hodges's decisive statement of the first two notes. It's one of the dreamiest records ever made.

"That's the Blues Old Man" is another blues with a secondary eight-bar theme, reversing the approach of "Things Ain't." This time the short theme is played twice, to open and close the arrangement, and the true theme, which sets up the solos, gets only one pass. This track also represents the last time Hodges featured his soprano saxophone. A disciple of Sidney Bechet, he had adapted the instrument to his own romantic disposition, playing it with his usual perfection of pitch and timbre—rarely heard to better effect than in this two-chorus solo. "Junior Hop" is an Ellington banquet. At first blush it appears to be a 32-bar AABA theme, except that each section is slightly different, not just in the initial chorus but in each one that follows, including a wily borrowing from "Beautiful Dreamer," which emphasizes the general feeling of summery nostalgia. What promises to be the last eight bars of the final chorus is foreshortened by half, and then flows into a recapitulation of the eight-bar intro—the only verbatim recap in a nearly through-composed piece that includes some of the most dazzling glissandos Hodges's alto ever had to execute. "Good Queen Bess" opens with two bars of "Christopher Columbus," and is notable not least for a hilarious entrance by Cootie Williams, who purrs and growls his way through eight bars. "Squatty Roo" is flat-out swing, and "Going Out the Back Way" is swing animated by the kind of swagger that prefigured r&b.

If Hodges walked the bounding line between blues economy and romance verging on decadence, Rex Stewart was a Cheshire Cat of vocalized antics, employing mutes and valving effects to create a panoply of personalities. The most infamous example is "Menelik (The Lion of Judah)," which instantly commands attention with its gnarly growls, then settles for a rhythmically charged riff that continues as Stewart introduces the actual tune. Way ahead of the curve in Afrocentricity, the performance peaks with a passage for trumpet and drums—including a reference to Harry James—and was considered so bizarre in 1941 that Victor would not release it until several years later. Stewart was an unusual figure in jazz, a premier stylist who was also a skillful writer-memoirist, and it's easy to read a degree of literate wit into his diverse voices.

Stewart plays two non-Ellington standards, "Linger Awhile" and "Without a Song." On the first, Carney makes one of his rare appearances on alto sax (he plays it again on "My Sunday Girl") and Ellington essays a splendid stride piano solo, except that he doesn't actually play the stride part, content to leave that to Blanton's incomparable bass walk, thereby anticipating bebop's "one-handed" pianists. Ben Webster raises the temperature as always, spurred by Greer's offbeat accents, after which Rex returns tightly muted, and the whole ensemble lifts off for a stop-time flight. "Mobile Bay" begins as a dilatory 32-bar song, in which Stewart pays homage to Cootie Williams, then, as Ben Webster enters, suddenly turns into a blues—Ellington plays a chord that announces the change in flavor—for one chorus, before finishing with a gospel-style passage, all interwoven as in a great short story. Webster never sounded sweeter than when discoursing with Lawrence Brown on "Some Saturday," or more lilting than on the threnody, "Poor Bubber," capped by some of Rex's most expressive mute work. (Lester Bowie begins here.) If "My Sunday Girl" is a lovely, inexplicably forgotten Ellington theme (surely there are lyrics somewhere?), "Subtle Slough" did, in fact, become an Ellington standard called "Just Squeeze Me," waiving the surprising riches of the original, including the animating shuffle beat; the 16-bar intro with trumpet breaks; a strange chorus in which the band plays a five-note riff and Stewart merely hints at the theme; a second chorus, where the theme is stated for the first time (the record is half over), including a savory bridge played by tenor and baritone saxes; and a reprise of the introduction—at which point one realizes that Ellington wrote practically every note.

When these 16 sides were initially released, they could be taken for granted as the kind of gemlike miniatures Ellington turned out without breaking a sweat. Sixty years later, we know how rare they are, how inimitable they would prove to be, even by Ellington himself. Those to whom they are uncharted territory will have their world enlarged.

[*The Absolute Sound*, April 2002]

114 ❖ *Continuing Education (Marian McPartland)*

Marian McPartland's learning curve is apparently infinite, an Escher-like, Velcro-covered loop that keeps picking up incremental details as it winds its way through jazz for six decades, turning what began as a generic approach into something personal. Her early '50s records, made at the start of her eight-year engagement at the Hickory House, reveal a gifted pianist with accomplished technique and a passable understanding of contemporary currents. But her playing was often polite—stylish without suggesting much individual style. Yet even by that time, Margaret

Marian Turner of Windsor, England, had wended her way through much music history, forging her approach with at least as much stubborn persistence as natural talent.

She was born in 1918, and began playing by ear; years of formal study followed, but in her early teens she discovered jazz and begin imitating records. "I just played everything," she told me a few years ago, on the occasion of her widely celebrated 80th birthday: "Duke Ellington was my big inspiration, and then I tried to play like Teddy Wilson." She won a few scholarships, including one that enrolled her in London's Guildhall School of Music, which she abandoned before graduation to go out on a tour in vaudeville. In 1944, while entertaining troops in Belgium, she met trumpeter and Beiderbecke acolyte Jimmy McPartland. Stationed deep in the Ardennes, he came to her rescue by commandeering a grand piano from a family of Nazi sympathizers so that she could play a concert. They married and settled in New York in 1946, and though her work with Jimmy was Dixieland, she instantly began to soak up the forces of modernism, asking and receiving advice from Bud Powell and Lennie Tristano, among others, and leading her own trio with Bill Crow and Joe Morello.

"Starting out with Jimmy was a great way to break into show business, so on any day I can play in his Dixieland style, but I'm also part Teddy Wilson, part bebop, part Bill Evans. I'd like to be part Wayne Shorter." By the 1970s, those parts and others had contributed to a redefinition of her playing—ballads slowed to a meditative crawl and parsed with extended rests; medium-tempo flourishes spelled with blues locutions and a near-rococo infusion of passing chords; uptempo aggression in which time is spiked with occasionally pugnacious syncopations. Her improvisations hadn't lost an iota of charm, but were no longer reliably decorous or even-tempered. She developed an unusually expansive book that included the expected standards, with a particular accent on Alec Wilder (her self-produced 1973 *Marian McPartland Plays the Music of Alec Wilder*, with bassist Michael Moore, marked a turning point), as well as originals and a plethora of jazz works that few others bothered to investigate.

McPartland's individuality accrued partly as a result of discriminating add-ons; she doesn't leap out like McCoy Tyner or Bill Evans, unmistakable from the first note. Yet like them, she plays with a clarity that allows you to hear her think. A relatively trite instance occurs at the end of "While We're Young," on her *Piano Jazz* entry with Evans, when she plays what you expect to be the penultimate note and sits on it, pondering whether or not to resolve it, and finally deciding not. A more telling example is her smashing 1991 *Live at Maybeck*, a rare instance of

McPartland alone. Her thought processes are on tap throughout a thoroughly engaging "Willow Weep for Me," the requisite funk tonality used sparingly, dressed in the finery of richly hued chords. A passage in "My Funny Valentine" gets down with a Dave McKenna–like bass line, but not for long, because she is more interested in a rhapsodic extension of the melody and harmonies. She revives Ellington's "Clothed Woman," which combines a striding melody (reminiscent of "Black Beauty") and modernist framework, and offers something similar on her own "Theme from Piano Jazz," mixing boogie woogie and dissonance. For an example of her clean, decisive, rigorous blues work, she chooses as her starting gate Ornette Coleman's "Turnaround."

Taking an opposite tack, she merged her trio with a 20-piece string orchestra in 1996 for *Silent Pool*, commenting at the time, "I was afraid people would say I sounded like Mantovani or something." Alan Broadbent's dark, stately arrangements of a dozen McPartland originals forestall that, but the main interest is the lucid way she navigates her part, taking stock every measure, a quality no less evident on her latest recording, *Live at Shanghai Jazz*, taped last year with Rufus Reid and Joe Morello; it begins with Mary Lou Williams's cheerful "Scratchin' in the Gravel" and settles into a vividly contemplative de facto trilogy of "Moon and Sand," "Prelude to a Kiss" (she's inhabited its harmonies for so long that she can bend them in any direction), and "All the Things You Are."

McPartland's running dialog with jazz has also taken shape in educational and literary pursuits—an anthology of the latter was published as *All in Good Time*. But the truest measure of her involvement is the incomparable *Piano Jazz* series, with which she has served NPR since 1978. Like many people who haven't turned on a radio in years, I know the show because dozens of installments appeared as CDs on Jazz Alliance—a wing of Concord Jazz, which released all the albums mentioned here. They've now gone out of catalog, but on August 27 Jazz Alliance will put out four volumes: reissues of Bill Evans (1978) and Oscar Peterson (1980) and, for the first time, Carmen McRae (1985) and Chick Corea (2001). They are oddly intimate portraits, combining music and conversation as McPartland and guest sit at two Baldwins (she has also done shows with nonpianists), exchanging pleasantries yet somehow getting to deeper levels of jazz talk than you expect. The courtliness of it all, and the focus on music-making with only scattered touches of biography, elicits an ingenuous desire to reveal and explain. McPartland, who has chatted and duetted with everyone from Eubie Blake to Cecil Taylor, never gets technical, though first-name references are not uncommon. The drama takes place during duets, as the game host attempts to blend in with the guest, soaking up the unusual chord or key change.

All are worth hearing, and the Evans is a classic. It begins with him playing the original written version of "Waltz for Debby" and quickly evolves into a demonstration of Evans's ideas about displacing rhythms. A born teacher, he discusses the need to know a tune's changes ("intuition has to lead knowledge, but it can't be out there alone"), while dismissing the need for group rehearsal—everything develops on the job, he says; in 20 years, the trio rehearsed maybe four times, usually before concert recordings. Most of the *Piano Jazz* shows have sent me back to records I'd forgotten or overlooked. For one example, while insisting he lacks the "dimension" to be a solo pianist, Evans laughingly refers to the endlessly repeated melody of his 1975 "People" (*Alone Again* on Fantasy); lo and behold, a performance I once thought dreary reemerges, "Nefertiti"-like, as a subtly impassioned tour de force—albeit not one I'm likely to play very often. He speaks of his early idols, of how he started off with boogie woogie, of the weddings and socials he played, including a polka band at Manville Polish Home, then plays Toots Thielemans's alternating-keys arrangement of "Days of Wine and Roses," transfigures Ellington's "Reflections in D," and raves about Marian's "While We're Young."

Peterson begins with a highly Tatumesque reading of "Old Folks," and shows how he uses minor seconds to "thicken" the harmony. McPartland picks it up and says, "See, already I copped something and it's only the first tune." He says most pianists are ambidextrous, at least in their thoughts. She says, "I am, in my thoughts, but watch me when I get to the piano." Peterson's in a stomping mood, demonstrating broken tenths as compared with striding octaves, telling funny anecdotes, chivalrously cradling McPartland's choruses, which are sometimes shaky though she adds pretty chords to "Like Someone in Love." He reveals that what she thought was his variation on "Satin Doll" is an interpolation of an old and obscure song: "You mean you don't recall 'Auf Wiedersehen'?" (Who knew he was a wit? Yet other examples abound in his remarkable memoir, *A Jazz Odyssey*, published by Continuum; his comments about Bud Powell are ludicrous, but his Lester Young stories more than compensate.) McPartland's best showing, not surprisingly, is her solo, "Willow Creek."

Carmen McRae was in great voice for her hour, and the sound balance and casualness underscore its crisp directness. Clearly enjoying McPartland, she is uncharacteristically genial. Though her piano is percussive and efficient, each note struck with confidence, it's no match for

McPartland's technique, which supplies her with a gently radiant boost. They talk about modern tunes and McRae pays homage to James Taylor ("Fire and Rain" is a "cute tune," McPartland avers); yet when asked to perform a new song, she prefers Jule Styne and Harold Arlen. Chick Corea's hour begins with platitudes ("music is life") and the through-composed "Brasilia," but grows deeper and more candid as he is encouraged to explore Monk and Waller and a few of his own early benchmarks. Blue Note has just reissued his masterly 1968 trio album *Now He Sings, Now He Sobs*, which had a huge impact in its day and stands up as well as anything he's done. It was a favorite of McPartland's (she concedes less interest in his fusion period), but although she can't get him to revisit "Matrix" or "Windows," her limpid version of "Crystal Silence" stimulates them both, leading to a completely free piece and a redoubtable capper in "Spain"—from which McPartland no doubt picked up a few more tricks.

[*Village Voice*, 14 April 2002]

115 ❖ *Fully Interactive (Bill Charlap)*

In making his brief for Kipling, Randall Jarrell wrote of those oppressively mighty figures in politics and art upon whose leave-taking the world—"tired of being their pedestal"—gives "a great *oof* of relief," only to elevate its own personage of equal weight. Jazz's last Napoleonic (or Kiplingesque) figure was Miles Davis, and no one since has offered a plausible succession—certainly not Wynton Marsalis, whose musical impact withered in direct proportion to his aspiration. Yet if jazz no longer presents an orderly chain of command, it holds out the possibility of contrasting empires. During the past couple of decades, the best and largest part of jazz struck with teeming, clamorous urgency: the legacy of hard bop as multiplied by the avant-garde, fusion, and the swinging strut of recycled repertory. The net effect was to drown out, marginalize, and even belittle middle-aged desires like Lyricism, Sentiment, and Nostalgia.

This was, more often than not, a good and necessary thing. The fragility of LS&N made it vulnerable to such horrifying mutations as New Age and Jazz Lite; and the talented middle-aged as well as the middle-aged young had their own enclaves and record labels where salutes to the sainted dead would always be welcome. For every Doc Cheatham or Ruby Braff, authentic sun gods, there were a dozen retired podiatrists ready to hit the stage—actually they were local pros who merely sounded like retired podiatrists. Mainstream exile was no more onerous than avant-garde door-money gigs and vanity labels. But lately, a renewed longing for the cooler precincts of melody and rhythm has become apparent, and not just in the fixation on blasé blonds and brunets with go-hither stares. It can be heard—not always, but often—in the music of Mark Turner, Stefon Harris, Dave Douglas, Ethan Iverson, Marc Copland, Jason Moran, and Matthew Shipp, as well as inveterate downtowners like Roy Campbell and William Parker, among others.

LS&N is the territory mined by Bill Charlap, the 35-year-old pianist who has been playing prominent sideman gigs for more than a dozen years, but recently clicked with something larger than himself: the Bill Charlap Trio. With bassist Peter Washington and drummer Kenny Washington, two mainstays of the New York circuit whose resumes include time with Tommy Flanagan, he has over the course of three albums and several engagements, including a recent week at the Jazz Standard, created something more than a stellar trio. He has himself a band, a unit, a trinity larger than its parts. They are all throwbacks. Peter W., at 37, favors the low, Paul Chambers register and is not only content to play one note where a dozen could be squeezed, but to repeat the note and let it reverberate; his concise and pointed phrases do the work of the bass while maintaining a subtle, almost reticent interest in their own right. Kenny W., at 43, has similarly no need to show off his technique except in the finesse with which he employs it; he has listened to Jo Jones and Kenny Clarke and his brushes have their polish, his sticks their crisp resolve—switching from one to the other, he jolts the group.

Charlap clearly enjoys listening to them and, willing to suspend his own considerable technique, allows whole episodes to pass with the mutuality of a Count Basie rhythm interlude. On "The Nearness of You," a slo-mo highlight of his new album, *Stardust*, the equitable mix gives the brushes a crackling, electric pizzazz; and on the bridge of the piano solo, Charlap suggests a phrase and lets the bass finish it. Conversely, on "Georgia on My Mind," he sometimes follows the bass's lead. One gets the impression that the three musicians are as intent on each other as on the tunes. That's how it's supposed to be and usually isn't. Most trios are content to play the arrangement. When the leader solos, the others back him. Charlap looks to the others for ideas he can spin. His m.o. includes a second chorus, after the head, in which he seems to noodle for several measures, looking for ground on which to build. Although unlike Ahmad Jamal he is a linear player and unlike Bill Evans a laconic one, he has borrowed from both the idea of a fully interactive band, albeit in a less formalized version.

That Charlap presently records for Blue Note is itself interesting. He has absorbed a great deal of the history of jazz piano, including aspects— block chords, ripe melodies, dilatory tempos—that lead you to expect him to record for specialty labels like Chiaroscuro, Progressive, and Nagel Heyer, for which he has indeed made memorable albums, which include among their tracks two strangely romantic versions of the knuckle-busting "Donna Lee." His breakthrough albums are on Criss Cross. The exceptional *Souvenir* (1995), with Scott Colley and Dennis Mackrel (an alert and sage drummer), opens with an assured Ornette Coleman blues, as if to obviate questions about how much piano he can play, then gets really interesting as he makes Benny Carter's rarely heard "Souvenir" sound like an Alec Wilder standard; begins "Confirmation" as though fooling around, skirting the tune while prodding the changes (a "Donna Lee"–type cascade, a fillip from Monk's "Criss Cross"— favorite tune? pun?), stating the theme only in the last 30 seconds for a *Memento* effect; voices "Godchild" with gracious, Mulliganesque harmonies (his big break was in Gerry Mulligan's 1988–90 quartet). An astonishing "Alone Together" opens with harplike a cappella arpeggios and evolves through Jimmy Rowles crushed chords; triangular interaction with melody, chords, and bassist; a chorus with a storming Tyneresque left hand, leading to a crescendo and a skittering arpeggio that gives pause as Colley begins his turn.

All Through the Night (1997) introduced the Washingtons and is in some ways a more mature if less startling effort (he stamps Wilder's "It's So Peaceful in the Country" indelibly). But the trio's rigors come to fruition on the two Blue Notes. I misprised *Written on the Wind* (the movie too, come to think of it) the first time around, hearing a cocktailish pithiness that, in light of *Stardust* and the Jazz Standard set, I now see as a core virtue in a stubbornly autonomous style that is at once beholden to and liberated from a '50s aesthetic. This style is exemplified by "In the Still of the Night," in which he refuses to hurry and finds his way from hesitant embellishments to puckish lightning-bug flight, winking in and out of the changes. He also makes "Blue Skies" romp, "One for My Baby" dawdle, and "Lorelei" twinkle the way they oughta.

One expects Charlap to know the jazz piano hierarchy from Wilson to Hancock. But what other young musician claims Jimmy Rowles, whose ironic fragments, touches of stride, closed chords, spare phrases, dynamic touch, and imperturbable patience he has assimilated? He lacks

Rowles's third-martini drolleries, but everyone does. Those qualities are evident in the imaginative accompaniment he renders Warren Vaché in their duets on last year's *2Gether* (Nagel Heyer), an engrossing jaunt for both, an object lesson in distinguishing sentiment from molasses; with "Dancing on the Ceiling," they attain conversational perfection—somehow the piano takes on a touch of the trumpet's glimmer, auguring Vache's perfect concluding note. On "Prelude to a Kiss," Charlap's rubato theme leads him to think the intro to Monk's "'Round Midnight," which he cuts off with a tremolo—I'm surprised they didn't start again, but it's a funny, human, spontaneous moment. On the other hand, "Nip-Hoc Waltz" (ad hoc Chopin) justifies Charlap's practice of usually leaving the composing to others.

Stardust should enlarge his audience. It's the quintessential well-made album, the Hoagy Carmichael songbook augmented by four guests—all, like Charlap, shrewd economizers. No one will be surprised that Tony Bennett and Shirley Horn are in their element on comfortably protracted ballads. But when has Frank Wess had a better showcase? Humming "Rockin' Chair" with a Ben Webster croon, he blends with the trio to create a plush groove, articulated by four-to-the-bar cymbals; this kind of playing comes with age, and the sentiment is historical only to the degree that few people dare play with such modesty anymore. Jim Hall opens "Two Sleepy People" with a loose solo variation that ends with a crafty phrase for Charlap to extend; a contrapuntal passage may remind you of Hall's two LPs with Bill Evans, but the net effect is quite different—a quietly jaunty chat between two self-possessed people at dawn's early light.

Hall sat in for Charlap's sold-out Wednesday set at the Jazz Standard and left the impression of playing a total of maybe 100 notes in the hour. Not that anything was missing. But if playing the bare minimum requires the same sense of adventure as kitchen-sink extravaganzas, then no one is more daring than this veteran guitarist who takes melody seriously enough not to overdress it. You get the feeling he'd rather unplug than play an unnecessary note. On tunes like "Without a Song" and "Blue Skies," as well as solid originals by Hall ("Bon Ami," "All Across the City"), they sparked polite dissonances and contrapuntal discourses that never descended to faux classicism. Refreshingly, Charlap didn't call a single song from the new album—they would have worked as well, but how novel that he wasn't thinking commerce.

[*Village Voice*, 30 April 2002]

Old recording artifacts die hard, their value increasing in ratio to the emotional coldness of their replacements. Last year, box sets of Billie Holiday and Charley Patton mimicked 78-rpm albums. Many CDs replicate original LPs, in cardboard or paper-modified jewel boxes—among them series from Savoy, Sony, Impulse, and Verve. Verve was the first to offer miniaturization with *The Complete Ella Fitzgerald Songbooks*, which remains one of the most delectable of reissues, a shrunken version of the original albums that seemed remarkably witty in 1993. Since then, Verve has specialized in amended versions of LPs in its Master Edition and By Request lines, which combine cardboard gatefolds with (breakable) plastic disc-holders. Now the label, which, due to recent mergers, owns Impulse, Decca, Mercury, A&M, Horizon, and other catalogs, returns to the miniaturization template for the LP Reproduction series. Unlike Savoy editions, which have inserts with the basic recording info that was omitted from the original jackets, Verve provides wraparounds that the unwary might (like me) inadvertently discard.

The wraparounds are necessary, because '50s producers, particularly Verve's Norman Granz, often failed to supply fundamental information, such as the identity of musicians, composers, and arrangers; the years when the tracks were cut; and even the order in which they were presented. The ethics of counterfeiting forbids adding those tidbits to the covers. And duplication does not extend to the disc itself, which reproduces the logo, though this would have been a handy place to include a track list with composer and player credits. Still, petite replicas grant a certain frisson to those who are partial to inner and outer sleeves, cheesy graphics, an average playing time of 35 minutes, and a reprieve from sundry takes. Moreover, they get neglected product back into catalog. Jazz discs must be moving so briskly that the industry can hardly keep up with the demand—hence an initial release of 20 LPs with another 10 scheduled for August. The choices are tres strange, reflecting neither consistent excellence nor commercial success, and running the gamut from Margaret Whiting to Alice Coltrane. Half are vocal or part-vocal, and a few groupings suggest themselves.

Carmen McRae's 1958 *Birds of a Feather* is a find: her last album for Decca, representing a transition from the sweet naïf to the edgy sophisticate she would become. It offers one of Decca's howl-inducing covers—two bluebirds examining her décolletage—and a saturated sound mix that sends McRae even more over the top than she was inclined to go. A few tracks ("The Eagle and Me," "Baltimore Oriole") are distorted by echo chamber; here is an instance where remastering might have undone the damage, but at the cost of fidelity to 1958. For contractual reasons, the LP identified the leading soloist as "a tenorman," though Ben Webster's sound is an unmistakable calling card, and his participation amounts to a full-scale collaboration. (Al Cohn also plays, but as a section man.) Ralph Burns's efficient charts employ four French horns on a few tracks but generally leave McRae and Webster unfettered. She is radiant: Note her left-field entrance on "Skylark," loose aggression on "Bob White," brief scat on "Bye Bye Blackbird." A choir and country-gospel chart by producer Milt Gabler on "His Eye Is on the Sparrow" suggests unfulfilled plans for a single.

Rosemary Clooney's *Swing Around Rosie* pretends to be a Coral recording (subsidiary of Decca) but actually consists of a dozen transcriptions from her radio show, backed by Buddy Cole's organ quartet. Again, the audio was maxed to fire the old hi-fi. Though Clooney's in hearty voice, Cole's buoyantly cute and often corny charts give her little room to maneuver. Her musicianship brooks no intrusions on "Do Nothing Till You Hear from Me" and "This Can't Be Love," but her finest work of the period was on RCA. Anita O'Day's 1960 *Incomparable!*, however, *is* her finest, or some of it, parsed in tight Bill Holman arrangements. She reveals an unusual glimmer of Billie Holiday's influence on "It Could Happen to You," and an appealingly raw edge to her top notes on a romping "Indian Summer." But she is always her own sexy, risk-taking self, adding canny embellishments on "Why Shouldn't I?" "Old Devil Moon," and "Easy Living." Her wordless "Slaughter on 10th Avenue" breaks the three-minute mold and shows off her accurate pitch, but all those doo-doo-doos recall Clem Kadiddlehopper. The several unacknowledged soloists include Bill Perkins, Conte Candoli, Frank Rosolino, and Lou Levy, with Mel Lewis keeping time.

Margaret Whiting is by no definition a jazz singer, but like most good pop singers of her day, she had solid time as well as a lovely vocal mask and exemplary intonation. Her *Jerome Kern Song Book* includes the verses and sustains an understated pulse. Only "D'Ye Love Me" is substandard Kern, and, among Russell Garcia's arrangements, only "I'm Old Fashioned" sinks to novelty level, though Whiting ignores its faux-baroque and works with the rhythm section. Her vibratoless whole notes are engaging on "Look for the Silver Lining" and she confidently canters through "Dearly Beloved" and the more improbable "You Couldn't Be Cuter." Ella Fitzgerald's *Whisper Not* (1966, her last Verve album) and Sarah Vaughan's *It's a Man's World* (1967, her last Mercury) are often overlooked. The former has resourceful golden-voiced ballads, notably "Thanks for the Memory," "Spring Can Really Hang You Up the Most," and "Time After Time," and the latter, despite oppressive strings, delivers many exceptional moments and one full-blooded masterpiece, "My Man," in which every syllable is discretely inflected. Mel Tormé's *Olé Tormé!*, arranged by Billy May, depicts Mel in toreador rig—it was that or a fruit-salad hat. The rock 'n roll intro to "Malaguena" screams 1958, though most of the tunes are well chosen and Tormé is in prime voice— "Baia" especially—if you like his prime voice. For some reason, the selections were programmed in a different order than listed on the jacket.

The Tormé leads to a second division, three albums recorded in the '60s, part of Verve's good-neighbor policy. Astrud Gilberto's *The Shadow of Your Smile* is whispery mood music, heavily arranged to exploit her "yearning innocence"—25 minutes worth. She is best with just guitar on a pleasing "Manha de Carnaval." According to *The New Grove Dictionary of Jazz*, she has "an economy of melodic line and a steady momentum akin to that of Basie, but its rhythmic drive is often devoid of contours." Got that? The title of Willie Bobo's *A New Dimension* refers to his singing, which is nondescript, but his fixed dance rhythms pack a punch (Freddie Waits on traps), and so do his soloists. Sergio Mendes & Brasil '66's *Equinox* is beyond the concerns, ken, and pale of this page.

As a bridge from bossa to boss instrumentals, Oscar Peterson's *Soul Español*, a 1966 Limelight, is overly familiar but effective. Adding three percussionists to his trio (bassist Sam Jones, drummer Louis Hayes), he spins each piece with rolling, hustling minor thirds and tremolos, mining romance from "How Insensitive" and "Meditation," and gusto from "Carioca" and "Mas Que Nada," which swing too hard to resist. *Stan Getz and the Cool Sounds* implies that he's playing with one of those '50s lounge trios, but, no, the title is generic, and he is left to his own devices, balladeering with great rhythm sections (Lou Levy, Jimmy Rowles, Max Roach, a spot of Tony Fruscella's trumpet) in peak form. Paul Desmond does his hat trick, entering with peculiar notes on "These Foolish Things" and "Star Dust," on *1975: The Duets*, but Dave Brubeck plods (he is stronger without Desmond, on "Summer Song"), and the absence of a rhythm section is no help. *Willow Weep for Me*, the posthumous Wes Montgomery album for which Claus Ogerman overdubbed orchestrations, should never have seen the light of day. This reissue is mind-boggling, especially since the type is so small that unsuspecting costumers are likely to note only the presence of a quartet. Montgomery's gleaming performances can be heard as he and Wynton Kelly intended, when they recorded them live at the Half Note, on *Impressions: The Verve*

Jazz Sides. If you see *Willow Weep for Me* in a store it is perfectly legal to stomp on it or set it afire.

The two remaining categories are big band classics and kitsch. Don't miss *Woody Herman 1963*, one of his all-time great ones, arranged almost entirely by members of the band, which helps explain the very cool choice of material—pieces by Horace Parlan, Horace Silver, Joe Newman, and Duke Ellington. The concerto for tenor saxophonist Sal Nistico, "Sister Sadie," is a high, but there are no lows—Jake Hanna's drumming is almost unbelievably on point throughout, and dig Woody's klezmer sound on "It's a Lonesome Old Town." The hot spots on Gerry Mulligan's *Concert Jazz Band at the Village Vanguard* are the Al Cohn charts for "Blueport" and "Lady Chatterley's Mother," and I hope this reissue won't hinder Verve's long-promised complete Concert Jazz Band. Count Basie's *King of Swing*, from 1953 to 1954, is motored by drummer Gus Johnson, and features the leanest riffing machine in jazz, with rocking blues arrangements and many superb solos; saxophonist Frank Wess erupts on Freddie Green's "Right On," and goes toe-to-toe with Frank Foster on Neal Hefti's "Two for the Blues." Dizzy Gillespie's *Afro*, from 1954, restores a major achievement that led to the rebirth of his orchestra. Chico O'Farrill's title suite is a deconstruction of "Manteca"—first the piece itself, then elaborations on the bridge ("Contraste"), the key rhythmic figure ("Jungla"), and the vamps ("Rhumba-Finale"). Gillespie's playing is exuberant.

Kitsch: Stan Kenton, *The Formative Years*, which includes "Concerto for Doghouse," with vocal by Howard Rumsey doing Tex Avery's Droopy (intentionality presumed); and Alice Coltrane, *Universal Consciousness*, which isn't as bad as it sounds if you have achieved nirvana or a reasonable state of inebriation.

[*Village Voice*, 21 May 2002]

117 ❖ *Personality*
(Houston Person)

One might argue, though not too strenuously, that three central tribes of tenor saxophonists emerged just after the war: those who played Lester Young hard, those who played him soft, and those who played Illinois Jacquet. All merged their primary influences with bebop's phrasing and shivered their timbres with leanings toward any number of other tenor saxophonists. Some even played Young hard *and* soft, or Young *and* Jacquet, who was himself obviously influenced by Young. Still, a distinction can be made, and part of it has to do with the fact that Young's disciples (and those of Coleman Hawkins and Ben Webster) grounded jazz's serious evolution, attracting serious listeners, serious critiquing, and serious pedagogy. Jacquet's brood, including the Lester-inspired Gene Ammons, leads to that presumably middlebrow school of tenors who often affix themselves to organ trios, name tunes after soul food, put semi-naked women on album covers, tour chiefly in black 'hoods, and like—really like—dancers. They attract listeners who clap in time, critics or at least annotators who fetishize simplicity and are really DJs anyway, and no pedagogues at all.

Jacquet, it must be emphasized, was a rugged, often brilliantly imaginative musician, who, though he scored one of the early slam-dunk rhythm & blues landmarks, playing "Flying Home" with Lionel Hampton (a bandleader who felt as much at home with r&b as swing), never followed the other swing renegades—Louis Jordan, Earl Bostic, Bill Doggett—into the groves of commercial dance music. Those three were nondescript jazz players and distinguished r&b players, whereas Jacquet could whittle any jazz virtuoso down to his own diminutive but muscular size. Yet he soloed with an aggressive, crowd-pleasing lucidity and excitement that Ammons advanced and helped pass on to tenors as varied as Arnett Cobb, Willis Jackson, Harold Ousley, King Curtis, Stanley Turrentine, and, of course, Houston Person, who, as Samuel G. Freedman wrote in a judicious Sunday *Times* piece, works "a circuit ignored by or unknown to much of the jazz intelligentsia." Lash me, daddy, eight to the bar.

After hearing an enlightening if interrupted Person set at Jazz Standard in early May, I found myself reevaluating my own prejudices. Mind you, I have always admired Houston Person for his huge tone, bluff humor, and pointed obbligato, and have seen him several times—but only with singers: Daryl Sherman once and Etta Jones the rest. Yet only in recent years, at their Vanguard gigs and through records, especially Jones's faultless 1997 *My Buddy* (HighNote), did the group they co-led from 1973 until her death last year really reach me. If I paid her any mind before the early '90s, it was as one of several OK heirs to Dinah Washington's crown. My ensuing raves, which were of the most-underrated-singer-alive sort, the best-by-comparison sort ("the disparity between the attention given blond youth and brunette maturity . . ."), and the they-are-a-New-York-institution sort, were Johnny-come-lately blurbs, holding actions while I tried to get a better fix on her and the band.

I'd invariably leave the Vanguard feeling good, but with a literary shortfall in puzzling out an effect that recapitulated all those liner note platitudes: simple, basic, direct, home cooking. Jones modified Dinah's defiant, trenchant attack, making it drier, in the sense of grainier mid-range and martini acerbity, with a combination of the ripening that was denied Dinah, coquettishly cracked high notes, and a contagiously poised comfort zone that was unmistakably boosted by Person's chivalrous obbligato and quilt-heavy solos. She and he invariably phrased on the beat and in pitch, swinging without effort and using only the notes they needed. They delivered a perhaps too tried if undeniably true repertory of blues and ballads and blue-ballads (she had sung with Buddy Johnson at 15 and never let the flame go out) with a slightly mocking infallibility, leaving nothing for me to say except amen and see you next time.

So I had never really taken the measure of Person, who, at 67, now tours with a quartet: Soul tenor is soul tenor, and I am the kind of fan who complains that jazz isn't more popular but has never much liked what passes for popular jazz. I attended his opening night at the Jazz Standard mostly out of curiosity, but midway through his opener, a Wild Bill Davis tune (Person has a large repertory of pieces by jazz composers, many of them rarely performed), his easy unruffled gait, whimsical insertions of "As Time Goes By" and other songs, fat straight-down-the-middle tone and equally hefty flaring high notes, not to mention a capable rhythm section led by pianist Stan Hope, who looks as though he were having the time of his life, transformed a high-tech club into the kind of room that's supposed to be Person's bread and butter—a neighborhood bar, with barbecue no less. I recalled sneering at music like this in the '60s (Person had a hit at the time, *Goodness!*, not one of his best), and (warning: food metaphor in progress) now scarfing it up and wishing everyone could share the dish, felt like the guest who arrives at a party when everyone else is leaving.

He then went almost without pause into "Tenderly," a tune that usually makes me blanch (Sarah Vaughan aside), and revived its jukebox glory with streaming blues locutions and a tone big enough to move into, come winter; Hope fed him plush, provoking chords while bassist Nat Reeves held the center and drummer Chip White snapped his brushes. Midway, the fire alarm went off—a mix of siren blasts and flashing lights, kind of like the Fillmore. Person played through it, finishing with a short, sweet cadenza and joking about the interruption. But the alarm tripped again during Tadd Dameron's "Lady Bird," this time for a long siege, as club personnel walked from table to table, assuring everyone there was no fire, buying a round of drinks for the house, and finally calling for an intermission until the problem was solved. The brief break seemed to energize Person, who returned roaring with "Don't Get Around Much Anymore," a display of Websterish economy and his own fuzzless timbre. Hope accounts for much of the group's familial pleasure; he plays spare and swinging solos that rarely surprise but never bore, affirming the idea of party jazz. Person underscored a feeling of jukebox reverie with "Where Is Love," from *Oliver!*, constructing a solo with high sighing notes, very different from his mid and bottom range.

The peak of the set, following a fast "Secret Love," was a slow and squally "Since I Fell for You," Buddy Johnson's signature tune. Riding the backbeat with every kind of blues lick and kicking up a storm in the upper register, he raged and caressed, then settled into a quick coda and out. And so it went, ending with a breakneck blues parsed by fastidious cymbal-slashing—Chip White is a drummer to watch—a chorus of "Happy Birthday" to his doctor, and Mother's Day wishes.

Converted, I dug out half a dozen long-unplayed and a few never-played Houston Person albums, and found confirmation for my new religion and old skepticism, sometimes on the same album, for example *Wildflower*. "Preachin' and Teachin' " is mostly rhythm and cliché, the backbeat as relentless as disco, and the tag-and-fade end is deadly conventional. The remarkable thing about Person at his best is the absence of cliché, as on the introspective "Dameronia." "My Romance" surprises: Person plays a handsome but hardly transformative head, and then, when you expect him to pass the piece to another player, embarks on an improv that makes the song his own, double-timing to pass the time but generally offering something much better—a diligent sense of melodic buildup and drama. The much neglected trumpeter Bill Hardman is also showcased, turning in concise, orderly inventions on "Dameronia," which he all but steals, and "Ain't Misbehavin'."

Person's several albums with pianist Cedar Walton are particularly good. He is inspired throughout *The Big Horn*, as are Walton (notably on "This Love of Mine," though "La Marseillaise" was evidently on his mind because he quotes it here and on "The More I See You," catching himself just as it almost slips in a third time), bassist Buster Williams, and drummer Grady Tate; Buddy Caldwell's congas do no damage. You expect Person to be in clover on "Gee, Baby Ain't I Good to You," yet he and the group are no less compelling on "Memories of You"—Walton's every note is articulated and given full weight (he doesn't appear to favor some fingers over others), and provides an attentive, rich, empathic accompaniment. "I Concentrate on You," despite yet another tag-and-fade, is a capacious performance, with a vividly alert Tate. The Walton-Williams teamwork is exemplified here: Williams responds to him with diverse textural ideas, including slides and double-stops, and Walton returns the favor, stabilizing the bass solo with a touchstone riff. Person lucidly rides the beat with figures you think you've heard but haven't. These are not merely recycled licks; they simply seem familiar, like family. Both of these albums were recorded in the '70s, yet, gray hair aside, Person is unchanged, as is evident in the more recent High Note albums, especially the casually crisp ballads on *In a Sentimental Mood* and *Soft Lights*, and the increasingly sage economy of *Blue Velvet* and the stark *Dialogues* with bassist Ron Carter. He remains an unmoved mover of valuable jazz essentials.

[*Village Voice*, 28 May 2002]

118 ❖ *Postwar Jazz: An Arbitrary Roadmap (1945–2001)*

The initial idea was to create an overview of jazz (and jazz-related) records from 1900 to 2001, by choosing one work to represent each year. After several weeks of revelatory listening to music from the dark ages—rags, marches, cakewalks, blues, minstrel and music hall turns—in an attempt to find appropriate tracks for 1900 to 1920, I realized that the project would have to be abbreviated. I had bit off more than I could chew or the *Village Voice* could accommodate. This particular fit of madness has now passed, and I don't expect to fill in the missing years any time soon. Even with the narrower scope of 1945 to 2001, I spent nearly five months groping for solutions to the labyrinth I was intent on building; the writing was, relatively, a snap as compared to the process of selecting representative recordings, given my self-imposed rules, about which more anon.

I wanted, for my own illumination, to posit a jazz map. By opting for one track (always a track, never an album, though albums on which the tracks are found are noted at the end of each entry) per year, I hoped to offer a purview that would balance achievement and innovation. Given my rules, however, I soon realized that nothing remotely like objectivity was attainable. An infinite number of maps was possible, all of them valid. Some years and periods—1928, 1936–41, 1957, 1961–65, 1980, 1988, and 1999, among others—were so bountiful that choosing was an exercise in frustration, even heartbreak. What I thought at first had at least a whiff of scholastic gravity revealed itself as a shameless parlor game. (Advanced classes might attempt lists made up entirely of non-Americans or guitarists or under-30s, and so on.) Though it gives me pleasure to look over this particular terrain, I refuse to defend it against others. When you're worn out ranting at the lunacy of my selections, try it yourself.

For me, the key reward was in exploring hundreds of records I hadn't revisited in years. Some records that I expected to include no longer sounded as good; others I had previously neglected now filled me with admiration. Since the final draft says more about me than jazz, it doesn't bear analysis, except to mention the obvious. In narrowing my options, I decided to stick with American jazz, an act of inexcusable chauvinism; also, the ages of musicians skewed older as I closed in on the new century—sorry, but it couldn't be otherwise. Choosing the best of anything, let alone the most important, is rarely possible. In the end, I simply settled on 57 tracks I cherish. That they also suggest how we got from there to here is of less interest to me than their consistent excellence, exuberance, and diversity. Of course, since I initially *believed* that I would be covering the century, I omitted those artists—Armstrong, Ellington, Hawkins, Basie, Young, Goodman, Tatum, Eldridge, and so forth—that I knew would fall into the earlier period; in many instances, I admire their later work no less than that which made them famous, so I was profoundly relieved not to have to take them into account.

If you want to play, you have to abide by the rules, mainly one big rule: A musician may be listed only once as a leader. The alternative is to allow a musician—an Armstrong or an Ellington or a Davis or a Coleman, etc.—to reappear over and over; that approach might be more suitable if the goal is to identify favorite or historically crucial performances, but I sought variety as well, which demanded frantic juggling and endless compromises. When I began, I dashed off paragraphs on random faves: Duke Ellington's "Harlem," Stan Getz's "Diaper Pin," James Moody's "Moody's Mood for Love," Ornette Coleman's "RPDD," George Russell's "All About Rosie," Sonny Rollins's "Three Little Words," Pee Wee Russell's "I'd Climb the Highest Mountain," Al Cohn and Jimmy Rowles's "Them There Eyes," Count Basie's "Little Pony," Dizzy Gillespie's "Emanon," David Murray's "Blues for My Sister," Thelonious Monk's "I Should Care," Lennie Tristano's "Becoming," John Lewis's "For Ellington," Cecil Taylor's "3 Phasis," Henry Threadgill's

"100 Year Old Game," and Arthur Blythe's "Sister Daisy," to mention just a few that survived the delete key; they were ultimately discarded because of conflicting dates when another record (not necessarily a better one) simply had to go into a particular slot. The only way to proceed was to organize an overall grid, plug in possibilities for each year, mix and match, and pray for the best.

Supplementary rules: Each work had to be tied to the year it was recorded, not released, which might create a disparity of a few years. Tracks that were not released for decades, however, were not eligible. I knew that I would cross generations, acknowledging masterly performances by older players amid new wrinkles by younger ones, but didn't make that a rule. Anyone who thinks that the following comprehensively depicts the postwar jazz era isn't paying attention. But are they worthy records? Every last one.

1945: Charlie Parker, "Koko." By no means the first bebop or modern jazz record, this is the one that cracked the firmament. Parker showed how to make music with advanced harmonies and tumultuous rhythms, creating a tuneful new lexicon in the process. He unleashed a virtuoso universe in which postwar musicians could reinvent themselves and their place in society. They could and often did play for dancing, laughs, and entertainment, but they no longer had to. For jazz, the noir years were golden. Not the least amazing thing about "Koko" is that it continues to overwhelm. Only after one has lived with it awhile, does Parker's blade-like articulation and incredible velocity give up its melodic secrets; his alto is nothing if not a melody maker. Built on the chords of "Cherokee," it opens with a jolting eight-bar unison theme, coupled with exchanges between Parker and Dizzy Gillespie. Then Bird flies: two choruses of staggering invention, his tone fat and sensuous, jagged and hard. Drummer Max Roach holds the fort for a chorus, before the head is reprised. In 2:50, the world is remade. *The Charlie Parker Story* (Savoy)

1946: Woody Herman, "Sidewalks of Cuba." After leading a band associated with blues for 10 years, Herman suddenly leaped to the forefront of swing's twilight years; like Gillespie, who had written for him in 1942, Herman's big band embraced the modernistic spirit with wit and daring. But where Gillespie turned to modes and Afro-Cuban rhythms, Herman looked to Stravinsky and r&b—and to Parker and Gillespie. Handed a prosaic '30s song, arranger Ralph Burns imbued it with the Herd's trademark fervor, reeds strutting as boldly as brasses and drummer Don Lamond on red alert. Herman plays clarinet and guitarist Chuck Wayne reveals the influence of Charlie Christian and bop. But the heart of the performance is a crazed "Bumble Bee"–break and half-chorus trumpet solo by Sonny Berman, whose drug-related death a few months later, at 21, was the wake-up call nobody heeded. Berman had absorbed Roy Eldridge and Gillespie while still in his teens and his phrasing is emphatic, personal, and wry. *Blowin' Up a Storm* (Columbia/Legacy)

1947: Dizzy Gillespie, "Manteca." No one accomplished more in the post-war era than its clown prince. Of the founding fathers, only Dizzy could have launched a hot-blooded big band—one that introduced saxophonist James Moody and a foursome later known as the Modern Jazz Quartet. And only he persistently sought ideas beyond U.S. borders. "A Night in Tunisia" established him as the most gorgeously spellbinding trumpet player in a generation and a composer of promise. With George Russell's "Cubana Be"/"Cubana Bop," he fused jazz, modalism, and Caribbean rhythms. The more accessible "Manteca," however, grounded an endur-ing Cuban-American merger. Percussionist Chano Pozo brought him the idea for a piece that employs three interdependent vamps, to which Dizzy added a contrastingly melodic 16-bar bridge and two short, break-neck solos. "Manteca" doesn't disguise its dual patrimony—the two cul-tures exist side by side with equal integrity. Gillespie continued to play it for another 45 years. *The Complete RCA Victor Recordings* (Bluebird)

1948: Tadd Dameron, "Lady Bird." When the Royal Roost, a Broadway chicken joint with music, switched from swing to bop, Dameron was installed as leader. The gig ran nearly 10 months, confirming the com-poser, arranger, and reluctant pianist as an original who knew how to spur musicians. "Lady Bird" is only 16 bars, but suggests—with its AABC form—a full-blown song. Unlike his unmistakable bop pieces ("Symphonette," "Hot House"), it has a suave, mellow theme that re-flects his apprenticeship with swing bands, yet sounds no less modern. After a tricky intro, the dapper drumming of Kenny Clarke guides the ensemble, which boasts two Lestorian tenors—celestial Allen Eager and earthly Wardell Gray. Dameron's greatest interpreter, though, was Fats Navarro, whose trumpet solo opens with a nine-bar phrase, soaring over turnbacks with matchless ease and grace and a tone of transporting beauty. The careers of Dameron, Eager, Gray, and Navarro were dev-astated by drugs; jazz was devastated by Navarro's absurd loss, at 26. *The Fabulous Fats Navarro, Volume 2* (Blue Note)

1949: Bud Powell, "Tempus Fugue-It." As much as if not more than Parker and Gillespie, Powell represents a line of demarcation for his instrument. The difference between pre-Bud piano and post-Bud piano is categorical.

He played impossibly fast or slow, with obsessive fury or meditative detachment; he used the left hand for bracing, kindling chords that fed the right, which expressed a percussive rage equaled only by his gentle raptures. In its economy, hurtling power, and infallible articulation, the minor-key "Tempus Fugue-It" (originally released as "Tempus Fugit") is a head-banging wonder: the crashing Lisztian chords in which the relatively conventional melody is swaddled, the close harmonies of the release, the thrilling riff configurations of the solo, the smashed arpeggio just before the out-chorus. Yet every detail rings clear as a bell, with sensational logic. It's not that he plays so fast, but that he thinks so coherently, balanced on a moonbeam. *Jazz Giant* (Verve)

1950: Sarah Vaughan, "Mean to Me." The voice that dropped a thousand jaws helped pave the way for bop in 1944–45 with her recordings of "East of the Sun," "Lover Man," and this song, backed by Parker and Gillespie; but they were just a whisper of where she was headed. At a 1949 Carnegie Hall concert, she introduced a second-chorus variation on "Mean to Me," a fantastic vocal swan dive that completely revamped the melody without retouching the lyric—without resorting to scat. A year later, she recorded it with a Jimmy Jones band, allowing Budd Johnson a noble half-chorus before embarking on her embellishments, egged on by Miles Davis's obbligato. Her voluptuous, resolute, winged phrasing adjourns high in the sky. By now management was grooming this formerly gawky, church-trained phenomenon for stardom; but they couldn't temper her musicality, much as they tried. *Sarah Vaughan in Hi-Fi* (Columbia/Legacy)

1951: Stan Getz, "Mosquito Knees." Having achieved glory with an eight-bar solo on Herman's "Early Autumn," Getz became an overnight star—one of many tenor saxophonists who brought the Lester Young template into modern jazz. He eschewed the heavier attack of, say, Wardell Gray (whose solo this year on Basie's "Little Pony" is itself monumental), in favor of a sighing dry-ice lyricism that was occasionally derided as a "white tenor" sound. Yet no one who heard his live 1951 sides could have failed to recognize that his breezy timbre was backed by heroic force. He was in peak form at Storyville, colluding with a dream team: guitarist Jimmy Raney, pianist Al Haig, bassist Teddy Kotick, and drummer Tiny Kahn. He was also armed with an impressive book, including six pieces by Gigi Gryce; a "Honeysuckle Rose" derivation, "Mosquito Knees," propels him into a blistering rampage, revealing a trove of melodic riffs, capped by exchanges with the rousing Kahn. *The Complete Roost Recordings* (Blue Note)

1952: Thelonious Monk, "Little Rootie Tootie." Lost between the Blue Notes that established him as a cult figure and the Riversides that would soon win him a popular following were the trio sessions that ought to have closed the case on him as a pianist of nerve and genius. Other pianists are obliged to make bad instruments sound good; Monk, with his clattering dissonances (consider the opening of the incredibly swinging "These Foolish Things") made good instruments sound unstrung. His train song is typical: funny, rambunctious, and starkly rhythmic, with three dissonant chords clanging at the end of alternate bars. He begins the last chorus with a bearded cliché—deedledee-deedledee up, deedledee-deedledee down—and brings it home with hilarious ingenuity. Art Blakey (dig him on the second bridge) was Monk's perfect drummer. *The Complete Prestige Recordings* (Prestige)

1953: Gerry Mulligan, "My Funny Valentine." Meanwhile, a new school was born on the left coast, and though much of the attention went to George Shearing's bop-lite and Stan Kenton's bop-ballistics, the prince of the realm was an exiled New Yorker who had taken a job at an LA club with a bandstand too small to fit a piano. Mulligan's love for big bands was apparent in his charts for Kenton and his own Tentette, but he became famous due to the pianoless quartet with Chet Baker, who never sounded more individual than in those early years, before he became enamored of Miles. The live, extended version of "My Funny Valentine," recorded at the cozy Haig, is more evocative than the studio hit of the year before. After a drum roll and an ominous two-note bass vamp, Baker wanders into the chords and by bar three (no baritone support either) is on the green; Mulligan follows suit, gingerly stepping through the clover. *The Complete Pacific Jazz Recordings of The Gerry Mulligan Quartet* (Pacific Jazz)

1954: Brown & Roach, Inc., "Delilah." The quintet founded by Max Roach and Clifford Brown in the spring of 1954 ended on June 26, 1956, when Brown, pianist Ritchie Powell, and Powell's wife were killed in a highway accident. Brown was 25, and he is still mourned. "Delilah," the most unlikely of vehicles (an undulating Hedy Lamarr prop), begins single-file—bass vamp, cymbals, piano vamp, tenor vamp—before Brown states the theme as though staring down the throat of the cobra he's charming. Harold Land, who had much of Wardell Gray's sandy sound and finesse, offers a bouquet of melodies; then Brown enters with a three-note figure that he develops through the bridge. He ends the chorus blazing and detonates the next one with a heart-stopping rip. Powell, who wrote the inventive chart, plays trebly chords, neat modulations, and a Grieg finish, followed by fours with Roach, who adds a melodic chorus of his own. *Clifford Brown and Max Roach* (Emarcy)

1955: The Jazz Messengers, "Prince Albert." For one year and one live recording, Art Blakey pretended non-leadership in the hope of creating a genuine cooperative, like the Modern Jazz Quartet, which had been picking up speed since 1954. With an ideal lineup—pianist-composer Horace Silver, trumpeter Kenny Dorham, saxophonist Hank Mobley, bassist Doug Watkins—the drummer press-rolled the Messengers into a new idiom that established itself as a permanent alternative to cool, modal, and avant-garde, and as a predecessor of soul jazz and funk. Dorham's much-played theme is a variation on "All the Things You Are," and Silver playfully introduces it with the requisite Charlie Parker vamp. Dorham's distinctly smoky tone and sleek phrasing are flexible enough to permit a "Camptown Races" joke, and Mobley's reedy authority steps evenly with the time, then doubles it. *At the Cafe Bohemia, Volume 1* (Blue Note)

1956: George Russell, "Concerto for Billy the Kid." A major theorist, instigator, and gadfly as well as one of the most original of jazz composers, Russell had been making his mark behind the scenes for a decade when he finally got the chance to record his own album. It was a turning point for him and the pianist for whom he conceived his dazzling mini-concerto. Bill Evans had appeared on a few sessions but was virtually unknown until he embarked on the avid, single-handed, stop-time whirlwind cadenza at this work's center. Russell, who preferred modes to chords and published several editions of his explanatory Zen-like treatise, *Lydian Chromatic Concept of Tonal Organization*, aligned each musician like a layer in a cake, making the sextet resound with startling freshness. He and Evans continued to collaborate ("All About Rosie," *Living Time*), and their first meeting—in the same year that Cecil Taylor debuted and Art Tatum bowed out—affirmed the rise of the new jazz intellectual. *Jazz Workshop* (RCA Bluebird)

1957: Charles Mingus, "Haitian Fight Song." After apprenticing himself in swing, bop, r&b, and pop, Mingus worked his way through a labyrinth of academic compositional techniques, which earned him the accusation of failing to swing. "Haitian Fight Song" was his response. A more thunderous bass intro has not been heard; he sounds like a giant plucking ropes against a tree trunk, albeit with perfect intonation. Leading a solid but hardly all-star quintet with written material that amounts to no more than eight bars (two canonical riffs), plus an orthodox blues for the improvisational grid, he herds (le mot juste) his men through double-time and stop-time rhythms for a riveting 12 minutes that feel more like three. Trombonist Jimmy Knepper makes his bones here; the others—altoist Shafi Hadi, pianist Wade Legge, and, in a fabled debut, drummer Dannie Richmond—play over their heads. Mingus's astounding solo obviated further criticism. *The Clown* (Atlantic)

1958: Sun Ra, "Saturn." In the year of Ornette Coleman's debut, no one paid much mind to the former Sonny Blount; critics sniffed at the eclecticism, the cultism, the garage sonics. Who can blame them? Compared to Coleman, Taylor, Russell, and Mingus, his bop was distilled with a touch of corn and more than a touch of doo-wop. He looked forward, back, and across the way to the r&b bars. He wrote painstaking charts and involved good musicians, but was a do-it-yourself type who bided his time until the mountain came to him. His theme song, recorded in different versions, combines a six-beat piano intro; a 14-bar contrapuntal 7/4 set-up melody; and the hooky main theme (in four and based on conventional changes). The latter may sound a bit too enchanted, but it generates energetic solos from tenor John Gilmore and baritone Pat Patrick, who along with the ensemble sway merrily. *Jazz in Silhouette* (Evidence)

1959: Miles Davis, "So What." The track (and album) opens with a hushed prelude, reportedly contributed by Gil Evans; Paul Chambers's bass prompts a three-note Bill Evans phrase, leading to a unison bass-like figure played by those two, followed by Evans's enigmatic Spanish-style chords and, finally, Chambers's introduction of a beat and a theme, which is punctuated by unison chords from the three winds. The head couldn't be more basic: a 32-bar AABA song. But instead of chord changes, it offers two scales for the improvisers—D minor with an E-flat bridge. Modalism has now found an accessible context and will soon be everywhere. Davis's solo sticks to the scales and is a lyrical marvel, immaculate in form and execution. Cannonball Adderley and John Coltrane are far more prolix, but they too are focused by the harmonic austerity, and Evans finishes with tightly ground chords, showing that Monk didn't have a patent on minor seconds. It's from the most enduringly popular jazz album of the LP era. *Kind of Blue* (Columbia)

1960: Gil Evans, "Le Nevada." Speaking of minimalism, Evans, nearing 50 and having gained some marquee value for his work with Miles, initiated a big band "head" arrangement, something that had rarely been heard since Basie's days in Kansas City. All he had for "Le Nevada" was a hooky four-bar riff and a tempo, yet after several unsuccessful tries, he eked out a 15-minute bobbing fantasia with exuberant improvs by Johnny Coles, Jimmy Knepper, and, chiefly, ageless tenor saxophonist Budd Johnson. Typically, Evans had strolled over to the trombone section while the recording was in progress and wrote on a matchbook a riff that sent the performance into high gear. Elvin Jones contributed, too, by shaking shakers throughout. In the year of Ornette's *Free Jazz* and Eric Dolphy's *Out There*, this performance walked a tightrope between old (which bop had become) and new, adumbrating the spontaneous big bands Evans perfected a decade later. *Out of the Cool* (Impulse!)

1961: John Coltrane, "Chasin' the Trane." Coltrane enjoyed an authentic hit with "My Favorite Things," and would soon foster the apex of boudoir crooning with Johnny Hartman, before achieving mythic standing with *A Love Supreme*. This 16-minute blues in F, though, was the Rubicon many of his old admirers could not cross. Coltrane's break with tradition didn't encourage dissertations on modes or free time; it elicited ecstasy or wrath. His battle, during 80 or so choruses, against the 12-bar structure that Elvin Jones and Jimmy Garrison maintain with yeoman determination, is a prodigal display of unbridled emotion: a howl, a mutiny, an invocation in the higher frequencies—the informal beginning of expressionism in jazz, and an unforgettable performance in a year brimming with them. Armstrong and Ellington, Bill Evans, Davis, Gillespie, Lee Konitz, Mulligan, Blakey, Getz and Eddie Sauter, and others all released classics. *Live at the Village Vanguard* (Impulse!)

1962: Dexter Gordon, "Love for Sale." In a prominent year for tenors— Sonny Rollins home from the bridge, Stan Getz at home with Brazil— Gordon, relishing one of his many comebacks, helped put the melodic, harmonic, rhythmic, and temporal restraints of bop back on the map, though he, too, was playing long and would soon find himself edging toward modes. He was at a personal peak for two sessions backed by a model trio (pianist Sonny Clark, bassist Butch Warren, drummer Billy Higgins), and though their music lacked the novel lilt of bossa nova, it had the catalytic power and rousing ingenuity of musicians brimming with ideas and having tremendous fun expressing them. Dexter had Coltrane's authority without the panic. "Love for Sale" is a fast hardball hit way out of the park, yet ringing with bemused and melodic details; Gordon's broadsword sound exudes dignity, and not one measure of his long solo is superfluous. *Go!* (Blue Note)

1963: Jackie McLean, "Love and Hate." McLean, a Parker acolyte who had proven his bop precocity in the '50s with pungent timbre and razor-sharp acumen, got caught up in and animated by the turbulence of the '60s. On one of his most dramatic albums, he recorded three works by trombonist Grachan Moncur III (whose *Evolution* is something of a companion disc). "Love and Hate" is the most ardent and compelling. It opens with a mourning gait, accented by Bobby Hutcherson's tamped vibraphone chords. After the memorable theme, McLean's caustic alto saxophone commences with a provocative phrase and then explores the harmonically spare terrain with wounded resolve. He sustains absolute emotional pitch, which is extended by Moncur and Hutcherson, while bassist Larry Ridley and drummer Roy Haynes steer a steady course. One way or another, almost everyone was responding to the new avant-garde. *Destination Out!* (Blue Note)

1964: Wayne Shorter, "Infant Eyes." Working his way through a Coltrane influence, Shorter demonstrated pensive originality as tenor saxophonist and composer with a stellar edition of Blakey's Jazz Messengers. Then he blossomed with Davis's bruising second great quintet, whose members enjoyed a life apart, mostly at Blue Note—a record label that enjoyed an unlikely flurry of hits with Herbie Hancock's "Watermelon Man," Horace Silver's "Song for My Father," and Lee Morgan's "The Sidewinder." "Infant Eyes," a ballad written for his daughter, brings out Shorter's raw, unaffected tenderness. It recycles a quote from Gershwin's "Soon" in a 27-bar ABA structure with one chord per measure. Shorter's improvisation ranges over three octaves, yet it consists of few notes and each one counts for timbre as well as melody. He later developed an equally expressive approach to the soprano sax, conspicuously evading Coltrane's shadow, while writing a body of sly tunes unlike anything anywhere. *Speak No Evil* (Blue Note)

1965: Archie Shepp, "Hambone." Shepp's militancy was too shrewd to be one-dimensional, his music too generous to be exclusively strident. The album that produced "Malcolm, Malcolm—Semper Malcolm," almost certainly the best poetry-and-jazz side ever made (some voice, some reading), also offered sextet arrangements of Ellington and bossa nova, a poised response to Buñuel's *Los Olvidados*, and the multi-themed "Hambone," based on a character in a kiddies show. It begins with a familiar Mariachi theme and proceeds to a passage that alternates measures in seven and five. The fine solos by trumpeter Ted Curson, altoist Marion Brown, and Shepp—with his raspy, skittery, anxious tenor sax sound—are subordinate to the ensemble, which comes on like a crazed marching band. Yet the new thing, new wave, new music, or new jazz, as it was variously called, was as much derided as Monk had been a decade earlier. *Fire Music* (Impulse!)

1966: Albert Ayler, "Our Prayer/Spirits Rejoice." He replaced notes with glossolalia and made a band music out of raucous disharmonies, folk melodies, marches, hymns, and bugle calls; his trumpet-playing brother, Donald, had an appropriately tinny sound for the latter. Ayler's grinding tenor saxophone threatened to burst asunder from the effusiveness of his playing. He scared the hell out of people, yet radiated a wildly optimistic passion. The optimism was manic. Dead at 34, in 1970, he never found the acceptance here that he won in Europe—some folks figured he was putting everyone on, among them true believers who were mortified by his later au courant compromises. Yet even in flower-child mode, he carried a cello and howled at the moon; he was never cut out for the Fillmore. Still, his mid-'60s bands electrify, and his medley of two original themes, complete with an interpolation of the "Marseillaise," suggests an old New Orleans parade band brought to a peak of revivalist hysteria. *Lorrach, Paris 1966* (hatOLOGY)

1967: Sonny Criss, "Willow Weep for Me." Few people noticed Lester Bowie's *Numbers 1 & 2* or acknowledged *Far East Suite* as one of Ellington's masterworks, both recorded this year. But for a brief span, modest attention was paid a blues-driven altoist who had created his own lapidary version of Charlie Parker, yet had not recorded at home in seven years. The third album of his comeback reflected a siege mentality by covering two hits (jazz musicians and producers always went for the most banal chart-toppers). Criss's creamy proficiency had no trouble riding roughshod over the Fifth Dimension, but he was in his glory with great tunes. The pitfall of drenching a ballad in minor thirds and other blues devices is the potential for cliché. Criss—alertly supported by guitarist Tal Farlow and pianist Cedar Walton—averts the danger with unerring taste and gleaming technique, producing a flawless gem, right down to the lustrous cadenza. *Up, Up and Away!* (Prestige)

1968: Jaki Byard, "Memories of You." Byard and Roland Kirk were made for each other—savoring the past as a cocktail of irreverence and sentiment. Byard contributed to Kirk's *Rip, Rig and Panic,* and now Kirk repaid the favor. The rhythm section brought together for Booker Ervin's *Book* series—Byard, bassist Richard Davis, drummer Alan Dawson—was present on all but one old tune by Eubie Blake, who, at 85, was a year away from his famous comeback. Kirk sticks to tenor and, whether soloing or backing Jaki, rarely pauses to breathe. Byard's ebullient take on stride piano is emboldened by his peerless, tumbling arpeggios: Tatumesque in concept, Tayloresque in touch. If the most ambitious release of the year was *The Jazz Composer's Orchestra*, this duet was perhaps the most serendipitous. Not much noted at the time, it exercised an influence that would be evident 30 years later. *The Jaki Byard Experience* (Prestige)

1969: Tony Williams, "Spectrum." As rock pushed jazz aside, a few musicians sought common ground not in dinky tunes or soul-brother affectations, but in energy, electricity, and coloration. Miles's *Bitches Brew* and Williams's *Emergency!* were as shocking to some as Ayler had been, yet for the drummer, born in 1945, fusion held the promise of destiny, if not of commercial salvation. He had joined McLean and Miles at 17, had recorded with cutting-edge players like Sam Rivers; to him, rock was a natural challenge and an opportunity. So he took the standard organ trio instrumentation and maxed it out, fusing free improvisation to blistering rhythms. It pleased hardly anyone—his Hendrixian singing was ill-advised—yet a track like "Spectrum," admittedly more jazz than rock, suggests exciting possibilities. The cymbals' lightning response to the first figure of John McLaughlin's guitar improv prepares you for the alert vitality that abides during Larry Young's organ spot as well as in their signature wrap-up crescendo. *Spectrum: The Anthology* (Verve)

1970: Art Ensemble of Chicago, "Theme De Yoyo." In perhaps the worst year ever for jazz records, two of the slyest of veteran swingers, Bobby Hackett and Vic Dickenson, played the hotel gig that eventually produced the album that launched Chiaroscuro; and the 15 or so sessions recorded by the little-known AEC in Europe began showing up stateside. The AEC's antic score for an obscure French film (shown here for a nanosecond as *Sophie's Ways*) treats Monteverdi to a second-line beat and, more predictively, ferments free and funk on "Theme De Yoyo." Lester Bowie pushes trumpet tonality beyond Miles's jurisdiction, proving along with reedmen Roscoe Mitchell and Joseph Jarman that this strangely theatrical troupe could be plenty pithy, while whitefaced bassist Malachi Favors and drummer Don Moye anticipate *Shaft*. For added measure, Fontella Bass croons, "Your fanny's like two sperm whales floating down the Seine." *Les Stances à Sophie* (Universal Sound)

1971: Mary Lou Williams, "What's Your Story, Morning Glory?" In another dour year for jazz records, Circle united Chick Corea and Dave Holland (they said they hoped to escape fusion) with Anthony Braxton;

Jimmy Rushing made his last stand, mobilizing a return of mainstream heroes; and Carla Bley waxed the "Overture" to *Escalator over the Hill*. No less striking was the latest comeback by Williams, who, like Earl Hines, had been playing since the 1920s and still sounded unequivocally modern. After building a following at the Cookery, she romped deliriously through the *Giants* concert with Dizzy Gillespie and Bobby Hackett and four months later started work on a more meditative solo LP. She begins her best-known blues (even better known as the plagiarized pop hit "Black Coffee") with a rhythmic vamp, and then plays seven comely choruses that combine slow-blues panache with fresh chords and a subtly metronomic beat—her penultimate chorus is a knockout. *Nite Life* (Chiaroscuro)

1972: Ornette Coleman, "The Men Who Live in the White House." Things looked up with Dave Holland's *Conference of the Birds*, Sonny Stitt's *Constellation*, and, in St. Louis, Julius Hemphill's self-produced *Dogon A.D.* But nothing could compare with Coleman's first and—to date—only recorded symphony. The somewhat compromised album was completed in nine hours under constraints that forbade him from using his band along with the London Symphony, which was the initial idea; it was ultimately edited for time and divided into 21 episodes. Yet its power ferments. Nearing the last leg, the orchestra introduces a six-note variation on "The Good Life," the gloriously ribald theme formerly called "School Work" and later adapted as "Theme from a Symphony" on the electrifying *Dancing in Your Head* (1975). Coleman's alto is round and warm as he lifts off for a cadenza that mines that same motif with his shamanistic cry, fading with fragile vibrato, until the spacious harmonies of "Love Life" lead him to the final, rustic urgency of "Sunday in America." *Skies of America* (Columbia/Legacy)

1973: Cecil Taylor, "Spring of Two Blue J's." Taylor's two magnificent Blue Note albums of 1966 were followed by a silence of nearly seven years, except for his collaboration with the Jazz Composers Association (and European concerts that weren't issued here until much later). Then, within a year, he released *Indent*, a solo recital from Antioch, where he had been teaching, and the second set of a Town Hall concert dedicated to Ben Webster. The latter has two sections: an epic if largely romantic piano solo, which offers an improvisational coherence his earlier work only hints at, and a meditative quartet variation that captures him in transition before the darker, deeper textures that followed when he launched his sextet. This was bassist Sirone's first recording with him and drummer Andrew Cyrille's last; both are fully committed, as is Taylor's most frequent collaborator, Jimmy Lyons, whose alto mirrors every pianistic conceit. *Spring of Two Blue J's* (Unit Core/OP)

1974: Modern Jazz Quartet, "Django." This was the piece that solidified international interest in its composer, John Lewis, and the MJQ in 1954, when Lewis, Milt Jackson, Percy Heath, and Kenny Clarke had been working together for nearly three years. It had been introduced at Clarke's last session; he would soon leave and be replaced by Connie Kay. Two decades later, all four called it quits (until 1981, when they reunited as if they had been enjoying a long vacation). But first they gave a series of farewell concerts. Despite its cool formalism, the MJQ was at its best in the freefall of live recording, and their triumphant evening in New York provided a definitive version of the cortege written in memory of Django Reinhardt—as definitive as possible for a piece Lewis never stopped revising. Here all the elements of his skill and the MJQ's interpretive power are as one: the evocative Gypsy feeling in the main theme, recalling the Adagio of Mendelssohn's Octet; the stout bass motif; the mixture of delicacy and force, discipline and spontaneity, tragedy and joy. *The Complete Last Concert* (Atlantic)

1975: The Revolutionary Ensemble, "Ponderous Planets." Their first studio album was their last; the group disbanded in 1977, ending a six-year run—impressive considering its inability to crack the cult ceiling. TRE often replaced a staunch beat with a mere pulse, suggesting a fusion between classical and jazz practices. But the reflexive interplay between Leroy Jenkins's spry violin, Sirone's redwood-heavy bass (and expert arco technique), and Jerome Cooper's fastidious, if often whimsical percussion was largely consonant and accessible, never more so than on Cooper's by-no-means ponderous opus. It begins with bowed strings and saw, achieves an unmistakably jazzy frisson with the entrance of plucked bass and cymbals, and finally, having made the case that impassioned improvisation can flourish without swing, swings like a thresher—in waltz time. A good year for Jenkins, who also introduced *For Players Only*, his daring Jazz Composers Orchestra spectacle. *The People's Republic* (Horizon/OP)

1976: Anthony Braxton, "Piece Three." Not exactly typical Braxton, but then, what is? And who else would have tried something as ironic and unexpected as this brazen send-up of a march—a piece, incidentally, that actually had everyone taking a position. The jubilant theme, which owes as much to the beer garden (dig that counter-theme by the reeds) as to military needs, modulates to a repeated oompah figure, as though stuck in a rut. Into this berserk stasis Leo Smith comes a-burning, playing only those trumpet tones of no use in a march. A surprising interlude introduces the aggressive trombone of George Lewis, who enters with a droll tailgate slide and is soon ripping and snorting, followed by the waspish, perhaps quizzical clarinet of Braxton, who fights against another static riff. Suddenly, the march is restored like a beam of sunshine, as the ensemble waddles cheekily down the pike. *Creative Orchestra Music 1976* (Bluebird)

1977: Hank Jones, "Oh, What a Beautiful Morning." Jazz records were bullish again, triggered by small labels that suited a horde of unknown talents from the West and Midwest, who also helped establish a loft alternative to nightclub venues. At the same time, there was an invasion of re-energized mainstreamers who required labels, too. Duets and trios were big: Jimmy Rowles serially encountered Al, Zoot, and Stan; McCoy Tyner and Tommy Flanagan tested diverse rhythmmakers; Konitz parleyed with Solal, Venuti with McKenna, and Hemphill with alter ego Roi Boye. Jones's best albums were with Tony Williams and Ron Carter, but it was at a session with Milt Hinton and Bobby Rosengarden that he was talked into going one alone and produced this neglected masterpiece—his quintessential performance. After a laconic vamp, the unlikely melody suddenly spills down in broken chords and is just as quickly dispensed with as Jones dives deep into its harmonies for a series of blues-driven variations that are infernally clever and utterly lovely. *The Trio* (Chiaroscuro)

1978: Sonny Rollins, "Autumn Nocturne." Jazz's preeminent concertizer disdains recording, where he usually keeps the lid on his id. So why not record all his concerts and cherry-pick them for albums? Maybe because the ferocity would alienate the faint of heart and leave no possibility at all for radio play. Happily, he does issue some live performances (meanwhile, his fans surreptitiously filch every note), preserving the most charismatic attack in the history of the tenor saxophone—a sound that, having already influenced the playing habits of two generations, reached extrovert heights in the mid-'70s. Indeed, not since "West End Blues" had there been a cadenza quite like this, which similarly begins on an odd note before plunging into a grove of euphoric convolutions. When Rollins finally attains the theme, after citations from "To a Wild Rose" and "Home Sweet Home," plus two vocal yawps, the sensation of release is overwhelming. From that point, he exhales a whoosh of melody, radiant and raunchy all at once. *Silver City* (Milestone)

1979: Bill Evans, "I Loves You Porgy." A musical dybbuk took possession of him in the last two years of his life, unleashing fresh, unexpected powers. The superb new trio with bassist Marc Johnson and drummer Joe LaBarbara revitalized him, too, and he played with the visionary conviction of a 19th-century romantic. Yet few knew about it until after his death, when a stream of concert recordings revealed that the impetuous "My Romance" or the extended "Nardis" you may once have heard were, in fact, chronic parts of his repertoire. These rhapsodies didn't quite dim the reverence for the old days, but did put them in perspective: Paris '79 was every bit as imposing as Vanguard '61. His unaccompanied "I Loves You Porgy" trumps the celebrated 1968 Montreux version, from the wary opening tones and patented Evans harmonies and touch to the downright zealous digressions that follow. He's captive to his own command. *The Paris Concert, Edition One* (Blue Note)

1980: World Saxophone Quartet, "I Heard That." Sometimes simple does the trick. At 3:23, Hamiet Bluiett's elementary blues could have fit on a 78, and it doesn't waste a moment. Most of the WSQ specialties were polyphonic or contrapuntal and encouraged collective improvisation; the most intricate were by Julius Hemphill and usually featured the quartet—himself, Bluiett, Oliver Lake, and the uncontainable David Murray, who also adapted some of his own best melodies. Here, Bluiett offers a showcase for Hemphill's roiling alto, his huge blistering sound buoyed by precision stop-time chords, as he renovates old licks and bonds them with biting asides and turnbacks. Hemphill sustains the churchy signifying and technical élan that too often took a back seat to his composing, posing, japing. This LP was in the can for two years and yet it still seemed a breakthrough when released in late 1982. *Revue* (Black Saint)

1981: Art Pepper, "Arthur's Blues." After 16 years of silence due to incarceration and drug addiction, one of the golden boys of 1950s L.A. came back in 1976, with a pressing need to be heard not only as a madly competitive altoist making up for lost years, but as a memoirist and nightclub seer. At first he battled his way through a Coltrane influence, but a year later the old facility returned, sharpened by a new urgency: Every solo was a bloodletting, whether backed with strings beautifully arranged by Bill Holman or loving piano by George Cables. The painstakingly slow but energetic quartet blues recorded a year before his death is typical: Throughout four choruses that Pepper plays before the piano and bass solos and three that he plays after, he constructs a narrative with barks, squeals, and 32nd-note asides, combining bravura technique, sheer guts, and a concentrated purpose. *The Complete Galaxy Recordings* (Galaxy)

1982: Air, "Do Tell." The most durable cooperative after the Art Ensemble, Air achieved nonpareil equity among its members, who could—playing Joplin and Morton or originals—undermine the beat without forfeiting it. Each member possessed grit and wit. Steve McCall's drums were plush and decisive, yet spare and understated. Fred Hopkins's bass fused audacious power with mercuric reflexes. Henry Threadgill wrote most of the material and played reeds, flute, and, briefly, a contraption made of hubcaps. Like Arthur Blythe, whose "Sister Daisy" (same year, *Elaborations*) is another model of loft-era swing, Threadgill's alto is ripe, raw, and focused. They had more in common with the restored Pepper than with the '60s avant-gardists. "Do Tell" has a mellow A-theme and double-time B-theme; each man helps to shore up the backbeat pulse until Threadgill launches a lusty climax. Air turned out to be a starter band for him, succeeded by such compound ensembles as Very Very Circus, Make a Move, and Zooid. *80 Degrees Below '82* (Antilles)

1983: Craig Harris, "Blackwell." In the year of James Blood Ulmer's *Odyssey*, when harmolodics ran the gamut from Shannon Jackson's Decoding Society to the acoustical Old and New Dreams, Harris's overlooked tribute to pioneering drummer Ed Blackwell offered a more obscure link to Ornette. More pointedly, it serves as a reminder that this trombonist and composer, who made a splash a year earlier with his "Nigerian Sunset," could conjure up striking, insightful themes in a neoclassical mode. This one alternates tricky syncopations in eight and six, which support a growly, ripping, timbre-changing trombone solo by Harris; a taut and pointed one by tenor saxophonist George Adams; and—connecting them—an upbeat Cecil-like offering by pianist Donald Smith, all of them kept on track by Fred Hopkins and Charlie Persip, who italicize every beat. Harris is probably the only trombonist ever to double on didgeridoo. *Black Bone* (Soul Note)

1984: Jack DeJohnette, "Third World Anthem." The drummer's Special Edition was big on saxophonists, and the tidy alliance of a reed trio (suggesting the influence of World Saxophone Quartet), machine-gun stickwork, and Rufus Reid's limber bass has a sharp state-of-the-art clarity. DeJohnette's music usually employs multiple themes and time signatures. This one begins with a staccato rhythm and moves through a sequence of tantalizing melodies and backup figures, welling and waning like a train now approaching, now receding. The alto, tenor, and tuba solos are vividly self-assured. John Purcell, whose alto captures some of the radius of Arthur Blythe's sound, welds short, acerbic phrases into a bold design; Howard Johnson, who doubles on baritone sax, lets loose a welter of double-time passages; and David Murray, whose woolly coilings on tenor personified the era, is enthused, funny, and succinct. *Album Album* (ECM)

1985: Benny Carter, "Lover Man." The most quietly productive career in jazz began in the '20s, when Carter helped formulate big band music and established a standard—rivaled only by Johnny Hodges—on alto saxophone; he later introduced his own suave orchestra, an introspective trumpet style, and major compositions, peaking in his seventh and eighth decades. His masterly "Lover Man" solo is a single chorus—32 bars; two minutes 20 seconds—that, with glancing phrases and melodious arcs, stands as a defining, sui generis statement. After a poised theme recitation by trumpeter Joe Wilder and guitarist Ed Bickert, Carter enters as the embodiment of lucid invention, doubling-up the slow tempo, pushing the beat, mixing mincing steps and flowing strides, disguising the melody with blues innuendoes, taut riffs, and half-moon melodies. Too bad a subtler pianist than Gene Harris wasn't on hand, but his glib soul-notes underscore Carter's ingenuity. *A Gentleman and His Music* (Concord Jazz)

1986: Wynton Marsalis, "Autumn Leaves." Looking to Marsalis for deep feelings is as pointless as looking to Miles Davis for easy laughs. The nature of his virtuosity is to stand slightly above the chords and rhythmic changeups, alighting in an expression of kinetic display. In a transitional juncture between the orthodox quintet that (along with classical side-trips) made his name and the self-conscious septet that fixed his direction, he appeared with just piano, bass, and drums, and revealed a lean, aspirate timbre that recalled Kenny Dorham rather than Miles, with whom he was widely compared. Even with a tune and speedy gait closely associated with Davis, he revealed a resolute inventiveness and stylish approach to time: The rhythm section gives the illusion of retarding the pulse, but Marsalis never flags during his seven hurtling turns, replete with raring turnbacks and rugged riffs, notably a 10-bar incursion in the fourth go-round. *Live at Blues Alley* (Columbia)

1987: John Carter, "On a Country Road." The last movement of the fourth of five suites in *Roots and Folklore: Episodes in the Development of*

American Folk Music shows how much ground Carter—who taught public school for more than 30 years before committing himself to a career in music—could seed with relatively chaste material. At heart it's a deceptively simple clarinet riff that burbles like a swallow yet requires consummate breath control, two-note chords, and register hopping. In a winning take on musique concrete, Carter employs a tape of his Uncle John telling a story. The cadences of John's voice and his nephew's appreciative laughter—not the tale—are what count. Fred Hopkins picks up on the clarinet riff and Andrew Cyrille (outstanding throughout the album) brings the rhythm home as the piece turns into a big city blues, featuring baying choruses by trumpeter Bobby Bradford, who is then superceded by a harmonica solo, which, ipso facto, returns us to the country. *Fields* (Gramavision)

1988: Don Pullen, "At the Cafe Centrale." The year belonged to the 11-volume *Cecil Taylor in Berlin '88*, despite its limited number and distribution—still the most extravagant single-artist achievement of the CD era. But another remarkable pianist associated with the outer fringe suggested a powerful detente with the center, when he teamed with Gary Peacock and Tony Williams. Pullen had journeyed from ESP-Disk to backing pop singers to Charles Mingus to co-leading a successful quintet with George Adams. He innovated a keyboard technique that obliged him to turn his palms up and rake the keys with his knuckles, while hewing to chordal boundaries and uncovering ecstatic melodies. His opening three choruses on "At the Cafe Centrale," a symmetrical 48-bar Flamenco stomp, are parsed in eight-bar segments, shadowed every step by Williams. The harmonic range is narrow, yet Pullen's percussive attack abounds with colors. *New Beginnings* (Blue Note)

1989: Muhal Richard Abrams, "Finditnow." Guru to the Association for the Advancement of Creative Musicians, Abrams relocated to New York in the '70s and sent the pigeonholers racing for cover. With every recording and concert a discrete project, he produced an immensely varied tableau of works that ranged from basic blues (not least his homage to Muddy Waters) to cultured orchestration and New Music fusions, often with humor. Along the way, he emerged as a major force in the preservation of big band jazz—in this instance as played by 18 pieces that trace the instrumental food chain from glockenspiel to synthesizer. Muhal brings out the best in everyone as "Finditnow" blends unadorned swing (the indispensable Fred Hopkins and Andrew Cyrille), four- and eight-bar exchanges (best are Abrams's piano and Warren Smith's vibes), a succinct flute and soprano sax passage, a Bach-inspired cello interlude (Diedre Murray), and rare voicings for xylophone and trombones. *The Hearinga Suite* (Black Saint)

1990: Abbey Lincoln, "The World Is Falling Down." It had been almost three decades since her last major record, when a French-produced album (with perhaps the only unflattering photographs of her ever published) affirmed her return as a matchless singer and songwriter working a terrain bounded by Billie Holiday and Bob Dylan. The title track throbs with backbeat fidelity, a gospelly stoicism that all but disguises the originality of her four-plus-eight-bar verses and a lyric worth hearing. With empathic support from Charlie Haden and Billy Higgins, she articulates every word, jolting the phrase, "We'll follow the breeze." Yet Lincoln accounts for less than half of the Ron Carter–arranged performance. Clark Terry and Jackie McLean abstain from their trademark licks as they exchange 20-bar trumpet and alto solos, plus a chorus of fours and twos (Terry's Schubertian insert is deft and telling) before she returns with the refrain: "The world is falling down, hold my hand." *The World Is Falling Down* (Verve)

1991: Joe Lovano, "Portrait of Jenny." The only bona fide jazz star in years to enjoy a serious big band apprenticeship, Lovano worked with Woody Herman and Mel Lewis, then shared center stage with guitarist Bill Frisell in Paul Motian's alluring combos. His consistency as a saxophonist is matched by an evidently limitless fund of conceptual ideas— every album is something new. An impetuous modernist with a mile-long romantic streak, he's an exceptional ballad player, aged and sagacious. His theme chorus on "Portrait of Jenny" recalls Coltrane, but for a warm, breathy vibrato that brings to mind Joe Henderson—who also had a breakthrough in 1991, playing Billy Strayhorn songs. Backed by pianist Michel Petrucciani, bassist Dave Holland, and drummer Ed Blackwell, Lovano totally stamps the song: the unwavering sustained note in the third bar; the trilling multiphonics as he comes out of his second bridge, propelled by Blackwell's cymbals; the cadenza, gently underscored by Blackwell's mallets. *From the Soul* (Blue Note)

1992: David Murray, "Flowers for Albert." He introduced this homage to Albert Ayler at his first performance in New York, in 1975. The 20-year-old then returned to Oakland long enough to drop out of college and was back in a flash—a poster boy for what became known as the loft era, playing in every context from unaccompanied tenor sax and bass clarinet to the greatly admired octet, followed by the big band, funk, rap, African percussion, etc. Murray may earn an entry in Guinness for the sheer number of albums he's made. A writer of engaging tunes and initiator of challenging projects (like an orchestral transcription of Paul Gonsalves's 27-chorus solo on "Diminuendo and Crescendo in Blue"), he developed an immense network of collaborators. For his fourth big band album, he reconceived his mascot tune as a mirthful dance, conducted by longtime associate Butch Morris, with elatedly cranky solos by Murray, Craig Harris, and (in an especially diverting turn) trumpeter Hugh Ragin. Just when you think it's winding down, Murray reappears for a two-minute cadenza that would've warmed Albert's cockles—Gonsalves's, too. *South of the Border* (DIW)

1993: Lee Konitz, "Exposition." If anyone rivals Murray in output and diversity, it's the venerable Konitz, whose widely noted solos with the Claude Thornhill band in 1947 (when he was 20) established him as the altoist who didn't sound like Bird. He was obviously the cool choice for Miles's nonet, and subsequent projects with his former teacher, Lennie Tristano. A committed improviser who shuns clichés and was playing long and free before long-and-free was a movement, Konitz was inevitably tagged a musician's musician, though his lilting if acidic timbre and casual swing, not to mention proto-repertory liberality, make him quite listener-friendly. Working with routine chord changes and like-minded fellows—clarinetist Jimmy Giuffre, pianist Paul Bley, bassist Gary Peacock—he makes "Exposition" a 19-minute meditation on instantaneous invention, conversational intrigue, and rhythmic equilibrium. *Rhapsody* (Evidence)

1994: James Carter, "Take the A Train." A reeds virtuoso who can play anything except subtle, Carter opened the year with a roar and closed it with a sigh—the former on behalf of eager little DIW (he looks like a jazz musician on the cover) and the latter for corporate stepchild Atlantic (he looks like a movie star). Both discs were mighty impressive, auguring his ability to make thematic albums. His raptor-like chomping of the Ellington band's theme is a splendidly heady prank. Soloing for nearly eight minutes, he uses every avant-garde technique Coltrane, Dolphy, and the other anti-jazz felons had employed to wreak havoc on the shaken '60s, only he swings like a madman and he never misses a chord. When he comes to ground, popping notes and closing with a screech, it's okay to guffaw. Craig Taborn continues in the same riotous vein on piano; perhaps the only prototype for this pair is Byard and Kirk. *Jurassic Classics* (DIW)

1995: Randy Weston, "Tangier Bay." In a solid year for records, connections with the Dark Continent were asserted in Hannibal Lokumbe's *African Portraits*, a stately oratorio that begins before the middle passage and ends after 52nd Street (and Hannibal's trumpet pyrotechnics), and circumnavigated in the animated techno-funk duets of Kenny Barron and Mino Cinelu's *Swamp Sally*. Weston, a pioneer in African American (or Moroccan-Brooklyn) synergy, inducted the best working band of his life, called it African Rhythms, and resuscitated his treasured older pieces, some of which had been around since the '50s. His seductive highflier "Tangier Bay"—A (16) A (16) B (16) C (a kind of eight-bar semicolon with first-beat drone chords)—opens with a suspenseful piano tableau by the composer, until a vamp fires the melody, stated by altoist Talib Kibwe with bebopping insouciance and plumy tone. Weston's two choruses can afford to flaunt his love of Monk, because his reflections soon turn to signature phrases that are pure Weston. *Saga* (Verve)

1996: Uri Caine, "Symphony No. 1, Third Movement." Other places and tribal rites also came into view: John Zorn at Masada, Tiny Bell in the Balkans, Roy Hargrove in Cuba, Don Byron on the Lower East Side, Steve Turre on the beach. Caine labored over the persistently fashionable Gustav Mahler and reinvented him as a suppressed Jewish klezmer. Mahler's soulful minor-key melodies, wrested from aggressive major-key opuses, engender a provoking midrash from the downtown elite, including Byron, clarinet; Dave Douglas, trumpet; Joey Baron, drums; a hand-drumming cantor; and many more. The third-movement themes from the Titan are ideal for Caine, demanding to be played "mit parodie" and offering a wistful canon, a dance tune that might have served *The Godfather*, and crashing cymbals (Baron may be the most strenuous drummer since Shannon Jackson). Caine adds a funeral march, bombshell eruptions, oy vey moaning, shrieking textures, a touch of "Autumn Leaves," and efficient solos by Byron and Douglas. *Primal Light* (Winter & Winter)

1997: David S. Ware, "Logistic." There are two themes. A short, repeated saxophone phrase sets off William Parker's teeming arco bass and Susie Ibarra's precise clickety-clack drumming; then an ascending hiccup figure leads to a galumphing melody, for which Matthew Shipp provides contrary piano chords, reminding us of the irony that strangely underscores the quartet's "godspellized" bliss. Ware's tenor had made an unforgettable impression in the '70s and '80s bands of Cecil Taylor and Andrew Cyrille, with its squalling timbre, its serrated edge—a sound that could rip phone books in half. If he often seems like a product of the Coltrane–Pharoah Sanders nexus, he is a phrasemaker of undeniable individuality, an avant-shocker whose control is never in doubt. Nor is the reach of his impulsively interactive quartet, or the freedom with which his bandmates head out for orbits of their own—alternative jazz of the past 20 years is unimaginable without Parker and Shipp. *Go See the World* (Columbia)

1998: Tommy Flanagan, "Let's." Suddenly, it was about the old Turks. Dewey Redman, Cecil Taylor, and Elvin Jones recorded the mesmerizing *Momentum Space* and John Lewis began preparing a stunning envoi— *Evolution*, two volumes. Flanagan had been one of many gifted Bud Powell-influenced pianists in the '50s. But not until the '70s, after a decade as Ella Fitzgerald's accompanist, did he create the trio that set him apart. He was now forging standards for group dynamics and discerning repertory. Who else would have revived Thad Jones's balmy caper? Based on standard AABA changes in a configuration that may have stimulated Coltrane's "Mr. P. C.," "Let's" veers into an old dark house digression with blunt chords and hesitations. In this definitive version, Flanagan bodes the antic hay with a descending phrase that recalls a song from *The Court Jester*. Then he goes to the races for half a dozen express laps. Bassist Peter Washington and drummer Lewis Nash cover him like white on rice. *Sunset and the Mocking Bird* (Blue Note)

1999: Keith Jarrett, "What Is This Thing Called Love?" Piano trios were bearish: Barry Harris assumed ever greater subtleties, Roy Haynes created a thrilling context for Danilo Perez, Cyrus Chestnut solidified his following, and relative newcomers—Bill Charlap, Jason Moran, Jacky Terrasson, Brad Mehldau—earned their own. After years of somber and extensive keyboard meditations (standing firm against the Fender plague), Jarrett turned to standards and convened a trio of extrasensory instincts. Sometimes he failed to sustain his shiniest conceits and one wished he had ducked out of a piece sooner. Yet in Paris, "What Is This Thing Called Love?" was by far the longest improvisation and he never falters. He begins alone, a firm left hand girding lively embellishments played with an oscillating rhythm between baroque and bop. Gary Peacock's bass knocks twice, followed by a whisper of Jack DeJohnette's cymbal, and very soon the trio levitates. *Whisper Not* (ECM)

2000: Ted Nash, "Premiere Rhapsodie." The achievement of a Flanagan or Jarrett derives in large part from logging numberless miles on the road, inducing among the players a synergy that borders on clairvoyance. Yet some projects may be better off as one-shots, conceived for the studio. Nash, the soul of sideman dependability, presented this memorable quintet in at least one New York concert, but it survives as a recorded feat of genre-defying eclecticism—a bright idea, brightly done. Debussy's clarinet exercise is augmented by Nash's resourceful voicing and an instrumentation that cannot help evoking tangents. Wycliffe Gordon's plunger trombone calls to mind Tyree Glenn's fruitful stay with Ellington and proves that bygone techniques can be revitalized without pomo condescension, while Nash's clarinet implies a rapprochement between France and Weimar and his tenor pushes at the parameters of free jazz—to say nothing of evocations summoned by accordion, violin, and drums. *Sidewalk Meeting* (Arabesque)

2001: Jason Moran, "The Sun at Midnight." A student of Byard and a protégé of altoist Greg Osby, who has mustered several important talents, Moran incarnates the state of a music that often seems weighed down by its own history. He has assimilated piano techniques of eight decades, from stride to free, devising a personal music that refuses to acknowledge stylistic prejudices. The past cannot suffocate him and musicians as varied as Stefon Harris, Mark Turner, Vijay Iyer, or the insatiably productive Matthew Shipp, among many others, because they've been there. Moran brought off a small miracle in specifically making common cause with the unwavering maverick, Sam Rivers. His "The Sun at Midnight," pretty in a stark and unsentimental way, is ideal for Rivers's flute, which amplifies the melody, forging ahead like a scout, spotted every step by drummer Nasheet Waits, bassist Tarus Mateen, and Moran, whose spiky, luminous elaboration continues the mood right through to a pedaled crescendo that brings Rivers home for the reprise. You might think that an individual keyboard attack is no longer possible, but you would be wrong. *Black Stars* (Blue Note)

[*Village Voice*, 11 June 2002]

119 ❖ How Not to Broaden the Jazz Canvas (Carnegie Hall Jazz Band)

The unceremonious booting of the Carnegie Hall Jazz Band from Carnegie Hall is old news, but hasn't been much addressed in or out of the jazz press, perhaps because George Wein, whose baby the CHJB was, capitulated without a fight to the hall's new executive director, Robert J. Harth. The public excuse, and it's a beaut, is that the hall wants to *expand* its presentation of jazz by looking to a wide variety of artists rather than one ensemble. Oh joy!—I so look forward to eating the words I'm about to deploy. Harth, the son of two concert violinists who was previously in charge of the Aspen Music Festival, where presentation of jazz was nonexistent, has told CHJB conductor and music director Jon Faddis that he intends no artistic slight. He just wants to broaden the jazz canvas. Apparently, the CHJB's four evenings a year were getting in the way. So much jazz, so little time.

Actually, not only hasn't Carnegie ever presented much jazz, it's not in the business of producing concerts; it leases its hall to producers and institutions for that purpose. One producer remarked last week that he had been asked to mount jazz concerts several years back precisely because, a Carnegie bigwig told him, the hall had been so inimical for so long to African American music. He suspects that the latest slight is nothing more than good old elitist disdain. I'm uncomfortable with the word *elitist*, which can apply to jazz connoisseurs as well as any other kind, but it would be hard not to conclude that a time-honored prejudice is at work. It is ludicrous to float a parallel: new boss comes to Lincoln Center, fires the New York Philharmonic to widen presentation of 19th-century music. For one thing, no director would ever be powerful enough to execute so draconian a decision—that's what boards of directors are for. It's different for a jazz orchestra that's survived barely a decade. One man controls the respirator. He flicks it off and an orchestra dies.

Ten years is not much time—not enough, in this instance, to become a treasured New York institution. The absence of protests proves that. Well, maybe it isn't a very good orchestra, maybe it contributes nothing to music. Yet no one has asserted that issues of quality were even considered. Perhaps something really obvious needs to be said about the nature of jazz orchestras. Every jazz lover has had to endure hugely ambitious concerts at which the conductor or producer boasts that the marvelous players on stage mastered the exceedingly complex scores in only three rehearsals. "Bravo!" we respond, meaning: "Close enough for jazz." And sometimes the performances are so good we applaud with genuine amazement. But as John Lewis used to say, there is no substitute for the long haul of experience.

After the debut performance by the American Jazz Orchestra, which Lewis introduced in 1986, he confided with unmistakable satisfaction, "In a few years, this will be a band." He liked to point out the discrepancies between classic discs by Duke Ellington or Woody Herman, when their bands recorded scores they'd first encountered in the studio the very day they were preserved for all time, with concert (usually bootleg) performances of the same works that were captured after road trips—for example, Ellington's Fargo concert, where the band sounds like it's breathing the music. The Lincoln Center Jazz Orchestra is light-years now from what it was in its early incarnation. The Vanguard Jazz Orchestra can do things now that would have been unthinkable when it was manned by bona fide jazz stars in its start-up years. The point doesn't need belaboring. You know how you get to Carnegie Hall. Practice, practice, practice. So the problem is not that Harth has greatly diminished the finances of its members, who did not depend on its handful of concerts to pay the rent, or even that he destroyed a band that by jazz standards had a pretty good run. In firing the CHJB he has trashed the 10 years of effort that went into making the CHJB just about the finest traditional jazz orchestra in the world.

If not the finest, then surely a contender with few rivals: Vanguard, Lincoln Center, Danish Radio Jazz Band, maybe one or two others in Europe (although they don't have our soloists), and Count Basie's ghost group. In a rare battle of the bands a few years back, the CHJB shellacked the LCJO, and I doubt the others would fare much better. That's partly because Faddis has invested much of his musical capital in dynamics; not even the Basie operation, which under its founder's gaze practically invented modern brass tuttis with unison shakes and decays, could outshine it, not without Faddis's trumpet to top those tuttis off. Competition aside, the CHJB took upon itself a direction broader than other bands, excepting the Danes. Although some of its most memorable achievements involved classic jazz repertory—Lalo Schifrin's *Gillespiana*, Maurice Peress's restoration of Ellington's *Black, Brown and Beige*—it preferred to commission new works, usually based on familiar themes.

Like Gerry Mulligan with his much shorter-lived Concert Jazz Band, Faddis developed a cadre of gifted writers, representing several generations of jazz, and allowed them to go for broke. Generally, they were invited to tackle and revise celebrated jazz works or pop songs. The inconsistent results were, strangely, one of the CHJB's charms: You were never too certain of what you were about to hear, and thus experienced the excitement of discovering big band music in the making, as an evolving art. Owing to thematic constraints, listeners had a grounding with which to evaluate variations: Can this hymn really be "Yesterdays" (it is, via Michael Phillip Mossman) or this mad labyrinth "Sing Sing Sing" (credit unpredictable Jim McNeely), and did Coltrane ever receive more disparate treatments than "Giant Steps" (the invariably swinging Frank Foster) and *A Love Supreme* (Slide Hampton slyly banishing solemnity)?

I agree entirely that Carnegie Hall ought to broaden its approach to jazz, and how better than with a resident crack orchestra that can handle virtually any challenge? In short, the CHJB ought to be encouraged to do more. For my money, it ought to do a lot more with classic repertory. No orchestra is better equipped to interpret a host of durable works that are no longer played, from Jimmie Lunceford and Mary Lou Williams to Bill Holman and Gil Evans. It's disgraceful that no orchestra (including the American Jazz Orchestra) has explored the works of George Russell (of course, Harth is probably planning to bring Russell himself to the hall, as part of his jazz expansion). In the meantime, here's a band growing like a pearl. Instead of tearing the pearl from the oyster, to which it brought much credit, Carnegie might insist on a board to oversee an enlargement of its mandate.

In that respect, I wish the CHJB's farewell, the first of seven intermittently jazzy Carnegie Hall concerts at this year's JVC Jazz Festival (ongoing as I write), had been two full sets, to more fully display its wares. After an hour of deconstructed ballads by the Brad Mehldau Trio, Faddis, clearly as angered as he was moved by the event, indulged a bit much in envoi speeches and ceremony (this has been the talkiest JVC in memory), before playing five of the band's commissions based on prewar standards. The chief pleasure of the CHJB is its ensemble esprit: You expect to be charred by high notes, jolted by dynamics, and caressed by snug voicings. Mossman's "Smoke Gets in Your Eyes" was an ideal opener, displaying the orchestra's polish, vibrant swing, and, in a two-note transitional screech, diverting virtuosity; Faddis's poised, mid-register solo was acutely gauged. Hampton's "Days of Wine and Roses" was a pastel: muted brass, flutes, and clarinet. Mossman's "I've Told Every Little Star" incorporated a mambo joke and rhythm before heading on to strong solos by his own trumpet and Ralph Lalama's tenor. Mike Abene's "You'd Be So Nice to Come Home To" introduced Terrell Stafford's trumpet and flute exchanges between the ageless (80, actually) Frank Wess and Jerry Dodgian. Frank Foster's thunderous "Fascinatin' Rhythm" laid out all the CHJB's strongest cards, powered by drummer Dana Hall.

Before Foster, Faddis supported Wess, on tenor, producing a warm purring sound, cozy as a stuffed animal, in a quintet reading of "Body and Soul." Faddis's willingness to allow small groups to emerge from the big one, a gambit at least as old as Benny Goodman's trio, gives the band a rest and the audience a change. But it takes a musician of uncommon aplomb to allow his own band a siesta while permitting an unannounced guest to steal the show. The infinitely hearty Carrie Smith belted "Blues in the Night," but she was really a beard for Clark Terry, who, at 81, is besieged by ailments and can't walk unaided. "The golden years suck," he announced, but, humor notwithstanding, the prospect of listening to him fumpher was not a pleasant one. Well, he didn't muffle a note; his tone was gorgeously unblemished, unmistakably lyrical and acerbic (including a few high-note Mumbles asides). I'm told he played as well at the recent Town Hall Eddie Bert tribute, but if I hadn't heard him I wouldn't have believed it. The only way to end was with the big band and Goodman's nightly farewell, "Goodbye." I hope not.

[*Village Voice*, 26 June 2002]

120 ❖ *Where's Waldo?*
(*JVC 2002*)

A brief July 9 press release about the flagship event that ran from June 16 to June 29 begins with an announcement from George Wein ("CEO of Festival Productions, Inc."): "The 2002 JVC Jazz Festival–New York was the most successful JVC festival ever held in New York." It was also the least jazz-like. JVC, whether good or ill or, per usual, in between, does not always reflect what is actually going on in the jazz world. This year it did—not musically, but culturally and economically as concerns what remains of jazz central in these United States. Fading away, like Uncle Tom in an episode excised from Duke Ellington's *Jump for Joy*, Uncle Jazz lies on his deathbed while producers and CEO's frantically administer adrenalin to keep him alive. It isn't necessarily his music they hope to preserve, but his name, a valuable brand on seven continents.

Never in my experience has JVC presented so little jazz, or so few thematic and imaginative concerts. Even re-creations, with which we are admittedly surfeited, vanished from the bill. There was nothing novel, original, or newsworthy. A cursory look at the events scheduled for The Hague, Montreal, and other international jazz sites reveals the singularity of New York's drought. Of eight concerts presented at Carnegie Hall, which according to a press release had a 90 percent ticket sale (that's the source of the "most successful" claim), only half were undeniably jazz. Of the others, Joao Gilberto and Eddie Palmieri remain tangential, though they have now become deservedly admired JVC traditions;

Michael Feinstein and Lauryn Hill were in on a pass. Of the four Beacon Theater concerts, only the one with Roy Haynes and Wynton Marsalis offered jazz, and it was a box-office disaster—probably in part because it was slated opposite a bona fide Carnegie jazz artist, Keith Jarrett. Of the mere three Kaye Playhouse shows, two were largely given over to cabaret.

True, much great jazz was heard nightly at Birdland and the Village Vanguard; but you can always hear great jazz there. Except for shorter stays (mostly one-nighters) and a two-for-one pricing gimmick that incorporated five other clubs and required a main-hall ticket stub, nothing about the JVC connection served to make those performances especially merry. At festivals in towns like Pori, Cork, Perugia, Nice, New Orleans, and San Francisco, as well as Montreal and The Hague and elsewhere, music lurks in many corners, often for the price of a beer or a general admission, and the small venues are essential pleasures. In New York, they suggest a guilt-edged Band-Aid for the cavernous hole into which jazz has disappeared; participating clubs get an official JVC banner and, if possible, more tourists than usual, and JVC can pretend comprehensiveness.

Since I spent most evenings at Carnegie, forlorn and confused, the thrill of hearing the Bill Charlap Trio with guests Phil Woods and Frank Wess at Birdland may have been intensified. If you count, as JVC did, isolated events at the Schomburg Center (jazz: a Mickey Bass quintet) and the Apollo (not jazz: The Roots and Living Colour), and a free afternoon of university bands at Bryant Park, this was the eighth day of the festival, and the first opportunity to hear unadulterated, urgent yet laid-back, small-band, bebopping, mainstream jazz. Having just experienced Joao, Lauryn, and a set of cabaret vaudeville, it was like coming home. Jazz!—ah, that grand old music. Birdland was packed tight with an audience conspicuously more attentive than those in the halls, where thousands of attendees apparently assumed 8:00 curtains would rise at 8:50. Charlap, a shrewd fellow, featured his guests on alternating numbers, demonstrating his masterly ability to comp with precision, drive, and originality.

With bassist Peter Washington and drummer Kenny Washington, he may have the best piano trio extant, a slot vacated by Tommy Flanagan. It swings so effortlessly and unselfconsciously you get the feeling that any top-flight soloist could have walked on and found himself comforted and encouraged. Woods, his sound bright with the sturdy glow that mixes beauty and defiance (still, at 70), brought Benny Carter's "A Summer Serenade" to gleaming life, signing off with a stately cadenza; Wess, his approach to flute kinetic and spry (still, at 80), enlivened an original based on "Exactly Like You." Joy turned to enchantment as the saxophonists (Wess on tenor) joined together for "What's New?" (alternating theme and obbligato every eight-bars) and the battle anthem, "Blues Up and Down," played super fast, both men roaring as Charlap thrust chords that shadowed and mimicked them, before essaying his own steely solo, building with abundant ideas. Even when indulging his rippling technique, he is never heavy-handed. And this was considered too rarefied for the customers on 57th Street?

For me, the festival got off to an enlightening start, but it had nothing to do with JVC, which is another problem with JVC. At the Knitting Factory, on the same night Michael Feinstein was crooning with a 70-piece orchestra, Cecil Taylor led his 27-piece Sound Vision Orchestra in a premiere of "With Blazing Eyes and Open'd Mouth." He was initially scheduled to play solo piano at Birdland but apparently decided late in the day that the club would either accommodate his orchestra or nothing—a poor way of doing business, perhaps, but the SVO was primed to go, the massed winds secure and resolute, pinning you to your seat with hurricane force. Like *Ascension*, it rotated solos and ensemble crescendos; unlike *Ascension*'s, the ensemble passages were written and varied. It went on too long—some soloists had little to say; others stood out, including altoist Bobby Zankel, singer Lisa Sokolov (whose volatile scatting and whooping made Taylor laugh aloud), one or two trumpet players I couldn't see, and tenor saxophonist Andrew Lamb, whose mellow, understated attack roused the pianist to full-throttle pianistic exuberance. The closing was inspired—a long, even winding-down, like a great beast giving its last breath.

As the Sound Vision Orchestra was followed, the next night, by the Carnegie Hall Jazz Band (discussed last column), optimism seemed warranted. But it dissipated. My third experience with Joao Gilberto was the anti-charm; his rite of performance, sure time, alluring voice, succinct guitar chords, and trance-inducing Portuguese seemed undernourished and repetitive. On a well-known piece, like "O Grande Amor," one could luxuriate in familiarity, but too many lesser-known (to me, unknown) pieces blended into soup. And is "'S Wonderful" the only North American song he considers worthy of his repertoire? He sang its chorus over and over (I lost count after seven), never altering the slightest nuance.

Lauryn Hill also took the stage with just voice and guitar, but where Gilberto said not a word, she paced her singing with a narcissistic volubility that circled her subject without tagging it, since she assumed that everyone present had spent at least as much time worrying about her travails as she has. Her music was '60s folk with a religious curve, much deftly handled melisma, and chugging Ritchie Havens–style guitar chords. Her occasionally pungent, even stirring voice and personal charm would have been better served had she maintained a few inches between microphone and lips—dynamics are not her strong suit. Perched tenuously on her stool, she felt obliged, more than once, to summon a servant to shift her footstool an inch one way or another or powder her hands—Minnesota Fats never used as much chalk. Her diatribe concerning the soulless cogs of the recording industry ranged from, "The person was shrinking and the corporation was growing, but I'm not a corporation, I'm an individual," to "People been saying they made Lauryn Hill, but God made Lauryn Hill." Intermittently audible lyrics also failed to elucidate, ranging from, "I'm way too individual to fit your groove," to "There's a reason for everything on Earth / [something, something] rebirth." Stardom is rough, but it beats pushing a footstool.

Teddi King was a minor '50s singer, modestly related to jazz and by all accounts a delightful lady, who died young of lupus and in whose name periodic concerts are mounted in support of lupus research. The hour I caught, before rushing over to hear Charlap and company, was surprisingly agreeable, a chance to reassess a couple of jazz-cabaret performers I don't often hear. But it was as talky as Lauryn Hill, as each performer said something about King before performing one song. Even Ted Mack was less brutal about time, and time ought to have been less pressing, because everyone said the same thing: She was a wonderful friend who chose good songs and focused on lyrics. Daryl Sherman, herself an ever-deepening interpreter of words and music, opened with a dependably expressive and snug "Isn't It a Pity." Marlene Ver Plank, usually a bit smooth for my taste, offered an obscure Berlin ballad, "Fools Fall in Love," revealing a precise intonation and radiant timbre that made me want to hear more. Barbara Carroll, with her disarming speakeasy voice, sang the Weill-Gershwin ballad "This Is New," coming to life as the time doubled, allowing herself a cunning, jaunty piano solo full of block-chords and rhythmic daring. Carroll, at 77, swings: If she worked downtown clubs, she might find a new if less moneyed audience than the one she long regaled at the Carlyle.

Lillias White, a Broadway actor I'd never heard, kept up the rhythmic juice, after conceding that she had never heard of Teddi King when hired, and demonstrated verve and control in a soaring "I Didn't Know About You" that flirtatiously threatened to go over the top, but never did; she allowed Bucky Pizzarelli a stunning chorus. She has taste and style, as well as voice, and I'd have hung around for a second helping. The rest was less appealing. Mike Abene played a drearily rubato "My Ship," Barbara Lea worked the words of "You Don't Know What Love Is" at the expense of a pulse, and Jackie Cain sang two songs with pianist

Roy Kral and, in church-lady mode, underscored the didacticism of "Look for the Silver Lining."

Patricia Barber, opening for Cassandra Wilson, was more convincing as pianist than singer, despite mannerisms that vie with Keith Jarrett's for unpersuasive theatricality—wincing at every minor third, as though the blues caused her terrific pain. If it hurts when you touch it, don't touch it! At it's best, her trio has a pleasantly cool jazz sound, without muscle—easy listening, complete with la-la-la vocalizing, best in the interplay between piano and guitar, worst in the aching cleverness of her original songs, including one that mentioned every thinker in Philosophy 101 and another that mentioned every artist in Art 101. A brief appearance by Dave Douglas did little to alleviate the artsiness.

Wilson, the only performer I saw at Carnegie who received an off-stage introduction, is one of the most compelling visuals in jazz: long white skirt, red top, bronze skin, golden hair, and megawatt smile that channels Faye Dunaway and Jeanne Moreau. Her primary gift is for adapting diverse material so completely that she makes it hers. She pulls it off with several songs on her recent CD, which provided the evening's material, but it's a mistake to make every appearance a plug for the latest product—you lose a signature repertoire and a long-term connection with the audience. The program could only have been enhanced with a few of her benchmark interpretations of Son House, Rodgers and Hammerstein, Miles Davis, or the Monkees—better those than originals that blend together, the words barely intelligible, the rhythms repetitive. When she sang her current revisionist triumphs, she glowed and the audience snapped to attention: "Wichita Lineman," "The Weight," "Hot Tamales," and best of all, "Darkness on the Delta," backed by bass and made languorously sensuous in her reading, especially on the bridge, and "Shelter from the Storm," enacting the refrain with a steady and sexy maternalism, before interpolating, medley fashion, a chorus of "I'll Remember April." The supporting trio was less cluttered than her recent groups. Geoffrey Haynes is an invigorating and distinctive hand-drumming percussionist, Mark Peterson an empathic bassist, and music director Marvin Sewell a clever and versatile guitarist, though his solos go on and on, riding the rhythm without bringing it to heel.

The sterling Keith Jarrett / Gary Peacock / Jack DeJohnette trio gave an even better performance than last year—indeed, virtually perfect, with a minimum of vocalizing and an exemplary selection of tunes that mixed standard standards ("I'm a Fool to Want You," "Smoke Gets in Your Eyes," "Summertime," "Last Night When We Were Young") with jazz standards ("Four Brothers," "Now's the Time," "Two Degrees East, Three Degrees West"), and a free improvisation. Why, however, does he

make the audience beg and beg and beg for the encores? After one belated bow, DeJohnette walked to the drums only to learn that there had
not yet been enough begging and then had to walk off stage; after the
next bow, Peacock made the same mistake. OK, it's a small price. Jarrett
and company, at least, know what they're doing. I'm not sure about JVC.
If this year's financial success breeds another year with as little resourcefulness, as little jazz, there won't be much point in covering it. We will
already have heard almost all of it worth hearing—year round, in the
clubs.

[*Village Voice*, 23 July 2002]

121 ❖ *Almost Peas in a Pod*
(Tony Bennett / Sarah Vaughan)

Tony Bennett is a pop singer who records extensively with jazz musicians but always comes off as a pop singer with a keen appreciation of
jazz. Sarah Vaughan was a jazz singer who made dozens of pop records
but always came off as a jazz singer who could never quite take pop
machinations seriously. I don't mean to use the terms qualitatively, not
here anyway, because Bennett and Vaughan are among my favorite singers and I'm less inclined to endorse their separate pigeonholes than recognize their many similarities. Although Vaughan's career is associated
with the obstetrics of modern jazz (1944) and Bennett with the post-noir
hit parade (1951), she was only two years his senior; both came of age
with the big bands and the seminal trinity of Armstrong, Crosby, and
Holiday. They sang the same songs and shared the same arrangers and
musicians, recorded for Columbia in the period of novelties and
schmaltz, worked with Basie on Roulette. They came from solid, New
York–area working-class backgrounds (he Astoria, she Newark) and
never lost an innate skepticism for the romance of stardom—she pro-
tecting herself with wicked irony, he with ingenuous geniality. Both
walked away from major record companies when they could no longer
abide compromises; both subsequently triumphed on their own terms.

Above all, they are the most operatic singers of their generation. It's
less a matter of technical range—many others have multiple octaves—
than of dramatic attack, dynamic disposition, a purple passion for song.
They concentrate on interpreting lyrics, but the listener gets something
more, not unlike the opera-goer who may know the story but not the

language yet is moved to elation. The power of Bennett's perfect verse-and-single-chorus on "I Left My Heart in San Francisco" is derived not from an image of little cable cars climbing halfway to the stars, but from the uninterrupted emotional arc that builds gradually from an appealing melody (stroked by a hooky piano obbligato) to an ascension so juiced with its own fervor that when it's over you feel as though you've been on a trip, and it wasn't to San Francisco.

Still, Bennett believes in—or makes us believe that he believes in—those little cable cars, while one knows that Vaughan wouldn't even pretend. Indeed, her 1967 recording of the song for Mercury is a rigorous medium-tempo swinger, classily arranged by Thad Jones, that goes full throttle for the big finish, with a jazzier but less overt effect than Bennett's. For her, the arc of a song is almost always a melodic/rhythmic construction that involves recomposition. It doesn't matter whether she is besieged with strings, as on "What Kind of Fool Am I?" in which her bold sideways attack is spookily inventive, or liberated with a guitar and bass on an open medium-tempo romp like "Just in Time," which begins straightforward. Having then drawn a breath after "I found you just in time," she refrains from taking another until she has completely reconstructed the next phrase: "Before you came my time was run-ninnnnnng low-o-o-ooooo[no break]I was lost" [breath]—at which point Barney Kessel's crisp big band–style chords drive her anywhere she wants to go. Bennett sounds rehearsed even when taking chances; Vaughan sounds spontaneous even when she's not. Bennett sings "The Best Is Yet to Come" as if he knows it for a fact; Vaughan warily picks her "plu-um" and grows more convinced as she proceeds. On an earlier take of that song, she rewired the melody from bar one—small wonder they made her do it again.

These records are available on two new reissues. *The Essential Tony Bennett* is a two-disc compilation covering familiar ground from his association with Columbia, 1951 to 2001, absenting his years (1971–85) in the wilderness when he started his own boutique label. The bulk of the selections were singles, and many were huge hits. A few ringers and omissions notwithstanding, it's an irresistible survey. The husky, emphatic emoting of "Because of You" and "Rags to Riches" ages well, and the best of his early recordings are decisive and well made, if sometimes frustratingly short. Microgroove had just come along to liberate musicians from the three-minute limit, but Bennett often produced deft showpieces that were two minutes and change, if that; "Firefly" is 97 seconds and sustains an outlandish high-energy roar, but one wishes it would go on. There is no more baffling side than "I Wanna Be Around"—Bennett at his peak, making the most of Johnny Mercer's sadistic lyric, building to a promising trombone solo that you expect to roar and trigger a hair-raising vocal reprise. Instead it fades suddenly at 2:10, an agonizing instance of cantus interruptus.

When rock commandeered the charts, his label grew desperate, adding more reverb, often atop knowing arrangements (for example, "Once Upon a Time," note the opening measures), instead of accepting the fact that Tony, like Frank and Ella, was essentially an LP artist. The stubbornness paid off with "San Francisco" and other hits through 1963, at which point the moneymen began to lose interest. But Bennett was no Eddie Fisher or Johnny Ray; for him the best really was to come. What age cost him in power and range, he made up in economy and time, swinging with imperturbable ease and enjoying one of the longest last laughs in show business history. (*Essential*'s last track is a blues duet with k. d. lang.) The recent passing of Rosemary Clooney and Peggy Lee leaves him the last one standing, the sole thriving remnant of a generation of pop singers who came of age with classic songs that were not yet classic and jazz principles that applied across the board.

Musicraft raised Vaughan's standing on the charts in 1948 with her cover of Doris Day's "It's Magic," and Columbia worked assiduously at keeping her there, achieving minor successes like "These Things I Offer You," in 1951. In 1959, however, Mercury scored big with "Broken-Hearted Melody," an atrocious anomaly that she loathed and refused to sing in concert. A year later, she leapt from the frying pan into the fire, signing with the mobbed-up Roulette and producer Teddy Reig, who loved jazz as played by Basie and dollars any way they came. That, at least, is the received wisdom about Vaughan's three years at the label, which she did nothing to dispel. At Basie's funeral service, she sat next to Billy Eckstine and giggled with mild embarrassment as he loudly encouraged Reig to rifle the coffin for any loot he might have overlooked. Aside from the masterpiece *Sarah + 2* (long unavailable) and two sessions with Benny Carter, most of her work was dismissed as meretricious, often deservedly. Yet Mosaic's *The Complete Roulette Sarah Vaughan Studio Sessions*, an eight-disc set that restores the original LP configurations, is filled with riches—funny, daring, intensely musical conceits as well as gorgeous, pulsating ballads and lingering notes that shine like full moons.

Bad news first: The 25 singles, which produced no hits, are worse than you can probably imagine. "My Dear Little Sweetheart" is imitation Patti Page, arranged by the same genius behind "Doggie in the Window," and "Let's" would have better served Annette Funicello (the melody weirdly adumbrates the score to *Lolita*). The low point in terms of Vaughan's singing, surprisingly, is the singles session with Billy May, which begins

with a faux-cowboy song; she sounds contemptuous of all the material—
her enunciation is off, even her pitch wobbles. The alto sax solo on
"Them There Eyes" is amateurish, and Vaughan goes so far over the top
on "Love," you wonder if she was determined to sabotage the session.
Her final Roulette albums are uneven, with little to treasure on *Star Eyes*
or *Snowbound.*

Yet *Sarah Slightly Classical* (arranged by Marty Manning with the same
echo he brought to Tony Bennett's "San Francisco" session) is so ludicrous a concept, weighed down by overwrought strings and Mario
Lanza's greatest hits, that the sassy one takes the opposite attack, choosing a delicate vocal mask that allows more nuance and color—notably
on the tympani-introduced "Ah! Sweet Mystery of Life," where her high
notes are pure as light. Far worse is "Alone," the Marx Brothers aria that
found its way to the album with Basie's band, which is crushed by it,
though Sarah attempts levity with interpolations ("make me make me
make me"). Much of *You're Mine You* is mediocre (Quincy Jones's best
writing is laden with strings and French horns, the worst is condescend-
ingly rhythmic)—its nadir the hopeless "Maria," which she essays
straight-faced; she is curiously uninvolved on "Moonglow" and
melodramatic on "Fly Me to the Moon." But she compensates on the
same album with several bright touches, including a hilarious Bea Lillie
break on the ersatz chart of "One Mint Julep," and in canny readings of
"The Best Is Yet to Come" and "Witchcraft."

The rest is mostly joy. Except for its opening track, an ooh-ridden "I
Believe in You," *The Explosive Side* rocks with ideas. The material is tried
and true, and Benny Carter's efficient charts are brisk showcases for the
singer, not the band. She brings sensuous irony to "Honeysuckle Rose,"
exercises her vibrato and easy swing to "Moonlight on the Ganges,"
improvises with abandon on "After You've Gone," and plots "I Can't
Give You Anything but Love" over a vamp. The three duets with Joe
Williams (and Basie) are less intimate but more intensely swinging than
previous encounters with Eckstine. *Dreamy* is as advertised, including a
sumptuous "You've Changed" (no one sings the word "blasé" like
Vaughan.) The little-known *Sarah Sings Soulfully* is a major rediscovery;
the title refers to the presence of generic organ, but it's part of a Gerald
Wilson sextet (Teddy Edwards underemployed, Carmell Jones offering
superb trumpet obbligato) and except for the dated "A Taste of Honey,"
it is dazzling, including a serenely impeccable "East Street," a definitive
vocal version of "'Round Midnight" (one of five jazz anthems), and, best
of all, a tantalizingly slow and thoroughly inspired "Baby Won't You
Please Come Home," quite unlike the one on *Sarah + 2.*

Of the two albums with just guitar and bass, *After Hours* is delightful; *Sarah + 2* is beyond words. A highlight of the latter (there are no low-lights) is "The Very Thought of You," which arcs ingeniously in the second half of the first chorus. Kessel then takes a nice twangy episode, followed by Vaughan's ornamented closer, complete with pretend stop-time phrasing. Compare it with Bennett's version on *Essential*, an equally daring interpretation because he is chaperoned throughout by the intri-cate and long-limbed shadow-play of Bobby Hackett's trumpet; they are at once independent and wedded at the hip, a trick I imagine they could have achieved only with Bennett focusing on the song and Hackett on Bennett. Played back to back, the Bennett and Vaughan versions of that venerable Ray Noble song from 1934 make for a double-bill of American vocalizing at its zenith.

[*Village Voice*, 13 August 2002]

122 ❖ *Lionel Hampton, 1908–2002*

Putting aside the probability that in the fullness of time every musician, from Palestrina to Perry Como, will be looked upon as a precursor of rock and roll, in the instance of Lionel Hampton the claim has much validity—indeed, it's surprising to discover that he isn't yet acknowl-edged in most reference works on the subject. Along with Lucky Millinder he practically invented orchestrated rhythm and blues. Both men arrived at Decca in 1941, two years after the label signed Louis Jordan, and restructured swing to accommodate voluble rhythms, rau-cous blues, and shameless showmanship. Millinder, however, had noth-ing like Hampton's breadth or appeal. Nor did he have "Flying Home": The moment Illinois Jacquet began his tenor saxophone solo with an extended quote from the 1847 opera *Martha*, jazz and pop were headed for a new kind of conciliation. The age of the honking tenor had arrived; on its heels came the JATP jousts, to one side, and, to the other, Tiny Bradshaw, Johnny Otis, Earl Bostic, and others, all (like Jordan) undis-tinguished veterans of swing bands who found their places in the sun with r&b. In 1954, Decca would seal the deal by signing Bill Haley.

In the interim and long before and long afterward, Hampton was everywhere, possibly the most schizophrenic force in American music. On the vibraharp, he was the very model of sophisticated improvisation, a lilting interpreter of ballads and furious purveyor of romping standards, girded with an intuitive sense of harmony that made him an ideal foil for Art Tatum, Oscar Peterson, and, for that matter, anyone of any generation who could play with anything like his sensitivity and spirit. Andre Hodier described Hampton's 1939 "When Lights Are Low," for which he assembled a reed section with Benny Carter, Coleman Hawkins, Chu Berry, and Ben Webster, plus Charlie Christian and Dizzy Gillespie, as the "apex of the ascending curve that symbolizes the evolution of swing." Yet on piano, he was the two-fingered madman of boogie woogie; listening today to his "I Found a New Baby" and "The Munson Street Breakdown," also made in 1939, it's hard not to hear the prescient marriage of swing and rock. On drums, his first professional instrument, he was just a madman plain and simple. Abbey Lincoln has recalled him playing at her high school and dancing on a drumhead until it broke. At a typical Hampton performance, he played the three instruments, sang, danced a bit, and said little beyond grunts and trademark Lionelisms like, "Thanks for those kind applause."

He was equally divided as a bandleader: This was the guy whose records helped establish Dizzy Gillespie ("Hot Mallets") *and* Earl Bostic ("Hamp's Boogie Woogie"), whose singers included in quick succession Dinah Washington, Betty Carter, and Little Jimmy Scott, whose originals in the course of a year ranged from "Hey! Ba-Ba-Re-Bop" to his oft-covered ballad "Midnight Sun" to the challenging "Mingus Fingers," by the then unknown Charles M. In the '50s, his reputation split as well. Welcomed as a prolific, masterly, apparently timeless soloist, he was largely dismissed as a bandleader whose orchestra became increasingly associated with "Live at the Apollo"–type soundies that were mostly fury and very repetitive. In the '60s, he triumphed at Newport by introducing the now much sampled funk team the Pazant Brothers, a ploy that worked better in person than on records. How bent on entertaining was he? There's the story of an aquacade double-bill at which Louis Armstrong cut him to the bone. Hampton climaxed his next set by having the drummer (or was it the brass section?) dive into the pool. Countless anecdotes involve producers struggling to get him off stage. He did not go gently into the wings—those applause were his sustenance. When he died Saturday morning, August 31, at 94, he got his first rest in a long time.

Hampton was born in Louisville, in 1908, raised in Birmingham, and educated in Kenosha and Chicago, where he began playing drums with the *Chicago Defender*'s Newsboys Band. He was a year older than Benny Goodman, though Goodman may have died thinking Hampton was younger (well into the 1990s, his presumed birth date was 1909 or 1913).

In the late-1920s, he moved to Los Angeles and played drums with the resident orchestra at the Cotton Club in Culver City, where Louis Armstrong appeared in 1930. Armstrong later recalled Hampton playing "some little bells which he kept beside his drums and he was swinging the hell out of them too." At his fourth recording session with the Cotton Club band, Armstrong wheeled a vibraphone from a corner of the studio, and on "Memories of You," Hampton recorded his first vibes solo.

He eventually became leader of the Cotton Club band, yet by 1936 he was reduced to leading a nine-piece group at a run-down sailors' haunt called the Paradise Club. Word began to spread about this human whirlwind, however, and soon celebrities began dropping by, including members of the Goodman band. One night Goodman drove out alone and was so elated by what he heard, he asked to sit in; they jammed until five ("that night, with Benny there, I was inspired," Hampton remembered), two hours past closing. The next night he returned with Teddy Wilson and Gene Krupa and invited Lionel to record. On August 21, the big band completed three numbers and then what soon became known as the Benny Goodman Quartet debuted with "Moonglow." After Wilson's four-bar intro, Goodman plays the theme and is suddenly buoyed by welling waves of vibraphone chords. The mallet sound was hardly unknown: Red Norvo had established it on marimba and xylophone, with Goodman himself playing bass clarinet on Norvo's 1933 "Dance of the Octopus." But Norvo preferred a concise bell-like sound and gave the electric vibes a wide berth until the damper pedal was introduced. Hampton showed what the new instrument could do, and Goodman gave him plenty of room—only Hampton improvises a full chorus on "Moonglow," complete with two-bar breaks, plus cadenza and final chord. Hampton had arrived in suitably dramatic fashion.

He worked with Goodman's small group through 1940, by which time Victor chose him to lead a series of all-star recordings to rival those that Wilson was making for Brunswick. Though Wilson's records became known for Billie Holiday's vocals, both men relied on the big bands as talent stables. Like field marshals assessing available troops, they recruited the best players from the bands of Ellington, Basie, Goodman, Calloway, Hines, and others for mostly impromptu sessions. Just as the Wilsons reflected the gentility of the leader, the Hamptons were bound to his volatile energy and peerless swing. Unfortunately, his producers endorsed showboating and faddish indulgences. More than half of the 90-plus tracks are weighted down with vocals, only a few of which are engaging (his reading of "Baby Won't You Please Come Home" is a knowing elaboration on the way George Thomas sang it with McKinney's Cotton Pickers) or given over to his piano stomps, some of which are quite mesmerizing—like "Wizzin' the Wiz" and "Rock Hill Special." What's left is an unfurling of masterworks.

These records are justifiably celebrated for the contributions of Hampton's guests. The run-down is pretty amazing: Johnny Hodges's original reading of "Sunny Side of the Street," Chu Berry's volcanic womb-to-tomb work on "Sweethearts on Parade," Coleman Hawkins's rhapsodic solo and Charlie Christian's chordal obbligato on "One Sweet Letter from You," Buster Bailey's nod to Jimmy Noone on "I Know," not to mention the aforementioned "When Lights Are Low" date, arranged by Benny Carter—plus significant work by Gillespie, Milt Hinton and Cozy Cole, Sid Catlett, Nat Cole, Budd Johnson, Herschel Evans, Ben Webster, Rex Stewart, Harry James, Ed Hall, Cootie Williams, and a lot more. Yet at his best, Hampton is equal to any of them. His melodic finesse is exemplary on "I Surrender Dear," his two choruses constructed on riff patterns that develop one to the next, powered with displaced accents and embellished in the second chorus by melodic bytes until a double-time passage dispels the mood. The single-minded deliberateness of that solo combines the watery flow of Lester Young with the cathedral might of Armstrong. On his own version of "Memories of You," he tracks a single motive—an inversion of the melody—through logical and decisive variations.

Of course, it will be these records and not his predictive role in rock nor his stage antics that will be most remembered. His jazz albums for Verve and other labels will continue to enjoy reissues, while his stupefying lounge albums for Brunswick have already disappeared from memory. On the other hand, it's no small achievement to monitor the pulse of musical fashion for nearly 75 years and ride it cowboy-like despite every twist and bounce. If he was ahead of the curve in the '20s, '30s, and '40s, he strutted alongside it in the decades that followed, never really falling behind—as secure and eager with Chick Corea as with Hank Jones. Nothing musical fazed him. His willingness to extemporize at the drop of anybody's downbeat suggested a talent so natural as to be elemental, but his ear was acute enough to see him through every harmonic labyrinth. Think of another career as long and ardent and constant. You can't—there isn't any.

[*Village Voice*, 25 September 2002]

123 ❖ Genius
(Charlie Christian)

"Legend" is the tribute we pay artists we'd prefer not to confront. A universe of legends and living legends inclines us to feel less awed than fatigued, and hyperbole ultimately masks indifference. In the absence of divinity and heroism, of a demiurgic unreality, even dictionaries surrender to fashion and concede that a legend may be merely a "superstar" or "celebrity." Thus we are brought short in the presence of the real McCoy. Charlie Christian, like other world-shaking artists who died absurdly young, radiates a mythological aura. It isn't that we lack biographical specifics. But the growing multiplicity of facts and dates do not bring us any closer to knowing the laconic, universally liked and admired, but strangely passionless Prometheus who took hold of electricity and gave it a voice. In a career of Orpheic brevity (23 months in the national limelight, 1939–41), Christian utterly transformed the DNA of jazz and popular music, and his innovations are matched by the still-waxing power of his art.

The ambiguity of legend was fostered not least by those who tried hardest to humanize him. In a typically defensive and non-musical essay, "The Charlie Christian Story," Ralph Ellison cites Christian, whose family he knew growing up in Oklahoma City, as an example of the "local, unrecorded heroes of jazz," who achieve broader acclaim late in life or not at all. Yet Christian was a jazz star at 23. Ellison justifies his privileged claim that renown was late in coming by pointing to his "skillful playing" in grade school, when he strummed guitars made from cigar boxes. The argument would appear preposterous but for the testimony of those who insist that he achieved professional standing at nine or ten. He is said to have begun on trumpet before taking on guitar, bass, and piano, in addition to singing and dancing.

Discovery was inevitable, as was competition for the credit. The public believed Benny Goodman was his benefactor; it was in Goodman's sextet that Christian became famous. John Hammond said that he scouted Christian and resorted to trickery to get Goodman to audition him. Mary Lou Williams pointed out that she brought Christian to Hammond's attention. In an account commissioned for the new four-disc Columbia/Legacy compilation, *Charlie Christian: The Genius of the Electric Guitar*, Les Paul casually claims that he heard Christian before Williams, in 1938, and helped get him his first real guitar—a tale omitted from Mary Alice Shaughnessy's *Les Paul: An American Original*, and partly contradicted by

Peter Broadbent's solid biographical account in the same Columbia/Legacy booklet.

It's strange but fitting that this mostly exemplary boxed set allows Paul slightly to muddy the water. Because even with its 17 previously unissued tracks, including entire rehearsal sequences, Christian manages to lie back in the shadows. At one point, Goodman asks him to lower his amplifier at the beginning of his solo, and then turn it up as the solo develops; Christian's muttered reply is mostly inaudible. Photographs show him smiling, sharp, serene, engaged. But those who knew him convey little beyond his dedication, his brilliant obsession with music. On December 1, 1939, a Chicago newspaper ran an essay credited to Christian: "Guitarmen, Wake Up and Pluck! Wire for Sound; Let 'Em Hear You Play." In it, Christian argues that the guitarist is "something more than just a robot plunking on a gadget to keep the rhythm going." He writes of how "electrical amplification has given guitarists a new lease on life," naming as examples Allan Reuss, teenager George Barnes ("who set the town on its ear"), and Floyd Smith of Andy Kirk's band.

Presumably, the essay was ghosted; if so, we may never know how much Christian contributed to it. In the March 1982 issue of *Guitar Player* that reprinted the piece, Barney Kessel, younger by seven years, spoke of jamming with Christian in their native Oklahoma for three days and compared his importance to that of Edison, but remembered him as "kind of street-wise" and inarticulate ("he didn't have very much of a vocabulary. He didn't even talk hip"). Only in his music is Christian a fount of clarity, his every phrase—inspired or not—enunciated, lucid, logical, and decisive.

As the Christian essay notes, he was not the first to plug into an amplifier. But he was the first to create a style for the electric guitar. His attack and tone are distinct, not a consequence of volume, but of a concept and control that define a new instrument. Influenced by Lester Young's riff-laden phrases and harmonic independence, he created an individual approach of lofty authority, of the Swing Era and slightly beyond. He embodies jazz history (note the climax of his "Honeysuckle Rose" chorus, the way he ping-pongs notes an octave apart in the manner of Louis Armstrong's 1928 "Muggles") while implying its future: His 1941 after-hours jam session solo on "Swing to Bop," often characterized as the birth of modern jazz, should be considered as an essential addendum to this set. Surrounded by the best musicians of the era—Goodman, Lionel Hampton, Cootie Williams, Count Basie, and, at one astonishing private session included here, Young—he stands out, his every chorus a floating casino of ricocheting rhythms, soaring melodies, and blues-bound epigrams.

As celebrated as the Goodman sextet sessions are, they've been blighted for six decades by discographical confusion. From the beginning, different takes vied for attention. A 1955 Columbia album (with front-cover essay: "This is the story of Charlie Christian . . .") included a striking warm-up, "Blues in B," and spliced versions of "Breakfast Feud" and "Airmail Special" that combined Christian solos from several takes. Only now has the label straightened out the mess, separating master and alternate takes, which reward scrutiny and comparison, and adding whatever breakdown scraps were found in the vaults. The audio mastering is exceptional, the clarity often bordering on revelation. Voyeurs will get their kicks from running-tapes for the "Benny's Bugle" rehearsal, though much of the conversation is difficult to hear and Columbia does not include a transcription. The sequencing is not ideal: the big band numbers are segregated on disc four (in proper sequence, they would vary the listening experience), and the labeling of every first issue as a master (e.g., the 1972 release of take five of "Breakfast Feud") is nonsensical. Those are minor annoyances. The failure to index the 21-minute, six-selection 1941 jam session is a maddening oversight; the only way to hear the famous "Blues in B" is to gun the fast-forward button through 19 minutes. Still, this set—produced by Michael Brooks and Michael Cuscuna—is a momentous achievement, fully confirming the wondrousness of Charlie Christian, jazz legend.

[*The Absolute Sound*, October 2002]

124 ❖ *At the Summit* *(Sonny Rollins)*

"Give yourself a gift," Marcus Aurelius advised, "the present moment." Aldous Huxley populated his island paradise Pala with parrots that fly around squawking, "Here and now, boys, here and now!" All the wise men agree: The key to a healthy life is alertness—a refusal to smother the brief candle with ruminations or apprehensions, an avowal to wake up and keep waking up. In art, the existential dilemma translates into devotion to the elusive light of inspiration, a challenge enacted nowhere with greater clarity and urgency than in jazz—where the composer composes in the arena, without benefit of eraser, white-out, tape dubs, or retakes—and by nobody with a more exhilarating sense of adventure than jazz's finest living practitioner, Sonny Rollins.

It was a remarkable week: Verizon colluded with the Jazz Standard to present five solo piano recitals; Jazz Alliance International jammed the same room with a dozen or so trumpeters in tribute to Fats Navarro, and Clark Terry proved it's what you play and not how much that wins the day; Tony Bennett sang his heart out for an hour and a half at Carnegie Hall (also for Verizon); Lincoln Center remembered Art Blakey; and Ted Nash reconvened Odeon. But when Rollins returns to town, after an all too typical two-year absence, time must have a stop; the present moment is suddenly lit in boldface italics, and after hanging on every measure for 95 minutes, one is disinclined to get the clock rolling again, even though it would trigger a dreamy post mortem on the immediate past. Because his records are sometimes rush-jobs proffering material that hasn't yet been (in his words) road-tested, and because spontaneity is his shield against cliché and ennui, a Rollins concert is a gift, and when he plays as well as he did at B. B. King's Blues Club and Grill on September 21, a miracle, too.

The most dilatory moment in the first set was one of the most perversely fascinating. Midway through an achingly slow and lovely reading of "You're Mine, You" (a fairly obscure John Greene ballad that Billy Eckstine and Sarah Vaughan recorded), he turned to his percussionist of the past couple of years, Kimati Dinizulu, and attempted, or so it seemed, to engage him in an exchange of phrases—fours, maybe. Well, who plays conga solos at that tempo? Dinizulu appeared at a loss, but Rollins nudged him with rhythmic and melodic figures, and Dinizulu tried to respond, and Rollins kept it up as the music banked into a cloud of suspenseful haplessness, until he decided he had gotten all he was going to get, and then returned to his suave blue-ballad interpretation of the 1930s song. On tape, this would be fairly stupefying, but in performance it was quirkily thrilling, since no one on stage or in the audience knew how it was going to play out. When he returned to the theme, people who had been leaning forward in their seats, now sat back, shaking their heads in wonder and thinking or murmuring—at my table, it was murmuring—"only Sonny." Jazz at its best is never entirely musical; it's also theater.

A minute into the opening number, "East of the Sun" (probably the only great standard written for an undergraduate show—in 1935, by a Princeton student, Brooks Bowman, who died in a car accident at 23 en route to his first job, with a movie studio), I was reminded that Rollins's genius is that of the instinctively discriminating editor. It's a talent that every artist possesses or strives for: knowing what to omit, recognizing when the canvas is finished. In jazz, there's no help, no second opinion, no second chance, except the next number and the next. Rollins has always had an uncanny sense of how to define a phrase, embellish it, erect a structure, cap it off; it's there in his earliest work—"There Are Such Things," from 1955, for one fantastic example. His mellow, fluent involvement with the melody of "East of the Sun" at B. B. King's made me wonder why no one else can play like that—an old tune, done to death, yet made ripe and timely, cagily swung with an authority that brooks no appeal. No one else soloed on it.

The band became prominent on "Global Warming," the recent original he plays most often, and a good raucous theme it is. One often complains about Rollins's bands, sometimes with good cause, but this one suits him. Trombonist Clifton Anderson is an uneven soloist, but he rides the time and is mostly charged with beefing up the heads, which he does in glistening unison. The rhythm section, four strong with the addition of Dinizulu, is of a piece. Stephen Scott is an ideal pianist for his rhythmic comping (rendered tinny by B. B. King's otherwise sensible sound system) and individual solo style, and drummer Tommy Campbell, who worked with Rollins in the '80s, is back with a more effective, understated style. The ageless Bob Cranshaw, who nonetheless will turn 70 before the year is out, feeds Rollins chords the way he likes to hear them; properly mixed, his nimble, concise phrases were unblemished by the buzz of his electric bass. And yet they are all at a disadvantage as soloists, because when Rollins isn't playing you hanker for his return, and when he is, you don't need to hear from anyone else. After a round of solos on "Global Warming," he pounced back with triumphant growls and tenacious riffs, two-note moans and ecstatic riffs, arpeggios pirouetting impudently through two octaves and staunch riffs: marathon man at the summit.

Then he went into ballad mode, always a titillating moment—especially in recent years, when he has consistently reached into the golden-age songbag marked, "Not standards, but worthy." In addition to "You're Mine, You," the choice surprise was "I'll Look Around," a song Billie Holiday recorded for Decca that I've never heard anyone else do. In Rollins's interpretation, the key phrase flirted with "I'll String Along with You," and the whole performance, much of it in his upper-mid register, mined a legato gentleness reminiscent of his '50s work and (in terms of singers) at least as suggestive of Nat Cole as Holiday. On an uptempo "Why Was I Born?" he returned to his current style of resolute paraphrase, spinning a zillion notes around the trellis of the tune yet never disguising it, this after a long drum solo that served only to spur him on. If he had a hammer—Sonny unflappable in black shades and white ascot, rocking in rhythm, playing all the notes in the chords and scales, and somehow still keeping the melody aloft.

After a 16-bar original that featured Cranshaw, whose rapid strumming eventually quieted those who consider bass solos a boon to conversation, Rollins opened up the floodgates on the oddest ballad to join his repertoire in recent years (or rejoin; he has recalled trying it out in the '60s): "Sweet Leilani." When he played it in New York two years ago, the antic strangeness suggested a provocation, however benevolent. His subsequent recording (on *This Is What I Do*) showed how smitten he was with a virtually forgotten 1937 Oscar-winning, gold-record-earning lullaby that bandleader Harry Owens wrote for his daughter and reluctantly refashioned for Bing Crosby and the movie *Waikiki Wedding*, inadvertently setting off a brief vogue for all things Hawaiian. That Rollins, who knows his radio singers, chose to invigorate a song that even in 1937 was considered treacly, speaks volumes about his lingering respect for the pop culture of his youth, as well as his exceptionally transfigurative powers. At B. B. King's, he went at it for 25 minutes, the definition of a tour de force, basking in the pretty tune, but with a familiar ardor unlike the quizzical romance of the stellar recording; then he rended it into its components, his tone growing darker and more rugged, until— around the 20-minute mark and in prelude to a long exchange with Campbell parsed in fours, threes, or both (confused the hell out of me)— he was chortling, growling, baying. Which is to say he was deep in a world beyond notes, rapt in the language of saxophonics that only he knows.

As they say at Passover, it would have been enough. But then he leaped into a cadenza that signaled his partying closer, the calypso "Don't Stop the Carnival," after which the crowd rose and roared long enough to merit a brief but generously lyrical encore, "Where or When." Afterward, I raced down to the Jazz Standard to hear Jason Moran, who I very much enjoyed, so I will not suggest that Rollins obviates the desire to hear anyone else. On the contrary, I think that total mastery helps sensitize one to the present moment with all its variety and options. Sonny Rollins gives a tremendous amount, and having taken it in, one stands a little straighter, breathes a little more deeply, and feels for at least a little while utterly in harmony with here and now.

[*Village Voice*, 9 October 2002]

125 ❖ *Purely Piano*
(Ethan Iverson / Vijay Iyer / Jason Moran)

Mid-September's 2002 Verizon Music Festival—note the absence of the J-word—offered little to the J-audience beyond McCoy Tyner and Tony Bennett, at least in the big halls. But a week of solo piano recitals at the Jazz Standard filled me with more optimism about the J-future than anything else this year. Though dramatically different from each other, three pianists born in the '70s indicated a united front in their unconventional approaches, filtering of influences, and involvement with the music of their time. Each has devised an emphatic solo style—a purely pianistic music, as opposed to trio music without the trio. Several times I wondered whether Ethan Iverson, Vijay Iyer, and Jason Moran were playing jazz at all, but I never really cared. This was no less true of 41-year-old Matthew Shipp, whom I will catch up with when *Equilibrium* is released in January. I assume it was also true of 47-year-old Fred Hersch (whom I missed), knowing his intermingling of jazz and classical techniques. But I doubt that Hersch accessed one ingredient connecting the other four, especially in their new or imminent albums: hip-hop beats.

It was just a matter of time. For more than a decade, jazz musicians seeking concord with contemporary pop hired rappers, who sometimes rapped about jazz, as if that would make their intrusions more palatable. The answer was as close as Miles Davis, who knew to cherchez the rhythm. Jazz musicians who know hip-hop or grunge as part of the wallpaper of their youths are neither intimidated by nor contemptuous of it. They follow a key principle of jazz aesthetics in stealing anything that works ("jazz is an octopus," Dexter Gordon said), which is different from mixed drinks that dilute both factors. When Herbie Hancock, a pioneer of monotonous fusion and electronic beats, argued for the acceptance of "new standards" (rock tunes), he had to superimpose harmonic patterns to make them playable—he might as well have stayed with Tin Pan Alley. The borrowings of the under-30s are so natural that you may not notice them unless signposts are erected: No one can miss the dubbed beats in Moran's version of Afrika Bambaata's "Planet Rock," but until I checked the sleeve I had no idea that the wildly effective fifth track of Iverson's *The Bad Plus* is a Nirvana cover.

Iverson, with shaved head and goatee, looks like a cross between Pete Fountain and Dr. Cyclops, and the latter's influence is the more prominent—in the microscopic attention to melody, the bombastic bursts of Lisztian fury, the patiently unpredictable bemusement while studying his captured song morsels. At the Jazz Standard, he opened with what might have been a John Ford soundtrack, the right hand picking "My Darlin' Clementine," "You Are My Sunshine," and "Red River Valley," while the left erected conflicting waves of dissonance or bounding ornamentation or a resolute ostinato, much of it foot-pedaled (the right pedal got a fierce workout all week). His control and plangent attack made the instrument roar, though an occasional rhythmic stiffness grounded him. He lightened up on standards, including a whirling "All the Things You Are" cadenza, but never relaxed for long, preferring to shake the rafters like the bell-ringer of Notre Dame.

The Bad Plus is a cooperative with bassist Reid Anderson and drummer David King, and no one will confuse it with an orthodox piano trio. The CD (on Fresh Sound) boasts an unmistakable jazz pedigree, but it also rocks, and even when they play theme and variations, they keep the theme in view, playing at and around it, never discarding melody or the equilateral rapport that gives the group its intensity. Nirvana's "Smells Like Teen Spirit" is a highlight, the chorus cued by a mad Cubano glissando in an arrangement that alternates permutations on the song's two themes, while the dynamic King steamrolls the beat, caroming into his marks. Abba's hopeless "Knowing Me Knowing You," however, a sorry opener for a good album, reminds us that jazzing pop can be as coy as jazzing the classics, and no amount of dissonance or artillery throttles the banality. Similarly, on "Blue Moon," the trio can't decide whether it likes the cloying tune or wants to humiliate it. Yet five originals do the trick. "The Breakout" begins and ends stormily and envelops a ripe ballad by Anderson; and Iverson's "Labyrinth" gets under way with a five-beat thumping before flowering as a concise meditation spurred by the natural momentum of inverted harmonies. One can imagine a jazz-to-grunge reversal here, a rock band laying claim to the piece—not that there's any need.

Vijay Iyer opened his Jazz Standard set with an elbow to the bass clef, followed by a dark drone balancing a light single-note tune and chiming treble chords, and sustained a rhythmic pulse without giving into four-square swing. An airless romanticism that blanketed his original pieces and one by Steve Coleman gave way to a stirring triptych of Ellington's "Le Sucrier Velours," Monk's "Epistrophy," and a Cecil-like barrage engineered around Hendrix's version of "Hey Joe." He is a stirring player who shares Iverson's penchant for fat chords and pedaled volume, compelling attention with long, confident phrases that race around the keyboard and avoid the usual stops. He, too, is involved in a cooperative, Fieldwork, with tenor saxophonist Aaron Stewart and another raging drummer, Elliot Humberto Kavee, whose rumble brings *Your Life Flashes*

(Pi) to instant life. Iyer wrote most of the music, but the pieces take their final form through an interactive serendipity. There's so much going on you never miss the bass. Rarely does anyone lay out for more than a few bars—this is all trio, all the time. In one passage, Iyer plays static chords in the extreme registers of the keyboard, and the effect is as if he has dropped out to favor a tenor-drums passage; he returns by claiming the middle register. Stewart's warm sound, reminiscent of Dewey Redman, adds to the intimacy. Only "The Inner World," one of two slow and moody pieces, derives conspicuously from generic '70s jazz; "Mosaic" alights with hip-hop accents. Most pieces are terse, spellbinding miniatures that never stand still.

In addition to being close in age and mixing their conservatory techniques with pop tropes, Iverson, Iyer, and Moran reflect the influence of pianists overlooked in the '60s and '70s, when every keyboard player seemed under the sway first of Evans, Tyner, or Taylor, and later of Hancock, Corea, or Jarrett. Now we keep hearing talk of and works by Jaki Byard, Andrew Hill, and Muhal Richard Abrams, plus the earlier stride hierarchy, not to mention Ellington, whose *Queen's Suite* evidently has a special resonance. Jason Moran's selection from it at the Jazz Standard was "Sunset and the Mocking Bird," during a set that never completely abandoned a jazz groove, or a sanguine originality even as he employed such devices as Horace Silver vamps, Monk dissonances, and partying stride; on the autobiographical "Gentle Shifts South," he added taped family voices. He doesn't use the tape for the version on *Modernistic* (Blue Note), but he has enough other rabbits in his hat. Indeed, this is one of the most rigorously unpredictable and rewarding solo piano albums in years.

Moran takes liberties, and the album has something to please or offend everyone. Consider four of the pieces he didn't write. The album title derives from James P. Johnson's 1930 recording, "You've Got to Be Modernistic," which the composer played at tremendous velocity, as a succession of 16-bar strains. Johnson is one of the founders of a jazz piano style that extends way beyond the Harlem tradition; it hews to melodic embellishments, something the players in the Jazz Standard series appreciate. They are as free as they want to be, yet incline toward variational fidelity. Thus Moran polishes Johnson's key theme even as he opens it up after each four-bar section with echoes of the last-played phrase, giving his reading an asymmetrical impulsiveness, with starts and stops, despite the stride underpinning. His "Body and Soul" may be the only genuinely new reading since Sarah Vaughan's 1978 duet with Ray Brown, which begins with the bridge. Working exclusively with the song's first melodic idea, Moran never plays the bridge at all. And so sure is he in working and reworking the hook, tied to an ostinato, that you don't mind its absence. Near the end, he suddenly erupts with a full-bore arpeggio, letting you know in that one gesture how much piano history he commands.

On "Planet Rock," Moran uses dubs and reversed tape—it's a different planet from Bill Evans's *Conversations with Myself*—to set up the melody, which he interprets almost as an anthemic lullaby, a radio tune stuck in your head. As an addendum, he adds a two-minute pensee on a beat he contrived for the arrangement. Covering all bases, he essays Schumann's "Auf einer Burg," from the second *Liederkreis* cycle, as a popular song—two 18-bar episodes with a four-bar transition. Moran plays the simple tune with a solemn loveliness, adding subtle variations in the harmony, which serves as a chord progression for his second chorus. At that point he embellishes the theme with rhythmic interest, yet never breaks the spell. He follows it with "Gentle Shifts South"; in this context his own melody emerges as an inversion of Schumann's, sustaining its crepuscular mood. *Modernistic* is a remarkable album.

[*Village Voice*, 23 October 2002]

126 ❖ *Point Counter Point* *(Dave Holland)*

Musical reductions are commonplace, expansions less so. Nineteenth-century virtuosos displayed their wares in keyboard adaptations of symphonies; Gershwin later created a player-piano version of his rhapsody. Occasionally, a Stokowski would reverse the process and make a chamber work symphonic. But either way the result tended to generate the dubious respect accorded gimmicks. In jazz, reduction and expansion seem more fluid, but only when the composer of the original is responsible. We don't give a second thought to Ellington taking a piece created for a small group, enlarging it for the big band (or vice versa), and additionally reworking it as a piano solo, piano-bass duet, or any other configuration that came to hand. But we can live without an augmented version of, say, the Miles Davis Nonet; many shuddered at the very notion of orchestrating *A Love Supreme*. Would Hal Overton's elaborations of Monk have been as readily countenanced if Monk had not been his pianist? Of course, adaptations of noted jazz solos by bands or vocalists are a part of jazz's requisite fuel and belong to a separate category that encompasses all of jazz history.

In an era of unceasing homages and remakes, we should probably count our blessings that more classics aren't recycled in fashionable outerwear. Yet two of the most exciting developments in big band music of the past 15 years have resulted from musicians resizing their chamber-size themes: first Jimmy Heath, and now Dave Holland. The wonder of Holland's 13-piece band, as recently heard at Birdland and on his outstanding new album, *What Goes Around* (ECM), is that the pieces don't sound reworked, even when compared with his small band or solo bass versions.

Like Heath, here is a brilliant instrumentalist in mid-life revealing not only a love of big band jazz, but a command of the idiom that indicates decades of (secret?) woodshedding. Unlike Heath, who began his career with an orchestra in an orchestral era, Holland has not been regularly associated with one since his student days, when he divided extracurricular time between the London Philharmonic and Ronnie Scott's house band, and doubled on electric bass, catching the attention of Miles Davis, who brought him to the United States in 1968. Holland appeared on the major Davis albums of the next two years—*Filles de Kilimanjaro, In a Silent Way, Bitches Brew*, and several live albums that followed. Yet in leaving Davis he also left fusion and moved toward the acoustic avant-garde, recording duets with guitarist Derek Bailey and bassist Barre Phillips and touring with Circle.

In 1972, Holland conceived *Conference of the Birds* (ECM), a durable statement for that era, paving an accessible middle road that sidestepped fusion and free jazz, and portended a modern mainstream in which such fearsome players as Sam Rivers and Anthony Braxton sounded uncompromisingly at home. Constantly in demand for his gorgeous sound, upbeat swing, and sturdily inventive and melodic accompaniment, Holland also managed to hold together a series of quintets. The present edition includes trombone (Robin Eubanks started with him in 1987, preceded by Julian Priester) and saxophone (Chris Potter joined two years ago, preceded by Steve Coleman and Steve Wilson) in the front line. More adventurous in his rhythm section, Holland has avoided piano, only rarely using any chordal instrument (briefly, guitarist Kevin Eubanks), but the 1994 addition of Steve Nelson's vibes magnified the group's spectrum and potential for interaction. Holland's bass represents clockwork dependability, while Nelson offers a free-associating commentary. Billy Kilson's drums turned up the heat; joining Holland in 1997, he offered a very different kind of percussion than predecessor

Marvin Smith, supplanting jaunty meticulousness with an incendiary restlessness that can blanket the room. The quintet, as heard on last year's *Not for Nothin'* (ECM), is alternately light-footed and precipitous, and if it resembles no comparable group, it doesn't really resemble the orchestra either.

Although the big band stems from the quintet, mass changes everything. Holland has thoroughly ingested three axioms of orchestral jazz: There's no point in having a lot of musicians if you don't employ them to accompany and counterpunch the soloists, devise interesting harmonies for them, and play loud. *What Comes Around* comes alive with the volume up, the troops in battle formation, the nuances splayed—ECM makes superb use of stereo range. It's a long album (25 years ago, it would have been released as two LPs), but something is always going on. Solos are set up and closed down with ensemble passages, and rarely do players get to breathe the air of the rhythm section alone—the winds shine like colored lights, shifting from one hue to another, and the vibes are everywhere, involved in a discrete shadow game. Most surprising about the harmonies is the frequent reliance on a '40s comfort-food sound, especially in the reeds, which places the writing in an Ellingtonian tradition even while it proffers a crazed polyphony—almost a free-jazz Dixieland.

Holland's favorite devices, which he is in danger of overdoing, are ostinatos and counterpoint, though he finds so many congenial ways to use them that it's hard to complain; they seemed more redundant live than on the record. He appears to have absorbed the entire tradition—certainly Ellington, Mingus, and Evans, but also Thad Jones's asymmetrical melodies and contrasting harmonies, and Bill Holman's contrapuntal inventions and unpredictable shape-shifting. Holland's deft ostinatos, which leverage soloists and ensemble, and the proliferation of themes—there's rarely a point without a counterpoint—help define a stylistic autonomy that subsumes the borrowings. A key indication of his success is the excellence of the soloists: Chris Potter doesn't play nearly as incisively on his own recent CD as he does here; Gary Smulyan, Antonio Hart, and Josh Roseman have never sounded more imposing; and given one shot to emerge from the anonymity of section work, Mark Gross plays an alto solo on "First Snow" reminiscent of the kind of star-making turns John Handy took with Mingus in 1959—he is anonymous no more. Sideman status has its advantages.

The title track, "What Goes Around," is the album's most ambitious piece. I don't know which came first: the small or big band version. The former, heard on *Not for Nothin'*, was recorded after the big band debuted at the 2000 Montreal Jazz Festival and only four months before the big band recording, so this is by no means a clear example of orchestral expansion. Yet the current arrangement is so formidable in design and execution that the other sounds like a clever reduction, working with the same material but lacking the conviction of size. Holland begins with a provocative bass figure, backed by a sprinkling of vibes, on which a mildly sultry brass theme intrudes; the saxophones counter with a stirring, expansively voiced theme that suggests postwar Ellington, as Nelson plies four-mallet chords; a joyous cascading multiplicity of instruments builds, as if each man were peeling away from the ensemble until the whole band is soloing, nurtured by Holland and driven by Kilson. The orchestra waxes and wanes before Potter embarks on one of his best tenor solos, a broad, gruff, pulsing flight energized with short bursts and a Rollins-like sonority (and a Rollins lick, too), until those '40s riffs rack up another ensemble interlude, setting up Eubanks, pushed relentlessly by Kilson, who soon unleashes his own firestorm—in all, 17 minutes and every one earned.

Mingus's mighty influence is more vigorously felt, in timbre and attack, on Holland's 1993 solo "Blues for C.M." (*Ones All*, Intuition) than on the 1987 quintet version (*The Razor's Edge*, ECM), but in both of those versions, the piece seemed little more than a crafty blues doubling as accomplished homage, suggesting Mingus's style (plangent sound, strumming) and melodic universe—especially in the ninth bar. The big band gives the piece new life, paying its respects by building on Mingus's precepts rather than mimicking them; the highlight is Nelson's spellbinding solo, played fast with a chilled-gin sound, letting the phrases breathe and breezing over the reeds. When the quintet recorded "The Razor's Edge" in 1987 and "Shadow Dance" in 1983 (*Jumpin' In*, ECM), it had the unison thrust of a big band, but the new versions exemplify the difference between augmenting parts and completely reconsidering a work. Paradoxically, the new "Razor's Edge," with its unison, thrusting theme, can easily be imagined in a small-band reduction, yet the brighter tempo and total deployment of instruments transform a reticent work into an aggressive one.

Although every composition is motored by Holland's bass—notably the first track, "Triple Dance," which begins deceptively bare with bass, vibes, drums, and Smulyan's adroit baritone—the leader never features himself until the closer, "Shadow Dance," which is radically remade, and masterly from top to bottom. He ignites it with a dramatic, carefully paced Mingusian solo of a sort that few other bassists are likely to try or bring off. Hart takes up the baton on flute, and after a while the band announces itself with modestly punching chords, no more than that, and suddenly the horizon fills up with cavalry—it's only a matter of time before they charge down the hillside. *What Goes Around* was recorded in January 2001, and a second volume is already in the works. On the evidence of the new music heard at Birdland—including the impressionistic ballad, "A Rio" (impressive Mark Gross), and the contrapuntal fanfares and astonishing Holland display of "Happy Jammy" (the last movement from his "Monterey Suite")—this looks like the start of something big.

[*Village Voice*, 6 November 2002]

127 ❖ *Christmas Gilt (Ella Fitzgerald / Johnny Smith / Grant Green / Others)*

The annual profusion of Christmas albums suggests a bottomless appetite for the same dozen or 15 songs done in every conceivable fashion, and a hapless record industry eager to oblige. When in doubt, shake up the backlist, develop a seasonal pun, and leave the rest to nostalgia. It is often noted that most of the good American Christmas songs, beginning with Berlin's "White Christmas" (1942, not so very long ago) are by Jewish composers. They have secularized the revelry to the·point where even unlapsed Catholics must at times struggle to recall that all the fuss commemorates their Savior's birth and not merely ASCAP and BMI annuities involving sleigh bells, drummer boys, chipmunks, reindeer, chestnuts, Santa, Frosty, and, most crucially, snow—of which there was a dearth in Galilee. Why those songwriters could not bestir themselves to write a decent Hanukkah song is a mystery for the ages. Hath not a Jew snow, snowmen, bells, singing animals, Buddy Rich?

Secularist that I am, I don't need chain-rattling Marley to muster my belief in miracles, for example, the sound of Ella Fitzgerald's voice in 1960, when she recorded *Ella Wishes You a Swinging Christmas*, recently reissued by Verve. Her instrument was pearly—perhaps at its apogee—and her time, well, what is there left to say of her time, a musical Greenwich Mean? "Have Yourself a Merry Little Christmas" is near perfect, so near that for the duration of her vocal I am inclined to close the book on singers and concede that paradise is lost. This, of course, is the Blane and Martin song from *Meet Me in St. Louis*, sung by Judy Garland to her kid sister, who then beheads the family snowman. Yule—sorry—shed no tears during the Fitzgerald reading, which lopes along on a springy, bass-driven vamp that heightens the endearing melody while taking nothing from her translucent high notes, each glimmering with the twinkling of a sigh. If only arranger Frank DeVol hadn't settled for a dreary instrumental interlude—his accompaniment, by contrast, is deft and congenial—and had given her more room to embellish a final chorus.

The generally upbeat tempos, chosen to fulfill the promise of the title, rob Fitzgerald of the balladic expansiveness she might have used to light up some of these evergreens. Her "Winter Wonderland" is tossed off too casually, leaving the field to Doris Day, whose 1964 rendering remains one of the most improbably erotic records ever made (available on Day's anthology, *Personal Christmas Collection*). That Fitzgerald was encouraged to keep the album brisk is made clear by alternate takes, including a slow and dreamy version of "The Christmas Song" that thoroughly supersedes the one chosen for the original album. On the other hand, it was unnecessary to release the jokey, rightly rejected take of "Frosty the Snowman," sung in her 1930s' "My Wubber Dolly" voice; does cleaning out the vaults preclude all discrimination? The LP's ringer is "Good Morning Blues," introduced by Jimmy Rushing in Basie's band, and adapted by DeVol for a triple-meter backbeat arrangement not unlike Cannonball Adderley waltzes from the same period. Though never a great blues singer, Fitzgerald bedecks the familiar phrases with her golden-throat ornaments, making them merry and bright.

The real end-of-year musical bounty lies mostly in box sets, and this season is rife with surprises, among them surveys of two guitarists who might be considered diametric opposites beyond their comparative obscurity: Mosaic's *Complete Roost Johnny Smith Small Group Sessions* (mail-order only) and Blue Note's *Grant Green Retrospective 1961–66*. Jazz has not produced many one-hit wonders, but Smith sort of qualifies. He was a phenomenal technician who invented a tight style of voicing chords and advancing seamlessly from one to the next, producing a mobile sound that at times resembles harp, organ, and steel guitar as well as the six-string electric guitar he was actually playing. Born in Alabama, self-taught, and apprenticed in hillbilly bands, Smith enjoyed a tripartite career in jazz, classical music, and anonymous studio work. His primary success in the first came in the 1950s, triggered by his 1952 quintet recording of "Moonlight in Vermont," a minor pop hit and instant jazz classic, at least among guitarists, who twisted and spread-eagled their fingers trying to replicate his harmonies.

Forever associated with him, "Moonlight" holds up beautifully, as does the entire session, which produced a similarly conceived "Where or When"—in both instances, sideman Stan Getz offers obbligato, brief solos, and a taut unison blend—and startlingly speedy versions of "Tabu" and an original, "Jaguar," in which the meshed instruments and lively swing confirm Smith's new wrinkle in cool jazz. If developed, it might have had a more enduring impact. Smith never considered himself a jazz musician, but he was a masterly improviser, launching his solos with jetting arpeggios, coloring them with thin chime-like harmonics, and sustaining lucid percussive phrases—his forceful transformation of "Stranger in Paradise" is typical. Most of the eight discs are taken up by short quartet and trio numbers, yet beyond a few commercial misfires (a *Flower Drum Song* album), Smith rarely falls short, combining blunt variations and an alluring, encompassing sound.

By contrast, Grant Green was a strictly one-note-at-a-time linear player, a direct extension of Charlie Christian. During his major period, the 1960s, he was considered an anomaly for his directness and constancy in both conservative and modernistic settings. Born in St. Louis, tutored by his father (Green, like Johnny Smith, began playing professionally at 13), and groomed in r&b, blues, and organ groups, he perfected an unfeigned steely tone and saxophone-like legato fluency. At a time when jazz guitar was occupied with the wonders of Wes Montgomery's octaves, Jim Hall's lyricism, and the up-and-coming dynamism of George Benson and Pat Martino, Green's greatest virtues—his incisive clarity and blues-grounded simplicity—undermined his stature, as did Blue Note's occasional input of '60s pop tunes and, far worse, Verve's subsequent accent on broad funk. The four-disc *Retrospective*, though heavy on the organ years and not fully representative (only one track from his masterpiece, *Idle Moments*; compiler Michael Cuscuna may have assumed you've got that, as indeed you should), is an engrossing survey of Green at the center of Blue Note's stock company, which provided him with such sidemen as Joe Henderson, Booker Ervin, Ike Quebec, Hank Mobley, Wayne Shorter, and Sam Rivers, just to mention the tenors.

The key, short-lived founders of jazz guitar were also documented this year: Eddie Lang in Mosaic's wonderfully comprehensive eight-disc *Classic Columbia and OKeh Joe Venuti and Eddie Lang Sessions*, and Charlie Christian in Columbia/Legacy's four-disc *Charlie Christian: The Genius of the Electric Guitar*, which consists entirely of his work with Benny Goodman, whose name is inexplicably omitted from the amplifier-shaped box, as is an indexing of tracks from the 1941 jam session that culminated with "Blues in B." But it straightens out, at long last, the mess of alternate takes and even adds a few—in Christian's case, never a surplus. Both sets are essential. I'm not sure the same can be said for two more collector-oriented packages, proof that there will always be more Frank Sinatra and Miles Davis than Santa can keep up with.

Frank Sinatra in Hollywood (1940–1964), a collaboration between Turner Classic Movies and Reprise, is a six-disc survey of movie-town desiderata for completists who want not only the tracks he recorded for films, but also the outtakes, promotions, running tapes, Oscar speech (honorary, 1946, for *The House I Live In*), pro forma interview with Louella Parsons, and new mixes designed to make the songs sound more like records than movies. The stocking is stuffed with several songs dropped from films, including one recorded for the soundtrack of *Advise and Consent*, and a pairing with Maurice Chevalier in which Sinatra indulges in the sheer baritoneness of his voice while the French guy is encouraged to swing. It's a time capsule, handsomely done, the best of it emphasizing not least the expertness of Hollywood's sound engineers.

I have not yet worked my way through all 20 volumes of *The Complete Miles Davis at Montreux* (Warner Music/Switzerland), but I will: No collection of previously unknown material released this decade has given me more pleasure while forcing me to unclog hardened aesthetic arteries. It begins with the Pete Cosey band of 1973, skips to 1984, documenting every set through 1986, and resumes with the shorter appearances between 1988 and 1991. The performances are unedited, and part of the consuming joy—these are mostly joyous sets—is indicated in the interaction between Davis and the audiences he transported. In the late '80s, I commented on differences between Davis's frazzled concerts in New York and the exhilarating ones that followed a couple of weeks later at European festivals. Q.E.D. The summer Montreux concerts in the '80s reveal a variety of material, communal dedication, and total commitment by the leader—Davis is determinedly on. Even when he begins with kitschy synthesized voices (1988), he's just setting up a stirring revision of "In a Silent Way," his trumpet stout and daring, verging on ebullience when it isn't ripping knifelike through blues, as in the 1986 Jack Johnson medley. One piece bleeds into another, bearing tidings most of us never knew: July in Christmas.

[*Village Voice*, 4 December 2002]

128 ❖ *Jazzman of the Year: 2002 (Clark Terry)*

Dear CT,

It's that time of year again—holidays, wrap-ups, and your birthday, number 82 on December 14, which undoubtedly seems more incredible to observers like me than to you, living with courage and style, and still playing with a gleaming ingenuity that spits in the eye of mortal ailments. I believe in choosing one's own savior, and this year, like it or not, I choose you. You inspire me, emboldening me with the desire to embrace and hear music anew. Since your phoenix-like recovery from serial ills—one of the more astonishing and upbeat stories of the year— I've found myself thinking a lot about what you have meant and continue to mean to jazz.

To be honest, last winter I feared you had finally put the flugelhorn away for good. The daughter of your great friend and mighty trumpet player Jimmy Maxwell had called to say she had heard you were in troubled health and was worried. You may not know that she and I were in college together. In fact, the first time I caught you live was when the Clark Terry–Bob Brookmeyer Quintet, or a version thereof, came to Grinnell, Iowa, during our freshman year. Anne later told me that until that evening (given the excited conversation that anticipated and followed it), she didn't realize that her father was famous or that you are one of the jazz gods. Of course, your casually infallible technique and comic esprit sometimes suggest that you don't know it either—but then true modesty is often inherent in true wit. I've never forgotten a moment that occurred after the concert, when the musicians were packing up. You and Bob had brought a pickup trio from Chicago, and they did their best. Right before leaving the stage, you walked over to the pianist, shook his hand with a wide smile, and said, "Don't think it hasn't been a gas just because it hasn't."

Maxwell passed on a few months ago—as you know, he'd been suffering a long time. But I cannot think of a more remarkable recoup than your appearance last summer with Jon Faddis's much lamented Carnegie Hall Jazz Band. When you were helped onto the stage and got a big laugh with your punchline ("The golden years suck!"), I thought: The last thing I want to hear is Clark Terry in less than sterling form. Not that it wasn't a joy to see you, but for some dumb reason I presumed that a weakness in your legs somehow connected to your embouchure. Well, holy Moses, man, when you started playing, my jaw hit my lap—I mean, you sounded as only Clark Terry can sound, every note robust, beaming, and shadowed with impish resolve and irony, the phrases whiplashing through the changes with the requisite trademark Terrytoons, floating on a raft of confidence. I had heard from Dan Morgenstern (remember his *Down Beat* essay, "Why Is This Man So Happy?"—it came out the same time as the Grinnell concert) that you played superbly at the Eddie Bert tribute weeks before, but if I hadn't seen you with Faddis and, months later, at the Fats Navarro memorial show, pressing half a dozen younger trumpet virtuosos to the wall (followed by a week at the Vanguard and last week's tribute to you at the Blue Note), I wouldn't have believed it possible that you are playing as well as ever. You are, after all, a beloved figure, and that induces a certain amount of sentimental forgiveness. None was needed.

A friend recently noted that you are the last of the major, unmistakable Ellingtonians. In truth, you are one of the last of the unmistakables, period. No one's likely to be fooled by you in a blindfold test: two bars and you know it's CT and that you're going to hear something good. As Benny Carter once said of Ben Webster, one can immediately tell "who it is and who he is." I've always wondered how you came to develop that distinctive, chortling style. On early records (with Basie, Barnett, and Dinah, and even in the beginning of your near-decade with Duke), it is not completely there. With hindsight, one hears the characteristic feints, the dramatically launched high notes, the terse, bent tones that round the corner from one note to the next like a motorcycle zooming around a curve—but not the full revelation of personality. It's certainly there by the late '50s, though, when you recorded with Monk. The brass radiance that so inspired your fellow St. Louisan Miles Davis suddenly takes on a three-dimensional disposition. Ellington definitely had your number when he cast you as Puck in *Such Sweet Thunder*. But you created your own alter ego on the first album with Oscar Peterson: the irrepressible, sometimes doddering, always mischievous vocalist, Mumbles. Incidentally, you must be one of the very few beings in music about which Monk and Peterson agreed.

And why not? The main thing you brought to jazz in the '60s was an ebullient style beyond style, beyond category, beyond definition (my God, you even cut a track with Cecil Taylor)—not bop or swing or mainstream or avant-garde, yet embraced by musicians across the board. Another thing you brought was the flugelhorn. Others had played it, notably Shorty Rogers, but in the mid-'50s you put it on the map and made it stick—eventually working up those inimitable solo duets, trumpet in one hand, flugel in the other. I guess 1964 was your breakthrough year: After being everyone's preferred sideman for more than two decades, you moved to the front. (Is that what you had in mind, in 1957, when you wrote "Serenade to a Bus Seat"?) Many fans probably don't recall Johnny Carson's role, and the part you played in breaking the color bar in New York's studio system. There you were, the first black player in the NBC studio orchestra, sitting in the *Tonight* band, and every time you were given a feature, which was pretty often, music lovers around the country asked, Who is this guy? At the same time, you were taking honors in Gerry Mulligan's Concert Jazz Band and filling the Half

Note with Brookmeyer. Inevitably, even record labels began to pay attention.

I've looked up the 1964 sessions. First you made *The Happy Horns*, on Impulse, a strutting sextet with Ben Webster and Phil Woods that included Bob Hammer's mini-suite arrangement of Bix's "In a Mist"; then came *Oscar Peterson Trio+One Clark Terry*, for Mercury, on which you debuted (spontaneously, at session's end) the Mumbles routine you had tested in clubs, and proved with a particular decisiveness—the theme statement on "Brotherhood of Man" alone would have done the trick— that you didn't sound like anyone else ever. Finally, for Mainstream, you recorded *Tonight*, the long-delayed debut album by the quintet, a perfect blend of Brookmeyer's light-gutbucket writing and your elfin, soaring variations. "Tete a Tete" has a quintessential rollicking CT solo, much as "Pretty Girl" opens with an archetypal ballad figure and "Hum" ends with a patented chortle. Your attack was so unambiguously original that the tunes echoed it; Roger Kellaway may have written "Step Right Up," but with your phrasing how could it sound like anything but Clark Terry? The same is no less true of Parker's "The Hymn" and Monk's "Straight No Chaser," to which you guys added a rather pointed tremolo. I get chills listening to your "Battle Hymn of the Republic" solo, on the quintet's second album—and, come to think of it, dizzy just thinking about the 1975 "Shaw Nuff" duet with Oscar, which must have set some kind of speed record.

Maybe nothing you've done was more quixotically impressive than leaving *The Tonight Show* in 1972 to launch your own Big B-A-D Band, an 18-piece, mostly all-star orchestra, which, it occurs to me now, may have offered Jimmy Heath his first opportunity to record his big band arrangements in a book that also included such durable charts as Woods's treatment of "Nefertiti." It's hard to believe that you toured with a band that had such talent as Duke Jordan on piano, and a reed section with Heath, Woods, Arnie Lawrence, Ernie Wilkins, and Charles Davis. Yet given your nerve, who could say no? Many indelible moments followed, including countless jam session appearances and weeklong gigs by your lustrous quintet of the past decade. Two recordings stand out for me: your sensitive support on Abbey Lincoln's 1990 *The World Is Falling Down*, and *One on One*, the magnificent piano duets you recorded for Chesky two years ago.

Clark, this has been another baleful year for jazz, with almost every week bringing news of another passing. And this is the season when we'll remember Peggy Lee, Walter Bolden, Wendell Marshall, Nick Brignola, Conte Candoli, Remo Palmier, Oliver Johnson, Shirley Scott, John Patton, Eileen Farrell, Buster Brown, Otis Blackwell, Truck Parham, Matt

Dennis, Curtis Amy, Russ Freeman, Nellie Monk, Rosemary Clooney, Ray Brown, Alan Lomax, Seymour Solomon, Edmund Anderson, Jimmy Maxwell, Phyllis Litoff, Roy Krall, Daphne Hellman, Idrees Sulieman, Larry Rivers, Lionel Hampton, Dodo Marmarosa, Peter Kowald, Ellis Larkins, Turk Van Lake, Eileen Southern, John S. Wilson, Adolph Green, Tom Dowd, Roland Hanna, Nancie Banks, Hadda Brooks, Mal Waldron, Bob Berg, Dolly Dawn, Arvell Shaw, and many others.

So my wish for you on this birthday and every one to follow is good health, good chops, and a full dose of the joy you have given the rest of us all these years. In the preceding century, jazz used to proclaim a succession of trumpet players as king. Right now, that's you—may your reign continue to flourish.

Warmest regards.

[*Village Voice*, 18 December 2002]

129 ❖ *Everything That Rises Must Converge (The Best Jazz Records of 2002)*

As the wheels of Capital grind remorselessly to the tune of impossible profit projections, jazz grows increasingly irrelevant to the dominant record labels. Atlantic vanished; Columbia recycled Miles; Concord Jazz did singers; BMG and Warner hardly mattered; and even Verve tightened the noose. Blue Note kept the faith, revived by the improbable triumph of Norah Jones in a non-jazz setting. Yet good jazz records proliferated, some better than good, and often on labels like Palmetto, Justin Time, Pi, Aum Fidelity, and others yet more obscure. Something like consensus coalesced around half a dozen titles. One dares to imagine the divided jazz tribes rising above ever-thinner layers of air to converge. For example, if the audience for *Bob's Pink Cadillac* were also to buy *The Music of Bob Haggart*, and vice versa, two little tribes might surprise themselves and turn into one with clout. Shhhhh—let me dream, albeit alphabetically. Five entries are asterisked: CDs that, like it or not, you must hear.

1. David Berkman, *Leaving Home* (Palmetto). Chris Cheek's take on Wayne Shorter underscores the Shorter-esque feeling of Berkman's writing on the title tune, yet the entire session—the sextet's third outing—resonates with understated clarity and deliberation, quickened by Brian Blade's drums.

*2. Arthur Blythe, *Focus* (Savant). In his most electrifying recording in a decade, the altoist's huge, ribald sound leaps out with renewed authority and abiding humor in the spectacularly empathic setting of marimba, tuba, and drums. "C.C. Rider" is the year's jazz rocker, but every track swaggers.

3. Ruby Braff, *Variety Is the Spice of Braff* (Arbors Jazz). The big band is better than the strings, but the latter inspire Braff—he sounds like an old friend whispering in your ear. On a highly imaginative "There's a Small Hotel," he reminisces about Bobby Hackett as only another original can, but it's pure Ruby from then on.

4. Dee Dee Bridgewater, *This Is New* (Verve). The Weill songbook, but not the faded Weill of Weimar cabaret. Pushing her vibrato, she weds theatrical flair, improvisational brio, and sexual provacateuring ("I'm a Stranger Here Myself") to take this repertoire in hand. "Bilbao Song" is vitalized, "Alabama Song" is as ham-on-wry hilarious as the composer intended, and "Poor Jenny" really struts her stuff. A parody/breakdown of "Mack the Knife" follows a minute of silence on the last track.

5. Bill Charlap, *Stardust* (Blue Note). "Jubilee" is a brilliant kick-off for an album with splendid contributions by Tony Bennett, Frank Wess, Jim Hall, and Shirley Horn, though the main attraction is the tight-as-a-fist trio—you may wonder who's leading whom through the darkest "Georgia on My Mind" since Ray Charles.

6. Von Freeman, *The Improviser* (Premonition). Life begins at 80. The tracks were culled from concerts, and the first is an unaccompanied ballad on which Freeman produces Rollins-like centered pitch. Three pieces with guitar trio and two with Jason Moran (quirkily whimsical on an "After Hours" blues) include breakneck "How High the Moon" variations ("Ski-wee") and a dreamy "Blue Bossa" that conveys the contorted melancholy of Albert Ayler.

7. Andrew Hill, *A Beautiful Day* (Palmetto). First listen for the plot, then go back for the nuances that animate the change-ups, as from the lowering clouds of "The New Pinocchio" to the swing-to-free acuity of "J Di." This is Hill's big band, recorded at Birdland, and more impressive than *Dusk* in its candid lyricism (especially the title piece, which cuts the sweetness of a tune verging on sentimental), disciplined solos (Marty Ehrlich is inspired on "Faded Beauty"), and shifting tonal centers. As ever, the pianist is stark and sure.

8. Dave Holland, *What Goes Around* (ECM). The other big band that recorded at Birdland, though this debut is a studio session. The voicings are bright as day and the solos damn near impeccable—Gary Smulyan's opening melody sticks in the brain. Holland's orchestra is built on the

foundation of his quintet, and he employs it strategically, allowing individual players breathing space while pumping up the ensemble, as in "Blues for C.M.," here rendered with a definitive luster.

9. Bireli Lagrene, *Gypsy Project* (Dreyfus Jazz). The recent *Gypsy Project & Friends* has more virtuoso éclat, but the sometimes plodding rhythm guitars are over-recorded, while the earlier album is leaner and more diverse—totally Django and yet a great modern guitar album.

10. Misha Mengelberg, *Four in One* (Songlines). Many soloists work better as sidemen than on their own sessions—Dave Douglas's muted, skittering phrases throughout this lively session contain some of his best work since Tiny Bell. His bee-loud trumpet buzzes through the first track, a "Freedom Jazz Dance" meets "Hot House" pastiche. Mengelberg's piano responds in kind and plies Monkian wit on a Monk triptych.

11. Mulgrew Miller, *The Sequel* (Maxjazz). Don't be put off by the high soprano-trumpet-vibes voicings or the disarming familiarity and relaxed ambience. Miller's tunes are shrewdly crafted to put his players in a groove. Subtle in design, they provoke subtle responses, including his own. Notwithstanding a tremolo habit, he never settles for rote phrases on "It Never Entered My Mind," and his lyricism fuels originals like "Holding Hands" and a deft reworking of "Dreamsville."

12. Roscoe Mitchell, *Song for My Sister* (Pi). The title track is the best hard bop tune in years—the kind of piece you think you've heard before, but would never connect with Mitchell, who solos politely at the end. Yet trust him, with his double rhythm section, to push other buttons as well, and remember that if you find it chilly at one point, the weather will shift before you have time to grab a sweater.

*13. Jason Moran, *Modernistic* (Blue Note). Jazz is not dead. Here's proof—a young pianist's first solo recital, with overdubs, tapes, a toy keyboard, and a repertory from stride to hip-hop, all undertaken with contagious invention. And the main thing is: there's no self-congratulatory cleverness, not to "Body and Soul" without the bridge, Schumann lieder with improvised variations, or conversations-with-himself on "Planet Rock."

14. William Parker, *Bob's Pink Cadillac* (Eremite). The bassist calls this his Clarinet Trio, and it may be the best record Perry Robinson has ever made—his sound liquid, his disposition relaxed yet buoyant. And what a kick to hear the veteran drummer Walter Perkins, who backed Roland Kirk so unforgettably on *I Talk with the Spirits*. The first disc was made in the studio, the second live at Tonic, where from the moment Robinson enters on a continuous five-part suite, Parker alights with Mingusian might.

15. Randy Sandke, *The Music of Bob Haggart* (Arbors Jazz). A coup for jazz rep. In 1958, Haggart arranged a Bob Crosby album released as *Porgy and Bess as Gershwin Would Have Liked It*. Especially with Gil and Miles on the case, no one took Crosby seriously, and Crosby didn't take the arranger seriously enough—Haggart was unidentified on the LP that he later declared his finest work. I've never heard that album, but the playing can't have been more ebullient than that of Sandke's crew. Lucid harmonies and polyphonic embellishments—Dixie-swing reborn.

16. Matthew Shipp, *Songs* (Splasc[h]). A highly personal hybridization of pop, jazz, and hymns treated with Calvinistic fury and heavy foot pedal. Bounding over genre lines, Shipp fractures each piece just enough to pull the cork and set free a world of secret spirits—"Con Alma" is one startling example, but the whole album unwinds in a combination of indignant passion and plainsong beauty.

*17. Wayne Shorter, *Footprints Live!* (Verve). Quartet music with a textural and compositional range that makes each measure count. Shorter is always front and center—it's his music, affect, tempo, respect for space—yet the solos are less exacting than the way the four men respond to each other and the moment. At least that's what I think now—every time I play it, I hear it differently. The only constant is that Shorter makes the tenor sound like breathing.

*18. Cecil Taylor, *The Willisau Concert* (Intakt). A magnificent solo tour de force (perhaps his best on records), and if I had to choose one, this would be my album of the year. Everyone for whom I've played the opening passage is instantly seduced. Unfortunately, not everyone wants to follow a 50-minute movement. Think of it, then, as a short opera, its variations coherent, broadly romantic, and often overwhelming.

*19. David S. Ware, *Freedom Suite* (Aum Fidelity). Doubling the length of Sonny Rollins's 1958 trio opus, and parsing the four themes into discrete movements, Ware has reconceived the piece as Rollins's *A Love Supreme*—even to its length, still a mere 39 minutes. The quartet is as tight as ever, but this is the leader's showcase, and though his style is obviously his own, he plays with a grace and well-being that invoke the composer's.

20. Cassandra Wilson, *Belly of the Sun* (Blue Note). After not hearing it for several months, I had forgotten how much fun it is, how original and varied, funny and melancholy.

[*Village Voice*, 8 January 2003]

130 ❖ Hot
(Louis Armstrong)

1. The Complete Hot Five & Hot Seven Recordings, Vol. 1

If Louis Armstrong had never lived, the world would be a different place—as radically different as if, say, Archduke Ferdinand hadn't been assassinated or the United States hadn't unleashed nuclear weaponry. In recounting those who shaped history, we invariably focus on conquerors or politicians. But cultural heroes also define our lives. Born to severe poverty in New Orleans, in 1901, and armed only with his cornet, voice, and personality, Armstrong conquered American music, erecting the foundation for the prevailing music of the last century.

Before Armstrong, jazz was perceived as a clamorous urban folk music, wedded to duple rhythms that had more in common with parade bands and African polyrhythms than the clear-sailing of what we call swing. It was a social music that favored collective embellishment over solitary virtuosity. To many, it wasn't an art at all, only a resource from which "legit" composers might borrow a thumping beat (as in *Rite of Spring*) or a blue note (as in *Rhapsody in Blue*). Jazz would surely have developed eminent soloists without Armstrong (it already had in Sidney Bechet), but its progress as an art in its own right would have been slow and chaotic. Armstrong was the visionary who grounded jazz as the music of a new world. In his hands, it became a calling of unlimited potential and universal appeal.

It was Armstrong who established blues tonality as jazz's harmonic bedrock at a time when many gifted musicians wondered whether the blues might be a mere vogue destined to fade away. He proved that pop songs did not weaken jazz, but rather broadened its possibilities; that a bold vibrato did not signal vulgarity, but rather a lively radiance that even symphony orchestras would soon adapt. With his love of comedy and lack of pretension, he helped erase hardened distinctions between high and low, serious and popular art. His gravelly, exuberant singing liberated America's vernacular voice. Above all, he taught the whole world to swing, instilling a new rhythmic tilt in body and soul. Without him, the Swing Era, modern jazz, mainstream pop, r&b, and rock and roll—assuming they came to pass at all—would be so changed as to be unrecognizable.

Armstrong broke down doors previously closed to African Americans, turned old minstrel stereotypes inside out, altered the thinking of millions of skeptical and downright racist whites and cultural mandarins. The jurist Charles Black has written of how his segregationist upbringing was undermined during a boyhood evening in Texas, when he saw Armstrong perform; Black went on to help litigate *Brown v. Board of Education*. Armstrong's impact on the integration of radio, film, TV, Southern theaters, and other aspects of American life is as immeasurable as the enduring genius of his music.

The quintessence of his early genius is crystallized in the three volumes of this series, which collects more than five-dozen selections made for OKeh Records between 1925 and 1928, by Armstrong units generally known as the Hot Five and Hot Seven. Classics do not wear out their welcome, certainly not these classics; the more you listen, the more ways you hear. As a personal example, I offer "You're Next," a track I'd previously neglected. Lil Hardin (Louis's wife at the time) channels her Fisk University classical studies for a delightfully inapposite intro that becomes the vamp from which Louis launches one of his great groove tunes, swinging deep and foreshadowing more accomplished works, like "Tight Like This." It has the savoir-faire of a very cool high: no pyrotechnics, just absolute command, as he plays the head with shapely understated flourishes, transforming the lineaments of melancholy into an insouciant meditation.

Armstrong was 24 when he inaugurated the Hot Fives and had been heard on records as a sideman for two years, from the time his idol, King Oliver, lured him to Chicago to play second trumpet with the Creole Jazz Band. In New York, in 1924, he worked with Fletcher Henderson's orchestra; backed such divas as Ma Rainey, Bessie Smith, and Sippie Wallace; and traded hot licks with Sidney Bechet on records organized by Clarence Williams. Returning to Chicago a year later, he was offered the chance to record as a leader, surrounded by hometown elders. Like Lil, Johnny Dodds and Johnny St. Cyr had worked in Oliver's band alongside Louis, who had previously played with Kid Ory—at 39, the old man in the group—in New Orleans.

The first session, in late 1925, begins almost shyly with Lil's "My Heart": Dodds is ornamental and stodgy, Lil rushes the tempo, and while Louis's breaks, two-note rip, and powerful lead are impressive, the record has neither the pneumatic complexity of Oliver's best records or the searing excitement of his own work with Bechet. "Yes! I'm in the Barrel," with its steady syncopated riff, allows him to expand (he builds to a lovely high note midway through his 16-bar solo), and Dodds has two solid blues choruses, but, yes, they're in the barrel, simmering and restrained. With "Gut Bucket Blues," however, Armstrong's self-confidence comes to the fore as he introduces the musicians and plays an elegantly intoned blues chorus; note how he echoes the dip in Ory's preceding solo.

When they resumed in February 1926, the band produced only one usable track, "Come Back, Sweet Papa," which starts like a lamb (Dodds plays the period melody on alto) and goes out like a lion, after Louis and Ory enter, injecting the element of swing along with breaks, riffs, growls, and slides. Another session, four days later, was more productive. "Georgia Grind," with Lil yelping the theme and her man responding, has little interest beyond an early display of Louis's blues singing (Ellington recorded the song days later), but "Heebie Jeebies" remains a benchmark. The tune was nothing much, a dance vogue adapted, oddly enough, from the B-strain of the Chauvin-Joplin rag, "Heliotrope Bouquet." Yet it put the Hot Five on the map, popularizing the New Orleans tradition of scat singing. Before he recorded as a leader, Armstrong had not been encouraged to sing, let alone scat—Fletcher Henderson had reluctantly permitted him one brief scat break on "Everybody Loves My Baby." Which may be why a balmy myth arose. It was said that the sheet music fell and that Louis scatted to save the take—an event the record itself disputes. His vocal spread among musicians like the Chicago fire.

While "Heebie Jeebies" encouraged singers to catch cold so that they could growl like Louis, "Cornet Chop Suey" had trumpet players striving for better health to emulate his virtuosity on brass. For all the bedazzling intensity of his 16-bar stop-time variation and lead work, there is also a charming rhythmic poise; he pushes the melody, but lets it sing, too. He similarly soars on "Oriental Strut." Despite the occasional cracked note, he's in total command, cushy and fat in every part of his range, merrily abandoning the quaint Tin Pan Asian strut to the alley where it belongs. "Muskrat Ramble" immediately became a jazz standard, more celebrated as a tune than for the run of solos—Armstrong is said to have written it, but Ory got the copyright.

The often-overlooked June 16 session shows the unit navigating between the revolutionary jazz it was inventing and coexistent pop. "Don't Forget to Mess Around" exploits the Charleston craze (its patented stop-time lick is sewn into the theme). Dodds solos on alto and clarinet, and Louis sings and leads the buoyant finale. "I'm Gonna Gitcha," with its 30-bar theme credited to Lil, prefigures by two decades Thelonious Monk's "Criss Cross"; each has a six-bar middle part that precipitously caroms into the final eight-bar section, keeping everyone alert. Too bad Armstrong permitted himself only a half-chorus on trumpet (replete with trademark phrases), presumably because he sings a full one that gets pretty wild. He also sings "Dropping Shucks," and drives the ensemble through a theme that briefly shines light on St. Cyr's banjo. "Who'sit," a true anomaly, begins with a musty trombone chorus, and then treads water with Louis's slide whistle. Maybe this was his response to the era's whistling vogue—Al Jolson and Morton Downey were famous for it, and Bing Crosby would take it up a notch a year later. French critic Hugues Panassié called "Who'sit" the weakest of the Hot Fives; yet heard in the right spirit, it has its moments—especially that long note with which Louis spirits the ensemble thru the final eight bars.

For sheer unpredictability, however, not much can compare with the first selection from June 23. "King of the Zulus" begins in Mardi Gras parade mode (the title refers to the Zulu Aid and Pleasure Club, which crowned Louis as king during the 1949 celebration), governed by an intriguing rhythm made up of sustained notes and three-beat rests. Ory enters with a moribund trombone passage against a three-beat riff (the play of three beats against four was a favorite strategy of young Louis) and is interrupted by one Clarence Babcock, who, affecting a Jamaican accent, demands a serving of chit'lins. Lil accommodates him, and the band proceeds. By this point, you may think you've stepped into a bad vaudeville act, but now comes Mr. Armstrong playing a full 32-bar chorus with a bluesy serenity and ingenuity that eclipses just about everything he had recorded to date; halfway, he launches a four-bar note, followed by a rip, before bringing the solo to ground. St. Cyr follows, breaking up the rhythm with arpeggios, until Louis returns to take the ensemble out in a blaze of glory—a thin joke turned into a masterpiece.

The rest of the session is anticlimactic. The mysterious Babcock, in his own voice, presides over a kind of square dance in "Big Fat Pa and Skinny Ma," which has a sweet-natured Dixieland theme. The ponderous "Lonesome Blues" is strange for having no trumpet until the end—it's mostly Dodds, unaccountably whiny at first, and an Armstrong vocal. "Sweet Little Papa" is the reverse, a cheerful piece, with Louis taking the first in a series of breaks and offering an uncharacteristic trumpet snarl.

The second half of the frisky November 16 session involved vocalist May Alix, but the first half offered the ensemble two singular selections. The upbeat "Jada"-type theme of "Jazz Lips" is given a touch-and-go punch by one-bar exchanges between Louis (supported by Dodds) and the group. His hilarious mouse-squeal high-notes precede an episode that suggests a classroom of kids, each trying to have his say, until Louis drives the ensemble home. "Skid-Dat-De-Dat" begins dark blue, and though the spirit revs up, the piece continues down and dirty, suiting Dodds's middle register and Louis's aggressive scat exchanges, which augur "Hotter Than That" and "West End Blues." A recurring four-bar theme binds the drama, as does Louis's concise and sure tone.

The famous stage-boast of Al Jolson, America's most popular entertainer when these records were made, provides a perfect set-up for volume two: "You ain't heard nothin' yet."

2. The Complete Hot Five & Hot Seven Recordings, Vol. 2

By 1927, when all but the first four selections on this volume were made, Louis Armstrong's records had attained real commercial viability. "Heebie Jeebies" had sold 40,000 copies, and the growing jazz audience now paid attention to each new release. In an era when million sellers were not uncommon, OKeh's sales were hardly earth shaking, but they suggested momentum beyond the confines of a cult music, especially given the absence of touring and live performances. Unlike almost every other major band in American music, these groups existed only to record. The Hot Five appeared before an audience just once, on June 12, 1926, at OKeh's "Cabaret and Style Show," a benefit for the black local of the Chicago musician's union. A *Chicago Defender* review and an OKeh ad for "Cornet Chop Suey" identified Armstrong as "the sensation" of that show. But he made his living as featured soloist in pit bands and floorshows, and some of these records reflect routines he polished before live audiences.

Despite their incalculable influence, little is known for certain about how the Fives came about. Was the instigator E. A. Fearn, head of OKeh's Chicago branch, or the ambitious Lil Hardin Armstrong, or OKeh's black recording director, pianist Richard M. Jones? Armstrong's most eloquent critic, Dan Morgenstern, opts for Jones; he notes that Louis could not have arrived in Chicago before November 4, 1925 (he recorded in New York on the 2nd), and was in OKeh's Chicago studio within five days (the 9th), backing singers alongside Jones. Two days later, Jones hired him as a leader for the first time, to accompany Hociel Thomas with a band that included Johnny Dodds and Johnny St. Cyr. Morgenstern continues: "On the NEXT DAY, the Hot Five make their first date. I don't need to point out that the presence of Dodds and St. Cyr on the previous day has got to be more than mere coincidence! And I'm almost certain that Jones was if not the mastermind then at least the facilitator."

By late 1926, however, other hands were involved, as becomes evident as we resume with the November 16 session. Armstrong was now performing at the Sunset Cafe, where Percy Venable staged the floorshows and created a couple of numbers for Louis and singer-dancer May Alix, which were quickly recorded. Given Alix's shrill vocals, they may seem mixed blessings, yet they endure as Armstrong landmarks. "Big Butter and Egg Man" has a flawless cornet solo (listen to how he develops the first phrase three times and that midway alarum), while "Sunset Cafe

Stomp" affirms his sublime poise with an apparently effortless brew of melodic logic, improvisational brio, and titanic swing. On November 27, Armstrong was sole entertainer on two more Venable numbers. "You Made Me Love You" (not to be confused with the Jolson hit) gets underway with a moaning Kid Ory and sanguine Johnny Dodds, only to be blown from its moorings by Louis's tempestuous vocal. His more serene cornet solo, which is no less robust, begins a measure early (a frequent ploy, as though he can't wait to get going) and unfolds with an intensifying riff and high-note break. By contrast, the winning "Irish Black Bottom" is rowdy farce, interpolating "When Irish Eyes Are Smiling" and "Black Bottom," as Louis claims Irish ancestry ("ha ha!—so imagine how I feel").

Then six months pass. OKeh had been taken over by Columbia Records—Richard M. Jones was out and a brash young Irish promoter, Tommy Rockwell, replaced him. At the same time, great strides had been made in electrical recording, encouraging Rockwell and Armstrong to try for a more opulent sound, beefed up by drums and tuba. At five sessions recorded in May 1927, the Hot Seven came to life to create 11 outstanding numbers, and then disappeared. Baby Dodds and Pete Briggs were the newcomers, along with John Thomas, who replaced Ory. At these sessions Armstrong retired the cornet once and for all in favor of trumpet.

The four-bar intro to "Willie the Weeper" ends with Baby's cymbals, letting you know right off that this is something new. The front line, brimming with enthusiasm, parts for a solid trombone solo (the little-remembered Thomas acquitted himself handsomely on these sides, especially here), followed by a magnificent Johnny Dodds chorus (his finest to date), a brief call from the leader interrupted by Lil Hardin, and a memorable guitar statement by Johnny St. Cyr. Then Pops goes to town with Baby slashing the cymbals and Briggs's tuba buoying him every step. Less an Armstrong outing than a collective ensemble shout, with each player responding instantly to Louis's perched high-notes and cunning pauses, this could be the greatest Dixieland record ever made.

Jelly Roll Morton's "Wild Man Blues" compresses that excitement in a superbly modulated blues, each phrase ending with a break that ranges from hoochie-coochie sensuousness to extravagant virtuosity. At once dazzling and moving, Louis rivets attention. Once again, Dodds is inspired—especially the closing episode of his stop-time chorus. Yet Armstrong functions on another level entirely. Musicians shook their heads in wonder when they heard this record in 1927, and still do: Who today improvises with as much force, economy, wit, and imagination?

"Chicago Breakdown," recorded two days later, gets in on a pass, since it's really a Hot Eleven—basically, the Carroll Dickerson band from the Sunset Cafe, which allows us an early glimpse of pianist Earl Hines (with whom Louis would achieve a new Nirvana in 1928), though Columbia didn't release it until 1940. Boyd Atkins (who co-wrote "Heebie Jeebies") is heard on soprano sax, Hines deconstructs time, and Louis stops it altogether. The Seven regrouped the next day for Fats Waller's "Alligator Crawl," which opens and closes as a blues yet makes room for an elaborate Armstrong solo on a different set of chord changes; and the irresistible "Potato Head Blues," with its abiding ensemble work (Dodds shadows and echoes Louis's melodic feints), a walloping theme, and kick-out-the-jams solos. A banjo transition starts Louis on his most daunting stop-time gambit yet, each phrase unfolding with infallible judgment, building to an ecstatic ride-out. After listening to this masterwork in the '50s, Miles Davis observed, "You know you can't play anything on a horn that Louis hasn't played—I mean even modern."

"Melancholy," which recalls "I Ain't Got Nobody" and was later outfitted with lyrics in its own right (as "St. Louis Street Blues"), boasts one of Armstrong's loveliest theme statements from this period, his timbre warm yet intense. He's melancholy only in the way great gospel is. Dodds's lower register shines on "Weary Blues," but Louis executes a flawed arpeggio that lands him in strangely high terrain from which he conjures a dynamic return. The arrangement of the generic warhorse, "Twelfth Street Rag," is fairly standard, yet Louis thoroughly refashions it with his first rip, toying with it like a cat with a ball of string.

"Keyhole Blues" is relatively ordinary, the highlights being Louis's riffing scat vocal and his risky high-note trumpet break. "S.O.L. Blues" was rerecorded the next day as "Gully Low Blues," and canned until 1940. Legend says that Columbia rejected it because of risqué lyrics and the shit-out-of-luck title, but titles can be changed and the words are rather tame. Louis's solo introduces the fierce descending arpeggios that he would later perfect in "West End Blues"—the solo is etched with greater finesse on the superior "Gully Low" remake, which permits him a second vocal chorus, too. "That's When I'll Come Back to You" is a damning portrait of marital hell, deriving a certain poignancy from the knowledge that Louis and Lil would soon divorce. Her part, stoutly sung, is violently self-abasing; his exudes an equally violent contempt.

After the final Hot Seven session, Armstrong didn't record for nearly four months, and then he reconvened the original Hot Five. "Put 'Em Down Blues" is not a blues; indeed, it's an ornate 48-bar song that Louis sings and plays for an uptempo and much-underrated tour de force. "Ory's Creole Trombone," another track suppressed until 1940, may have been rejected for being so candidly old-fashioned—Ory had recorded it in 1922, and his tailgate trombone breaks had seriously dated in five years; also, the ride-out is clumsy. Yet it's a fascinating example of how things had changed, at times suggesting the dialogue between a patriarch and his impetuous son. "The Last Time" is of interest for the vocal, which shows Louis gaining control of pop material. Armstrong was probably suffering embouchure trouble because he didn't record again for another three months.

He returned breathing fire. "Struttin' with Some Barbecue" is possibly the most famous of all the Hot Fives, and for good reason. The glorious theme, with its unusual use of a minor seventh, became an instant classic, as did Louis's widely imitated solo. The group is absolutely primed, with Ory and Dodds twining through Louis's lead at the pinnacle of their New Orleans game. The stop-time trumpet episode, despite a couple of cracked notes, is ravishing, blinding—a peerless example of improvised bravura melody. "Got No Blues," like it says, is no blues, but it has Armstrong's rugged lead, another stop-time extravaganza, and a yeoman attempt by him to straighten out a faltering last chorus. We end this volume with the first of two pieces recorded the next day, "Once in a While"—high-note breaks, stop-time episode, and a surprise (almost Haydenesque) ensemble-chord before the clarinet solo.

But wait: Armstrong was on an ascending arc, and he's about to take his music to still grander heights.

3. *The Complete Hot Five & Hot Seven Recordings, Vol. 3*

The journey Louis Armstrong traveled between late 1925 and late 1928, as documented in this three-volume series, now reaches its final stage, accelerated by the input of three powerful talents, all of whom absorbed Armstrong's influence and then challenged him with what they made of it: Lonnie Johnson, Earl Hines, and Don Redman.

"I'm Not Rough," the second tune recorded at the December 10, 1927, session, was the first of three for which Armstrong recruited Johnson, who went on to enjoy a trifecta of careers (1920s jazz guitarist, 1940s r&b star, 1950s bluesman). Johnson's striking chorus opened his own portal into the future; it is played almost entirely in triplets, a rhythmic conceit that would become pandemic during the genesis of rock and roll. He is the sole accompanist to Armstrong's memorable vocal, and an ideal partner during the trumpet solo, bearing down with fourth-beat accents. "Hotter Than That," based on a strain of the New Orleans anthem, "Tiger Rag," is a succession of marvels, including one of Armstrong's best-ever scat solos, with its devious cross-rhythms beginning at bar 16; an

Armstrong-Johnson dialogue; and Louis's break and solo, culminating with 12 high-Cs parsed over seven bars.

Johnson replaced Johnny St. Cyr on those two numbers, but both men are present on "Savoy Blues," a lesson in rhythm. It begins with a zany oom-pah figure, accenting first and third beats and suggesting a countryish air emphasized by Louis's opening solo and the commiserating ensemble. Then Johnson plays a four-bar transition, changing the time to a jazzy four and triggering an episode by the two guitarists that has the effect of crossing a period blues record with a cutting-edge jazz disc. Enter Armstrong, so harmoniously you want to hug him, understated and lyrical through two blessed choruses (as the guitarists come down hard on the two and four). Ory's trombone slide guides the ensemble chorus, and the captain steers the ride-out with the stamping swing he virtually invented.

The December 13 session was at once a pinnacle for the old Hot Five and a harbinger of the radically remodeled one to come, after an absence of six months. By June 1928, the New Orleans clique had been dispersed; the new Hot Five, with six musicians, was drawn entirely from the Carroll Dickerson band with which Armstrong appeared nightly. Trombonist Fred Robinson, a workmanlike musician by the standards Jack Teagarden and Jimmy Harrison forged for the instrument, played with a clarity that kept him working through the swing era. The often harsh-sounding clarinetist Jimmy Strong was no Johnny Dodds, but proved adequate for an ensemble that usually rejected polyphony. Mancy Cara (or Carr) deftly handled the banjo, which was subordinate to the drumming of Zutty Singleton, a veteran of New Orleans bands who proved sufficiently flexible to enjoy a vital career until 1969, when a stroke retired him.

Most important, Armstrong installed the ingenious Earl Hines on piano. Born in 1903, in Pennsylvania, Hines transfigured jazz piano on these records and others made in the same period. He was said to play "trumpet style," in deference to his assimilation of Armstrong's linear attack, captured by Hines in rapid arpeggios, vibrato-like tremolos, and staunch octaves. Hines and Armstrong had worked together in clubs and formed a mutually inspiring bond powered by a genuine competitive spirit.

How better to announce a new dawn than with "Fireworks," in which the New Orleans texture is streamlined into unison riffing, rigorously paced by Singleton's blocks and cymbals (he was apparently asked not to use the snare and bass drums). Louis climaxes a string of solos, coursing over stop-time rhythm and brimming with joyous aplomb. On "Skip the Gutter," Singleton applies the cymbal not to beat time, but for coloration—like an arranger's flourish. The hot spot, though, is the piano-trumpet exchange, where, finally (and for the first time, since Sidney Bechet in 1924), we hear a musician give Armstrong a run for his money. Strong and Robinson are tiresome, but Hines engineers a delightful return to push the rhythm and to platform Armstrong's concluding chorus. Louis pays Hines and Zutty a serious compliment in invoking their names on "A Monday Date" (he hadn't done that since "Gut Bucket Blues"), a new number by Hines that became a jazz standard. Note the blithe reference to Prohibition, as Armstrong suggests that some homemade gin might lighten Hines's mood, and the melodious vocal—quite a contrast to the wild-man singing of, say, "I'm Gonna Gitcha."

The fabled June 28 session began indifferently with "Don't Jive Me" (possibly the first record to use "jive" in the title), which was canned until 1940; it's not hard to hear why. The attempt at polyphony is as awkward as Strong's clarinet solo. Incredibly, they segued from that to "West End Blues," far and away the most celebrated number in the series. The opening cadenza is the electrifying call to arms of a new world-shaking art, unmatched to this day in its concise power and relentless invention. Each subsequent chorus is different: sober trombone backed by woodblocks; enchanting voice and clarinet duet; dreamy Hines; and the leader's momentous return, sustaining one note for four bars, then detonating an impeccable series of descending arpeggios (an idea first explored on "S.O.L. Blues"). Singleton, who signs off on clop cymbal, comes to the fore on "Sugar Foot Strut," his hand-cymbal breaks invoking a tap dancer. Louis's audacious vocal sets up a superb Hines solo and his own risky attempts to play a couple of gambits that don't quite succeed.

"Two Deuces" is a fine 20-bar melody that deserves to be rediscovered; it has Cara's best banjo spot and an odd double-time interlude, after which Hines restores sanity and Louis lovingly finesses the close. The popular "Squeeze Me" was Armstrong's second pass at a tune by Fats Waller, whose work soon became a significant part of his repertory. Armstrong is in clover, quoting the New Orleans warhorse, "High Society," in his break, then improvising a lyrical chorus with banjo support and singing with mellow graciousness—backed by crooners Hines and Cara, who prefigure countless doo-wop groups. "Knee Drops" is a breakneck "Tiger Rag" variation (cf. "Hotter Than That"), with Strong on tenor sax and Armstrong saving the day with a 32-bar solo that could serve as a definition of swing. The weirdly protracted ending sounds as though no one wanted to stop—that's probably why it came in at 3:23.

Armstrong did not record for the next five months, but he came back with a vengeance, producing ten amazing numbers between December 4 and 12. On these sides, the New Orleans sound all but disappears and we witness the establishment of the soloists' art and the unison section work that would dominate jazz throughout the 20th century. Even a basic blues like "No, Papa, No" adumbrates the future: consider Hines's horn-like backing of Louis, and the varied unison riffs supporting the sequence of wind solos. "Basin Street Blues" is a masterpiece of tension, deep feelings, and release. Hines sprinkles pixie dust with a celeste, after which a sotto voce Louis leads the ensemble, almost trembling in the primeval repose of the still-prancing celeste. Louis then asserts himself with a melodic, eloquent blues chorus—the only one in the performance—and Hines sets up the exquisite vocal chorus. Yet it is Armstrong's inspired reprise that raises gooseflesh, beginning with a double-time phrase and continuing for three eight-bar episodes that peak midway and ultimately retire to the peace of celeste and silence. Many people think his more ecstatic 1933 version for Victor is even better. It may be as good, but *nothing* is better.

The next day brought a different kind of milestone, as Louis invited two arrangers to join the party, now billed as Louis Armstrong and His Savoy Ballroom Five. Don Redman, a key draftsman of big band music, had changed the direction of Fletcher Henderson's orchestra by incorporating Armstrong's style in his writing. A noted saxophonist, he now replaced Strong, while Dave Wilborn made a one-time appearance subbing for Cara. Redman's clean ensemble phrases and graceful transitions distinguish "No One Else but You," as do the savvy trumpet solo and vocal, each a free abstraction of the melody. The bursting-at-the-seams "Beau Koo Jack" is the work of 22-year-old Alex Hill, who died young, never fulfilling the promise of this gem. Its "Black Bottom"–type theme suggests a saxophone concerto at first, but that's merely a prelude to the whiplash trumpet breaks (Armstrong nails an antic that tripped him up on "Sugar Foot Strut") and careening ensemble figures that take it over the top.

Redman's relatively easygoing standard, "Save It, Pretty Mama," sports an exceptional Hines chorus and a cogent Armstrong-influenced one by the composer. With the written scores out of the way, Armstrong dismissed the other musicians and turned his sights on Hines. "Weather Bird," their only duet, remains the gold standard for off-the-cuff encounters. Instead of a sonata approach, where one musician plays lead and the other accompanies, this is a true duel in which the composition (a three-strain rag) is simply the backdrop for a swinging scuffle packed with abrupt tempo changes, shifty jabs and feints, one-note exchanges, and, at last, a beautiful rapprochement. The superlative "Muggles"

represents the final meeting of the Hot Five without arrangers, and eschews ensemble playing in favor of successive solos. It meanders pleasantly until Louis takes off, suddenly turning into a turbojet as he
launches himself with a dramatic four-bar break into a 24-bar rhythm
fantasy and a thrilling half-time, 12-bar resolution.

The last Chicago session took place five days later. Armstrong's "Heah
Me Talkin' to Ya?" was the only upbeat piece of the day and its jaunty
verve elicits thoughtful playing by Hines, Redman, and a very cool
Armstrong. "St. James Infirmary" exemplifies Louis's singing as he in-
fallibly gauges high notes and propels the chorus with rhythmic emotion
(cannily backed by Hines). He produces a catchy counter-melody to the
trombone solo, and a gloriously authoritative finale. The Savoy Ballroom
Five ended the day and its existence with "Tight Like This," a matchless
record and a thumbed nose to those who would "sivilize" genius. The
subject is sex—if the title and repartee (with Redman's falsetto) don't
make it clear enough, there's always Louis's interpolation of the hoochie-
coochie jingle, "Oh, the girls in France." Yet the mood verges on religious
rapture. Armstrong had never been more expansive than here, playing
three choruses that spiral up in an immaculate architectonic curve (he
sets the scene with a two-note figure, E to B, played five times), so that
even the risqué jingle adds to the cumulative range and passion.

It's a perfect conclusion to the most influential musical experiment in
recording history. The next time Louis recorded, it would be in New
York with an all-star, integrated jam band. The days when he was the
property of a small audience of jazz lovers were just about over. Soon
the world would hear of him, and take him to heart for all time.

[*Louis Armstrong: The Complete Hot Five & Hot Seven Recordings,*
Columbia/Legacy, 2003]

131 ❖ *Out of the Territories (Steven Bernstein)*

Steven Bernstein has been so much a part of the downtown cultural
exchange, through which the usual suspects are transmitted from one
band to another in an endless game of musical chairs where the last man
standing has to get a real job, it was surprising to learn that his early-
January appearance at the Jazz Standard was his first in an upscale joint

midtown—that is, north of Houston. Leading his nine-piece Millennial Territory Orchestra, he noted, repeatedly, what a novelty it was to work in a place with heat. Sporting earrings, a loopy smile, and lavender trousers, he relished the role of refugee at the ball, mocking midtown manners. Management made its customary request for minimal conversation, to which Bernstein remonstrated that conversation was encouraged: "If you're on a date it could be important; if you're married, talk loud, 'cause she isn't listening." Funnier was the way he used boho irascibility to sell an honorable dose of jazz repertory.

Bernstein is a card-carrying card carrier. If the band wore uniforms and the leader annunciated his introductions (not a bad idea), his crew might do battle with, say, the spit-and-polish squad of Vince Giordano's Nighthawks. For despite the holy-roller eclecticism, the playful attitude toward pitch, the we-make-it-up-as-we-go front, the faux-insecurities of do-you-wanna-hear-more and are-you-having-a-good-time and well-I-dunno-we've-never-played-a-place-like-this, not to mention muttered whimsies concerning politics, dope, and other unmentionables, when the time comes, Bernstein clicks an invisible switch and the band pops into semi-flawless unison. At that point, you may imagine yourself in Harlem in 1929, listening to Lloyd Scott (obscure enough for you?) or W.C. Handy, except that there's no room to dance and, besides, at any moment the unison could turn south. In truth, it isn't Harlem Bernstein recreates but the fanboy joy of late-night listening sessions to old records. He's the R. Crumb of jazz.

"Dju recognize that solo?" he asked, referring to an interpolation in a piece that began with Delta guitar, pizzicato violin, and clarinet over stop-time bass. "NO?!" he wailed, more in sorrow than in anger. It was Don Byas's opening tenor spot on Basie's "Harvard Blues." The whole class flunked and I was sobbing in shame when the orchestra snapped into Preston Jackson's "It's Tight Jim," casually introduced. I had to look that one up: Jackson, a trombonist remembered for his work with Louis Armstrong in the early '30s, though he had a long career, recorded it in 1926 for Paramount. I envision the Millenialists sitting around the phonograph late at night, Bernstein holding the 78 to the light to assess scratch-damage. Or has it been reissued? In any case, this was the best piece of the set. The leader offered a strong trumpet lead against trombonist Clark Gayton's trills; Peter Apfelbaum played a gracious half-time tenor solo over ensemble chords and Ben Perowsky's rumbling drums; violinist Charles Burnham soloed with country-like multiple stops over Ben Allison's bass, until the full rhythm section returned, the band barked staccato chords, and the piece transformed into a slow, harmonious "All

You Need Is Love" with improvised overlay—which was as left-field as Preston Jackson, but made for a compelling closer, complete with bird-like peeping and a unison high-note finish.

For all his fish-out-of-water ingenuousness, Bernstein is not entirely unknown to the upper precincts, or vice versa. As a leader, his big act is Sex Mob, a quartet that established his irreverent attack, marrying gentility to up-yours while keeping the jokes subordinate to the music. But he has also directed the Lounge Lizards, worked on a couple of high-visibility film scores (*Get Shorty*, *Kansas City*), and backed Aretha, Mel Tormé, Lou Reed, and Sting, among others. Still, he seems genuinely uncontaminated by breeding or stardust, and his enthusiasm is catching. He presides over a band that interprets ancient jazz as an old-time religion, only without the solemnity—more like old-time paganism really.

One indication of his impiety is that he doubles on soprano trombone, usually called slide trumpet, an instrument whose jazz pedigree is almost exclusively pictorial and negative: Armstrong famously posed with one, which encouraged skeptics to accuse him of playing one to affect his astounding glissandi on such records as "Lazy River." For 70 years its renown involved Armstrong's never playing it. Bernstein does not go in for much tailgating although he's aces at growling into a derby, but his use of the archaic horn suggests the kind of insider authenticity that reverberates throughout the band. Take, for example, Erik Lawrence, who plays baritone sax solos that chug and groan as though Harry Carney, let alone Gerry Mulligan, never lived; or former Lounge Lizard clarinetist Doug Wieselman, who grows his sound to full pre-swing weight (limning the melody of "Happy Hour Blues," by Lloyd Scott, brother of the slightly more famous Cecil Scott); or Apfelbaum, who savors quarter-tones, reaching into a bag no one has opened since Prince Robinson. If all this sounds like a heavy course in jazz arcana, the orchestra itself does not. At its best, it achieves a balance between slap-happy repertory and raucous excess. At its worst, the excess takes over, glee turns rote, and we're not having as much fun as we're supposed to. Best outnumbered worst about eight to one.

The band's spirit is such that it gets away with what a few years ago might have seemed borderline minstrelsy: a performance of "You'se a Viper," boldly sung at a leisurely tempo by the banjoist-guitarist Doug Wamble. Music belongs to whoever cares enough to play it, and Wamble, who exudes instrumental élan and sings with plangent openness, knows this stuff cold. But while prettifying the title phrase would be as barbarous as, say, "Bess, You Are My Woman" or "You Are Nothing More than a Hound Dog," phrases like "I got to gets" paint the lily a coat darker than Jonah Jones did on the original 1936 Stuff Smith record (which, incidentally, was taken way up in tempo and has one of Jones's best trumpet solos). Wamble also belabored the ending, drawing it out with tremolos and shtick that worked well enough at the club, but underscored the challenge the band will face when it records. The MTO has yet to release a CD, but it taped the Jazz Standard sets with that in mind. Although a live performance captures a degree of spontaneity, interaction, and laughs that may or may not travel well, the clarity and discipline of a studio might make the stronger case for its repertory.

Either way, the Millennial Territory Orchestra is a band with much promise and should be making frequent trips across Canal to various heated venues. The immensity of arcane jazz promises a limitless book, and Bernstein's arrangements draw out the musicians in the kind of flattering cameos that are a virtue of largish ensembles. It was a particular pleasure to hear Charlie Burnham away from Odyssey and other downtown bands, demonstrating elaborate chops and witty reflexes, and to hear Apfelbaum go deep inside and circumspectly outside, as the circumstances permitted. I want to hear more of Wamble singing, too. Bernstein knows the strengths of these musicians and the others well enough to indulge in his own variation on what Butch Morris calls conduction— controlling sudden changes in dynamics, sending one contingent in while having the other lay out, and conveying withal the notion that this music is so much fun it can hardly contain itself.

[*Village Voice*, 22 January 2003]

132 ❖ *Aqui Se Habla Espanol (David Murray)*

No career in jazz during the past 30 years has proven more consistently unpredictable and rewarding than that of David Murray. When he first showed up in New York—a 20-year-old student on furlough from Pomona College, playing "Flowers for Albert" in Stanley Crouch's Bowery loft—he had two big things going for him. First, he didn't sound like anyone else, certainly not Albert Ayler, though one could imagine that Ayler's example encouraged his penchant for the split-tones and squeals of the so-called hidden register. The classic Texas tenor Buddy Tate, who also favored upper-register cries, once advised young musicians to find their own sound, which isn't only easier said than done but almost impossible to do. The sound is you and not something out there awaiting discovery.

But Tate came up in the '20s, when every saxophonist—every musician—of note had a distinctive sound. That Hawkins, Webster, and Young existed in the same world indicated the tenor saxophone's extraordinary range; if those three and others (like Herschel Evans, Bud Freeman, and Chu Berry) represented unmistakably distinctive attacks, the spaces between them offered all kinds of possibilities. Tate, for one, started out blending Evans and Hawkins before finding his own place. The '70s offered a parallel challenge: the post-war tenor hierarchy had handed down alternatives no less distinct in the work of Gordon, Gray, Getz, Rollins, and Coltrane. Yet for a while it looked as if the tenor would be buried in a welter of Coltrane imitators. Murray, however, proved to be merely the youngest in an influx of musicians who demonstrated that many "sounds" were yet to be had—especially, for some reason, on alto sax (no fan could confuse Anthony Braxton, Arthur Blythe, Julius Hemphill, and Oliver Lake), but that's another story.

Murray paired Ayler and the habitually underrated Paul Gonsalves. Nobody raises an eyebrow at that now, but in 1975, a young saxophonist choosing Gonsalves as his North Star was a chin-scratching wonder. In short, Murray's inclination to play free and even ecstatic was tempered by a desire to play pretty; he produced a smooth yet aspirate lyricism that practically trembled with shy aggression. A second attribute also set Murray apart, although over time it was largely abandoned: an exceedingly legato approach to time, the obverse of the usual free-jazz assault, that tended to underscore the shyness. He held the tenor with a veteran's authority, physically floating it on the beat, yet placed his tones just behind it, playing catch-up and consequently drawing the listener into the drama. Now he commands attention with the richness of his sound and his ability to hit the beat whenever he wants.

Murray had a third thing going for him, though no one knew it until 1976, by which time he dropped out of school and made New York his stamping ground: a fierce ambition to play everything, be everything, do everything. In no time, he was leading a quartet, an octet, a big band, co-leading the World Saxophone Quartet and Clarinet Summit, collaborating with Butch Morris, working with musicians from every generation, grooming some of the hottest rhythm sections of the era, crossing over into other idioms, and all the while composing, arranging, and transcribing (not least, all 27 choruses of Gonsalves's legendary Newport solo). During the next 15 or so years, he made so many records as to become a punchline; no one could keep up—indeed, some of his best work was hardly heard here at all (e.g., *South of the Border*). Yet in 1997, after incredibly productive stays with Black Saint and DIW (while also getting in licks on other labels), Murray signed with Montreal's Justin Time, and began releasing one disc per year; in effect, the old Murray—which is to say the young Murray—faded away and was replaced by a musician who recorded less, but with a pronounced involvement in a larger domain of music.

Even so, one of his liveliest ventures never got recorded: "The Obscure Works of Duke Ellington and Billy Strayhorn," a big-band venture arranged in part by James Newton which started in Paris, where Murray relocated several years ago, occasioned a sumptuous concert at Aaron Davis Hall—it was perhaps the most memorable of all the centennial Ellington projects. A private tape was made for friends, but no one wanted to finance its release. For a while, it looked like another large-scale undertaking, his Latin big band, might also disappear without proper documentation. Murray first went to Cuba with three long-standing partners (Craig Harris, Hugh Ragin, and Hamiet Bluiett) to organize and record a 30-piece orchestra in 2001. An advance of the CD, *Now Is Another Time*, went out that year, but wasn't released: *Yonn-Dee*, a Guadalupian album with the Gwo-Ka Masters, came out instead. Meanwhile, Murray returned to Cuba, formed a smaller version of the Latin Big Band (without the Americans), and recorded two new originals, replacing two earlier works, completing the CD to his satisfaction.

It was worth the wait. Murray's Justin Time series persistently (pick one) tests the patience or enlarges the horizons of his fans. When he commits to an idiom, he embraces it fully. So while his graying followers could only be pleased with *Like a Kiss That Never Ends*, one of his most appealing quartet sessions, and *Octet Plays Trane*, a giddily original take on pieces usually played with palpitating reverence, explorations into other worlds required a shared interest in his passing obsessions, some of which weren't so passing: *Speaking in Tongues* was not his first and won't be his last look at gospel, to which he has strong personal ties, but it is the most wide-ranging and intensely engaged; his fascination with Guadalupian rhythms and voices has produced two albums, the multifarious, multicultural jazzmen-in-a-newfound-land *Creole* and the voice-heavy *Yonn-De*. *Fo Deuk Revue*, which initiated his Justin Time contract and indicated his impatience with standard jazz formulae, reflected the world of transplanted Africans he had found in Paris, and combined Senegalese rhythms, hip-hop beats and recitations, poetry, and jazz.

What one misses in some of these collaborations is Murray himself. He hits a couple of pro forma grand slams in *Yonn-De*, notably "On Jou Maten" and "Moman Colombo," yet even when he is fully launched, as on "La Pli La," the rhythms are often less stimulating than restraining, less empathic than jazz rhythms supple enough to follow his lead and oscillate accordingly. *Now Is Another Time* is a lesson in rhythm, and not necessarily Cuban rhythm; much of its interest stems from the sly often imperceptible swinging between jazz and Latin beats. In Geraldo Piloto, Murray has found a drummer happy, even eager, to shadow him, so that the timbales and congas may signal one culture while soloists, drummer, and arrangements aim for another. Murray may have gone to Cuba to play Cuban, but the Cubans he found wanted to play modern jazz, and the most exciting moments on the album derive from the mutual understanding that exoticism really isn't the point—it isn't even on the menu.

Which isn't to say that it's easy. At his January opening night at the Knitting Factory, Murray's clanging rhythms and bumbling winds shared few ports of call during the opening "Blue Muse," while the soloists strained to be heard. The band began to cohere on "Crystal," with its baritone voice-leading, a bewitching rhythmic figure that doubles the third beat in every eight, and bold brassy finish reminiscent of the kinds of things Johnny Richards used to write. But it was during the aptly titled "Break Out" that the band really came to life, the fast sinuous theme pulling the rhythm into its own free-bopping orbit, the riffs provoking the soloists, and the rhythms building to a contagious dancebeat that begged for a ballroom. After that, "A Sad Kind of Love," a long string of improvisations with broad orchestral backdrops, and "Aerol's Changes," a characteristic Murray melody framed in mambo elation and finishing with Abraham Burton's tenor caroming into staccato orchestral chords, seemed almost as convincing as the album.

Murray wrote and arranged all seven pieces (foolishly, the label did not update liner notes that were written for the disc's original version and say otherwise); they are mostly long, eventful, and given to change-ups. No one will complain of a paucity of Murray, who is the key soloist and in righteous form. His almost Websterish entrance on "Crystal" is as comforting as a quilt, and though his eventual rising into the stratosphere—the equivalent of trumpet high notes, each one articulated with clarity—has the flavor of inevitability (on "Mambo Dominica," you may wish he had curbed it), he mostly earns his way. His middle register has never sounded more warmly capacious, and some of his low notes, as on the marathon solo that dominates the first half of "A Sad Kind of Love," distend into fat two-note chords. His equally distinctive bass clarinet is heard on "Blue Muse," which is also notable for an attractive written interlude.

The best pieces are architectural. "Crystal" and "A Sad Kind of Love," open with piano prologues, the former adding a transitional baritone sax theme—baritones are rising: Dave Holland's big band does something similar on "Triple Dance"—and subsequently generating a blitz of free polyphony en route to the final crescendo. The most traditional pieces, "Mambo Dominica" and "Giovanni's Mission," are sequenced in the CD's middle, providing a respite of modulated lyricism. The latter has an exceptional trio of solos by Hugh Ragin, who in his mellow yet idiosyncratic approach to melody recalls Booker Little; altoist Roman Feliu O'Reilly, who by contrast, is roundly boppish; and Murray, working in middle range and splitting the difference. How much *Now Is Another Time* ultimately adds to the endless stream of Latin jazz and jazz Latin albums is anyone's guess, but its raging individuality—flamboyant writing and candied excesses—cannot be denied. After more than 25 years, David Murray shows no signs of settling down.

[*Village Voice*, 19 February 2003]

133 ❖ *French Music, Not Necessarily Freedom Music (Louis Sclavis)*

A certain kind of melody is embedded deep in the DNA of silent movies. It's a melancholy diatonic waltz, the love child of "After the Ball" and Charlie Chaplin, whose genius extended to sentimental themes that nudge us to smile through our tears. The living master of the idiom, which is not so much composed as recycled, is the born-and-bred New Yorker Carl Davis, a workhorse of '70s British cinema who scored several new films while finding his true métier in re-scoring silents and TV series about the silents. The last place you expect to find an outstanding example of that kind of melody, which has done more for Kleenex than the flu, is in the work of a musician and composer closely associated with the European jazz avant-garde. And my first response to Louis Sclavis's *Dans La Nuit*, his commissioned score to Charles Vanel's long-forgotten 1929 film, was indifferent disappointment.

Arriving after the double-whammy 2001 releases of *Les Violences de Rameau* and *L'affrontement des prétendants*, its retrograde nostalgia seemed peripheral, a Gallic detour or ECM indulgence. Many jazzmen have scored films and prepared corresponding albums, yet in this case there was neither an available film to boost interest nor enough elaboration to give the album a life apart.

Then, on March 7 and 8, Sclavis and his new quintet debuted in New York, accompanying a screening of the film at the French Institute Alliance Française and playing selections from *L'affrontement* at Tonic. The latter confirmed and expanded my admiration. The former, however, puts me in the odd situation of wanting to praise a score that can exert only limited enchantment on those who cannot see the film. Still, I find myself listening repeatedly to the 16 concise episodes that vividly recapitulate key events in an exceptional "lost" movie—for which Bertrand Tavernier has loyally campaigned, wisely recruiting Sclavis (who had scored one of Tavernier's pictures). I can suggest how *Dans La Nuit* fits into Sclavis's growing canon, amplifying melodic ideas in his earlier work and rounding out an intense scrutiny of French music that makes him a formidable figure in French jazz and not merely an imitator of American customs. (Can I hear an amen?) What I cannot do is argue that the film is incidental to the CD, or vice versa.

If Vanel's name doesn't ring a bell, his face might. He starred in hundreds of movies, including several international productions: A favorite of Henri-Georges Clouzot, he was the craven Jo in *Wages of Fear* (named best actor at Cannes) and the proto-Columbo police detective in *Diabolique*, which may have led Hitchcock to cast him as Cary Grant's betrayer in *To Catch a Thief*. *Dans La Nuit*, a meditation on fate, infidelity, fear, and loneliness, pays homage to his father's Lyonnais mining village and to Soviet-style montage, wielded with brio and auguries that emerge more clearly on a second viewing. With the advent of sound, a silent film had no chance; Vanel directed one other picture (*Le Coup de Minuit*, 1935) but never recovered from the fate of the first, which he had financed himself. It belongs to the realm of fascinating one-shots by actors—among them, Laughton's *Night of the Hunter*, Lorre's *The Lost One*, and Brando's *One-Eyed Jacks*—and, though little seen, portends set-ups, images, and ideas in 1940s Hollywood films as varied as *How Green Was My Valley*, *The Face Behind the Mask*, *The Woman in the Window*, and *Phantom of the Opera*.

Sclavis scored the film for his clarinet and bass clarinet; Dominique Pifarély's violin; Vincent Courtois's cello, outfitted with a Hendrixian reverb attachment; Jean Louis Matanier's accordion; and François Merville's drums and marimba. At the French Institute's Gould Hall, they sat in a semicircle before the screen, following the action with the mostly through-composed score. Aside from an introductory air, which Sclavis borrowed from an earlier work (called "Dia Dia" on the CD), the movements were newly composed to complement the action, either by explicit musical rhyme (a percussive train-like rhythm in synch with the mechanics of the mining machinery) or in deliberate contrast (a rubato moodiness to underscore an astonishing fight between masked doppelgangers). The recurring title theme is Sclavis's diatonic waltz, a 32-bar melody arranged by Pifarély, whose violin adds a glimmer of dissonance in the variation chorus; the brisk tempo and combination of accordion and clarinet places it in the tradition of French scores that milk a jazzy banality—that is, a melodicism unrelated to jazz proper though influenced by its rhythms, economy, and instrumentation (think Tati). Sclavis, who has called nostalgia "a beautiful prison," skirts that and other traditions, as he did the Baroque in *Les Violences de Rameau*, juicing the DNA to better emphasize the film's provoking modernism. In a sequence that occurs as the nightmare mounts, the title theme is recast with enveloping, ominous gravity.

At Tonic, Sclavis and his musicians were unfettered, and the change in personnel from the recording of *L'affrontement des prétendants*—violin and accordion instead of trumpet and bass—dramatically cast the selections in a new, at times unrecognizable light. The first set included the chamber improvisations of "Distances" and the rocking hard bop complete with cello reverb of "Contre Contre" and closed with an elaborate performance of the album's flashpoint, "Hommage à Lounés Matoub," involving backbeat rhythms, Middle Eastern rhythms, and eggbeater rhythms (also rhythms played with little bells and what appeared to be ping-pong balls), and instrumental techniques that ranged from violin col legno to a grunting bass clarinet cadenza, topping out with Sclavis's rapturous soprano saxophone improvisation and nifty accordion-cello exchanges, before the abrupt precision ending. The overall effect conveyed the pleasure the five musicians derive from the freedom of virtuosity and how content Sclavis is to give them all room; at one point, when Pifarély hit a fresh vein of ideas, Sclavis postponed his own solo, glanced at his watch, and squatted on the floor to listen.

At 50, with five ECM CDs recorded over the past decade and others as leader and sideman that are generally impossible to find here (including a highly regarded Ellington survey—an isolated look at standard American material—on IDA), Sclavis has become an increasingly uncategorizable light in European jazz, devoting as much energy to pure composition as to extended improvisation. He breaks down rhythms so that swing or rock or a kind of static Morse-code repetition (heard at the top of *L'affrontement* and in passages of the film score) become options designed to stimulate specific emotional grounding, and stakes out his own precinct from which to explore the jazz muse by exploring the often neglected legacies of French music. His sound and attack on soprano sax, clarinet, and bass clarinet are distinct, and have been for at least 15 years—since his ensemble and solo work stood out amid the fireworks of Cecil Taylor's all-star 17-piece European Orchestra on *Alms/Tiergarten (Spree)*, recorded in Berlin in 1988. His bass clarinet in particular, fat and saturated in every register, is the most consistently imposing since Eric Dolphy's, and he adds an effective trick, if sparingly used: blowing into the bore without a mouthpiece.

He has yet to repeat himself in the ECM cycle. The already hard to find *Rouge* (1991) is a quintet with Pifarély and a conventional rhythm section—including bassist Bruno Chevillon, an impressive, longtime Sclavis associate. The consonant chord periodically asserted in the dark "Nacht," along with its yearning closing melody, and the waltz interpolated into "Rouge," look forward to the film score's melodic candor. "Les Bouteilles" showcases Sclavis's sensuous bass clarinet sound and comfortable phrasing along with the graininess he uses to emphasize certain notes. His ability to sustain drama is apparent on "Face Nord," where his clarinet is backed by Christian Ville's attentive spaced-out drums and François Raulin's synth chords. *Acoustic Quartet* (1993) is more chamber-like, with guitar, violin, and bass used to craft plush backgrounds for solos—opulent on "Bafouée," tense on "Rhinoceros."

Most impressive are *Les Violences de Rameau* (1996), an ardent recomposition of themes from the Baroque composer's obscure opera *Les Boréades*, and *L'affrontement* (1999), which appears to be a companion, not because they were both released in this country two years ago, but because the violence of the first is underscored in the second—and not by the usually strenuous perorations of avant-garde blowing, but through the scrupulous structural designs that blend free jazz, rock, and composition in a montage of jump cuts that suit the twitching quick-change aspects of Rameau as well as Sclavis. It might be noted that another musician who did an album of Rameau is Bob James, the jazz-lite guru who overdubbed electric keyboards on a 1984 LP comprising performances he initially recorded to give as Christmas tapes. To Sclavis, Rameau is not Christmassy, but a key to the violence below the surface of Baroque classicism's merry zeal. That violence underscores the political passion at the heart of "Hommage à Lounés Matoub" and other works on *L'affrontement des prétendants*, and can even be gleaned in the subverted nostalgia of *Dans La Nuit*. It's an inescapable part of a musical world that isn't quite as pretty as it sounds.

[*Village Voice*, 19 March 2003]

134 ❖ Equilateral Chamber Jazz (The Bad Plus)

Traveling from the completely sold-out Cassandra Wilson gig at the Jazz Standard to the completely sold-out Bad Plus gig at the Village Vanguard, one could jump to the conclusion that jazz had, at long last, been blasted out of the doldrums. The winds blew emphatically from the audience, which seemed renovated and primed, aglow in anticipation and on its feet at the curtain, though some of us may need remedial repertory catch-up. Sonny Rollins plays "Sweet Leilani" because that's what he grew up with, which is the same reason Wilson sings "Lay Lady Lay" and the Bad Plus (or two-thirds of them) covers Blondie. It's a sign of prime-time preparedness that the Bad Plus's covers are rarely as good as its original pieces; indeed, the part of one's brain wired for cynicism might conclude that they choose cloying pop tunes because their originals seem so much more compelling by comparison—whiskey to wipe away the taste of grenadine. That would even explain why they call themselves the Bad Plus.

On the other hand, since the Bad Plus's few covers are chosen less for melodic or harmonic grounding than for hooks—those repeated morsels or sweetened riffs that nag the memory like nursery tunes or '50s commercials—they serve the same useful function as standards, orienting and flattering the audience. This falls under the rubric of admirable commercial savvy, and undoubtedly contributes to the increasing enthusiasm for a group that has the disarming appearance of an adventurous jazz piano trio. In truth, it's an equilateral chamber group that merges jazz, pop, and the conservatory in a heady and original way, accessible and seriously playful.

The Bad Plus consists of pianist Ethan Iverson (the third who never heard of bands like Nirvana), drummer Dave King (the third who is better known in Midwest rock circles than in East Coast jazz), and bassist Reid Anderson (the third who seems to choose most of the repertory). They've played together on and off since 1989, and the difference between the Bad Plus and a piano trio is instantly evident in a comparison of the collective's new CD, *These Are the Vistas* (Columbia), and the best of Ethan Iverson's trio CDs, *The Minor Passions* (Fresh Sounds, 1999), with Anderson and rough-and-ready drummer Billy Hart.

Everything from the recording mix to the division of solos and tunes heightens the ensemble's cooperative ethos. But the distribution of work isn't what turns the trick as much as the collective rising tides. Even during an ostensible solo, the listener is always conscious of the trio, and the arrangements are so bent on making the most of dynamics and change-ups that a solo never gets too far before turning abruptly into a group conceit. In its early days, the Modern Jazz Quartet occasionally appeared as the Milt Jackson Quartet, which some wags insisted was the true meaning of MJQ. Yet a vibes quartet wouldn't have lasted two years with the same personnel—we know what it would have sounded like from Jackson's many albums. John Lewis's textures prevented the MJQ from becoming routine. The Bad Plus's longevity will depend on how long it can thrive amid group textures.

Bill Evans's 1961 Vanguard records upped the ante on trio interaction, though the listener was never in doubt as to who the leader was or whose turn it was to solo. Before Evans, Art Tatum and Nat Cole explored trio interplay in groups with guitar and bass, while other pianists favored one partner over another—Ellington his bassist, Monk his drummer—and Ahmad Jamal created a trio-centric music that, paradoxically, gave his sidemen little freedom. Miles Davis's '60s rhythm section suggested a near-total autonomy of attack, as does David S. Ware's '90s rhythm section, in which Matthew Shipp, William Parker, and a series of drummers have enjoyed immense improvisational latitude. Still, one knows who is leading and who isn't. The Bad Plus are closer to the MJQ template, and arrives at a time when equilateral trios are blooming. Bill Charlap and Jason Moran are undeniably the leaders of their trios, but Charlap's proclivity for thoughtful rests and Moran's for compositional gambits, as well as their shared responsiveness to trio dynamics, define their groups as interdependently rigorous.

In taking chamber unity up another notch, the Bad Plus create high-energy tableaux while sacrificing some of the jazzier pleasures of elaborate solos; sometimes, for example, you want Iverson to stretch out for another chorus or two, unequivocally leading the others. At the Vanguard, a greater sense of improvisational freedom suggested itself than on the CD, yet *These Are the Vistas* fulfills the promise of 2000's *The Bad Plus*, (Fresh Sound) and may be a hard act to follow. The simplest piece reveals the group's design. Iverson's "Guilty" is a blues based on a brief figure with an ambiguous tonal center, developed over a very deliberate backbeat and substitute chords. It consists of a four-bar intro and six choruses: theme, bass solo, piano solo, theme. But the solos aren't just solos and the rising and falling from head to head arcs in a sustained curve. As Anderson's solo peaks, Iverson adds to the intensity and then takes over with dissonant chords before retreating into single-note blues figures; in his second chorus, Iverson's left hand counterpunches the blues figures, augmenting a crescendo of surprisingly ripe melodic character and feeling, before coming to earth as he approaches the head. The performance is too well grooved to permit an extra chorus by anyone. That's not true of Iverson's "Boo Wah," an impressive piece that opens with a kind of tribal drum thumping and develops in call-and-response phrases requiring piano-drums unison, piano-bass unison, and trio unison; it includes a fast secondary theme and an explosive improvisational interlude, but because it's basically composed rather than elaborated, it feels more like a conservatory exercise than a developed performance.

One of the most appealing pieces is King's "Keep the Bugs off Your Glass and the Bears off Your Ass," with its memorable Monk-like hook introduced on bass, and a theme that rebounds between the players. Straggling accents and drumming that engages the beat and never merely underlies it increase the Monkian character, as does Anderson's powerful bass solo. The once ubiquitous Eddie Gomez–type of bassist whose every solo raced to the bridge to plunk buzzy high notes has disappeared in the William Parker era, and Anderson recalls Parker and Mingus in his driving control of the low register. The brief piano coda adds a Wallerian (as in Fats) touch of frou frou. This piece might get covered in its own right. King's other number, "1972 Bronze Medallist," contrasts a head-banging backbeat with almost blithely lyrical piano—the crashing rhythm gets wearying, but the solo and the threadlike line between the preconceived and serendipitous compels attention.

Anderson is a fascinating writer, not as dry as Iverson but perhaps more ambitious, which makes his appetite for hooky pop the more unexpected. "Big Eater" gets under way with drums and combines a tricky tick-tock figure that implies five or the superimposition of five over four with a swinging four-beat bridge, a contrast sustained in the ad-lib section. Nothing could be more unlike it than "Everywhere You Turn," which, with its sotto voce opening and tapping rhythm, sounds as though it were waking from a Chopin nocturne it can't quite recall. It waxes in volume, yet remains slow and stately over a swinging backbeat four—an apparently through-composed drill in dynamics and ghost of a tune that tiptoes into the room and then backs out again. Anderson's "Silence Is the Question," the album's longest performance, is a ballad redolent of magnolia or the score of a Civil War movie, yet it avoids sentimentality in an arrangement that grows denser as the trio gains organic mass, peaking with foot-pedaled glissandi and heavy block chords—a candelabra romanticism in the context of rock and roll drums.

Of the covers, the irresistible "Smells Like Teen Spirit" may come to be the Bad Plus's theme song as much as it is Nirvana's. Their new version is more focused and dramatic than the one on the first Bad Plus CD. The ominous scene-setting piano chords taken up by bass and drums, the suspenseful buildup as the drums add an emotional fervor, and the release of the eight-note hook and climactic glissando are of a piece, as is the ad-lib interlude, which at first is a trio endeavor and then a piano invention with Iverson's left and right hands moving in discrete yet complimentary directions—a specialty of his. For the recap of hook-and-climax, the trio is blown as large as an acoustic trio can be, short of Cecil Taylor, whose own liberating glisses are oddly recalled. "Flim" passes for sweetness and light in the world of Richard D. James's alter ego, Aphex Twin; the Bad Plus's version marries unison piano-bass to resourceful drums more suggestive of Tony Williams than constructed techno beats, but the music-box melody sits there and never gets the improvisational obliteration it deserves. They briefly decimate Blondie's "Heart of Glass," with King's drums leading the tumultuous onslaught, yet the tune's trite vamp reasserts itself quickly, and is much repeated until King ends it with a marchlike paradiddle. The Bad Plus are worthier than that.

[*Village Voice*, 5 March 2003]

135 ❖ *Satchuated*
(Louis Armstrong)

Years ago, watching a clip of bungee jumpers, I thought, It's just like writing a biography—the long drop into the abyss, then the sudden jerk of salvation. Later I realized that was wishful thinking. There is no jerk, except yourself, plunging into the depthless mire of research, until finally you are obliged to concede, "Hold, enough!" However many bones you unearth, you know there are more, buried a little deeper. And when the boneyard is truly bare, bones already baking in the sun will be endlessly re-excavated. Otherwise there wouldn't be hundreds of biographies of Alexander, Napoleon, and Lincoln, each presuming to varnish or grind into dust its predecessors. I have never attempted a full-dress biography of Louis Armstrong, but I have written a short life and several essays, enough to feel some confidence in understanding him, his genius, and his times. Yet seconds after curator Michael Cogswell ushered me into the Louis Armstrong House & Archives for a recent visit, I felt I was plunging down the rabbit hole.

In the short time I spent there, examining maybe .05 percent of the holdings, I found no dramatically new information. But facts and factoids have a limited appeal. What you really hope for is a better purchase on the man, a jarring of the imagination that enables you to see what you already know in a clearer light. A few steps into the archive I was stopped dead by a pasteboard blowup of a photograph that had never been published, showing Armstrong and his adopted son, "Clarence Hatfield." I had never given Clarence much thought, having heard he was mentally retarded and died a long time ago, hidden away.

But here he was: beaming backstage at the Band Box, a club in Chicago, in the 1940s, nattily dressed in a double-breasted suit not unlike the pinstripe tailored for Armstrong, who also beams, with unmistakable paternal pride. Clarence and their relationship sprang to life, sending me back to Armstrong's account in *Satchmo: My Life in New Orleans*, to appreciate for the first time its affectionate candor regarding his only venture into paternity. Clarence was born in 1915 to Louis's teenage cousin, Flora, apparently after she was molested by an old white man her father felt powerless to challenge. Louis's first sight of the baby washed "all the gloom out of me." He took it upon himself, at 14, to get a job hauling coal (immortalized in the 1925 "Coal Cart Blues") to support the baby and the ailing mother, and assumed full responsibility after Flora's death, marrying his first wife and adopting the three-year-old at 17. In that period, Clarence fell off a porch and landed on his head; doctors judged him to be mentally impaired. When Louis married Lil Hardin in Chicago, Clarence joined them, and Louis never forgave Lil—who claimed that Clarence was never legally adopted—for her impatience with him. When he left Lil for Alpha, he brought Clarence along.

Eventually, Clarence was set up in the Bronx, where he was married in an arrangement of convenience financed by Louis. Clarence's surname is something of a mystery. According to Armstrong's friend, photographer Jack Bradley, he was listed in the phone book as Clarence Hatfield—but this may have been an expediency to keep nosy fans and biographers at a distance. Before Flora died, she evidently anticipated Louis's involvement and renamed her son Clarence Armstrong. He lived a full life, dying in August 1998, and endures in Armstrong's memoir as the happy athletic boy everyone called, much to Louis's pleasure, "Little Louis Armstrong." You sense the father's attachment in the photograph; had I seen it 15 years ago, I would have made every attempt to find and interview "Hatfield."

Other photos are no less revealing. Apocryphal stories concerning Armstrong's meeting with Pope Paul VI (in one, the pope holds out his hand, and Pops slips him some skin) are belied by a sequence of six or seven snapshots. They offer no proof as to what exactly took place, but suggest the utter absence of levity; indeed, I have never seen Armstrong look as stricken by the solemnity of an event. Everyone in the photos, including the pope, looks relaxed and unaffected—except Louis, whose downcast eyes seem to glisten with gravity.

Documents also fill out the portrait. Armstrong's private journals and letters (he was an amazingly prolific writer) are prizes of the archive that are already well known to researchers. But there is more. A letter to E. A. Fearn of OKeh-Odeon Records testifies to the popularity of his records in Italy; he is featured on the cover of a Fonotopia-Odeon catalog dominated by Rossini, Puccini, and Verdi. What makes this intriguing is the date: September 1926, at which time Louis had been recording as a leader for 10 months. Armstrong's scrapbooks preserve writings about himself in black newspapers of the '20s and '30s. Another document, recently found, is Armstrong's book-length collection of jokes and sayings, most of which were unprintable at the time he collated them.

But the most fascinating treasure is in the 650 reels of tape Armstrong made over a period of some 15 years, each housed in a box lovingly designed with a collage—a medium he explored contemporaneously with Romare Bearden, who first signed a collage in 1961. In 1991, when Cogswell was hired to oversee the Armstrong collection, there was some question as to whether the tapes—recorded on four tracks at slow speed and kept in a heated room—were salvageable. The Louis Armstrong Educational Foundation gave the collection to Queens College with the provision that it be preserved and made available to the public; it has continued to provide annual grants that have enabled Cogswell and his staff to scrupulously document and enlarge its holdings. Much of their effort has been devoted to transferring the tapes (two-thirds are done and relatively little proved unrecoverable) and creating archival reconstructions of the boxes. The Louis Armstrong House in Corona, which the foundation gave to New York, will finally open this fall after a $1.6 million restoration; at the same time Collectors Press will publish Cogswell's *Louis Armstrong: The Offstage Story* (with royalties assigned to the archives), which reproduces many pictures and documents for the first time.

But the question remains: How can the tapes be made available? Several anthologies could be culled that are funny, heartbreaking, and revealing beyond strictly scholarly appetites. Many tapes consist of records Armstrong wanted to take on the road, but his anecdotal introductions weren't intended for his ears only—he's clearly speaking to an imagined audience. Few artists have been more conscious of posterity. Sometimes he plays trumpet with records, never more movingly than on King Oliver's "Tears," where he essays his original part in letter-perfect unison for the entire recording. I was nearly in tears myself during the episode of two-bar breaks, when he exchanges passages with his old self—it's like nothing else I've ever heard. He plays as though time has stood still, his out-chorus borne on a tide of inspiration. After which he says, "That was just for kicks and to show the difference in the lead and modern recordings and things," and then plays the record by itself, so you can "dig how this was Satchuated."

He recounts with laughter the making of *High Society*, when the director wanted him to swing his cigarette holder until the smoke irritated his eyes and "I was sitting up here like Art Tatum." Meanwhile, everyone in the band is trying to steal the scene: "Trummy Young mugged so much, folks, I'm telling you, when the director was explaining the scene, he was mugging *listening*." Another term he uses for mugging is Tomming, with no pejorative intended, merely a realistic appreciation for what black entertainers do. One morning, he has the wife of critic Hugues Panassié in France on a phone and Cozy Cole on another, trying to get them to hear each other. He tells her, "Cozy's gonna come up in a minute, and I tell him he and Red Allen's the only two that's staying on Broadway a long time, so you know they got to be the greatest Toms in the world."

In another passage he inadvertently explains why no one who saw King Oliver's Creole Jazz Band in 1922–23, when Louis played second trumpet, commented on Armstrong overpowering or upstaging Oliver. It never happened. He and friends are reading a magazine account of Rocky Marciano knocking out Joe Louis. Armstrong says (this is inexact and much abridged):

"It says here the saddest moment [was] Joe Louis flat on the canvas after being KO'd by young Rocky Marciano, see. And you know that boy hated like hell to see that happen, how 'bout that. That's something like [James 'Coatsville' Harris], my drummer, one time I had the big band, and we was in Eugene, Oregon, and we're in this ofay hotel and [its] raining out there and ain't nowhere to go no how so I'm horsing Coatsville to shoot some dice on the bed. Coatsville don't have but two dollars, see, now he didn't want to win my money. You know, he's my boy and he just thinks a lot of me and I'm the leader and he said, 'Pops, I don't want to shoot. I don't want to,' you know. 'Aw, shoot the dice, man! Why don't you shoot?' Bam! 11, 11, 11, 11 . . . [he] won $750. But I'm just showing you how this boy admired Joe Louis so that he didn't even want to hit him but he had to bat him a couple, see. It's one of them things when you admire somebody so. Same as when I was playing second trumpet with Joe Oliver. And you think I'd, uh, blow for him? Like hell and I was [a] New Orleans little old young country sumbitch, strong as an ox, but I always respect Joe Oliver and that was that. He was the man and I wasn't the one to moo him, no no. When I blew that horn, I got away from Joe, believe that. Didn't blow it until I left him, you know? Yeah and every other page in my story is Joe Oliver, man. That's the respect this Marciano had for Joe Louis. [King Oliver] was a great man, you know, and I wouldn't let nobody play him cheap right today. When them ofay writers and all them cats, you know, want to make my situation, they say, 'Didn't Bunk Johnson teach you?' I say, 'Bunk didn't teach me shit!' Any similarity of tone or whatever it is, it's accidental. Joe Oliver was the man that would stop and show the kids in New Orleans anything they want to know about their music. Bunk didn't have time on the way to the Eagle Saloon. But Joe Oliver would stop. So this is the respect this Marciano had for Joe Louis and I think a lot of it. Bet your life."

[*Village Voice*, 16 April 2003]

136 ❖ The Academy's Pulitzer
(Jazz and the Pulitzer Prize)

Two days after the Pulitzer Prizes were announced, the *New York Times* ran a story by Anne Midgette, "Dissonant Thoughts on the Music Pulitzers," in which John Adams, who had received the award for *On the Transmigration of Souls*, expressed astonishment at winning, and ambivalence bordering on contempt. The prize, he said, has "lost much of the prestige it still carries in other fields," because "most of the country's greatest musical minds" are ignored, "often in favor of academy composers." He specified the Pulitzer's neglect of mavericks, composer-performers, and "especially" the "great jazz composers." His point was hardly surprising; that a recipient made it was. He had said aloud what countless American composers grumble privately every year, most of them shy of going public and courting accusations of sour grapes.

In 1967, when Edward Albee won a make-up Pulitzer for *A Delicate Balance*, he said that friends urged him to refuse it; four years before, the drama jury had chosen to present no award rather than recognize *Who's Afraid of Virginia Woolf*. In effect, Albee argued that his dissent would have more meaning as a winner. He went on to win more Pulitzers, and if he contested them at all he kept it quiet. So Adams took a nervy stand, opening himself to allegations of biting the hand that massaged him.

Not many winners have publicly questioned the process since Sinclair Lewis spurned the prize in 1926 (as well he should, *Arrowsmith* having beaten *The Great Gatsby*, though that wasn't his reason). And Adams loosened other lips. John Corigliano, the 2001 winner, told Midgette, "The Pulitzer was originally intended to be for a work that is going to last, to mean something to the world. It changed into another kind of award completely: by composers for composers"—mired, he added, in a pool of rotating jurors.

The Pulitzer Prizes, launched with a fourth of Joseph Pulitzer's $2 million bequest to create the Columbia University School of Journalism, began presenting laurels in journalism and literature in 1917. The music prize was instituted in 1943, the year Ellington premiered *Black, Brown and Beige*; the prize, however, went to William Schuman's *A Free Song*, a respectable choice by an important composer who was already a magnet for prizes. In the jazz world, the Pulitzer is shrugged off as just another establishment club (from the Grammys to the Kennedy Center Honors) that routinely ignores composers working in the idiom that most consistently and articulately proclaims "America" to the rest of the world. Yet many civilians are amazed to learn that in its 60 years, the Pulitzer in music has never acknowledged a single figure in popular music and only once gave the nod to a jazz work—Wynton Marsalis's *Blood on the Fields*, in 1997. Gunther Schuller and Mel Powell have also won, but for pieces entirely unconnected to their jazz work.

The most infamous pas de deux between the Pulitzers and jazz occurred in 1965, when the jury unanimously voted to override the standard rule of honoring a single work premiered the previous year, in order to hail Duke Ellington for his lifetime achievement. The jury, to its dismay, was overruled by the advisory board, which chose instead to present no award. A Pulitzer spokesman would later argue that the single-work rule could not be broken; but if they had wanted to make it right at the time, they could have given it to Ellington the next year for the premiere of his masterpiece, *Far East Suite*—or for subsequent suites debuted before his death in 1974.

Yet had the advisory board acknowledged any of those works, it would have done little more than apply a Band-Aid to a triple-bypass. The real problem went to the heart of Pulitzer politics and the rule itself. The jury that desired to honor Ellington understood something about indigenous American music—it is different; it plays a different game. The board would look foolish giving it to one new song by Bob Dylan or one typical concert by Sonny Rollins. The congregate achievement is almost always what counts. Lester Young was a great composer not because of his riff tunes, but because he created an utterly original and hugely influential canvas in American music; as instantly recognizable as an Aaron Copland ballet, Young's canvas was as amorphous as *Leaves of Grass*, his every improvisation another leaf, some greener than others, all part of a visionary achievement. It is easy to retrospectively find jazz compositions that ought to have been recognized within the constraints of the Pulitzer rulebook, but to say that *A Love Supreme* is eligible, and not John Coltrane's lifework is to force jazz to conform to the very 19th-century Eurocentric model it supplanted. Similarly, Irving Berlin or Woody Guthrie songbooks are not only more popular than Pulitzer compositions, they also answer Corigliano's call for "work that is going to last, to mean something to the world."

The Pulitzer is not averse to Band-Aids. It has a separate category called Special Awards and Citations, which has, in 73 years of occasional prize-giving, acknowledged three pop or jazz figures: Scott Joplin in 1976 (59 years after his death), George Gershwin in 1998 (61 years after his death), and Duke Ellington in 1999 (25 years after his death). The Ellington presentation was made "in recognition of his musical genius, which evoked aesthetically the principles of democracy through the medium of jazz and thus made an indelible contribution to art and culture." In short, it was a lifetime achievement award. And that's the right idea. The trick is to honor the recipient while he or she is still breathing, and in the Music category proper, rather than a remedial "duh" division. Ironically, on the one occasion when the board approved a jazz award, the jury played a shell game with its unbreakable edict, recognizing a 1997 "premiere" at Yale University, although the work had been recorded in 1995.

Adams, in listing a few non-winners for the *Times*, mentioned John Cage, Morton Feldman, Harry Partch, Conlon Nancarrow, Steve Reich, Terry Riley, Philip Glass, Meredith Monk, Thelonious Monk, and Laurie Anderson, as well as the wide category of "great jazz composers." He would like to impose a more radical sensibility on a historically conservative institution. (Consider fiction: *Laughing Boy* beat *The Sound and the Fury* and *A Farewell to Arms*; *Years of Grace* beat *As I Lay Dying*, *The Maltese Falcon*, and *Flowering Judas*; *Now in November* beat *Tender Is the Night* and *Appointment in Samarra*; and the board could find no worthy fiction in the years that *For Whom the Bell Tolls*, *Native Son*, *The Hamlet*, *The Adventures of Augie March*, *V*, *Idiots First*, *Losing Battles*, and *Gravity's Rainbow* were eligible.) But the issue as it regards jazz is no longer about radical or conservative views of culture; the influence, constancy, and genius of American music is denied nowhere—and none of it is represented in the Pulitzer rolls.

Does it matter? Of course it does. Owing to its long history and the press's psychic investment in the journalistic (and primary) wing of its prize-giving, the Pulitzer has a visibility and cachet beyond other cultural awards. The *Times* doesn't phone recipients of National Book Awards or American Music Center Letters of Distinction for human-interest reports on how they felt when they heard their names called. The Pulitzer, like it or not, is America's big award, a kind of official sanctioning. Only rank stubbornness can rationalize prolonging a slight that should have been rectified decades ago.

A couple of weeks after the Pulitzers were handed out, the American Music Center awarded Letters of Distinction to George Crumb, the *Voice*'s Kyle Gann (an accomplished composer as well as a critic), Steve Reich, Wayne Shorter, and the late music publisher Ronald Freed. Though Shorter is the ringer in this group, he has plenty of company among previous AMC recipients, who include—in addition to most of Adams's mavericks and many who've won Pulitzers—Randy Weston, Max Roach, Modern Jazz Quartet, Dizzy Gillespie (posthumously), Muhal Richard Abrams, Cecil Taylor, and Ornette Coleman. All but Gillespie and most of the MJQ are living, and it is hard to imagine anyone questioning the appropriateness of awarding any of them Pulitzers. There are others deserving of consideration, among them Rollins, Dylan, Benny Carter, George Russell, Lee Konitz, B. B. King, Henry Threadgill, Abbey Lincoln, Art Ensemble of Chicago, Ray Charles, Jim Hall, Andrew Hill, Chuck Berry, Roy Haynes, James Brown, and David Murray.

Should the Pulitzer board decide to rejigger its rule book or expand its grasp, it will have to overcome the embarrassment of a necessary mea culpa, something on the order of: "The Pulitzer Prize in music has decided to accept the reality of American music and will no longer dismiss out of hand all composers who swing or sanction improvisation." But the real difficulty would be administrative. The divides among jazz and pop and the academy remain so vast that in selecting its jurors in any given year, the committee will have virtually decided which area to favor; accordingly, word would have to be leaked that the barriers have come down, because few non-academics bother to submit nominations. Put a couple of jazz people on the jury and the dice are loaded for jazz. Better to switch loaded dice from one year to the next than to use—as is now the case—the same loaded pair every year.

[*Village Voice*, 6 May 2003]

137 ❖ Savooooy Be Gooood
(Jazz Jive)

Bill Milkowski's entertaining encyclopedia of jive, *Swing It!*, attempts various explanations of the word, but when push comes to shove settles for a definition that seems inclusive enough to silence debate: "Coded speech of the jitterbug scene." Yet Milkowski defines a jitterbug as "a swing fan," while many of his jivesters are devoted to bop or r&b. So clarification is in order. I suggest: a wacky, usually "inside" mode of humor associated with but not exclusive to African American musical idioms generated between World War I and the Korean War. Even that embrace, however, fails to account for the 18 tracks on the Savoy collection *All That Jive*. And neither does the subtitle "Jazz Classics with a Swinging Sense of Humor," unless straight readings of "'Round Midnight" and "The Way You Look Tonight" crack you up.

Few catalogs have been reissued and repackaged more frequently than Savoy's, which includes various short-lived indies like National, Dee Gee, Parrot, and Hi-Lo. A succession of owners have done complete editions, best-of anthologies, and facsimiles of the original LPs, which were infamous for their weird covers and sometimes semi-literate but always useless liner notes. In recent years, excellent editions—handsome packaging, restored sound, informative notes—have recycled the label's stars: Charlie Parker, Lester Young, Erroll Garner, Billy Eckstine, Stan Getz, Dizzy Gillespie, and others. *All That Jive* is a negative image of all those virtues. I won't complain about the selection by the usually reliable Billy Vera, except to note the absence of jive titans Stuff Smith and Big Jay McNeely, insufficient Slim Gaillard ("Flat Foot Floogie" is a flat choice when they've got "Ding Dong Oreenee," "Dunkin' Bagel," and "Oxydol Highball"), and the surprising absence of jive monuments like Dusty Fletcher's "Open the Door, Richard" and Gillespie's "Swing Low, Sweet Cadillac." But the musicians are unidentified and the notes don't come close to compensating. In short, the disc looks like a tossoff. But it's great company on a plane, always lively and occasionally surprising.

Like all such compendiums, *All That Jive* redefines its selections by the company they keep. For example, I've always thought of Gillespie's "Oh! Lady Be Good," a Joe Carroll feature, as nothing more than egregiously out-of-tune vocalizing. But now I wonder if Carroll's excruciating pitch isn't the joke in the jive—not intentional, surely, but sort of a found treasure, like the unrehearsed spill of a baggy-pants comedian. When he sings "Well IIIII'm all alone in the city" (twice), he merely gives way to immoderate enthusiasm, but the final "Myyyyyyyyyy lovely lady be good, ladyyyy be gooood to meeeeeeee" is alarming. Yet now instead of wincing I find myself laughing aloud. Maybe they laughed in the studio too. That would certainly explain why they didn't try another take.

And then there's "The Old Masturbator"—I mean "The Old Master Painter," a peculiar concoction by the Havens and Smith team that wrote "Lucky Old Sun." They evidently liked cosmic themes, and the old whatever is clearly meant to be God, but I had to reach for the CD case to convince myself I wasn't hearing what I thought I was hearing. I concluded that the only reason the song was sung by Jackie Paris and included here is its 12-year-old's sense of humor, especially as Paris fails to enunciate the last consonant in "master." But a little research shows that the song was a big hit in 1949, not for Paris but for one Richard Hayes (top of the hit parade, Christmas week), and quickly covered by Frank Sinatra, Snooky Lanson, Peggy Lee and Mel Tormé, Phil Harris, and Dick Haymes. (How many songs have been sung by both Phil Harris and Dick Haymes?) And even if my Freudian slip is showing, how solemnly is one to take this lyric? "Captured the dreamer with a thousand thrills/The Old Master Painter from the faraway hills./Then came his masterpiece and when he was through/He smiled down from heaven and he gave me you."

Paris is also represented by "'Round Midnight" from the same session (backed by saxophonist Eddie Shu and the swing-to-bop rhythm section of Dick Hyman, Johnny Collins, Tommy Potter, and Roy Haynes), which remains one of the best vocal interpretations to date. Jive it isn't, but it's as pleasantly dated as the other selections—a nostalgic reminder of the white vocal style of the late '40s, struggling to be born in a shotgun marriage between Sinatra and bop. Paris, who despite a long nightclub career never broke through on records, employs enough slides, turns, and mordents to border on idiosyncrasy, but he never crosses the border. Protected by good taste, time, and intonation, he keeps the performance interesting and compelling measure for measure. It was his last record date for three years, an oversight, as is Paris's entire discography—which I'm now inclined to pursue.

Carroll shows up on other tracks with Gillespie, most notably "Pops' Confessin'," in which his intonation is straightened out through his devastatingly funny impression of Louis Armstrong. I know I should say that the record was made in fun and with great affection (the liner notes call it an "homage"), and repeat how much Dizzy venerated Pops and how amused Pops was by it all, but successful satire requires no apology, and unless you are offended by the very notion of anyone taking a shot at jazz's genius-saint, you have to concede that this one nicks its target. Otherwise it wouldn't be funny. Carroll's delayed entrance, which requires him to rush to the first of many "mmmmmmmmm"s, is an inspired opening, and he sustains the joke by exaggerating familiar elements of Armstrong's style just enough to puncture its power. Dizzy, on the other hand, has it both ways: his trumpet solo begins as a beautiful imitation, his tone huge and timing precise, until a break, which he subtly retards, turning it into travesty. He ends with an easy joke, a ladder of high notes that climaxes in a dog whistle, as Carroll and he mimic Louis's studio banter and laughter.

Billy Eckstine gets two cuts: "(I Love the) Rhythm in a Riff," arranged by Budd Johnson and featuring, in addition to the leader's supple baritone scat, a dynamic Gene Ammons tenor solo monitored by a young and chipper Art Blakey; and "Oop Bop Sh'Bam," which has Eckstine's most effective valve trombone solo and more Ammons, backed by screaming brasses and decaying glissandi. Gillespie's "Sunny Side of the Street" has an impetuous Stuff Smith violin solo, a low-key cup-muted solo by the leader, and a vocal chorus that presumably qualifies it as jive ("life could be so fine/fine as Manischewitz wine"). The high, patronizing singing by Gillespie and Carroll on "Oo-Shoo-Bee-Doo-Bee" (on which Milt Jackson plays piano) reminds me of Mingus's remark that he never heard a black person say "groovy." This track appears to be belittling ofay shooby-doobies, but Babs Gonzales (the former Lee Brown, who changed his name because Cubans met with less prejudice) is here to dispute any racial scat divide, shoobying himself into a lather and adding a new wrinkle to Ebonics ("I must have was touched in the head"), backed, as usual, by great players, including Hank Jones and Buddy Tate, who gets a tenor solo (following Maurice Simon's baritone) on Gonzales's sexist version of "Ornithology," "The Boss Is Back."

Annie Ross also has a hot band with Milt Jackson (on vibes), Blossom Dearie (piano only), Percy Heath, and Kenny Clarke, and is in good voice on two standards, offering a variation on "Between the Devil and the Deep Blue Sea" and raising the tempo on "The Way You Look Tonight"; she ain't jiving, though. The obscure Emitt Slay Trio is vaudeville jive— "Mail Call" consists entirely of a letter, read with organ accompaniment, in which a soldier in Korea learns that his wife has a new friend. In compensation, we get Eddie Jefferson's entire 1952 Hi-Lo session with the Walt Harper Quintet (including drummer Cecil Brooks, father of CB III). In addition to his original take on "Honeysuckle Rose," with its rash fade, he does three vocalese adaptations of solos James Moody recorded in 1949: "The Birdland Story" (from "Blue and Moody"), "I Got the Blues" (from "Lester Leaps In"), and "Body and Soul," a clever companion piece to Jefferson's better-known adaptation of Coleman Hawkins's version. As with Ross, his pitch isn't unerring, but it's on target more often than not and his feeling for bebop is uncanny. I don't know why I find his pronunciation, in "The Birdland Story," of the name Charlie so appealing; it's the beginning of a vivid snapshot of a bandstand incident in which Moody steals the show—"That's when the Yard looked round and said, go ahead and swing it Moody." It's neither ha-ha funny nor particularly jivey. But it's way cool.

[*Village Voice*, 28 May 2003]

138 ❖ Swashbuckler (Erroll Garner)

Conversation with a clerk at a megastore, May 2003:

"Do you carry a DVD of Erroll Garner?"

"Oh, I know that, it's like, um, adventures of Erroll Garner, right?"

"Uh, I don't think so, I think it's something like Erroll Garner in concert."

"No, my boyfriend showed it to me. He, like, fights pirates and stuff, right?"

"Excuse me?"

"What kind of movie is it?"

"He's a jazz musician. It's a concert film."

"Oh, right. I'm thinking of Errol Flynn."

Actually, it's called *Erroll Garner in Performance*, and consists of two 35-minute sets taped in 1964 for the BBC series *Jazz 625*. In fairness, Garner's attack does indicate a swashbuckling fortitude, a piratical confidence, an adventurer's audacity. Still, not long ago—OK, 25 years ago—every record store clerk in the nation knew Erroll from Errol, simply because of the volume of records he moved, as suggested by an earlier tête-à-tête. Having first encountered Garner at a 1964 concert in Queens, I had bicycled the next morning to a record store and looked in vain for a Garner bin or, failing that, Garner albums in the miscellaneous G section. I asked an employee, "Is it possible you don't have a single record by Erroll Garner?"

"No, it's not possible. We have lots of Garner. Where did you look?"

"In jazz."

"We don't keep him there," he said, leading me to the section for pop pianists like Roger Williams, Ferrante and Teicher, and Carmen Cavallaro. Perhaps sensing my embarrassment even to be seen in this vicinity, the clerk reached into the large Garner bin, pulled out *Concert by the Sea*, and said, "This is what you're looking for." He explained that no guilt by association was intended; it was just that a large part of Garner's tremendous following had no interest in jazz. He was wrong about associative guilt, though. Although many jazz critics acclaimed Garner as a giant, many others dismissed him as middlebrow: One *Down Beat* critic likened him to a can of soup, and another argued that he had been in decline since 1948. How good can he be if everyone understands what he's doing?

Or rather, how bad can he be if he routinely holds the interest of the great unwashed with six- and eight-minute improvisations in a totally original style that influenced practically every jazz and pop pianist alive—if not to play like Garner, then at least to express his joy. John Coltrane's line about Stan Getz ("We'd all like to sound like that if we could") applies emphatically to Garner; no matter how dreamy, rhapsodic, or laggardly his playing may be, it always radiates contagious delight, gaiety, energy, exuberance. Imagine feeling as good for one hour of each day as Garner apparently felt every time he played piano. The consistency alone is anti-jazz, to the degree that jazz reflects manifold feelings—even Fats Waller recorded sorrowful laments—and normal people are usually less than ebullient.

But who said that Garner was normal? Picking out complicated melodies at age three and broadcasting professionally at age 10, he created a style so much his own—without learning to read a note of music—that it has abided as a kind of jazz orphan, without ancestry or descendants. Yet one recognizes multiple seasonings in the compound—Lisztian rhapsody, Debussyan harmony, Wallerian stride, big-band riffs, Powellian involution, Monkian rhythmic displacement—despite the self-contained singularity that inclines other pianists to take on the Garner gestalt. Midway in, say, a Jaki Byard solo, a Garneresque passage has the effect of a Jimmy Cagney impression interrupting a dramatic monologue. On his own, Garner can be plenty dramatic; cited by others, he represents humor or well-being. Garner wrote 200 songs in addition to "Misty," on which he probably could have retired early, many of them conceived spontaneously at the piano while the tapes were rolling. "Afternoon of an Elf" merges Debussy's harmony, Willie "The Lion" Smith's rhythm, and a melody either man might have claimed, yet it's pure Garner—dreamy nostalgia brimming with affirmation.

Beyond emotional constancy, the stylistic ingredients that make up the Garner approach are easily tallied: droll abstract introductions, metronomic time, flashing octaves, strummed or broken or cascading chords, winsome variations, impressionistic harmonies, guitar- or harp-like arpeggios, extreme shifts in dynamics, orchestral pounding, and quirkily protracted or abrupt closings. The rhythmic independence of his hands suggested a disconnect bordering on twin personalities; indeed, an associate pointed out that Garner could sign autographs with either hand. For all his fabled spontaneity (he once recorded three albums' worth of material at a single session, and frequently barged into a number with no preconception of what he would play), Garner developed a standard format. The intro leads to a theme statement, a single-notes variation (frequently beginning with a pianissimo right hand), a storming block-chord episode, a reprise of the theme, and a coda. The variations might be one chorus or several, and he might alternate the linear and block-chord inventions until exhausting his interest in a piece. What he rarely exhausted was his audience's patience.

His playing does not avert predictability. The stabilizing nature of Garner's style can become tiresome if you know the drill, and a surplus of rote Garner defines the limits of joy when it lacks inspiration. Yet as the DVD shows (the first set is mostly excellent, the second starts brilliantly and then flags), he could almost always sustain an audience's fascination. Two things invariably keep the train on track. First, he swings hard enough to allay reservations; if he has charge of your foot, he can get to your mind. Second, and more impressively, he improvises with a matchless lucidity that allows people who glaze over at the thought of improvisation to follow Garner's most fanciful inventions. One way he pulls this off is by introducing a motif or secondary theme; its recurrence has a subliminal effect not unlike rhyming verse. He also intersperses notes or chords from the theme—usually at turnbacks, like road markers—to keep it in plain sight. A typical example is "How High the Moon" (1950): The improv begins with a phrase played twice, which is echoed in the first two bars of each of the succeeding eight-bar segments. Add contrasting dynamics, a device few jazz pianists other than Cecil Taylor and Ahmad Jamal have explored before or after Garner, and you have a music so spellbinding it could be dangerous in the wrong hands.

If this counts as easy listening, it's the sort that carries an emotional wallop and reveals increasing intricacies and intimacies over time. I speak from modest experience, having seen Garner on two occasions, a decade apart. The first time he opened for Lionel Hampton at the New York World's Fair in September 1964. I had come to see Hampton and groaned upon learning that I'd have to sit through an hour of someone

I expected to be as deep as Tyrone Power playing Eddie Duchin. He walked out with the Manhattan phone book under his arm, placed it on the piano bench (this was standard practice for the man who wrote "Afternoon of an Elf"), and for the next hour, without a break or a word (also standard practice—he never introduced tunes or musicians), shook the Singer Bowl. I left before Hampton arrived, not wanting anything to trample the reverberations of that music.

Given his high-priced celebrity (he was the only jazz musician regularly presented by Sol Hurok), Garner stopped working New York jazz clubs by the late '60s, and so a generation of jazz lovers never got to see him. But as a fledgling writer, I was comped for a set of what turned out to be his last New York engagement, at the St. Regis's Maisonette Room, in May and June of 1974. He had added congas to his usual bass and drums backing, but everything else was the same—the phonebook, the lack of speech, the driving intensity. He did nothing to entertain the well-heeled crowd except play with everything he had; nor did anything in his tune selection or treatments imply pandering. Yet he had the room in his thrall, not a whisper anywhere.

Garner died two years later, of cancer, at the age of 55, still a major attraction throughout the world. But people and record companies forget. While many Garner CDs are available, some of the best are not; Columbia has yet to release a decently mastered edition of *Concert by the Sea*, reputedly jazz's first million-selling album, and an abiding example of Garner at his peak. The DVD—two sets succinctly introduced by critic Steve Race, taped in 1964 and broadcast in early 1965—is a time machine. It offers close-ups of Garner's expressive hands and insights into the ways of the rhythm section (bassist Eddie Calhoun and drummer Kelly Martin, like their predecessors and successors, never solo; the drummer usually uses brushes; neither man knows what tune an intro may spark; Garner cues arranged episodes with slight nods), as well as a reminder of how engaging a performer he was—his perspiring face rolling to the beat and reacting to various conceits, though his eyes are usually set on the middle-distance, whether twinkling, buggy, or transported. Garner is superb on "Just One of Those Things" (fast and witty), a "Spring" medley (extended intro and theme statement of nearly vocal timbre), "Laura" (an early hit that suited him uncannily well), "Sonny Boy" (he'd just recorded *At the Movies*), "Honeysuckle Rose" (a good example of his expeditious stride, plus a boogie-woogie episode), "Jeannine (I Dream of Lilac Time)" (convoluted and surprising), and a robust "I Could Have Danced All Night" that salvages a trite "On the Street Where You Live." The audio is thin, but an audio-only performance of "Misty" captures

Garner's resonant sound; a video component for "Misty" is shown on the menu screen, but is inexplicably cut off after a minute or so.

Garner recorded between 1944 and 1973, almost always with just a rhythm section, though there was a famous date with Charlie Parker, a jam with Wardell Gray, several solo sessions, and the occasional anomaly, notably the unjustly forgotten *Music for Tired Lovers*, with vocals by Woody Herman. *The Complete Savoy Master Takes* collects the romantic '40s records that made him famous, as well as a Slam Stewart session. The 1954 *Contrasts* is an excellent set of mature Garner, including the original "Misty," the ingeniously relentless "7-11 Jump," and a rare blues. Telarc issued several '60s and '70s albums as twofers—the enchanting *At the Movies* is coupled with the much less endearing brass section of *Up in Erroll's Room*. Previously unreleased material collected on five discs in Emarcy's "The Erroll Garner Collection" amounts to an unmitigated gift, especially *Easy to Love* and *Solo Time*, which offers a striding "The World Is Waiting for the Sunrise" that turns into "Our Waltz" and "I Can't Escape from You"—no one had a larger repertoire of obscure songs. But much of the best Garner was recorded for Columbia, between 1950 and 1958, when he successfully sued the label for releasing what he considered substandard material. A couple of anthologies were released more than a decade ago with dreadful sound, leaving much work to be done in restoring such masterly performances as "Girl of My Dreams," "Caravan," "Avalon," "The Man I Love" (great drumming by Specs Powell), "Will You Still Be Mine," "Love for Sale," and many others, not to mention albums like *Paris Impressions* and *Concert by the Sea*, all of which could be prescribed as over-the-counter antidepressants. Guaranteed: no side effects.

[*Village Voice*, 4 June 2003]

139 ❖ *Deep Easy Listening*
(Jim Hall / Cyrus Chestnut)

Call it a taste for opposites, but in taking note of the nearly simultaneous appearances by Jim Hall at the Village Vanguard and Cyrus Chestnut at the Jazz Standard, it occurred to me that they might sound wonderful together—the former's tight asymmetrical phrases and careful timbres coursing through the latter's buoyant chords and gospel preachments.

They play as they look: Hall is lean and deliberative, Chestnut rotund and effusive. Heard on their own, they underscored the breadth of contemporary mainstream jazz. They're both reliable club draws with hard-earned yet largely undeserved reputations for middle-of-the-road easy listening. What I mean is, yes, they are readily enjoyed, but you do have to pay attention, and though that is true of any music worth your while, Hall and Chestnut—separated in age by more than 30 years—violate many of the very conventions they appear to embody.

Of the two, Hall is the more radical. Long associated with players and composers on the edge (Chico Hamilton Quintet, Jimmy Guiffre Three, Sonny Rollins Quartet, John Lewis, Gunther Schuller, Ornette Coleman, Paul Desmond, Joe Lovano, Greg Osby; duets with Bill Evans, Ron Carter, Dave Holland, and others), he is now less well known as the writer of pliant melodies like "Romain" than of idiosyncratic third-stream conceptions in which each member of the ensemble is accessed as a distinct voice, occasionally reflecting a guileless sense of comedy (one charming example, "Circus Dance" on the inspired *Textures*) that is otherwise more apparent in his stage patter than his solos. Yet it's Hall's soloing that most persistently defies the orthodoxies of jazz improvisation.

In escaping the guitar player's rut of playing all the notes all the time, Hall established texture, timbre, and voicing as the equals of linear phrasing. Coolly modifying his sound (he seems to turn up a new timbre or two every time I see him), he improvises short sovereign phrases that sustain interest largely for the way they sound; his solos unfold statically, like tableaux, favoring the present over the future. Most jazz solos are assembled out of eight-bar phrases that imply their resolutions the moment they are launched. Hall doesn't do that; he plays as though he doesn't know how his aural sculptures will look until they're done. In short, he plays the changes; the changes never play him. The same can be said of his relationship to the guitar and electricity. Though he continues to switch between acoustic and electric instruments, no guitarist sounds more electric. Electricity is never merely a means of amplification for him. It has its own glowing aura, an exacting integrity, which he manipulates for a broad range of shades and colors. I can think of no musician who makes me more conscious of atomic particles and the humming alternate world obtained through a wall socket.

To this, add two other virtues. As was strikingly clear opening night, his swing is diabolical. No matter how few notes he plays—a phrase may be no more than a wave of chords bleeding into each other, or one sustained tone that the bassist fleshes out—they intensify the rhythm. He avoids clichés as if they simply aren't in his vocabulary. At the Vanguard, accompanied by the warm-toned, pitch-accurate bassist Steve

LaSpina and the unerringly empathic drummer Lewis Nash, Hall played two original blues and two routine standards, none dampened by familiarity or requited expectations. "All the Things You Are" and "My Funny Valentine" morphed as harmonic and melodic abstractions, riveted by the constancy of the beat. Yet the highlights of the set were Billie Holiday's "Don't Explain," in which he followed a decorous bass solo with a shimmering chorus of phrases so disparate you had to accept on trust that they'd add up to something, and Joe Lovano's "A Message from Blackwell," from *Grand Slam*, during which Nash switched to mallets and the two evolved a duet, Hall hand drumming the guitar strings.

Cyrus Chestnut's subversiveness is more obvious and less startling. As he wryly notes in a liner squib for his forthcoming *You Are My Sunshine*, he is often told what his influences are, but resists making "repertory driven" albums. If you hear his music as jazz, gospel, soul, or classical, it's all the same to him as long as you like it. It's an old story, this business of crossing the great divide of church and state. It wasn't that long ago that Ray Charles was pilloried for taking gospel techniques into the outside world, substituting "baby" for "Jesus"; and more recently, David Murray has recalled having to sneak around in order to play the devil's music in the early 1970s. Yet Louis Armstrong, to his sister's chagrin, had hits with spirituals in the 1930s, and many church-bred soul groups and singers mixed the two, from the Golden Gate Quartet and the Charioteers to Aretha Franklin and Al Green.

Still, it's a novel experience to hear a contemporary jazz trio blithely turn from jazz to gospel as if the barriers never existed, which is precisely what Chestnut accomplishes with his disarming smile, calming élan, and roly-poly authority. When he wants to bop, he bops. When he wants to play hymns, he goes straight to the Trinity Hymnal. In this aesthetic, Stevie Wonder and Thomas A. Dorsey are not only brothers under the skin, but de facto collaborators. And when he wants to play classical, he feels no need to rig the time to suit swing purists—he just goes for it, an extended two-part invention while bassist and drummer look on. On the new CD, Chestnut plays a triple-meter soul-jazz-gospel original called "Hope Song," which is built on four bars from the adagio of Beethoven's "Pathetique." The attitude is take it or leave it, and you'd be a fool not to take it. Chestnut exudes Garneresque satisfaction in having so much music to play—or play with.

In the nine years since his debut album, *Revelation*, Chestnut's basic approach has remained consistent—the diverse repertory, the contrast between outgoing jazz and the solemnity of old hymns, and the omnipresence of his trademark technique, the tremolo, which takes on the character of whatever attitude he's trying to convey and complements his use of modern harmonies. The 1996 *Earth Stories* is an especially good sampling, perhaps his best to date. But an increased complexity enriches his recent work, bringing the various idioms closer and sometimes fusing them, and that nexus is the defining aspect of his style. At Jazz Standard, his trio opened with a fresh paraphrase of "East of the Sun," the improvisation accented with Tatum-esque flash and robust 1950s chords (he remembers Red Garland), but the overall approach was individualized by the tremolos and glissandi, which impart punctuation, feeling, and dramatic tension. He has a way of playing energetic phrases that change dynamically—as if someone had turned down the volume for, say, two out of six bars.

Wonder's "Can't Help It" was too limited harmonically to hold much interest—sometimes the rhythm in a riff isn't enough. But Chestnut recouped with Dorsey's "Precious Lord," a highlight of the new CD, introduced by a rock-steady vamp. Michael Hawkins's two chugging bass choruses prepared the way for Chestnut, who was appealingly unaffected as he casually plotted his moves at a fast tempo, resisting undue exertion or flash. With Neal Smith marking every beat on a choked cymbal, the trio mined the kind of earthbound groove that always seems easy when pulled off, making you wonder why it isn't pulled off more often. Midway in the set, Chestnut extemporized a Bach-inspired cadenza with blues shadows, a stride interpolation, and climactic tremolos of the sort that once accompanied silent movies—all of it treated more with a deliberation worthy of Hall than the broad comedy usually employed for such eclectic capers. The trio then embarked on a backbeat "Body and Soul" that, despite a fizzled finish, demonstrated yet another way to ride that most traveled of warhorses.

You Are My Sunshine (Warner) begins with its dimmest number, "God Smiled on Me," a bland tune from a Whoopi Goldberg movie that Chestnut perks up with a few nice touches, but not enough to justify its inclusion, let alone its starting position. Then the CD comes roaring to life with the staccato chords that set up Cole Porter's "It's All Right with Me." There's no denying the benefit of a great tune, and Chestnut puts his thumbprint on this one with an odd time signature (in seven, I think) and comprehensive use of the whole keyboard; when the trio takes up a straight four, he breaks out like a thoroughbred, as if relieved that he no longer has to count beats. An original, "For the Saints," is a bravely slow backbeat gospel meditation, girded with tremolos and blues notes, rocking from side to side and beautifully controlled. "Precious Lord" has a modified second-line beat and disarmingly fresh voicings—it's one of the several arrangements that cast old material in a new light. By contrast the title tune relies on an all too familiar arrangement, complete with tambourine shaking. At best it's a hearty transition to the darker material that follows.

But first comes "Errolling," a funny ABAB Garner pastiche with an Ellingtonian transition; the solo, strewn with octaves and reminders of the theme—a folklike melody that suggests "I've Been Working on the Railroad"—never flags, and the abrupt finish is just right. Richard Small-wood's "Total Praise" is contemporary gospel, covered first by Destiny's Child and played straight by Chestnut—the way William Walford's 1840s hymn, "Sweet Hour of Prayer," is on *Revelation*. Walford's tune, however, is now resurrected in a trio arrangement with plush chords and a rhythmic kick, restating it as a jazz piece. For 19th-century gospel authenticity, the peak moments are "What a Fellowship" and especially "Pass Me Not O Gentle Savior," a deep-dish blues improvisation with a climactic crescendo. For jazz authenticity, the originals, "Lighthearted Intelligence" and "Flipper" are outright swingers, the latter constructed with a standard bebop lick and a pretty bridge. Chestnut's repertory is every bit as unorthodox as Hall's inventions, and whether or not they ever play together, the fact that they have loyal and attentive audiences says a lot about how nondenominational modern jazz has become.

[*Village Voice*, 11 June 2003]

140 ❖ Masters of Time (Roy Haynes / Max Roach)

At 78, Roy Haynes is only a year younger than Max Roach, yet jazz history pigeonholes them, respectively, as second- and first-generation bebop drummers. Each was a wunderkind who initially made his rep-utation with swing titans: Roach with Benny Carter, Haynes with Lester Young. But Roach was the first to assimilate Charlie Parker's radical redesign—"Koko" was as much a coming out for him as for Parker and bop itself—and by 1949, when he asked Haynes to replace him in Par-ker's quintet, a chair Haynes held until 1952, Roach's influence was per-vasive and absolute, as Haynes readily acknowledges. Roach had changed everything. It took nothing away from Sid Catlett's rolling au-thority or Buddy Rich's heart-stopping stickwork or Jo Jones's majestic hi-hat tattoos to realize that they were all inadequate to a music that demanded the drummer's increased collaboration in shaping themes and propelling soloists. Stylish timekeeping was now supplemented by simultaneous rhythms (and independent limbs that made them possible), which redefined and deconstructed time while keeping it steady and resolute.

Roach wasn't alone—Kenny Clarke had worked out many of the same ideas, and there were others—but he was the most ingenious, resourceful, venturesome drummer of his generation. Even drummers who didn't want to play bop envied his reflexes, panache, freedom, and adamant musicality. As Burt Korall points out in the illuminating *Drummin' Men: The Heartbeat of Jazz: The Bebop Years*, even Buddy Rich, who knew he could paradiddle Roach or anyone else into oblivion, was obliged to reconsider the limits of supersonic paradiddling. Korall justly observes that Rich "ran Roach out of the recording studio" when they recorded together in 1959, but an earlier unspoken contest tells a different story: the records each man made with Parker, where Roach is exalted and Rich frequently at sea.

Haynes was never at sea during a singular career that ranges from Louis Armstrong to Pat Metheny and includes prominent alliances with Young, Parker, Bud Powell, Lennie Tristano, Sarah Vaughan, Stan Getz, John Coltrane, Eric Dolphy, Thelonious Monk, Jackie McLean, Chick Corea, and David Murray, among many, many others. One reason traditionalists and avant-gardists as well as modernists like working with him is that, as Korall writes, musicians "find it difficult to coast" when Haynes is monitoring every bar with the "broken rhythms, provocative syncopation, and improvisatory, Haynes-tailored techniques that no one ever has been able to duplicate." One reason Haynes was often relegated to Roach's (and Art Blakey's) shadow is that he put off becoming a leader. In the mid-'50s, when Roach found Clifford Brown and created one of the era's glorious bands, Haynes was exhibiting an unequaled meld of restraint and aggression as Vaughan's drummer. As the ideal accompanist, he received less attention than his peers or even the most prominent of the musicians he decisively influenced, including Elvin Jones, Tony Williams, and Jack DeJohnette. Yet not even Roach could match him for pure spontaneity.

Haynes's brash watchfulness keeps his music in a state of suspended agitation—he makes listeners and musicians feel secure and wary at the same time. He commands the drums and the rhythm like a general looking over a field, apparently willing to try anything and confident he has the discipline to make it work. Haynes has never lacked confidence or felt obliged to direct his virtuosity toward the obvious fulfillments of speed and flash. As a soloist, he lets his music breathe, storing ideas during rests and following through with great exhalations of ingenuity. In his taste and control, he recalls Roach, but his playing has more immediacy and wit. On some level, Roach is a fundamentally more serious player; his solos sometimes exude a calculated gravity, as if he has a point to make and is intent on seeing it through. Haynes more often indicates a playful impulsiveness, a carefree emotionalism. (Yes, there are exceptions both ways.) Roach is known for drum solos written in homage to Catlett and Jones that never wear out their welcome; it's hard to imagine Haynes playing the same solo twice.

All of which is intended as prelude to two stunning new CDs, recorded last year for a subsidiary of Sony Music Japan called Eighty-Eight's, and now released here by Columbia. The happy few who remember the mid-'70s as a golden moment in jazz history may remember the stylish Japanese label East Wind, which teamed Hank Jones with Ron Carter and Tony Williams, and Art Farmer with Cedar Walton; its founder, Yasohachi Itoh, is behind the new venture, which has released four discs heavy on drumming. Eddie Henderson's *So What* is burdened by its Miles concept, though Billy Hart and Victor Lewis rise above it. Ravi Coltrane's *Mad 6* is more rewarding and impressively launches drummer Steve Hass. The Haynes and Roach discs, however, are must-haves, each borderline miraculous.

Only Haynes could have made *Love Letters*, involving two all-star units of younger players—Kenny Barron alone was born within two decades of him. It isn't the talent pool that makes the disc (recorded in two days) momentous, but the relieved delight that informs the playing, the absence of bandleader fretting and record-making indecision. In responding to Haynes's nonstop challenges, the participants cavort with the heedless joy and friendly one-upmanship that brought them to jazz in the first place. If you were bewildered by the recent Christian McBride, bored by the recent Joshua Redman, exasperated by the recent John Scofield, you get to hear them make their bones all over again, in company with Dave Holland and David Kikoski. Unburdened of the responsibility of devising a concept or a selling point or a novelty, they go with the flow, which with Haynes paddling must have felt more like white-water rafting.

The first seconds are killing: Irving Berlin's "The Best Thing for You," introduced with eight two-bar exchanges between Haynes and McBride—fast, exciting, competitive, like-minded. The ingenuously merry tune, propelled by slashing cymbals, inspires Redman and Barron, who are no less involved in displacing the beats than the rhythm players. The sense of unbridled enthusiasm continues with "That Old Feeling," as Scofield starts directly with the head and the leader inserts his first soft-shoe commentary in the fourth bar. Ever aware, ever kinetic, ever plush, Haynes lifts the ensemble in tandem with Holland's pneumatic and lyrical bass. During Scofield's third solo chorus, Kikoski plays a few chords, then lays out as Haynes pushes the beat, and at the first turnback of Kikoski's solo, Haynes turns the rhythm around so forcefully you think he's about to solo himself; later he gets into a rhythm that sounds like bucking and winging. For all his aggression, he never intrudes. When he goes for broke throughout Scofield's run on "Afro Blue," he elicits the guitarist's best playing of the session.

"Que Pasa?" makes up in fireworks for what it lacks in the drama of Horace Silver's original record, especially when Barron—brimming with provocative ideas behind Redman—takes over. The pianist is completely unleashed on "How Deep Is the Ocean," playing a middle-of-the-keyboard variation with harmonic surprises, and buoyant fours with Haynes (fitting payback for the powerful support Haynes gave him on *Wanton Spirit*). Always enlivened by exchanges, Haynes trades fours with Scofield on "Love Letters," which has a mischievously protracted ending; and Redman and Barron do eights and fours on "My Shining Hour," which also ends with a freely improvised episode. The penulti-mate cut, "Stomping at the Savoy," is relatively easygoing, while Haynes's closing feature, "Shades of Senegal 2," the only original, pivots on a three-note mallets figure and shows off his extended dynamic range, concluding at a whisper.

Friendship, by Roach and 82-year-old Clark Terry, recorded (in one session) when neither of them were expected to record anytime soon, is less consistent, but its peaks are in the clouds. They had played together with Monk, and in the intervening years Roach did some of his most accomplished work in duos, notably with Dizzy Gillespie and Cecil Tay-lor. This reunion is short and mostly sweet, its release coming on the 60th anniversary of Max's first recording date. On a quartet version of Monk's "Let's Cool One," with pianist Don Friedman and bassist Marcus McLaurine, Roach stays in the pocket, prodding the beat with an econ-omy that recalls Catlett. But he's best on the duets, including "Brushes and Brass," a blues with Clark using a mute to get an unusually high piping sound and playing two breathless choruses (his lungs are unim-paired: One phrase is 12-bars long) while Roach shows off the different colors of percussion—a completely satisfying performance under two minutes. "Simple Waltz" is a blues in six that suggests a New Orleans funeral parade, with Roach freely supporting Terry through a beautifully timed fade—they march down the road as the last chorus comes to a close.

Terry's tone is gorgeously solvent on "I Remember Clifford" with bass and piano, but no Roach, who in his absence inevitably becomes a subject of the tribute; Terry finishes his lovely coda with a note Bobby Hackett might have played. Terry is also in clover on a quartet reading of "But Beautiful," his timbre shining (note the foxy turnback after the bridge), with and without mute, and his phrasing utterly free of his patented licks. "The Profit," a duet, is a static blues riff with solos and fours verging on free jazz. Two ballads are unaccompanied trumpet solos—shades of Lester Bowie—as compared to one Roach solo, and on "To Basie with Love," he plays lissome flugelhorn responses with one hand to the muted trumpet in the other. A couple of the later tracks reveal weariness—familiar licks crop up on "For Dancers Only" and, except for Friedman, "Makin' Whoopee" is lackluster, with Roach overindulging a tympani effect on tuned drums, though the rendition manages to avoid the usual whimsy. Terry winds it up with "The Nearness of You" and a battle-cry cadenza.

Friendship is an unexpected addition to two brilliant careers. *Love Letters* ought to be the first in a series—Haynes presiding over jazz players playing jazz for jazz lovers.

[*Village Voice*, 25 June 2003]

141 ❖ *Ornette and Others (JVC 2003)*

And it must follow, as the night the day, that whenever JVC is as false to its calling as it was last summer, it will direct its next installment toward the true light. Look it up: The JVC Jazz Festival never scrapes bottom in consecutive years. With the return of Ornette Coleman (imperial), Wayne Shorter (tapped to elation by Savion Glover), and Dee Dee Bridgewater (an incendiary "Fever" for Peggy Lee), Carnegie Hall once again shone with star power, while diverse programming at Kaye Playhouse and inspired bookings at participating clubs added to a sense of citywide satiation. As usual for recent programs, it skewed to one age group—this year, elder statespeople. Boomers, so recently dominant, were in short supply (especially loft grads), and the young were virtually absent. I assume impresario and first-time author George Wein doesn't do this deliberately; it just happens, like the rainy season and hot spells.

JVC got off to a terrifically festive start at Kaye with the kind of no-brainer that almost always works, though not at this level. The recipe is simplicity itself: a couple of beloved veterans as objects of homage, and reliable mainstreamers to combine jam-session zest, pointed anecdote, and pulsing esprit. Joe Wilder and Frank Wess, recent editions to the octogenarians' club, hardly said a word all night but were involved in just about every segment, their trademark brews of eloquence and economy as potent as the sometimes ecstatic salutations played in their honor. From the first—Wilder, Wess, rhythm section, "Just Friends"—it was evident that the indispensable drummer Winard Harper would not tolerate flagging spirits; marking time on the hi-hat, shuffling over the snares for encouragement, and working the ride cymbal for incitement, he buttressed every measure.

The concert switched from pleasing to memorable when Phil Woods and Antonio Hart weighed in with their twin altos on "My Shining Hour," the former venting with his customary electric charge, the latter modifying his Cannonball proclivities with a strong jolt of Woods, showing off the consequences of serious woodshedding. A promising player for what seems like forever, Hart held his own and stayed in tune. So many privileged moments ensued that singling out a few seems unfair to the abiding euphoria, but that's what we're here for: Jimmy Heath constructed a solo as lucid and intricate as an architect's blueprint on "Bag's Groove"; Bill Charlap found in Stephen Sondheim's "Uptown Downtown" an anthem that combines stride rhythms and dramatic shifts in dynamics; Wilder engaged Charlap on "It's Easy to Remember" and dapper Benny Powell on "Squeeze Me"; Jon Faddis outclassed Roy Hargrove on a Basie riff, but came in second on a ballad medley in which Hargrove's Brownian lyricism ("Never Let Me Go") showed his real forte; Wilder and Warren Vaché locked horns on a contrapuntal "It's You or No One," preferring polyphony to the usual fours; Wess and Heath mined the deepest and mellowest swing groove of the evening on "What Is This Thing Called Love?"; and everyone scored on a stunning finale of "Lester Leaps In" that was talked about all week—not least for the rapid-fire piano exchanges between Charlap and Renee Rosnes. It demands a sequel. I suggest "Over the Heath and Into the Woods." No charge.

Ted Rosenthal's "Piano Starts Here" scored more often than not once a thudding triptych of technicians was out of the way. Eliane Elias's Gershwin medley showed that she can play breezy and her duet with Kenny Barron showed that she can play fast, but she brings little to a jazz party. Joey Caldarazzo brings nothing at all, beyond endless arpeggios, a consuming self-importance, and riff routines designed to make stadiums cheer (didn't work at Kaye). It's never seemed fair to me to review child prodigies the way they do in classical music, chiefly because so few of them get it, so suffice it to say that the 16-year-old relocated Siberian, Eldar Djangirov, played more notes faster than anyone else and that it behooves his tutors to tell him about John Lewis and Tommy Flanagan. A little Tatum is a dangerous thing.

There was much to admire. Barron dug into "Yardbird Suite" at the swinging medium tempo that brings out his best. Charlap, uncharacteristically hyper (a few times he clapped his hands as if impatient of finding the right chord), played tunes by Michel Legrand and the Bergmans with economy and purpose, as well as duets with Rosenthal ("Rocker"—they had each worked with Gerry Mulligan) and Cedar Walton. Rosenthal revisited numbers from *Threeplay*, "Forever Young" and Monk's "Let's Cool One," with his gentle touch, pretty bass-clef harmonies, and astute time. Kenny Werner just about stole the show, deftly supported by Peter Washington, with his contemplative, ariose improvs, the last of which gradually revealed itself as a fantasia based on "Giant Steps." Cedar Walton closed with just the right touch of maturity, revealing the ideal proportion of technique, swing, vamps, blue notes, and rests on J.J. Johnson's "Lament" and his own classic "Bolivia."

Randy Sandke and Richard Sudhalter organized the centennial repertory tribute to Bix Beiderbecke, which managed to insert a few surprises amid careful re-creations and adaptations that included transcribed Bix and Frank Trumbauer solos played by trios of trumpets and C-melody saxophones, sometimes incorporating solos from alternate takes. The key surprises were the shrewd inclusions of little-known arrangements by the Whiteman and Goldkette arranger Bill Challis, and a couple of modern interpretations of Bix material by Tom Talbert and especially Gil Evans, whose "Davenport Blues" was a highlight. Yet it underscored a problem that stifled some of the early transcriptions: the idea that the drummer can do no more than politely ping the cymbal as directed by the score. Trombonist Wycliffe Gordon and clarinetists Dan Levinson and Ken Peplowski were not asked to play down to the level of Bix's gang, so why must the rhythm section? Drummer Joe Ascione showed on the Evans arrangement that he has a lot more feeling than a metronome, and that feeling would have enlivened the creakier charts.

Sandke, who per usual played with sparkling articulation, did not make the mistake of including a passel of singers, as he did on a recent Bix CD (pianist Mark Shane handled the few appropriate vocals tolerably), but longueurs intruded, including an Eastwood Lane relic and, oddly, a plodding "Singin' the Blues" that suffered from the same excessive reverence that, in the earlier pieces, reproduced the divide between Bix's gems and his gang's faded velvet. On "Riverboat Shuffle," Gordon's growling ensemble work and kickass solo showed how encompassing this music can be and set the stage for the Bixian climax; Gordon was slyer, waving his plunger like Vic Dickenson, on Levinson's scoring of "Blue River," though his tailgating on "Clementine" seemed a tad patronizing. The ensemble fired up "At the Jazz Band Ball" with such burly confidence you could almost forget it was jazz repertory.

Terence Blanchard's misguided Carnegie concert of music he wrote for Spike Lee movies began with a brief chat between composer and director, who soon left, perhaps for a basketball game—he wore his jersey and surely had better things to do than listen to film cues accompanied by a slide show. What were they thinking? Isn't the JVC JAZZ Festival an ideal opportunity for a gifted JAZZ musician like Blanchard to create JAZZ adaptations of the tunes he writes for movies? Backed by a chamber ensemble, with the occasional guest dropping in for a song, Blanchard presented the scores as heard in the movies, where they do their job. The drummer was so stiff he must have thought we were still in Bixland, and the music was almost uniformly sad, moody, oppressive, ominous, and nostalgic. Blanchard came to life once during the first half, on "Mo' Better Blues," which Jacky Terrasson treats more creatively on his new CD. I left at intermission, feeling bamboozled.

The tribute to Peggy Lee deserves more attention than I can give it. If one can believe that everything that occurred was intentional down to the last intonational wobble and the final clip of Peggy emoting the lethal "Is That All There Is?" in the manner of Olivier's Hamlet soliloquies (lip-synching the chorus, closed-mouthed and thoughtful-looking through the rest), one might compare it as a drama to, say, *Follies*. Alas, Michael Feingold was not present and I was, and I'm obliged to review the music. It started well, with a montage of TV clips, a robust orchestra conducted by Mike Renzi, and Nancy Sinatra doing a thoroughly respectable— I was happily stunned—"Why Don't You Do Right?" Things began to go strange as two dancers in white gloves emerged from the wings to distract Anne Hampton Calloway, who was having enough trouble with "Mañana," a tasteless period piece no matter how benevolent Miss Peggy's intentions (as most songs were Lee originals, "I'm Gonna Go Fishin'" would have been a better choice). Producer Richard Barone had gone and revived the worst aspect of '50s TV variety shows—bad choreography.

There was an exception. Dee Dee Bridgewater, who needs no choreographer, radiated confident musicality on "Black Coffee" and returned wearing the last of Salome's seven veils to strut her long legs on the most daringly erotic "Fever" imaginable; when male patrons at Carnegie Hall rearrange their coats and playbills on their laps, you know you are witnessing a historic event. She received the evening's sole standing ovation, and it came before the intermission. Petula Clark and Chris Connor, who are respectively 70 and 75 (just an interesting tidbit), had pitch problems. But Connor had the range and spunk to try a difficult song, "Where Can I Go Without You." Clark, who had neither, mentioned that unlike her friends, who grew up listening to Vera Lynn, she preferred Peggy—and then sang, as ever, like Vera Lynn. Deborah Harry apparently thought they were saluting Mae West, as she camped cluelessly and tonelessly around the stage, and Jane Monheit did her own version of sexy, which meant patting her hair and touching her breasts, first one, then the other, for the duration of her song. Thank goodness for Maria Muldaur, who salvaged Act Two with a good-natured touch of rock 'n' roll ("I'm a Woman"), and the redoubtable Shirley Horn, who required a crib sheet for "There'll Be Another Spring" and *still* got more from the lyric than most of the others.

I hope Charlie Haden's gotten "American Dreams" out of his system now that he's performed the album at Carnegie; an exercise in bland democratic solemnity, it does carry the seed for what might be a great project. His inclusion of Ornette Coleman's "Bird Food" suggests that he and Kenny Barron might profitably explore the Coleman oeuvre—just the two of them, no strings, no tenor saxophone, although Michael Brecker did have one bright moment, sounding tearily emotive on "Young and Foolish." But enough of that. Art Blakey famously said that music washes away the dust of everyday life, and so it was when Ornette Coleman took the stage with his new quartet.

He went at it for close to 90 minutes, stopping, after a one-minute encore in response to a five-minute ovation, at the stroke of 11. That kind of precision characterized the entire set, not just the variational logic and magically timed endings, but the hairpin turns as the quartet sustained the leader's expansive, combustible playfulness. With Denardo Coleman's drums behind Plexiglas, the sound balance (better overall this summer than at any JVC festival in memory) gave each man his due, preventing the basses from getting muddied. Sometimes Greg Cohen asserted a thumping pizzicato bedrock as Tony Falanga employed his bow for melodic incursions; sometimes they plucked together, usually with Falanga suggesting the lead; and at one point Cohen laid out while Coleman and Falanga exchanged phrases. At all times the group seemed to breathe together, rising and falling like a pair of lungs, locked together with an emphatic rhythmic integrity that, in the Coleman manner, is less propulsive than fixed in the present—a perpetual-motion machine that swings in place, spotlighting the momentum of Coleman's improvised melodies.

Nothing in jazz is more moving than the purity of Coleman's sound and conception. Essentially, it has remained the same since 1959, when Shelly Manne marveled at how he could make the alto saxophone laugh and cry—never in a mimetic way, but through the natural effusiveness of his inventions. His compositions reach into an unguarded place where we store the most elemental tunes of childhood, and embody their universality, encompassing every kind of emotion. His solos chortle, sigh, exult, and dream, and when he's finished you get sent back to the dust of everyday life. Small wonder the audience wouldn't let him leave. Every Coleman concert is an event, but on this night he was preaching from the mountain and the clean air was exhilarating.

Meanwhile, there was much action in the clubs, including the return of Carla Bley's big band. On opening night at Iridium she performed the current *Looking for America* in the first set, and began the second with an alternate, unrecorded version of the Overture to *Escalator over the Hill*, continuing with a jolly Monkian piece called "Hip Hop" and excerpts from the 1996 *Goes to Church*. Gary Valente, a distinctive and robust trombonist who disappears from view when Bley isn't around, was featured, along with Vincent Herring, Gary Smulyan, Steve Swallow, and other familiars, but it's the stirring unity of the orchestra and Bley's decisive writing that floats this mighty ensemble. At Birdland, Ira Gitler introduced respectful but hardly reverent repertory bands in tribute to the Tadd Dameron and Charlie Parker units that played the Royal Roost. Don Sickler, not an exciting trumpet player but an appealing one with his confident timbre and lyrical phrasing, straw-bossed the Dameron band, with Jimmy Heath outstanding on "If You Could See Me Now" and in tandem with Jimmy Greene, who played a knockout solo on "Our Delight." The rhythm sections for both bands were in the reliable hands of Kenny Washington, Peter Washington, and pianist Michael Weiss, who is rarely more commanding than when reaching into his bop bag— especially in the Parker band, which featured Jim Rotundi, an accomplished trumpet player who played too close to the mike, and altoist Jesse Davis, who is back in New York after five years in New Orleans and approximates Parker's sound with fidelity, verve, and invention. Davis is long overdue for serious attention on the club circuit.

The festival climaxed at Carnegie with "Wayne Shorter: Life & Music," a program as concise and wary as Coleman's was effulgent and generous that nevertheless came to a smashing conclusion. Personally, I liked the first set, which was 45 minutes long and involved Shorter's quartet and one duet with Herbie Hancock, yet feel obliged to report that many colleagues grumbled. Though Shorter's sound was as light as a flute and his group a model of aggressive interaction, many fans want him to play conventional quartet music with coherent solos that have at least the vitality of his recent quartet album, if not the fabled might of the Miles Davis or Weather Report eras. Shorter, however, prefers at times a kind of hide-and-seek call-and-response with Danilo Perez, John Patitucci, and Brian Blade. In this mode, the band reminds me of Count Basie rhythm interludes, where instead of a piano solo you get a four-way immersion in timekeeping. With Shorter, the issue is less about rhythm than rests and retaliations—indeed, rhythm was nowhere to be found in the precisely executed, almost Debussyan duet with Hancock.

In any case, no one complained after the second set, which was dominated by tap dancer Savion Glover, whose lack of universal recognition amazes me—though I feel the same way about Ornette Coleman. With intermittent contributions from a chamber orchestra conducted by the histrionic Robert Sadin, he leaped to his platform and beat out so riveting a tattoo of complicated rhythms, with such finesse, that no one minded and some failed to notice that he often had his back to the audience. His music is that compelling—from any angle. After his initial solos and involvement with the arrangements, he kicked new life into Shorter, challenging him in a kind of standoff that had the tenor saxophonist wailing like a banshee or, better still, the old Wayne Shorter. Then he challenged the others, and one measure of his ingenuity was that Brian Blade, the sharpest drummer of his generation and one of the most restlessly stimulatingly since Roy Haynes, was hard-put to match him. It was over by 10, a satisfying and fitting conclusion to a festival that felt like a festival, breaking little ground but sprucing up the old homestead just fine.

[*Village Voice*, 9 July 2003]

142 ❖ *Overview and Meditation (Art Ensemble of Chicago)*

Nearly four years ago, Lester Bowie blew his last blat and took with him a sensibility that is as much mourned as his trumpet playing. With no worthy heir to his white lab coat, jazz suffered an irreplaceable loss in theatrical wit, surgical strikes, massed brasses, pan-generic repertory, and nostalgic caprice. The Art Ensemble of Chicago, however, refused to lay down its little instruments, appearing periodically as a trio and, with the return this year of founding member Joseph Jarman, a quartet. Ending the post-Lester recording drought, two new CDs, one by each configuration, have now shown up at the same time. True believers will want both; those, like me, with limited patience for plunking and grinding percussion melees, will rejoice without cavil at the arrival of the majestic *Tribute to Lester* (ECM).

Recorded two years ago, it is unlike anything else in the AEC's catalog, beginning with a compact summary of the band's first 30 years. Famoudou Don Moye's "Sangaredi," first recorded in abbreviated form in 1987, is treated to a definitive rendition, its African rhythms smartly bubbling from the start and quickly weighted with bass, gongs, and bass saxophone. Percussion feature though it is, the piece builds with compositional discretion until the chiming close, which suggests Big Ben tolling for the dead. An extended silence leads to Roscoe Mitchell's "Suite for Lester," a tripartite masterstroke of concision that opens with an allusive, poignant soprano saxophone melody reminiscent of his "For Lester B," recorded in three variants in 1997, most memorably as a hymn on Mitchell's *Nine to Get Ready*. This melody, backed by empathic drums and the bowed bass of Malachi Favors Maghostut, gives way to a serene full-bodied flute invention in the manner of Bach, complete with variation, that is in turn supplanted by a partying swing number on bass sax—all this in little more than five minutes.

"Zero/Alternate Line" is just what it says—Mitchell's revision of Bowie's "Zero," a forceful 32-bar ABAC theme introduced by the group (Bowie punched home an impressive solo) on *The Third Decade*. Mitchell announces the theme on alto in whole-note phrases at a dirge tempo, bringing out the melody's belly-dancing provenance, then jaunts into tempo, working chord changes that give the tune the feeling of infinite circularity; his long, freely sonorous phrases are pumped with connecting triplets. Favors's "Tutankhamun" recalls the AEC's genesis, having debuted as a bass solo on *Congliptious*, by Roscoe Mitchell's Art Ensemble, which also introduced Bowie's "Jazz Death?" Its marchlike descending cadences were interpreted a year later in a tour de force ensemble version (introduced by Mitchell with a poem in Joycean jabberwocky), and a few years after that in Mitchell's unaccompanied bass saxophone rendition. Mitchell retains that instrument as he swaggers over a loping rhythm, imparting a eulogistic mood maintained in the bass and drum solos before returning with a madhouse soprano saxophone episode cast with impossibly long if patented phrases that avoid sounding forced or mechanical. This is stirring, virtuoso stuff that sets up a powerful return to the theme, with sax and bass echoing each other and the theme.

The second half of the album comprises two payoff group improvs that illuminate the AEC's emotional extremes. "As Clear as the Sun" is a stunner. Mitchell's soprano erupts after a bass and drums passage and within four minutes enters a plane of intensity so profuse you have to laugh or at least reel at the joy of it all—endless loops of sound and relentless piping, like an aviary on uppers. It's a miraculous display of lung control, a protracted thrill ride in which the phrases sustain interest and energy, achieving a furious stasis and finally swelling and decreasing in volume like an ambulance circling the block before stopping on a dime. Not for every mood (it's like watching someone do 300 pushups, a friend noted), but nice to have when you need it. "He Speaks to Me Often in Dreams" is a little-instruments meditation that should lower the blood pressure and encourage quiet time for those so inclined.

I'm less enchanted by *The Meeting* (Pi), recorded in Wisconsin during several studio sessions last spring and documenting Joseph Jarman's anticipated return to the band after a decade. As at a concert, Mitchell's percussion cage gets more of a workout here, along with assorted whistles and recorders. Indeed, *Tribute to Lester* feels like a record qua record, while *The Meeting* may well require the empathy of a throng rather than the fidgeting of an unevolved individual like myself. Still, there are moments.

The CD begins with a bang: Jarman's song "Hail We Now Sing Joy," a hooky eight-bar melody that cleaves to the brain and inspires both reedmen to raucous flights. The brawn of their saxophones produces bewilderingly busy textures (one may suspect dubbing, though there's no mention of that) on Mitchell's herky-jerky "Tech Ritter and the Megabytes" and his whirling "The Meeting," in which the interplay is teeming and diverse. That cannot be said of the combined half-hour of "It's the Sign of the Times" and "Wind and Drum," which are spacey, still enclaves populated by ghostly fragments amid tinkling, jangling, buzzing, pealing, and altogether too much tranquility. Missing is that sensibility lamented and reclaimed in *Tribute to Lester*.

[*Village Voice*, 17 September 2003]

143 ❖ *All Duke's Chillun Got Melody (Gerry Mulligan)*

At long last, Gerry Mulligan's five Concert Jazz Band albums, recorded for Verve between 1960 and 1962, have been collected, though not by Verve. Mosaic (the mail-order company in Stamford, Conn.) has done a consummate job with *The Complete Verve Gerry Mulligan Concert Band Sessions*. These much-loved but long unavailable records have never sounded better—even the muzzy Milan sides gleam. The integrity of the original LPs is preserved, with unreleased takes placed at the end of appropriate discs. From the first measures of Al Cohn's arrangement of

"Sweet and Low," you know you are on enchanted ground, and the feeling of discovery and triumph never subsides for long, partly because each album's personality is distinct from the others.

Mulligan became an overnight sensation with his pianoless quartet in the early 1950s, but big bands remained his first love and the CJB was his boldest attempt to initiate a venturesome orchestra: The very name warned dancers to go elsewhere. It was to be a workshop ensemble, an expanded version of the Miles Davis nonets (for which Mulligan had scored most of the music), allowing him and other writers to show what a full complement could do. His celebrity, plus the willingness of members to work cheap and Norman Granz's deep pockets, made the undertaking possible. Another crucial component, as Bill Kirchner demonstrates in his notes, was the steady instigation of Bob Brookmeyer, the Mulligan quartet's valve trombonist and ultimately the CJB's most prolific arranger and deputy soloist.

Eighteen months after the start-up, Granz sold Verve, dooming the project but for one last hurrah in late 1962, but the CJB's influence was immediate and lasting. The first big band to play the Village Vanguard, it engendered what is now known as the Vanguard Orchestra amid a tide of rehearsal or Monday-night bands. Its method of building orchestral constructions from combo outlines helped Mulligan retain a limber spontaneity; among the many bandleaders who elaborated on the idea were Charles Tolliver* (a neglected trumpet player and composer whose

---

*Charles Tolliver initially staked his claim as a rugged hard-bopper on two 1964 Jackie McLean LPs, then freelanced widely (memorably on Horace Silver's *Serenade to a Soul Sister*), until 1969, when he introduced a daring quartet, Music Inc. Two years later he and pianist Stanley Cowell launched Strata-East, which issued many strong records, including a lavish and ignored 1975 big band album, *Impact*. The label and Tolliver vanished. Since reemerging in New York, he has kept a low profile, teaching at the New School. At 61, Tolliver is ripe for act two. His trumpet retains the vigorous tone, diligent logic, and controlled fury of his early playing. But his most powerful achievement may be as a composer-conductor. At Jazz Standard, he had the band solidly in hand, his dramatic semaphore directing intricate section work in long numbers that balanced pace, color tones, and excitement. His reed section, like the one convened on *Impact*, is a dream team: Gary Bartz, Jesse Davis, Craig Handy, Gary Thomas, and Howard Johnson.

Tolliver has expanded the fast version of "'Round Midnight" that capped his 1973 quartet album, *Live in Tokyo*; the orchestra arrangement blends bass/baritone-range lows and screech trumpets, followed by musing trumpet backed by Cowell, until unison brasses pick up the last two bars of the theme and throttle the tempo as Jesse Davis and Cowell aim for the bleachers. Also impressive is a detailed revision of "Mournin' Variations," originally recorded with big band and string octet; this time flutes, bass clarinet, and trumpet intone the Japanese-flavored theme, in contrast with fat dissonant orchestra chords. A succession of robust solos (Bartz in clover) and exacting riffs dominate the middle section, and the reprise is expanded by a Billy Drummond drum break for what Gerry Mulligan would have called a "capital E ending."

recent appearance at Jazz Standard ought to signal the resumption of a career that peaked in the 1970s), David Murray, and, most recently, Dave Holland. But Mulligan's band had something no other band could rival—his stubborn, frequently inspired, occasionally cloying passion for melody.

Mulligan was so preoccupied with the mechanics of leading the band that he wrote nothing for it beyond an unreleased update of his Kenton classic "Young Blood" and a majestic "Come Rain or Come Shine," twice recorded to feature Zoot Sims and, more successfully, himself. So in addition to Brookmeyer and Cohn, he recruited composers Bill Holman, George Russell, Johnny Mandel, and an unknown Gary McFarland. Mulligan and Brookmeyer handled most of the solos, spelled by Sims, Clark Terry, Gene Quill, Jim Hall, Willie Dennis, forgotten tenor Jim Rieder, and the group's unsung hero, trumpeter Don Ferrara, whose bursts of invention on "Out of This World," "Barbara's Theme," "I'm Gonna Go Fishin'," and "All About Rosie" place him in the Hasaan category of lost jazz noblemen, though he isn't listed in any jazz reference work.

A benign Olympian hovers over this material, and it isn't Apollo. The blessings of Duke Ellington are everywhere; no other group of writers paid homage with more candor and creativity. The original notes to the CJB's last LP specified Ellington's impact on those pieces, but it was apparent from the start: symbolically in the first recorded number, "I'm Gonna Go Fishin'" (from *Anatomy of a Murder*), and wittily in the Ellington-meets-Clyde-McCoy passages of "Sweet and Low." Hats are also tipped to Evans-Thornhill, Basie, Goodman, and Herman, while Russell's "All About Rosie"—a superior update of his original 1957 version—flies in its own orbit. Yet Ellington is invoked constantly, in voicings that include clarinet and in the interplay between soloists and ensemble.

There is so much to admire, not least the rhythm sections, especially the team of Mel Lewis and Bill Crow, which emphasize a relaxed capering that reflects Mulligan's easeful swing. The contrast between Mulligan's smoothly gruff lyricism and Brookmeyer's gruffly smooth barking, hissing, chomping solos typifies the good humor that often rises to the top—as in anything by Cohn, notably the matchless double windup of "Lady Chatterley's Mother," or the last bar of Brookmeyer's "You Took Advantage of Me" (a solo sigh that was played by the ensemble at a European concert released on European labels), or Mulligan's whimsical "Emaline" intro to "Come Rain or Come Shine," or his breakaway interpolation of "Blues in the Night" and Brookmeyer's asthmatic entrance on "Sweet and Low," or John Carisi's orchestration of Miles Davis's two choruses on "Israel," to say nothing of Mulligan's impetuous

exchanges with Clark Terry on "Blueport" and Holman's 6/8 arrangement of "I'm Gonna Go Fishin'," which turns it into a rocking counterpart of Davis's "All Blues." The *On Tour* album qualifies as a de facto
Zoot Sims concerto and a definition of mercurial wit.

Rumors of hours of unreleased material have proven untrue; the Vanguard tapes are apparently lost, and the 11 new alternates and otherwise
unreleased items don't add much, except for "Young Blood." Mulligan
would undoubtedly be relieved; he rankled at the release of discarded
takes. This is desert island manna, returned to life after more than two
decades, in a limited pressing of 7,500 copies, which ought to catch the
attention even of Verve, its long unappreciative landlord.

[*Village Voice*, 15 October 2003]

144 ❖ *Midlife Bloom*
(Dianne Reeves)

Of the 70-plus tunes attributed to Thelonious Monk, the ballads occupy
a singular plateau, none more so than "Reflections," which he introduced
at a magnificent 1952 Prestige trio session alongside "Trinkle Tinkle,"
"Bemsha Swing," and a riotously swinging "These Foolish Things" that
begins with a condign borrowing of Johnny Ray's "Please Mr. Sun."
Though acclaimed as an evocative melody, "Reflections" failed to attract
a lyricist and so never found traction with singers. It is classic, paradoxical Monk, beautiful and memorable yet a minefield of odd intervals,
each essential to its bricks-and-mortar structure. It gives the illusion of
being readily singable but isn't.

In the 1980s, Jon Hendricks wrote an impressive, poetic lyric for the
tune as part of Carmen McRae's last major project, *Carmen Sings Monk*.
McRae takes it at a medium tempo, cannily interpreting the lyric from
the vantage of a worldly lady who has seen it all; she rushes the tag,
"Thank God I'm one girl who knows," as if relieved to have made it
safely to journey's end. She also finesses the tune, gliding over some of
the knottier intervals. Well, that's what jazz singers do, and when they
embellish a pop song and make it better, we cheer. But like Ellington's
trickier melodies, "Reflections" ought to be sung as written.

Fifteen years later, Dianne Reeves has made the Monk-Hendricks song
a focal point of her new, best-ever CD, *A Little Moonlight* (Blue Note). It
also shone at her October 21 concert at Zankel Hall. If singers continue

to neglect "Reflections" from now on, it may be for fear of not matching her standard. At her best, Reeves has always been candid in channeling Sarah Vaughan and McRae; on the first cut of *A Little Moonlight*, "Loads of Love," she suggests a serendipitous meeting between them, scatting the first chorus à la Vaughan, and reading the lyric ("I never have demanded much") with a touch of Carmen. But she also exudes a quality of her own—a positive, midlife, blossoming, open-to-experience womanhood. This is poignantly expressed on "Reflections," where, backed only by piano, she applies her good time and flawless pitch to a slow Monkian tempo fraught with pregnant pauses—none more effective than in a bold assessment of that tag line: "Thank God I'm a woman [pause] who knows [long sustain]."

For an indication of how successful this disc is, consider that Monk's tune and Richard Rodgers's "Loads of Love" both sound made for her, as does Hoagy Carmichael's "Skylark," handled in an unexpectedly high key and making the most of the bridge, an adventure unto itself. Sinatra once faulted Ella Fitzgerald because one can hear her breathe; the champion of sentence-like phrasing would doubtless disapprove of the gulps of air Reeves draws in a line like "won't you [breath] tell me [breath] where my love [breath] can be." Not being a jazz singer, he would be unlikely to appreciate the parallel rhythmic effect she gets from those breaks. Then again, that Reeves is herself a jazz singer has not always been easy to ascertain.

Earlier this year, Blue Note released *The Best of Dianne Reeves*, which, excepting a few tracks from her potholed Vaughan tribute, *The Calling*, serves as a sampler of the contrived, dated, and overarranged work that delivered her from astonishing youthful promise to virtuoso entombment. That she was recording beneath herself became thrillingly apparent when she stopped the reconstructed "From Spirituals to Swing" concert at JVC in 2000, singing two Ida Cox blues with a slow, cagey, sexy humor and rhythmic bravura and then chiming with Dr. John on "Come Rain or Come Shine."

She stopped her Zankel Hall performance, too, with a slow grab bag of blues lyrics ("got the blues in the morning," "got rocks in my bed"), storing every phrase in the pocket, drawing appreciative laughs in all the right places, using melisma with a sultry and (here's a novelty) sparing cool. She is a tremendous blues singer, a natural—maybe she undervalues the knack because it comes too easy for her. Yet during that performance and during the 16 a capella opening measures of "You Go to My Head"; a duet with brushes on "What a Little Moonlight Can Do"; an authoritatively inventive mid-range scat solo on "I Remember Sarah"; her original evocation of childhood, "Nine"; and an even more expansive

"Skylark" and an even more reflective "Reflections" than on the CD, one had the sensation of being in the presence of a pantheon jazz singer.

Reeves's trio—pianist Peter Martin, bassist Reuben Rogers, and drummer Greg Hutchinson, whose restraint in this context was as impressive as his full-throttle attack with Joe Henderson—was discreetly employed in full and in part, undulating with the singer's every impulse. The arrangements are scrupulous, and Reeves respects what doesn't need fixing. In concert and on the CD, she indulged a Vaughan-like Brazilian jones with guitarist Romero Lubambo, eschewing a samba rhythm only on "Lullaby of Broadway," which, though it overdoes a wordless refrain, achieves a fresh deliberation of words and melody. It took Vaughan and McRae years to escape industry compromises. It would be nice to think that if Reeves continues in this vein, middle-sized middle-Earth Zankel Hall will no longer be sufficient to contain her audience.

[*Village Voice*, 19 November 2003]

145 ❖ Flee as a Bird
(Weather Bird)

As Groucho Marx used to sing, "Hello, I must be going." It's time to move on when you begin to calculate a job's duration the way children do their ages. Whereas I used to think in round numbers, lately I found myself muttering, "29 and a half years," "30 years, two months," "30 years, seven months, two weeks, five days"—which is correct as of today. Or am I confusing children with convicts? This was the hardest decision I've ever made, and like Artie Shaw, who has a different answer every time he's asked about quitting clarinet, I'm not sure why—except that I want to focus on books, I dislike writing short to suit a new layout, and it is time. In jazz, time is all.

Shortly after I joined the *Voice,* Martin Williams swore off criticism for a long spell (and produced a series of albums for the Smithsonian that forever altered jazz education). When I asked him why, he answered, "I've said everything I had to say." Tough-minded fellow. I don't feel that way at all. I'm as besotted with jazz as ever and expect to write about it till last call, albeit in other formats. Indeed, much in the way being hanged is said to focus attention, this finale makes me conscious of the columns I never wrote.

John Lewis and I had a joke about the end of projects. I once told him that I held certain musicians, about whom I knew very little, in abeyance—that when I ran out of everyone else, I would turn to them and then know I was done. I cited, as an example, Stan Kenton. One day when we were planning American Jazz Orchestra programs, he said, "You know, we'll have to get to Stan Kenton. He's important." I gave him a look. He said, "Maybe just one set." I kept looking. He said, "Then we'll know we're done."

It amazes me to realize that in all these years I never wrote a column on Booker Ervin, a great and neglected tenor saxophonist, and the subject of one of the first articles I ever published (elsewhere). Every time a new reissue came out, I'd swear I was going to write about it, and something else always intervened. I had the pleasure of meeting Booker shortly before his death, when I was a student and he was working midtown with Ted Curson's quintet. I asked him about the "hidden register," those squally high notes that were the rage of the 1960s, and presumed to be the result of ardent virtuosity. He said, "That's easy. You bite the reed"—and, sitting at the table, gave a numbingly funny demonstration.

I never wrote a column about Charlie Rouse—can't explain it. When I first got to know Stanley Crouch, we bonded over our mutual outrage at how three favorite tenors had been critically disrespected when we were growing up: Rouse, George Coleman, and Paul Gonsalves. We set out to render justice. Rouse's pithy, almost epigrammatic phrases; sandy timbre, by way of Wardell Gray; and uncanny ability to blend with the tones of Thelonious Monk's piano amounted to a rare oasis in a frantic era. For that matter, I never wrote a long-planned column on Wardell Gray either. What the hell was I doing? Nearly 650 Weather Birds, maybe 400 Riffs, yet no Rouse, no Gray, no Ervin, no Tristano, no Dameron, no James P., no Teschmacher, no Lee Morgan. Mea multiple culpas.

Or blame Robert Christgau. The Dean made it a point of professional pride that we write essays and not tethered briefs. Some musicians (not those mentioned above) only merit briefs, but the beauty of the *Voice* is that we had our page and could stretch out—less now than once upon a time, but still. Occasionally, exhausted, I'd rankle and hand in "Twelve Albums with Strange Covers" or "Five Bands I Heard Last Week," though rarely more than once a year, not including holiday wrap-ups. Essays require a deep immersion, the inhalation of an artist's life and work. There's also an obligation to concentrate on musicians who are alive; you can do only so many historical pieces without morphing into the ghost of jazz past.

Unexpectedly, 2003 closes a circle in that regard. The early '70s were weak on new recordings, but provided a bonanza in excavations: Lester Young rehearsing with Benny Goodman, Duke Ellington in Fargo, Roy

Eldridge at the Arcadia, Art Tatum and Hot Lips Page after hours—practically every week something old that was new. (At this point, you might stop reading, get Clifford Brown's *The Beginning and the End*, and play the first 4:53 of "A Night in Tunisia," the Dead Sea Scroll of trumpet solos.) Three of the best albums this year were similarly buried: *Bossas and Ballads: The Lost Session of Stan Getz* (Verve, 1989), Jaki Byard's *The Last From Lennie's* (Prestige, 1965), and Andrew Hill's *Passing Ships* (Blue Note, 1969), to say nothing of the deconstruction of Miles Davis's *Jack Johnson* (Columbia/Legacy, 1970). Hill's inspired December 8 Merkin Hall duets with Jason Moran (before an uncommonly musician-heavy audience), provided ample proof that yet another torch has been passed and that—despite label mergers, a corrupt FCC, and a Congress that misprizes the public domain—jazz ascends. Weather Bird sees no paucity of subjects for continued exploration.

[*Village Voice*, 17 December 2003]

146 ❖ How Come Jazz Isn't Dead? (Music's Four Stations)

The question is facetious, though not entirely. At times even dedicated boosters like me begin to wonder if jazz isn't edging into the museum's marble tomb. In a 1968 recording, "Jazz Death?" the then-little-known Lester Bowie posed effetely as a *Jism* magazine critic to inquire, "Isn't jazz, as we know it, dead yet?" After an unaccompanied trumpet solo, he answered, in his own mocking voice, "Well, that all depends on what you know." Bowie was responding to debates that were rife during the summer and winter of love. Miles Davis had said that calling him a jazz musician was no different than calling him "nigger"; jazz journals were filled with barbarians-at-the-gates prognoses. One authority confidently proclaimed that so long as Louis Armstrong lived, jazz lived, settling the matter in his mind until July 6, 1971, by which time—or shortly after—the arrival of dozens of gifted musicians like Bowie made it irrelevant.

Today, "Jazz Death?" is more frequently accessed for backup than music—a smirking rejoinder to those who believe that jazz is moribund, and an inadvertent example of the defensiveness that is a certain sign of bad times. We do well to remember that jazz coroners have been hanging crepe since the 1930s. In those years, reactionaries horrified by big-band swing and its damning popularity argued that authentic jazz was the

exclusive province of small, unschooled, polyphonic ensembles with relatively fixed instrumentation and repertory. They encouraged primitivism of a kind that was southern and Negro, reversing the initial
assumption (stated in Osgood's *So This Is Jazz,* 1926) that black bands,
however accomplished, could not compete with white concertizing orchestras. Serious jazz lovers rejected mannerly dance bands and symphonic elaborations as advocated by king-of-jazz Paul Whiteman
(making "a lady out of jazz" was an approving catch-phrase) in favor of
highly rhythmic, down-and-dirty, blues-drenched improvisations by the
likes of Jelly Roll Morton, King Oliver, Bessie Smith, Bix Beiderbecke,
and especially the valiant Armstrong; they belonged to an exclusive club
of advanced thinkers—but not for long. Some grew to detest Armstrong's ensuing success. They were too politic to say "we resent the interest of the masses" or "we hate to see our beloved primitives grow
rich." So they waved the flag of authenticity. Armstrong, they alleged
(Blesh, *Shining Trumpets,* 1946), sounded the first death rattle when, in
1929, he adapted white pop from Tin Pan Alley.

For half a century, each generation mourned anew the passing of jazz
because each idealized the particular jazz of its youth. Countless fans
loved jazz precisely *because* of the chronic, tricky, expeditious jolts in its
development, but the emotional investment of the majority audience—
which pays the bills—quickly metamorphosed from adoration to nostalgia. Mid-Depression America gave its heart and feet to swinging big
bands and later rejected the modern postwar school in which mostly
urban listeners found their own mirror images. Buffs in the booming '50s
accepted jazz as cool (West Coast), funky (East Coast), and mainstream
(enduring swing heroes, including vocalists like Ella Fitzgerald and
Frank Sinatra), while shunning the burgeoning avant-garde, which a
dwindling '60s fan base would embrace as a reflection of political and
social unrest.

The avant-garde and its small, loyal coterie proved virtually impreg-
nable, ultimately emerging as a permanent alternative to the changing
but constant (and consonant) center. Over four decades, it, too, evolved
diverse factions—free jazz, new music, harmolodic, freebop, and cross-
cultural fusions of every kind, which taken together suggest a kind of
parajazz or jazz in exile (downtown, in Europe, out of the way). The
avant-garde intersects with the center no less than Dixieland, swing, bop,
cool, hard bop, third-stream, soul, and the rest intersect with each other.
But every idiom has its own adherents, and when we refer to a "jazz
audience," we are really conjuring up a nation of tribes that speak different dialects and rarely marry out of faith. The combined tribes ought
to add up to a sizable commercial force. Yet not long after Ken Burns's

Jazz roused a patriotic fervor for "America's classical music," record industry accountants say that the jazz business is in free-fall. Jazz discs account for 3 percent of total sales, including jazz-lite (a slanderous term). What's going on?

Every enduring art has to face the issue of outlasting the world of its genesis—has to confront the day-to-day plight of sustaining and growing an audience despite a mass media consumed with mass appeal. How can we evaluate the importance of an art with a following so cult-like that it barely creases national consciousness? At what point does a vital form of expression become a museum to celebrate vital forms of expression? Born as outlying cults, musical traditions that achieve popular success invariably end as establishment cults, generating international infrastructures of subsidy and scholasticism to replace a once-clamorous public.

Jazz, at the dawn of its second century, affirms a template for the way music is born, embraced, perfected, and stretched to the limits of popular acceptance before being taken up by the professors and other establishmentarians who reviled it when it was brimming with a dangerous creativity. Duke Ellington was denied a Pulitzer Prize in 1965 because the jury commended him for his overall achievement rather than a specific work; in 1999, when he lay 25 years in the grave, he was awarded the prize—for his overall achievement. The jazz template, although not new (while the Three Tenors bellow the music of Lord Webber, consider that no American record label has a symphony orchestra under contract), may have a singular prognostic relevance for rock. It has four stations.

The first station might be called "native." Every musical idiom begins in and reflects the life of a specific community where music is made for pleasure and to strengthen social bonds: New Orleans fraternal societies, Appalachian fiddlers, Bronx high school doo-woppers, and so forth. The fable that recounts how jazz came up the river from New Orleans to Chicago and then leaped to New York and the world is crude, but it will do to set the stage. Jazz was brewed in a cauldron of music, including marching bands, spirituals, ragtime, blues, African drum choirs, Spanish and French dances, slave chants, minstrelsy, opera, and anything else that could be heard in New Orleans at the turn of the 20th century. It developed a distinct and local character, applicable to every kind of social occasion from picnics to funerals. Stalled at station one, traditional or Dixieland jazz might have remained one of the world's great folk musics, achieving its formulaic apex in King Oliver's Creole Jazz Band, which came to Chicago in 1921. One reason it didn't stall is that a year later, Oliver elected to bolster the ensemble with a second trumpet, and wired his protégé Armstrong to join him.

Those who experienced the exhilaration of Oliver's band during its residency at Chicago's Lincoln Gardens wanted it to go on forever. But the ailing Oliver knew how fickle sophisticated audiences are. Biting the bullet of progress, he soon exchanged his incomparable ensemble for a larger, mediocre, New York–style orchestra. As the "native" period faded into history, critics sentimentalized it while attempting to hold the fort. Authenticity reared its baleful head. "Printed scores are not a part of jazz," historian Rudi Blesh declared. Armstrong, he said, had abandoned jazz; "West End Blues" "narrowly misses banality," with its "dark romanticism foreign to jazz." Ellington's "tea dansant music" had no jazz content whatsoever.

Blesh was neither the first nor the last critic to proclaim his love of an art by telling its artists what to do. On a radio program with Blesh, Alan Lomax introduced New Orleans clarinetist George Lewis as an example of jazz in its Arcadian purity. Lewis, an affecting musician with a fat-boned sound but limited technique, had gained attention playing with Bunk Johnson, the ancient trumpet player recently outfitted with new teeth and paraded (falsely) as a mentor to Armstrong and beacon of true jazz. Lomax told his audience that in Lewis it would hear jazz as it was before commercialism mucked it up. He repeated the claim after Lewis's solo, unaware—unlike all of his teenage listeners (including future critic Martin Williams)—that Lewis, eager to show New York he was no dinosaur, had played the latest hot licks from Woody Herman's "Woodchopper's Ball."

By 1940 it was easy to mock "moldy figs" like Blesh and Lomax (though they had a sizable following, including novelist James Jones, who wrote a short story, "The King," about the thrill of finding Bunk), because jazz had long since reached its second and most important station, which might be called "sovereign." Here, music ceases to be the private reserve of any one place or people. No longer a communal craft with relatively few technical demands and a myopic outlook, it metamorphoses into a universal art with the "potential to compete with the highest order of previously known expression" (Schuller, *Early Jazz*, 1969). For Gunther Schuller, Armstrong's introductory cadenza on "West End Blues" was the alarum; some would choose other and earlier Armstrong performances. But virtually no one contests Armstrong's genius as the triggering agent. A transitional moment is caught on Oliver's 1923 "Chimes Blues." Armstrong was assigned the trio episode, a brief, written melody, played twice. It offered him no improvisational freedom, yet his brilliant tone, confident phrasing, and robust swing all but capsized the ensemble. Within a year, he would cause New York's best players and arrangers to rethink everything they knew about jazz; a year after that, in Chicago, he would initiate sessions by the Hot Five (a band that existed only to record), restructuring jazz as an art in which individual vision meant everything.

I don't mean to imply that Oliver, Morton, and others who brought the New Orleans style to full flower failed to achieve a profound level of expression. But Oliver inspired musicians to play Oliver's music; Armstrong inspired musicians to discover their own. Armstrong was the one great tributary to spring directly from Oliver. Tributaries that sprang from Armstrong ranged from the Swing Era ("orchestrated Louis," it was called) to modern jazz (Miles Davis: "You know, you can't play anything on the horn that Louis hasn't played—I mean even modern") and beyond. Armstrong's singing unleashed America's vernacular voice; his rhythmic and melodic liberties reversed the balance of power from song (and song publisher) to performer. Everything he did bolstered individuality as indicated in the jazz axiom, "It ain't what you do, it's the way that you do it."

The genie was out of the bottle, and no one—certainly not its liberator—could put it back. Armstrong did not initially like the extravagant intricacy of Dizzy Gillespie's playing, but as Gillespie observed, "No him, no me." The music would now go wherever individual genius took it, and the status quo would never be static for long. When jazz became capacious enough to include Dixieland, boogie-woogie, swing, and modern jazz (or bop), the word *jazz* grew too large for the comfort of most listeners. Jazz had accrued a history, a chain of events, but in reality each link would attract its own followers and only a handful of critics and listeners would care to track them all. For more than half a century, music lovers had been arguing Brahms or Wagner, Tchaikovsky or Debussy, Stravinsky or Schoenberg. Now jazz enthusiasts could join in the fun. The jazz wars of the 1940s and after produced some of the most intemperate spats in all cultural criticism.

The second station is the hardest to leave, and bitterness was inevitable. For little more than a decade, 1935 to 1946, jazz had been America's pop music—to a point. *Swing* was the byword, not jazz. True, the great bands of Ellington, Basie, Goodman, Hines, Shaw, Lunceford, Herman, Dorsey, Webb, Calloway, Krupa, and many more, played jazz; they enjoyed success with dancers and recorded many of the most profitable and artistically accomplished and innovative platters of the era. But all of them, to one degree of another, at times tamped down the jazz for arrangements that allowed them to keep larger audiences. A typical Benny Goodman session would produce two jazz instrumentals and two pop vocals. "Flamingo" bought Ellington time to compose *Black, Brown and Beige*. To many Americans, none of those names meant as much as

Glenn Miller, Hal Kemp, Guy Lombardo, Larry Clinton, Kay Kyser, and the other leaders of novelty or sweet bands that flourished as swing but had little or nothing to do with jazz. For that matter, the average Basie fan had no more interest in searching for old sides by Oliver and Bix than in contemplating the flatted fifth—bebop's preferred blue note.

And yet, only in 1939 could Coleman Hawkins have scored a hit with "Body and Soul," a peerless two-chorus saxophone improvisation with scant reference to anything resembling familiar melody. Only in the "sovereign" period could jazz have so utterly taken hold of the world's imagination. It penetrated the Soviet Union and China, where listening to jazz was an offense, and was adopted by occupied nations as a statement of defiance—in response, the Nazis recorded imitation jazz records to lure listeners to its own broadcast channels. The immediate postwar explosion of modern jazz, from the release of Charlie Parker's "Koko" in the first weeks of 1946 to the economic failure, in 1948, of the Basie, Herman, and Gillespie bands, also belongs to the second station. The jazz wars—trad versus swing, swing versus bop—had created a public consciousness of jazz that contributed to the rise of bop clubs and concert series. The nation never took bop to heart, but it knew something was up if only because of the frequent radio and movie gibes. *Life* explained bebop (the moniker alone made it seem trite, like hip-hop) as a clownish society of ritual handshakes, dark glasses, berets, and goatees—the humorous pretensions of Negro artists (Parker was not mentioned). Armstrong recorded "The Boppenpoof Song" and Bing Crosby and Patti Andrews followed with "Bebop Spoken Here." In *Appointment with Danger*, Alan Ladd asks, "Bop? Isn't that when everyone plays a different tune at the same time?" Maybe he was thinking of Dixieland, but the comment (in a 1951 flick) demonstrates the widening gap between jazz and the public's understanding of it.

Jazz was now sweeping inexorably toward the third station, which might be called "recessionary." This occurs when a style of music is forced from center stage. The floating orchestras that had recently crisscrossed the nation fell victim to postwar economics and changing tastes. Swing was now associated with the hardships of Depression and war. In Denmark, jazz, which had become a popular obsession during the Occupation, suddenly fell out of favor after the Liberation—it reminded people of evil times. In the United States, the turnabout was not as abrupt, but returning servicemen did not expect to resume the old party, and young people wanted something to call their own. Rhythm and blues and later rock and roll gave it to them, after a transitional period in the early '50s, when the pop charts were dominated by novelties that implied an optimism and faux-innocence verging on idiocy. In that environment, the undercurrent of rebellion and excess that had always been part of jazz slid into the shade, where it flourished with fewer constraints. Young musicians who wanted to play jazz didn't look to swing veterans for inspiration, but to the rebels who were remaking jazz as emotionally introverted concert music. (The distinction between concert and nightclub lessened as wartime cabaret taxes forbade dancing in most small clubs). Ballroom habitués weren't necessarily the types to seek music in the relatively genteel setting of a concert hall.

Of course the issue of gentility disappeared as new rites of passage, like the long-running Jazz at the Philharmonic tours, introduced a level of rowdiness rivaling the Savoy during Battles of the Bands; now battling tenor saxophonists generated the screams. Yet the gap widened between jazz and an increasingly uncomprehending public that was taught to associate modern jazz with characters like TV beatnik Maynard G. Krebs, who incarnated a white, lowbrow version of *Life*'s report on bop. In movies of the early '50s, modern jazz meant jukebox platters by ineptly raucous big bands playing stock riffs overlaid with dissonance. They drive Marilyn Monroe to murder in *Niagara*, Sam Jaffe to lechery in *The Asphalt Jungle*, and Marlon Brando to sentimental malingering in *The Wild Ones*. Meanwhile, swing was now as sentimentalized as Bunk Johnson; in *The Glenn Miller Story*, Miller's swing charts are engulfed in strings to diminish the rhythms. Between stodgy swingsters and pathological boppers, one thing was sure: Jazz was off the beaten path. By the time Chuck Berry sang, "I have no kick against modern jazz unless they try to play it too darn fast," everybody sort of knew what he meant, though he didn't mean anything at all.

Yet it's a mistake to think that the distancing of jazz from the commercial center resulted in a great decline in popularity. "Recessionary" means a retreat from marketplace power but not bankruptcy. As jazz began to sacrifice commercial self-reliance for the perks and miseries of classicism, it busied itself with mining the past—reissues complete with rejected takes, biographies, treatises, discographies—as well as forging an extremely exciting and diverse present, one that has never ceased growing in stature. The fan base may have been reduced and localized, but it was stable. New stars with cutting-edge personalities appeared: Miles Davis, Thelonious Monk, Gerry Mulligan, Dave Brubeck, Charles Mingus, Art Blakey, Clifford Brown, Jimmy Smith, Ahmad Jamal, and as many others as there had once been great orchestras for dancing. The jazz business prospered with a renewed luster: smart music for smart people. The masses don't get it? That's OK—1928 all over again: We're hip and you're not.

For the next 15 years, as youth music blanketed the culture and rock and roll's sovereignty in the marketplace brooked few incursions, jazz qua jazz—as opposed to jazz qua swing or jazz qua bop—achieved a success that, in some respects, trumped anything in its past. The factions seemed to fade and the flag of authenticity was raised only to banish the shamelessly commercial, the hangers-on. True, a lot of the great pre-bop soloists fell on dark times, but everyone at least paid lip service to their greatness. The main thing is that jazz had come to embody the sleek, affluent, postwar adult world. It was the original New Frontier, not just smart and hip but also socially adventurous, patriotic, and incredibly sexy. Everybody said so, from Lenny Bruce to Jack Kerouac to Norman Mailer to Steve Allen to Leonard Bernstein to James Baldwin to Hugh Hefner to Peter Gunn. Received wisdom says different. Ken Burns's *Jazz*, for example, is predicated on the glorious cresting in the 1930s, when swing bands resuscitated the recording industry and fueled a national craze. No one can doubt that—for the country at large—jazz peaked in those years, as (mostly white) jazz stars became famous enough to warrant Hollywood cameos and mainstream magazine covers. Yet in terms of financial rewards and cultural respect, jazz made immense strides between 1951 and 1964.

This was the era when Hollywood produced most of the jazz-themed movies and virtually all jazz-themed TV programs. These were the great years not of live radio broadcasts, which had all but disappeared, but of canned radio stations devoted to jazz on disc. Consequently, it was also the peak period for independent labels that focused on modern jazz as well as classic jazz. They proliferated: Blue Note, Prestige, Verve, Emarcy, Fantasy, Cadet, Riverside, Bethlehem, Atlantic, and Impulse, for starters. Jazz hits, of which there were many, did not figure in most sales charts because they were LPs. Yet they often sold more units than the hits of the 1930s. Sales between 1931 and 1938, when many assumed that the record business was on its last legs (radio offered music free to a cash-ravaged country), were negligible by the standards of the 1950s. In 1936, a disc that sold 40,000 units wound up in the top-20, 25,000 in the top-100; 100,000 was almost unheard of. In the 1920s, sales had often topped a million, as they began to do again in the '50s. The reasons for the upsurge were not entirely musical.

After impressively rebounding from the Depression in the late '30s, the record industry had been on hold during the war—a victim of the rationing of vinyl, the drafting and disbanding of orchestras, union strikes, and the focus on transcription recordings for the armed forces. Then came the revolution of tape and microgroove, which proved especially suitable for jazz and classical music. In a contest of patents, RCA and Columbia divided the business: the donut-hole 45 rpm disc replaced the 78 rpm disc as the vehicle for pop singles, while the 12-inch 33 rpm LP replaced the multiple-78s album and offered an expanded slate for more ambitious projects. Almost instantly, jazz labels encouraged artists to record longer works. Ellington was the first to compose extended pieces for the new medium—tone poems that, unlike suites, couldn't easily be divided into three-minute movements. Sonny Rollins extended his solos into tours de force of thematic improvisation. Sinatra, designing his fabled comeback, continued to concentrate on three-minute arrangements but now presented them in theme-based sequences, like moody novels. Satisfied with dominion over the singles market, rock and roll was content to use the LP for anthologizing hits, until the Beatles introduced *Sgt. Pepper.*

Jazz's concept albums and live recordings sold reasonably well: Fitzgerald's songbooks, Miles Davis's concerti, Oscar Peterson's trios, Brubeck on campus, Cannonball Adderley in nightclubs, Jimmy Smith at the chicken shack (which inaugurated a new genre of Hammond B3 organ combos), and others scored better numbers than most hit singles of the '30s. Benny Goodman's 1938 Carnegie Hall concert, first released in the early 1950s, outsold the 78s that had made him a megastar 15 years earlier. Many jazz LPs were so successful that tracks were released as singles, and several ranked high on the pop charts—Brubeck's "Take Five" (three months, 1959), Dinah Washington's "What a Difference a Day Makes" (five months, 1959), Etta Jones's "Don't Go to Strangers" (seven weeks, 1960), Stan Getz and Charlie Byrd's "Desifinado" (four months, 1962), Vince Guaraldi's "Cast Your Fate to the Winds" (18 weeks, 1962–63), Louis Armstrong's "Hello, Dolly!" (number one, 1964), Ramsey Lewis's "The 'In' Crowd" (four months, 1965). Yet most of the action was in the LP market, where jazz radio boosted unlikely recordings to a prominence that superseded the presumed marginality of its audience: John Coltrane's "My Favorite Things" is a famous example, as are the consecutive hits (1963–65) Blue Note enjoyed with Herbie Hancock's "Watermelon Man" (covered by Mongo Santamaria), Horace Silver's "Song for My Father" (covered by James Brown), and Lee Morgan's "The Sidewinder" (adapted for a Gillette ad). There were others, as well as frankly meretricious bonanzas like Wes Montgomery's *A Day in the Life.*

Jazz continued to infiltrate pop throughout the '60s. By the '70s, imitators of Coltrane and Montgomery were everywhere, and jazz was commonplace in movie scores and on TV talk shows. Sadly, those uses generally amounted to little more than background music. The kinds of jazz that pressed hardest for serious attention were the avant-garde, which required a lot of concentration, patience, and blind trust (Cecil Taylor might be a genius, but a four-hour concert is a serious investment, and Taylor himself took a Joycean stand, expecting preparation from his audience), and fusion, which required the same, plus a willingness to accept loud electrical instruments (Miles might be a genius, but the repetitions and lack of melody—from him, of all people—were as provoking as the funny clothes and tape loops). Suddenly, the traditional history of jazz, from Dixieland to avant-garde, could be encapsulated in one odd word, "acoustic," and in the years 1968–1972, acoustic jazz bottomed out. Many key figures left for Europe, the studios, teaching, pit bands, and fusion. Jazz had sunk into such a slough of despond that no one bothered to argue authenticity—except as regarded producer-generated fusion, where established players were inveigled into overdubbing solos over rote funk arrangements; and there wasn't much debate there either, since everyone seemed to agree it was a thoroughly disreputable business. This was the moment when Bowie recorded "Jazz Death?" for one of the Chicago labels that were documenting a new approach to acoustic jazz— a broader, wittier, looser avant-garde. Jazz was now pulling into the fourth and final station.

The situation in which jazz is presently found might be called "classical," not to denote an obeisance to orthodoxies and traditions (though, yes, there's plenty of that), but because even the most adventurous young musicians are weighed down by the massive accomplishments of the past. In the space of a lifetime, jazz history has progressed from a carton of King Oliver 78s stored in the attic to a grand labyrinth of idioms and artists that one can hope to master only with years of commitment. For the first time, a large percentage of the renewable jazz audience finds history more compelling than the present, and young musicians, who once aimed above all else for an original voice, are now content to parrot the masters. Pundits ask the reasonable question: If a young fan enters the huge jazz section at Tower, should he buy Wynton Marsalis's rehash of Monk or an actual Monk classic? The answer is implicit in the question, which would not have been posed in any other period. (Monk or Tatum? Both, of course.) The parity between old and new no longer exists. History keeps jazz alive in the Cultural Treasure sense—like opera—while making it almost impossible for new artists to get a hearing.

Perhaps the "recessionary" station's last hurrah was the "loft era" that peaked between 1975 and 1985. The previous decade, as noted, was rife with compromise and despair, bleak efforts to adapt psychedelic attitudes and electric instruments (remember the Varitone sax?), when even

John Lewis and Bill Evans recorded on Fender Rhodes. As jazz once again raised its head as an uncompromising art in the banner year of 1975, it faced up to the reality of occupying a small and isolated section of cultural real estate. Yet the sheer number of new players and re-emerging old ones engendered a liveliness that had been absent for years. A wave of major musicians who had been riding out the storm away from the limelight regenerated their careers, among them James Moody, Hank Jones, Tommy Flanagan, Dexter Gordon, John Carter, Cecil Taylor, Don Pullen, Art Pepper, Johnny Griffin, Red Rodney, Phil Woods, Frank Morgan, Jimmy Rowles, Jackie McLean, and Benny Carter. The young and not-so-young (but little known) musicians from the West and Midwest who turned up in New York as members of collectives, cooperatives, or rehearsal bands included Lester Bowie, Muhal Richard Abrams, Henry Threadgill, Sirone, Roscoe Mitchell, Leroy Jenkins, Fred Hopkins, Steve McCall, Julius Hemphill, Oliver Lake, Jerome Cooper, Leo Smith, Anthony Braxton, Hamiet Bluiett, David Murray, Arthur Blythe, James Newton, Marty Ehrlich, James Blood Ulmer, Shannon Jackson, and many more. They eschewed the mainstream (or vice versa) and transformed New York's jazz scene by organizing concerts, producing records, and gentrifying low-rent lofts into performance venues.

Most of them carved out successful professional niches in the world arena. But the world closed in on them and their audience became true believers. Still, they were strong individualists, and the one thing that did not close in on them was jazz history. No one posited a marketplace competition between David Murray and Dexter Gordon. The younger players drew on the past; they did not mimic or recycle it. Which is precisely what has happened in the "classical" phase. In 1981, Wynton Marsalis came to town. Working with Art Blakey, he personified the promise of a neoclassicism he hoped would restore a virtuoso élan that predated the avant-garde but still had a lot of life to it. As his renown spread, however, Marsalis reawakened the old Rudi Blesh debate about jazz authenticity: If you didn't swing his way, you didn't swing; if you didn't play the changes, you weren't playing jazz. The ensuing jazz war was probably inevitable. In a sense, the "classical" station is defined by the question: Who will inherit the music—the classicists or the renegades? What Marsalis was slow to learn is that the audience is less inflexible. By 2002, he was without a label and asking for incredible sums when his records sold no better than those he claimed were killing jazz. Marsalis is very likely the most famous living jazzman—everyone knows him. He writes books and appears on TV and in magazine ads. He is a genial, generous, and increasingly mellow spokesman for jazz, and his educational programs and big band tours merit and receive much praise.

Yet his orchestra could not function without the sponsorship of Jazz at Lincoln Center (the most successful fund-raiser in jazz history), his music exercises decreasing influence, and his record sales are modest. He is the quintessential superstar for an art overwhelmed by its past.

For most jazz artists, fame will always be circumscribed. Establishment—as opposed to marketplace—recognition is in short supply. Jazz has virtually no standing with Brahmin networks like the American Academy of the Arts or the Pulitzer. The Kennedy Center Honors, which have acknowledged Chuck Berry, Johnny Cash, Bob Dylan, Paul Simon, and Paul McCartney, have been far less generous to jazz innovators of the past half-century: Do not expect them to ring up Sonny Rollins, George Russell, Ornette Coleman, Max Roach, Horace Silver, Cecil Taylor, Charlie Haden, McCoy Tyner, Clark Terry, or the rest any time soon— Brubeck or Peterson maybe, Marsalis surely, in time. (A representative of the Kennedy Center Honors once asked me to recommend a jazz musician. When I stumped for Benny Carter, she laughed: This is for television and the TV audience has never heard of Carter. A petition mounted in Hollywood eventually got him the honor.) The idea of jazz as a stately, classical art—less stuffy than European classicism yet more dignified than rock—remains an attractive one, and cities around the world are eager to launch jazz festivals, each with its own definition of jazz. Dixieland thrives in New Jersey, swing in Florida, soft-funk at Newport. In 2002, the New York JVC Jazz Festival offered its lowest quotient of bona fide jazz ever; its impresario insists there are no longer jazz stars to pack the big halls. In fact, there are a few—Sonny Rollins never fails to draw one large flank, Chick Corea another, Diana Krall a third. The one musician who unites the diverse tribes, if only in contumely, is Kenny G—the Lord Webber of jazz. Several years ago a widely repeated joke underscored the sense of desperation: You are given a gun with two bullets and placed in a room with Idi Amin, Saddam Hussein, and Kenny G. Only two bullets. What to do? Shoot Kenny G twice.

Jazz as a business is in deep trouble, despite steady sales of archival classics and various commercial uses of those same beloved records, often rendered anonymous in TV ads. How could it be otherwise? Jazz musicians have virtually no access to the machinery of capitalism, and multinationals have no patience with leisure pursuits that supply insignificant profits. Furthermore, the appalling copyright extension, sanctified by the Supreme Court in 2003, prevents smaller jazz labels from fleshing out their catalogs with competitive editions of classics that, in many cases, the majors refuse to reissue anyway. I am not convinced that the issue of commercial marginality cannot be effectively addressed and alleviated. But it will take a dot.com billionaire jazz lover. Such an individual could work wonders by creating a national jazz radio network or cable station; or by organizing an agency to plan and produce jazz tours, reviving the campus circuit and the kind of excitement that attended Jazz at the Philharmonic; or by erecting a national jazz temple equal to those that exist for country music and rock and roll. Barring that, a new Miles or Monk or Rollins could come along and attract as much excitement as the originals. Anything *could* happen. In lieu of pipe dreams, however, jazz will survive as a permanent alternative music, like the 19th-century symphonic repertory, sustaining its audience through word of mouth and a constant replenishing of the talent pool.

One of several remarkable musicians to appear in the last few years is pianist Jason Moran, who records for Blue Note and works regularly in New York. New York has no commercial jazz radio station; nor is there a jazz outlet on the hundreds of cable stations. Yet he is committed, inspired, prolific, and by no means alone. A critics' darling almost from the first, he achieved something rare in contemporary jazzcrit: a consensus regarding his 2002 solo album, *Modernistic*. Much of the excitement stemmed from the way he approached the wider world—that is, the jazz past (stride pianist James P. Johnson), the pop past ("Body and Soul"), the jazz present (avant-garde guru Muhal Richard Abrams), the pop present ("Planet Rock"), a probable future (originals that combine improvisation and swing with hip-hop beats and prepared tapes), and even a circumnavigation that adapts Schumann lieder as a harmonic grid for ad-lib variations. With minimal self-consciousness, Moran asserts himself as a gifted jazz artist and as a musician of his generation. He may have little if any chance of cracking the multinational monopolization of mass media, but he embodies a way of negotiating the margins without succumbing to traditionalism and nostalgia—something rock musicians will have to master when the mantle of classicism falls on them.

Ailments granted, jazz could never be sick unto death. There is no indication that the music or the desire to master it will vanish, any more than cinema or literature will vanish. A stream of new blood enters the jazz body annually. The best young musicians invariably learn to make a living at it. The constancy of jazz's past (in 2001, Columbia Records revealed that Miles Davis's 1959 *Kind of Blue* sold, on average, 5,000 units a month) guarantees an unending succession of players who want to master the idiom and get plenty of encouragement in school and from the media's occasional obeisance to America's Classical Music (a phrase that doesn't seem so flattering now that the evidence is QED and jazz players are less in need of respect than work). They aim to make their own contributions and extend jazz history. If they differ from their forebears in having learned jazz from records and in classes rather than on the street or as apprentices in big bands, they embody the same spark of obstinate originality and defiant pleasure. The notion that jazz is dead or could die in the foreseeable future is predicated on one of two ideas: It is a narrow musical style with fixed parameters, or a passing fashion that has had its day. A century of development puts paid to both.

Indeed, the jazz press seems more upset by the obstacles than the musicians, whose optimism ensures jazz's endurance as something more than a museum treasure. For them, authenticity isn't an issue of style but of competence and imagination, as summed up by an observation once made by John Steinbeck. "Great reward can be used to cover the loss of honesty [among other artists] but not with jazz players," he said, adding: "Let a filthy kid, unknown, unheard of and unbacked sit in— and if he can do it—he is recognized and accepted instantly. Do you know of any other field where this is true?" Put another way, it all depends on what you know.

[*This Is Pop*, edited by Eric Weisbard, Harvard, 2004]

Index